DWG.3

Credits

Executive Editor
Chris Nelson

Development Editor
Jennifer Eberhardt

Managing Editor
Sarah Kearns

Copy Editor
Audra McFarland

Technical Editors
Robert Reinhardt
Andy Shafran

Cover Artwork
Bruce Heavin
bruce@stink.com

Designer
Ali Karp
Alink Newmedia
alink@earthlink.net

Proofreader
Sheri Replin

Indexer
Cheryl Jackson

Lynda's Bio

Lynda Weinman has written six books on Web design, many in second editions. She has been teaching digital design and animation since the late 1980s, and recently opened her own training center in Ojai, California (http://www.digitalartscenter.com). She has a line of video training tapes, and regularly teaches at her center. Lynda has written for numerous magazines, including *Step-by-Step Graphics*, *MacWorld*, *MacUser*, *DV*, *How*, *Web Techniques* and *Adobe*. She has taught at Art Center College of Design, UCLA, American Film Institute, and San Francisco Multimedia Studies Program. Lynda lives in Ojai with her husband, daughter, 3 cats and her 74-year old dad (who has a Web site!).

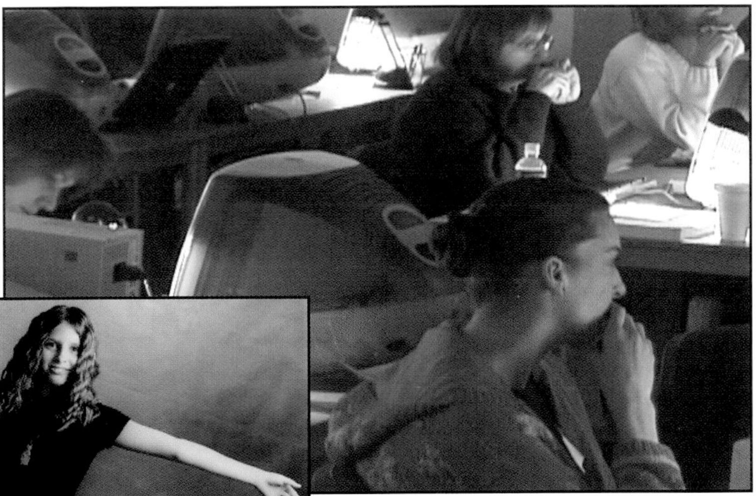

Thanks to all the wonderful students who've attended our classes at the Ojai Digital Arts Center (http://www.digitalartscenter.com).

Thanks to the love of my life—my beautiful daughter Jamie.

Thanks to my favorite book designer, Ali: Always searching for artistic inspiration. Even while on vacation in Norway, she's caught in the act of stealing a well designed museum poster advertisement .

Thanks to my favorite man—my husband, partner, and true love Bruce!

ics.3>

th... ...tion

Words: Lynda Weinman
Design: Ali Karp

Designing Web Graphics.3

Lynda Weinman

New Riders Publishing
201 West 103rd Street
Indianapolis, Indiana 46290

International Standard Book Number: 1-56205-949-1
Library of Congress Catalog Card Number: 98-85805
Printed in the United States of America
First Printing: March 1999

Trademarks

All terms mentioned in this book that are known to be trademarks or service marks have been appropriately capitalized. New Riders Publishing cannot attest to the accuracy of this information. Use of a term in this book should not be regarded as affecting the validity of any trademark or service mark.

Warning and Disclaimer

Every effort has been made to make this book as complete and as accurate as possible, but no warranty or fitness is implied. The information provided is on an "as is" basis. The author and the publisher shall have neither liability nor responsibility to any person or entity with respect to any loss or damages arising from the information contained in this book.

Lynda's Acknowledgements

So many people have helped me over the course of writing this book that I only hope I remember to list all of them here!

First and foremost, **my husband Bruce**, whose belief in me is unending, and whose love and humor get me through each day.

Second and foremost, **my daughter Jamie**, who has to put up with a Mom who loves her work, which sometimes means I work long hours and don't have as much time for her as she'd wish.

To **my collaborators at lynda.com, LLC**: Garo Green, Chris Deutsch, Tony Winecoff, Heidi Goodspeed and Phillip Latham. You make it possible for me to do so much more than I could do on my own—it's great to work with each and every one of you.

To my book agent, **David Rogelberg**, who knows how to negotiate a great deal, and has made many of my dreams a reality this year.

To **my book designer**, Ali, who is always there for me, who puts heart and soul into these books and it always shows.

To **my family**, who also miss seeing me much of the time, but understand that I love what I do and support me fully.

To **Jennifer Eberhardt**, thank you for your commitment and dedication to the quality of my projects.

To **my contributors** (directly or indirectly) to this book—Christopher Schmitt, Michael Macrone, Mike Shuey, Doug Olson, Doug Meisner, Tom Hale, Diana Smedley, David Mendels, David Baldeschwieler, Matt Brown, Suzanne Porta, and Joy Silverman.

To **my readers**, without whom there would be no new books, videos, classes or conferences. You propel me forward, and I thank you for it!

Table of Contents

2 HTML Editors 17

3 Strategy 29

4 Web Authoring Environments 41

6 Low-Bandwith Graphics 77

16 Web Typography 249

17 Alignment & Tables 269

22 JavaScript: Rollovers & More 347

25 Flash & Shockwave 395

26 HTML for Visual Designers 411

Designing Web Graphics.3

TOC at a Glance

Introduction

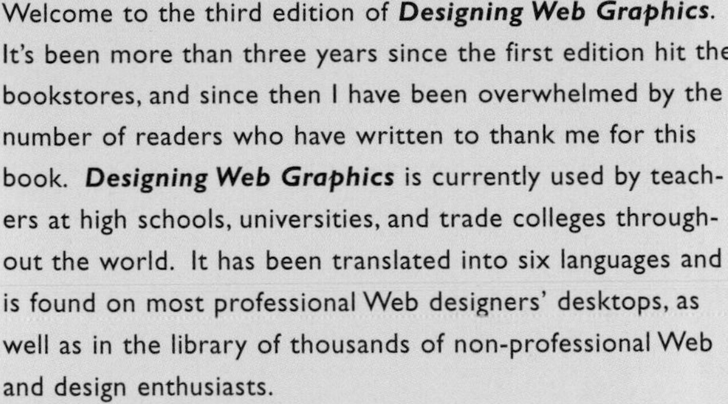

Designing Web Graphics.3

Chapter Contents

Welcome to the third edition of ***Designing Web Graphics***. It's been more than three years since the first edition hit the bookstores, and since then I have been overwhelmed by the number of readers who have written to thank me for this book. ***Designing Web Graphics*** is currently used by teachers at high schools, universities, and trade colleges throughout the world. It has been translated into six languages and is found on most professional Web designers' desktops, as well as in the library of thousands of non-professional Web and design enthusiasts.

The Ever-Changing Web

What compels me to return day after day to the computer to write about the ever-changing Web? The Web is a phenomenon on so many levels that I still find myself awestruck by it. I am still amazed when someone from Europe or Asia enters my guestbook. I am still amazed that, as an individual using a little box that shines back at me, I can communicate with others on a global level. I am still amazed when I see a URL on a billboard, the side of a truck, or a T-shirt. I am still amazed that the Web grew up to be such a big thing to so many people. I imagine that at some point, I'll become jaded by the Web; but for the moment, I think it's an exhilarating time to be alive and witnessing the emergence of this medium.

I'm an educator, and nothing pleases me more than to teach others. Teaching people about the Web is not an easy task however, because there are so many unfamiliar constraints and rules. For me, designing for the Web is not about dogmatic ideas and rigid principles. It's about harnessing the power of design to enhance ideas and communication.

The term "Web site" is a bit of a misnomer because "Web site" can mean so many things. There are sites for educational, entertainment, commercial, informational, vanity, and experimental purposes, as well as sites for a hybrid of many purposes. How could you possibly apply the same rules to all these different types of sites? I wouldn't presume to know the one "right" way to make a site for all these different purposes.

Instead, I believe that knowledge is power. If I can share with you the knowledge about how to do things, the repercussions of certain decisions and strategies, or the penalties of using certain technologies, you can make decisions about what is right or wrong for your site.

I've been creating computer graphics for the past 13 years and have watched tools and computer hardware come a long way. Even so, it's truly amazing at times how frustrating computers can be and how much time can be eaten up by things that don't work right or by wrestling with inefficient tools.

My goal is to spare you some of the pain by sharing my favorite tips, tools, and techniques, as well as the ever-present "gotchas" that plague those of us doing this work. Don't forget that Web design is still in its infancy. Anyone who claims to be an expert has been doing this work for maybe three to five years—at the very most!

My attitude is that we are all new at this stuff, even those so-called "expert" folks. I consider myself both a student and a teacher of Web design. There's never been a reason to understand file compression, navigational techniques, color palettes, animation, and sound in one visual design discipline. And visual design should not be entirely separated from information design and/or programming design. Great sites work on all levels, not just visual design. The Web makes it possible and necessary to combine many different disciplines at once, and it's one rare superhuman who can do it all well.

I hope this book is helpful to you. If it is, I have done my job.

What's New in DWG3

If you own an older edition of this book, you might be wondering what is new in this edition and if you should buy anew. For that reason, I thought it would be valuable to share a list of what's new so you can make your decision easily and decide if these new additions are of value to you.

- Design strategies
- Working with clients
- ImageReady tips
- Fireworks tips
- Dreamweaver tips
- Flash tips
- Shockwave tips
- Photoshop 5.0 tips
- DHTML chapter
- QuickTime 3.0 chapter
- JavaScript chapter
- Frames
- CSS chapter
- Color aesthetics

How DWG.3 Works

It's always tricky to write about Web design, because there are so many overlapping principles and concepts. For example, tables can be used for layout and alignment, or for cutting apart images to save on file size and downloading time. Teaching about linked graphics and navigation involves both image creation techniques and HTML or CGI. Sometimes, making the decision about which chapter to put with which subject is difficult! For this reason, I have intentionally structured this book so that readers can approach it in a nonlinear manner. Whenever a subject is mentioned in more than one chapter, it is clearly noted.

Those who use the Web for information often wonder if they need to buy a book, when so much information is available for free right on the Web. Indeed, the Web is an invaluable resource, and this book is not meant to be a substitute for it. Few will dispute the advantages to having all the information you need in a compact, transportable, and easy-to-read format. Books have not lost their importance in the age of networked information, but must work in tandem with electronic resources to be as effective as possible. This book (of course!) has a sister Web site–check it out at http://www.lynda.com/dwg3.

Although it might be possible to read or skim this book in a single day, the information inside is far too overwhelming to absorb in a single sitting. It took me many months to write this third edition. Even with that many months, I could not have possibly understood the task at hand without many more years of experience under my belt as a computer graphics artist and teacher. The task of collecting all this information in one place is enormous and, frankly, never feels finished. The Web changes and evolves constantly, but once the ink is dry on this book's pages, it will forever be there.

That's why there are many references to outside information sources in this book. Everything from other URLs, other books, magazines, conferences, newsgroups, mailing lists, and CD-ROMs are offered as support resources whenever a new subject is touched upon. I wrote this book with the full understanding that information will change and evolve, and gave you outside channels to get to that new information. Updates and errata will be posted at my Web site as well. Just remember how to spell my name—with a "y"—and you'll be able to email me or check in on my Web site at any time. I can't promise to answer everyone, but I do whenever time permits.

lynda@lynda.com
http://www.lynda.com

Enjoy the book, and I hope to see you on the Web!

What the Chapters Cover

1 Getting Started
- Career Advice
- Training Advice
- Skills Assessment
- Portfolio Advice
- Pricing Advice
- Hardware Advice
- Software Advice

2 HTML Editors
- What Is HTML?
- HTML Versus Design
- Should You Learn HTML?
- WYSIWYG Editors
- HTML Terminology Explained
- Choosing an HTML Editor

3 Strategy
- Defining Your Goals
- Storyboarding
- Flowcharting
- Brainstorming
- Navigation Approaches
- Site Structure
- Metaphors

4 Web Authoring Environments
- Browser-Safe Color
- Guidelines for Compatibility
- AOL Browsers
- Cross-Platform Color Calibration
- Gamma Differences
- Type & Size Differences
- WebTV

5 Web File Formats
- Bitmap or Vector?
- Lossy or Lossless
- GIF
- JPEG
- PNG
- Digital Watermarks
- MNG

6 Low-Bandwidth Graphics
- File Size and Downloading Speed
- Making Small JPEGs
- Making Small GIFs
- Anti-Aliasing vs. Aliasing
- Dithering & Banding
- Hybrid Images
- Batch Processing

7 Color Calibration Issues
- RGB Versus CMYK
- What Is sRGB?
- What Are ICC Profiles?
- Gamma Issues
- sRGB in Photoshop 5.0
- Accurate Web Color Solutions
- Helpful URLs

8 Browser-Safe Color
- Browser-Safe Colors Defined
- When To Use Them, When Not To
- Hexadecimal Color
- Safe Color Picking
- Browser-Safe Swatches
- Ensure Safe Colors
- JPEGs, Never Browser Safe!

9 Color Aesthetics
- Color Vocabulary Terms
- Color Schemes
- Contrast
- Color Relationships
- Readability
- Color Hierarchy
- Balance & Harmony

10 Color HTML Tags
- HTML Color Attributes
- BODY Colors
- LINK Colors
- Color Names
- FONT Color
- Coloring TABLE Cells

11 Linking Basics
- Creating Links
- Turning Off Borders
- WIDTH and HEIGHT
- ALT
- Thumbnails
- Linking to Other Media

12 Background Tiles
- Tiling Backgrounds
- Pattern Sizes
- Full-Screen Backgrounds
- Background Code
- Seamless Tiles
- Photoshop Techniques
- ImageReady Techniques

13 Transparent Artwork
- What Is Web Transparency?
- Faking Transparency
- GIF Transparency
- Problems with Glows
- Tools & Techniques
- PNG Transparency

14 Rules, Buttons & Bullets
- Rules with HTML
- Rules with Graphics
- Clip Art Rules
- Bullets with HTML
- Bullets with Graphics
- Using Layer Effects
- Button Clip Art

15 Imagemaps
- What Are Imagemaps?
- Client-Side Imagemaps
- Server-Side Imagemaps
- Using Both Server- & Client-Side
- Imagmaps in Fireworks
- Imagemaps in ImageReady
- Imagemap Resources

notes

Designing Web Graphics.3

Getting Started

Introduction

This chapter takes a look at the various issues surrounding the setup of a Web design studio and outlines different choices for getting started. It covers career decisions, pricing standards (or lack thereof), educational resources, and hardware/software guidelines.

Not all readers of this book want to be professional Web designers. Many people have personal Web sites and want to improve their graphics and design skills for the sole reason that it is gratifying to make a great-looking site. Some of you are already making a living through Web design, or are setting up a design studio as a business for the first time. Feel free to skip around and just read the sections that apply to your interests and goals.

Chapter Topics

- Career Advice
- Training Advice
- Skills Assessment
- Portfolio Advice
- Pricing Advice
- Hardware Advice
- Software Advice

Lynda's Career Counseling

If you were to take a poll of professional Web designers and query them about their backgrounds before they became involved with the Web, you would be amazed at how many disparate specialties you would find. We're in an era where Web design is so new that very few people knew this was what they wanted to be when they grew up.

Therefore, if you are new at this (and all of us are really, considering that the Web is only a few years old), you are not alone. Basically, almost everybody is in the same camp. Those who excel in this industry are always self-taught in something, be it design, programming, or project management.

Schools and universities are finally starting to offer classes, certification, and degrees in Web development, but very few professionals in the workplace are products of formal Web education. Even if you have had the luxury of Web-specific training, the industry is in constant flux, and the skill of teaching one's self will always be at a premium.

The questions to ask when heading down the Web design career path are:

- Where do I get training?
- What skills will employers expect?
- What kind of portfolio should I build?
- How do I know what to charge?
- Should I start my own company?
- How do I find a job in this field?

The following sections will help you answer these questions and will direct you to resources for further exploration.

Training

The term "training" has evolved over the years to include books, seminars, lectures, hands-on classes, certification, and online courses. Everyone has different learning styles, and it might be helpful to answer some questions about yourself before you embark on a training path.

- Do I learn best by "doing"?
- Do I learn best by "being shown"?
- Do I learn best by "studying"?
- Do I learn best by "examining other's work"?

You might learn best through combining all these means, but my experience as a teacher has taught me that most people have different learning styles. It's important to identify what type of "learner" you are and to choose training that best suits your learning style. If you can first identify what type of learner you are and accept that the most important aspect of training is that you actually learn something, then you can make intelligent choices about how to get the best training for your learning style.

If grade point averages and/or certification are important to you, make sure they are important to your prospective employer. My experience has proved that most employers care more about the competence and quality of actual work than about grades or degrees. This is not to dismiss the value of a course that offers certification or grades. It is simply to forewarn you that it's often more important that you actually have a portfolio and real experience than a degree or high grade in a class.

When I taught full-time at Art Center College of Design, I used to tell my undergraduate and graduate students that it really didn't matter what grade they got in my class. It mattered much more if they actually learned and retained the information and could produce results in a real-world situation. Many of my students, based on a single class, went on to successful Web design careers, and I'd like to think it was because the emphasis of my training was on practical results instead of grades.

Before you take a class, do a little research into the teaching methods of the teacher and see whether it fits your learning style. If it's possible, see if you can talk to other students who have taken the same class. There are lots of classes out there that aren't effective; it would be a shame to waste your time and money on one of them.

For a listing of schools and training resources, refer to Chapter 27, " Web Graphics Resources."

Teach Yourself!

Very few people who are good at their fields learned everything they know in school. That is especially true of the Web. Here are some resources and ideas to help teach yourself Web design and general design:

- Read Web design and development books—It's often hard to tell the good from the bad, so try to find a review before you buy! Many online book resellers offer reader-generated reviews of books. (I also offer many personal recommendations throughout chapters of *Designing Web Graphics.3*.)
- Reverse engineer sites—If you find a site you like, view the source code! Chapter 2, "HTML Editors," will teach you how.
- Web design magazines—See Chapter 27, "Web Graphics Resources."
- Online Web design and HTML resources—See Chapter 27, "Web Graphics Resources."
- Join UseNet groups or listservs.
- Attend conferences or take seminars.

Improve Your General Design Skills

- Read design books—Go to a bookstore and camp out in the design section, not the computer area!
- Read design magazines—See Chapter 27, "Web Graphics Resources."
- Attend design conferences or seminars.
- Join a design association like AIGA (http://www.aiga.org).
- Go to museums and galleries for inspiration.
- Find your muse—look to things in nature and life that inspire you artistically.

What Skills Are Important?

If you want to market yourself as a Web designer, you will find that almost every employer you talk to expects a different set of skills. At times, it will feel as if there is no end to what you need to know and learn in order to be marketable. In one sense, there is no end to what you could learn, but you do need to keep in mind that no one person can learn everything. So the question becomes, how high should you set your goals?

In my opinion, the following are skills that you will need day in and out as a Web designer: You might notice a similarity between these lists and several more chapter names in this book! :-)

Web Design Skills	
Core Skills	**Additional Skills**
Image Optimization	Storyboarding
Transparency	Flash
Background Tiles	Shockwave
Animation	Director
Layout	HTML
Color	DHTML
Type	JavaScript
Photoshop Layers	CSS
Alignment	

First Career Steps

Most first jobs in Web design are what I would label as "production" jobs. You might not get asked to do anything more creative than to mass produce a bunch of images to fit into someone else's design. I highly recommend that you take these first jobs in your stride and have patience in climbing the career ladder. You will get an education you couldn't find elsewhere.

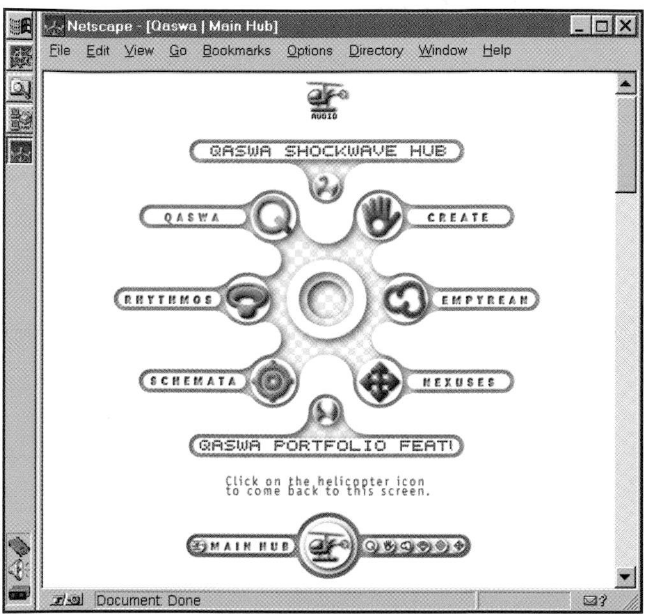

Ammon Haggerty owns his own Web design firm and creates some of the coolest Web graphics around. He started his career doing production grunt work, just like you probably will!

In my book *Deconstructing Web Graphics.2*, (co-written with Jon Warren Lentz), one of my favorite Web designers, Ammon Haggerty (http://www.qaswa.com), described his first job in multimedia design where he spent three months cutting masks in Photoshop. If you pay some dues doing grunt-like production work, you will share good company with many people like Ammon! It's a myth to think you will walk into the world and become a highly paid art director of a mainstream Web site.

The Importance of a Portfolio

Nothing is more important than a portfolio of examples to show a prospective employer. A good portfolio is more compelling than all the degrees and good grades the world has to offer. Building a portfolio can accomplish much more than good job prospects; it can also serve as an experimentation ground to teach yourself new skills.

As you read through this book, or browse the Web, you will likely get all kinds of neat ideas to try. Use your own Web site as a playground for exploring this field. An employer is going to like that you are a self-starter and that you possess initiative. There will be plenty of times in your professional life when you'll get asked to do something you've never done before. Start practicing this on your own first!

If you're interested in getting hired to design rollover buttons, be sure you have a lot of different rollover buttons on your Web site. If you want projects where you get to choose the colors, experiment with different color schemes to prove this is something you're good at. If you hone into what you like to do best, and make sure you have plenty of examples that promote that skill, your chances of being hired to do what you love are much greater.

In addition to publishing your own Web portfolio, nothing beats having real clients to list on a resume. If you are new at Web design, see if you can design a site for a friend, relative, local company, or non-profit cause. Even if it never gets published to a real working URL, it will show a future employer that you've worked with other people's needs and ideas, and that you have some real world experience.

Knowing What to Charge

I've heard of prices for Web site design ranging from $20 to 2 million. It can be that crazy; I swear! Of course, there are different levels of Web sites—the cost of a two- or three-page site versus that of a thousand-page site is obviously going to be different.

A huge number of factors go into pricing. If you are trying to get a job at a Web design firm, you will typically get the most money if you freelance and use your own computer. Of course, that is also the least secure method of employment! By accepting a salaried in-house position, you might make less but learn a lot more.

If you do plan to start your own company, there are lots of hidden costs. I always recommend that students get a job before they decide to start a business. You'll quickly see that there is a lot more to creating a successful company than knowing the technical or design side of Web publishing. Try adding accounting, bidding, public relations, marketing, advertising, office outfitting, business taxes, and health care costs to the list, and you'll start to get my drift!

It would be a big mistake for me to quote prices in this book because for every pricing rule, there will be always someone out there to break it. You will always have your big name Web design firms pricing their work higher than a new upstart company. You will always have famous illustrators who get paid more than recent art school graduates. There will always be inequities and a wide variation of pricing ranges.

If you're going to bid on building an entire site, it might help to know what other companies charge. **I**nternet **S**ervice **P**roviders (ISP) often double as Web design firms, and it's helpful to check out their pages to see what their pricing strategies are. Hint: They are often also a good source of work for freelance Web designers!

For an ISP list, check out http://thelist.internet.com/. It might help to find ISPs that are in your local area (or areas within which you'll be freelancing) to get a good idea of what pricing your specific market will bear.

In addition to knowing what the market rates are, it's important to understand and state your own boundaries. It's often not clear to clients that Web sites are "designed," "programmed," and "maintained." You must be very clear about what services you are providing for the money, or you may discover that their expectation of what you owed them was different than yours.

Legal contracts are a very good thing. Either invest in a lawyer to write up a contract template for you, or use those that are available from professional groups, such as the **Graphics Artists Guild** (http://www.gag.org) or the **HTML Writers Guild** (http://www.hwg.org/services/jc/).

When I ran my own freelance motion graphics design company before my daughter was born, I learned firsthand how tricky bidding could be. It helped that I had worked in the field for many years before going out on my own. I knew how long it would take me to finish a given task, and therefore knew how to charge so I'd be properly compensated. It took years of learning assessment skills to be good at my own business; some clients were easy, and others were a nightmare. So many factors go into bidding—it involves good people and negotiation skills in addition to good technical skills.

How to Find Jobs in Web Design

Often, the best way to find a job is first to find a Web design firm that you like. As you browse the Web, start visiting the "contact" or "credits" area of sites you like. Many sites post job listings or the name of the Human Resources contact.

You might also consider subscribing to a listserv related to Web design. Job listings are often posted, as well as invaluable tips and commentary about Web design. Important warning: If you do subscribe to a listserv, you can expect a lot (a lot) of extra email! A listserv is an email-based exchange to which many people subscribe. Some of these lists have thousands of subscribers, and hundreds of email messages are passed within a single day. You might consider subscribing to the archived versions of these lists or getting an email program that allows you to write filters so that the listserv email is stored separately from your personal email.

Favorite Web Design Listservs:
http://www.webmonster.net/lists
http://www.highfive.com/core/babble.html
http://www.wwwac.org/#mailing_list

Web/Design-based Headhunters:
http://www.wertco.com

Online Job Listings:
http://www.monster.com

It might also help to post your resume and portfolio to your own Web site. That way, you can list your URL at the bottom of a printed resume, and prospective employers can check you out online. This way, search engines can list your resume, too, if someone is doing a search for your specific skills. Which leads us directly to the next section...

tip

Pricing Resources

An established industry pricing resource can be purchased from the Graphics Artist Guild (http://www.gag.org):

Graphic Artist Guild Handbook: Pricing and Ethical Guidelines, 9th Edition
North Light Books
ISBN: 0-932102-09-3
$29.99

This book has historically set pricing guidelines for many areas of design, including print publications, merchandising, cartooning, animation, and technical illustration. They are starting to touch upon Web design pricing, but this area is still too new to have reliable guidelines.

You can also visit their Web site to learn about joining the Guild. They offer legal assistance for Web designers and other types of artists, as well as chapter meetings, newsletters, and Guild events.

Use Search Engines!

The Web has more information and leads than any other resource in the universe. Your key to locating information about jobs, tips, techniques, software, and hardware (and just about anything else in the universe!) can be found by using search engines.

Search engines are Web sites that offer URL listings to you based on keyword queries. In order to use a search engine, you must first understand that there are two different types of search engines: spider-based and directory-based.

A **spider-based search engine** gets its information from a software robot (also called a spider or crawler) that automatically visits and revisits Web sites and catalogues their contents. A **directory-based search engine** gets its information from submissions.

Search Engines		
Site	**Spider**	**Directory**
http://www.altavista.com	x	
http:/www.yahoo.com		x
http://www.hotbot.com	x	
http://www.excite.com	x	
http://www.lycos.com	x	
http://www.webcrawler.com	x	x

A spider-based search engine is good when you want to find every possible resource on a given subject. But sometimes, you'd rather find the information based on a more narrow search. For example, I used Alta Vista, a spider-based search engine to help my daughter research her bird report for school, which yielded a few hundred Web page addresses for us to choose from. When I went to research family vacations, however, Alta Vista would have yielded way too many results. I instead chose Yahoo, a directory-based search engine. I only saw family vacation listings from companies that had submitted their URLs to Yahoo, so there were less to choose from, and I had an easier decision.

In addition to knowing which type of search engine to use, it's also beneficial to know how to use a search engine. For example, when I typed Lynda Weinman into Alta Vista, the response yielded a whopping 47,905 results! Instead, if I put Lynda Weinman in quotes ("Lynda Weinman") or placed a plus sign (Lynda+Weinman), it yielded a more accurate result of 2,000 Web pages that included a reference to me.

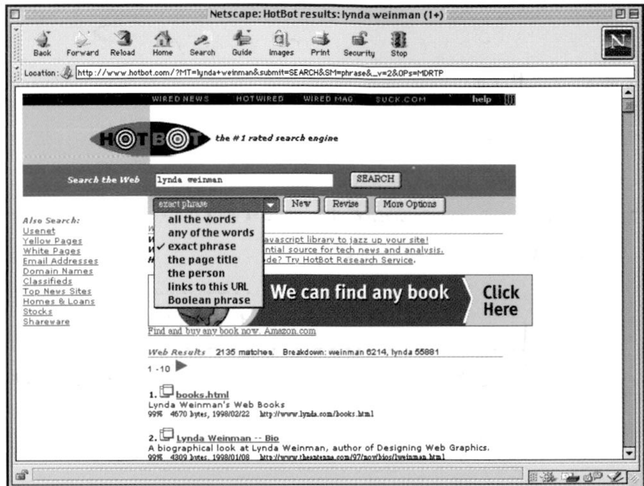

http://www.hotbot.com makes it easy to navigate through the use of a pull-down menu that offers search options.

If you'd like to learn how to use **search engines** (highly recommended!), visit these educational URLs:
http://searchenginewatch.internet.com/facts/powersearch.html
http://www.webreference.com/content/search

note

Don't Believe Everything...

With all this talk about search engines, I thought it might be important to point out that not all information on the Web is accurate or reliable. The Web reflects many societies and cultures, many viewpoints and ethics. Ya gotta be careful not to trust everything and browse the Web with a skeptical eye toward the truth. Don't believe everything you read.

Hardware Choices

In a day and age where each computer manufacturer is boasting faster, cheaper, and better computers than the next, you might wonder what type of system is suitable for your Web publishing and design needs. I might shock you to state that Web design is one of the least taxing activities you can perform on a personal computer. Of course, it's positively dreamy to work on a fast machine loaded with RAM and hard disk space, but truth must be known that a high-end system is not necessary.

Macs and PCs are going to have the widest range of Web-design tools. Most of your Web audience will be on Macs or PCs. So, even if you're lucky enough to work on a high-end UNIX platform, you might consider getting one of these lower-end platforms to author Web pages. At the very least, it will give you a reality checkpoint.

Which Flavor: Macintosh or Windows?

Chances are, you already have a computer. If you don't and are considering getting one to use for Web design, then you have a challenging decision to make. Be forewarned that this is a topic of great passion and controversy. This subject is known to stir up more trouble than a political or religious debate. On the other hand, many people do regard this subject as sacred as religion!

Macs Versus PCs

Let me first state my own bias clearly. My first computer was an Apple II+ running CPM. My second computer was a Macintosh that I bought in May 1984. I bought my first PC in 1995, and currently own numerous Macs and PCs. (I'm a computer packrat; why sell 'em when the old ones aren't worth anything?)

My bias is toward graphics and design (probably obvious to you), and I have taught design professionals for the past nine years mostly using Macintosh computers. Most design professionals who have been into digital imaging for very long own Macintoshes because it used to be that it was the only computer platform that supported graphics. This is no longer true, though there is still a huge user base of Macintosh loyalists who grew up using their Macs and don't have any desire to switch to Windows.

This has created a great irony in Web design: Many professional Web designers and art directors use Macs, but most of the audience they design for is on PCs. I am not suggesting that you buy a Mac instead of a PC, or that PCs are inferior. I am simply stating that for historical reasons, more visual designers use Macs.

It is a fact that there are many more PCs in circulation than Macs, and most of your audience will likely be using PCs. So, if you want to see your Web site as most of your audience will see it, you will want to consider owning a PC. I think it's beneficial to have both platforms if at all possible. Virtually all professional Web design firms and many independent Web designers have both. Even if you buy one state-of-the art computer for work and a used, older computer for testing, you'll be in better shape than if you only own one platform.

Some Mac Advantages

You'll find that the majority of design-based software comes out on the Mac and the PC. Even so, most service bureaus that deal with desktop publishing are biased toward Macs, not PCs. Most likely, you'll find more support among other artists and designers if you are on a Mac.

Some PC Advantages

Most end users are on PCs. Most browser software comes out first for the PC, and often never fully supports the Mac. The PC has a bigger market share than the Mac, so equipment and peripherals are often less expensive. If you're technically inclined, you can build your own PC much easier than you can a Mac. This can not only save you money, but it allows you to put your resources into the aspects of the computer that are most important to you.

Which Platform Is Best?

There is truly no wrong or right platform. Regardless of which platform you buy, you will be able to design Web pages. I strongly suggest that you try out the software and equipment you want to get before you buy it. Ask around. Find sites that you admire and ask the developers what equipment and software they recommend. There's no wrong decision here; just make sure your choice fits your budget, needs, and style.

It's always important to check your site on platforms other than that from which you authored. If you are lucky enough to own two platforms, this can be done in the luxury of your own office, studio, or home. If not, make sure you locate another system where you can preview your site. As future chapters describe in detail, what you see on one platform isn't necessarily what you see on others. This is a universal problem that you will encounter, regardless of which platform you decide to own.

System Requirements

The key components of a computer system are processor speed, RAM, hard disk, video and sound cards, monitor, CD-ROM drive, modem, and scanner. I have evaluated their importance for Web authoring in the following list:

Processor speed: These days, we often hear about fast processor speeds, sometimes even in excess of 500 megahertz. How important a factor is processing speed in terms of Web design? Not very. Processing speed helps with 3D graphics rendering and the speed of rendering television or film-sized movies. It really helps when you're working with a huge, high-resolution image that's being prepped for printing. Making images for the Web requires that you work with low resolution. Processing speed helps with complex, math-intensive computer operations. Unless you are planning to use your computer for those types of projects in addition to Web design, a fast processor is going to buy you very little advantages.

RAM: Most computer veterans will assure you that you can never have too much **RAM** (**R**andom **A**ccess **M**emory). Extra RAM means that you can run simultaneous applications and with less likelihood of crashing. It lets you keep an HTML editor, imaging program, and Web browser open at the same time. This will save you more time (and isn't your time worth money too?) than you may imagine. Never skimp on RAM if you can possibly avoid it. Try to get at least 64mb and more if possible. Seriously, you can never have too much RAM! Many Web browsers require a minimum of 16 to run at all, and imaging software (especially Photoshop!) requires even more.

Hard disk(s): This is the other resource you can never have too much of. I highly recommend getting a removable storage system in addition to a permanent hard drive. Iomega (www.iomega.com) makes two excellent removable drive systems: Zip drives (100mb) are great and Jaz drives (1gb) are even greater! If you are going to be working regularly with a computer service bureau or outside company sharing files, be sure to see what they have so your removable storage system is compatible with theirs.

Video card: Most computer systems ship with a video card pre-installed. For this reason, many new computer buyers aren't even aware of their video card's features or capabilities. The video card is what dictates how many colors your monitor can display. Most of the Web audience will have 8-bit color (256 color) or less (more about this in Chapter 7, "Color Calibration Issues"). Images look much better with millions (24-bit) or thousands (16-bit) of color displays. If possible, go for a card with the highest bit depth (24-bit). This allows you to design for everyone—those with the lowest and highest common denominators. Sometimes, it's possible to own a card that can be upgraded with additional video RAM (V-RAM) to upgrade its bit-depth capabilities. If you don't know how to check your video card's bit depth, Chapter 4, "Web Authoring Environment," will show you how.

Sound card: If you plan to work with sound, you will need a sound card. Again, many contemporary computers ship with these cards built in. The Web today offers mostly 8-bit sound because the files are smaller and faster to download. Just like with video, you'll get better results if you start with the highest quality and downscale for your audience later.

Monitor: The majority of your audience will be on standard 12–13" monitors or 640×480 (that's the number of pixels) monitors. Even though we recommend that you design your site to work within a small screen (more on this in Chapter 16, "Tables & Alignment"), it's much easier to design on a larger monitor because you have more room for all the menus, windows, and palettes that most popular imaging programs sport these days. Almost any kind of monitor will do (make sure it will work with the kind of video card you get), but bigger is better for ease of use with design.

CD-ROM drive: A lot of software these days ships on CDs, which makes owning a CD-ROM drive a necessity. Installing software off a CD-ROM is very handy, but if you're using your CD-ROM drive for this purpose only, speed doesn't matter much. If you're going to play games or look at CD-ROM titles, however, you'll want 4X speed at the very least. (Fortunately, 8X and faster CD-ROM drives are available for less than $100 as of this writing.) Since most CD drives are now faster than that, speed is probably not a problem.

Modem: Picking a modem is often based on price versus performance. I suggest you choose one based on the latter and not the former. The faster, the better. If you're uploading files to a Web site, you will be grateful to transfer at the fastest possible speed. Getting a high-speed modem is not something to skimp on if you're planning on doing this kind of work seriously. You might also consider ISDN or a cable modem if your community supports it. Though more expensive than the standard modem solution, if your time is worth money, then this solution might be more economical in the long run.

Scanner: Because you'll be working with low-resolution imagery, dots per inch and image quality are not your primary considerations when choosing a scanner for Web design. Speed is the primary concern, so pick a scanner that can scan in color quickly. I used to own a multiple-pass scanner, which would take separate scans for each color channel: red, green, and blue. I finally broke down and got a one-pass scanner, and the time savings is worth every penny that I spent on it. For the resolution of Web images, speed is the only factor that will make any difference in your production flow.

tip

Shop for Discounts!

You may be frightened off by the prices of software, but don't pay retail! Look into the many mail order catalogs for great discounts. Some of these catalogs have online resources as well:

Surplus Direct
http://www.surplusdirect.com/

Mac Zone
http://www.zones.com/Mac_Zone/Default_Mac.htm

PC Zone
http://www.zones.com/pc_zone/default_PC.htm

Also, if you take a class in Photoshop, sometimes you can get an impressive student discount. It might just cover the expense of the class and the software! Before you enroll, be sure to see if the school of your choice sells student-priced software and if you qualify.

Software

Software is a huge part of your investment in a Web design studio, both in terms of money and time. If you haven't been around computers long, you might not realize that software changes all the time. If you buy version 1.0, next year you'll have to decide whether or not to upgrade to version 2.0, and that process will go on for years and years.

The truth about software is that it almost always improves with future versions. You may get along just fine with a version of software that you already own and decide against upgrading even if there are improvements. The point is that software is fluid by nature. If it stayed the same, we would complain. It doesn't make for the most comfortable purchasing decisions, however!

How many other professions or hobbies do you know of where the tools change and evolve constantly? You can bemoan this fact, or embrace it. If you plan to participate in the digital arts, though, changing software is a fact of life.

There are three categories of software: commercial software that you buy in the store, free software that you download off the Net, and shareware that you download today and pay for tomorrow (http://www.shareware.com is a great place to start).

Most likely, you will have to buy software sooner or later, even though at times it seems that everything anyone would ever want is found on the Web. The next section lists resources, makes recommendations, and helps you weigh some of these challenging software decisions.

Imaging Programs

To create graphics for the Web, you need some image-making software. This book concentrates primarily on Photoshop, Paint Shop Pro, ImageReady, and Fireworks techniques. The Web has brought about a new era in software publishing since most Web imaging editors offer free trial versions from their Web sites. This makes it possible for you to try tools before you buy them. Those of us who have been into computing since before the WWW really appreciate this fact, as I'm sure any newcomer will as well.

Adobe Photoshop (http://www.adobe.com) is the most popular imaging software among professional designers on any platform for almost any purpose—not just Web design. Not surprisingly, Photoshop also has the most depth and features of all the imaging software reviewed in this book. I primarily use Photoshop, and this book is weighted in its favor. This book will show examples using Photoshop 5.0, though many exercises will work on older versions of Photoshop as well.

Paint Shop Pro (http://www.jasc.com) is available as shareware and is one of the better all-around imaging programs available outside of Adobe Photoshop. It has many of the same features as Photoshop, such as layers and filters, and is a fraction of the price. Still, most professionals use Photoshop, and if you're looking to find a job or interface with other artists, you might not find as many prospects with this solution.

ImageReady (http://www.adobe.com) is a new software tool that looks and feels like Photoshop, only is geared toward Web and screen-based imaging instead of print-based imaging. You can download a trial demo version from their site.

Fireworks (http://www.macromedia.com) is another new Web graphics software package that is a very strong image editor which uses vectors and bitmaps to do the job. It also writes JavaScript rollovers and includes image optimization features. You can download a trial demo version from their site.

Of course, other software tools will be mentioned in other chapters in this book, and tips, techniques, and training resources will be listed then. A discussion of HTML editors is found in Chapter 2, "HTML Editors."

summary Getting Started

Getting started in Web design can present an overwhelming number of decisions and choices. This chapter focused on some guidelines to help you make those decisions. To summarize, these were the key points:

- If you're going to purchase formal training, make sure the class you choose best fits your personal learning style.
- Most great Web designers are self taught in one area or another. Learning to teach yourself is a key skill in this field.
- A Web-based portfolio is more important than any grade, degree, or certification.
- Web sites are not created equally; you'll find different pricing strategies for different types of sites.
- It's best to own a Mac and PC for authoring Web pages and for checking compatibility.
- Try out software before you buy it by visiting software company's Web sites and downloading trial versions of their software.

HTML Editors

Introduction

Chapter Topics

- What Is HTML?
- HTML Versus Design
- Should You Learn HTML?
- WYSIWYG Editors
- HTML Terminology Explained
- Choosing an HTML Editor

2

I am devoting an entire chapter in this book to HTML and HTML editors because these issues are as critical to a Web designer's livelihood as choosing the right image editor or hardware platform. I often get asked the questions "Do I really need to learn HTML?," "If so, can I use an HTML editor?," and "Which editor should I buy?" Unfortunately, there are no simple or universal answers to any of these questions.

There are two camps of people who are reading this book: those who are just starting out and those who have been blazing trails in HTML and Web publishing for a few years. Most Web designers, regardless of skill or experience level, will find valuable information in this chapter. I find that most people who already know HTML still have lots more to learn about it, and those who are just getting started have many confusing decisions to make.

Deciding "how much HTML to learn" and which, if any, HTML editor to use is a choice you will not know how to make without understanding a few of the issues this chapter covers. Inside, you'll find a short synopsis of HTML, an explanation of why HTML is counter–intuitive to design, an overview of the language, a debate about whether to learn to code from scratch or not, tips and resources about how to learn HTML, and an overview of HTML editors.

HTML in a Graphics Book?

At this point, some of you might be wondering why this book need contain any discussion of HTML at all. Didn't you buy this book because you wanted to understand how to make graphics for the Web?

Well, for the moment, HTML and graphics are inextricably joined at the hip. If all you learned was HTML, you would have boring text-laden pages that contained no images. If all you learned about was Web graphics, you'd have no understanding of how to incorporate them into a Web page without HTML.

HTML is one of those necessary evils in life. Some people love programming, but I am not one of them. I am as anxious as the next person to see HTML disappear into history as part of the early playing curve of Web publishing. Those days aren't here yet, however, so if ya wanna play today, ya gotta deal with the beast. Most people don't find HTML difficult to learn; I swear!

What Is HTML?

HTML stands for **H**yper**T**ext **M**arkup **L**anguage, and breaking apart the acronym somewhat explains its meaning:

Hypertext is one of the most revolutionary things about the Web. It is what enables Web pages to contain links, which when clicked on, take you to other Web pages, sites, or parts of a single Web page. Even though the word Hypertext is used, its meaning pertains to visuals whenever a graphic contains a link.

Markup stands for marking up how the Web page content will look. In HTML, this markup is accomplished with the use of bracketed tags that define how something is displayed. For example, in HTML, if I write <STRONG>This is cool!</STRONG>, the words "This is cool" will appear inside a Web browser in bold. The markup tag <STRONG> is what instructed the browser to alter the appearance of the words.

Back when I started using computers in the early 1980s, there was no such thing as a WYSIWYG (**W**hat**Y**ou**S**ee**I**s**W**hat**Y**ou**G**et) word processor. Computer programs and monitors couldn't even display bolded text! You would mark up things like italics, bold, and underlined text in your word processing document with tags that closely resemble HTML tags today, and when the document would print you would see the formatting results. Hard to believe HTML has thrown us backward in time a couple of decades, but after reading the next section perhaps you'll be more forgiving of that.

The **Language** element of the HTML acronym is the only part that doesn't really make sense since HTML is really not a programming language at all. Most computer languages are capable of writing programs, and Web pages are not programs. The HTML language simply defines the syntax of how to format a Web document.

HTML has grown well beyond its earliest specifications, and Web pages have grown in complexity as a result. Today you'll hear about a lot more than just HTML, but this is the starting point of Web publishing regardless.

Why Is HTML So Troublesome for Design?

For starters, it's important to understand that HTML was not created to be a design language, which would offer precise control over presentation of content. It was created as a display language, with the intent that results might display differently on different machines and operating systems. Ever notice how browser software enables you to change your fonts and their sizes, and whether images and links are turned on or off? HTML was supposed to be a transportable language that could be customized to the end user's liking.

This is a good and bad thing. The fact that Web pages are customizable is precisely what makes it a global communication medium. It enables blind people to have pages "read" to them through automatic processors and people with poor vision or large monitors to increase the size of their fonts. It also enables different computer platforms to view the same content, and it provides automatic translation capabilities from English to other languages.

In my early days of exposure to HTML, I used to wonder why anyone ever developed such a dumb programming language for designers. This attitude reflected my ignorance about what the role of HTML was in relation to the goals of the Web. I now understand and respect the trade-off that HTML affords because I understand its need to be flexible.

I am a Web publisher because I love the fact that I, as an individual, can publish content for a wider audience than any other publishing medium in history. In order to accomplish this goal, the language with which Web pages are created has to make very few assumptions about its audience, as it must support as many platforms, foreign languages, hardware restrictions, and end users as possible.

I recognize that HTML is counterproductive for many design tasks. Part of what compels me to write about this medium is to help people figure out ways to turn those limits into opportunities for creativity and expression. At its heart, effective design should aid communication. Design and accessibility can be combined in harmony, but not without extra education and effort on the part of designers and programmers.

If you, like me, understand that the Web must stay accessible in order to thrive and evolve, then you might be more forgiving of HTML's limits. My philosophy is to embrace the medium for what it is, and take the challenge to work with its quirks and shortcomings, because the end result is worth the effort.

Whenever I lecture in public, I often say that the Web is the largest beta software experiment unleashed upon the public in the history of computing. It's important, in my opinion, to recognize that today's Web publishers are participating in the infancy of an important communication medium. HTML is one of the casualties of the grand experiment. It's weird, it's foreign, it's frustrating, and it's limiting, but HTML is here to stay for a while, and without it we wouldn't have the Web we know today.

Should You Learn HTML?

If you never "wanted to be a computer programmer" when you grew up, and the idea of writing HTML is intimidating, unappealing, or just plain loathsome to you, the Web might be a good reason to change your attitude. HTML is a bit of a nuisance, but it isn't nearly as difficult as learning a real programming language. The rewards are much greater than the pain; I promise.

If you compare the Web to the early days of desktop publishing, HTML is a lot like the PostScript language. You used to have to write in PostScript to produce computer typesetting. Today, we have programs like QuarkXPress and PageMaker, which write PostScript behind the scenes, without ever seeing the code or even needing to know it exists. No one, except a die-hard PostScript programmer, would need or want to learn to write PostScript today.

So how is HTML any different from yesterday's PostScript? Because up until recently, HTML has gone through several iterations and revisions, and PostScript is a stable programming language that works for any PostScript-enabled imaging device.

In the few short years I've been involved with the Web, HTML has gone through massive changes. Some of these changes were sanctioned by the **W3C** (**W**orld **W**ide **W**eb **C**onsortium—the official standards committee for the Web), but many were not. Browser vendors such as Mosaic, Netscape, and Microsoft have actually changed the course of HTML development by introducing proprietary enhancements to the code. For these reasons, HTML cannot be compared to PostScript or any other programming or markup language because it is still in development.

So, am I saying that to be a Web publisher today that you must learn HTML? Yes and no. Frankly, some of the best Web sites I've ever seen were developed by artists who didn't understand a line of HTML code and who teamed up with an HTML programmer. It is possible to divide the line and leave art to artists and code to programmers. You may fall into the camp of artists who don't want to learn HTML, and that is totally valid. Just be forewarned—you will feel powerless, and you will not like the feeling.

Is there a middle ground? Yes, and it is discussed later in this chapter in the "HTML Editors" section. These software programs write HTML invisibly, just like QuarkXPress and PageMaker write PostScript, and you don't have to understand a line of code to use them. I still issue the same warning, however; if you don't learn the basics of HTML, you will at times feel powerless and you will not like the feeling.

Most artists, by definition, are control freaks. We like to pick the exact right color, make the exact right shape, see the exact right layout. Throughout this book, I will discuss when HTML affords this type of exacting precision and when to give up on the control freak stuff.

Their are a few major penalties one suffers to skimp on an HTML education. The first is that someone else will be in the position to tell you whether you can or cannot do certain effects, and you will probably regard them suspiciously. The other is that if you are called upon to troubleshoot something you have designed, you will not know how. This could cause you to lose credibility in a work situation, or could simply result in being frustrating to you. If you have the time and inclination, you should at the very least get comfortable viewing HTML code and understand its basic structure.

How to Learn HTML

There are a many ways to learn HTML, and many great resources exist online. You will find a list of them in this chapter and in the Web Design Resource Appendix at the back of the book.

The View Source command, which is found within most browsers should be your premiere guide. If you like something you see on the Web, view its source code. You can copy and paste someone else's source code into your own word processor or HTML editor. This is done all the time, and is not frowned upon by the Web authoring community. In fact, most of the HTML jockeys I've met tell me this is exactly how they taught themselves the markup language.

Studying HTML may seem intimidating. But most people will find it is very simple to learn the basics. It's not necessary to write every line of code by hand, but if you learn to write a little, it will help your comprehension of the more difficult programming tasks.

HTML can be written in a simple word processor or in a dedicated HTML or WYSIWYG editor. The key to writing HTML is that it must be saved in ASCII format (text only mode) and include the file extension .html or .htm (either will work). The Windows file management cannot store four-letter extensions, which is why .htm is used on many Web pages.

tip

Shameless Self Promotion

Frankly, I didn't wholeheartedly like any of the HTML books out there, so I enlisted my programmer brother to coauthor one with me. Our book is much like a class, which walks readers through hands-on exercises and contains all the necessary course materials on the CD-ROM.

My book agent, David Rogelberg, calls this book a reftorial—because it is half reference book and half tutorial. Our book covers many topics, including how to fix bad WYSIWYG HTML editor generated code, a full HTML 4.0 reference of tags and attributes, and many design tips.

Creative HTML Design
Lynda & William Weinman
New Riders
ISBN: 1-56205-704-9
$39.99

If you want to check out the book and read a sample chapter, check out http://www.htmlbook.com.

Online HTML References

As well as the View Source trick, and reading a book, there are plenty of fantastic online resources for learning HTML. Here is a list of some of my favorites:

NCSA: A Beginner's Guide to HTML Home Page
http://www.ncsa.uiuc.edu/General/Internet/WWW/HTMLPrimer.html

HTML: An Interactive Tutorial for Beginners
http://www.davesite.com/webstation/html/

The WDVL: HTML—The Hypertext Markup Language
http://www.stars.com/Tutorial/HTML/

Webmonkey: An HTML Tutorial
http://www.hotwired.com/webmonkey/teachingtool/index.html

NCDesign: An HTML Design Guide v4.0
http://www.ncdesign.org/html/

Index DOT HTML: The Advanced HTML Reference
http://home.webmonster.net/mirrors/bloo-html/

HTML Writer's Guild: A resource list
http://www.hwg.org/resources/html/intros.html

Important HTML Terms

When I first learned HTML, I thought everything inside the brackets was called a tag. When I wrote *Creative HTML Design*, my coauthor (brother William Weinman) corrected me. If you want to know how to speak about HTML properly, here's a handy terminology list:

Tag: Everything between the "<" and ">" symbols. For example, <FONT> is a tag.

Container: Some tags require containers, also known as closing tags. For example, <FONT> requires the closing tag </FONT>, known as a container.

Content: Everything that falls between the open and close tags of an HTML document is called content.

Attribute: An attribute is a modifier to a tag. In the example <FONT FACE= "verdana">, FONT is the tag and FACE is the attribute.

Value: A value usually follows an attribute. In the example <FONT FACE= "verdana">, the above, "verdana" is the value of the attribute.

Element: An element describes a collection of tags, attributes, values, and/or containers. For example, the entire string "<FONT FACE="verdana">" is called an element.

What Does HTML Look Like?

HTML is a markup language that has a pretty simple structure. Here is a very basic example, with key elements that you should understand:

code

```
1 <HTML>
2 <HEAD>
3 <TITLE>name_of_document
4 </TITLE>
5 </HEAD>
6 <BODY>The stuff that goes on the page goes inside the body tag.
7 </BODY>
8 </HTML>
```

code deconstruction

1. All HTML documents must begin with the HTML tag.

2. The HEAD of the document contains all of the header information.

3. The TITLE element contains the name of the document, which will appear at the top of the browser window.

4. It's necessary to close the TITLE tag, which is indicated by the slash.

5. It's always necessary to close the HEAD tag, which is indicated by the slash.

6. Everything that is visible inside the HTML document is inside the BODY tag.

7. Ya gotta close the BODY tag.

8. And ya gotta close the HTML tag, too.

Of course, there are lots and lots of other tags, attributes, and values for an HTML document. This book will cover many of them in its later chapters. This is just the absolute, most-basic page you could ask for, just to show you that it is pretty understandable if you break it down in simple chunks.

HTML Editors

There might come a day when understanding HTML is not critical to creating Web pages. That day is already here if you are a casual Web publisher and don't want to exercise a great deal of control over the look and feel of your content. My father, for example, has a Web page. He didn't care about learning HTML, making his own graphics or anything beyond putting his content online (favorite TV shows, political rants, news about his cat and granddaughter, etc.). Using an HTML editor was the perfect choice for him to create a Web page, and I don't think he really needed to care much about HTML at all to do so.

There are all types of HTML editors—from the type that would satisfy my father to the type that would satisfy the most persnickety programmer. As mentioned earlier, some types of HTML editors allow you to work in a WYSIWYG (**W**hat**Y**ou**S**ee**I**s**W**hat**Y**ou**G**et) mode. This means that you can type directly in the editor and instead of seeing HTML code, you'll see whatever you typed. These types of editors give you the freedom to change a font style, font size, or alignment, or drag and drop images into position. If you view the source code the WYSIWYG editor produced, it will show all the HTML elements that were hidden from your view.

There are disadvantages and advantages to using HTML editors. When I taught full-time at Art Center College of Design, I used to forbid my students to use HTML editors until a few weeks had passed so they could learn to code by hand. This wasn't because I don't think HTML editors are great; I do, and I use them all the time! It was because editors shield you from the HTML learning process, and I think it's important to understand the process before turning it over to an editor. Even the best editors at times require troubleshooting, and you will be powerless to do so if you don't understand what you're doing.

Another disadvantage to HTML editors is that things change quickly in this industry, and sometimes they do not keep pace. You want to make sure you know how to add to your code in the event you want to implement a new technique or technology. The other bummer about HTML editors is their tendency to add proprietary tags, which have no use other than to the editing program itself. HTML is getting more strict than it used to be, some of these proprietary tags may not fly in the future.

There are many varieties of WYSIWYG editors. Some are consumer-oriented and some professional. We're entering an era of second- and third-generation HTML editors, so the software is improving and bending to the needs of ever changing specifications. I'll put it this way, it has only been recently that I could recommend these types of editors at all. The early versions were too immature to be very useful. If you tried an HTML editor a few years ago and threw your hands up in disgust, try some of the new breeds. They are much better than they used to be.

The advantages of using an editor are profound. Editors can be a tremendous timesaver, allowing artists and non-programmers to easily mock up pages and get ideas out quickly. Then there are those people who just don't want to learn HTML or can't. Your ability to learn HTML has less to do with your intelligence than your aptitude for this task. I know many bona fide brilliant individuals who cannot make their minds think in HTML. Why should they have to? They don't.

That said, the next question to ask is what type of HTML editor best suits your needs. Some are good for designing individual pages, others for site management, and still others for advanced design with DHTML using JavaScript, CSS, and/or Object Models.

tip Try Before You Buy!

One of the best things about most HTML editors is that you can typically download demo versions to "try before you buy." I highly recommend that you do this to ensure that the editor meets your needs. Often, the HTML editor's site has lots of very helpful tutorials, and sometimes even user groups that offer email-based subscription lists.

GoLive
http://www.golive.com

Dreamweaver
http://www.dreamweaver.com/

Claris Home Page
http://www.filemaker.com/products/homepage3.html

BBEDIT
http://web.barebones.com/products/bbedit/bbedit.html"

Homesite
http://www.allaire.com/products/HOMESITE

FrontPage
http://www.microsoft.com/frontpage/default.htm

PageMill
http://www.adobe.com

NetObjects Fusion
http://www.netobjects.com

HTML Editing Features

Deciding on HTML software has everything to do with the scale and scope of your Web site, your budget, your programming aptitude (or lack thereof), and your expectations. I am not going to recommend any specific software because everyone's needs will be different. Instead, I thought it would be helpful to outline some features, and then you can pick an HTML editor that contains the features you want.

Roundtrip HTML: The term "roundtrip" HTML was coined by the Macromedia's Dreamweaver product team. It means that the HTML editor writes HTML without adding any of its own proprietary tags. One of the dangers of using an HTML editor is the fact that it adds its own code to the HTML. In many HTML editors, if you remove the proprietary tags, and then re-import the files for maintenance or changes, the program will re-insert them! Roundtrip HTML means the code stays like you typed it, regardless of whether you save the file and re-import it.

DHTML (Dynamic **HTML):** A collection of technologies that work together to produce more interactivity and dynamic content than HTML alone can offer. It usually involves the use of HTML 4.0, CSS, JavaScript and a document object model (DOM). HTML 4.0 is the most current specification for HTML (as of when this book was written!), and DOM can mean the additional use of plug-ins or other types of scripting languages (such as ActiveX or VBasic.)

CSS (Cascading **S**tyle **S**heets**):** Cascading Style Sheets are used for specifying specific layout properties, such as font size, font family, leading, indents, and much more. Individual style sheets can be included in individual Web pages, or a Web site can reference a single CSS document. (More about this in Chapter 19, "Cascading Style Sheets.") Some HTML editors support the creation of CSS, although this is usually reserved for high-end, professional HTML editors.

JavaScript support: JavaScript is a scripting language that extends the capabilities of HTML. Popular uses of JavaScript include rollovers, specifically sized browser windows, and browser detection. (More on JavasScript can be found in Chapter 22, "JavaScript: Rollovers & More.") Some HTML editors support the capability to add or append a JavaScript, while others actually write Java-Script functions. These features are usually found in high-end and professional HTML editors.

Plug-In support: Plug-ins are separate files that must be installed in a browser in order for plug-in content to be visible. Common plug-ins that you might be familiar with include RealAudio, Flash, and Shockwave. (More information on plug-ins is in Chapter 25, "Flash & Shockwave.") Some HTML editors don't support the capability to code plug-in content, but most professional-level editors do.

Frames: Frames create regions of a Web page that are stationary while other regions can change. If you plan to use frames, I highly recommend that you test the HTML editor for this feature before you buy it. Many HTML editors handle frames poorly, meaning that they are difficult to previsualize and set up. More information about frames can be found in Chapter 18, "Frames."

Fonts: Just about all HTML editors allow you to set fonts, and change size and style. This is standard fare. More information about font tags and workarounds are in Chapter 16, "Web Typography."

Alignment: Some HTML editors are better at alignment than others; again, it's always best to try before you buy! More information about alignment can be found in Chapter 17, "Alignment & Tables" and Chapter 18, "Frames."

Tables: Tables are very important for layout and images, and some HTML editors create tables better than others. More information about tables can be found in Chapter 17, "Alignment & Tables."

Site management: Some HTML editors will include site management features. This is extremely handy, since you can typically change a link and the change will ripple through your site.

Database integration: Some HTML editors interface well with databases. If you plan to run your site using a database, this should be a consideration.

Button rollovers: The latest and greatest HTML editors will write JavaScript rollovers for you.

Browser conversion: Some HTML editors will convert pages that utilize DHTML and CSS to alternative pages that use HTML that is supported by earlier browsers.

Browser Feature Comparison Chart								
	Go Live	**Dreamweaver**	**Claris**	**BBEDIT**	**Homesite**	**FrontPage**	**PageMill**	**NetObjects Fusion**
Roundtrip HTML		X		X	X			
DHTML	X	X						X
CSS	X	X		X				X
JavaScript Support	X	X				X		X
Plug-In Support	X	X	X				X	X
Frames	X	X	X			X	X	X
Site Management	X	X						X
Database Integration	X	X				X		X
Button Rollovers	X	X						X
Browser Conversion	X	X						X
Platform	M	M,W	M,W	M	W	M,W	M,W	M,W

summary HTML Editors

This chapter reviewed many of the issues surrounding HTML and HTML editors. Here's a synopsis:

- HTML makes it difficult to control exacting design because it was developed to be accessible to many computer platforms, languages, and devices.
- It's best to understand the basics of HTML so that you will be able to troubleshoot problems if and when they arise.
- If you plan to use an HTML editor, try it before you buy it. This chapter contains many URLs for HTML editing software.
- There is no best HTML editor, just ones that are best for you and your needs. Read up on the features to help you decide which one is right for you.

Strategy Introduction

Chapter Topics

- Defining Your Goals
- Storyboarding
- Flowcharting
- Brainstorming
- Navigation Approaches
- Site Structure
- Metaphors

3

In previous editions of this book, I didn't have a strategy chapter. With the Web's growing maturity, however, the need for a strategy is not only more obvious, but more necessary. Developing a strategy involves defining your goals, your audience, your limitations, and your methodologies.

This chapter focuses on how you can develop a strategy that fits your Web development needs. We will look at planning, storyboarding, establishing goals, as well as design themes and how to profile your user. By answering certain questions and developing a plan at the front end, you can save yourself a lot of catch-up work down the road.

Strategies are as varied as types of Web sites, which include vanity, educational, experimental, entertainment, commercial, and information-based sites, as well as many hybrid combinations thereof. The truth is, there is no one correct method for developing a strategy. And, as strange as it might sound, there is danger in developing a strategy that is too rigid. Web sites evolve; it is the nature of this medium. If you control your plan too tightly, those happy accidents that befall most of us at times won't have the opportunity to happen.

This chapter will expose you to the issues at the heart of Web site planning, without pushing inflexible rules that might not match the needs or goals of your site. It's important for you to understand that there are too many types of sites to apply one set formula to all of them.

First Steps

It might seem obvious, but the first step toward developing a Web-site strategy involves answering a few practical questions:

- Who is my target audience?
- What does the site need to communicate?
- Does my client have any special goals or needs?
- Have I asked my client what sites he or she likes and why?
- What is the scope of my site?
- Is there print material I can match or borrow from?
- What other sites are similar to mine in scope and intent?

The answers to these questions will provide a road map for you to follow that could not be achieved in any other manner. Let's break apart the questions and weigh some of the solutions.

Target Audience: Do you have a narrow audience or a broad audience? My husband Bruce, for example, is a professional illustrator. His Web site (http://www.stink.com) is geared toward promoting his work to sell to art directors. He can assume that art directors have nice systems with more than standard amounts of RAM, larger than usual monitors, and full-color displays. They might be willing to download a plug-in or wait a little longer for a large image to appear. Contrast this with one of my students who was the Web designer for the Library of Congress (http://www.loc.gov). Her government agency had mandated that over the next three years, all the images in their collection must be available online. Her audience is quite a bit broader than my husband's. You might imagine that keeping her site accessible to everyone is key to the goals and intent of her site.

Communication Goals: Some sites want nothing more than to spread the good name of their product. Levi's Web site (http://www.levi.com), for example, is not a place where you can buy blue jeans; instead, it sets a tone, ambience, and point-of-view, just like a television commercial might. On the other hand, if you go to Amazon's site (http://www.amazon.com), you'll see that their goal is to sell books. They aren't pushing any one aesthetic or impressing you with their good humor. It serves their site well not to have a personality, but to be neutral to ensure that anyone who visits the site will feel comfortable and included.

Helpful Links:
http://info.med.yale.edu/caim/manual/intro/purpose.html
http://wwwwseast2.usec.sun.com/styleguide/tables/Purposes.html
http://www.ibm.com/ibm/hci/guidelines/web/web_guidelines.html

Client's Needs: If you have a client (I realize some of you are your own clients!), it really pays to listen carefully to what he or she wants. Sounds obvious again, but you'd be amazed at how many firms and individual designers complete an entire Web site that didn't address what the client really wanted. It pays to ask a lot of questions of your client and to listen carefully to the answers. I can't tell you how many times I've heard a Web designer complain that the client wanted something that he or she didn't understand about in advance. Figure this out at the front end, not when the site is finished and you're seething mad because you have to make major changes at no charge. And leave your design ego at the door. Sometimes clients make really dumb choices, but they do hold the purse strings. Unreasonable clients are sometimes part of the reality of this business, and your ability to deal with it is a component of your success. Not everyone is lucky enough to have ideal clients all the time. If you're in this business, it's often your job to educate your bosses and clients because they are probably even more new to this Web stuff than you are!

Client's Favorites: Ask your client (if you have one) to submit a list of his or her favorite sites. Spend some time going through them with the client, and ask a lot of questions along the way. Figure out why he or she likes and dislikes certain sites and features. It will give you valuable information about how to structure your own work so it meets your client's expectations and taste.

Site Scope: Defining your scope is tricky, but very important. Do you want to educate, entertain, create interaction, distribute information, collect information, or support commerce? This step is similar to defining the site's goals, but it has more to do with services offered than visual design. Are you going to need a guest book, a database, a shopping cart, a listserv, an email contact form, or frames? You may not be able to answer these questions if you're brand new to Web design, but if you can plan ahead, it will help you build the correct team and estimate your time much better.

Be User-Centric, not Designer-Centric: Equally important to your goals are the goals of your users. Many developers often overlook this, which can ultimately cause the failure of a site achieving its goals. After all, we are designing the site for the users, not us, right!? The goal(s) of your site should be focused around what the user wants, not just what you want to give them. For example, you want to "sell," but your user wants to "buy." Put yourself in the shoes of the user, and make it easy for them to find merchandise and buy it if that is your site's goal.

Print Presence: Does your client or your Web venture already have a print presence? If so, you might be able to borrow ideas for the Web site design. If you already have a logo or a colored brochure to work with, it can help you pick type faces and color strategy. You might choose to create something altogether different for the Web, but if you don't know where to start for color themes or design direction, this can be a great launching device. (**Warning:** Electronic print files are often difficult to translate into Web images and color. More on this in Chapter 20, "Scanning for the Web," and Chapter 7, "Color Calibration Issues.")

Other Sites: It's very important that you research other sites before embarking on your own. Catalogue what you like and don't like and it will help you decide on a direction for your own work. Sometimes you might like a piece of a site, like a button design or a background tile. Most visual designers keep an "inspiration" file, which they refer to when they're stuck or looking for ideas. And don't limit it to other Web sites! Many artists find inspiration from unexpected sources. This is not to suggest you should steal another person's artwork or ideas. I am simply stating that inspiration is important, and defining your likes and dislikes is critical to refining your own vision. Many people think Web design is a separate discipline that has no history. Although the Web is certainly new and different from other media, there is a lot history can still teach us. Look to other sources such as books, magazines, libraries, and outside experiences to spark an idea for your Web site.

Storyboarding

Once you've established the goals, the scope, and the audience of your site, it's time to start producing ideas, and you might find the need to create storyboards. The term "storyboard" is borrowed from the film industry. That industry, just like ours, has a very loose definition of what a storyboard is. It can be a scribble on a napkin or the most beautiful full-color renderings you've ever seen. Storyboards have to communicate an idea of what your Web site is going to accomplish. If you're doing this for yourself, scribbled napkins will work just fine. If you're doing this for a client, storyboards might also serve as presentation boards, which communicate your idea and the art direction of your idea.

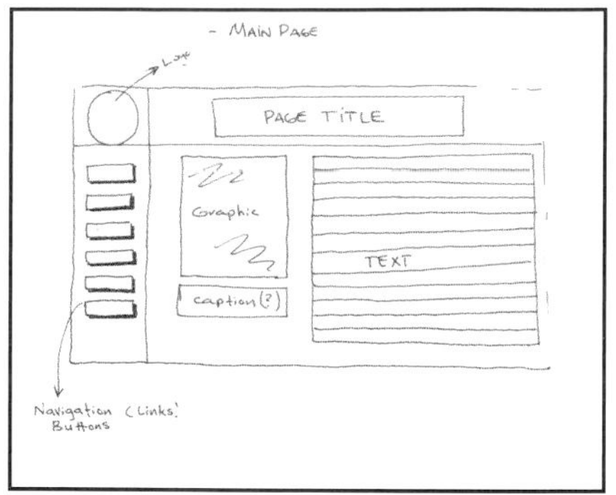

Storyboards can be as basic as sketching out placement ideas, like this example. A simple sketch like this can help you solve all kinds of issues before you start, such as the size for your graphics, and how much text to write.

Elisabeth Roxby, who designed the National Design Museum's site for the **Cooper-Hewitt Museum** (http://www.si.edu/ndm/), took a screen capture of her browser window and made photocopies as templates for her storyboards. If you want to take a screen capture of something on your screen (like a browser window, for example), press **F13** on a PC or press **Command+Shift+3** on a Mac. I recommend that you do this anyway so you can measure the interior and get a sense of the size of the space you're working with in the first place.

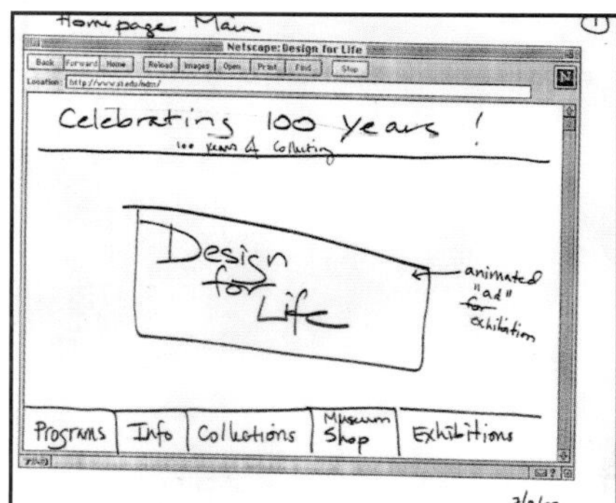

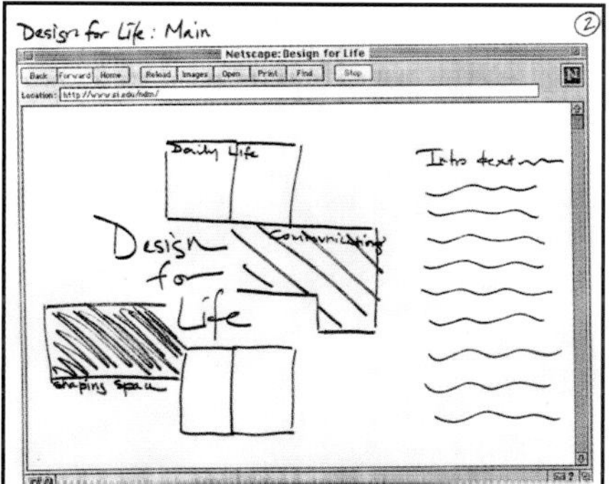

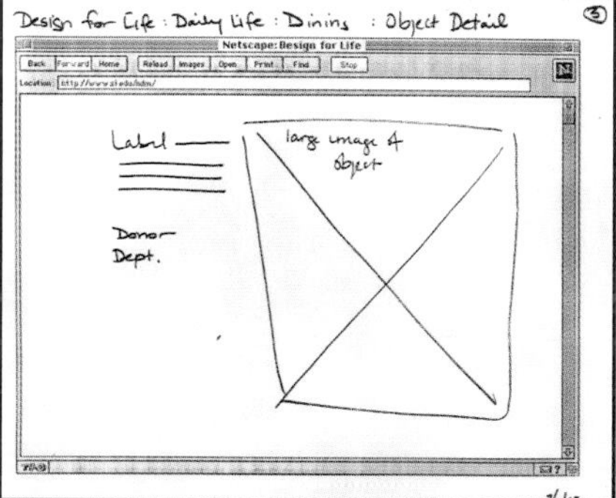

Using a photocopy of the browser window is a good idea. It helps give context and the correct format and scale to your visual idea.

I was once asked to consult on a design magazine's redesign of its Web site, and the art director sent me color printouts of the storyboards. They were created in QuarkXPress and fit an 8 1/2 x 11 inch sheet of paper perfectly. The trouble was, unlike paper, most computer screens are wider than they are tall. My first suggestion was that the designer make a dummy window in the shape of a browser and lay out everything again. This might seem obvious, but if you're new to the field, it isn't.

Case Study: From Storyboard to Production

Graphic designer and educator **David Cabrera** came to one of my workshops having never done Web design before. He had already designed many brochures and invitations for his client, so he had a solid design direction in mind for his first site.

He made a wonderful presentation storyboard in Photoshop, using fonts and imagery familiar from his print campaign. But once he settled on the design, he was unable to figure out how to get his design onto the Web. This was totally understandable, because he was inexperienced with Web design. I thought it would benefit the readers of this book to see how his storyboard was broken down into Web-ready elements and then reassembled using many HTML and imaging techniques.

David's original Photoshop storyboard.

David made the background a separate element, and sav-ed it as a JPEG. For information on background tiles, see Chapter 12, "Background Tiles."

[ArtPace]
A FOUNDATION FOR CONTEMPORARY ART | SAN ANTONIO

He made the main logo a transparent GIF file. For more information on transparent GIFs, see Chapter 13, "Transparent Artwork."

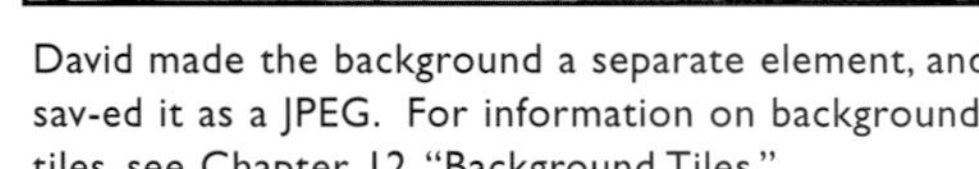

Each name was a transparent animated GIF file, so that the names appeared and disappeared on the front page in random order. For more information on animation, see Chapter 21, "GIF Animation." They were positioned on the front page using tables. For more information on alignment using HTML tables, see Chapter 17, "Alignment & Tables."

This points out a problem: Unless you've done Web design before, it's hard to know how to design for the Web. Even though it makes sense to start out with a storyboard, you might lock yourself into a design that you don't know how to execute. If you are in this position, I highly recommend that you show your design to an experienced Web designer before submitting it to a client. Potential problems that you aren't even aware could happen might be avoided! Of course, reading through all the chapters in this book will help you as well.

Flowcharting

The term "flowchart" refers to a visual representation, or chart, showing the flow of a site. It's a wonderful idea to chart your site before you get too far into its design. However, take heed that your flowchart will change over time! It's dangerous to lock yourself into a rigid site flow because you may invent a new category or realize the need for a missing one along the way.

One of the best ideas I've ever heard for this process was from **Margaret Gould Stewart**, Creative Director of http:www.tripod.com. She shared her process with me, and I will pass it on to you:

- Put all your Web site categories on separate index cards.
- Spread them out on the ground and arrange them logically.
- Give the same pile of cards to other members of your design team or your client and see if they arrange them differently.
- Pick the best ideas from everyone.

I love this approach because it offers the freedom for input from multiple sources regarding the flow of the site. You'd be amazed at how valuable it is to open these types of difficult decisions to others (including your clients). It's important to recognize that the function of a site is to work for many people. On some decisions, it's great to get feedback from many people.

Another great way to storyboard is with an invaluable product called **Inspiration**. Visit http://www.inspiration.com and http://www.conceptmapping.com/ to see if you might like to add this tool to your current set.

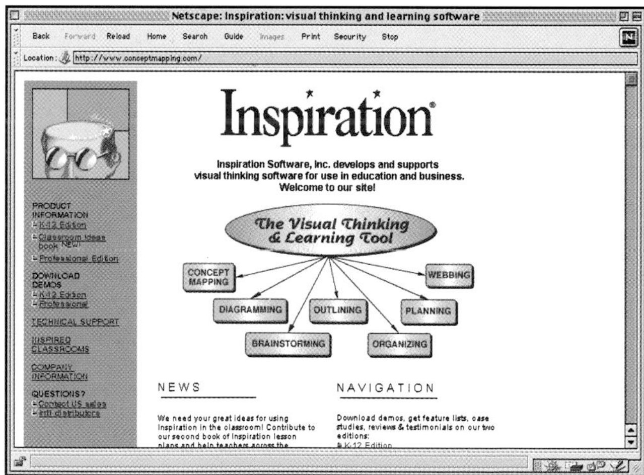

Inspiration software (http://www.conceptmapping.com) allows you to brainstorm in outline form or with graphics, and is a great tool for mapping a site structure.

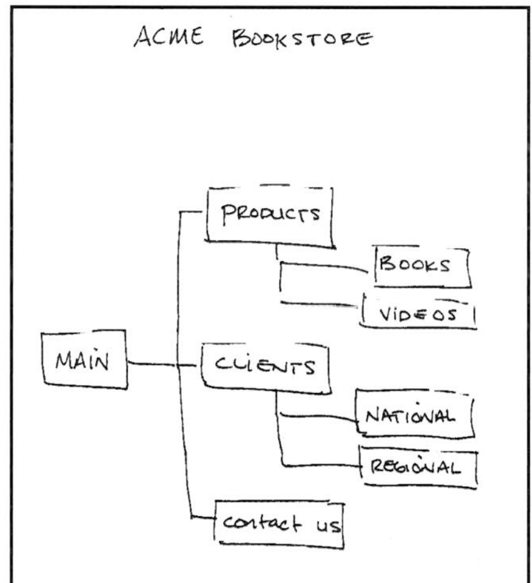

Flowcharts, like storyboards, can be scribbled on paper or be perfectly laid out using a program like Inspiration. It only matters that it helps you define the navigation of your site.

Navigation Approaches

The term "site architect" refers to the person who oversees the process of designing navigation and information flow of a Web site. Some Web design firms are so large that they have someone who fills this position. Other Web sites are so small that a single person might wear the hat of "site architect" sometimes and many other hats at other times.

It's hard to design the flowchart of a site without some understanding of the different types of navigation choices. This subject is addressed in this chapter in a theoretical sense; it's addressed in a practical sense in Chapter 18, "Frames," and Chapter 11, "Linking Basics."

There are many possible types of navigation approaches, but my warning to you is that you make navigation choices available from every page within your site. If you rely on the browser's Back button, for example, you may not have great results. For example, many people bookmark an interior page of your site instead of the home page. If this is the case, a person might enter your site on a page that has no reference to the front page of your site, and he may never see your site as you intended.

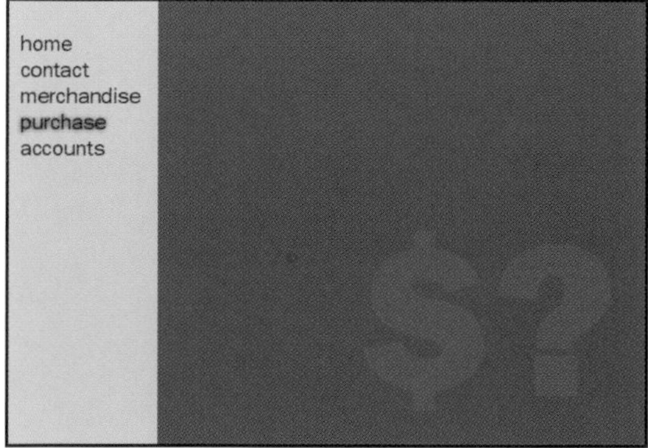

Frames (see Chapter 18, "Frames") enable you to display a common navigation bar throughout the site. This can be done with HTML text or a graphical imagemap (see Chapter 15, "Imagemaps").

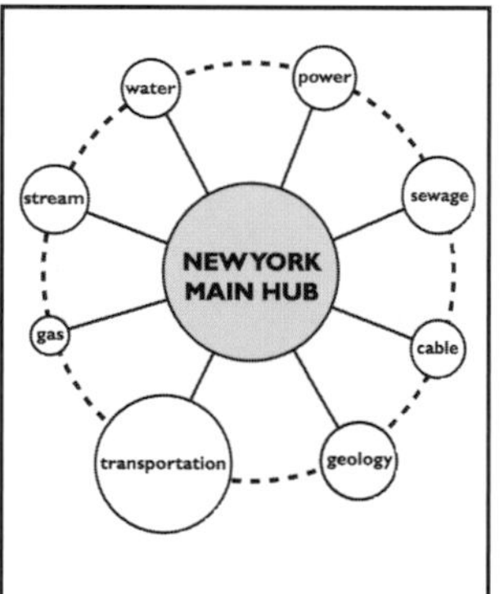

A "**hub and spokes**" style architecture relates to the idea that users should return to a "hub" in order to visit other parts of the site. In **National Geographic's New York Underground** site (http://www.nationalgeographic. com/ features/ 97/nyunderground/), such a navigation system was used. If you click on any of the links on this image map you go to a "spoke." You must click back to the "hub" (depicted on the left) to access other navigation points.

More Navigation Approaches

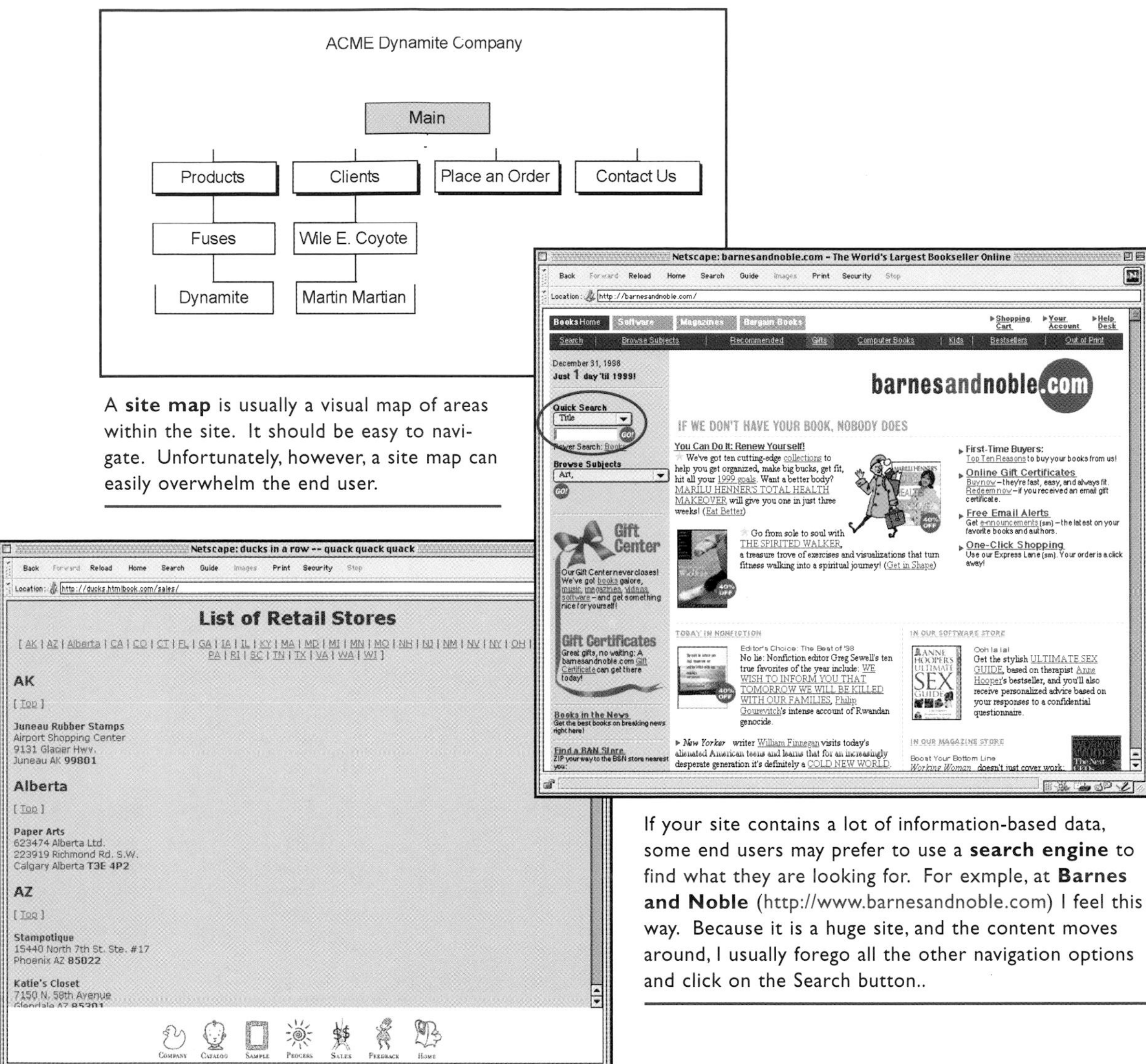

A **site map** is usually a visual map of areas within the site. It should be easy to navigate. Unfortunately, however, a site map can easily overwhelm the end user.

If your site contains a lot of information-based data, some end users may prefer to use a **search engine** to find what they are looking for. For exmple, at **Barnes and Noble** (http://www.barnesandnoble.com) I feel this way. Because it is a huge site, and the content moves around, I usually forego all the other navigation options and click on the Search button..

An **index** is helpful for sorting through large lists. Of course this isn't foolproof; it only works if the end user knows the name of where he or she wants to go.

Site Structure

Although you can draw flowcharts by hand, a few HTML editors offer flow-chart features which display your site structure. It's important, however, to define your site struture before you enter an HTML editor. Using the methods described so far will help you define your navigation catagories. Once you've got that done, it's time to map out the structure of the site.

Many HTML editors support site management features; it's possible to plan your site architecture as well as spawn actual HTML Web pages from the original chart.

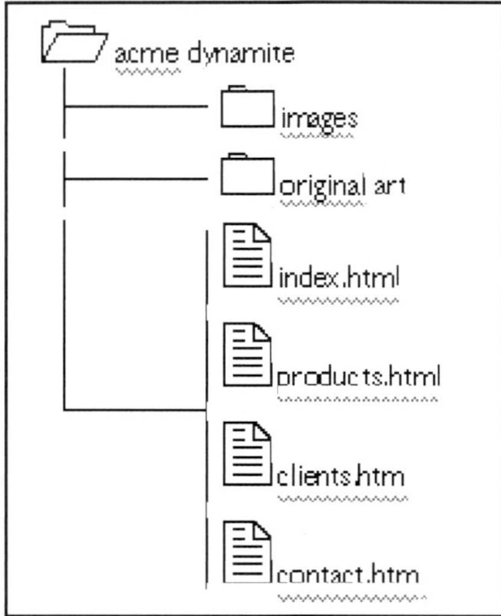

You can figure out your own site structure—this one was created with the drawing tool from **Microsoft Word**!

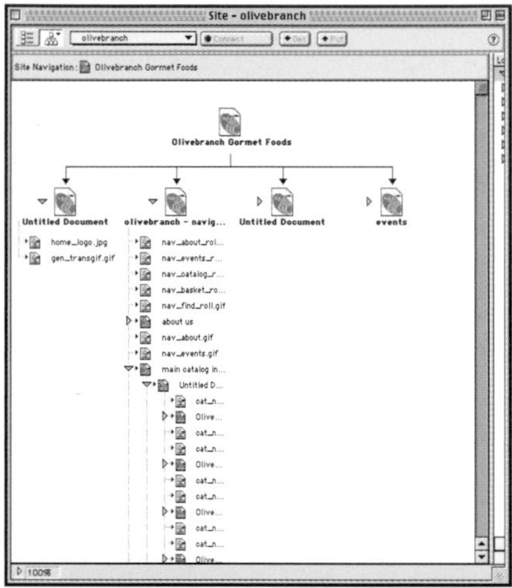

Dreamweaver 2.0 site mapping feature.

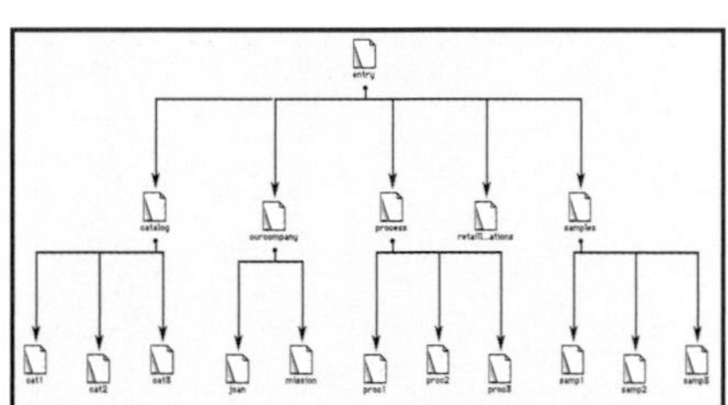

GoLive CyberStudio site mapping option.

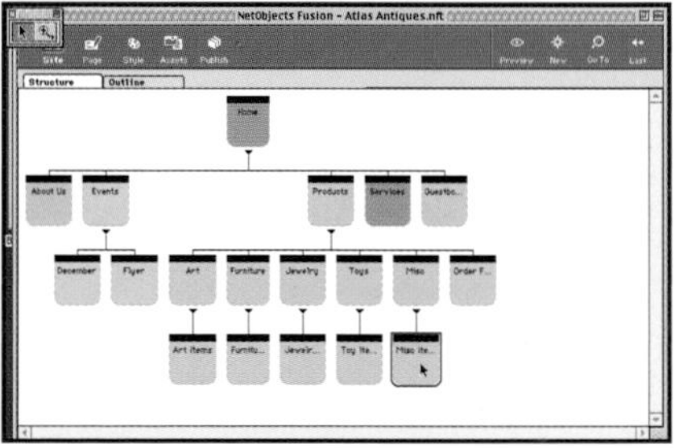

NetObject Fusion (http://www.netobjects.com) site mapping option.

tip

Recommended Reading

The subjects of site architecture, navigation, flowcharting, planning, and brainstorming are broad enough to fill a book. Here are a few such books that I have read and recommend:

Web Concept and Design
Crystal Waters
New Riders
ISBN: 1-56205-648-4
$39.99

Web Navigation Studio: Designing the User Experience
Jennifer Flemming
O'Reilly and Associates
ISBN: 1-56592-351-0
$34.95

Metaphors

When planning a site, it's helpful to draw up a list of metaphors that build on free associations of objects or ideas. Helpful metaphors for Web building can relate to sounds, images, or movement. When my brother and I developed the **Ducks In A Row** Web site for a rubber stamp company (http://www.ducks.htmlbook.com), we came up with this list of free associations. Our list contains nothing too unexpected or earth-shattering, which is precisely the point. You should be able to throw out ideas quickly when brainstorming this way.

Ducks in a Row Brainstorming List		
Sounds	**Visuals**	**Animation**
quack	water splashing	animated stamps
water	water ripples	swimming ducks
paper folding	rubber ducks	pond ripples
splashing	yellow	quacking ducks
rain drops	actual stamps	wings flapping

A brainstorming list—in a formal chart or just scribbled out—can feed you ideas while you create your animations, sounds, rollovers, navigation, and images.

Metaphors: Help or Hindrance?

Sometimes metaphors can help your site design, but sometimes metaphors can hurt. It's often a matter of taste because sometimes metaphors can be heavy-handed or too cutesy to be practical. Let's take www.yahoo.com for example. You could make a huge issue out of the "search" metaphor with a giant magnifying glass for each button or a telescope on the masthead. The thing is, people who go to www.yahoo.com don't need lots of graphics to aide their search needs. For a site like this, I'm not convinced that a metaphor is necessary.

It's hard to know when to use a metaphor and when not to. My advice is don't use it unless it reinforces both your message and the end user's experience. Often it won't.

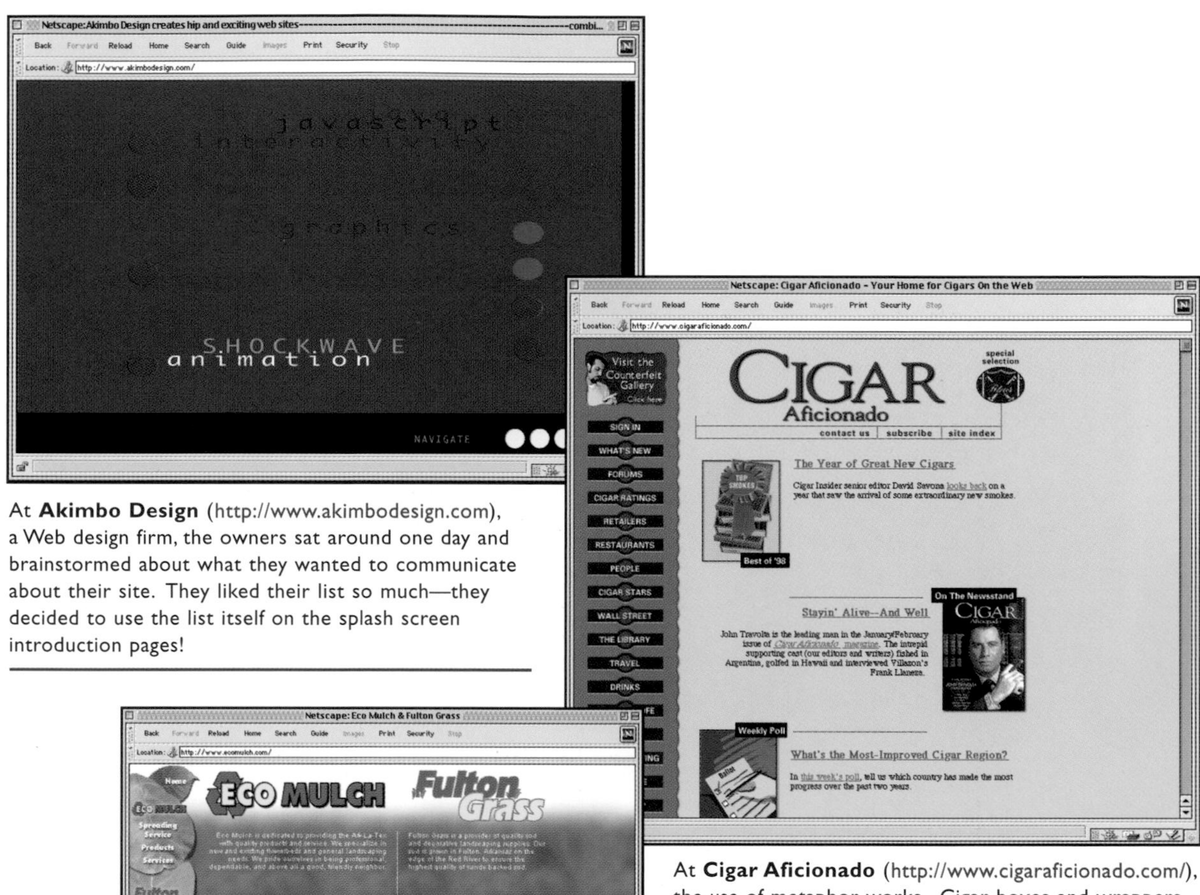

At **Akimbo Design** (http://www.akimbodesign.com), a Web design firm, the owners sat around one day and brainstormed about what they wanted to communicate about their site. They liked their list so much—they decided to use the list itself on the splash screen introduction pages!

At **Cigar Aficionado** (http://www.cigaraficionado.com/), the use of metaphor works. Cigar boxes and wrappers are beautifully designed, so the use of them on the Web site provides an appropriate visual reinforcement.

Eco Mulch (http://www.ecomulch.com/) uses metaphor effectively. There's no doubt what this site is for!

summary Strategy

The success of a Web site involves a lot of planning and forethought. This chapter outlined many principles and techniques for site planning that might prove useful to your type of Web site. Here are some highlights:

- Cover the bases when determining a strategy: Set your goals and expectations, and define your needs, scope, and target audience before you begin.
- Communicate with your clients and make sure you account for their special needs, likes, and dislikes.
- Storyboarding can be as simple as scribbling an idea on a napkin or as complex as creating a full-color printed presentation. Which you choose depends on the purpose of the storyboard.
- Metaphors can be helpful to site design, or they can be heavy-handed and interrupt communication.
- Brainstorming is essential to determining the important areas of focus in your site.
- Don't be too rigid with your strategies; leave room for flexibility and last-minute solutions.

Introduction

Web Authoring Environments

Chapter Topics

- Browser-Safe Color
- Guidelines for Compatibilty
- AOL Browsers
- Cross-Platform Color Calibration
- Gamma Differences
- Type & Size Differences
- Web TV

The very thing I most love about the Web—the fact that it is a global-publishing medium that can reach people regardless of geography or computer preference—is exactly what I hate the most about the medium. Most of us have never encountered a design environment where people see what's published differently depending on what device it is viewed from. This fact makes it necessary to change your mindset when designing for the Web. It means that a lot of us have to let go of trying to have absolute control, and we have to alter our expectations about what is possible and what is not.

The Web is unusual in that no other type of design has ever required such an understanding of cross-platform differences and compatibility issues. As evidence, it's very common to see separate aisles for Macs and PCs in the CD-ROM section of your local software store. And computer stores usually don't even have aisles for UNIX platforms! When authoring for Internet-based Web sites, however, regardless of which platform you own, you are creating material for every platform on the planet.

Compatibility problems are definitely at the top of the list of things that most Web publishers hate about this medium. This chapter references many of the compatibility problems and issues, including browser differences, gamma differences, monitor differences, HTML editor differences, bit-depth differences, resolution differences, and font size differences. I may not have a solution for each of these problems, but at the very least, I will help you gain a deeper understanding of the issues in order to make informed choices.

Browser Differences

The browser plays a huge role in your experience of visiting a Web site. It interprets the HTML code, the colors, the graphics, and the layout of a page. This means that someone viewing your site is subject to a completely different result depending on which browser version he is using. In addition, the exact same browser version might behave differently on Macs, PCs, and UNIX workstations, which increases the variables again.

In the first edition of *Designing Web Graphics*, I compared identical Web pages inside 11 different browsers on Macs and PCs. There were close to 21 different results. Some differences were subtle; some were not so subtle. Years later, there are no longer 11 browsers to contend with. For the most part, we're dealing with three browsers: Netscape's Navigator/Communicator, Microsoft's Internet Explorer, and AOL. Sure, some people still use Mosaic and Lynx, but those numbers are much smaller than they used to be, and much much smaller than those of the big three.

It's very important that you answer some of the questions the last chapter posed before developing a browser strategy. Who is your audience? Is your audience more likely to have newer machines and browsers or older equipment and outdated browsers? How important is it to you to reach people with older equipment and browsers? For many sites, it is very important to reach that audience.

Some of you will want to go the route of the lowest common denominator. Others will want to take the high road, with the expectation that most end users will have current browsers, will have plug-ins loaded, and will be capable of faster connections. Both paths of action are valid and acceptable, but you need to make the decision of which path to choose.

In addition to evaluating your audience, you should also know which features are more forgiving than others. Some features are non-destructive, even when viewed on older machines and browsers. Other features result in a broken image icon or messed up pages. Other chapters in this book will warn you when a graphics or HTML feature will degrade gracefully on older browsers.

Resources for Tips on Browser and HTML Differences

http://www.threetoad.com/
Screen captures of browser comparisons and an excellent tips section.

http://www.browsercaps.com
Interesting surveys that you can view and participate in. You can even suggest a survey of your own liking.

http://www.tue.nl/bwk/cheops/via/maker/html4/char.htm
HTML Entities in Different Browsers.

http://www.tue.nl/bwk/cheops/via/maker/html4/html.htm
Comparison of all HTML Tags from HTML 4.0

http://developer.netscape.com/docs/manuals/htmlguid/tags_complete.html
Netscape HTML Tags by Browser Version. A list of all the tags ever supported by Netscape, sorted by version. Thus, there is a long list for 1.0 and a few tags for every version thereafter, which provides a good general picture of HTML evolution.

http://developer.netscape.com/docs/manuals/htmlguid/contents.htm
Netscape HTML Tags Understood by Navigator 4.0. Lists all the tags supported by Communicator 4.0.

http://www.webdeveloper.com/drweb/19970811-drweb.html
Getting Tables to Display Correctly in AOL Browsers.

http://www.microsoft.com/workshop/author/ie3html/ie3dtd.asp
SGML DTD for MSIE 3.0.

http://www.htmlcompendium.org/index.htm
HTML Tag Compendium. Contains info on which browsers support each tag.

http://developer.netscape.com/docs/technote/dynhtml/css1tojs/css1tojs.html
CSS1 Manipulation from JavaScript. Although both Netscape and Explorer allow CSS stuff to be done via JavaScript, they do it differently! It has code that detects which browser is being used and contains examples of the differences between the two.

http://developer.netscape.com/docs/examples/javascrip/browser_type.html
The Ultimate JavaScript Client Sniffer.

http://www.webreview.com/guides/style/mastergrid.html
Table of CSS Implementations in Netscape and MSIE.

http://www.webreview.com/guides/style/safegrid.htm
The "safe list" of CSS stuff that you can use without [much] fear.

http://www.webcoder.com/reference/2/index.html
Table of JavaScript Implementations. Outlines inconsistencies between Netscape's and MSIE's implementations of JS.

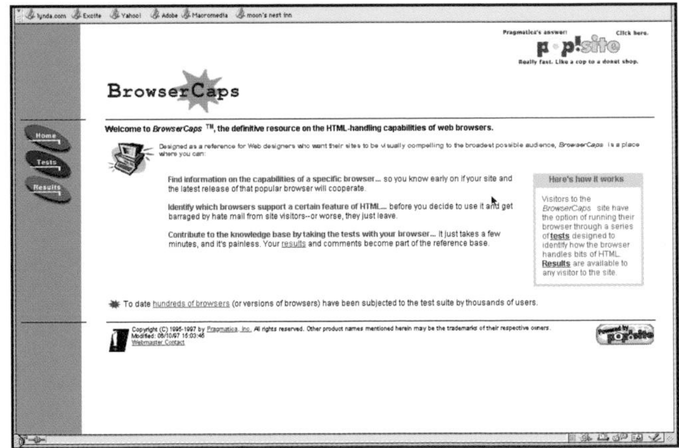

Guidelines for Compatibility

Following a few general guidelines will help you avoid serious browser incompatibilities with your site. Here are some suggestions:

Test on multiple browsers. Most professional Web design studios have testing workstations and a host of older browsers. It absolutely pays to have an older machine, a slow modem, and older browsers to test your pages on. You can pick up older equipment at garage sales or through the classifieds for very little money. If you want to download an older browser, go to this Web site: ftp://ftp.nvc.cc.ca.us/pub/internet/AntiqueBrowsers/index.html.

Use standard tags. If you have the choice of using a proprietary tag or a standard tag, use the standard. Netscape and Explorer are infamous for inventing their own tags. For example, you can make type bold by using the Netscape-originated tag B, or you can make text bold by using the standard STRONG tag. The standard HTML specifications are located at http://www.w3c.org. You will also find a printed directory of HTML 4.0 tags and attributes in my book *Creative HTML Design* (which I co-authored with my brother).

Provide navigation options. If you will use a graphical navigation bar, be sure to include a text-based alternative as well. Imagemaps work differently on older browsers, and you never know how someone is going to find your site. You'll learn how to implement these solutions in Chapter 11, "Linking Basics," Chapter 15, "Imagemaps," and Chapter 22, "JavaScript: Rollovers & More."

Use the NO tags. Many tags have a NO alternative. For example, the alternative to the FRAMES tag is a NOFRAMES tag. You would put alternative content into the NOFRAMES tag for browsers that don't support frames. You will learn how to implement these solutions in Chapter 11, "Linking Basics."

Enable browser detection. If you want to provide alternate content for different browsers, you can use a browser detection script to determine what browser your end user is using. Browser detection scripts are often used in conjunction with redirect scripts, which first determine the brow-ser version and then serve the appropriate page for the end user. This can be an extremely time-consuming approach to Web publishing and should be used only when you have the time and resources to generate multiple content. In my book *Deconstructing Web Graphics.2*, I wrote a very interesting case study in which the browser detection script loaded one of four possible external CSS resources, which applied different styles to the same Web pages. More about these solutions are included in Chapter 19, "Cascading Style Sheets" and Chapter 22, "JavaScript: Rollovers & More."

Wait six months. If you want to make sure that a new feature is widely supported, wait six months before you use it. This rule doesn't apply to all Web publishers, especially those who are pushing the Web as an experimental medium. I waited two years to use tables on my main page, but I am often more conservative than many designers because my goal is to reach the most people that I can and still produce a good-looking site.

The Dreaded AOL Browser

Millions of people—myself included—have been introduced to the Web and email via AOL. I was an early subscriber to the service (before the Web) and loved the ease of use, the user forums, and the chat forums. Because AOL is a closed and proprietary system, they are able to implement a user interface that makes a beginner's life on the computer a breeze. I know many people who are not "into" computers like I am, and who want nothing more than to easily view and find content. AOL can be the perfect solution.

Unfortunately, in order for AOL to offer its own custom interface, it has created its own Web browser. The trouble is, its Web browser is much less robust than that of Netscape or Explorer. While any AOL user can download a custom version of Netscape or Explorer to use, many don't know how or don't bother.

It is impossible to estimate how many users are browsing the net via the AOL browser because AOL uses a proxy server instead of allowing its users to freely access the Internet. A proxy server stores data from other servers. In AOL's case, instead of allowing AOL subscribers to freely roam the Internet, it dispenses outside sites from its server. Let's say an AOL user comes to my site. If she or he is the first AOL subscriber to ever come to my site, my site is downloaded to AOL's proxy server and then served to that AOL user. The next AOL user who wants to visit my site doesn't hit my server at all; instead, that request hits AOL's proxy server. That means that I might serve hundreds of pages to AOL users yet see only one request from that initial AOL user on my Web statistic logs. This means that AOL users may not see updated information (from a news or stock site, for example) as quickly as someone using another ISP.

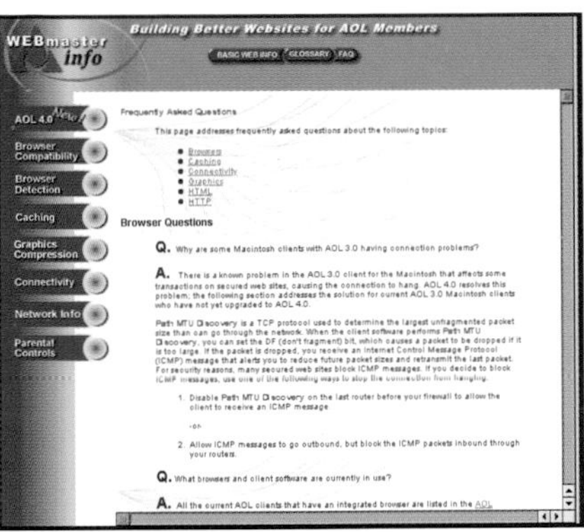

For more information on how the AOL proxy server works, visit this site: http://webmaster.info.aol.com/.

Another casualty of filtering sites through the AOL proxy system is the fact that all the graphics are converted from JPEG and GIF to the Art format. Unfortunately, the Art format works better for photographs than for graphics. Very little is published about this proprietary file format that is owned by AOL.

GO inside

Discovering the ART Image Format

by Joyce Kohl

April 7, 1998

On my Yorkie's Web site (Yorkies Dot Com), visitors may apply for a "Yorked by Mandy" award. If their pages qualify, then I give them permission to grab the image of their choice. The image is usually in JPG format, but can also be in GIF format. Once the image is actually up, then I add the the URL to the recipient list. Last weekend when checking the URL before adding the link, I discovered many of the graphics appeared to be broken and did not appear in Netscape Communicator. A quick view of the source revealed several images with the extension of "ART."

What is ART?
I began searching the Internet for ART. Nothing turned up. I then searched graphics programs and read the features list for each and found none included ART. The next step was inquiring of the webmaster using ART images why she wasn't using the original JPG. Her answer: "The program I use on AOL, pp2, converts the images to ART. I've asked other AOL members about the images and they see them just fine. It must be your browser that has the problem." Well! The nerve, I thought! So, okay, I quickly swallowed my pride and off I went to check her site with AOL. Sure enough, every single graphic showed up. Hmmmmm.... I then tried using Microsoft Internet Explorer. All the graphics were visible with it, too. Knowing that AOL also uses MSIE as its internal browser, then a plethora of questions began racing around in my head.

Where is ART Information?

A couple of AOL users have written interesting commentaries and advise about the ART format. See http://goinside.com/98/4/ art.html (shown above) and http://www.rdwebworks.com/MamaBear/aol.htm.

At the moment, not all plug-ins are supported by the AOL browser. Before version 3.0, plug-ins were not supported at all. At this point in time, plug-ins have to be custom written to work with AOL's browser, which results in a rather limited number of choices. When this chapter was written, the only supported plug-ins were Shockwave, RealAudio, and VOL. To see if this list has increased, make a visit to their site: http://multimedia.aol.com/internal/plugins.htm.

Cross-Platform Color Calibration Issues

One of the problems with color on computer screens is that few monitors are calibrated accurately to one another. Shades of a color often vary wildly from computer to computer and from platform to platform. (If you've ever owned two television sets, you know how the color can vary from set to set.) Anyone who works for a company with more than one computer knows that the colors shift between systems—even between identical operating systems with identical hardware.

Color calibration is a distressing problem for Web designers who expect the colors they've picked to look the same on every system. Macs, PCs, SGIs, and Suns all have different color cards and monitors, and none of them are calibrated to each other.

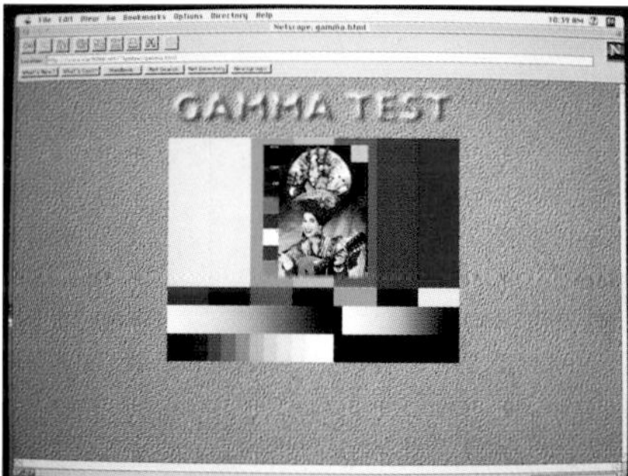

MAC

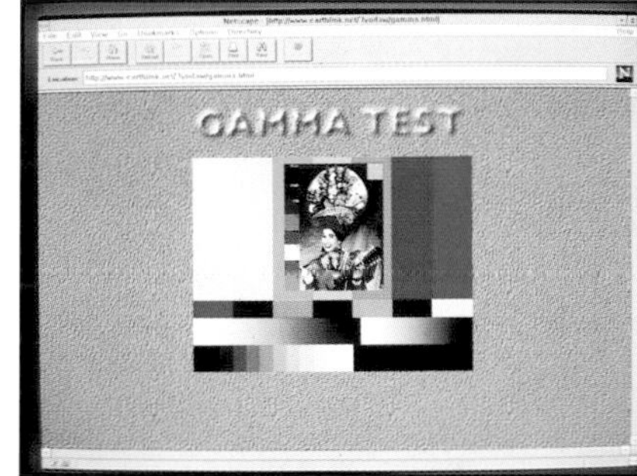

PC

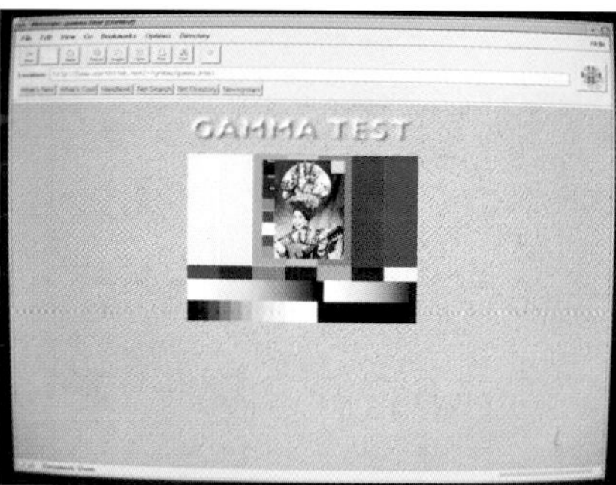

SGI

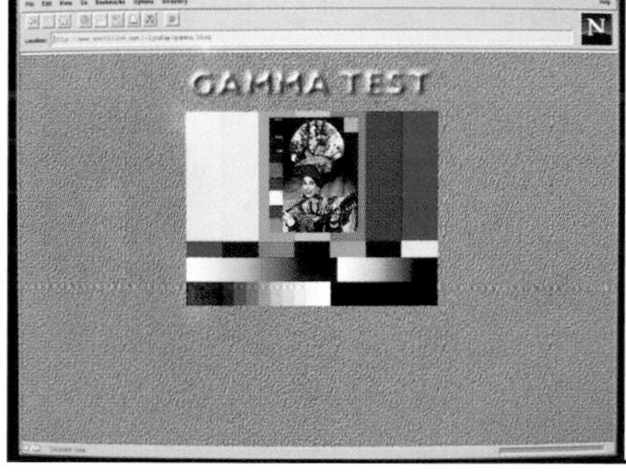

SUN

Gamma Differences

Another thorn in many a Web publisher's side is the awful dreaded gamma difference between Macs, PCs, and UNIX machines. Gamma settings dictate brightness and contrast of your computer's display. Unfortunately, factory presets are different for Macs, PCs, and UNIX systems.

Average Factory Settings	
Mac	1.8 gamma
PC	2.2 gamma
UNIX	1.7 gamma

Currently, there is no solution for gamma differences; however, some are in the works. These new solutions are documented in Chapter 7, "Color Calibration Issues." For the moment, it is just important for you to understand that your images will most likely appear lighter on Macs than on PCs. While this might sound relatively minor, it can wreak havoc on images that are created on Macintoshes and displayed on PCs.

Although there are no true solutions for this problem, you can follow some suggestions to increase your awareness of the problem. As stated earlier, always check your site out on other platforms and systems. If you catch a serious problem, you can correct it by lightening or darkening the image. Techniques for adjusting image brightness and contrast are discussed in Chapter 20, "Scanning for the Web."

ImageReady has a wonderful function that allows you to preview gamma differences. On a Mac, choose **View:Windows Gamma**, or on a PC, choose **View:Mac Gamma**. This temporarily lightens or darkens your screen to simulate the other platform's gamma settings. It enables you to catch serious problems before you publish your images.

Other proposals for dealing with gamma differences are in the works right now, but none of them are implemented effectively quite yet. The PNG file format (which is discussed in greater detail in Chapter 5, "Web File Formats") is capable of recording a gamma profile. Unfortunately, Web browsers cannot read the profile, so even though the image could be adjusted appropriately in theory, that day hasn't arrived yet.

Some file formats (such as Photoshop 5.0) contain ICC profiles (**I**nternational **C**olor **C**onsortium—http://www.color.org/), which "tag" the image with gamma information so it can be interpreted by printers and display mechanisms (monitors). Unfortunately, these profiles are often larger than compressed Web files themselves, so ICC profiles are not that practical for Web delivery.

Another future solution might be sRGB (http://www.w3.org/Graphics/Color/sRGB.html), a new color space standard for the Internet. This subject will be discussed in more depth in Chapter 7, "Color Calibration Issues." The idea, in a nutshell, is that there would be a universal color standard that would apply to Macs or PCs to resolve the current differences between platforms. The drawback to sRGB is that monitors and printers must understand it, and because the specification is so new, it will be many years before it truly solves any of today's problems.

Gamma is a much more complex subject than you might imagine. For those of you who want to know more than this chapter has explained, visit http://www.inforamp.net/~poynton/Poynton-articles.html. Charles Poynton is one of the foremost scholars on this subject and has written many articles of interest.

Understanding Value and Contrast

Now that you've seen for yourself that you have no control over the calibration of the systems your work will be viewed on, what can you do to make good-looking graphics that look good everywhere? What becomes more important than the colors you pick and what is stressed throughout this book is the contrast and value of a graphic. If you achieve contrast and value balance, the brightness and darkness, or color differences, on various platforms are going to be less objectionable.

Value is especially important in the context of Web graphics. Differences in computer platforms, gamma settings, or a monitor's calibration can wreak havoc on the readability of images. A dark image created on one machine may come out black or appear tinted on another. Macintosh computers are generally lighter than Windows-based machines. Web pages can now also be viewed over television screens, which are calibrated differently from computer monitors.

So how do you know if you are creating an image with values that will be displayed properly on other machines? You can start by making sure your images have a good range from black to white. Don't place all the important information in the dark areas because they might go to black and fade out on someone's PC. And the same goes for light areas. You can't have absolute control over how someone will see your images, so making them as readable as possible in terms of value should be your highest priority. Always view your images on other platforms to see whether your images achieve their intended value.

A great exercise is to temporarily throw your monitor into grayscale mode and then view your image to see whether its values are displayed as you expected. This converts all the color data to blacks, whites, and grays. This change of settings yields much better feedback about brightness and contrast than a color display can.

Colors are notoriously deceptive when you're judging brightness and darkness because variables such as a fluorescent color or subtle hand tinting are overpowering when you're judging value.

Here's the original image.

When you view it in grayscale, it almost disappears—it's because the values (lights and darks) are too close together.

Here is the corrected color version of the image.

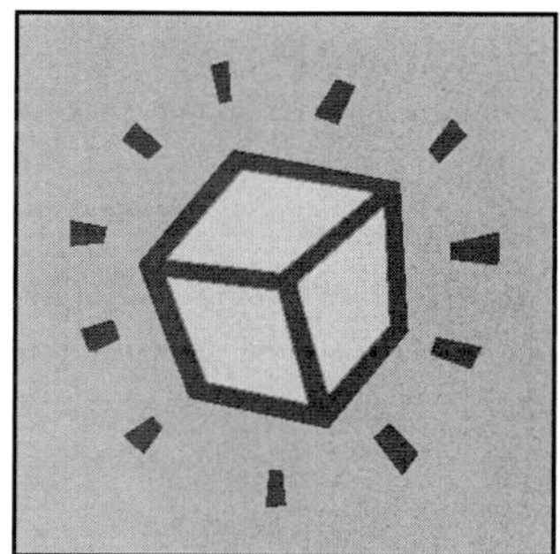

See how readable the grayscale version looks.

High Resolution Versus Low Resolution

Because your delivery medium is a computer screen and not a printed page, high-resolution files serve no purpose to Web designers. High-resolution graphics are intended to be printed on high-resolution printers, not displayed on standard computer monitors. A typical screen resolution is 72 dpi, and a high-resolution image is often 300+ dpi. You should always work at "screen resolution" when authoring images for the Web (or any other screen-based medium, such as television or interactive multimedia). The accepted measurement of "screen resolution" is 72 dpi, or 72 dots per inch. On a 72 dpi monitor, one inch of space contains 72 pixels.

For those of you who have worked with high-resolution files before, you may remember that in order to view them 1:1, you generally have to use the magnifying glass tool many times, which results in a huge cropped image on your computer screen. The reason for this is that a computer screen can't physically display a high-resolution file. If you put a high-resolution file on the Web, it can display only at 1:1 magnification, meaning that it will appear much bigger than you intended. Most likely, your goal for working in high resolution is to ensure the highest possible quality for your image; in actuality, however, you would defeat that purpose.

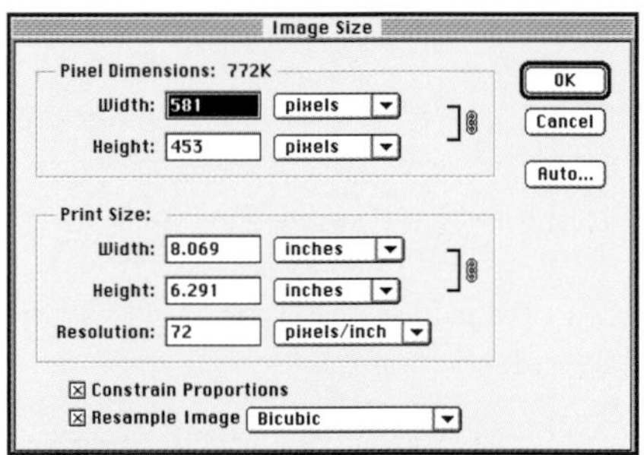

In Photoshop, you can find out the resolution by opening the Image menu and selecting Image Size. In this case, it's 72 dpi.

Here's the 72 dpi image in Netscape. It appears exactly the way you want it to.

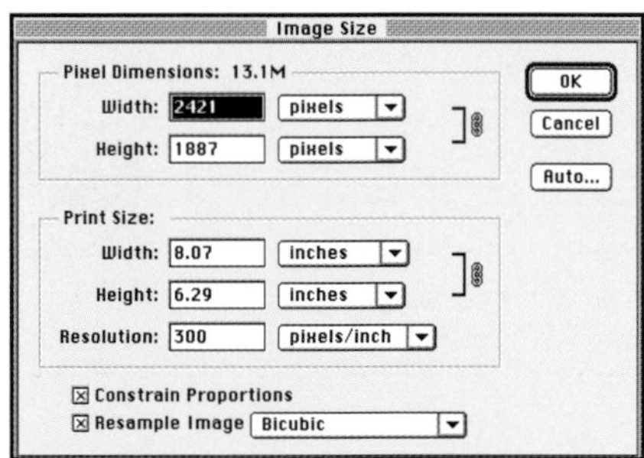

Here, the resolution is set to 300 dpi. In print graphics, this would improve the appearance of the image significantly. In Web graphics, it makes the image way too big for the screen to display.

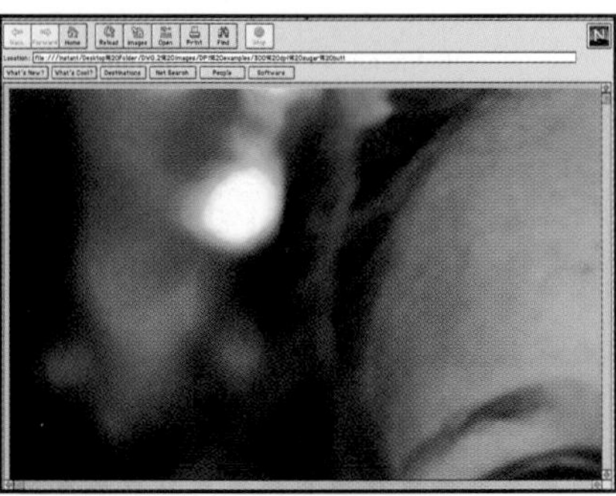

Here's an example of the 300 dpi image displayed in Netscape. Get the picture?

tip

Setting Photoshop Preferences

When you're working on images for the Web, set your graphics to be measured in pixels, not inches. Inches are needed when creating artwork that will be printed on paper, pixels are the standard unit of measurement for screen-based bound images.

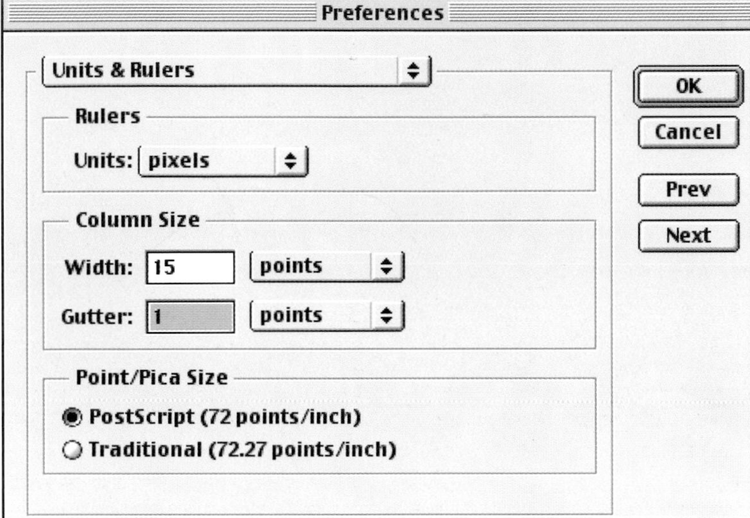

It's extremely useful for you to select **Edit:Preferences:Units & Rulers** and set the Ruler Units setting to pixels. If you use grids to align Web graphics, or if you cut apart images for insertion into tables, you must always set this preference to pixels.

Bit Depth

Understanding bit depth is extremely important to understanding Web graphics. Bit depth can refer to the number of colors in an image or the number of colors a computer system is capable of displaying. To "calculate" bit depth, you figure that one bit equals two colors, and then multiply 2 times 2 to arrive at each higher bit depth. Below is a chart of numbers that identify various bit depths.

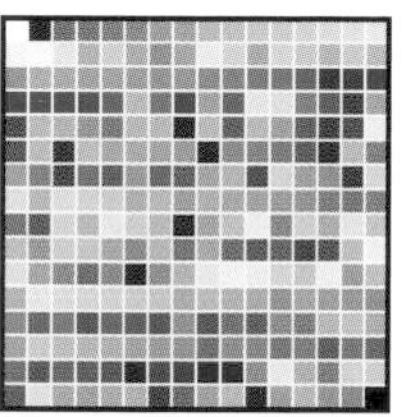

8-bit • 45.3k • 256 colors

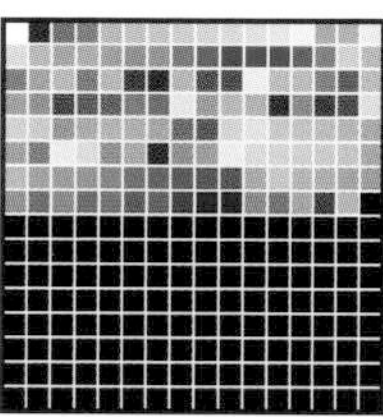

7-bit • 38.2k • 128 colors

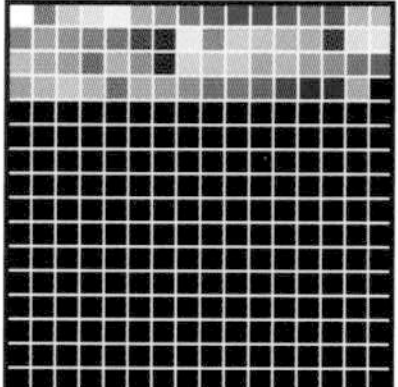

6-bit • 32k • 64 colors

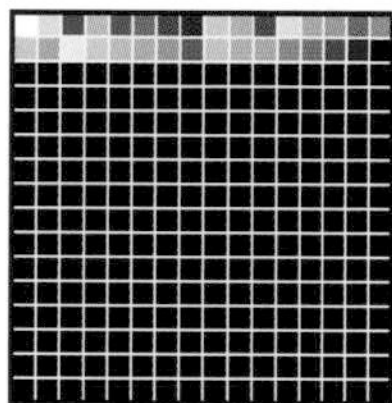

5-bit • 26.7k • 32 colors

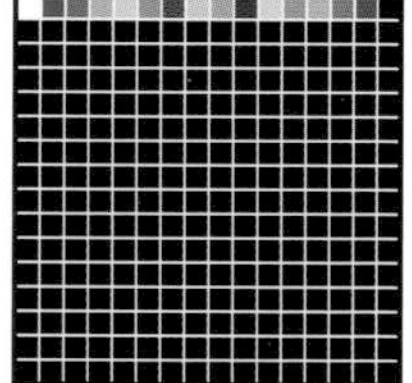

4-bit • 21.4k • 16 colors

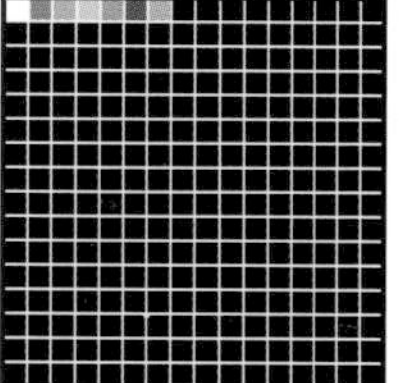

3-bit • 15.9k • 8 colors

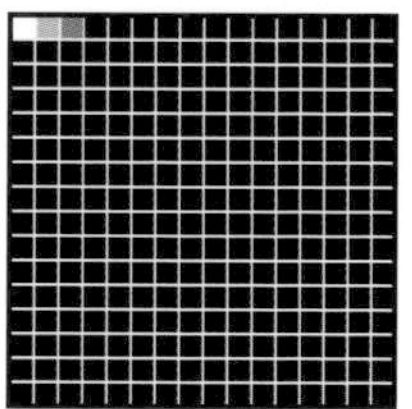

2-bit • 10.7k • 4 colors

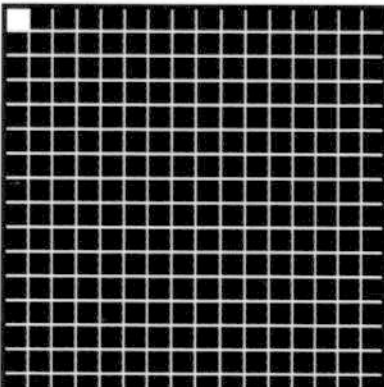

1-bit • 7.2k • 2 colors

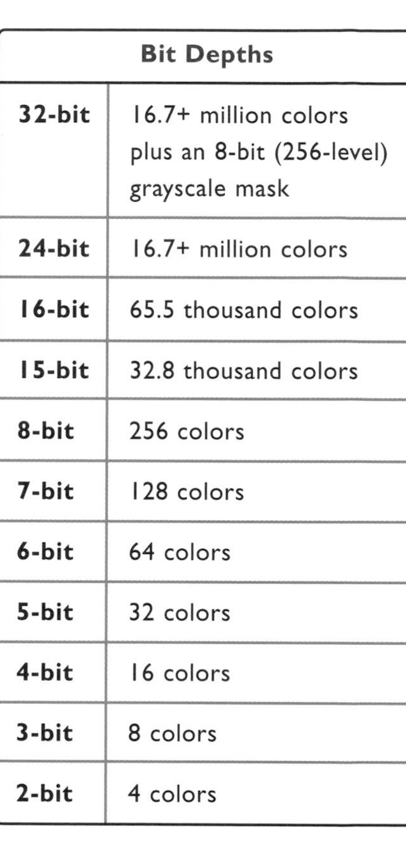

Bit Depths	
32-bit	16.7+ million colors plus an 8-bit (256-level) grayscale mask
24-bit	16.7+ million colors
16-bit	65.5 thousand colors
15-bit	32.8 thousand colors
8-bit	256 colors
7-bit	128 colors
6-bit	64 colors
5-bit	32 colors
4-bit	16 colors
3-bit	8 colors
2-bit	4 colors

Did you notice that as the bit depth decreases, so does the quality and the file size? You will find much more information about how to choose the bit depth for your Web graphics in Chapter 6, "Low-Bandwidth Graphics."

Monitor Bit Depth

So far, bit depth has been defined as it relates to images. There are actually two areas in which understanding bit depth is important. The first is to understand the bit depth of an image, and the second is to understand the bit depth of your end user's monitor. In this section, you'll learn about the monitor's bit depth, not the bit depth of images.

Most professional digital artists have 24-bit video cards, which can display up to 16.7 million colors. Many average computer users have 8-bit video cards, which are limited to displaying 256 colors. This makes sense if you consider that most computer monitors are owned by average people who bought the least expensive version of their computer system, not professional graphic artists who might have greatly enhanced systems.

Herein lies a huge problem. The majority of the people who create artwork for Web sites are viewing the artwork under better conditions than the average end user. This makes for a communication gap—one this book hopes to bridge rather than skim over (or worse, ignore).

If a computer system has only an 8-bit color card, it cannot physically display more than 256 colors at once. When a person with a 256-color system views your Web screens, she cannot see images in 24-bit even if she wants to. She can't change it, and neither can you. Chapter 6, "Low-Bandwidth Graphics," and Chapter 7, "Color Calibration Issues." provide specific advice for working with 8-bit color and files

How to Change Your Monitor's Bit Depth

I recommend that you always run a bit-depth preview test on your Web pages before you send them out for the world to see. Change your monitor setting to 256 colors, and you'll see how your artwork translates under those conditions. **Tip:** Be sure to change your monitor setting, quit the browser, and re-open it. If you change the setting while your browser is open, you will not get an accurate rendition of the effect.

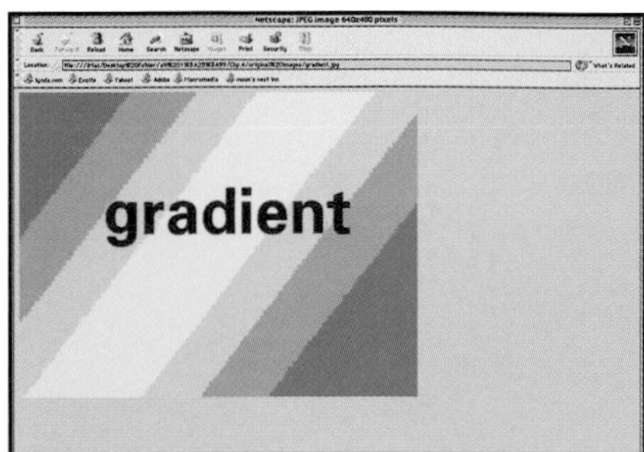

The result of switching to 256 colors in the middle of a browsing session.

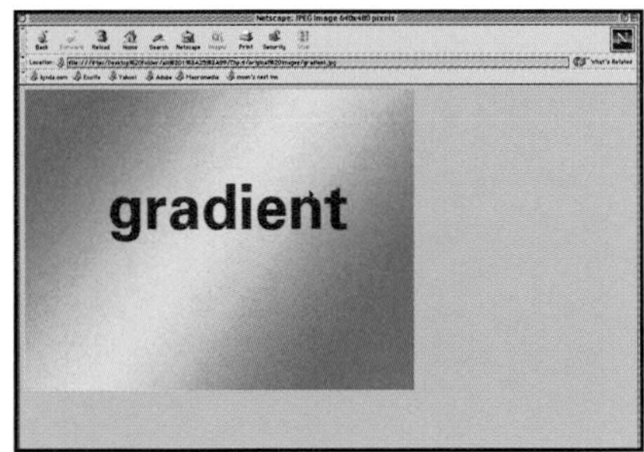

The result of quitting the browser first and then switching to 256 colors. This is the accurate way to preview Web sites in 256 color mode.

Following are instructions on how to change your computer's monitor to display in 256 colors so you can preview the bad news before others do.

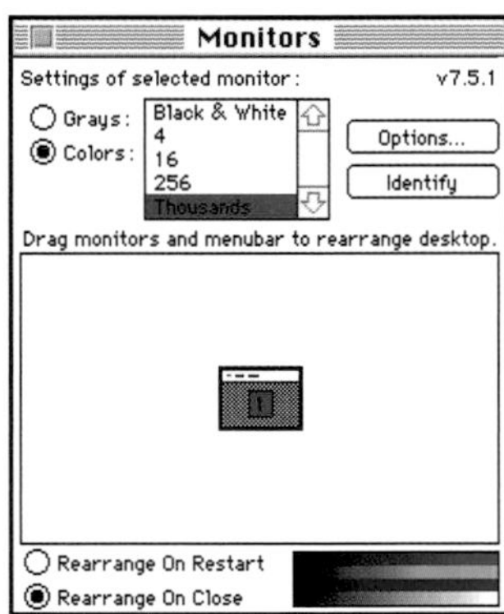

Macintosh: Open the Control Panel called Monitors or Monitors and Sound. (Control panel items located in System folder.)

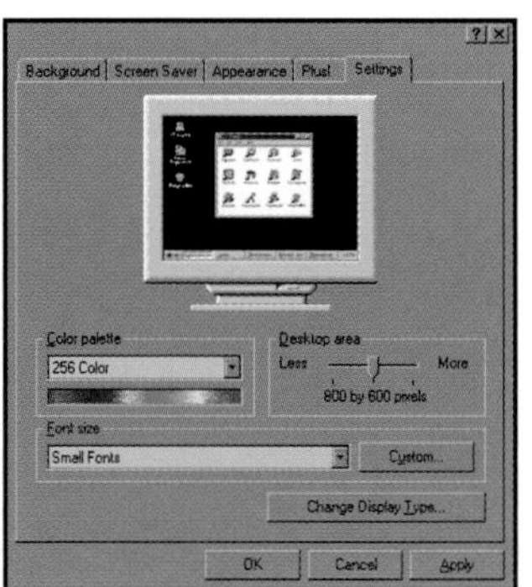

Windows 95 and/or Windows 98 PC: To access your display properties, right-click any empty area of the desktop (area not occupied by an icon) and select **Properties** from the pop-up submenu.

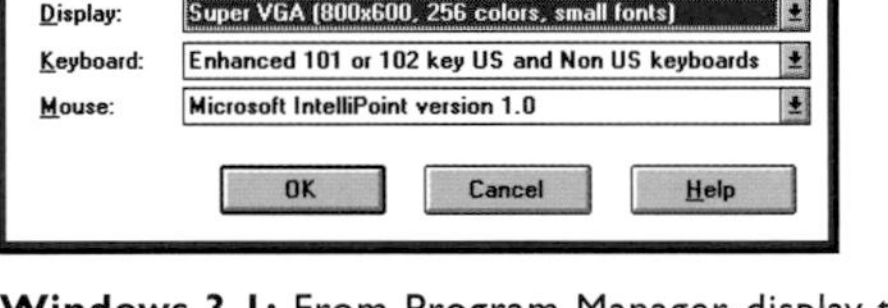

Windows 3.1: From Program Manager, display the Change System Settings dialog box by double-clicking on the Windows Setup icon (found in Main program group). Choose **Options:Change System Settings**.

Type Differences

To add to the long list of frustrations, type is displayed differently on Macs and PCs. Macintoshes display type at 72 dpi, and PCs display type at 96 dpi. To demonstrate the problem, I took a screen shot of my site on a PC using 12pt. type and on a Mac using 12pt. type. Besides the fact that the two systems use different default fonts (Macs use Times Roman and PCs use Times New Roman), notice that 12pt. type is displayed differently on the two systems. That's because of the dpi difference between the two platforms.

MAC

PC

MAC/PC Combination

Notice how the images are the same size on the two monitors, but the type is different? This illustrates the different measurement standards between Macs and PCs.

Solutions for the problem, such as CSS, type embedding, and using images for type, are addressed in Chapter 16, "Web Typography." However, I can offer one overriding bit of advice: Don't use small fonts when designing on the PC. They will be miniscule on Macintoshes. Like every other problem this chapter lists, it's imperative that you check the results of your page design on multiple platforms so you can correct any serious problems.

Monitor Size Considerations

One of the hardest things to address when you're trying to design an effective layout for your site is the fact that a Web page has no fixed size. Some browsers have predefined sizes that the viewing window fits into; others let you size the screen to fill your monitor. Some of your audience will see your page through tiny portable computer screens. Others will have 21" monitors.

My friend, **Mike Kuniavsky**, who works at **wired.com**, is responsible for their usability studies. They have a system in which they study people who are new to Web surfing in order to gauge their responses to the Hotwired site's navigation. Their studies proved conclusively that many newcomers to the Web don't understand that you can scroll beyond the first screen. This study reinforced my intuitive sense that your site's opening screen should fit within a window without requiring any scrolling.

No method enables you to detect what monitor size your viewer is using. You can make assumptions about your audience based on some of the guidelines in Chapter 1, or you can choose the lowest common denominator method, which is what I do for my site.

I tend to err on the conservative side when suggesting width restrictions for graphics on a Web page. The width of an average computer monitor—even many portables—is 640 pixels, and I think there should be some breathing room around that. On the Macintosh, Netscape's opening screen defaults to 505 pixels across. I've picked 480 pixels as a good width for an opening graphic or headline. That's the approximate width of the menu bar for Netscape's home page. This rule is not cast in stone. I'm simply describing the sizes of some of the environments your page will be viewed in and arriving at a size based on how I would want my graphics to be viewed.

If you have decided to use plug-ins on your site, you might consider creating a Flash-based site. Flash is described in greater detail in Chapter 5, "Web File Formats," and Chapter 25, "Flash & Shockwave." It is a vector-based graphics format that will actually scale to whatever size window the site is viewed from. Version 4.5 of Netscape supports Flash without a plug-in, and it is rumored that Explorer support will soon follow.

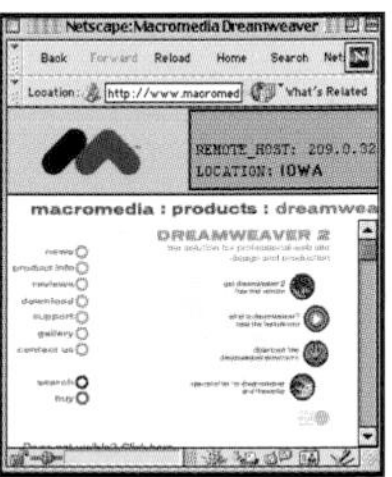

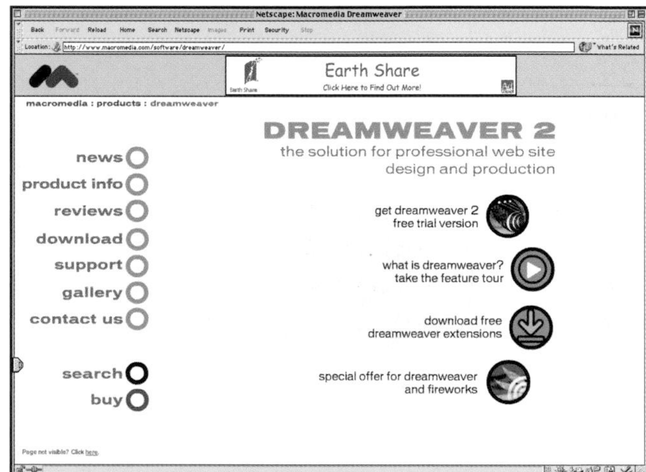

Macromedia's Flash-based site (http://www.macromedia.com) scales to whatever size browser window from which it is viewed.

WebTV

The advent of Web delivery via television screens introduces a new audience to our pages, as well as a new can of worms for our authoring concerns. As you can see by the set-up screen below, WebTV allows the end viewer to set up his or her preferences for text size and size adjustments. Here's one more area where you have to relinquish that precious design control most of us crave.

Television is a very different medium than the computer. It has lower resolution: A standard computer monitor displays 640x480 pixels, while a standard television monitor displays 544x378. Television uses NTCS color space, which is very sensitive to highly saturated colors, such as pure reds, greens, blues, yellows, cyans and magentas. Television is interlaced, meaning that it displays two alternating images to create a single image. This can cause single pixel lines to jitter. The Web TV system uses a convolution filtering system to reduce flicker, and it works quite well.

WebTV screen dimensions are 420x560 pixels. Some of this space is reserved for the WebTV interface and navigation bars:

- 6 pixel margin at the top of the screen
- 8 pixel margin at the left and bottom of the screen
- 36 pixel area at the bottom of the screen for title bar

The majority of people who have actually viewed Web TV (go to your local electronics store to check it out) are impressed at how well their pages translate. One difference is that the font tags you use (for more information on HTML font tags, check out Chapter 16, "Web Typography") will be altered to a larger typeface, as shown below.

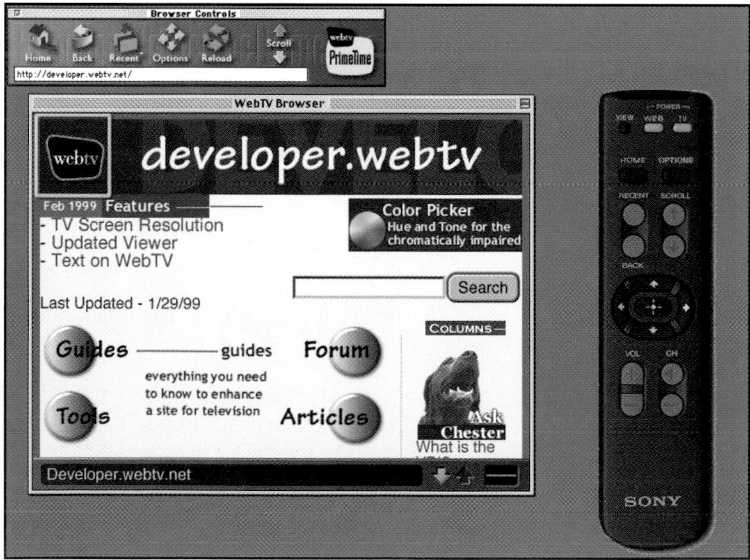

If you download the WebTV viewer, you can simulate how your site will fare on WebTV. Nothing is as accurate as really viewing your site with a terminal, but this is the next best thing. You can download the viewer from http://developer.webtv.net/design/tools/viewer/Default.htm.

Web TV Supports
Animated GIFs
Tables
Background Color
Colored Text
Background Tiles
Sound (RealAudio v2, AU, WAV, VMF, AIFF, ShockWave audio, GSM, MPEG II audio, and layer 3 MPEG I)
Inline JPGs, GIF89a
Frames
Shockwave
Flash (Make sure Flash movies do not exceed 100k in size)
Web TV does not support
VRML plug-ins
JavaScript
QuickTime movies
Proprietary Plug-ins
Java
Frames

Note: Many of the plug-in-based and streaming movie technologies are too RAM intensive. Remember, Web-TV is not a computer, and has a price-point that doesn't support high-end dedicated hardware.

Unsupported HTML Tags
HTML Committee
<APPLET>
<A TITLE REL REV URN>
<DFN>
<DL COMPACT>
<FORM ENCTYPE>
<FRAME>
<FRAMESET>
<IMG ALT LOWSRC>
<META NAME>
<NEXTID>
<OL COMPACT>
<PARAM>
<PRE WIDTH>
<SCRIPT>
<STYLE>
<TABLE HEIGHT>
<TD NOWRAP>
<UL COMPACT>
<TEXTAREA WRAP>
Netscape
<BLINK>
<BODY ALINK>
<EMBED>
<ISINDEX PROMPT>
<lI VALUE>
<SERVER PUSH>
<WBR>
Internet Explorer
<FONT FACE>
<IMG DYNSRC LOOP>
<PLAINTEXT>

If you're curious about designing for WebTV, check out their developer docs at http://developer.webtv.com.

WebTV Design Tips

A list follows that offers design tips for WebTV friendly sites. This was culled from the Design Tips list on the WebTV site. It includes my comments, annotations, and tips as well (http://www.developer.webtv.com).

- You will be warned not to use full red or full white; both cause screen distortion. Many sites use pure-white backgrounds for their Web pages however, and so far those that I've personally viewed over Web TV have looked acceptable.
- Use client-side imagemaps instead of server-side imagemaps; it works better with a remote control. See Chapter 15, "Imagemaps" for details on programming client-side imagemaps.
- You will be warned to avoid small text sizes in HTML. The truth is, if you do use small text sizes, WebTV will convert them to a larger font on-the-fly. You don't really have to redesign your pages, it's just that WebTV will go in and change your small typefaces for you.
- Avoid small type in in graphics. The resolution of a TV screen does not produce as crisp a display as a computer monitor, and small type is much more difficult to read.
- Avoid narrow columns; images are scaled and text will wrap frequently.
- Try to reduce the number of items on your page because television audiences are used to looking at one focal point.
- Use light-colored text against dark-colored backgrounds; television audiences find it easier to read. Contrast is very important; subtle color changes that would display on a computer screen might not even appear on TV.
- Don't use horizontal single pixel lines because they flicker on television sets.
- Use images with size hints (the IMG width and height attributes) to speed up load time.
- The best way to ensure your page looks good on WebTV is to view it on a WebTV Internet terminal. The WebTV site has just recently released a viewer that you can download from http://developer.webtv.net/tools/viewer/Default.htm.
- If you're going to use a browser detection script to serve different pages to WebTV, its User Agent information is: "~/WebTV". More information on browser detection and user agent information can be found in Chapter 22, "JavaScrip: Rollovers & More."

Comparing WebTV to the Net

The following examples show how WebTV translated my site. I used the WebTV viewer to take these screen captures.

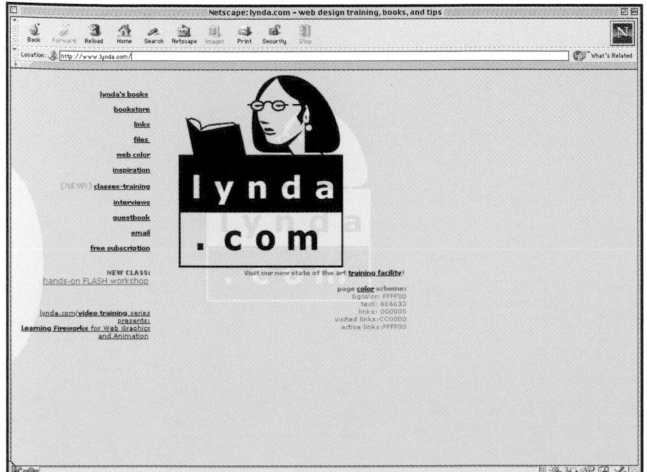

Here's http://www.lynda.com viewed through Netscape.

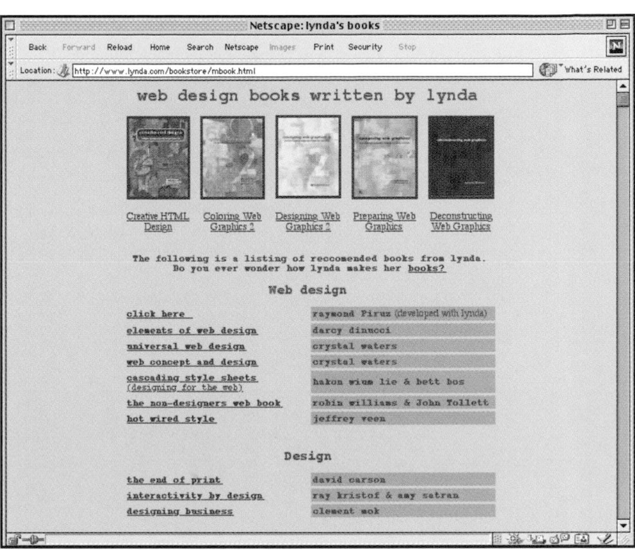

Here's http://www.lynda.co/bookstore/ viewed through Netscape.

On WebTV, there are no scrollbars. Instead, the system pages down to each screen using an arrow key. The type will be enlarged by the WebTV browser to enhance readability on a television monitor. **Note:** Links are highlighted in yellow bounding boxes.

summary Web Authoring Environments

The Web environment is one of the most challenging mediums in computing today. Cross-platform authoring is possible on the Web, but that doesn't necessarily mean it looks good. Take the following items into consideration, and you'll be able to make the best of a difficult design situation:

> Assume that your site will look different on different computer monitors and platforms.

> Work in 72 dpi and pay attention to the size monitor you are designing for.

> Test your pages on other platforms and make informed decisions for changes if necessary.

> Pay attention to the brightness and contrast of your graphics so they will look their best, even when viewed under poor monitor conditions.

> Don't design with very small font sizes. Test your type to verify that it is readable on multiple computer platforms.

> Create your opening screen to fit inside a monitor window without using the scrollbars.

Introduction

Web File Formats

Chapter Topics

- Bitmap or Vector?
- Lossy or Lossless
- GIF
- JPEG
- PNG
- Digital Watermarks
- MNG

5

Most of us have never cared a hoot about file formats. A file format is something that is in the background of daily tasks—a formality for saving computer files, but nothing beyond that. You might be used to saving files as BMP, PICT, TIFF, EPS, or Photoshop (PSD), but it's not like any of those file types have any special place in your heart.

The Web has introduced some new file formats which, beyond formality, directly affect the performance of your Web site. That starts to get a little closer to the heart, right? Maybe not, but trust me. If you understand a bit about the various Web file formats, your site will perform better for it.

This chapter offers the inside scoop on Web file formats, hopefully without getting too nerdy on you. As usual, I've tried to condense the information to the interesting essentials, in order to spare you from technical overload. Still, I can't in good conscience spare you entirely, or my mission to help you make faster and better looking Web sites would fail.

There are many file formats in the world to write about, but this chapter provides an overview of the main Web-based file format contenders; Chapter 6, "Low-Bandwidth Graphics," offers detailed instruction on how to make the smallest possible graphics.

Bitmap or Vector?

File formats for computer graphics typically fall under two categories: bitmap or vector. If you have worked at all in computer graphics already, some familiar bitmap formats might be Photoshop (PSD), PICT, BMP, or TIFF. Common vector formats include Illustrator, QuarkXPress, FreeHand, EPS, and PostScript. None of these formats are used for the Web because they produce files that are too large to download.

The most widely supported image formats on the Web are GIF, JPEG, and soon-to-be PNG. Part of the reason why they are so widely supported is because these file formats are native MIME types to most browsers. This means that end viewers see these types of graphics easily, without changing any settings in their browser or doing anything special beyond typing in an URL. Web developers like us can publish GIFs and JPEGs (and soon-to-be PNG) to our hearts content, without fear that they won't be seen. As you can imagine, getting a file format accepted as a recognized MIME type by the browser vendors or W3C (**W**orld **W**ide **W**eb **C**onsortium) can make or break a file format's viability.

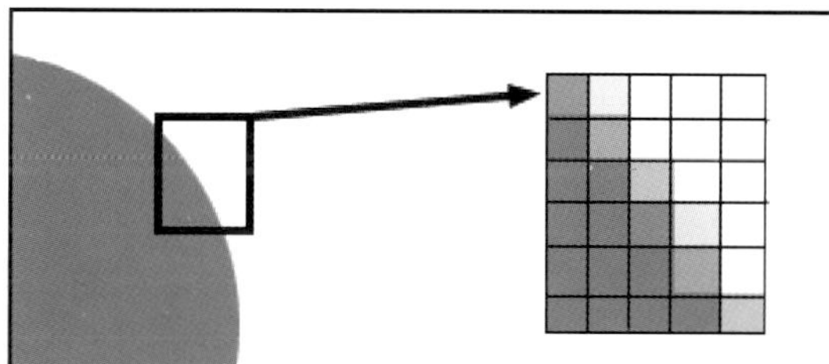

Raster, or bitmap, artwork is stored as a series of values.

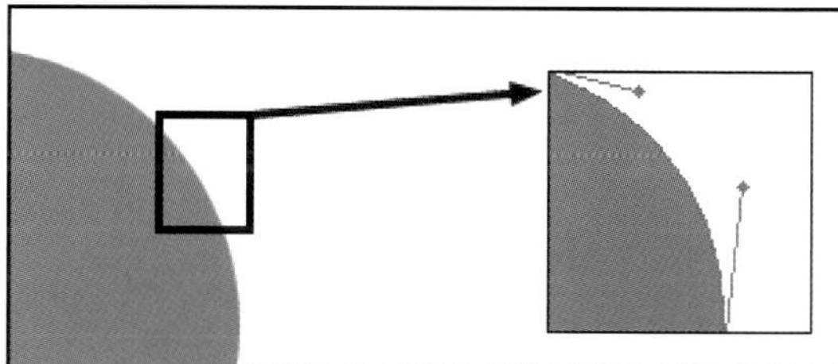

Vector artwork is stored as mathematical instructions.

GIFs, JPEGs, and PNGs are all bitmap formats, also known as "raster graphics" in some circles. A bitmap file is stored by the computer as a series of values, with each pixel taking a set amount of memory. That is why the same exact image that is scaled at 100% will take more memory than one that has been reduced to 50%. Every pixel counts for a set amount of memory.

Vector graphics are a different story. Vector graphics contain a series of lines, curves, and splines that form different shapes through mathematical instructions. A very simplistic explanation follows: Suppose you had an image that contained a line that was 20 pixels long. In a bitmap format, this image would take 20 pixels to describe, while the same line in a vector format might only take one mathematical instruction, such as a start and end location of the line. Unlike raster formats, vector formats take the same amount of memory regardless of whether they are scaled big or small.

Vector formats are resolution independent, meaning they will scale according to the output device, without affecting the amount of disk space they take up (or in Web terms, without affecting the amount of downloading time they require or the size of the browser window!). In the print world, the same 100k vector graphic image will print at 300 dots per inch on a home printer or 2,400 dots per inch on a professional imagesetter printer. The vector format prints at whatever resolution the printing device allows, as all it really contains is a set of mathematical instructions that are interpreted by the printing device.

Bitmap files are the opposite. If any of you has ever created bitmap images for print graphics, you will testify to the need to work with huge file sizes. It is not uncommon that a Photoshop image for a magazine might be over 100 megabytes. Since the file savings and device independence of vectors is indisputable, you might start to recognize the efficiency a vector format would bring to the Web.

It should be strongly noted that vector graphics are more suited for line art, illustrations, type, and flat-style artwork than bitmaps. Bitmaps are better suited for continuous tone images, such as photographs, blurry images, soft edges, glows, and drop shadows. While you can succeed at presenting line art in a bitmap format and can attempt to simulate a continuous tone image in a vector format (with lots of complex fills and gradients), ideally each format is best suited for specific types of content.

Vector formats can typically scale to any dimension and still retain perfect resolution. It's because they are resolution independent.

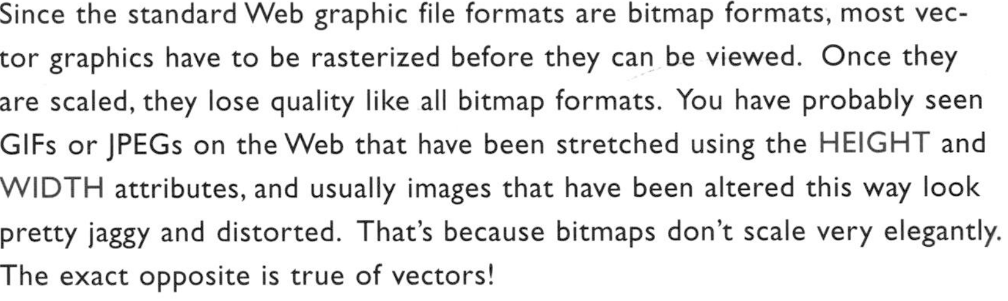

Since the standard Web graphic file formats are bitmap formats, most vector graphics have to be rasterized before they can be viewed. Once they are scaled, they lose quality like all bitmap formats. You have probably seen GIFs or JPEGs on the Web that have been stretched using the HEIGHT and WIDTH attributes, and usually images that have been altered this way look pretty jaggy and distorted. That's because bitmaps don't scale very elegantly. The exact opposite is true of vectors!

Common imaging tools which create vectors are CorelDraw, Illustrator, FreeHand, QuarkXPress, and PageMaker. Common imaging tools which create bitmaps are Photoshop, Paint Shop Pro, Image Composer, and Macromedia Director.

At the moment, the only vector format with much browser support is Flash, distributed by Macromedia (more in-depth information about Flash is covered in Chapter 25, "Flash & Shockwave"). Adobe has a proposal into the W3C for Web-vector format PGML (**P**recision **G**raphics **M**arkup **L**anguage), which has not yet been accepted. My hope is that vector formats will become widely supported in the future, because it is a much smaller and smarter way to deliver certain styles of artwork, such as typographic art, line art, and certain illustrations.

Bitmap formats, such as GIF and JPEG, look terrible when scaled. The number of pixels stay the same but because they get enlarged they look distorted and jaggy.

Lossless or Lossy?

What do all file formats for the Web have in common? Compression. Compression is the key which creates small graphics. Compression is not a necessary feature in other computer graphic file format specifications, which is why the file formats you'll find on the Web might be new to you. Web-based image file formats have to implement impressive compression schemes in order to transform large images to small file sizes. Unfortunately, at times, with compression comes loss of quality.

Before going too heavily into formats, it's necessary to define some terms. Lossless compression means that even though the file is compressed (enjoys a smaller file size than an uncompressed image), it will not lose any quality. A lossless image will contain identical data regardless of whether it is compressed or uncompressed. The popular file format GIF uses lossless compression.

Lossy compression is the opposite of lossless compression. Data is removed from the image in order to achieve compression. Often, this loss of data is not visible because the compression algorithm was designed to reduce data that wasn't essential. The popular JPEG file format uses lossy compression.

note

GIF Pronunciation

GIF is officially pronounced with a soft *G* as in **"jiffy."** Many people pronounce it with a hard *G* as well. I pronounce it both ways, depending on my mood. Since the word is an acronym for **G**raphics **I**nterchange **F**ormat, you would think it should have a hard *G*. But it doesn't. Some people don't care, and pronounce it the way it should be pronounced grammatically instead of the way it was pronounced back in its CompuServe days. Some people don't know it should have a soft *G* and pronounce it with a hard *G*. Some people don't care either way.

GIF Compression

Unlike most other computer graphic file formats, GIF (**G**raphic **I**nterchange **F**ormat) was designed specifically for online delivery because it was originally developed for CompuServe in the late 1980s. GIF uses a compression scheme called LZW, which is based on work done by Lempel-Ziv & Welch. The patent for LZW compression is owned by a company called Unisys, which charges developers such as Netscape and Photoshop licensing and royalty fees for selling products that use the GIF file format. End users, such as ourselves (Web designers) and our audience (Web visitors), do not have to pay licensing fees or worry about any of this.

There is some speculation that the GIF file format may be less prevalent at some point because of the fees, but we hope not. GIFs are accepted by all browsers, GIFs are small, and GIFs do things that many other file formats do not, such as animation, transparency, and interlacing.

The GIF file format, by definition, can contain only 256 colors or less. This is not the case with JPEGs, which by definition contain millions of colors (24-bit). Because GIFs are an indexed color file format (256 colors or less), it's extremely beneficial to have a thorough understanding of bit-depth settings and palette management when preparing GIF images.

There are two different flavors of GIF: **GIF87a** and **GIF89a**. GIF87a supports transparency and interlacing whereas GIF89a supports transparency, interlacing, and animation (more information on these features follow). As of this book's printing, the major browsers (Netscape, Internet Explorer, and Mosaic) all support both GIF format specifications. You don't really have to refer to the names GIF89a or GIF87a unless you want to sound nerdy. Most of us simply call these files by the features used, be it a transparent GIF, animated GIF, or plain vanilla GIF.

GIF compression is lossless, meaning that the GIF compression algorithm will not cause any unwanted image degradation. The process of converting a 24-bit image to 256 or fewer colors will cause image degradation on its own, however, so don't get too excited!

Interlaced GIFs

If you've toured the Web much, you've encountered interlaced GIFs. They're images that start out blocky and appear less and less blocky until they come into full focus.

These examples simulate the effect of interlacing on a browser. The image starts chunky and comes into focus over time. This allows the end viewer to decide whether to wait for your graphic to finish or just click onward.

Interlacing doesn't affect the overall size or speed of a GIF. In theory, interlacing is supposed to make it possible for your end viewer to get a rough idea of your visuals and to make a decision whether to wait or click onward before the image finishes rendering. Again—in theory—this is supposed to save time. Unfortunately for the end viewer, being forced to wait for the entire image to finish coming into focus to read essential information is often a frustrating experience. In other words, interlaced images save time if you don't have to wait for them to finish.

My recommendation is that you do not use interlaced GIFs for important visual information that is critical to viewing your site. An imagemap or navigation icon, for example, must be seen in order to fulfill its function. Although interlaced GIFs serve their purpose on non-essential graphics, they only frustrate end users when used on essential graphics.

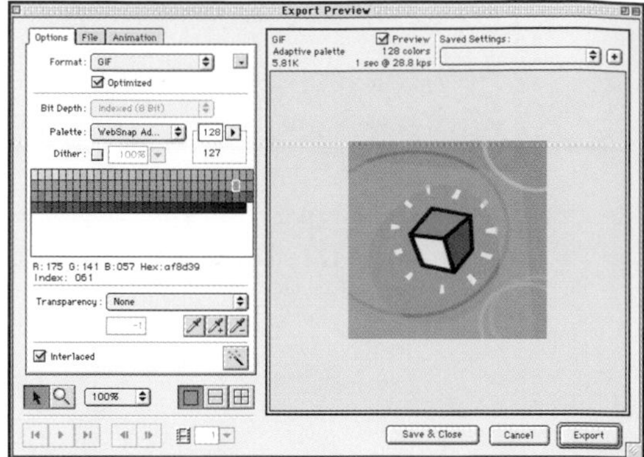

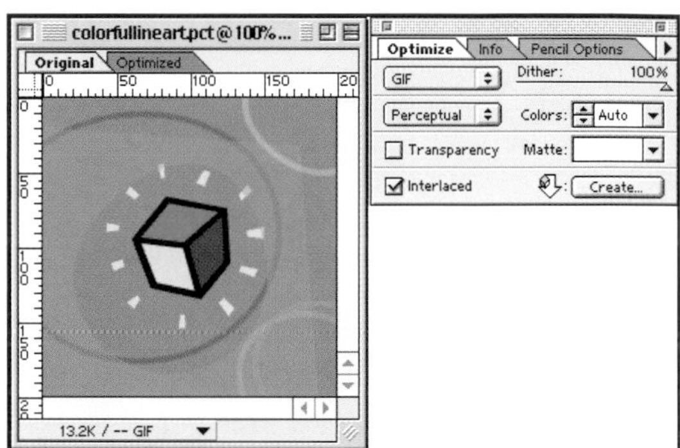

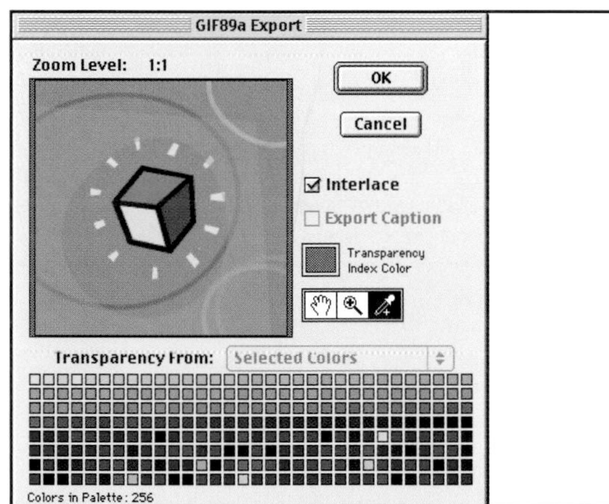

You create an interlaced GIF in an image editing program. In Photoshop, ImageReady, and Fireworks, all you do is click an Interlaced GIF check box and the file is written this way automatically. You won't see the results in any software application except a browser.

Transparent GIFs

Transparent GIFs are used to create the illusion of irregularly shaped artwork. All of the computer-made images end up in rectangular-shaped files; it's the nature of the medium. Certain file formats, such as GIF, can store masked regions, which create the illusion of shapes other than rectangles. This "masked region" appears to be transparent. Creating transparent GIFs is discussed in Chapter 13, "Transparent Artwork."

This screen shows the transparent artwork in context. Once the GIF transparency is recognized within browser software, the browser enables the rectangular artwork to appear irregularly shaped.

Animated GIFs

Animated GIFs are part of the GIF89a specification. They are often called multi-block GIFs because multiple images can be stored as separate blocks within a single GIF document. When the GIF document is viewed, the multiple images display, one at a time, and produce a slide show effect. Once the animated GIF file has finished downloading, it can play very fast and look more like animation than a slide show.

Animated GIFs can include custom palette information and be set to play at different speeds. They can also include interlacing and transparency settings. The beauty of animated GIFs is that they require no plug-ins, and the authoring tools to create them are often free and easy to learn. As well, major browsers (Netscape, Internet Explorer, and AOL) support them, so you can include them in Web pages without worrying about compatibility or accessibility. Specific instruction on how to create animated GIFs and apply custom palettes is available in Chapter 21, "GIF Animation."

Here's a 30-frame GIF. It's hard to tell the subtle changes from frame to frame when viewed in sequence, but once the frames are played in motion over time the '50s man appears to be bobbing his head and waving his finger, and has little lines flowing from the side of his head. It totals 64k in size. Why? It's only two colors, with no anti-aliasing.

JPEG

The JPEG (pronounced jay-peg) file format offers a 24-bit alternative to the 8-bit GIF file format. This is especially great for photographic content because 24-bit photographs will always look better than 8-bit photographs. One added advantage to dealing with JPEGs is that they don't need you to define the palette for them, unlike GIFs. Whenever an image format includes millions of colors (24-bit), palette and color mapping issues disappear. This is because enough colors are allowed to rely on the original image's color information, and substitute colors are no longer necessary.

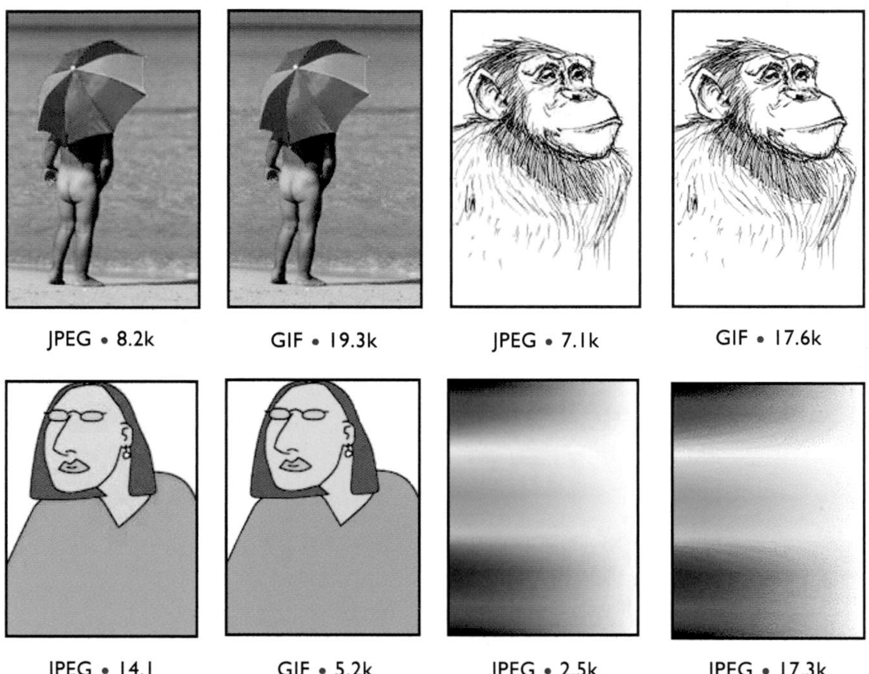

JPEG handles images with subtle gradations beautifully. This is in part because the file format enables the image to remain in 24-bit. Compare the JPEG images to the left to the 8-bit GIF images to the right. The JPEGs compress photographic style images better than graphic style images and look better too!

JPEG was developed specifically for photographic-style images. It looks to areas with subtle tonal and color changes and offers the best compression when it encounters that type of imagery. It actually does not compress solid color well at all!

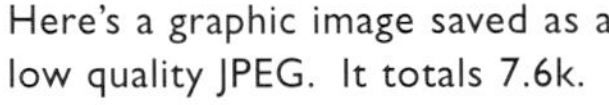

Here's a graphic image saved as a low quality JPEG. It totals 7.6k.

A close-up of JPEG artifacts.

The GIF looks better (no artifacts!), but it is larger at 17.6k.

JPEG is a lossy compression algorithm, meaning that it removes information from your image and, therefore, causes a loss in quality. JPEG does a great job of doing this, so the difference in information data is often not visible or objectionable. It does introduce artifacts in some instances, especially where it encounters solid colors. This is a byproduct of its lossy compression methods.

Unlike the GIF file format, JPEGs require both compression and decompression. This means that JPEG files need to decompress when they're viewed. Although a GIF and a JPEG might be identical sizes, or sometimes even when the JPEG is smaller, the JPEG may take longer to download or view from a Web browser because of the added time required to decompress.

Another difference between GIF and JPEG is the fact that you can save JPEGs in a variety of compression levels. This means that more or less compression can be applied to an image, depending on which looks best.

Progressive JPEGs Versus Standard JPEGs

Progressive JPEGs support interlacing (where the graphic starts chunky and comes into focus). They were initially introduced by Netscape and are now additionally supported by MSIE. Progressive-JPEG-making tools for Mac and PCs are listed at http://www.in-touch.com/pjpeg2.html#software.

One disadvantage to progressive JPEGs is that many older browsers do not support them. A progressive JPEG will appear with a broken image icon on these browsers, which is a penalty many of us are unwilling to suffer.

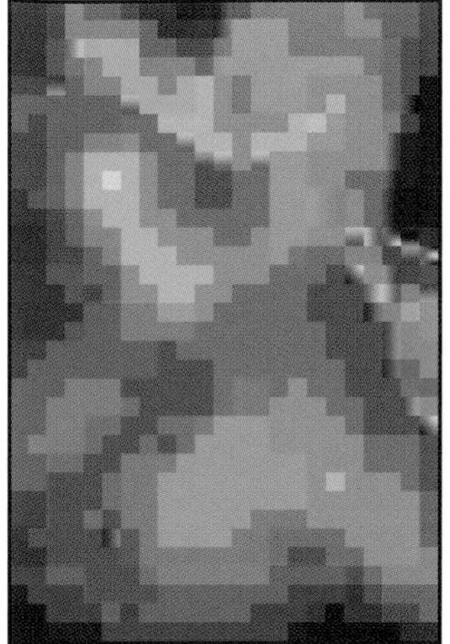

Low • 8.7k

Med • 10.5k

High • 12.4k

Max • 28.9k

PNG

PNG (**P**ortable **N**etwork **G**raphics, or more fondly known as PNG Not GIF) holds fantastic promise as a new Web file format. The W3C (**W**orld **W**ide **W**eb **C**onsortium at http://www.w3.org/pub/WWW/Press/PNG-PR.en.html) has made a formal endorsement of PNG, which has, in turn, caused Netscape and Explorer to partially support the format.

PNG uses a lossless compression method, meaning that no quality loss is incurred when it's applied to images. PNG is compressed using any number of pre-compression filters and is then decompressed when viewed. This enables PNG to retain every original detail and pixel, with no loss of quality.

Unlike GIF or JPEG, PNG can be stored at many different bit depths using different storage methods. GIF, for example, can be stored only in 8-bit or lower bit depths. JPEGs must be stored in 24-bit and no lower. PNG can be stored in either 8-bit or 24-bit or 32-bit. This makes PNG one of the most flexible formats available for Web images and also one of the more difficult formats to program for developers. For this reason, PNG support for browsers and imaging software has been slow coming.

PNG was developed by Thomas Boutell (visit his amazing site at http://www.boutell.com, and the W3C spec pages for PNG at http://www.boutell.com/boutell/png/). Unlike JPEG and GIF, PNG was created to be a cross-platform file format and contains information about the characteristics of the authoring platform so that viewing software can automatically compensate and display the image correctly.

Gamma Correction

Gamma correction enables an image to display properly on different platforms without losing contrast or brightness in the translation. Differences in gamma between different platforms can make an image seem darker or lighter on a platform other than the one it was created on. PNG has the capacity to store a value that represents the gamma of the system on which the image was created. This value can then be used by the displaying system to correct for its gamma value, if known.

The only caveat for gamma correction to work is that both the creating and displaying systems must know their own gamma, and this is usually not the case in today's Web world. Here's a case of a good idea with little to no browser or tool support.

Alpha Channel Transparency

The PNG format has the capacity to store a variable transparency value known as alpha-channel transparency. This allows your images to have up to 256 different levels of partial transparency (or translucency).

My misconception about PNG images was that you had to use a 32-bit palette to use alpha-channel transparency, which was not true. The PNG format allows any entry in any palette to represent any channel, either Red, Green, Blue, or Alpha (these palettes are called RGBA instead of RGB).

note

PNG Resources

The Siegel & Gale PNG Live plug-in for Netscape 4
http://codelab.siegelgale.com/solutions/pnglive2.html

The PNG Specification at W3C
http://www.w3.org/TR/REC-png-multi.html

Digtal Watermarks

The term watermark is traditionally used to describe special printed paper that guarantees proof of authenticity and ownership. Dollar bills are a good example of watermarked currency, which has special information embedded in the paper stock to prevent counterfeiting.

Digital watermarks are a new technology that follow a similar principle, only the embedded copyright information is not visible until loaded into a computer that can read it. Watermarking technology can embed copyright notification, ownership, audience (adult or general interest material), and usage information (restricted or royalty free). The watermark signature can be read by Photoshop and Digimarc.

Digimarc (http://digimarc.com/) offers a digital watermarking service that offers watermarking software and a database/retrieval service for professionals. Their fee structure is listed on their site.

The **PictureMarc** plug-in for Photoshop is digital watermarking software that enables you to embed watermarks into digital documents for print- or Web-based submission. When PictureMarc is invoked, you are given the opportunity to obtain your own creator ID, which links your images to up-to-date contact information that is stored on the Digimarc site.

Every time an image is opened or scanned into Photoshop, PictureMarc performs a quick detection and adds a © to the Image window's title bar. By clicking on the © on the title bar, PictureMarc launches your Web browser and displays detailed information about the image and lists whatever contact details you have provided.

This service supports CMYK, RGB, LAB, Grayscale, and Index Color color spaces, and it works with any file format type that Photoshop supports on NT, Win95, Win3.1, and Mac (68000 and PPC) platforms. A minimum image size of 256×256 pixels is required, which makes its usefulness for the Web limited to larger images, thereby unfortunately excluding navigational graphics, buttons, bullets, and rules.

MNG

We've already discussed PNG and that it is inferior to the GIF format only in its lack of animation features (and widespread browser support). A new proposal has been submitted to the W3C for a file format called MNG. Glenn Randers-Pehrson, a research physicist at the U.S. Army Research Laboratory and one of the developers of the PNG format, is leading the MNG development effort.

He has posted an interesting article about MNG on the W3 Journal site: http://www.w3j.com/5/s3.randers.html. (By the way, the W3 Journal site is pretty neat on its own. Take off all the end slashes of the URL, and give it a visit when you have time to read a slew of interesting articles and commentaries.) The latest version of the MNG proposal from the PNG Development Group is available at ftp://swrinde.nde.swri.edu/pub/mng/.

MNG stands for **M**ultiple image **N**etwork **G**raphics, and is being positioned as an additional member of the PNG file format family, which will be used for storing and presenting multiple image animations.

Advantages to MNG

Because all the images within a MNG file are PNG files, MNG has the same advantages of PNG. For visual designers, these advantages include:

- Alpha Channel Transparency—the ability to have subtle opacity changes and overlays, creating much more professional looking animation than GIF can provide.
- Platform-independent color fidelity, because the files store gamma and chroma information which travel with the document and display accurately wherever viewed from.
- Single-image GIF (**G**raphical **I**nterchange **F**ormat) files can be losslessly converted to PNG.

In addition, MNG adds the following features:

- It will stream (play back quickly over modem connections).
- Includes the ability to set loops and variable interframe delays.
- Uses "sprites" so that separate movies can be combined. For example, there could be a "background movie" and foreground objects which move. The file format would only store the moving data values, as opposed to re-rendering each frame as an entire image.
- Can implement frame-differencing, meaning similar data will be subtracted from changing data, resulting in smaller file sizes.
- Includes the capability to be scripted in JavaScript and other DHTML-based extensions to HTML, so that movies, timing, and playback can be dictated externally.

Disadvantages to MNG

The primary disadvantage to MNG is that it is in proposal stage only! It will be years before this spec is finalized, implemented by the browser vendors, and supported by toolmakers. I have heard rumors that MNG takes a very long time to decompress, which would impair its capability to stream or compete with GIF animation, even if the files themselves were very small.

summary

Web File Formats

It's important to understand some of the basics of file formats to choose which one to pick for Web delivery. Each file format has strengths and weaknesses and is best suited for certain types of images or delivery. Here is a brief summary of each file type that was reviewed in this chapter:

- For line art, vectors are much smaller and faster to download than bitmaps. Unfortunately, the only vector format for the Web that has gained much acceptance (Flash) still relies on plug-ins for most browser versions. Adobe has proposed a new vector markup language called PGML, but it has not yet been accepted by the W3C.
- GIF uses a lossless compression scheme, but is limited to 256 colors or less (8-bit). It supports interlacing, transparency, and animation.
- JPEG uses lossy compression and is limited to 24-bit. It supports interlacing in its progressive format, but does not support transparency or animation.
- PNG can use lossy or lossless compression, and is capable of storing gamma and alpha channel information. Unfortunately, older browsers cannot render PNG images without a plug-in.
- MNG is in proposal stage right now, but would extend PNG file capabilities to include animation and scriptable actions.

Introduction

Low-Bandwidth Graphics

Chapter Topics

If you look through a book or magazine and see a compelling picture, who cares if the file was eighty gazillion megabytes or one kilobyte? In the print world, there is no experiential penalty to viewing images with large file sizes. On the Web, the exact opposite is true, because large files can cause your audience to leave your site in frustration, regardless of how alluring your pictures promise to be.

It has never been the job of an artist to care about the file savings of a graphic before. If learning to make small and speedy Web graphics is new to you, you are not alone; it's new to lots of people. Fortunately, since the last edition of this book was written, there are lots of great new tools that make the job of optimizing images much easier than ever before.

This chapter reviews the most popular file formats—GIF, JPEG, and PNG—and shows you how to squeeze every kilobyte out of your graphics to ensure they're small, fast, and lookin' good. This is accomplished through understanding compression principles and how to use Web image optimization tools.

If you read the last chapter, you are already familiar with lossy versus lossless compression methods, and you have the background to delve a little further into the nuances of file size savings. This chapter reviews some brand-new tools for image optimization, including Adobe ImageReady and Macromedia Fireworks, as well as some tools with more history, including DeBabelizer, Boxtop Software plug-ins, Digital Frontiers plug-ins, and GIFWizard.

File Size and Downloading Speed

So you know images on the Web have to be small, but how small is small? If you are a digital print designer, you probably don't blink at large file sizes and work on images ranging from tens to hundreds of megabytes as a common, everyday fact of life. Even if you aren't working in graphics or print, you've been hearing that Web graphics have to be small—but again, how small is small?

For those of you who are mathematically challenged (I include myself in this group!), a kilobyte is 1,024 bytes, a megabyte is 1,048,576 bytes, and a gigabyte is 1,073,741,824 bytes. The myth of the Web is that every kilobyte takes 1 second to download. This measurement method would mean that a 30k image would take 30 seconds and a 80 megabyte file could take weeks.

The truth of the matter is that there are many different connection speeds. Universities and large corporations usually have connection speeds that exceed well beyond those of most home users. On a **T1 line** (available at most universities and large companies), a graphic might take a second or two, whereas the same image could take a minute or longer on a slower connection. Unfortunately, your Web images can't sense what type of connection speed your end user has. This is one case where it pays to make small graphics for everyone.

We are a remote-control culture. As soon as Web surfing speed matches channel surfing speed for television, the Web will become a much more viable distribution, entertainment, and information medium. Until bandwidth issues are solved, the pressure is on us as publishers to keep files small so that they download quickly over slow connections.

tip

There's More to Downloading Speed Than Small Images

My site has very small images in terms of file size, yet there are times when it is still slow. This has nothing to do with my images at all, but with the speed of my Web server or the unforeseen bottlenecks of the Internet on any given day.

Many newcomers to Web publishing subscribe to a large service, such as AOL, Earthlink, or GeoCities. They accept the 15mb free Web space as the location for a first Web site. This can work out well for small sites, but for a large, professional site, it pays to go with a service that is dedicated to hosting Web Sites (a presence provider) as opposed to a service that also hosts Internet connection (an **I**nternet **S**ervice **P**rovider, or ISP).

Sometimes, there just isn't anything anyone can do about connection speeds. There was a two or three week period last year when the Mae West router connection failed in San Jose. My Web site crawled, as did my email access. Sometimes, speed is out of everyone's control, and it's one of the wild cards of this medium. Still, you do have control over a big part of the equation, which is to make your images as small as possible. If you do your part, then the Web will be a more tolerable place for all of us.

What Size Your File Really Is

How can you tell how many kilobytes an image is? You would think to look to your hard drive, but even that can be deceptive.

Macs and PCs differ in terms of file size reporting. On a Mac, if you look at your hard drive for the file size of an image, you'll notice that the file size numbers are all nicely rounded figures: 11k, 33k, and 132k. Your computer rounds up the size of a file to the next largest number depending on how large your hard drive partition is. Have you ever had a file read two different file sizes on a hard drive and a floppy? That's because the computer rounds off the size of the file depending on what size storage medium it's on.

radiopict.get info Info

radiopict.get info

Kind: Adobe Photoshop™ 3.0.4 document
Size: 44K on disk (36,152 bytes used)

On a Mac: The only way to get information about the true byte size of a file is to do a Get Info command. First, highlight the file you want to check in the Finder, go to the File menu, and then choose Get Info.

On a PC: The file size shown in the menu is very close to the actual file size, with rounding to the next lowest number occurring. Under DOS, you can get a more accurate reading of the file size, but it is not much different from what you see in Windows.

Most Photoshop users think the readout in the lower left corner of a document informs them about the file size. Not true! These numbers relate to the amount of RAM Photoshop is allocating to your image and its scratch disk virtual memory scheme. The only way to tell what size your Photoshop document truly is, is to look to your hard drive on a PC or to Get Info on a Mac.

tip

Photoshop Icons Take Space

Photoshop typically saves images with an icon. The icon is a small, visual representation of what the image looks like, which the file references. Photoshop icons take up a little extra room on your hard drive. This ultimately won't matter because when you send the files to your server, you'll transmit them as raw data, which will strip off the icon anyway. But if your goal is to get a more accurate reading of the true file size, you should set your preferences in Photoshop to not save an icon.

Personally, I like to leave my Photoshop icons turned on. I deal with so many images on my hard drive that it's very helpful to me to see the icons. I trust the file size increase to disappear once I post the images to a Web site, and enjoy the luxury of a visual representation of my images on my hard drive. Unfortunately, PC operating systems cannot display image icons inside directories, so this is one reason why I prefer doing creative work on my Macintosh system.

To set your preferences to not save the icon, choose **File:Preferences:General**. In the General dialog box, set the Image Previews to **Ask When Saving**.

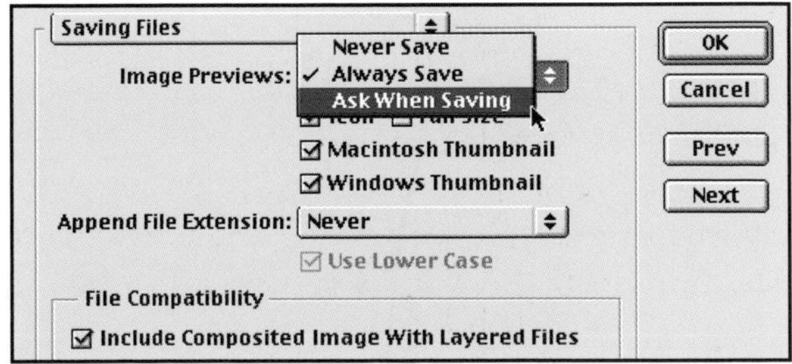

File Size Reporting in ImageReady and Fireworks

Both Fireworks and ImageReady give better feedback about file size than Photoshop. These tools were developed as Web graphics tools, as opposed to Photoshop, which was developed originally for print graphics. Here are some examples of how to read the image size of files in both new products:

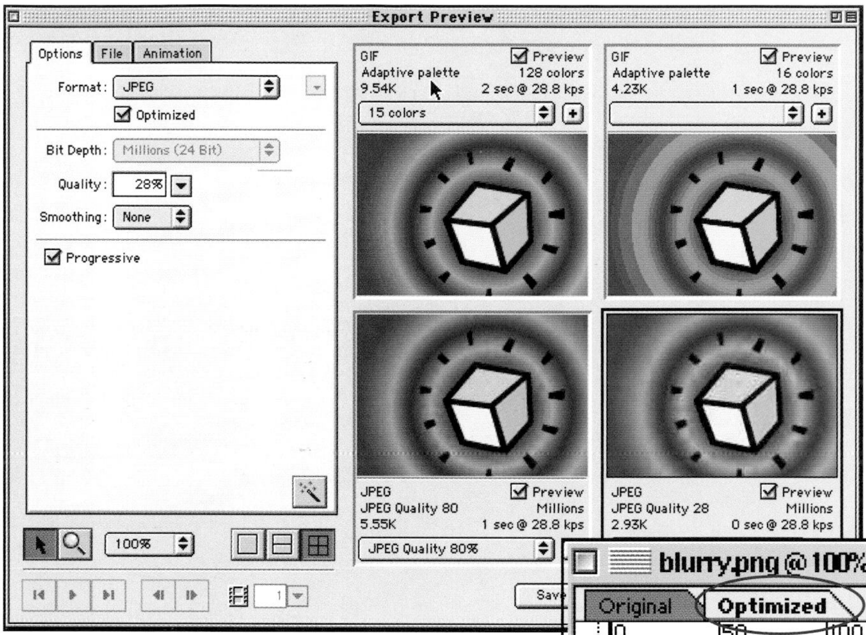

To see the file size of an image while working in Fireworks, choose **File:Export**. By setting the compression choices, the program will interactively display the file size values. The file is actually not compressed or saved until you click the Export button.

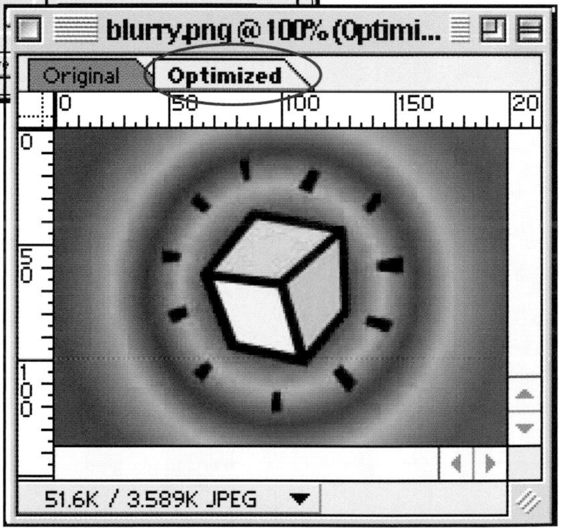

To see the file size of an image while working in ImageReady, click on the **Optimize tab** of the Dual Image window. You can view the image size information, downloading speed, or image dimensions on the bottom Image Info pop-up menu, depending on which choice you select.

Evaluating the Style of Your Image

Throughout this book, you'll notice that I reference different styles of images. Line art is the style that contains a lot of solid colors and lines, such as what you would find in a graphic, illustration, or logo. Continuous-tone art is the style that contains subtle gradations or tones, like those found in photographic content. Hybrid art is a combination of both styles.

LineArt

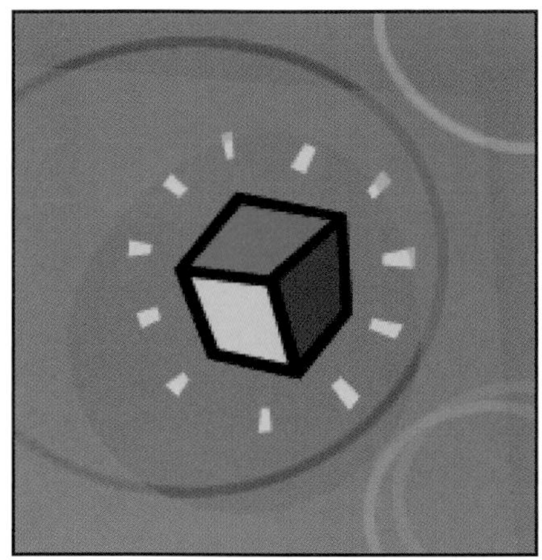

Continuous Tone Artwork

Hybrid Artwork

Different compression types are designed for different style images. GIF compression works much better on line art than photographs. JPEG compression works much better on photographs. Hybrid imagery will work better with JPEG or GIF, depending on the image.

Identifying the style of the image in question will help you make the decision of where to start on your quest for image compression. Keep in mind that the acronyms of GIF (**G**raphic **I**nterchange **F**ormat) and JPEG (**J**oint **P**hotographic **E**xpert **G**roup) describe what types of files these compression algorithms were designed for: GIFs for graphics and JPEGs for photographs.

Saving Photographs as GIFs—None Dither Method

8-bit GIF • 78.5k

7-bit GIF • 66.9k

6-bit GIF • 54.8k

5-bit GIF • 41.9k

4-bit GIF • 32.7k

3-bit GIF • 18.6k

2-bit GIF • 13.3k

1-bit GIF • 8.7k

Saving Photographs as JPEGs

Max • 51.4k

High • 36.2k

Med • 28.3k

Low • 24.8k

Saving Photographs as GIFs—Dither Method

8-bit GIF • 81.1k

7-bit GIF • 69.1k

6-bit GIF • 56.1k

5-bit GIF • 44.2k

4-bit GIF • 34.4k

3-bit GIF • 22.9k

2-bit GIF • 17.7k

1-bit GIF • 12k

While some of the GIF files produced smaller file sizes, the quality was not as good as the smaller JPEG. This example demonstrates clearly that JPEG is the superior compression method for photographic content.

Saving Graphics as GIFs—None Dither Method

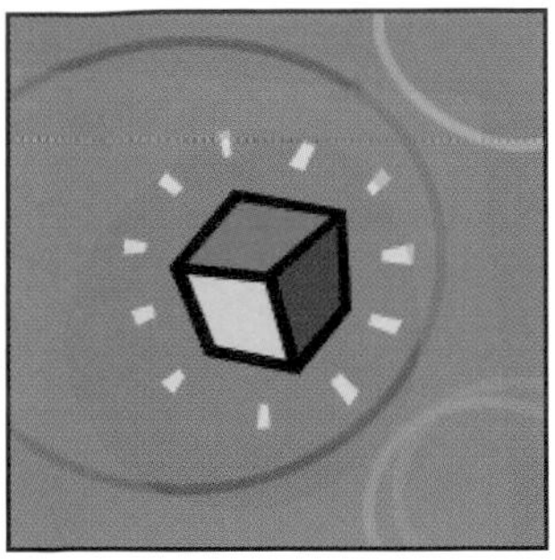

8-bit GIF • 15.3k

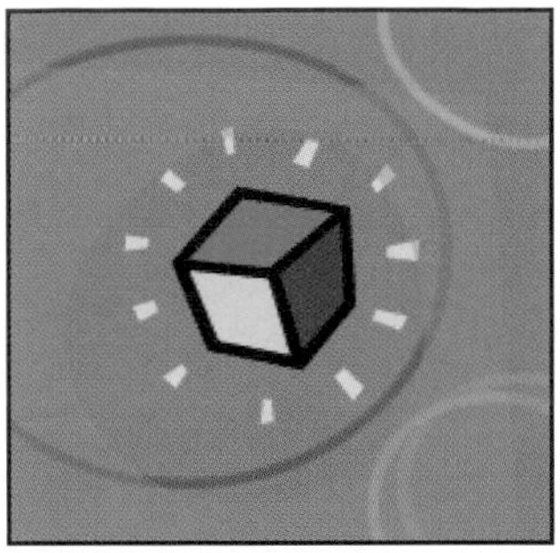

7-bit GIF • 15.3k

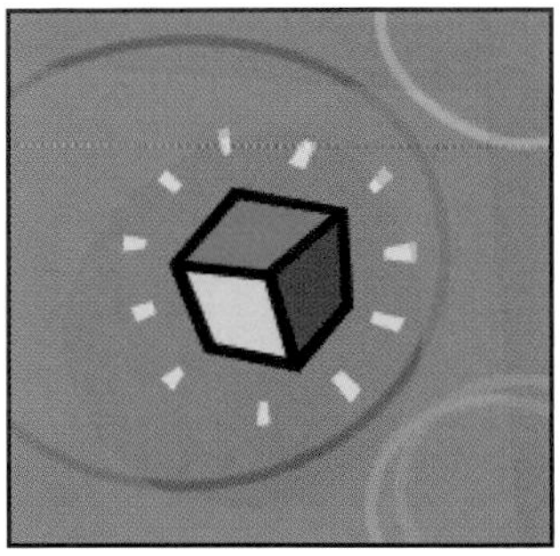

6-bit GIF • 14k

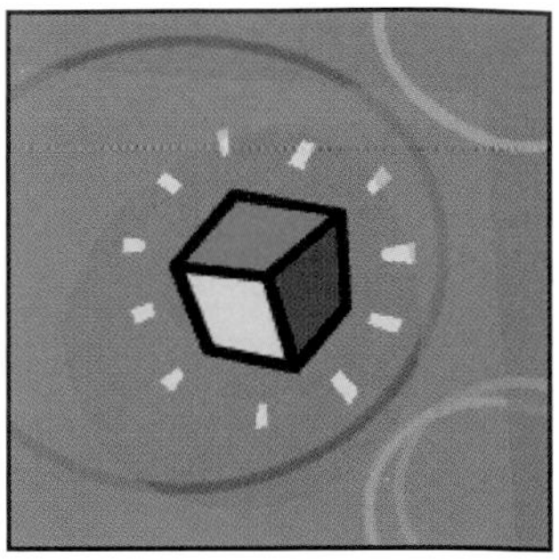

5-bit GIF • 12.8k

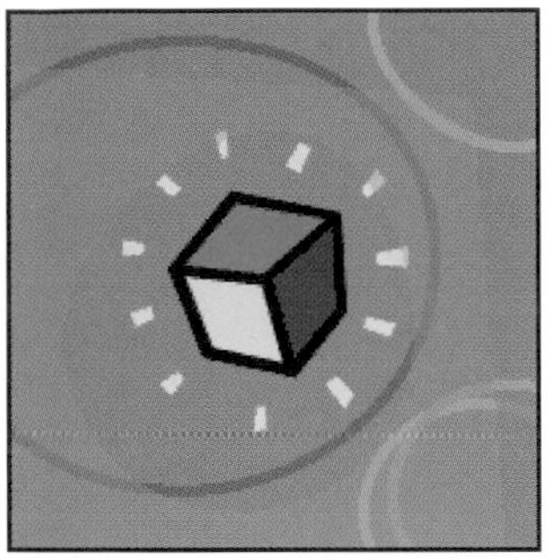

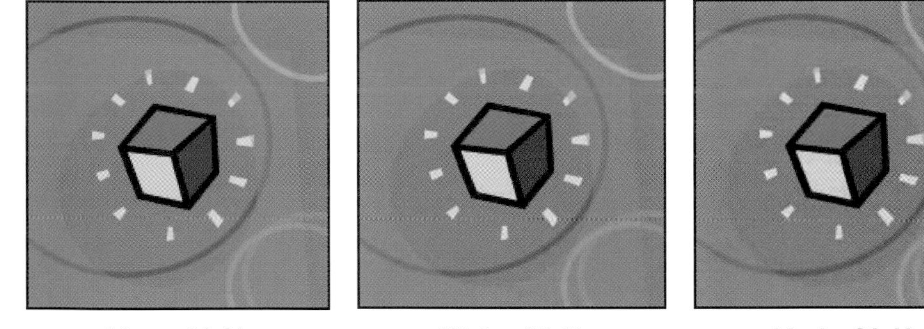

4-bit GIF • 11.5k

3-bit GIF • 9.8k

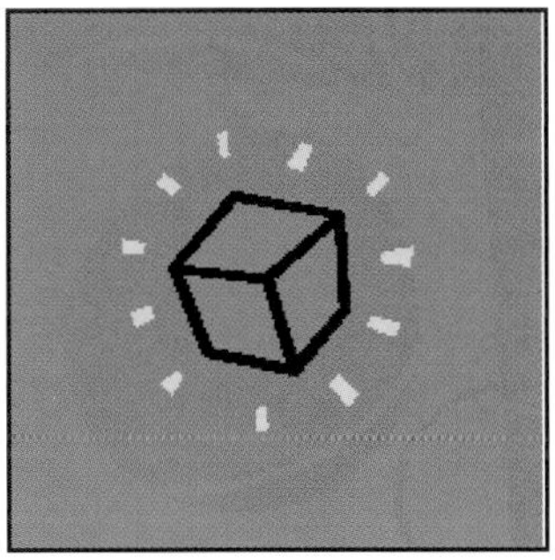

2-bit GIF • 9.1k

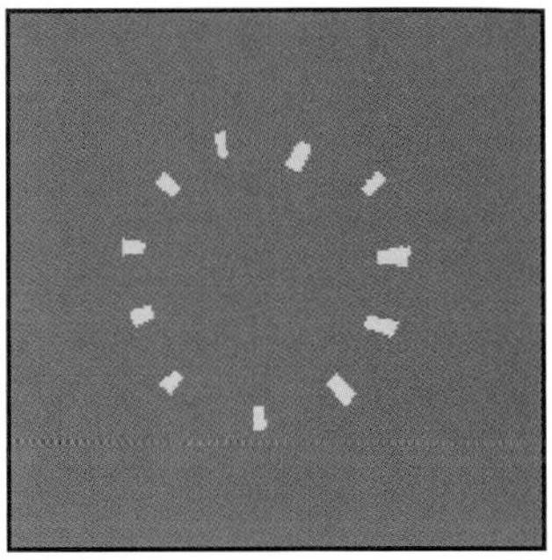

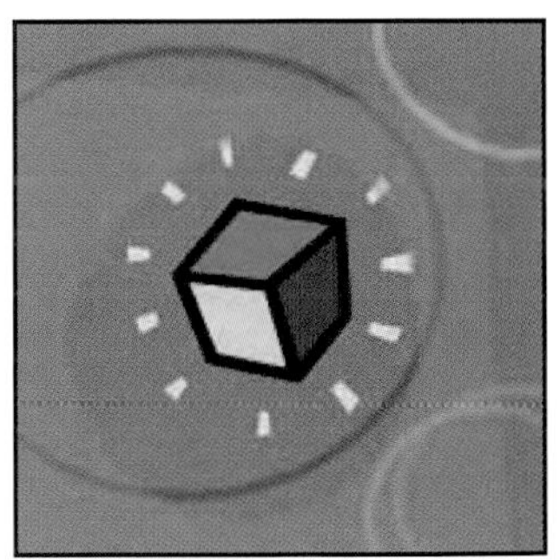

1-bit GIF • 4.7k

Saving Graphics as JPEGs

Max • 28.3k

High • 23.9k

Med • 21.1k

Low • 20k

Saving Graphics as GIFs—Dither Method

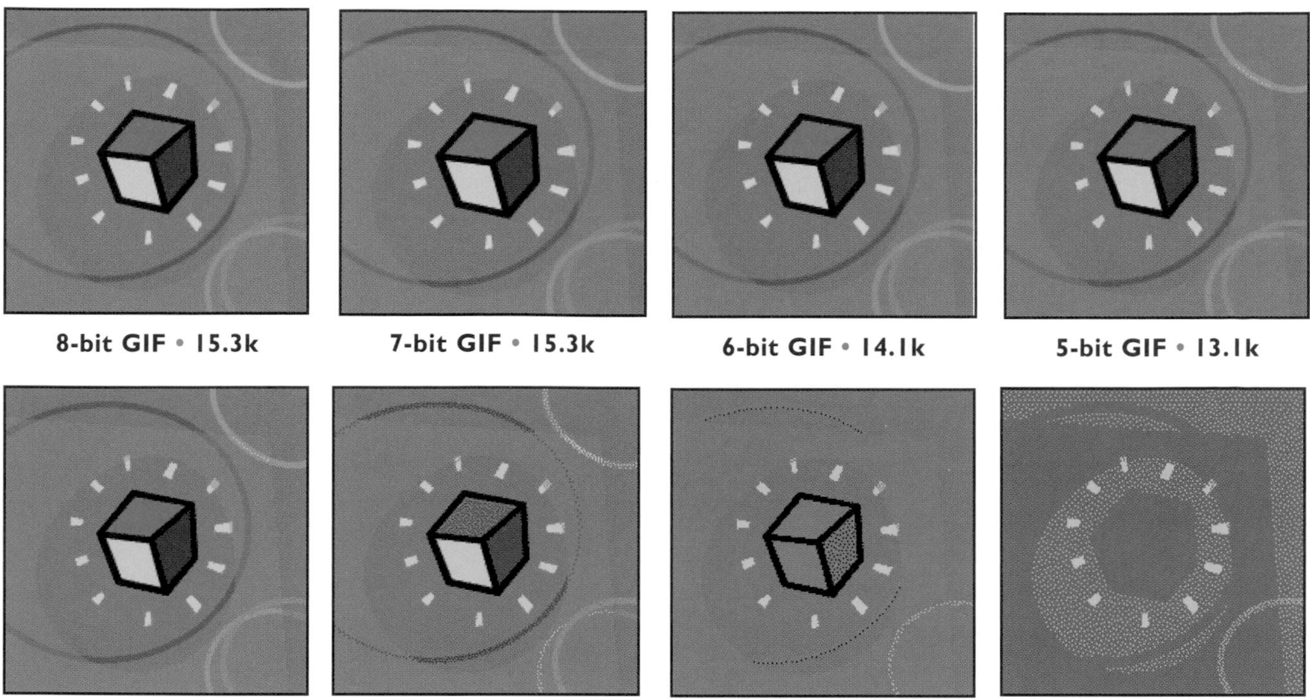

8-bit GIF • 15.3k | 7-bit GIF • 15.3k | 6-bit GIF • 14.1k | 5-bit GIF • 13.1k

4-bit GIF • 11.7k | 3-bit GIF • 11k | 2-bit GIF • 9.8k | 1-bit GIF • 10.5k

These examples demonstrate clearly that the GIF file format produces smaller files for graphic based content.

Making Small JPEGs

The good news is that making small JPEGs is infinitely easier than making small GIFs. There are no palettes, dithering, indexing, or color-depth issues, which are described later in this chapter. It's fairly simple: JPEGs are best for photographs or continuous-tone images. JPEG compression is applied to an image when you save it and appears as a file format choice in Photoshop and other imaging applications that support Web graphics.

JPEG files can be saved in RGB, CMYK, or grayscale. I have crashed my Web browser when displaying CMYK-based JPEG files, so don't try that at home! All Web files should be prepared in RGB or grayscale (See Chapter 7, "Color Calibration Issues" for more details).

JPEG compression uses a lossy method, meaning it eliminates data. This means that the more compression you apply to an image, the lower the file size and the quality. It is your job to judge that fine line between a small file size and sufficient quality.

Photoshop implements three types of JPEG compression: Baseline Standard, Baseline Optimized, and Progressive. Here is a summary of each format:

Baseline Standard: JPEG compression can be set at different levels. The more compression you add on a scale from 1–10, the smaller the file will become. The scale applies to quality, so a setting of 10 would result in the highest quality, the least amount of compression, and the largest file size.

Baseline Optimized: Baseline Optimized JPEG compression can result in slightly smaller JPEG files.

Progressive: Progressive JPEG files might be slightly larger than those using Baseline Standard methods, but this format supports interlacing, meaning the image will appear chunky before it comes into full focus as it finishes downloading. The Progressive JPEG format is not supported by older browsers.

warning

Older Browser Concerns

I only use Optimized JPEG compression on my Web site because Baseline Standard and Progressive JPEGs are not supported by older browsers (any browser before Netscape 2.0 and IE 3.0). The penalty of using these other types of JPEGs will result in a broken image icon. That's too steep a penalty for me. If you are using browser detection (see Chapter 22, "JavaScript: Rollovers & More.") or some other method of distributing multiple sets of pages to your audience, then the advantages of Baseline Optimized and Progressive JPEGs might be attractive to you.

JPEG Examples

A major difference between GIF and JPEG is the fact that you can save JPEGs in a variety of compression levels. This means that more or less compression can be applied to an image, depending on which looks best.

The following examples were taken from Photoshop. Photoshop employs the JPEG compression settings of max, high, medium, and low. In Photoshop, these terms relate to quality, not the amount of compression.

Baseline Standard

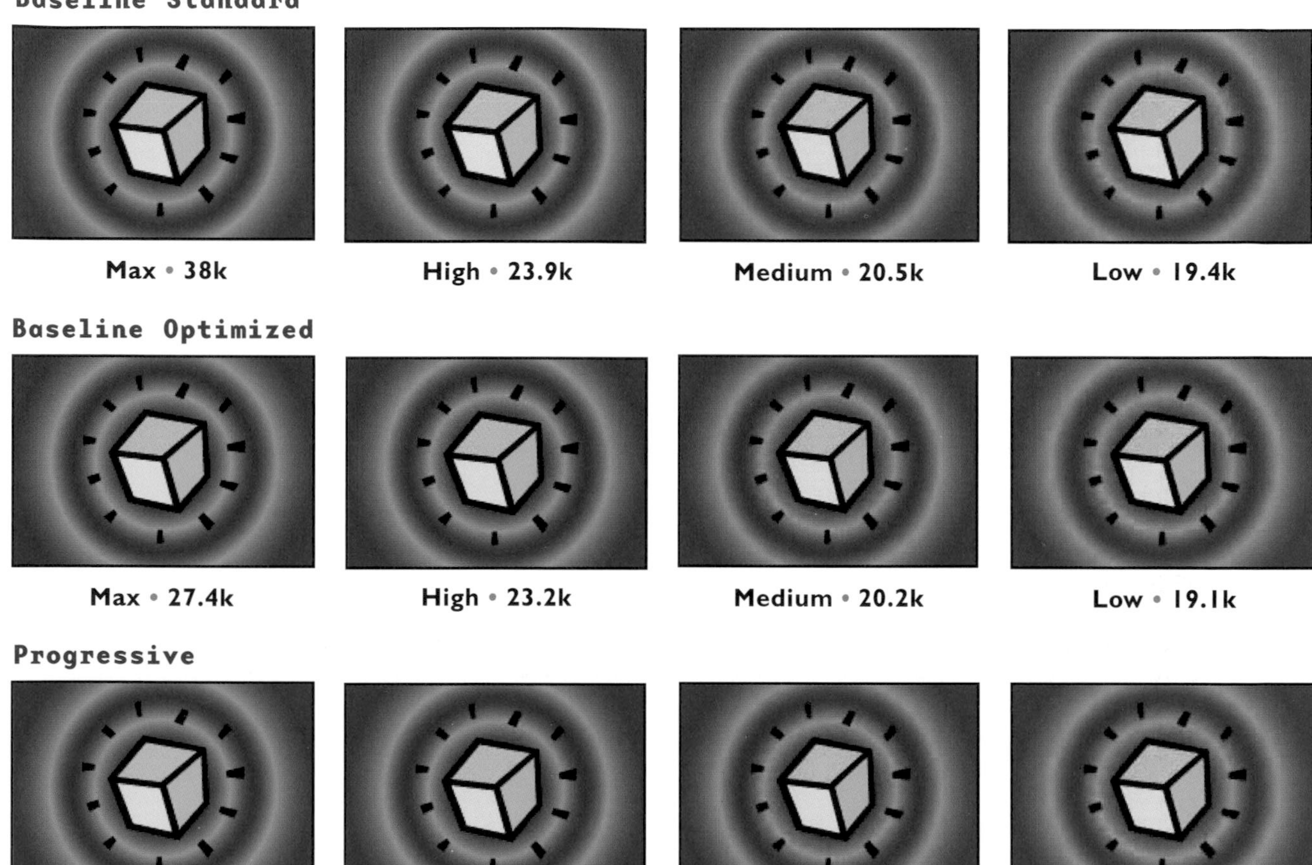

Max • 38k | High • 23.9k | Medium • 20.5k | Low • 19.4k

Baseline Optimized

Max • 27.4k | High • 23.2k | Medium • 20.2k | Low • 19.1k

Progressive

Max • 27.2k | High • 23.2k | Medium • 20.2k | Low • 19.2k

You can see by this test that there is not a whole lot of difference between low-quality and high-quality settings, except for images with a lot of line art or solid colors. As I've said, leave graphics for GIF and photographs for JPEGs. Although there are good reasons for saving photographs in the GIF format (animation and transparency), there are no good reasons for saving graphics in the JPEG format unless the graphics are combined with photographs. With photographic content in general, don't be afraid to try low-quality settings. The file-size savings is usually substantial, and the quality penalties are not too steep.

Photoshop Plug-Ins for Making Small JPEGs

If you plan to stick with Photoshop as a Web graphics tool, then there are two plug-ins that make much smaller JPEGs than Photoshop. These products are **ProJPEG** (http://www.boxtopsoft.com) and **HVS Color JPEG** (http://www.digfrontiers.com). These products get placed inside the Photoshop Plug-Ins folder in order to function.

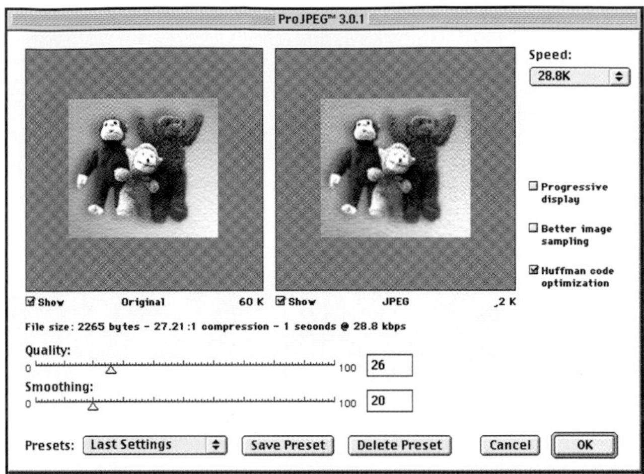

To access the ProJPEG plug-in, choose **File:Save As:ProJPEG**, and this dialog box will appear. It's very handy to have the before-and-after preview, which will help you decide where to set the quality slider interactively. When you're happy with the setting, click OK, and your file will be saved as a JPEG file.

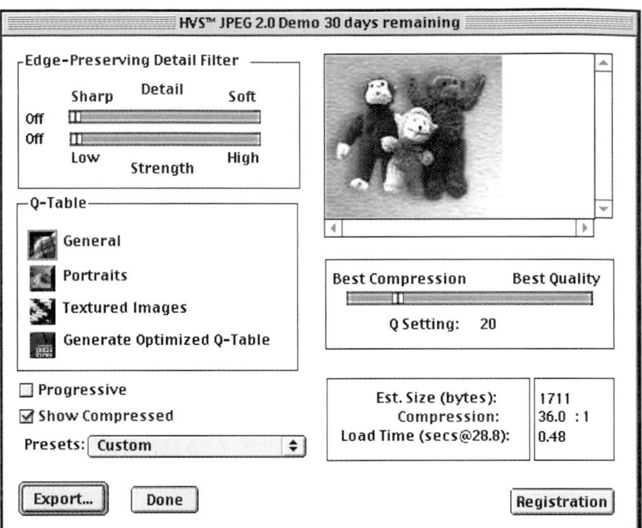

To access the HVS JPEG plug-in, choose **File:Export:HVS JPEG**, and this dialog box will appear. The Q-Table represents different compression algorithms for different types of images. Way cool. The file savings are totally impressive, too.

warning

Don't JPEG a JPEG!

Don't apply JPEG compression to a file that already has it. Each time you add JPEG compression, the image will lose quality. The first time, it won't be noticeable, but multiple JPEG applications will degrade the image beyond repair. Save your files as Photoshop files, or in other non-destructive formats (PICT, TIFF, EPS, BMP, or TGA), to ensure that saving the image as a JPEG is the last step.

Making Small GIFs

The GIF file-compression algorithm offers impressive file-size reduction, but the degree of file size savings has a lot to do with how you create your GIF images. Understanding how GIFs compress is the first step in this process.

GIFs use a compression scheme known as LZW compression, which seeks out patterns of data. Whenever it encounters areas in an image that do not have changes, it can implement much higher compression. This is similar to another type of compression called run-length compression (used in BMP, TIFF, and PCX formats), but LZW writes, stores, and retrieves its code a little differently. Similar to many types of run-length compression, however, GIF compression searches for changes along a horizontal axis, and whenever it finds a new color, adds to the file size.

Here's an original image saved as a GIF image that contains horizontal lines. It is 6.7k.

Here's the identical image, only flipped on its side so that the lines are vertical. It's 72% bigger at 11.5k!

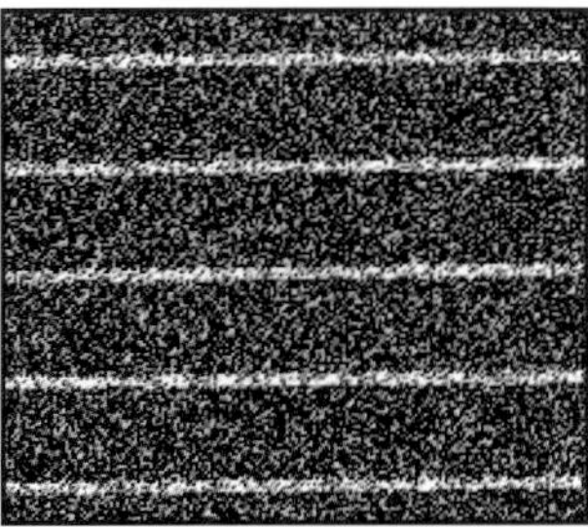

Try adding noise to the original. You'll be expanding the file size by more than eight times to 56k!

So what does the line test really teach? That artwork that has horizontal changes compresses better than artwork that doesn't. That anything with noise will more than quadruple your image's file size. That large areas of flat color compress well, and that complicated line art or dithering does not.

BitDepth Affects Size

Aside from the visual complexity of the image, there are two additional factors that affect file size: bit depth and dithering methods.

With all GIFs, the fewer colors (lower bit depth), the smaller the resulting file. GIFs can be saved at any bit depth from 8 bits down to 1 bit. The bit depth refers to how many colors the image contains. Generally, the lower the bit depth, the smaller the GIF.

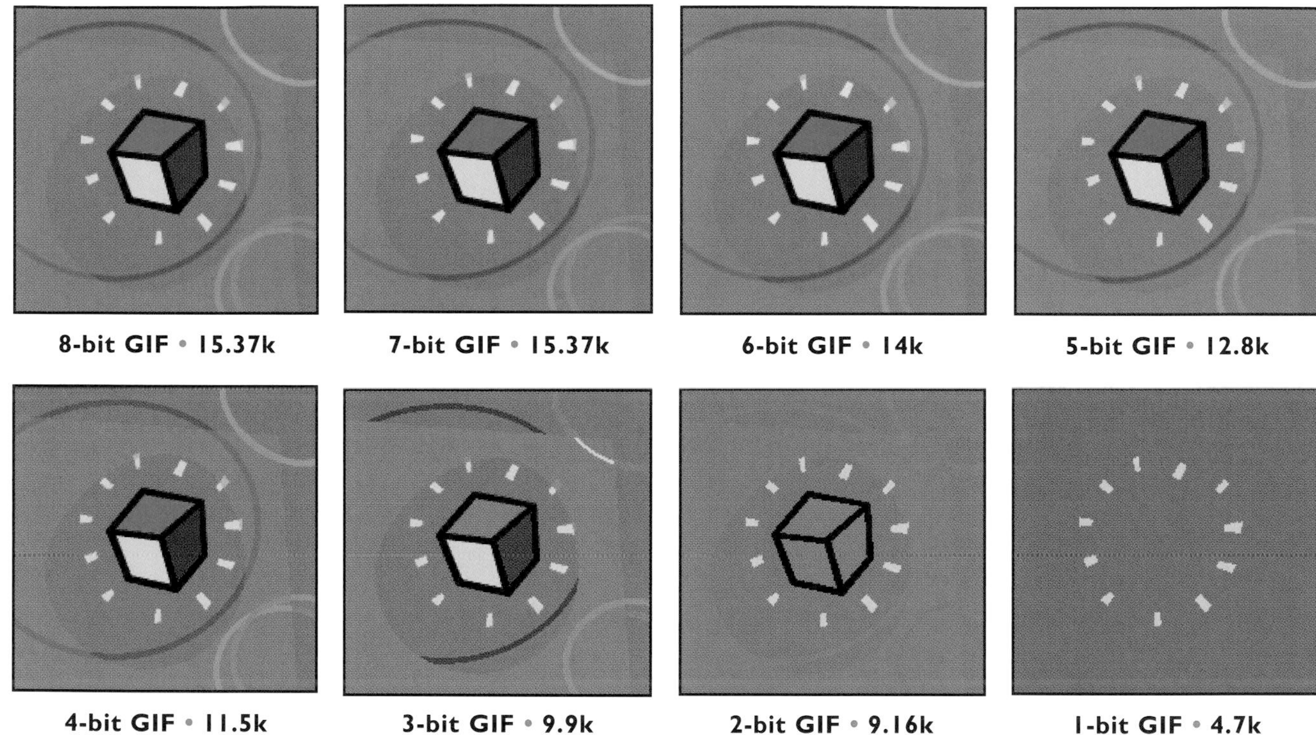

8-bit GIF • 15.37k | 7-bit GIF • 15.37k | 6-bit GIF • 14k | 5-bit GIF • 12.8k

4-bit GIF • 11.5k | 3-bit GIF • 9.9k | 2-bit GIF • 9.16k | 1-bit GIF • 4.7k

Your job when preparing a GIF is to take it down to its lowest bit-depth level and still maintain acceptable image quality. Depending on how important this image is, acceptable quality falls at 4-bit, which offers a 25% file size reduction over the 8-bit version.

Anti-Aliasing Versus Aliasing

ALIAS or ANTI-ALIAS

Here's an example of aliased text. It resulted in a file that totaled 5.78k when saved as a GIF.

ALIAS or ANTI-ALIAS

Here's an example of anti-aliased text. It resulted in a file that's 7.5k when saved as a GIF. The anti-aliasing caused the file to be 23% larger!

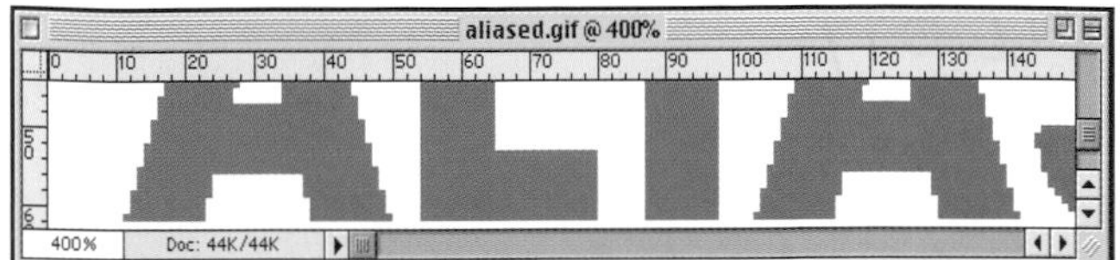

Close-up view: Aliasing doesn't disguise the jaggy nature of pixel-based artwork.

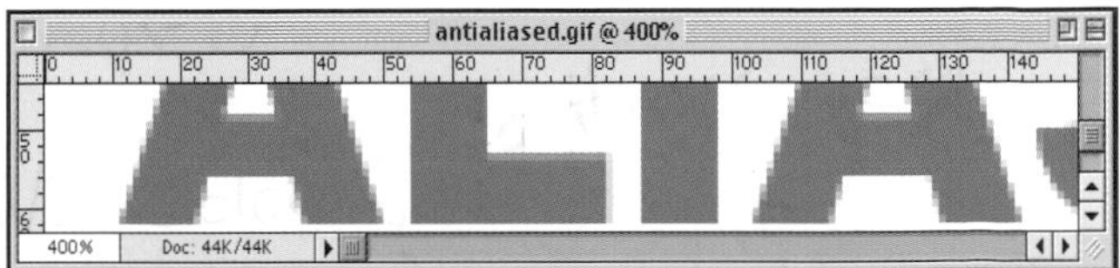

Close-up view: Anti-aliasing creates a blended edge. This blending disguises the square-pixel-based nature of computer-based artwork.

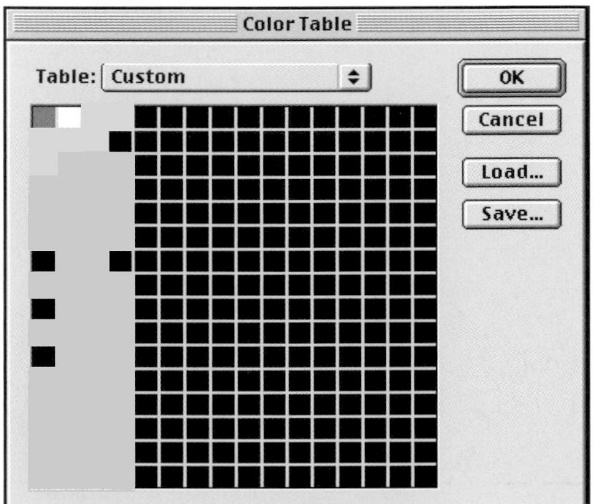

The aliased artwork used only 2 colors.

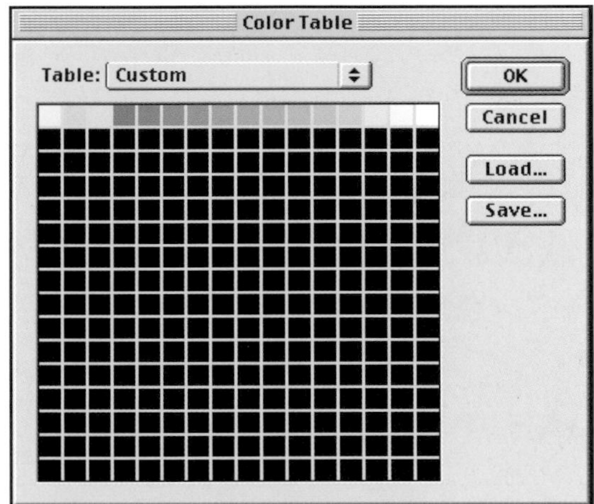

The anti-aliased artwork used 16 colors.

Anti-aliasing can affect bit depth. If you work with aliased images instead, the file sizes will always be smaller. Aliased artwork doesn't always look good, so this is a decision you'll have to weigh depending on the imagery.

Aliased Artwork

Most computer artists have never considered working with aliased artwork. It's assumed that artwork will always look better if it has anti-aliased edges. This is simply not true! Artists have never had to factor size of files into their design considerations before. Having something load 23% faster is nothing to balk at. In many cases, aliased artwork looks just as good as anti-aliased artwork, and choosing between the two approaches is something that Web designers should consider whenever possible.

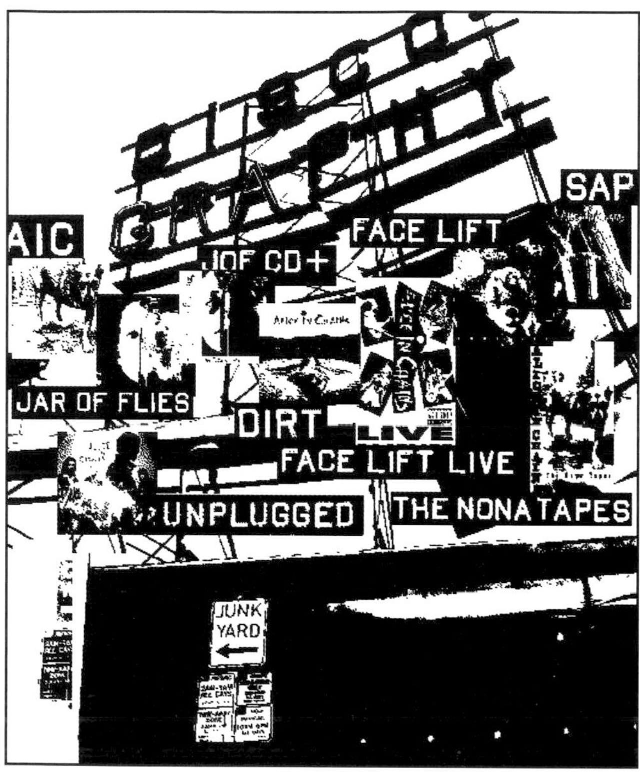

Part of the charm of the Alice in Chains site is the fast download and rough graphics (which are aliased!). To visit this site: http://www.sonymusic.com/artists/AliceInChains/discog.html.

This background tile is aliased, and looks great. To check this, and other aliased background tiles, visit http://www.donbarnett.com/tilesets/set1.htm.

As well as considering whether to use aliased or anti-aliased graphics, you should also always work with browser-safe colors when creating illustration-based artwork for the Web. Examples of how browser-safe colors improve the quality of illustrations are demonstrated in Chapter 7, "Color Calibration Issues."

GIFs for Line Art-Based Imagery

GIFs work much better for graphics than photographs. By graphics, I am referring to line art, illustrations, cartoons, or logos. Such graphics typically use areas of solid color, and GIFs handle compression of solid color better than the varied colors found in photographs. Because the GIF file format is lossless, illustrations with limited colors (less than 256) won't lose any quality. Because JPEG is a lossy method, it actually introduces image artifacts into solid color.

The left image is saved as a GIF file, and weighs in at 15.3k. The right image is saved as a JPEG and weighs in at 20k. Not only does the JPEG look worse, but it's also bigger. Moral of the story? Use the GIF file format for line art.

GIF Color Palettes

Color mapping refers to the colors that are assigned to a GIF image and can be taken from either the image or a predetermined palette of colors. Photoshop calls palettes that are derived from existing colors adaptive palettes. It enables you to apply external palettes (system or browser-safe are two examples) or makes a best-guess palette (adaptive) based on the content of your image. While the number of colors in an image (bit depth) affect the size of the graphic, the palette additionally affects the quality of your image. Some images can endure fewer colors, while others cannot. If you understand how color affects size and quality, you will create better looking and faster loading Web pages.

Adaptive palette

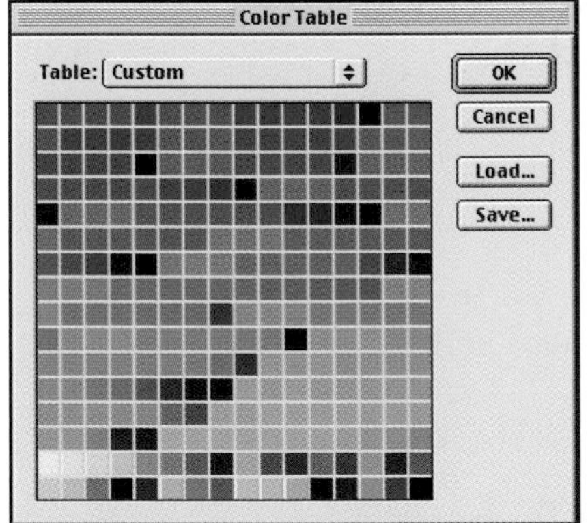

The adaptive palette looks the best because the colors are based on the content of the image. Paint Shop Pro calls this type of palette a Nearest Color palette. Photoshop calls it an adaptive palette.

Mac system palette

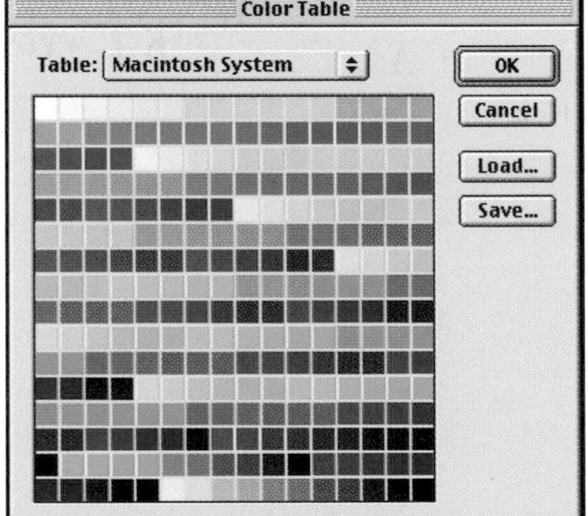

The system palette image looks much worse. Although it has the same number of colors as the adaptive palette, the colors are unrelated to the image and detract from the quality.

216 browser-safe palette

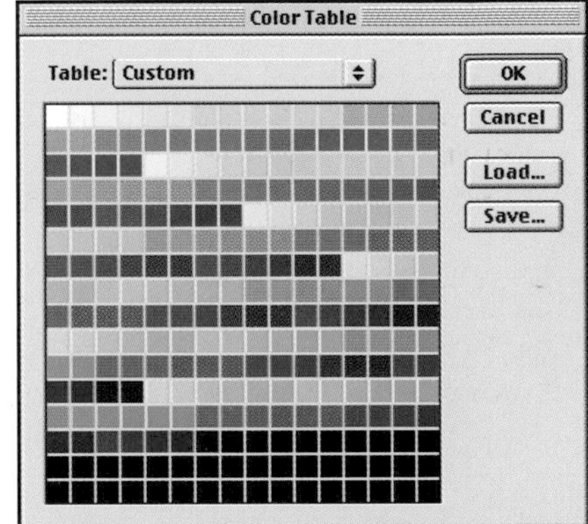

The browser-safe palette looks worst of all. Not only does it use fewer colors, but just like the system palette, the colors are unrelated to the image.

Dithering and Banding

When an image with millions of colors is converted to an image with 256 colors or less, image quality is lost. Basically, when colors are removed from the image, some sacrifices have to be made. This can take place in two forms: dithering or banding. Here are some definitions to remember:

Dithering is the positioning of different colored pixels within an image that uses a 256-color palette to simulate a color that does not exist in the palette. A dithered image often looks noisy, or composed of scattered pixels.

Adaptive palette is used to convert the image to 256 colors based on existing colors within the image. Generally, adaptive dithering looks the best of all dithering methods.

Screen dithering is what happens when a 24-bit or 16-bit image is viewed on a computer with a 256-color video card. The image's color is reduced to 256 colors, and the dither looks uniform, as if a pattern was used.

Banding is a process of reducing colors to 256 or less without dithering. It produces areas of solid color and generates a posterized effect.

Understanding the terminology of dithering and banding is important in Web design because these are often effects that are undesirable. Bringing down the quality of images is necessary at times for speed considerations, but riding the line between low file size and good-enough quality means that you will often encounter unwanted results. These new terms help define the problems you'll encounter when creating Web graphics and will be used throughout the rest of the book.

Screen dithering takes the form of a repeated pattern and as a result creates a moiré appearance.

This is an example of **image dithering** using an adaptive palette. It will typically look a lot better than screen dithering because the dither pattern is based on the content of the image, not a preset screen.

The **banding** in this image is very obvious. It resembles a posterization effect.

The dots in a **screen dithered** image look uniform, they are based on a generalized screen pattern.

Even though the **image dithering** example is composed of pixelated dots, they are less obvious and object- ionable because there's no obvious pattern or screen.

Here's a close-up of the **banding**. Instead of the dots you'll find in dithering methods, the computer takes the image and breaks it into regions of solid color.

Dare to Dither

Dithering sometimes gets a bum rap. While it is true that dithering adds file size to GIF images, sometimes you have to use dithering in color-reduction processes or the image will look terrible.

GIF saved with **dithering** 40.7k.

GIF saved in Photoshop's **dither none** 37.2k.

There's almost no perceivable difference between these two images, regardless of whether a dithering method is used to convert to 8-bit color or Photoshop's Dither None method was chosen. Why? This image has a lot of solid areas of color to begin with. The file savings between 40.7k and 37.2k is not huge either, but the nondither method still yields a smaller file size.

GIF saved with **dithering** 17.6k.

GIF **without dithering** 14.5k.

In this example, the GIF that did not use dithering is an impressive 17% smaller. The only problem is, it looks awful! Sometimes file savings does not warrant loss of quality. Whenever a photograph contains glows, feathered edges, or subtle gradations, you will have to use dithering when converting from 24-bit to 8-bit in order to maintain quality.

Instructions for how to set up dither and no-dither methods for **Photoshop**, **ImageReady**, and **Fireworks** are described later in this chapter. All of these programs offer the capability to set the dithering or no dithering method.

note

Four Rules of GIF Compression

To summarize, there are four rules to making smaller GIFs:

- Try to save the file at the lowest possible bit depth (use the fewest number of colors), while monitoring quality
- Try to avoid dithering, if the image can withstand it
- If possible, create images with lots of areas of solid color, and avoid noise, gradations, and/or photographic content
- Avoid anti-aliasing, if the image can withstand it

There is never one pat answer for making the smallest possible GIFs. Choices between bit depth and dithering methods should always be based on the image's content. In general, images with subtle gradations will need to be dithered. Images with areas of solid color will look fine without dithering.

Reducing Colors in GIF Files Using Photoshop

The Indexed Color dialog box has three important functions: setting the **color depth,** the **palette**, and the **dither**. The **resolution** affects the bit depth of the image; the **palette** sets which colors are used; and the **dither** tells the program which color reduction method to use—dithering, screen, or no dithering.

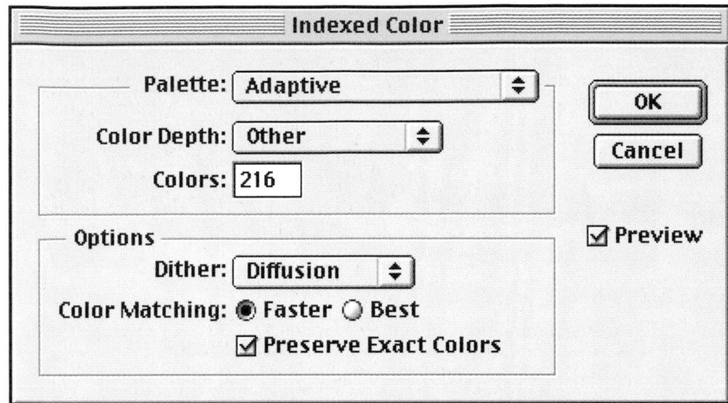

Step 1: An RGB image must be converted to Indexed Color mode before it can be saved as a GIF. Under the Mode menu, choose **Indexed Color**.

Step 1: You can type any number into the Colors field. Try to go so low that the image looks bad, and then back off a step. This ensures that you've pushed the limits to how few colors are needed in order to make a small file that still maintains acceptable quality.

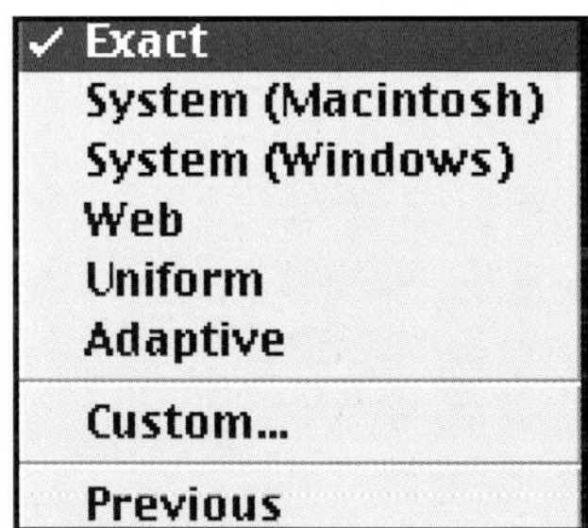

Photoshop Palette Options

Choosing a palette is dependent on your type of image. Here is a definition of Photoshop's palette choices:

Exact: This option is only available if you have fewer than 256 colors in your original image. Because there is no reason for the program to reduce the number of colors, you will not have access to any dithering choices and the file will not be dithered.

System (Windows): Applies the Windows palette.

System (Mac): Applies the Macintosh palette.

Web: Applies the 216 browser-safe palette to the image (more on this in Chapter 7, "Color Calibration Issues").

Uniform: Applies a palette using all the colors in the spectrum in uniform increments. Not very useful for Web graphics.

Adaptive: Chooses colors from the original image, and biases the palette colors toward those colors. For example, an image of autumn leaves might have reds, browns, oranges, and yellows; it would not likely contain blue, aqua, magenta, or lime green.

Custom: If you have saved a Photoshop palette (instructions on how to do this are in Chapter 7, "Color Calibration Issues"), you can load it as a custom palette by choosing this setting.

Previous: Applies whatever palette was last used in the previous image to the current image.

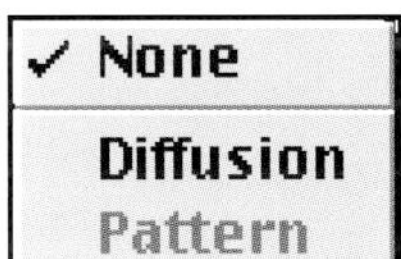

Dithering Options

- Choosing **None** will produce no dithering. On images with lots of solid colors, this is recommended as it will produce smaller GIF files.
- Choosing **Diffusion** will produce dithering. On images with lots of tonality, such as photographs or graphics with gradients, shadows, and glows, this is recommended to increase image quality, even though it might result in a larger GIF file.

Reducing Colors in ImageReady

Reducing colors in ImageReady is fairly simple; it involves typing a new value into the Optimize palette, making sure that GIF is selected. If you click on the Optimized tab in the LiveWindow view, you will see the changes to the image update instantly. This allows you to hone in on a color-reduction, palette, and dithering setting while seeing the results interactively.

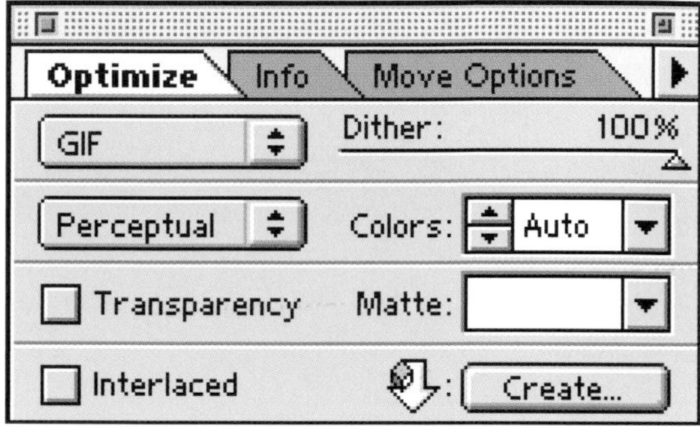

ImageReady Palette Options
ImageReady has slightly different palette behavior than Photoshop. Here is a definition of ImageReady's palette choices:

Perceptual: The perceptual palette uses colors from the original image, just as Photoshop's adaptive palette does. The difference is that the colors are chosen based on visual perception as well as from colors from the image. If an original image contains browser-safe colors (see Chapter 7, "Color Calibration Issues"), those colors might shift when reduced using the Perceptual palette.

Adaptive: The only difference between Photoshop's adaptive palette is that ImageReady will not shift browser-safe colors. This is a great boon to Web designers who use this product.

Web: The Web palette is identical to Photoshop's Web palette.

tip

Auto Setting in ImageReady

The Auto setting in the color-depth field of the Optimize palette will automatically reduce the number of colors to the fewest necessary.

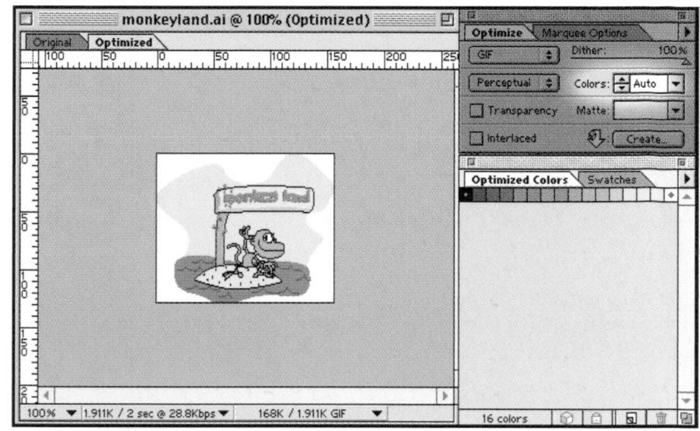

To check how many colors the Auto setting has selected, make sure the **Optimized tab** and **Optimized Colors tab** are active so you can view the results.

Reducing Colors in Fireworks

All color reduction takes place in Firework's Export module. Select **File:Export** to access this module.

You can enter custom values into the **numbers of colors** pop-up settings.

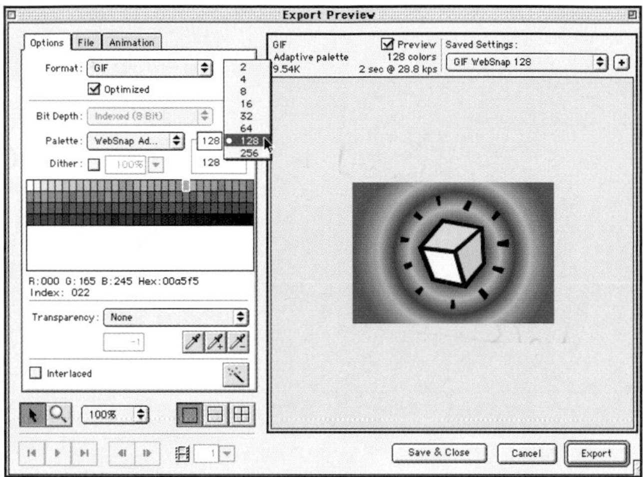

Fireworks Palette Options

Adaptive: Similar to Photoshop's adaptive palette, the settings are derived from actual colors in the image.

Websnap Adaptive: An adaptive palette that shifts colors that are near in value to browser-safe colors to the nearest browser-safe color.

Web 216: The 216 browser-safe colors discussed in detail in Chapter 7, "Color Calibration Issues."

Exact: If your original image is less than 256 colors, this palette setting will preserve the exact colors used.

System (Windows) and System (Macintosh): The palette used by each operating system.

Grayscale: A palette of 256 or less grays, which when applied to a full color image results in a grayscale image.

Black and White: Converts a color image to black and white (no grays!, no colors!).

Custom: It is possible to save a custom palette in Fireworks, reload it and apply it to any Fireworks image.

Reducing Colors in Paint Shop Pro

Decrease Color Depth - X Colors
Palette
Number of colors:
128 (2-256)
Reduction method
Nearest color
Error diffusion
Options
Boost marked colors by
1 (1 to 10)
Include Windows' colors
Reduce color bleeding
OK
Cancel
Help

Paint Shop Pro Palette Options

Number of Colors: Dictates the depth of the image.

Nearest Color Reduction method: Is the same as Dither None in Photoshop and Photo-Paint. It creates a banded appearance.

Error Diffusion: Will create dithering based on the image itself.

Boost Masked Colors: Allows you to select colors within the document and have the palette weigh toward favoring those colors.

Include Windows' Colors: Ensures that the 16 colors within Windows are reserved in the image's color table. See note on this page.

Reduce Color Bleeding: Reduces the left-to-right color bleeding that sometimes occurs with the Error Diffusion settings.

note

The Windows 16 Palette

Sixteen colors are reserved for a native palette found in all Windows machines. Unfortunately, only the last six colors are browser safe. There are some cases in which you might want to use these colors in a Windows-based Intranet, where cross-platform compatibility is not an issue.

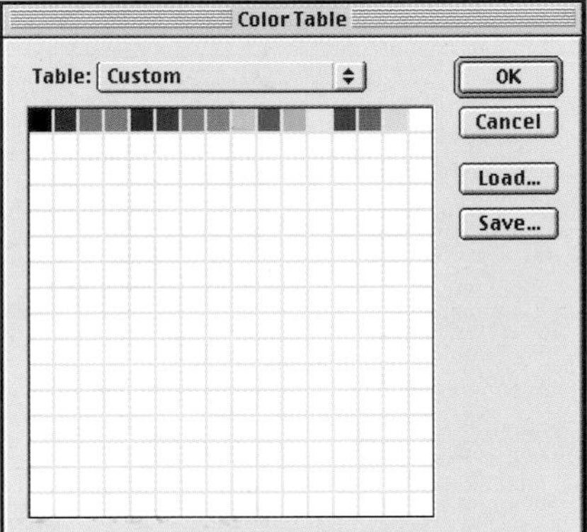

Here are the 16 reserved native colors for Windows systems. Only the last six colors are browser safe.

Hybrid Images

As mentioned earlier, sometimes your image doesn't fall into the continuous tone or the line art category, because it contains both. This is where choosing a compression method gets its trickiest. The only way to deal with an image like this is to try compressing it with GIF and JPEG to see which method produces a smaller file.

Many imaging programs support the ability to create GIF and JPEG files, but when you want to compare compression methods, it's great to have a dedicated image editor that is devoted to Web tasks. Two such products have been released recently: Macromedia Fireworks and Adobe ImageReady. Here is how you would compare compression methods in Fireworks and ImageReady:

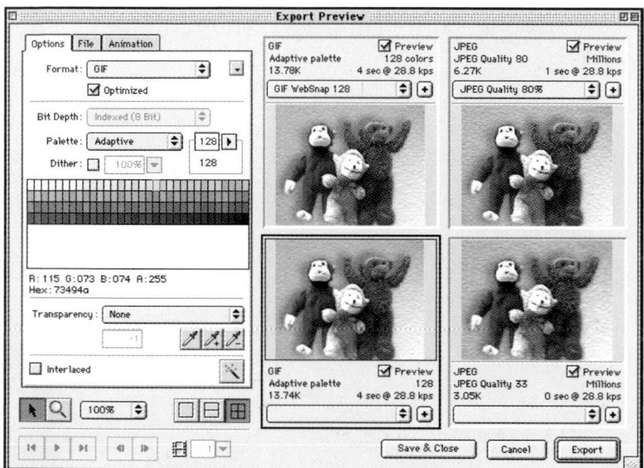

Fireworks has a feature called Split View, which allows you to see the same image compressed up to four different ways on the same screen. You would implement this feature by choosing **File:Export** and clicking on the **Split View tool**.

ImageReady allows you to set the compression within the Optimize palette and then view it by clicking on the Optimized tab. You can tear off the Optimized tab and create multiple versions with different compression settings. Each time you tear off one Optimized view tab, a new tab appears in which you can enter new settings.

Photoshop Plug-Ins for GIF Optimization

For those users who don't want or plan to buy a separate Web graphics application, there are a few noteworthy plug-ins that will optimize GIFs much more effectively than Photoshop. Two are mentioned here: **Boxtop Software's PhotoGIF** (http:/www.boxtopsoft.com) and **Digital Frontier's HVS ColorGIF** (http://www.digfrontiers.com). These plug-ins work with Photoshop and are installed inside the Photoshop Plug-Ins folder.

BoxTop Software

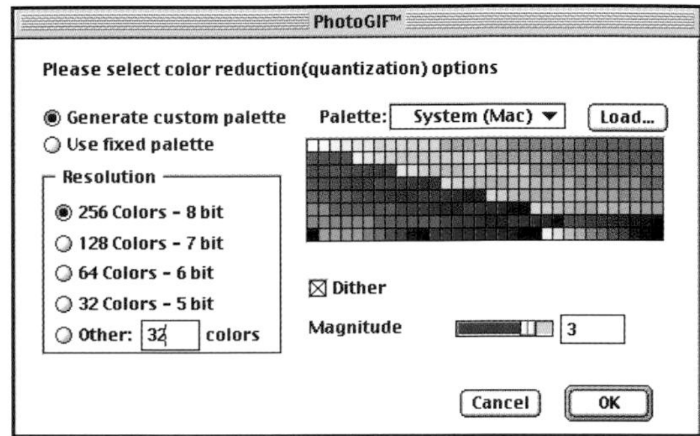

Step 1: Using PhotoGIF is a two-step process. Once the plug-in is installed, it shows up in the menu when you **Save As**. You choose your color depth and palette settings in the first dialog box.

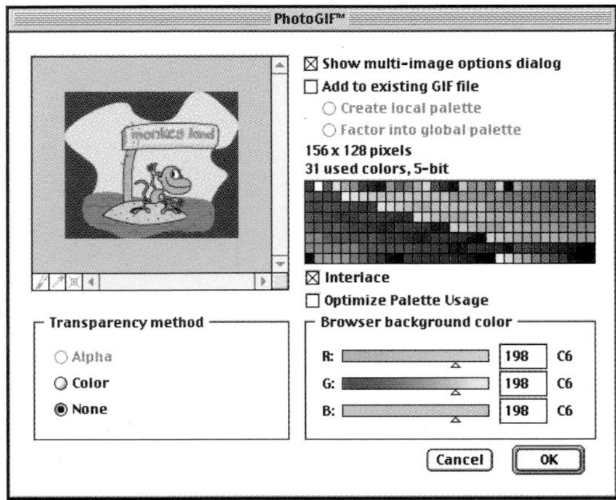

Step 2: After choosing your depth and settings, a preview appears before you finalize the file by clicking **OK**.

HVS ColorGIF

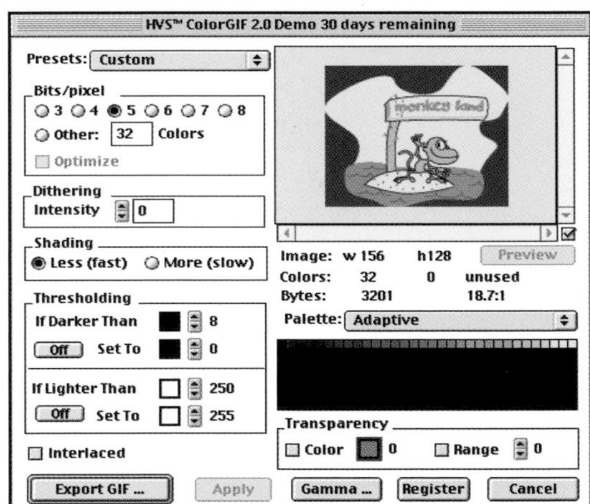

Step 1: The HVS Color method is one-step. Choose **File:Export:HVS Color GIF**, and this dialog box appears. Enter your own settings (the preview is quite handy!), and choose **Export GIF** when you're finished.

Reducing File Size Online: GIFWizard

Another trend in GIF optimization can be found online at http://www.gif wizard.com. If you visit this site, you can sample the compression rates by submitting a URL of choice, and watch GIFWizard do its magic to the file size savings. This service is not free.

GIFWizard, at http://www.gifwizard.com, will compress your graphics online, on any platform, at a variety of price points. Visit the site for the pricing guide, which ranges from year-long licenses to one-time usage.

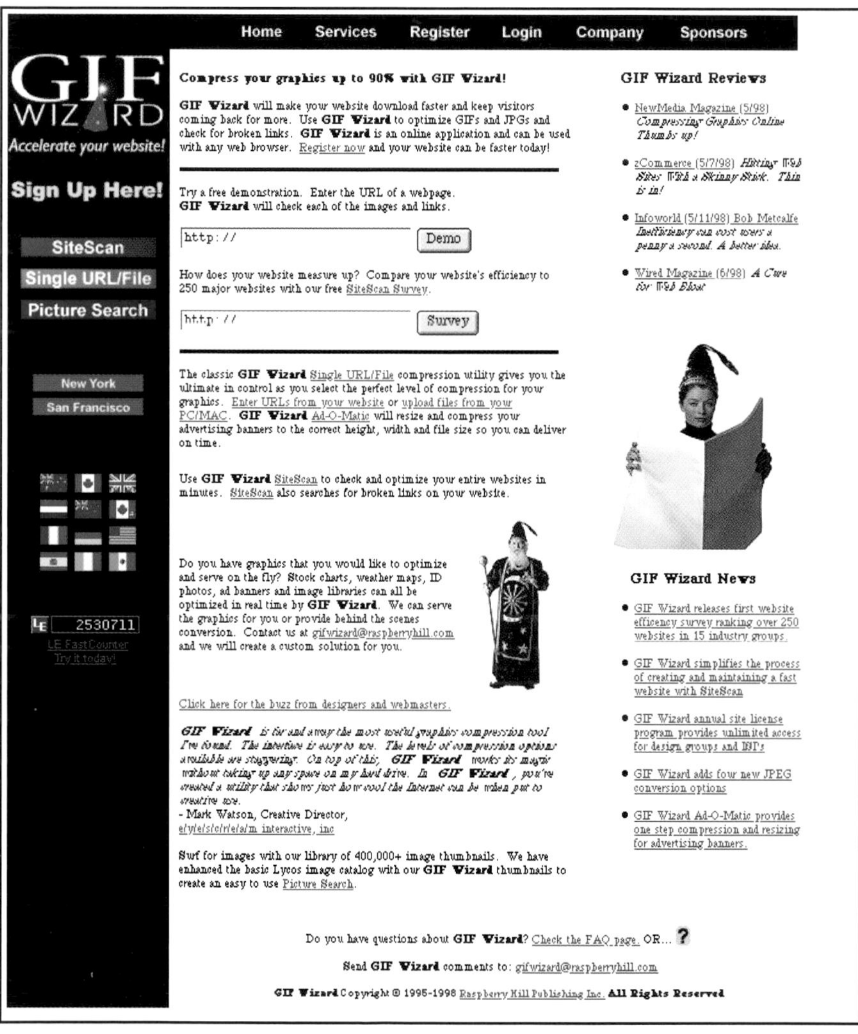

Animated GIF Issues

Just like other GIF files, the number of colors and amount of noise in the frames affects the overall file size. If you have a 100-frame animation with each frame totaling 5k, your animated GIF will be 500k. It simply multiplies in size according to how many frames you create and the file size of the individual frame of artwork. On the other hand, your end viewer is really waiting for only 5k servings at a time, so it's nothing like the painful waiting that a static 500k GIF would incur!

If you want to learn about controlling palettes for animated GIFs and/or techniques for optimization, turn to Chapter 21, "GIF Animation."

This animation, http://www.lynda.com/bookstore/process.html, is only 15.k. Each frame is 1k! Why? Lots of flat color and no anti-aliasing.

Making Small PNG Files

PNG is difficult in the abstract because it has so many different permutations. You can save PNG files in 8-bit or 24-bit; the 8-bit mode resembles GIF whereas the 24-bit mode resembles JPEG. Therefore, all the complexities of GIF and JPEG are rolled into one ultra complex format!

Since you have to evaluate between many settings, I highly recommend ImageReady and Fireworks over Photoshop or other imaging tools for compressing PNG files. The added interactivity that these two products lend to this process is extremely helpful. Neither ImageReady or Fireworks give you access to the filters for PNG that Photoshop does, but many of the filters are relatively useless, so this is really not a drawback.

To evaluate PNG settings in Fireworks or ImageReady, refer to the preceding section. If you only have **Photoshop**, however, here are the **PNG settings** and a description of what they mean:

Interlace

None: No interlacing

Adam7: Interlacing

Filters

None: Like the name says, this offers no filter. Strangely, this is the setting Adobe recommends as the best setting for Web images. I'm not clear what the filters do if they don't compress, but go figure...

Sub: Compares and averages pixel values next to each other on a horizontal axis.

Up: Compares and averages pixel values next to each other on a vertical axis.

Average: Averages all the pixel values in the document.

Paeth: Uses linear calculations to average and compare the different pixel values.

Adaptive: Best guess. Use this one if you want to use a filter, and it will pick the best of the above methods depending on which style of image you're using.

Batch Processing

Batch processing allows you to use a single setting over multiple files. Let's say you have a folder or directory filled with images that are in CMYK at 300 dpi. You want to use them for the Web, but you know they're in the wrong color mode and way too big. You could set up a script that would change the color mode to RGB, 72 dpi, and reduce the files to 50% of their original size. If you had 100 images, imagine doing this process 100 times? No way. This task is tailor made for batch processing.

Many tools support batch processing, and unfortunately I am not familiar with, nor do I have enough space to write about, all of them here. I will concentrate on four: **Photoshop**, **ImageReady**, **Fireworks**, and **DeBabelizer**.

Photoshop Actions

The Actions palette, found in both Photoshop and ImageReady, records "macros," or small scripts, that can be replayed. These scripts can be used on individual images or in batch processing mode, where they play over hundreds of files.

Here's how we would record an action in either program.

Step 1: Open the file that you wish to alter. Click on the **Create New Action** icon to begin a recording.

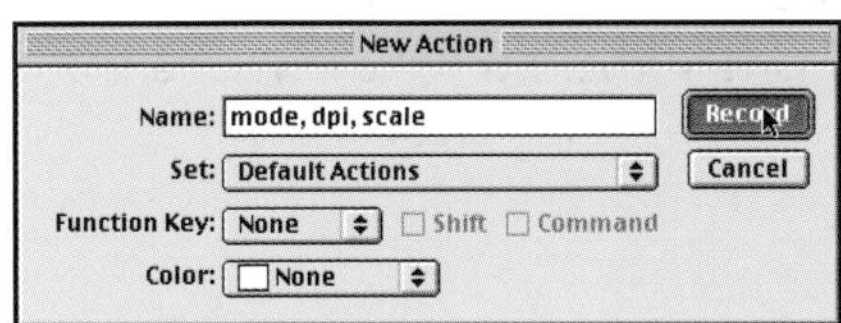

Step 2: Name the action.

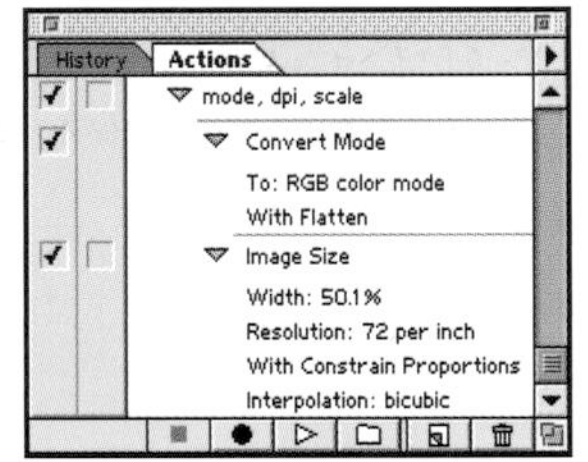

Step 3: Perform the changes. In this case I changed the mode to RGB, 72 dpi, and scaled the image 50%. When you are finished, click the **Stop** button and twirl down the arrows to see if everything recorded properly.

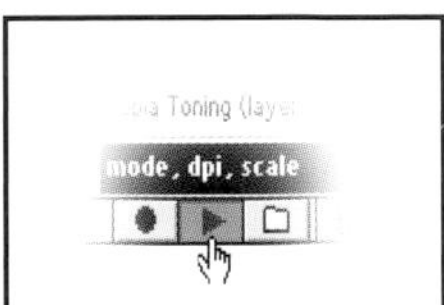

Step 4: Click on the **Play** button at the bottom of the Actions palette to test the macro on any image.

Photoshop and ImageReady's Batch Processing

To run the preceding action over many images requires batch processing. This is accomplished differently through Photoshop and ImageReady.

In Photoshop 5.0

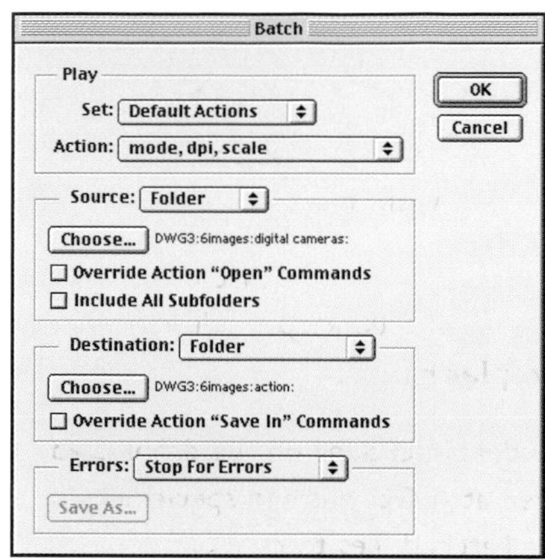

Step 1: Choose **File:Automate:Batch**.

Step 2: Fill in the settings. If you want to choose a Source and Destination folder, click on the respective Choose buttons to select the appropriate directories.**Important Tip:** Always work on duplicates in the event that your action might damage important files.

In ImageReady 1.0

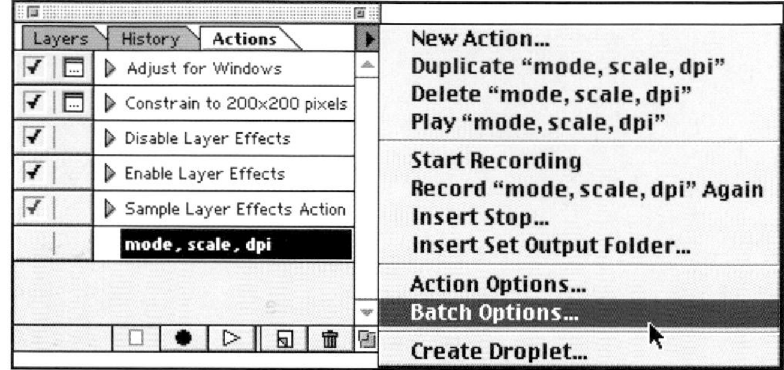

Step 1: You access the Batch Options menu item from the pop-up menu on the upper-right corner of the Actions palette.

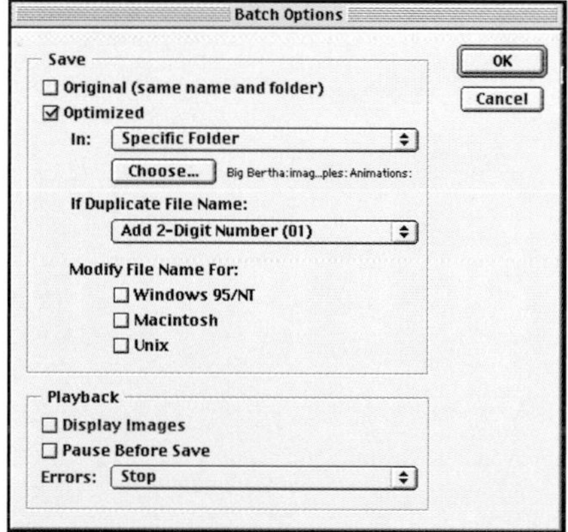

Step 2: The Batch Options dialog enables you to select different menu items from the **In: pop-up** menu and the **Duplicate File Name**: pop-up menu.

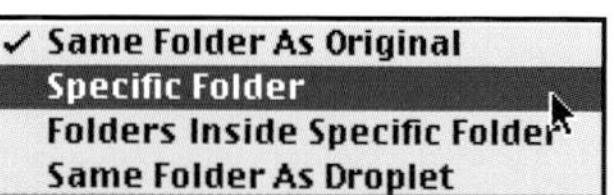

Step 3:The In: menu items are much more in tune with Web graphics than Photoshop's Batch options. The ability to add **numeric extensions** to batch processed items is also better than Photoshop's naming capabilities.

ImageReady's Droplets

Droplets are a new type of batch processing capability, which ImageReady has pioneered. A droplet can be made from an **action** or the **optimize** palette.

The term droplet refers to the fact that you can drop files or folders on to the icon, and it will perform the operations it was scripted to execute. Droplets can be created from the Actions palette or the Optimize palette. The following steps explain how to do it:

From the Actions Palette

Tip: Before you begin this process, make sure you have set the optimization settings in the Optimize palette; otherwise, the droplet will use the default compression setting.

Step 1: Create an action based on the preceding instructions.

Step 2: Drag the action from the Actions palette to the desktop.

Step 3: Any file, folder, or directory you drop on the droplet will perform the action.

Note: You can double-click on the droplet to see the contents of the action.

From the Optimize Palette

Step 1: Open an image and select the type of optimization you wish to apply.

Step 2: Drag the droplet icon from the Optimize palette to your desktop or click on the **Create droplet** button.

Step 3: By double-clicking on the droplet, you can edit the Batch Options and specify a location for the batched files to reside.

The icon for an ImageReady droplet can sit on your desktop, which allows you to drag files or folders on top of it.

Firework's Batch Processing

Firework's batch processing allows you to apply any Preset (optimization setting information) and scaling information to a folder or directory of images. The first step is to establish a Preset.

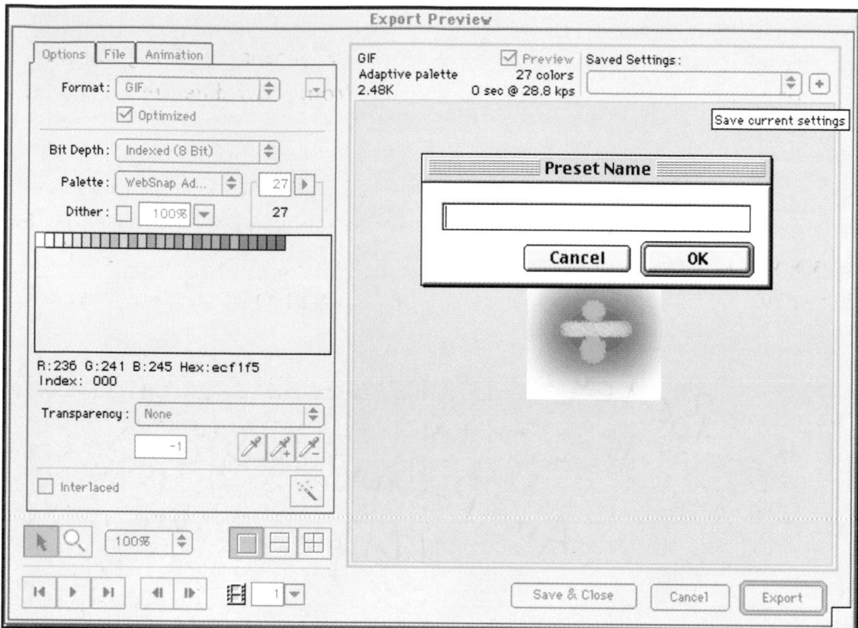

Step 1: Open an image and choose **File:Export**. Choose your settings. In this case, I chose Websafe Adaptive Palette with 27 colors. Once I was happy with my settings, I clicked the plus symbol in the upper right-hand corner below the words **Saved Settings**. This launched the **Preset Name** window. As soon as you make a preset you're happy with, or choose to work with one of the existing presets, you are ready to batch process. Click on the lower right-hand button, **Save and Close**.

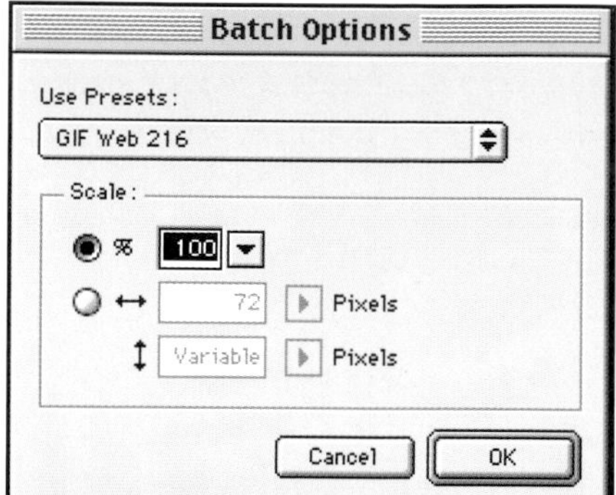

Step 2: Choose **File:Batch**. You will be prompted to locate a folder to apply the batch processing to. Once that folder is selected, the dialog box Batch Options will open. You can select from any Preset in the pop-up menu and choose to scale by percentage or values. Whatever settings are entered into this dialog box will apply to the folder or directory you preselected.

DeBabelizer's Batch Processing

Most serious multimedia and Web professionals who deal with large volumes of images use DeBabelizer (available for Macs or PCs) for batch processing. While Photoshop, ImageReady, and Fireworks all offer this capability, none of them are focused on this as the most important purpose of their product.

DeBabelizer has a feature called a Batch List, which enables you to set up a list of files to process. Although all the other programs only work on a single folder or directory, DeBabelizer can cull its list from many different hard drives, folders, and directories.

It also has scripting functions that can perform advanced operations, such as including conditional script parameters such as If, Then, Else, and Loop statements. This means you could instruct the script to perform different functions for different images in your batch script. Let's say you instructed the script to compress all images with the letter X in the file name to save as GIF files and all images with the letter Z to save as JPEGs. This sort of thing is way over the head of other batch processing products.

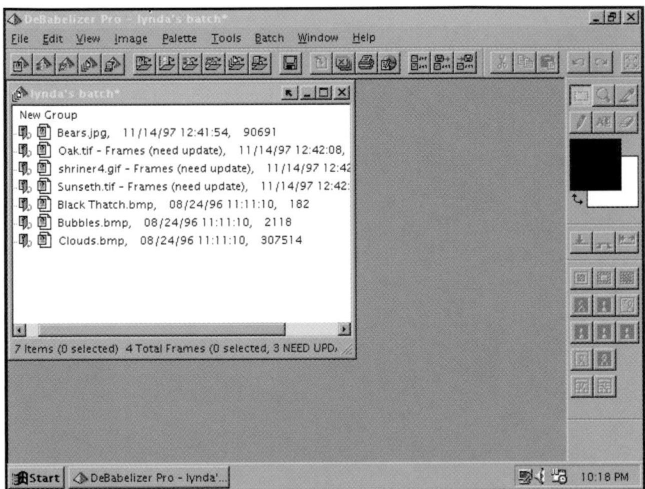

The Batch List function in DeBabelizer is valuable because it can take images from any hard drive, folder, or directory. Once the images are in this list, any number of scripts can be run on them.

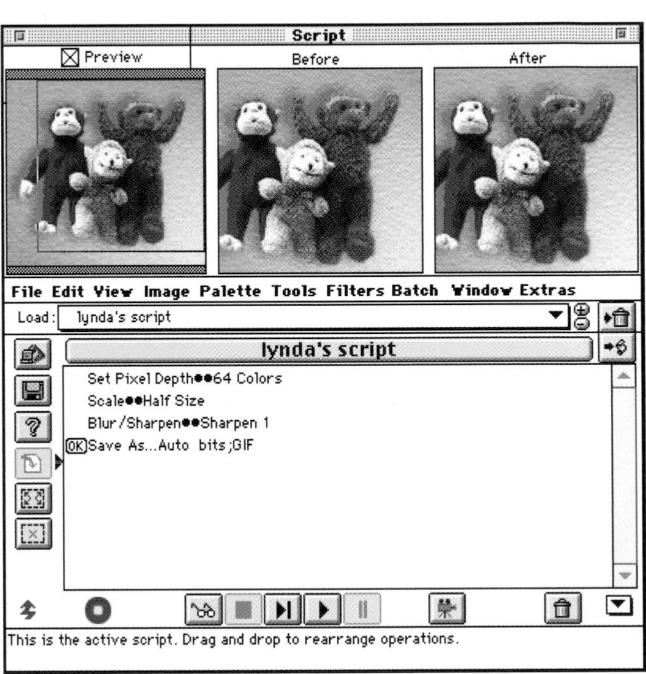

The Script window is where you can set up all the scripting functions, including the conditional scripts that can respond to **If**, **Then**, **Else**, or **Loop** functions.

tip

Image Optimization Resources

The Bandwidth Conservation Society
http://www.infohiway.com/faster/index.html

Web Reference
http://www.webreference.com/dev/graphics/

summary Low Bandwidth Graphics

An important part of Web design is making sure images are small in file size so that they download more quickly. The tradeoff for speed is quality, so it's your job to evaluate where to draw the line. There are many tools to choose from for this process, but here are the principles to remember regardless of which tool you choose to use:

- JPEG compression is best applied to photographic images or continuous-tone artwork.
- Quality settings in JPEG affect file size. Find the lowest-quality setting that still looks good, so the file size will be as small as possible.
- Never apply JPEG compression to a file that has already been saved as a JPEG. The lossy compression method will degrade the image.
- GIF compression is best applied to graphics or images that contain line art.
- You can optimize the size of a GIF by reducing the number of colors it contains. Fewer colors translate to smaller file sizes.
- Dithering adds to the file size of a GIF, but should be used anyway for images that contain gradients or soft focus elements. If your image has a lot of solid colors, it will not require dithering and will be smaller if you don't use dithering methods in your file saving procedure.
- With hybrid images (images that include line art and continuous-tone graphics) it's best to save as both GIF and JPEG and then compare the results.

Introduction

Color Calibration Issues

Chapter Topics

- RGB Versus CMYK
- What Is sRGB?
- What Are ICC Profiles?
- Gamma Issues
- sRGB in Photoshop 5.0
- Accurate Web Color Solutions
- Helpful URLs

7

Until the Web, most computer graphic artists created artwork for print, not for screen delivery. If you come to the Web from print, you might be familiar with the color space called CMYK. CMYK is a color system developed for computer graphics so the color on the screen can be accurately translated to printing inks. On the Web, our printing inks are phosphors and pixels, and we are subject to all kinds of variables that don't exist in print, such as monitor calibration and gamma differences between platforms.

In many ways, working with screen-based color can be more fun than working with printed inks. There is no waiting for color proofs or working with CMYK values (which are much less vibrant than RGB), no high-resolution files, and no dot screens to deal with. Although working on the computer for computer delivery is a lot easier in some ways, don't be fooled into thinking that what you see on your screen is what other people will see on their screens. Just like its print-based counterpart, computer screen-based color has its own set of problems and solutions.

This chapter will focus on some of the color gremlins associated with Web design from the perspective of color calibration. We will examine RGB versus CMYK, gamma, and sRGB and ICC profiles. Several hardware and software companies are hard at work trying to solve some of the many problems related to using computer color. This chapter offers concrete advice, as well as an overview of all the various technologies associated with Web color.

RGB Versus CMYK

The color of a pixel is made up of three projected colors of light that mix together optically. The projected light colors are red, green, and blue. Mixed together, these three colors create a color space called RGB. You might also hear about a CMYK color space, which is formed from cyan, magenta, yellow, and black. On a computer, the CMYK color space simulates printing inks and is used commonly by print designers. On the other hand, the work of Web designers is screen based, so we have typically used RGB color space only.

CMYK colors are subtractive, meaning that mixing multiple colors creates black. This color space was created for computer graphics that will be printed on paper using a four-color process.

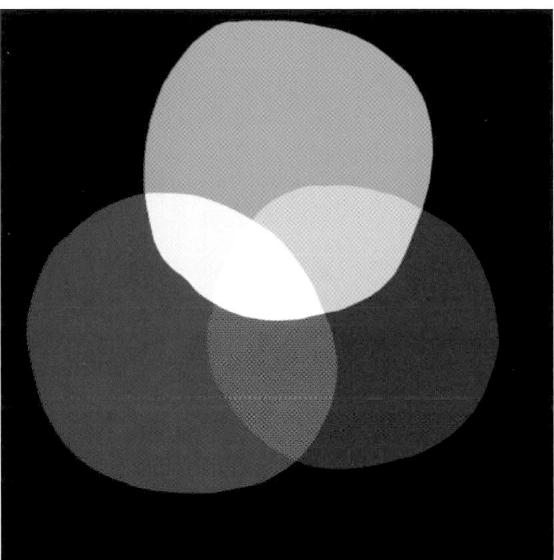

RGB color is additive, meaning that mixing multiple colors creates white. This color space was created for computer graphics that will be viewed only on computer screens.

RGB and ICC Profiles

Have you ever looked at one image on two different computers and seen its color or contrast shift? This happens because there is no universal calibration model for screen-based color.

The problem of non-predictable color is currently being addressed in a number of ways by hardware and software manufacturers. There are two camps working on two different strategies. The first is sRGB, which proposes a more tightly defined color space that is tailored for on-screen delivery; the second involves ICC profiles, which travel along with a file and instruct the device (a printer or monitor) to display colors accurately.

The following section reviews these two approaches and describes how they will affect your Web publishing color methodology.

What Is sRGB?

On August 5th, 1996, Microsoft and Hewlett-Packard proposed a new color space standard called sRGB. This standard was accepted by the W3C and is going to find its way into many software and hardware packages in the future.

The proposal describes the problem that CRTs (**C**athode **R**ay **T**ubes, otherwise known as computer monitors) can be set to a nearly infinite combination of calibration settings. The core principle of sRGB is to produce a reliable and repeatable method of describing color that can be understood by CRTs and that would pick one calibration, based on an average monitor, to be used as a default for everyone.

Browsers and imaging software would benefit from a single description of RGB because they wouldn't have to support every possible flavor of RGB (like what we have today with no calibration standard). Because sRGB is based on an average monitor, many users won't have to recalibrate their settings. The users most affected are non-PC users, such as those creating graphics using Macs and UNIX systems (SUN, SGI, and Linux on Mac.)

Instead of relying on color profiles (which you'll learn more about in the next section) for accurate color management, sRGB represents a more tightly defined color space than RGB. The idea is that imaging software would allow developers to create artwork in an sRGB color space, and monitors and browsers would understand how to accurately display the results. Because the specifications of sRGB are more rigorous than RGB, the unpredictable color differences we see today would be eliminated.

The **sRGB proposal** listed a **call for action**, which will give you a good idea of what has to happen before sRGB is widely supported:

- OSs and authoring tools must support sRGB calibration.
- Authoring tools should enable the use of the operating system is color management tool to transform incoming images into sRGB.
- Authoring tools should enable users to view and edit text in sRGB.
- Web page creators should publish content in sRGB.
- Browser vendors should support style sheet extensions that use the OS color management tools.
- Organizations that create and support file formats should ensure that the file formats are capable of declaring their color space.
- Of course, it will take some time for this to really work well. It will take time, for example, for imaging programs to support sRGB (more on this later) and for hardware devices to recognize it.

The three issues at the heart of **implementing sRGB**:

- The original image should be created in sRGB.
- The display device (monitor) should recognize sRGB.
- The browser software should display sRGB.

Here are some **possible scenarios** if the imaging software, browser, or CRT is not aware of sRGB:

- Image is not created in sRGB, and system doesn't recognize sRGB. This is the state of things today; colors vary wildly between platforms and monitors.
- Image is created in sRGB, but system doesn't recognize sRGB. On non-sRGB compliant monitors, colors will most likely appear darker than they did in the original. (This is similar to creating an image on a Macintosh today and displaying it on a PC.)
- Image is created in sRGB, and system recognizes sRGB. The colors will display accurately on all devices that recognize sRGB.

The sRGB proposal suggested that Web developers create images in sRGB. I'm not certain I agree with this hypothesis or if it even matters whether I do or do not. The truth is that most average Web publishers haven't even heard of sRGB, so it is unlikely that it will be widely adopted soon. Because the sRGB standard is dependent on participation of software, hardware, and Web publishers, it will probably be many years before this solution is truly a solution.

What Is an ICC Color Profile?

The ICC (**I**nternational **C**olor **C**onsortium) was founded by Adobe, Agfa, Apple, Kodak, Microsoft, SGI, Sun, and Taligent and has since grown to include 29 different software and hardware vendors. The purpose of the organization is to create and adhere to a device- and platform-independent color management system. If this sounds similar to the goals of sRGB, it is. The means of achieving the goal are different, however.

sRGB is a color space that exists exclusively for CRT and on-screen display. ICC device profiles are targeted more toward the printing industry but can be used by monitor devices as well. Ideally, you would create an image on your machine that would always look the same whether it was displayed on a computer monitor or printed on paper.

ICC color profiles are embedded into a file format as additional data that specifies the color characteristics of an image. For example, an RGB image profile specifies the gamma (lights and darks), white point (a "cool" or "warm" white), and phosphor colors (because monitors don't have perfectly pure lines of red, green, and blue). These measurements and settings remain with the file, and any device the image is ultimately viewed from can accurately interpret the data.

One of the problems with ICC CMS (**C**olor **M**anagement **S**ystems) is that it increases the file size of a document. This is not practical for Web delivery because the color profile alone could take up to an unbelievable 750k for a full-blown profile, which is many times larger than an optimized Web image.

The list of color profiles that ships with Photoshop 5.0 is so long it scrolls right off the screen. The idea is, you should select the output device as you work on your image, so when you save it the correct color profile will be tied to that image.

My Thoughts About ICC and sRGB

It's great that the major industry powers-to-be are establishing standards that will ultimately result in more accurate color calibration. The problem is, until the new standards are widely adopted, they won't be effective.

RGB has the disadvantage of not yet being widely adopted by imaging programs or display devices. The likelihood that an image has been authored in sRGB and will also be displayed in sRGB is slim. For images that are created in RGB, colors will be unexpectedly altered if they're displayed in sRGB.

sRGB is based on a simple assumption: In the absence of a color profile, software that knows how to do color compensation will assume one "lowest common denominator" flavor of RGB, which is based on a typical Windows screen. It also assumes that even if the software doesn't know how to implement color profiles, your results will be close to the original if your monitor settings are standard (a pretty good assumption for everyone except Macintosh users).

The ICC color profiling method doesn't translate your original image into another color space; it simply adds a description of the color assumptions to the file. It is then up to other devices and software applications to read and compensate for the description. However, browsers, for example, do not read color profiles. In addition, the Achilles heel of this approach is that color profiles significantly increase the file size—a kiss of death for Web graphics.

Frankly, neither option is very helpful to Web developers—yet.

note

Helpful URLs

sRGB Proposal
http://www.w3.org/Graphics/Color/sRGB

ICC Color Profile Specification (in PDF)
ftp://sgigate.sgi.com/pub/icc/ICC34.pdf

Color Management for the WWW
http://www.color.org/wwwcolor.html

Adobe Support for Photoshop 5.0 Color Management
http://www.adobe.com/supportservice/custsupport/TECHGUIDE/PSHOP/main.html

Apple's Colorsync Site
http://www.apple.com/colorsync/

More Gamma Issues

Of the three major color calibration variables (phosphor color, white point, and gamma), the phosphor color is quite subtle in its effect (designers with highly tuned color sensibility will be able to see the difference, but typical users will not). The phosphor color is the only variable that is unchangeable, and that is because it has to do with hardware, not software. White point and gamma, however, are completely adjustable and can be modified using a freeware calibration utility such as Adobe's Gamma utility. Gamma, by far, is the most noticeable variable, and it varies the most between a PC and other platforms.

One key component of sRGB is the fact that it calls for a standardized gamma setting of 2.20. Currently, RGB can be displayed at a variety of gamma settings. Most Macintoshes are set to a gamma reading of 1.80, most SGIs are at 1.70, and most PC systems are set to 2.2. This is why Macintosh images typically appear much darker on PC systems.

Because the majority of people who view the Web are using PCs, it makes sense to me to widely adopt the 2.20 gamma setting as the standard. It is possible to alter a Mac to use PC gamma if you want to do so.

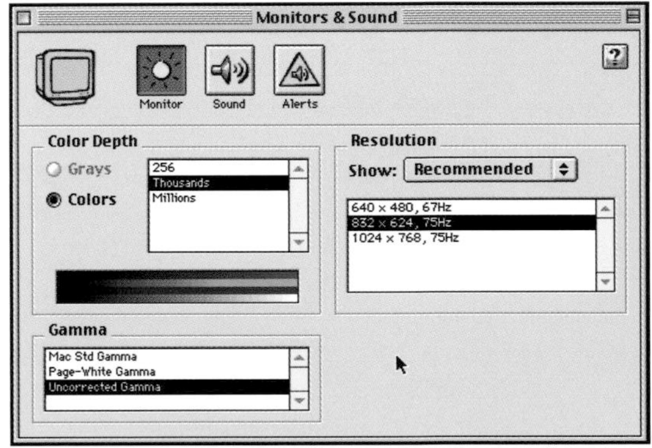

Go to **Control Panels:Monitors & Sound** and choose **Uncorrected Gamma**. This will make your entire display appear darker, but it will more closely resemble the standard that most netizens see.

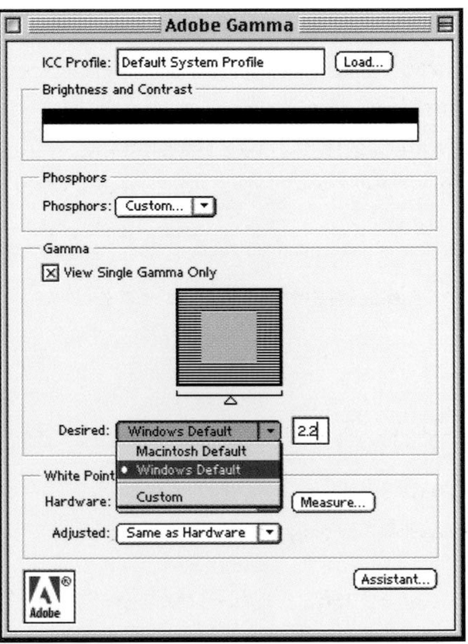

You can also use the Adobe Gamma utility that ships with Photoshop to change your Macintosh gamma to **Windows Default**. This utility is located inside the **Goodies/ Calibration** folder of the Photoshop directory. To my knowledge, there is no way for a PC user to specify Mac Gamma.

sRGB in Photoshop 5.0

To my knowledge, Photoshop 5.0 is one of the first imaging programs to use sRGB. In fact, it ships with sRGB as the default color space (though this is fixed in Photoshop 5.01). In my opinion, this is not good for Web development because files will be modified and will appear differently based on each specific monitor is settings. The difference will be most noticeable for Macintosh users who do not reset their gamma to Uncorrected. This means that images will appear differently in Photoshop than they do in other applications.

Here is a side-by-side comparison of the exact same image in Adobe Photoshop 5.0 and Adobe ImageReady. Photoshop 5.0 ships with sRGB as the default color space, whereas ImageReady and other Web applications use the old undefined flavor or RGB.

I don't know about you, but it drives me crazy to have my colors altered between applications. You can turn off sRGB in Photoshop, and I recommend that you do.

How to Turn Off sRGB in 5.0

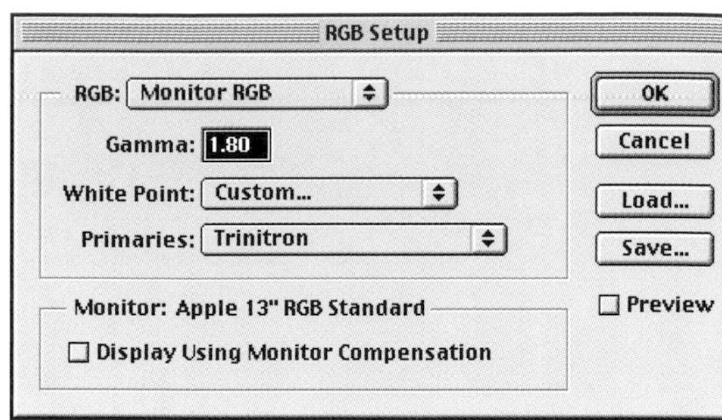

Step 1: Under **File**, choose **Color Settings: RGB Setup** and set RGB to **Monitor RGB** (**"Simplified" Monitor RGB** on Windows).

Step 2: In the RGB Setup screen, *uncheck* **Display Using Monitor Compensation**.

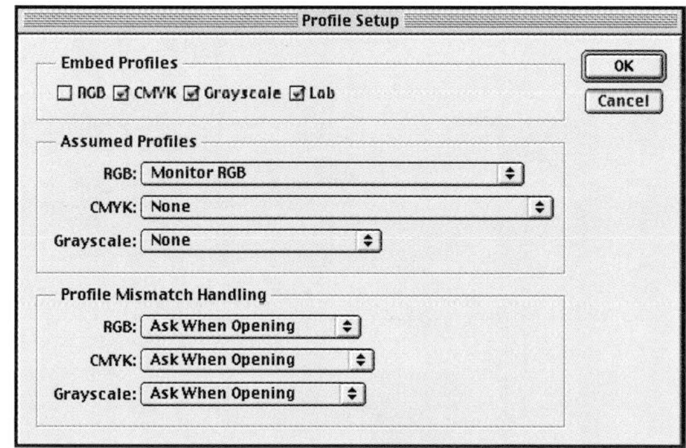

Step 3: Under **File**, choose **Color Settings: Profile Setup** and change Assumed Profiles to **Monitor RGB**.

Step 4: Change Profile Mismatch Handling to **Ask When Opening**.

Step 5: Under **Embed Profiles**, *uncheck* **RGB**. These settings change Photoshop settings back to the old days, before sRGB.

Web Sites That Need Accurate Color

Certain Web sites require accurate color, even at the expense of requesting visitors to load a plug-in. Let's say you have a clothing catalog Web site or a car site where someone is choosing a color. It is mighty important in those types of situations that you can display dead-on correct color.

Pantone has a product called Personal Color Calibrator that ensures screen-to-screen and screen-to-print color accuracy. It requires a Pantone Color Reference card and the use of an ICC profile that describes the characteristics of your monitor. The profile is then used to ensure screen-to-screen and screen-to-printer color accuracy. To learn more about this tool, visit http://www.pantone.com/catalog/p2c2ss.html.

Apple Computer is licensing a technology called **ColorSync**, and many vendors such as Adobe, Kodak, and GoLive CyberStudio are integrating it into their software. ColorSync is a color calibration system that involves downloading a plug-in from Apple. For more information on this tool, visit http://www.apple.com/colorsync/.

GoLive CyberStudio recently announced its support of Apple's ColorSync. This image was taken from Apple's Web site (http://www.apple.com/publishing/ama/0102s/golive.html) with instructions on how to set it up inside Photoshop and CyberStudio.

summary Color Calibration Issues

sRGB, color profiles, and gamma settings make Web life interesting to say the least. Ultimately, the proponents of ICC and sRGB will create standardized color calibration, but for the moment, these new standards confuse Web publishing more than they help it.

Here is a review of what this chapter covered:

- sRGB is a proposed color space that will be adopted by image editors and CRT manufacturers in the future. This will benefit the industry when the support is widespread. Until then, it is not a good idea to be an early adopter because you will be working with a largely unsupported color space.
- ICC profiles ensure that images are displayed correctly on different devices. Unfortunately, the profiles are too large to be Web savvy, so they aren't useful to Web developers yet.
- Gamma settings differ on the PC, Mac, and SGI. Because most of the Web audience uses PCs, if you author content on the Mac (as I do), you might consider changing your gamma settings to that of a PC.
- On sites that require accurate color, you might need to turn to plug-in solutions, such as Pantone's Personal Color Calibrator. But be aware that these are based on the assumption that your site's visitors have accurately calibrated their screens.

Introduction

Browser-Safe Color

Chapter Topics

- Browser Safe Colors Defined
- When to Use Them, When Not To
- Hexadecimal Color
- Safe Color Picking
- Browser Safe Swatches
- Ensure Safe Colors
- JPEGs, Never Browser Safe!

You might have heard of the browser-safe palette, Netscape palette, 216 palette, Web palette, and/or 6x6x6 color cube. All these terms refer to the same set of colors, which this chapter will describe in detail. I will outline techniques for working with browser-safe colors in a variety of software applications and situations in order to help you understand when to use the palette and when not to.

There's a strong irony in Web design in that most developers have more advanced computer systems than the end users for whom they are developing content. This is especially true of visual designers. Most of us have big monitors, lots of RAM, lots of colors, and big hard drives. The trouble with this is that it's easy to create artwork that works on your system, but not on a less advanced system.

Most people who view the Web are not visual designers or Web developers. Many of them have older systems and video cards that support only 256 colors. There are no statistics on this subject because there is no detection mechanism in place to query video card components. What this means is that you will never have any idea what percentage of your audience has a problem seeing all the colors your system can display.

My goal in teaching this subject is to help you make informed decisions about when and when not to use this palette. Using the palette is covered in-depth, with examples showing detailed techniques in many software applications. If you decide to work with browser-safe color, as I suggest you do under certain conditions, this chapter should provide all the necessary reference material to help you produce good-looking compact images that won't dither or shift unexpectedly.

What Is the Browser-Safe Palette?

Let's say you've created images with millions of colors (JPEGs) or GIF images with custom colors of your choosing. What happens in a browser encounter on a system that is limited to 256 colors (8-bit)? It converts all your colors to its own fixed palette. On an 8-bit color system, even though your end user wants to see all the colors on your Web page, they can't. It's both a hardware limitation and a browser software limitation.

The hardware limitation is based on your end user's video card. An 8-bit video card cannot display any more than 256 colors. The question is, which 256 colors will the video card display when it encounters an image with thousands or millions of colors? That's where the software comes in. The browser software makes a decision about which colors to display. Instead of pooling colors from the Web image, it chooses colors from its own fixed palette. There is no way it can display a color outside of this fixed palette. Honest.

Fortunately, the three most popular browsers (Netscape, Mosaic, and Internet Explorer) all share the same fixed palette. It contains a core of 216 colors and allows 40 additional colors, which differ from platform to platform. Most prefer to work with these 216 common denominator colors when necessary. I refer to this palette as the browser-safe palette throughout this book. This means that if you stick to the 216 common colors, they will be honored universally across all browsers, operating systems, and computer platforms.

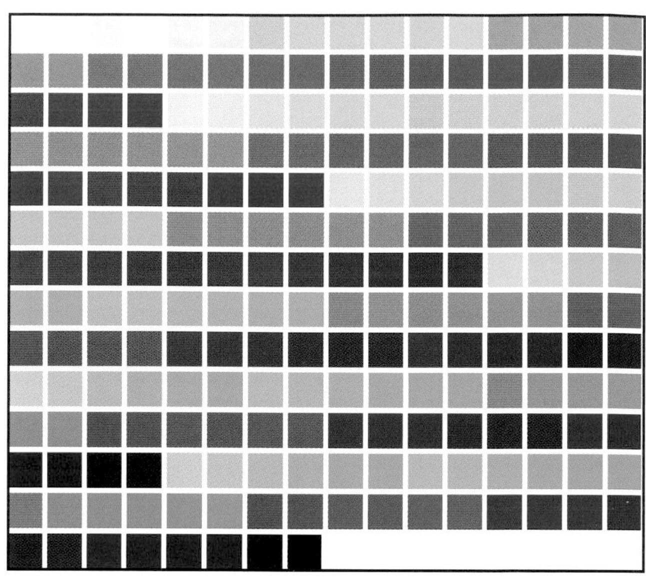

Browser-safe colors were picked by math, not beauty. Here is a version of the browser-safe palette, straight out of the computer.

Notice how these colors have no sense of organization? They are organized by math, not beauty.

On pages 126-129 you will find the same 216 colors, organized in a more useful way: by color (hue) and value (lights to medium tones to darks).

The browser-safe palette is composed of mathematical color combinations, and if you are math phobic like many people, you might think you have to memorize 216 different numeric combinations to understand it. You don't. There are really only six numbers to remember. In fact, this color system is sometimes referred to as the 6x6x6 color cube because it contains six possible values of red, green, and blue (RGB).

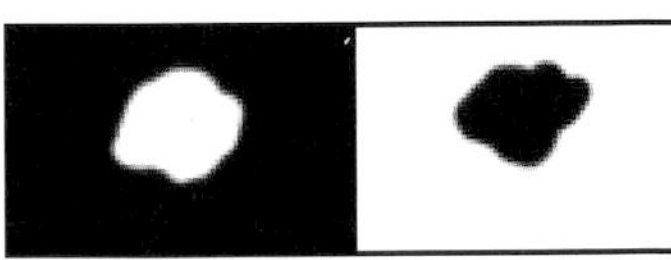

	R	G	B
white	255	255	255
black	0	0	0

255 is the value that is the highest intensity, and 0 is the value that is the lowest intensity. Pure white would contain the value of 255 across all three channels of R, G, and B. Pure black would contain the value of 0 across all three channels.

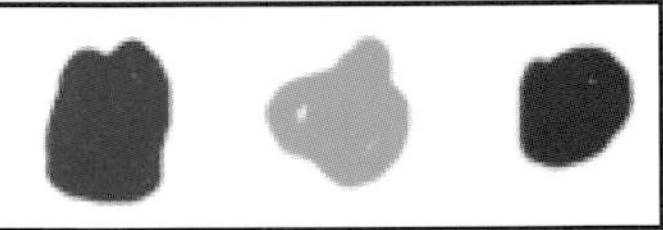

	R	G	B
red	255	0	0
green	0	255	0
blue	0	0	255

To form red, green, or blue, a single color would be turned on while the other two are turned off.

	R	G	B
yellow	255	0	255
cyan	0	255	255
magenta	255	255	0

Yellow, cyan, and magenta are formed by turning on different combinations of RGB.

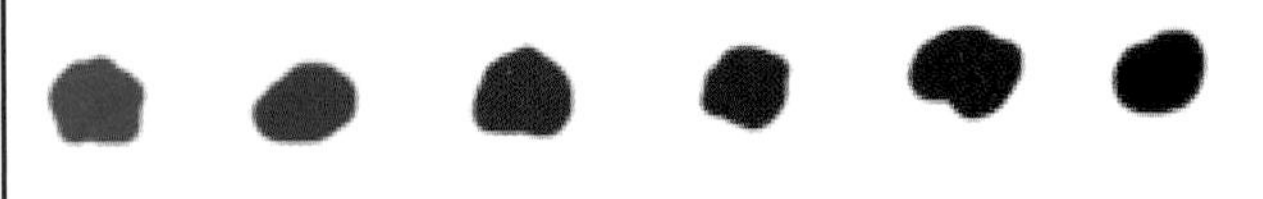

R	G	B
0	0	0
51	0	0
102	0	0
153	0	0
204	0	0
255	0	0

The six RGB values are 0, 51, 102, 153, 204, and 255, from dark to light. Notice how they are separated by 51 numbers? To understand the principle behind achieving a ramp in color values, you can examine the math for one color. Here are the numbers for a value ramp using red.

Note: I realize this is an abstract way to look at color, but if you understand the principle of these colors, you will realize that browser safe colors follow mathematical logic. The following sections explain why the palette was developed and when and when not to use it.

Browser-Safe Color Charts Organized by Value

FFFFFF R=255 G=255 B=255	FFFFCC R=255 G=255 B=204	FFFF99 R=255 G=255 B=153	CCFFFF R=204 G=255 B=255	FFFF66 R=255 G=255 B=102	CCFFCC R=204 G=255 B=204	FFFF33 R=255 G=255 B=051	CCFF99 R=204 G=255 B=153
99FF99 R=153 G=255 B=153	CCFF00 R=204 G=255 B=000	CCCCFF R=204 G=204 B=255	66FFFF R=102 G=255 B=255	FFCC66 R=255 G=204 B=102	99FF66 R=153 G=255 B=102	CCCCCC R=204 G=204 B=204	66FFCC R=102 G=255 B=204
33FFFF R=051 G=255 B=255	CCCC66 R=204 G=204 B=102	66FF66 R=102 G=255 B=102	FF99CC R=255 G=153 B=204	99CCCC R=153 G=204 B=204	33FFCC R=051 G=255 B=204	CCCC33 R=204 G=204 B=051	66FF33 R=102 G=255 B=051
FF9966 R=255 G=153 B=102	99CC66 R=153 G=204 B=102	33FF66 R=051 G=255 B=102	CC99CC R=204 G=153 B=204	66CCCC R=102 G=204 B=204	00FFCC R=000 G=255 B=204	FF9933 R=255 G=153 B=051	99CC33 R=153 G=204 B=051
9999FF R=153 G=153 B=255	33CCFF R=051 G=204 B=255	CC9966 R=204 G=153 B=102	66CC66 R=102 G=204 B=102	00FF66 R=000 G=255 B=102	FF66CC R=255 G=102 B=204	9999CC R=153 G=153 B=204	33CCCC R=051 G=204 B=204
00FF00 R=000 G=255 B=000	CC66FF R=204 G=102 B=255	6699FF R=102 G=153 B=255	00CCFF R=000 G=204 B=255	FF6666 R=255 G=102 B=102	999966 R=153 G=153 B=102	33CC66 R=051 G=204 B=102	CC66CC R=204 G=102 B=204
FF6600 R=255 G=102 B=000	999900 R=153 G=153 B=000	33CC00 R=051 G=204 B=000	FF33FF R=255 G=051 B=255	9966FF R=153 G=102 B=255	3399FF R=051 G=153 B=255	CC6666 R=204 G=102 B=102	669966 R=102 G=153 B=102
996699 R=153 G=102 B=153	339999 R=051 G=153 B=153	CC6600 R=204 G=102 B=000	669900 R=102 G=153 B=000	00CC00 R=000 G=204 B=000	CC33FF R=204 G=051 B=255	6666FF R=102 G=102 B=255	0099FF R=000 G=153 B=255
339933 R=051 G=153 B=051	CC3399 R=204 G=051 B=153	666699 R=102 G=102 B=153	009999 R=000 G=153 B=153	FF3300 R=255 G=051 B=000	996600 R=153 G=102 B=000	339900 R=051 G=153 B=000	FF00FF R=255 G=000 B=255
CC3333 R=204 G=051 B=051	666633 R=102 G=102 B=051	009933 R=000 G=153 B=051	FF0099 R=255 G=000 B=153	993399 R=153 G=051 B=153	336699 R=051 G=102 B=153	CC3300 R=204 G=051 B=000	666600 R=102 G=102 B=000
6633CC R=102 G=051 B=204	0066CC R=000 G=102 B=204	FF0033 R=255 G=000 B=051	993333 R=153 G=051 B=051	336633 R=051 G=102 B=051	CC0099 R=204 G=000 B=153	663399 R=102 G=051 B=153	006699 R=000 G=102 B=153
9900CC R=153 G=000 B=204	3333CC R=051 G=051 B=204	CC0033 R=204 G=000 B=051	663333 R=102 G=051 B=051	006633 R=000 G=102 B=051	990099 R=153 G=000 B=153	333399 R=051 G=051 B=153	CC0000 R=204 G=000 B=000
990033 R=153 G=000 B=051	333333 R=051 G=051 B=051	660099 R=102 G=000 B=153	003399 R=000 G=051 B=153	990000 R=153 G=000 B=000	333300 R=051 G=051 B=000	3300FF R=051 G=000 B=255	660066 R=102 G=000 B=102
330066 R=051 G=000 B=102	0000CC R=000 G=000 B=204	330033 R=051 G=000 B=051	000099 R=000 G=000 B=153	330000 R=051 G=000 B=000	000066 R=000 G=000 B=102	000033 R=000 G=000 B=051	000000 R=000 G=000 B=000

FFFF00 R=255 G=255 B=000	**FFCCFF** R=255 G=204 B=255	**99FFFF** R=153 G=255 B=255	**CCFF00** R=204 G=255 B=102	**FFCCCC** R=255 G=204 B=204	**99FFCC** R=153 G=255 B=204	**CCFF33** R=204 G=255 B=051	**FFCC99** R=255 G=204 B=153
FFCC33 R=255 G=204 B=051	**99FF33** R=153 G=255 B=051	**CCCC99** R=204 G=204 B=153	**66FF99** R=102 G=255 B=153	**FFCC00** R=255 G=204 B=000	**99FF00** R=153 G=255 B=000	**FF99FF** R=255 G=153 B=255	**99CCFF** R=153 G=204 B=255
FF9999 R=255 G=153 B=153	**99CC99** R=153 G=204 B=153	**33FF99** R=051 G=255 B=153	**CCCC00** R=204 G=204 B=000	**66FF00** R=102 G=255 B=000	**CC99FF** R=204 G=153 B=255	**66CCFF** R=102 G=204 B=255	**00FFFF** R=000 G=255 B=255
33FF33 R=051 G=255 B=051	**CC9999** R=204 G=153 B=153	**66CC99** R=102 G=204 B=153	**00FF99** R=000 G=255 B=153	**FF9900** R=255 G=153 B=000	**99CC00** R=153 G=204 B=000	**33FF00** R=051 G=255 B=000	**FF66FF** R=255 G=102 B=255
CC9933 R=204 G=153 B=051	**66CC33** R=102 G=204 B=051	**00FF33** R=000 G=255 B=051	**FF6699** R=255 G=102 B=153	**999999** R=153 G=153 B=153	**33CC99** R=051 G=204 B=153	**CC9900** R=204 G=153 B=000	**66CC00** R=102 G=204 B=000
6699CC R=102 G=153 B=204	**00CCCC** R=000 G=204 B=204	**FF6633** R=255 G=102 B=051	**999933** R=153 G=153 B=051	**33CC33** R=051 G=204 B=051	**CC6699** R=204 G=102 B=153	**669999** R=102 G=153 B=153	**00CC99** R=000 G=204 B=153
00CC66 R=000 G=204 B=102	**FF33CC** R=255 G=051 B=204	**9966CC** R=153 G=102 B=204	**3399CC** R=051 G=153 B=204	**CC6633** R=204 G=102 B=051	**669933** R=102 G=153 B=051	**00CC33** R=000 G=204 B=051	**FF3399** R=255 G=051 B=153
FF3366 R=255 G=051 B=102	**996666** R=153 G=102 B=102	**339966** R=051 G=153 B=102	**CC33CC** R=204 G=051 B=204	**6666CC** R=102 G=102 B=204	**0099CC** R=000 G=153 B=204	**FF3333** R=255 G=051 B=051	**996633** R=153 G=102 B=051
9933FF R=153 G=051 B=255	**3366FF** R=051 G=102 B=255	**CC3366** R=204 G=051 B=102	**666666** R=102 G=102 B=102	**009966** R=000 G=153 B=102	**FF00CC** R=255 G=000 B=204	**9933CC** R=153 G=051 B=204	**3366CC** R=051 G=102 B=204
009900 R=000 G=153 B=000	**CC00FF** R=204 G=000 B=255	**6633FF** R=102 G=051 B=255	**0066FF** R=000 G=102 B=255	**FF0066** R=255 G=000 B=102	**993366** R=153 G=051 B=102	**336666** R=051 G=102 B=102	**CC00CC** R=204 G=000 B=204
FF0000 R=255 G=000 B=000	**993300** R=153 G=051 B=000	**336600** R=051 G=102 B=000	**9900FF** R=153 G=000 B=255	**3333FF** R=051 G=051 B=255	CC0066 R=204 G=000 B=102	**663366** R=102 G=051 B=102	**006666** R=000 G=102 B=102
663300 R=102 G=051 B=000	**006600** R=000 G=102 B=000	**6600FF** R=102 G=000 B=255	**0033FF** R=000 G=051 B=255	**990066** R=153 G=000 B=102	**333366** R=051 G=051 B=102	**6600CC** R=102 G=000 B=204	**0033CC** R=000 G=051 B=204
003366 R=000 G=051 B=102	**3300CC** R=051 G=000 B=204	**660033** R=102 G=000 B=051	**003333** R=000 G=051 B=051	**330099** R=051 G=000 B=153	**660000** R=102 G=000 B=000	**003300** R=000 G=051 B=000	**0000FF** R=000 G=000 B=255

Browser-Safe Color Charts Organized by Hue

330000 R=051 G=000 B=000	660000 R=102 G=000 B=000	990000 R=153 G=000 B=000	CC0000 R=204 G=000 B=000	FF0000 R=255 G=000 B=000	663333 R=102 G=051 B=051	993333 R=153 G=051 B=051	CC3333 R=204 G=051 B=051
CC0033 R=204 G=000 B=051	FF3366 R=255 G=051 B=102	990033 R=153 G=000 B=051	CC3366 R=204 G=051 B=102	FF6699 R=255 G=102 B=153	FF0066 R=255 G=000 B=102	660033 R=102 G=000 B=051	CC0066 R=204 G=000 B=102
CC0099 R=204 G=000 B=153	FF33CC R=255 G=51 B=204	FF00CC R=255 G=000 B=204	330033 R=051 G=000 B=051	660066 R=102 G=000 B=102	990099 R=153 G=000 B=153	CC00CC R=204 G=000 B=204	FF00FF R=255 G=000 B=255
FF99FF R=255 G=153 B=255	FFCCFF R=255 G=204 B=255	CC00FF R=204 G=000 B=255	9900CC R=153 G=000 B=204	CC33FF R=204 G=051 B=255	660099 R=102 G=000 B=153	9933CC R=153 G=051 B=204	CC66FF R=204 G=102 B=255
330099 R=051 G=000 B=153	6633CC R=102 G=051 B=204	9966FF R=153 G=102 B=255	3300CC R=051 G=000 B=204	6633FF R=102 G=051 B=255	3300FF R=051 G=000 B=255	000000 R=000 G=000 B=000	000033 R=000 G=000 B=051
666699 R=102 G=102 B=153	6666CC R=102 G=102 B=204	6666FF R=102 G=102 B=255	9999CC R=153 G=153 B=204	9999FF R=153 G=153 B=255	CCCCFF R=204 G=204 B=255	0033FF R=000 G=051 B=255	0033CC R=000 G=051 B=204
3399FF R=051 G=153 B=255	6699CC R=102 G=153 B=204	99CCFF R=153 G=204 B=255	0099FF R=000 G=153 B=255	006699 R=000 G=102 B=153	3399CC R=051 G=153 B=204	66CCFF R=102 G=204 B=255	0099CC R=000 G=153 B=204
00CCCC R-000 G=204 B=204	33CCCC R=051 G=204 B=204	66CCCC R=102 G=204 B=204	99CCCC R-153 G=204 B=204	00FFFF R=000 G=255 B=255	33FFFF R=051 G=255 B=255	66FFFF R=102 G=255 B=255	99FFFF R=153 G=255 B=255
006633 R=000 G=102 B=051	339966 R=051 G=153 B=102	00CC66 R=000 G=204 B=102	66CC99 R=102 G=204 B=153	33FF99 R=051 G=255 B=153	99FFCC R=153 G=255 B=204	00FF66 R=000 G=255 B=102	009933 R=000 G=153 B=051
009900 R=000 G=153 B=000	339933 R=051 G=153 B=051	669966 R=102 G=153 B=102	00CC00 R=000 G=204 B=000	33CC33 R=051 G=204 B=051	66CC66 R=102 G=204 B=102	99CC99 R=153 G=204 B=153	00FF00 R=000 G=255 B=000
66CC33 R=102 G=204 B=051	99FF66 R=153 G=255 B=102	66FF00 R=102 G=255 B=000	336600 R=051 G=102 B=000	669933 R=102 G=153 B=051	66CC00 R=102 G=204 B=000	99CC66 R=153 G=204 B=102	99FF33 R=153 G=255 B=051
333300 R=051 G=051 B=000	666600 R=102 G=102 B=000	666633 R=102 G=102 B=051	999900 R=153 G=153 B=000	999933 R=153 G=153 B=051	999966 R=153 G=153 B=102	CCCC00 R=204 G=204 B=000	CCCC33 R=204 G=204 B=051
CC9900 R=204 G=153 B=000	FFCC33 R=255 G=204 B=051	996600 R=153 G=102 B=000	CC9933 R=204 G=153 B=051	FFCC66 R=255 G=204 B=102	FF9900 R=255 G=153 B=000	663300 R=102 G=051 B=000	996633 R=153 G=102 B=051
CC3300 R=204 G=051 B=000	FF6633 R=255 G=102 B=051	FF3300 R=255 G=051 B=000	333333 R=051 G=051 B=051	666666 R=102 G=102 B=102	999999 R=153 G=153 B=153	CCCCCC R=204 G=204 B=204	FFFFFF R=255 G=255 B=255

FF3333 R=255 G=051 B=051
996666 R=153 G=102 B=102
CC6666 R=204 G=102 B=102
FF6666 R=255 G=102 B=102
CC9999 R=204 G=153 B=153
FF9999 R=255 G=153 B=153
FFCCCC R=255 G=204 B=204
FF0033 R=255 G=000 B=051

993366 R=153 G=051 B=102
FF3399 R=255 G=051 B=153
CC6699 R=204 G=102 B=153
FF99CC R=255 G=153 B=204
FF0099 R=255 G=000 B=153
990066 R=153 G=000 B=102
CC3399 R=204 G=051 B=153
FF66CC R=255 G=102 B=204

663366 R=102 G=051 B=102
993399 R=153 G=051 B=153
CC33CC R=204 G=051 B=204
FF33FF R=255 G=051 B=255
996699 R=153 G=102 B=153
CC66CC R=204 G=102 B=204
FF66FF R=255 G=102 B=255
CC99CC R=204 G=153 B=204

9900FF R=153 G=000 B=255
330066 R=051 G=000 B=102
6600CC R=102 G=000 B=204
663399 R=102 G=051 B=153
9933FF R=153 G=051 B=255
9966CC R=153 G=102 B=204
CC99FF R=204 G=153 B=255
6600FF R=102 G=000 B=255

000066 R=000 G=000 B=102
000099 R=000 G=000 B=153
0000CC R=000 G=000 B=204
0000FF R=000 G=000 B=255
333366 R=051 G=051 B=102
333399 R=051 G=051 B=153
3333CC R=051 G=051 B=204
3333FF R=051 G=051 B=255

3366FF R=051 G=102 B=255
003399 R=000 G=051 B=153
3366CC R=051 G=102 B=204
6699FF R=102 G=153 B=255
0066FF R=000 G=102 B=255
003366 R=000 G=051 B=102
0066CC R=000 G=102 B=204
336699 R=051 G=102 B=153

33CCFF R=051 G=204 B=255
00CCFF R=000 G=204 B=255
003333 R=000 G=051 B=051
006666 R=000 G=102 B=102
336666 R=051 G=102 B=102
009999 R=000 G=153 B=153
339999 R=051 G=153 B=153
669999 R=102 G=153 B=153

CCFFFF R=204 G=255 B=255
00FFCC R=000 G=255 B=204
00CC99 R=000 G=204 B=153
33FFCC R=051 G=255 B=204
009966 R=000 G=153 B=102
33CC99 R=051 G=204 B=153
66FFCC R=102 G=255 B=204
00FF99 R=000 G=255 B=153

33CC66 R=051 G=204 B=102
66FF99 R=102 G=255 B=153
00CC33 R=000 G=204 B=051
33FF66 R=051 G=255 B=102
00FF33 R=000 G=255 B=051
003300 R=000 G=051 B=000
006600 R=000 G=102 B=000
336633 R=051 G=102 B=051

33FF33 R=051 G=255 B=051
66FF66 R=102 G=255 B=102
99FF99 R=153 G=255 B=153
CCFFCC R=204 G=255 B=204
33FF00 R=051 G=255 B=000
33CC00 R=051 G=204 B=000
66FF33 R=102 G=255 B=051
339900 R=051 G=153 B=000

CCFF99 R=204 G=255 B=153
99FF00 R=153 G=255 B=000
669900 R=102 G=153 B=000
99CC33 R=153 G=204 B=051
CCFF66 R=204 G=255 B=102
99CC00 R=153 G=204 B=000
CCFF33 R=204 G=255 B=051
CCFF00 R=204 G=255 B=000

CCCC66 R=204 G=204 B=102
CCCC99 R=204 G=204 B=153
FFFF00 R=255 G=255 B=000
FFFF33 R=255 G=255 B=051
FFFF66 R=255 G=255 B=102
FFFF99 R=255 G=255 B=153
FFFFCC R=255 G=255 B=204
FFCC00 R=255 G=204 B=000

CC6600 R=204 G=102 B=000
CC9966 R=204 G=153 B=102
FF9933 R=255 G=153 B=051
FFCC99 R=255 G=204 B=153
FF6600 R=255 G=102 B=000
993300 R=153 G=051 B=000
CC6633 R=204 G=102 B=051
FF9966 R=255 G=153 B=102

Why Does the Browser-Safe Palette Exist?

Why was the browser-safe palette developed by browser software manufacturers? Because the easiest solution to the 8-bit hardware limitation is for the browser software to impose a fixed palette.

Those of you who have authored multimedia using Macromedia Director before have been able to assign custom palettes to specific pieces of artwork using palette channels. HTML has no means with which to do this. There is no "change palette" tag, and color lookup tables (CLUTs) are not of a MIME type recognized by browsers. Because of this, the browser has to deal with the issue instead of depending on your input.

If a browser created 256 color palettes based on the colors within images, it would quickly run out of colors anyway. Then it would have to map all the rest of the images to whatever palette it established based on the first few images. It's actually better that the browser use a fixed palette, because at least you can identify it and work within its constraints.

tip

Do Browser-Safe Colors Really Matter?

You may think that all this hubbub over browser-safe colors does not apply to you. If you think your site will be viewed only from millions-of-color monitors (24-bit), you might be right. It's always important to decide who your audience is before you design a site and create artwork that is appropriate for your viewers.

The most common tasks performed on personal computers are word processing, spreadsheet calculations, database work, and games. None of these activities requires more than 256 colors, hence many people who own computers for these purposes have no reason to set their monitors to higher color depths or even have video cards capable of displaying more colors.

My recommendation is that if you are going to pick colors for backgrounds, type, text, links, or illustrations, you should choose cross-platform compatible colors. There may come a day years from now when everyone has video cards that support more than 256 colors, but most systems today do not.

When To Use the Browser-Safe Color Palette

You might think that I advocate using the browser-safe palette at all times. I do not, and I am alarmed when I see the palette misused. To explain when to use this palette, I will define the four possible scenarios that relate to browser-safe colors:

- **Hexadecimal-Based Color:** Within the HTML code, when you specify colors for your background, text, links, visited links, or active links, you must use hexadecimal code.
- **Line Art:** Graphics that contain solid colors or lines.
- **Continuous Tone Art:** Graphics or photographs that contain blends, gradients, tones, and soft focus.
- **Hybrid Art:** Art that combines continuous tone and line art.

The following sections go into greater depth about when and how to the browser-safe colors.

When To Use Browser-Safe Colors?	
Hexadecimal Colors	Yes, always.
Line Art Images	Only for areas of solid color.
Continuous Tone Images	No, never.
Hybrid Images	Only for areas of solid color.

Hexadecimal-Based Colors

If you want to add colors on your site—such as colored text, colored links, colored backgrounds, and colored borders—describing them by their hexadecimal values is the only way HTML lets you do it.

#	0	1	2	3	4	5	6	7	8	9	10	11	12	13	14	15
HEX	0	1	2	3	4	5	6	7	8	9	A	B	C	D	E	F

What on earth are hexadecimal values, you may well wonder? Hexadecimal values are based on base–16 mathematics. Here's a little table that shows how hexadecimal numbers translate from our standard base-ten counting system.

RGB	0	51	102	153	204	255
HEX	00	33	66	99	CC	FF

Here's a very handy chart that shows how to convert browser-safe RGB values to hexadecimal values. Notice that the hex values never exceed two digits, unlike the RGB values, some of which are three digits long. This makes hexadecimal code a more uniform system than RGB numerics.

Let's say, you want to describe a pure browser-safe red in hexadecimal code. The RGB value would be 255, 0, 0. According to the chart to the left, this setting would translate into hexadecimal code FF0000.

More information on how to select and convert RGB to HEX follows later in this chapter. For the moment, let's stick to the question at hand: Why should you use browser-safe colors for hexadecimal colors in your HTML?

If a browser on an 8-bit system encounters a Web page with color codes that are not browser safe, it converts the colors to browser-safe values for you. This sounds polite and all, but the problem is, you can't control which color the browser will shift. I have received letters from people complaining that when they uploaded their site, their client couldn't see any of the text. Why? Because the client had an 8-bit system, and the browser shifted their text color to match their background color.

There is no reason for you to risk such a disaster on your site. Simply follow the rule to always use browser-safe colors for your hex values, and this will never happen to you. Instructions for picking and implementing these colors follows later in this chapter.

Non-Safe Colors Shift!

Here's an example of what can go wrong if you don't use browser-safe colors in your HTML code. The following code will shift on 8-bit color systems:

<BODY BGCOLOR="#090301" TEXT="#436E58" LINK="#CF7B42" VLINK="#323172" ALINK="#FFFFFF">

You should be able to tell just by looking that these colors are not browser safe! Remember, browser-safe hex combinations are always formed from variations of 00, 33, 66, 99, CC, and FF.

Mac 8-bit display

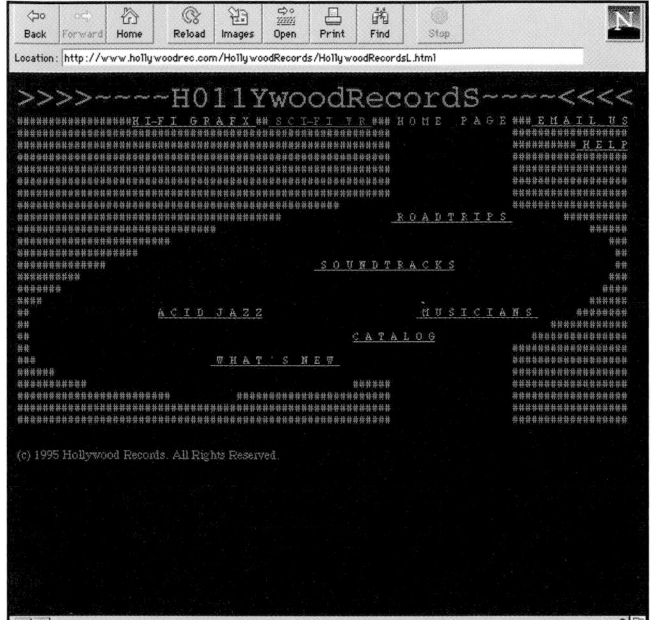

PC 8-bit display

This comparison demonstrates the kind of color shifting that occurs with hexadecimal-based artwork on 8-bit systems if the colors used are not browser safe.

Illustration-Based Artwork

With illustration-based artwork, if you create logos, cartoons, or drawings in colors outside of the 216, the browser converts your colors. Instead of shifting the color, which is what happens with hexadecimal-based color, it dithers the artwork. Here are some examples of the unwanted effects of dithering.

On a millions-of-color display, you might not notice any differences between these two illustrations. The one on the left was created using non-safe colors and the one on the right was created using browser safe colors.

On an 8-bit display, look at what happens to the left version. It is filled with unwanted dots caused by dithering. Why? The colors in the right logo are browser safe, and the colors in the left are not.

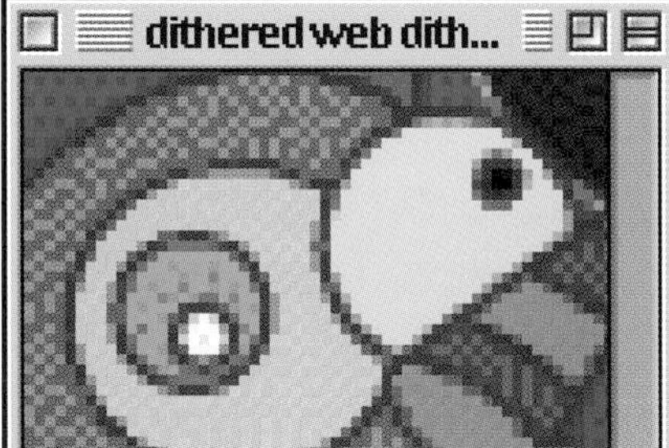

Here's a close-up of the dithering that occurs in the nonbrowser-safe version of this illustration when viewed on an 8-bit (256-color) system.

The close-up of the version created with browser-safe colors will not dither, regardless of which bit depth the end-viewer's system supports. The moral of the story: Always create this type of artwork using browser-safe colors.

Photograph-Based Artwork

Continuous tone artwork (photographs) is the one type of image that really does not benefit from using browser-safe colors. The reason is that the browsers convert photographs, but do a great job of it, unlike the terrible job they do with hexadecimal-based color and illustration-based artwork.

It is not necessary to convert photographic-based images to the browser-safe palette or even an 8-bit palette. The browser does it's dithering dirty work, regardless of how you prepare the image. It's best to leave the image in an adaptive palette or 24-bit file format because photographs look better in 24-bit browser environments. JPEGs will always produce the smallest file size for photographs, and JPEG is a 24-bit file format, unlike GIF, which cannot save images at higher bit-depths than 8-bit (256 colors). More information on how to save JPEG and GIF images with adaptive and Web-safe palettes follows later.

Here are some comparisons:

Viewed in 24-bit	Viewed in 8-bit
 JPEG	
 Adaptive GIF	
 Web-safe GIF	

Notice how every image in the 24-bit column looks better than the 8-bit column? People with better video cards see the Web in better color. Look carefully however, and notice that all the 8-bit images look the same, while the JPEG and adaptive GIF look much better. This shows that the browsers convert 8-bit images no better than you could convert them yourself. So why not let your more fortunate audience see your images with better fidelty? The moral of the story—don't use browser-safe colors on photographs!

How to Use Browser-Safe Colors

Okay, now that you know when to use browser-safe colors, the bigger question becomes "How?" The following sections share my favorite tips and techniques for applying browser-safe color to hexadecimal color choices and to images. We've identified three possible scenarios for using browser-safe color: hexadecimal color, line art images, and hybrid images. Let's start with hexadecimal color first.

Browser-Safe Hex Color Picking

Picking a color scheme for your site's background color, text, link, active link, and visited link settings can be done using a variety of tools. Many HTML editors include color pickers and browser-safe color palettes. Imaging tools also include browser-safe color pickers. Rather than focus on any particular tools at this point, let's look at the principle.

Step 1: Pick the colors you want to use. (More information on aesthetic concerns and choices follows later in this chapter.) You can choose the colors off the chart printed on pages126-129 or by downloading the **nhue.gif** or **nvalue. gif** from my Web site: http://www.lynda.com/files/. The electronic files will be more accurate, since the chart is printed with CMYK inks and cannot accurately portray the colors.

Step 2: If necessary, convert the RGB values to hexadecimal values. Some imaging and HTML programs use percentages instead of RGB. Here's the translation:

RGB	PERCENTAGES	HEX
0	0%	00
51	20%	33
102	40%	66
153	60%	99
204	80%	CC
255	100%	FF

Step 3: Write the HTML for the BODY tag of your document. The BODY tag is where the color information for your Web page is stored. Let's say I picked the following color scheme:

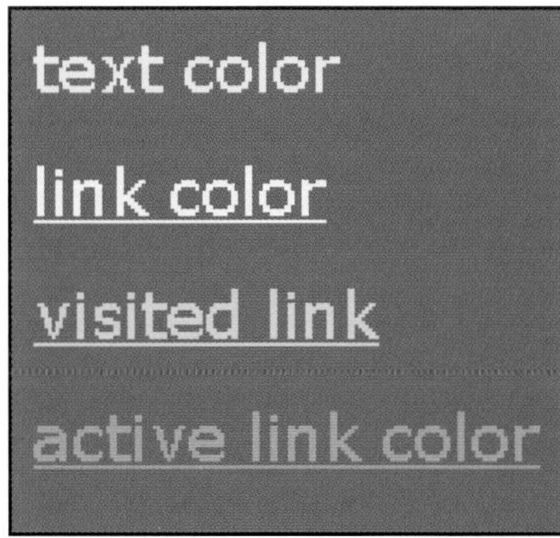

This is what my HTML code for the background, text, link, visited link, and active link colors would look like:

```
<BODY BGCOLOR="#336699"
TEXT="#CCFF99" LINK ="#CCFFCC"
VLINK="#99CCCC" ALINK="#9999CC">
```

Note: The hash mark (#) is not required, but it is part of the formal HTML 4.0 specification. At this point in time, browsers do not require it. But if future browsers become more strict, this mark may be required. Try to get in the habit of using it, to protect your site from potential problems in the future. The trend of HTML is leaning towards more strict syntax.

Other Conversion Methods

Here is a chart for dealing with the conversion from RGB (0—255) to hex. The browser-safe colors are highlighted.

00=00	01=01	02=02	03=03	04=04	05=05	06=06	07=07	08=08
09=09	10=0A	11=0B	12=0C	13=0D	14=0E	15=0F	16=10	17=11
18=12	19=13	20=14	21=15	22=16	23=17	24=18	25=19	26=1A
27=1B	28=1C	29=1D	30=1E	31=1F	32=20	33=21	34=22	35=23
36=24	37=25	38=26	39=27	40=28	41=29	42=2A	43=2B	44=2C
45=2D	46=2E	47=2F	48=30	49=31	50=32	**51=33**	52=34	53=35
54=36	55=37	56=38	57=39	58=3A	59=3B	60=3C	61=3D	62=3E
63=3F	64=40	65=41	66=42	67=43	68=44	69=45	70=46	71=47
72=48	73=49	74=4A	75=4B	76=4C	77=4D	78=4E	79=4F	80=50
81=51	82=52	83=53	84=54	85=55	86=56	87=57	88=58	89=59
90=5A	91=5B	92=5C	93=5D	94=5E	95=5F	96=60	97=61	98=62
99=63	100=64	101=65	**102=66**	103=67	104=68	105=69	106=6A	107=6B
108=6C	109=6D	110=6E	111=6F	112=70	113=71	114=72	115=73	116=74
117=75	118=76	119=77	120=78	121=79	122=7A	123=7B	124=7C	125=7D
126=7E	127=7F	128=80	129=81	130=82	131=83	132=84	133=85	134=86
135=87	136=88	137=89	138=8A	139=8B	140=8C	141=8D	142=8E	143=8F
144=90	145=91	146=92	147=93	148=94	149=95	150=96	151=97	152=98
153=99	154=9A	155=9B	156=9C	157=9D	158=9E	159=9F	160=A0	161=A1
162=A2	163=A3	164=A4	165=A5	166=A6	167=A7	168=A8	168=A9	170=AA
171=AB	172=AC	173=AD	17=AE	175=AF	176=B0	177=B1	178=B2	179=B3
180=B4	181=B5	182=B6	183=B7	184=B8	185=B9	186=BA	187=BB	188=BC
189=BD	190=BE	191=BF	192=C0	193=C1	194=C2	195=C3	196=C4	197=C5
198=C6	199=C7	200=C8	201=C9	202=CA	203=CB	**204=CC**	205=CD	206=CE
207=CF	208=D0	209=D1	210=D2	211=D3	212=D4	213=D5	214=D6	215=D7
216=D8	217=D9	218=DA	219=DB	220=DC	221=DD	222=DE	223=DF	224=E0
225=E1	226=E2	227=E3	228=E4	229=E5	230=E6	231=E7	232=E8	233=E9
234=EA	235=EB	236=EC	237=ED	238=EE	239=EF	240=F0	241=F1	242=F2
243=F3	244=F4	245=F5	246=F6	247=F7	248=F8	249=F9	250=FA	251=FB
252=FC	253=FD	254=FE	**255=FF**					

This chart shows how RGB values, which range from 0–255, convert to hexadecimal mathematics.

Hex Color Aides

A variety of hexadecimal color aides are available, from mousepads to hexadecimal calculators:

Christopher Shmitt of christopher.org created a Web-safe color mousepad in the round. You can easily order yours from http:// www.christopher.org/NETWORK/ webdesignpad.com/.

Raymond and **Dante Pirouz** have a Web design supply company at http:// www.r35.com. You can order a mousepad or poster showing the browser-safe palette from them if you'd like to keep a handy printed reference nearby your computer. One caveat applies to those items and the printed color charts in this book as well: It is impossible to re create RGB colors with CMYK inks. For this reason, the truest color guides are found in electronic form instead of printed form (such as those found at http://www.lynda.com/files/). Nevertheless, having the chart in print can save a lot of time, even if the chart isn't 100% accurate.

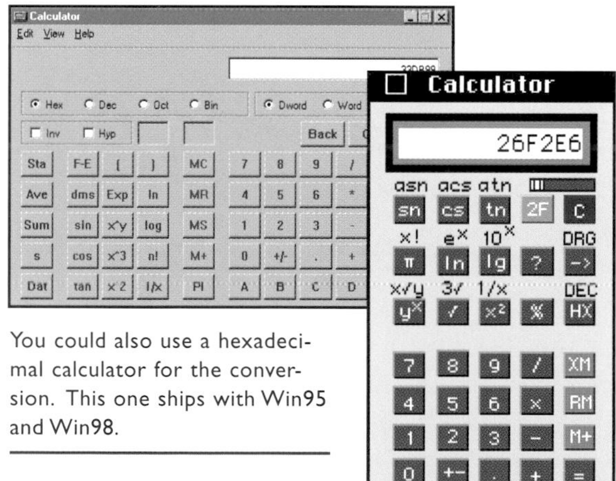

You could also use a hexadecimal calculator for the conversion. This one ships with Win95 and Win98.

If you use a Macintosh, you need to download a hexadecimal calculator. My favorite is available at ftp://ftp.amug.org/pub/mirrors /info-mac/sci/calc/calculator-ii-15.hqx.

Pantone's Browser-Safe Solution

Pantone has come to the browser-safe rescue with a Mac-only product called ColorWeb and ColorWeb Pro (http://www.pantone.com). Both products include an Internet-safe color picking system that consists of a printed swatch set and a System Color Picker that displays the 216 safe colors in the Apple Color Picker dialog box.

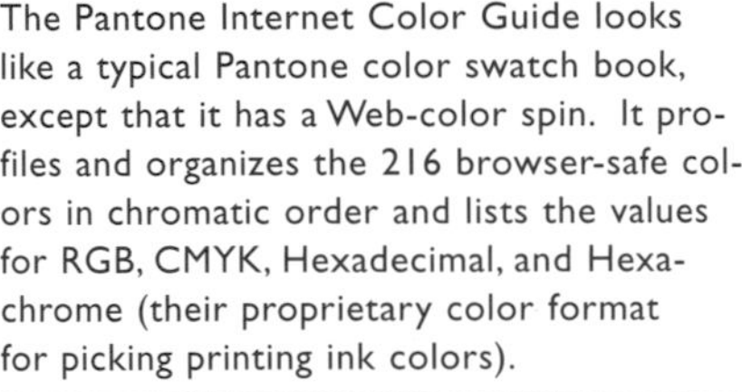
The Pantone Internet Color Guide looks like a typical Pantone color swatch book, except that it has a Web-color spin. It profiles and organizes the 216 browser-safe colors in chromatic order and lists the values for RGB, CMYK, Hexadecimal, and Hexachrome (their proprietary color format for picking printing ink colors).

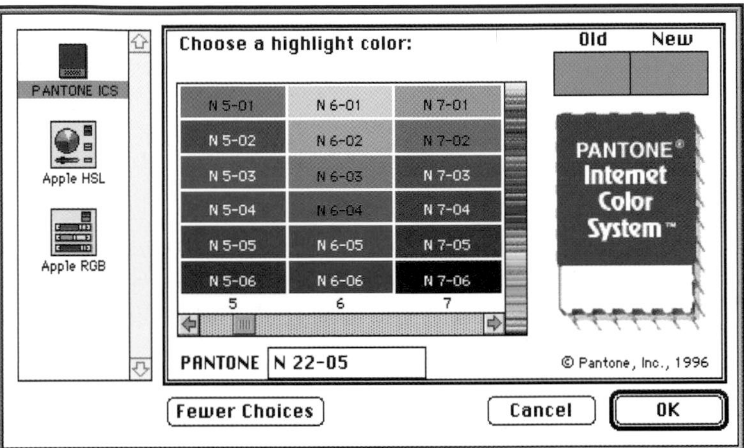

If you install Pantone's ColorWeb software, it will add another entry, called Pantone ICS, into the Apple Color Picker choices. Pantone ICS will enable you to pick from the 216 browser-safe colors.

warning

CMYK Is Not Browser Safe

It should be noted that there is no perfectly accurate way to convert CMYK values to RGB. The numbers that the Pantone Internet Color Guide cites for CMYK Internet-safe values are ballpark approximations and do not yield browser-safe colors when converted to RGB. The two color spaces—RGB and CMYK—do not share common colors consistently. Some RGB colors are outside of the CMYK color gamut, and nothing can be adjusted to create a reliable conversion method.

ColorWeb Pro adds an additional color picker that displays 1,024 Pantone colors and allows you to locate the closest browser-safe color to it. It also ships with a printed fan book that contains all 1,024 colors. This book is a beautiful and useful tool, even if you aren't a print designer! Pricing and order information for ColorWeb Pro is available at the Pantone Web site.

Browser-Safe Color Picking

In order to create artwork with browser-safe colors, you must learn to select the correct colors, paint and fill with them, and shift existing documents to contain them. The first step is learning how to load the palette into your image editor, and the next step is learning to paint, fill, and shift to it.

Unfortunately, there are so many image editors on the market that I don't have space to include all of them. Of all the tools, I favor ImageReady because it has the best color management features of any Web graphics product I know. You can download a demo version of ImageReady (Mac or PC) from http://www.imageready.com/ to try these techniques yourself. As space allows, I will cover other tools as well.

tip

What Is a CLUT and What Do You Do with One?

CLUT is an acronym for **C**olor **L**ook**U**p **T**able. A color lookup table is the file that assigns the specific colors to any 8-bit or lower bit-depth computer image. Photoshop and ImageReady use CLUT files in two different ways. You can load a CLUT into the swatches palette for color picking, or you can assign colors to an image using a CLUT. In Photoshop, a CLUT file is also called a swatch, a palette, or a color table. Other imaging programs use CLUT files, too, but sometimes they have no way of viewing them or accessing them. Anyway, now you know what CLUT means, so you can continue reading with more terminology comfort than before...

How to Load a Browser-Safe Swatch Palette into Photoshop

The method to reset, load, replace, and save swatches in Photoshop 5.0 and 4.0 is to go to the Swatch palette and hold down the triangle in the upper-right corner to access the menu selections, which are described next.

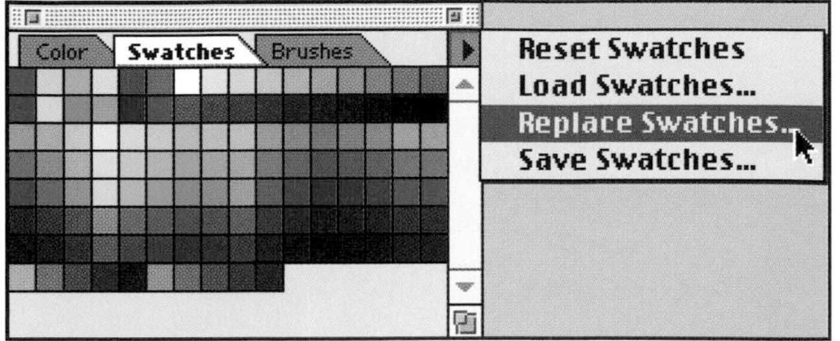

Reset Swatches: Choose this if you've loaded other swatches and want to return to the default swatch set.

Load Swatches: Choose this setting if you wish to load other swatches to the current swatch set. It will append the display and you can load many swatches at once with this feature.

Replace Swatches: Choose this setting if you want to replace the existing swatch with a new one. I recommend this setting most often for working with browser-safe colors. That way, you know that you don't have any non-safe colors in your Swatch palette display.

Save Swatches: Choose this setting if you've created your own swatch set (instructions follow later) and want to save it so you can load it later or distribute it to other Photoshop users (such as a Web design production team working on your site!).

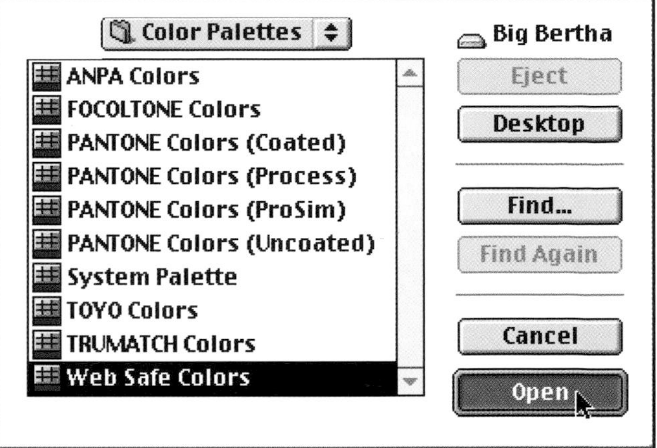

Photoshop 5.0 ships with a Web Safe Colors palette. You can load this palette by choosing **Replace Swatches** in the **Swatch palette** menu. You can locate the palette in your Photoshop 5.0 folder or directory by choosing **Photoshop:Goodies:Color Palettes** and then selecting **Web Color**.

For earlier versions of Photoshop, you can download the file **bclut2.aco** from my Web site—http://www.lynda. com/files/. You can load it into the Photoshop Swatch palette by using the upper-right triangle in the Swatch palette and choosing **Replace Swatches** from the pull-down menu.

How to Load the Browser-Safe Palette into ImageReady

Because ImageReady was developed as a dedicated Web graphics tool, the browser-safe palette is part of ImageReady and doesn't have to be imported or loaded. Simply go to the Swatch palette, and it's already loaded! Not only that, but it's much more nicely organized than the Photoshop 5.0 version, don'tcha think?

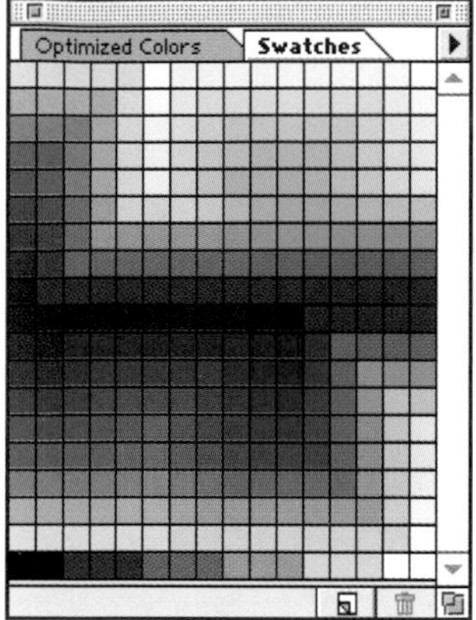

ImageReady goes many steps further than Photoshop in that it has added a browser-safe color picker to its other Color palette.

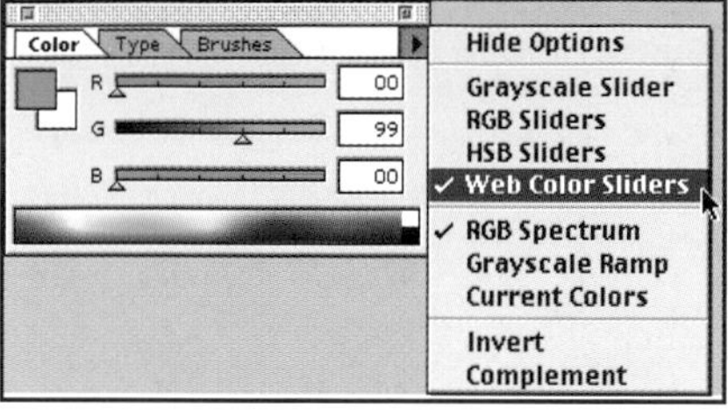

This means that you can move the RGB sliders and know that any color you snap to will be within the browser-safe selection range.

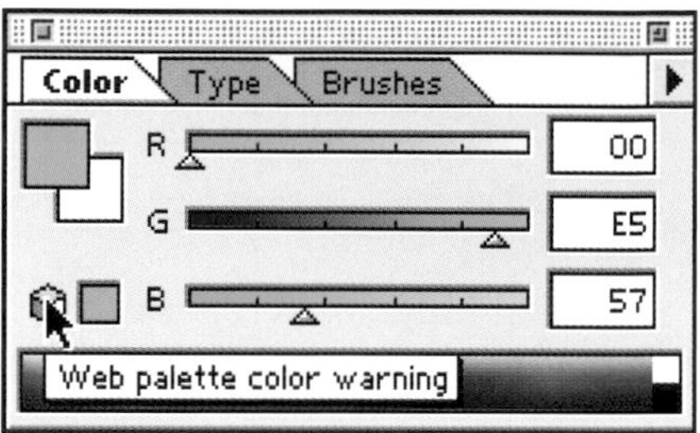

Let's say you want to use the RGB Spectrum picker located below the sliders. This effectively lets you select from millions of colors. If a color you select is not browser safe, the warning cube will appear in the lower-left corner of the Color palette. Click on the cube icon, and the non-safe color you selected will shift to the closest browser-safe color.

Another great feature in ImageReady is the ability to select a color within the swatch or within color palette and copy the color as hexadecimal code into an HTML editor. All you do is pick a color and select **Edit:Copy Color as HTML**. When you paste, the code it will look something like this: COLOR ="#009900"

Photoshop's Info Palette

ImageReady's Info Palette

Unlike in Photoshop, the Info Palette window in ImageReady shows hex values in addition to RGB. ImageReady, on the other hand, could care less about CMYK information!

How to Load the Browser-Safe Palette into Fireworks

Because Fireworks was also developed specifically as a Web graphics application, it also has better Web color support than Photoshop. The browser-safe palette is the default palette here, too.

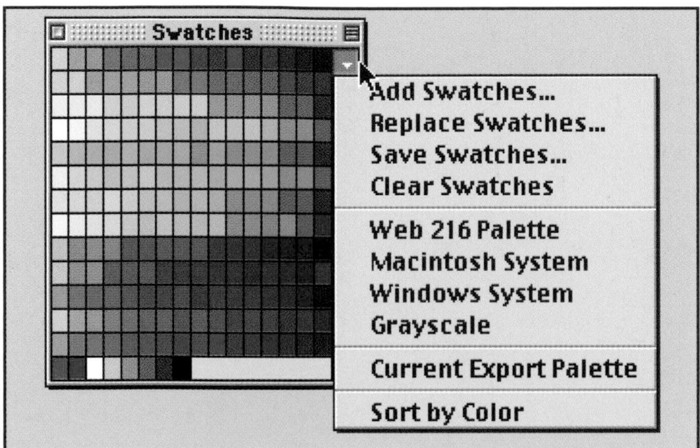

You can add, replace, save, and clear swatches in Fireworks. The Swatches palette displays browser-safe colors by default. You can also **Sort by Color** (shown above) to arrange the colors in a more pleasing array than you get from Photoshop's mathematical sorting.

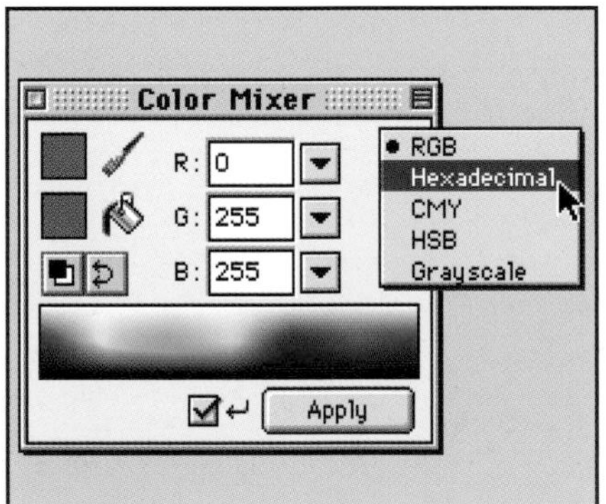

The Fireworks Color Mixer palette defaults to the RGB spectrum. You can change it to the Hexadecimal palette by accessing the popup menu available in the upper-right side.

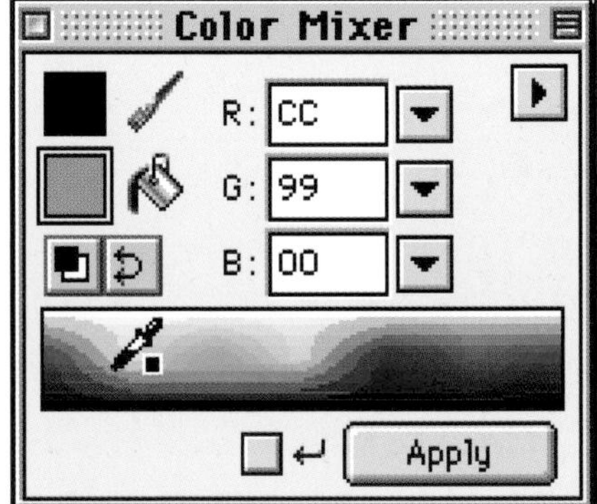

The Hexadecimal setting limits the spectrum colors to browser-safe values, and the numeric readouts display hexadecimal code instead of RGB values.

How to Ensure That Your GIF Artwork Stays Browser Safe

If you work with browser-safe colors when you create artwork, you still have the important task of ensuring that those colors remain browser safe during the file format conversion process to GIF. This is easy in ImageReady and Fireworks, but it's cumbersome in Photoshop. The following sections review this process for each of these applications.

Safe GIF Files in Photoshop

Unfortunately, Photoshop does a very poor job of this, so you must learn workarounds to ensure that your artwork holds the safe colors. Even if you create an image using browser-safe colors, they can be lost during the saving process! Here's how to prevent this from happening to your graphics:

Step 1: Open or create an image that contains browser-safe colors (it must be a **.psd**, **.pict**, **.tiff**, or **.bmp** to begin with).

Step 2: Choose **Mode:Indexed Color:Web**. This converts the image to include only Web-safe colors. Notice that the color table includes all 216 of the Web-safe colors. That is unnecessary and will make the GIF file much too large.

Step 3: Choose **Mode:RGB**. This converts the image back to RGB color. Next, choose **Mode:Indexed Color:Exact**. In this example, the exact palette has only 21 colors, but they are all browser safe. This will create a browser-safe image and will remove all the unused colors.

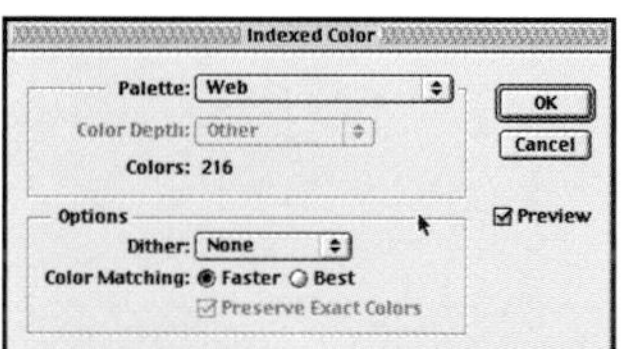

Here is the Indexed Color dialog box in Photoshop, when Web Is selected.

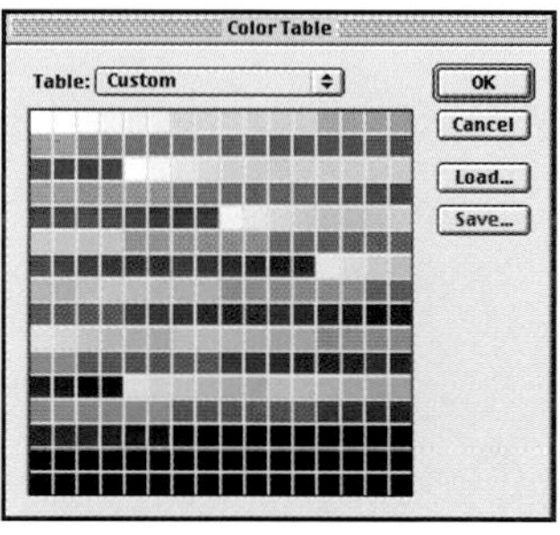

The resulting color table.

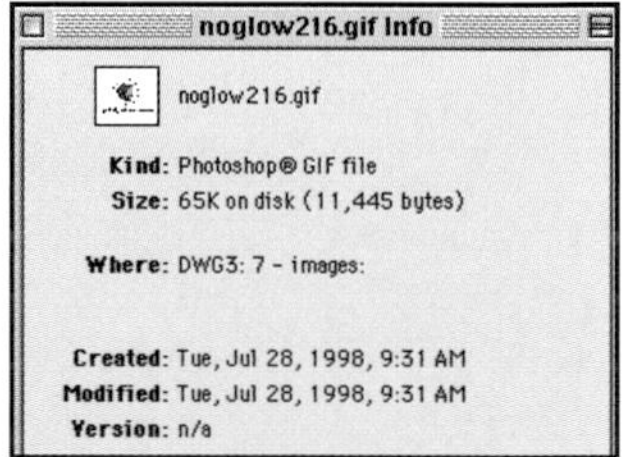

The resulting file size—11.4k—is too big!

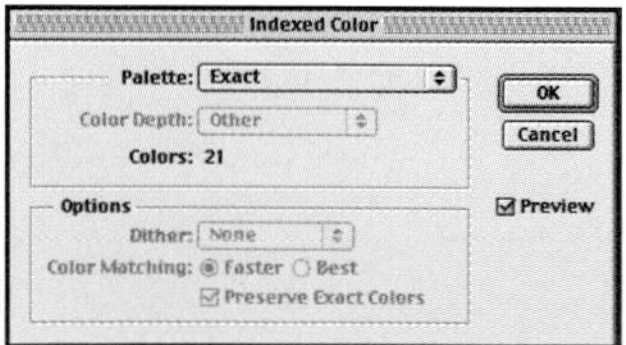

Here is the Indexed Color dialog box in Photoshop, when Exact is selected after Web was applied.

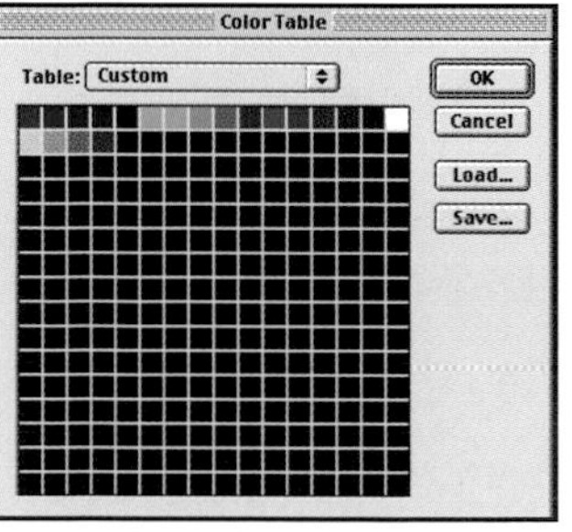

The resulting color table has fewer colors; all are browser-safe.

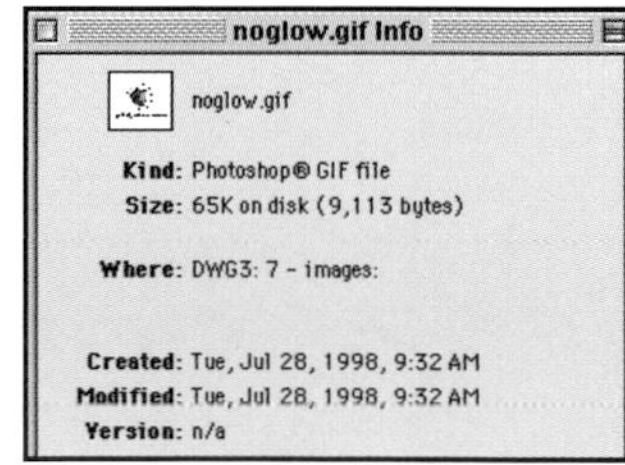

The resulting file size —9.3k—is much better!

Safe GIF Files in ImageReady

ImageReady accomplishes what Photoshop does but in fewer steps and with better file saving results. When the GIF format is set to Web and Colors are set to Auto, the program knows to eliminate all unused colors. Look at the file size too—an impressive 2.271k—quite a bit smaller than what Photoshop delivered, even with the Exact color palette trick.

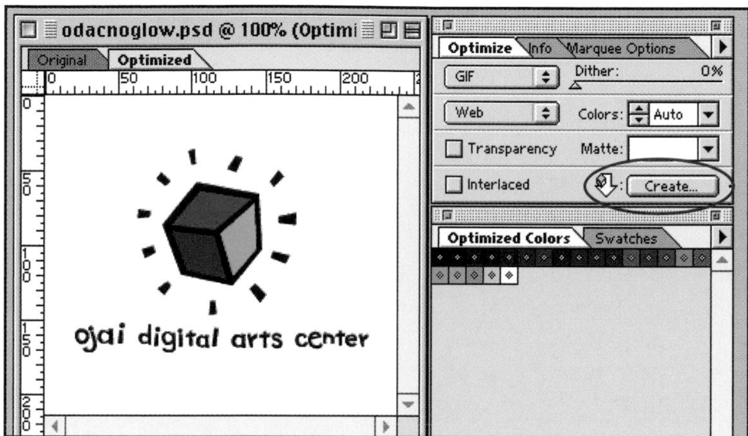

The Auto setting figures out the fewest necessary Web safe colors for the file.

Safe GIF Files in Fireworks

In Fireworks, choose **File:Export** to see this Export Preview dialog box. If you apply the GIF Web 216 to your Saved Settings, the program also eliminates unused colors automatically. Notice also that Fireworks has found only 21 browser-safe colors, and the resulting file size is 2.33k—smaller than both Photoshop and ImageReady!

The optimize button chooses the fewest necessary Web safe colors.

Vector-Based Software: Illustrator and FreeHand

Most vector-based software packages were designed for print mediums, not the screen-based Web. For this reason, many vector-based programs support only CMYK and not RGB color.

Browser-Safe Colors in Illustrator 8.0

Like many other computer graphic programs, Illustrator was originally engineered to generate artwork for print projects and functioned only in CMYK. With the popularity of the Web and because so many Illustrator customers use this product for Web graphics, the product finally supports the RGB color space. Woo hoo! Unfortunately, any versions of Illustrator before this did not support RGB color, so it is impossible to work with browser-safe colors in older versions.

How to Work with Illustrator 8.0 Swatches

Illustrator 8.0 ships with a Web palette, but it doesn't work the way palettes do in Photoshop. If you install Illustrator with its Swatch Libraries folder, you simply open the folder and open the document named Web in the Mac version or **Web.ai** in Windows version. This loads the browser-safe colors into the Swatches palette automatically.

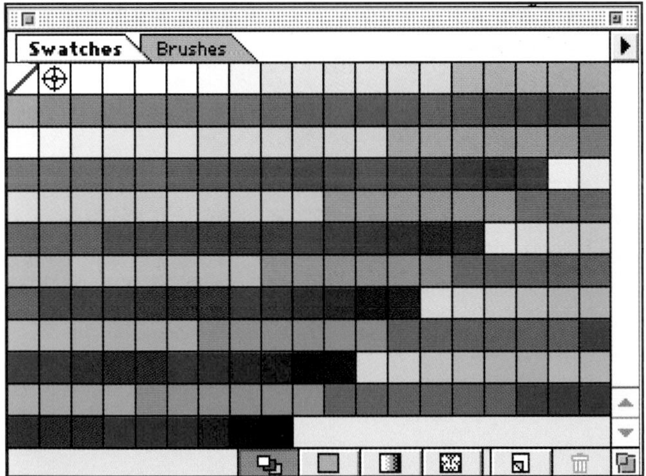

The Swatches Palette in Illustrator 8.0 with the Web palette loaded. Swatch palettes cannot be loaded or saved in Illustrator as they can in Photoshop. Basically, any colors that you use or mix in any Illustrator 8.0 document become part of the Swatches palette.

warning

Illustrator 7.0 and 8.0 CMYK Problem

Make sure the colors you pick from the swatches palette are in RGB! If the colors are CYMK colors, they will shift into non browser-safe colors when the image is rasterized in RGB. Check your color palette to see if your values read in CYMK as pictured below. One clue that the colors are CYMK is that the color amounts are given in percentages. Also, make sure to check the fill as well as the stroke when changing color. In fact, check every element and change it to RGB so that none of your colors stray.

A few other things to keep in mind:

> Illustrator 7 will rasterize your images to RGB in the program; however, the artwork will come out cleaner and crisper if it's rasterized with the place function into Photoshop.

> Gradients between browser-safe colors aren't browser safe.

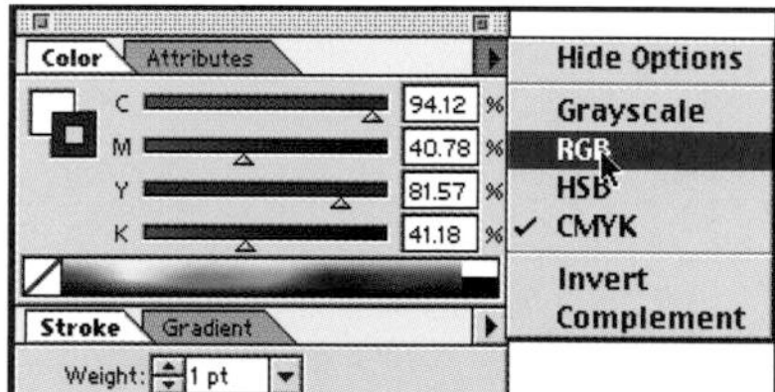

If the value readout shows CYMK, change the CYMK color to RGB. Use the triangle button in the upper-right corner to switch to RGB. The color readout will then range from 0 to 255.

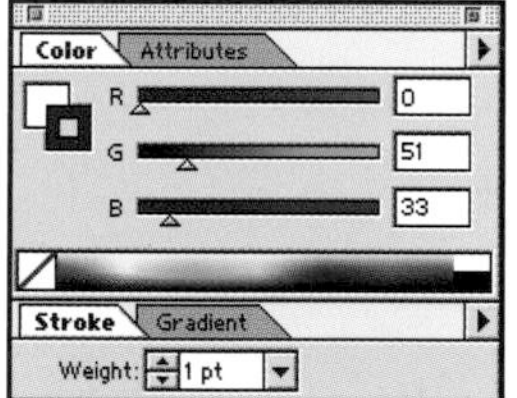

Restrict your color picking for browser-safe colors in Illustrator to six values. The values are 0, 51, 102, 153, 204, 255 for the red, green, and blue channels. If you want to use the color palette to mix colors yourself, round off the colors you pick to the nearest numbers to achieve browser-safe versions of them.

Working with FreeHand 8.0

Artists who use FreeHand for its excellent type-handling tools and vector-drawing tools are in luck! FreeHand allows users to work directly in RGB and includes a Web safe color palette.

FreeHand works with RGB percentages instead of specific RGB values. It's possible to mix browser-safe colors right in RGB within FreeHand. Just remember these conversions:

Percentage	RGB	HEX
100	255	FF
80	204	CC
60	153	99
40	102	66
20	51	33
0	0	0

The following steps will enable you to access the Web safe color palette in FreeHand 8.0:

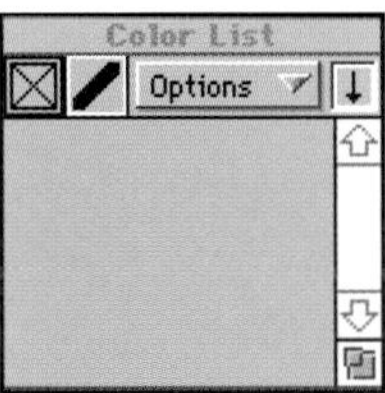

Step 1: Open the Color List Palette. Under **Options**, choose **Import**. Locate the Web Safe Color Library.

Step 2: Select **Web Safe Color Library**.

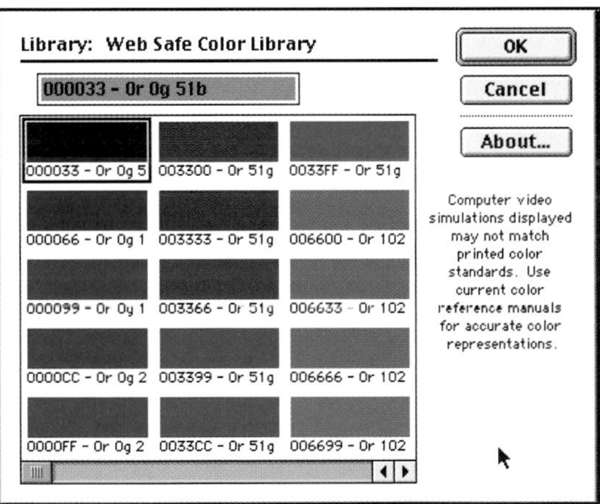

Step 3: If you use these colors to paint with, you can Choose **File:Export** in the GIF file format. Click on the Options button to set dithering (or not!) and also to set GIF transparency.

JPEG Artwork Cannot Retain Browser-Safe Colors

Unfortunately, files that are converted to JPEGs do not retain precise color information. The lossy compression method that's used throws away information and introduces compression artifacts, even though they are often not easily visible. Because of this, there is no way to accurately control color using the JPEG file format.

Here's an example of a solid browser-safe color, with the hex readout of 51, 153, 153.

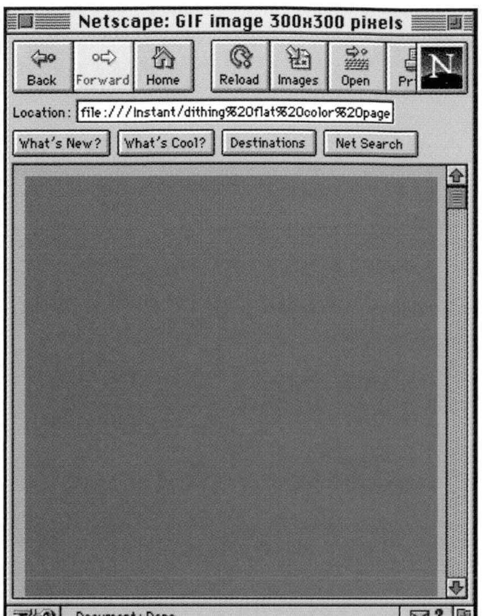

When saved as a GIF file, this color stayed browser safe.

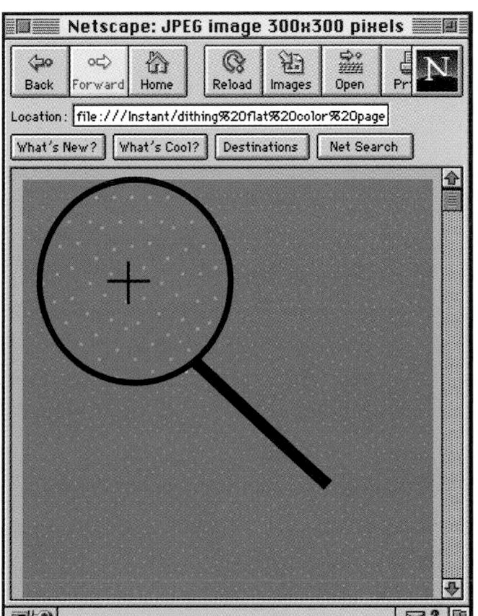

When saved as a JPEG, the color shifted from 51, 153, 153 to 154, 154, 156. It is no longer browser safe, as is evident by the dither that appears when it's displayed in Netscape under 8-bit monitor conditions. Note: If you use the highest quality JPEGs, color inconsistency can be avoided, but you will have to deal with larger files sizes. Seems like if one thing doesn't get you, something else certainly will!

What this means is that you cannot accurately match foreground GIFs to background JPEGs or foreground JPEGs to background GIFs. Even if you prepare images in browser-safe colors, they will not remain browser safe when converted to JPEG—no matter what you do. We've already established (in Chapter 3) that JPEGs are not good for solid colors. This is one more reason not to use JPEGs when dealing with flat-style illustration, logos, cartoons, or any other graphical image that would not lend itself to having unwanted dithering.

Hybrid Image Challenges

Like most things in life, there are exceptions to the rules. When you have an image that combines line art and continuous tone art, you have to combine browser-safe colors and non-safe colors. If you map the continuous tone artwork to browser-safe colors, it will look terrible; and if you leave the solid colors in non-safe colors, they will dither. It is possible to combine techniques to achieve a hybrid image, but only in the GIF and PNG formats. There is no way to lock a browser-safe color in the JPEG format. Instructions for creating hybrid images as GIFs in browser-safe and non-safe colors follow.

Hybrid Image as GIF in Photoshop

Whenever you deal with hybrid images that contain solid and continuous tones, it's best to save in an adaptive GIF palette instead of the Web-safe palette.

Photoshop 4.0 adaptive | **Photoshop 4.0 web** | **Photoshop 5.0 adaptive**

This row of images shows the differences between saving with an adaptive palette (left and right) and a browser-safe palette (middle). You can see that the adaptive palettes look better than the Web.

Photoshop 4.0 adaptive | **Photoshop 4.0 web** | **Photoshop 5.0 adaptive**

When viewed on an 8-bit system, all these images look identical. The browser converts the adaptive palettes to the browser-safe palette as expected.

So what's the moral of the story? Use an adaptive GIF palette with hybrid images. It will usually (though not always) retain the browser-safe colors and will produce a much better looking continuous tone image. On 8-bit systems, it will look the same as if you had forced it into the browser-safe system yourself.

There is one potential disadvantage to this technique. If you use adaptive palettes, you will often use more colors than if you stick to browser-safe colors. This sometimes results in larger file sizes. It's that "beauty versus size" thing again, and it all boils down to your own personal preferences.

Hybrid Image as GIF in Fireworks

Fireworks allows you to save in GIF with an adaptive palette. It has presets at 256 and 128 colors.

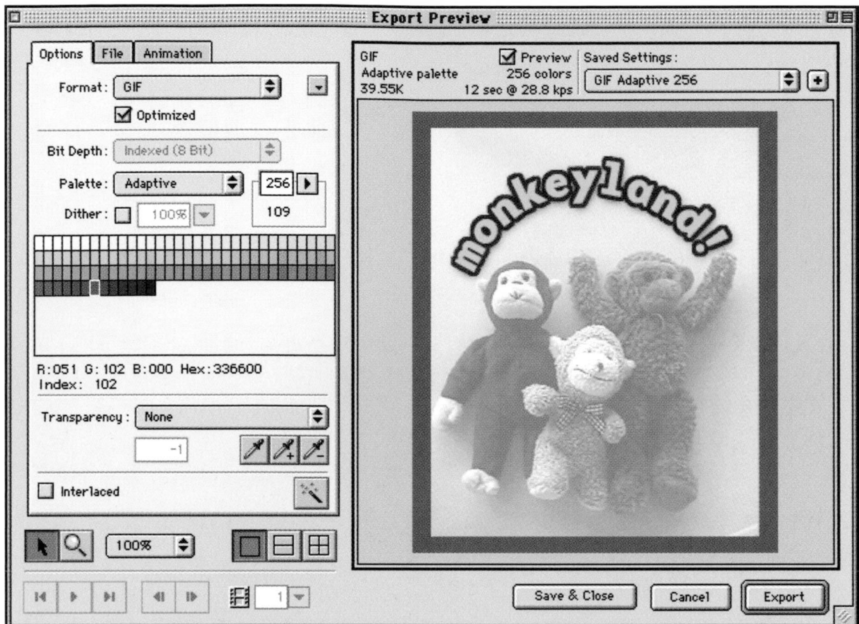

To access this dialog box, choose **File:Export**. The adaptive palette is best for hybrid images and will not alter browser-safe colors.

Hybrid Image as GIF in ImageReady

ImageReady has three different types of adaptive palettes: Perceptual, Adaptive, and Selective.

Each of these algorithms works slightly differently, but all preserve solid browser-safe colors as a priority. The only reason to try the different types of adaptive palettes is to see if you like the image quality of one better than another.

Perceptual

Adaptive

Selective

Non-Safe Images with Solid Colors

What about images that weren't created with browser-safe colors but should have been? Fireworks has a nifty feature called the WebSnap palette. This shifts colors towards the browser-safe colors when it encounters solid areas of color that are not safe.

To access the WebSnap Adaptive palette, choose **File: Export**. This palette will shift non-safe solid colors to safe ones.

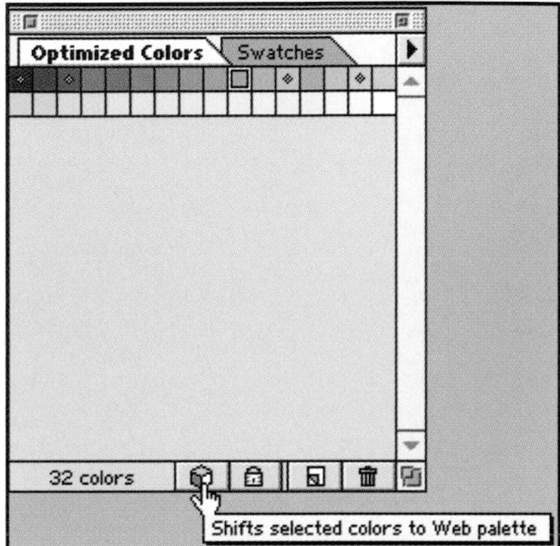

ImageReady allows you to select individual colors within your document with the eye-dropper and then shift a non-safe color to a safe one by clicking the cube icon.

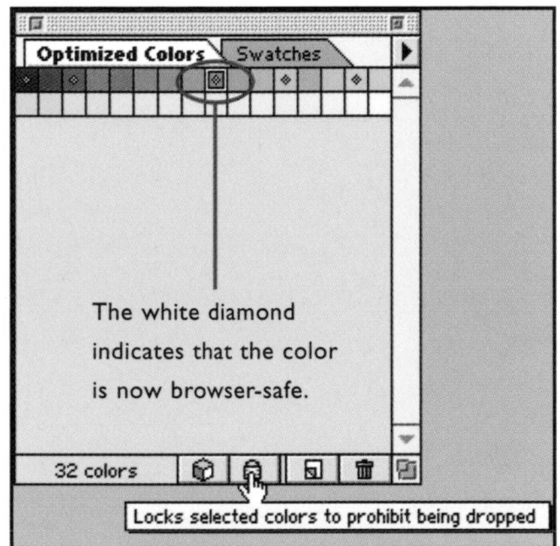

After you shift a color, you can lock it so that the color will not disappear if you reduce the colors within your GIF.

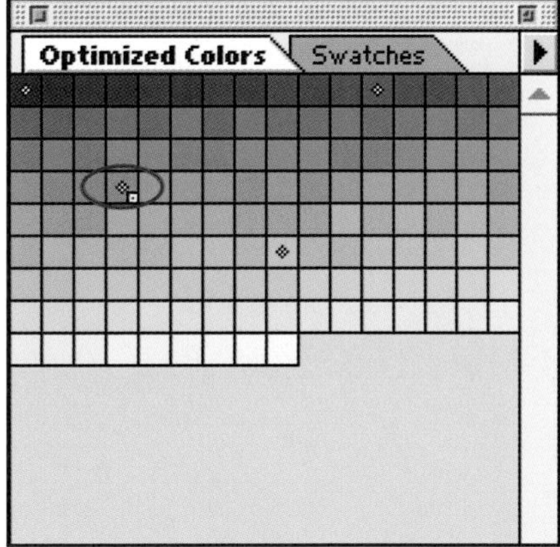

When a color is locked in ImageReady, a little white box appears in the palette display.

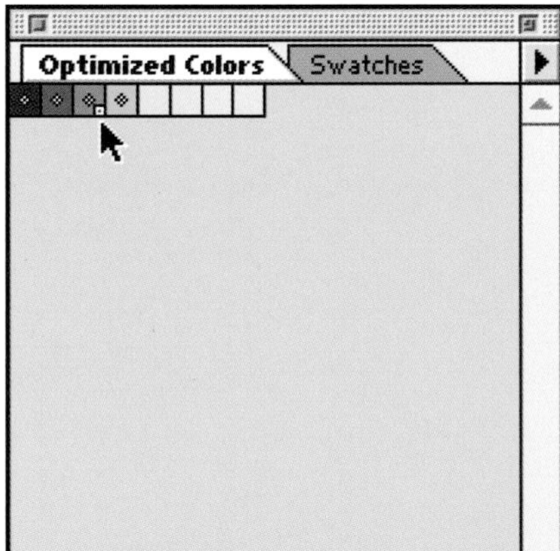

When you reduce the color depth to fewer colors, the locked colors remain.

summary Browser-Safe Color

Browser-safe color is a huge subject, with lots of variables and different implementations. This chapter covered the what, why, where, and how of browser-safe color, outlining the specs and software tools for producing safe graphics and safe HTML code. Here's a summary of the main points in this chapter:

- Always use browser-safe color with HTML-based schemes, such as your background, text, links, visited link, and active link colors.
- Always use browser-safe color for graphics that include areas of solid color.
- Don't use browser-safe colors on photographs.
- Save photographs in the JPEG format when possible.
- If you have a hybrid image that has areas of solid color and continuous tone imagery, use the GIF format with an adaptive palette.
- You can shift solid color artwork to browser-safe colors using Fireworks or ImageReady.
- Never save browser-safe colors in the JPEG format.

Color Aesthetics

Introduction

Chapter Topics

- Color Vocabulary Terms
- Color Schemes
- Contrast
- Color Relationships
- Readability
- Color Hierarchy
- Balance & Harmony

If you are reading this book, you obviously care about improving your graphics and Web site appearance. One of the most overlooked areas of improvement on most sites is color. A pleasing and effective color scheme can be more powerful than animation, interactivity, or clever graphics.

Few people are well trained in color theory, and most Web developers, even seasoned artists, are insecure about their abilities to choose pleasing color schemes. You would think color theory would be a fun and creative subject. Unfortunately, it is approached in a very dry and technical manner in most color theory books. This chapter approaches color theory with a distinct Web focus. It's my goal to back away from overtly technical explanations and gravitate toward easily identifiable principles and techniques.

I cannot, however, take credit for most of the ideas in this chapter; I can take credit only for the way in which the ideas are presented. My talented husband Bruce Heavin, who painted the wonderful cover to this book and all my others, is my color mentor. He has shared his color picking methods with me, which has greatly enhanced my own color picking abilities. I hope to pass down his pearls of wisdom to as many people as possible; hence, the approach of this chapter.

This chapter covers hybrid color, Web color schemes, and color identifiers such as hue, saturation, value, and contrast.

Color Vocabulary Terms

In order to describe color, we must first establish some common vocabulary terms. Here are the most important terms covered in this chapter:

Spectrum: All the possible colors in a color space, such as RGB or CMYK.

Hue: Defines a specific location on the color wheel or in the color spectrum. In this example, a green hue has been selected.

Value: Describes the range from light to dark. In this example, a red hue is shown at varying values from dark to light.

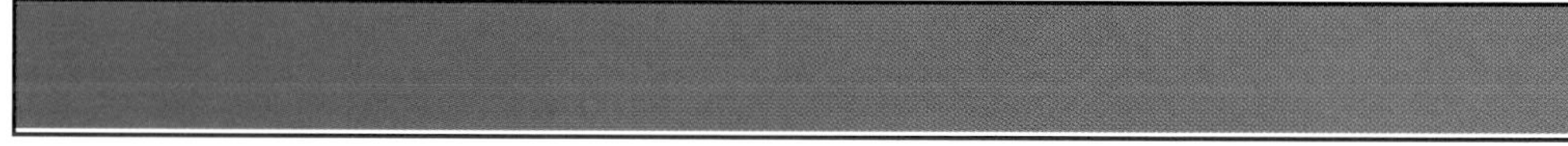

Saturation: Defines the intensity of a color.

Muted: When people describe muted colors, they often refer to colors that have very little saturation.

Low Contrast **High Contrast**

Contrast: Separation between values.

Readability: Relates to contrast.

Tint: The process of adding white to a color.

Tone: The process of adding black to a color.

Choosing Color Themes

In order to choose pleasing color themes for your Web pages and sites, it's necessary to learn a bit about color relationships. This next section will familiarize you with some terms that will later be shown in the context of Web pages.

Many books on the market describe the emotion of color. Some might say that purple is for passion, red is for anger or attention, and blue is for tranquility. I don't believe anyone can or should project what a color means to someone else. It is totally subjective, regardless of what any book might tell you.

Some clients might use pre-existing color schemes for their logos, printed brochures, or corporate identity. In such cases, you will need to work with their colors in a pleasing manner that is suitable for the Web. This might mean that either you'll convert their colors to hybrid-safe or browser-safe equivalents, or you'll work with variations of their colors using hexadecimal code.

Other times, you might have total freedom over a color scheme. Sometimes freedom is a dangerous thing in the hands of someone who doesn't know what to do with it! Rather than focus on the subjective and intangible aspects of color emotion, I've chosen here to focus on harmonic relationships of color.

Color Relationship Terms

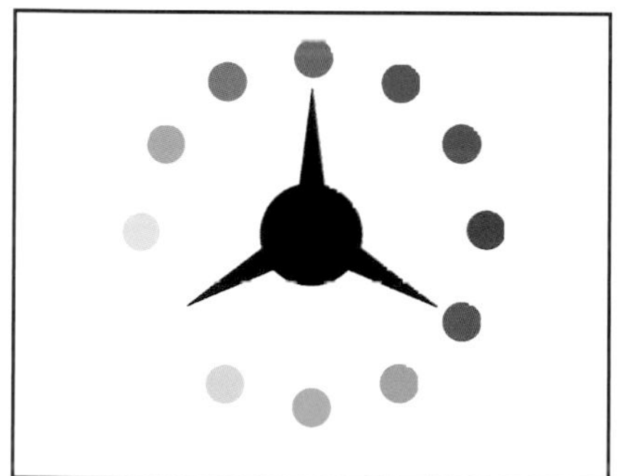

Primary colors

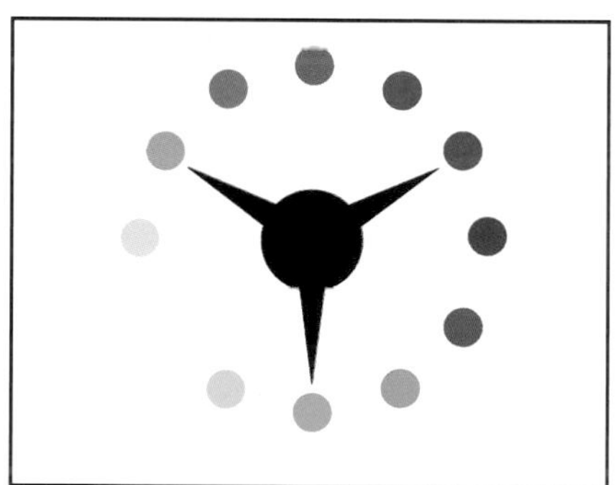

Secondary colors

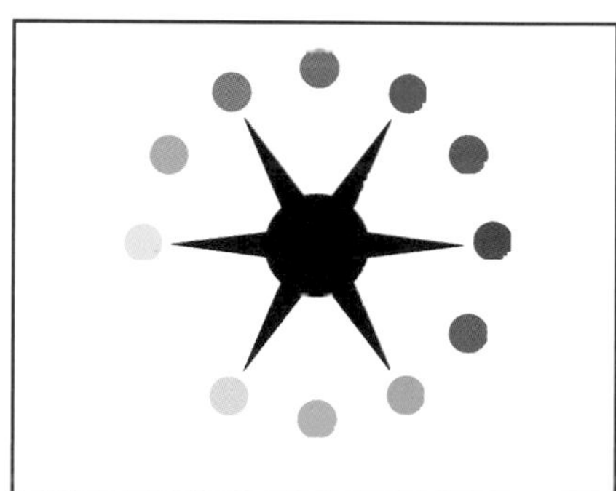

Tertiary colors

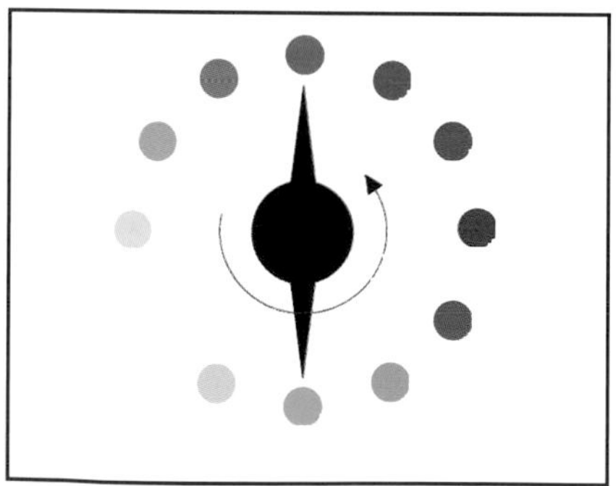

Complementary colors (can be rotated in any direction on the wheel)

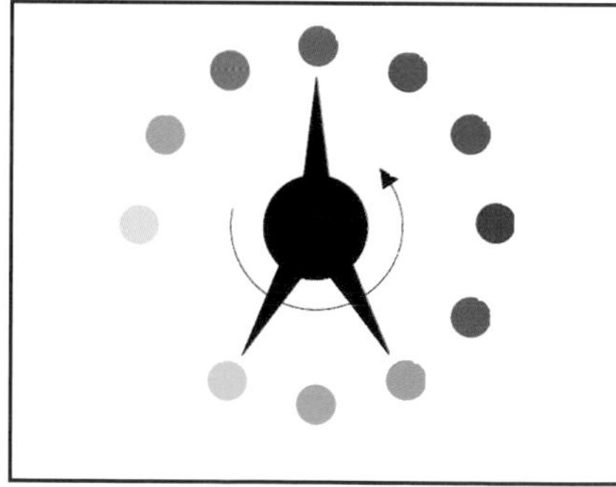

Split complementaries (can be rotated in any direction on the wheel)

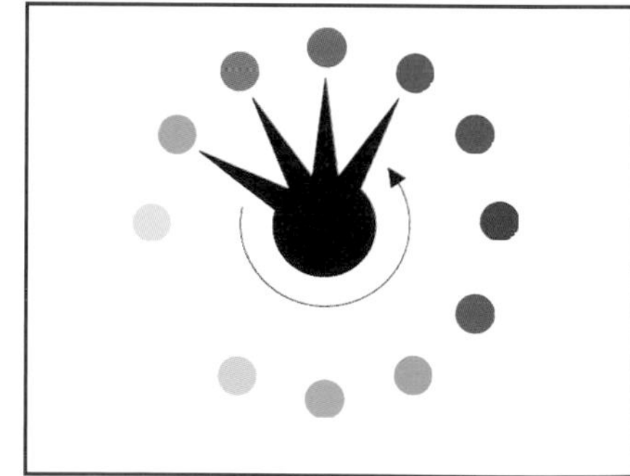

Analogous (can be rotated in any direction on the wheel)

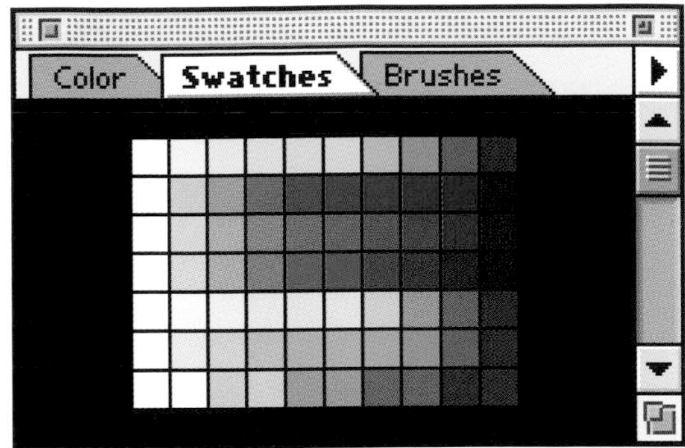

Monochromatic browser-safe color swatch (Monochromatic color schemes take a single hue and use different values of that hue)

A **monochromatic color** scheme in effect using cyan.

Warm colors

Cool colors

Applying Color Relationships to Web Design

Perhaps you can impress your clients or colleagues by knowing a complementary color from a tertiary color, but unless you can put that knowledge to dynamic use on your own site, it's not going to result in practical knowledge. The color relationship terms that were just established all have to do with choosing hues. But what about saturation and value? They are equally as important as hue, if not more so in most cases!

Horrible

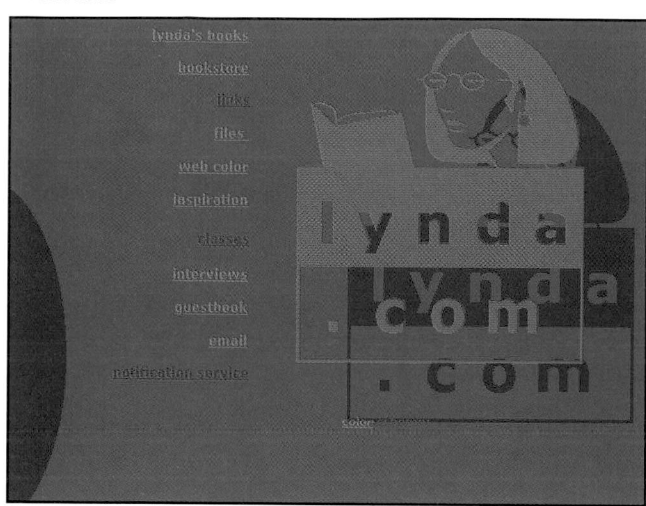

Better

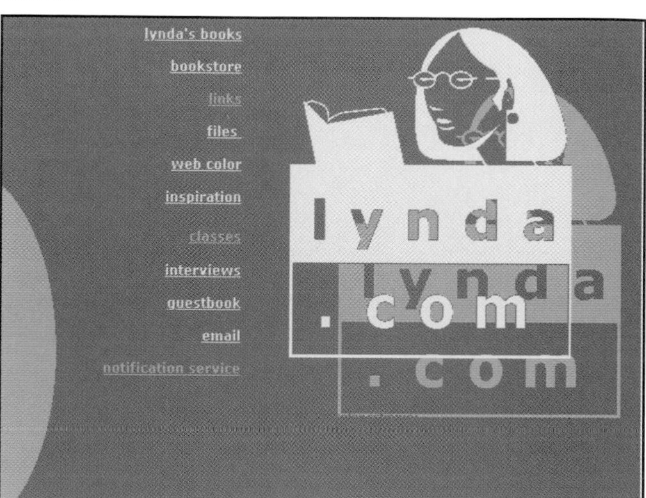

In the **Horrible** example, the color scheme is analogous, using blue, red, and magenta hues. The readability is indeed horrible, if not impossible. On the right side, the example labeled **Better** uses the same analogous color scheme of blue, red, and magenta, but it also uses varied values and saturations. What a difference! It is not enough to choose a type of color palette (like analogous, or complementary, or monochromatic); you must also learn to balance values and saturation of color at the same time for readable color relationships.

Looking at the horrible color combination, you'll notice that all the colors are fully saturated and close in value.

Looking at the better color combination, you'll notice that there is variety in saturation and value.

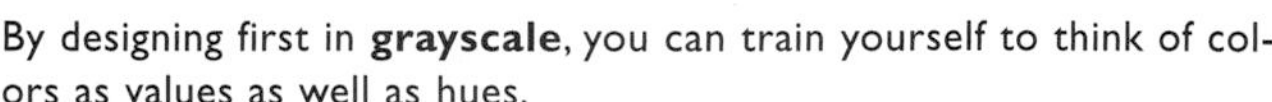
By designing first in **grayscale**, you can train yourself to think of colors as values as well as hues.

Hues have replaced grays, and I'm getting the exact read I want with my colors.

If you understand the balance between hue, value, and saturation, you can force the read of your image to highlight what's important and subdue what isn't. It's quite empowering to grasp this concept. Applying it to your designs puts you in control of your color so it will no longer be left to chance.

A great exercise to force yourself to think in these terms is to previsualize your Web site, as I have, in Photoshop using layers. Try filling the layers with shades of gray instead of color to make the information you want to "pop" work correctly. After you've designed the page using grays, replace the grays with colors. You'll be amazed at how effective this is as a learning exercise.

Color Relationship Tools

If you are trying to communicate effectively by using color, it really pays to work with some good tools. Looking at the browser-safe palette again, notice it has no aesthetic organization. The same colors can be viewed in a different order and offer much better clues to color relationships.

Coloring Web Graphics.2

Coloring Web Graphics.2 is a book and CD-ROM that Bruce Heavin and I wrote together (now in its second edition). It offers hundreds of palettes for use in Photoshop and every other imaging program, and they are organized by color relationships instead of by math logic. Examples follow of how a palette from that book's CD-ROM could help you more effectively design with color.

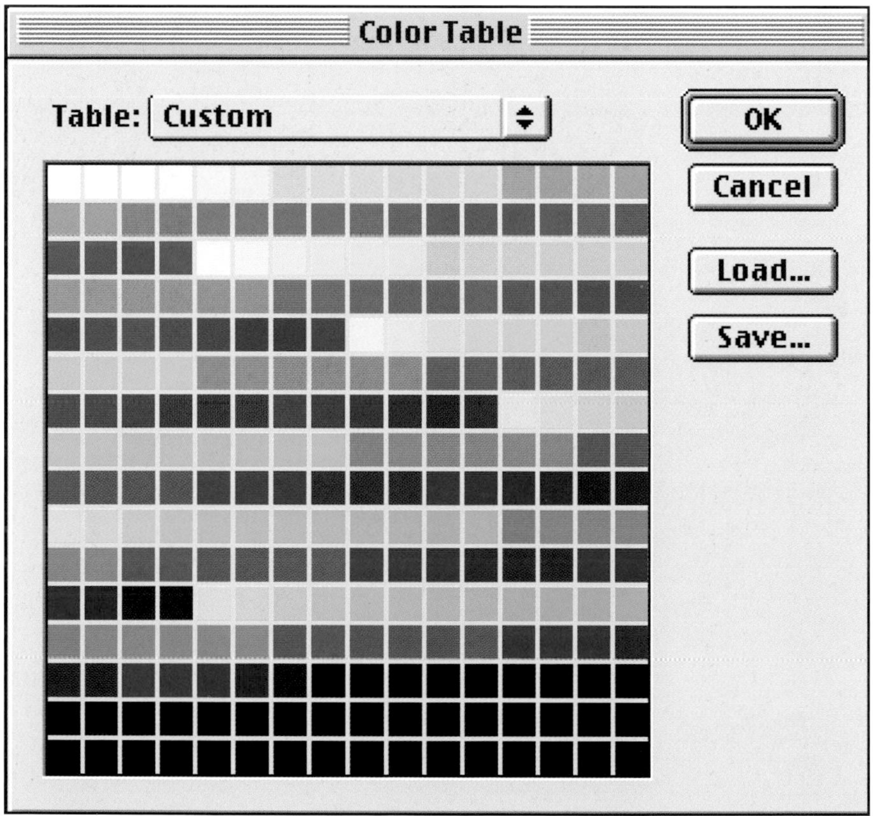

The browser-safe color chart is organized by math logic, not aesthetic logic.

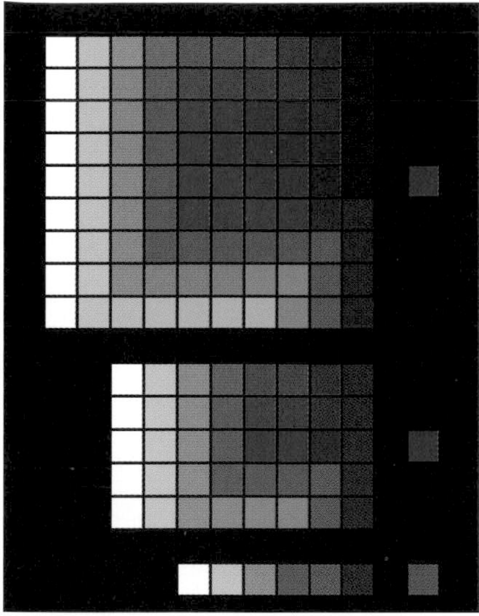

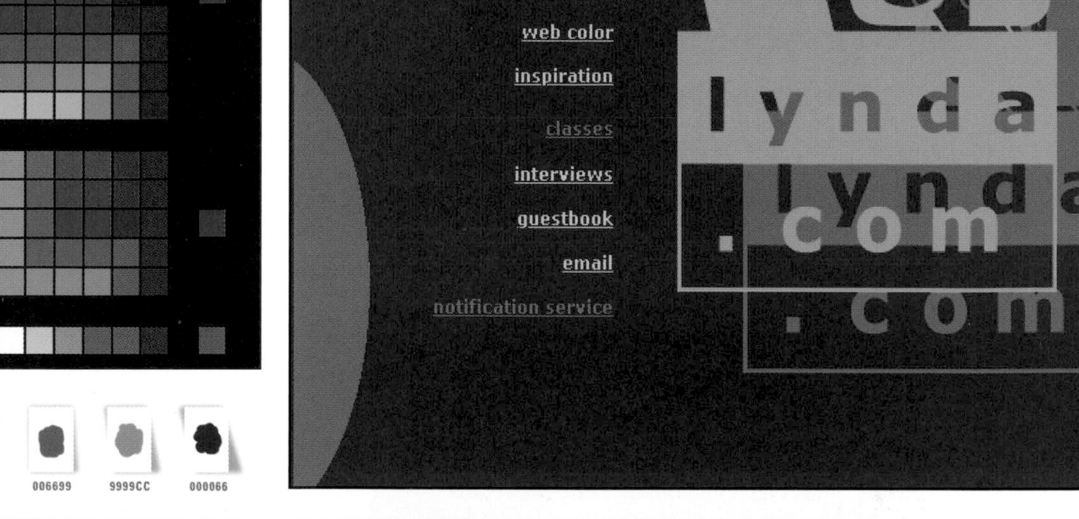

99CCFF 6666FF 006699 9999CC 000066

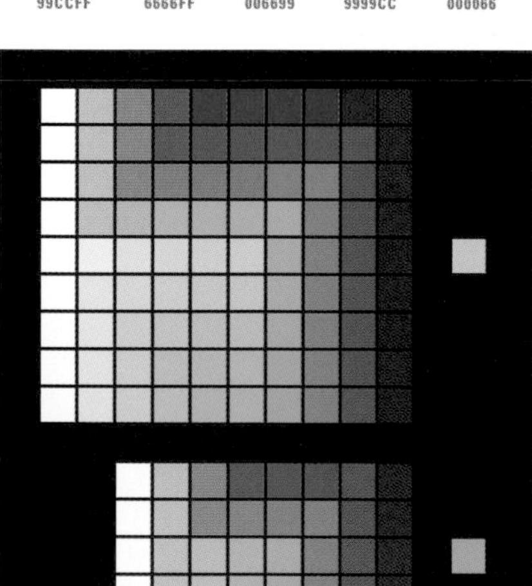

CCCCFF 99FF99 009999 33FF99 006666

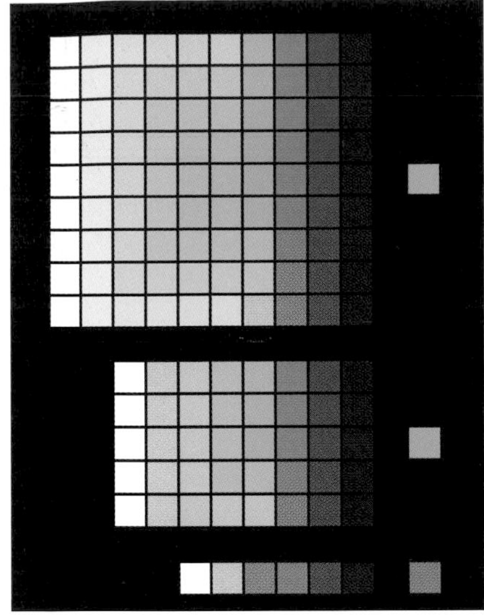

CCFF99
99FF99
009966
33CC33
006600

lynda's books
bookstore
links
files
web color
inspiration
classes
interviews
guestbook
email
notification service
lynda
lynda
.com
.com

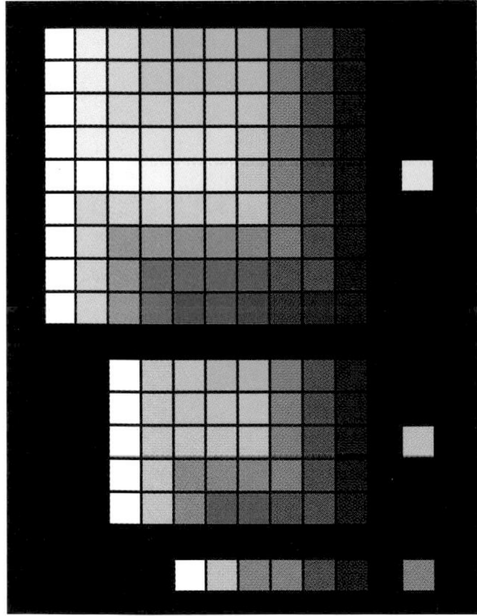

996600
339900
FFFF00
FF9900
CCCC00

lynda's books
bookstore
links
files
web color
inspiration
classes
interviews
guestbook
email
notification service
lynda
lynda
.com
.com

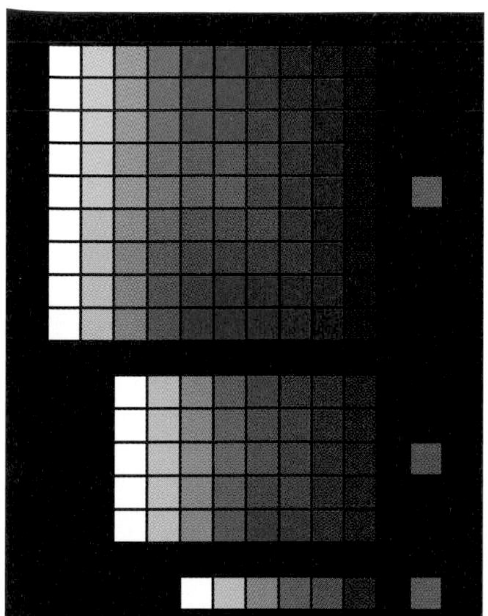

CC99CC FF9999 990066 FF99CC 660066

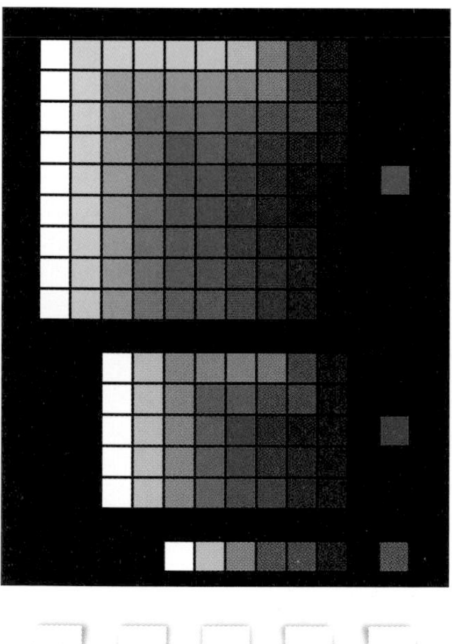

FFCC99 FF9933 663333 996633 990000

Color Harmony Photoshop Plug-In

A remarkable Photoshop plug-in that came to my attention and relates to this subject is called **Hot Door Harmony**. You can download a trial version from http://www.hotdoor.com. At the time this chapter was written, the product was Mac-only, but a PC version is supposed to be out soon.

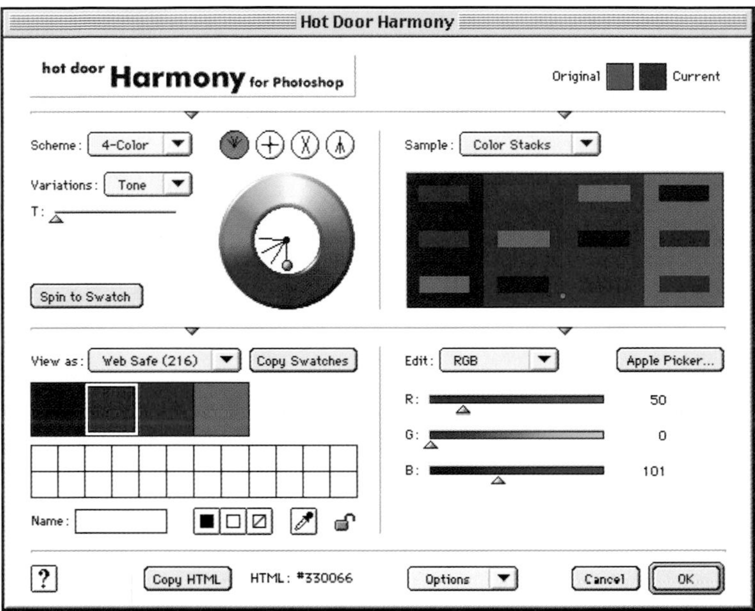

Hot Door Harmony let's you pick colors through harmonic relationships. You click on which type of color scheme you want (I have analogous selected) and then spin the ball. The program shows you color selections within the browser-safe spectrum. You can increase the Tint (lighten) or Tone (darken) settings to access different values, and you can copy the hexadecimal code for any color. I highly recommend that you download this tool for a test spin.

Readability

Making a Web page read the way you want is the key to effective communication. You want to draw your end user to the areas of your site that are most important, and you can do that in a variety of ways. Because this is a chapter about color, let's look at some examples of using color as a device for creating visual importance or hierarchy.

If I want my logo to be the most important element of this page, I can make it pop with color.

If my navigation element is more important, I can choose to make that pop instead.

A very important exercise that you should try before you develop your opening page is to identify what the first, second, third, and forth reads should be. Armed with a specific order of importance, you should be able to use many of the principles covered in this chapter to achieve your communication goals using color.

Color Gallery

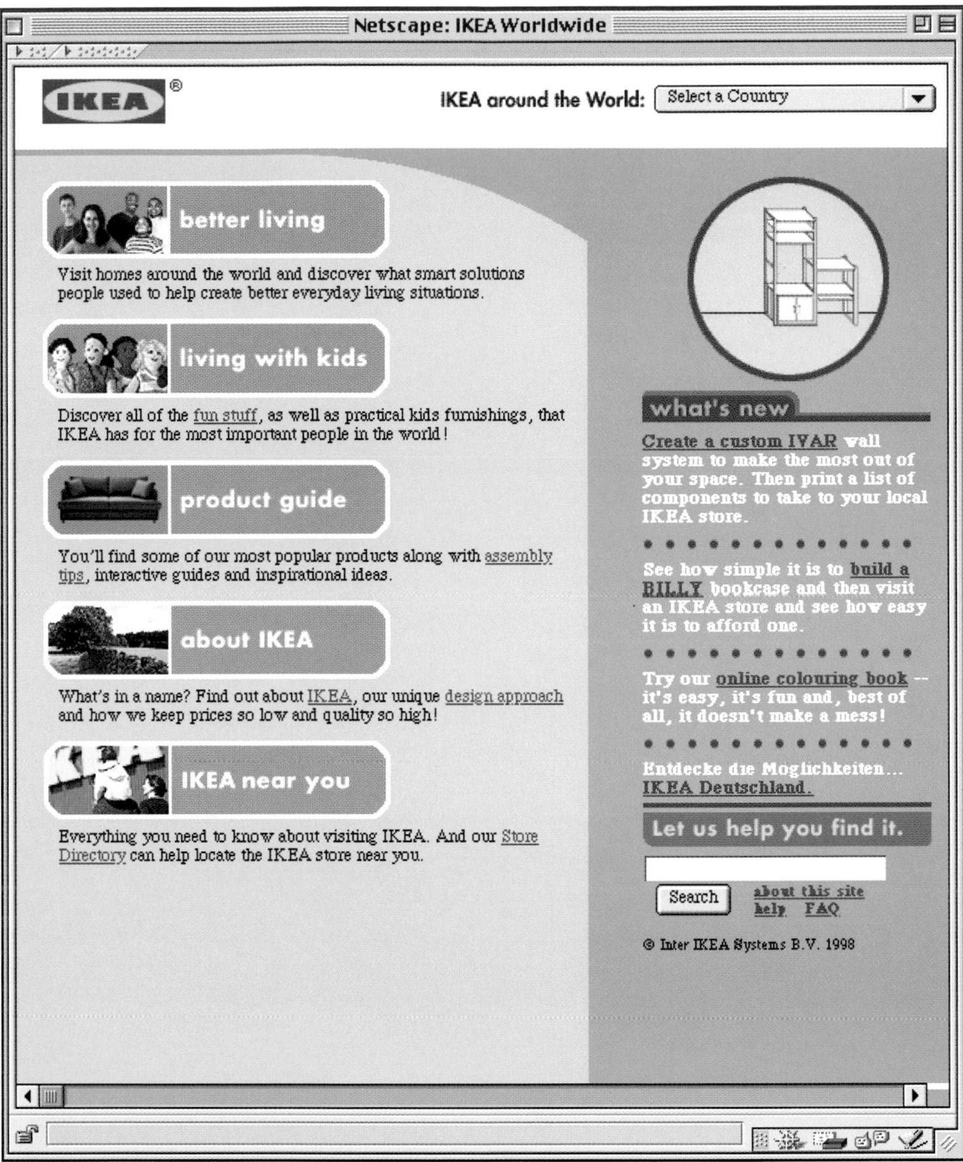

Ikea (http://www.ikea.com) uses a warm analogous color palette. The white that's used is the brightest value, and red is the darkest. The designer could have created the site using the company's corporate colors of blue and orange (complements) but didn't. I prefer their warm analogous palette over their corporate colors as it is more harmonious and offers a greater range of unified colors.

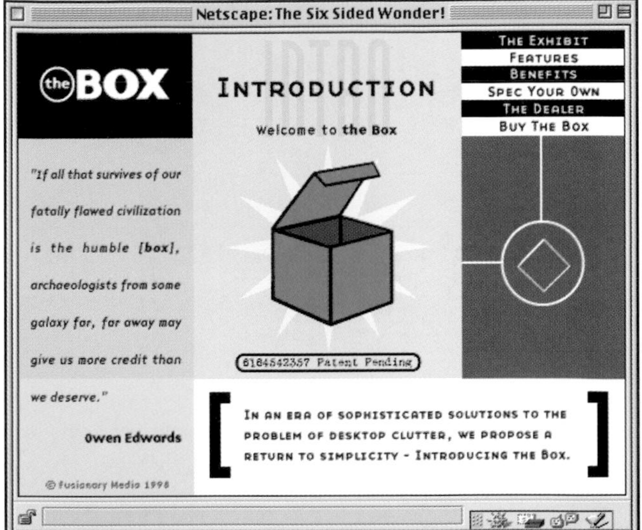

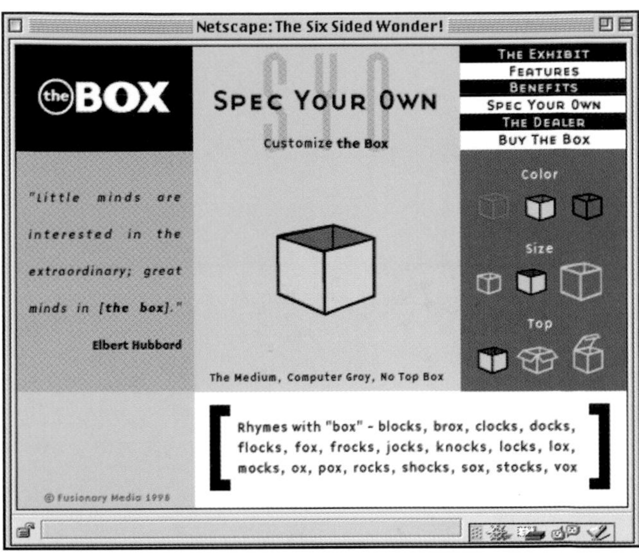

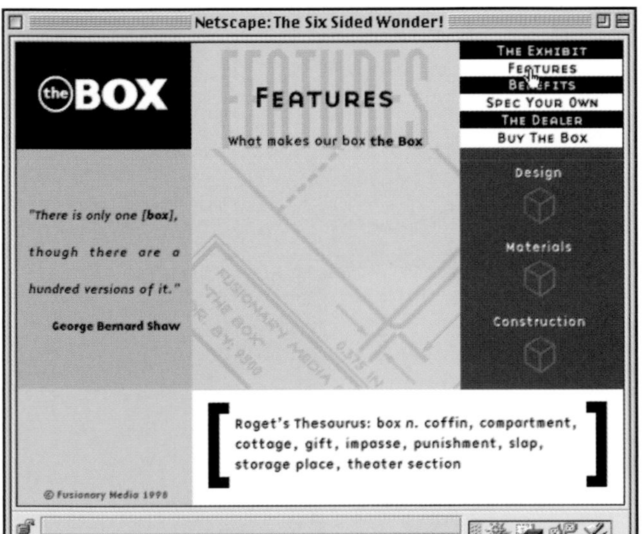

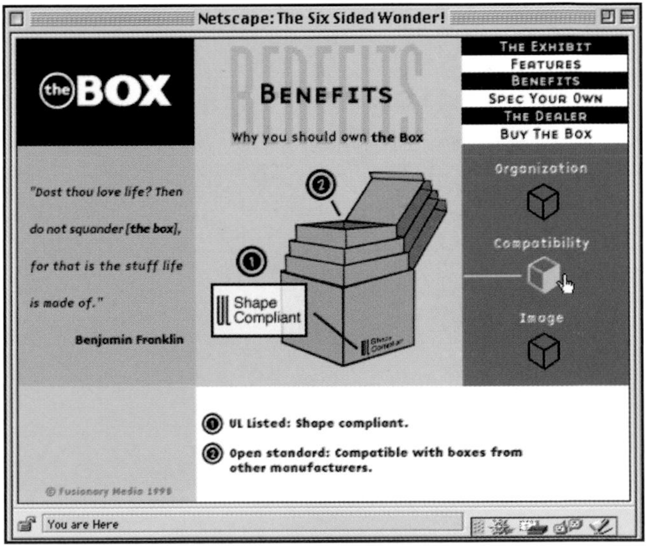

The Box (http://www.sixsides.com) uses a combination of analogous color and split complementary colors. Each area of the site is branded by color, which achieves a dual purpose of looking good and reinforcing navigation.

Communication Arts (http://www.commarts.com) shows a great example of how to use a monochromatic color scheme effectively. A monochromatic color scheme that uses blacks, whites, and grays can work very effectively with a single color or two.

IMAX Everest: Roof of the World Film (http://www.mos.org/Everest/home.htm) is a great example of using complementary colors in an effective manner.

r35 Direct's site (http://www.r35.com) uses a black background to effectively carve out graphic shapes and color accents.

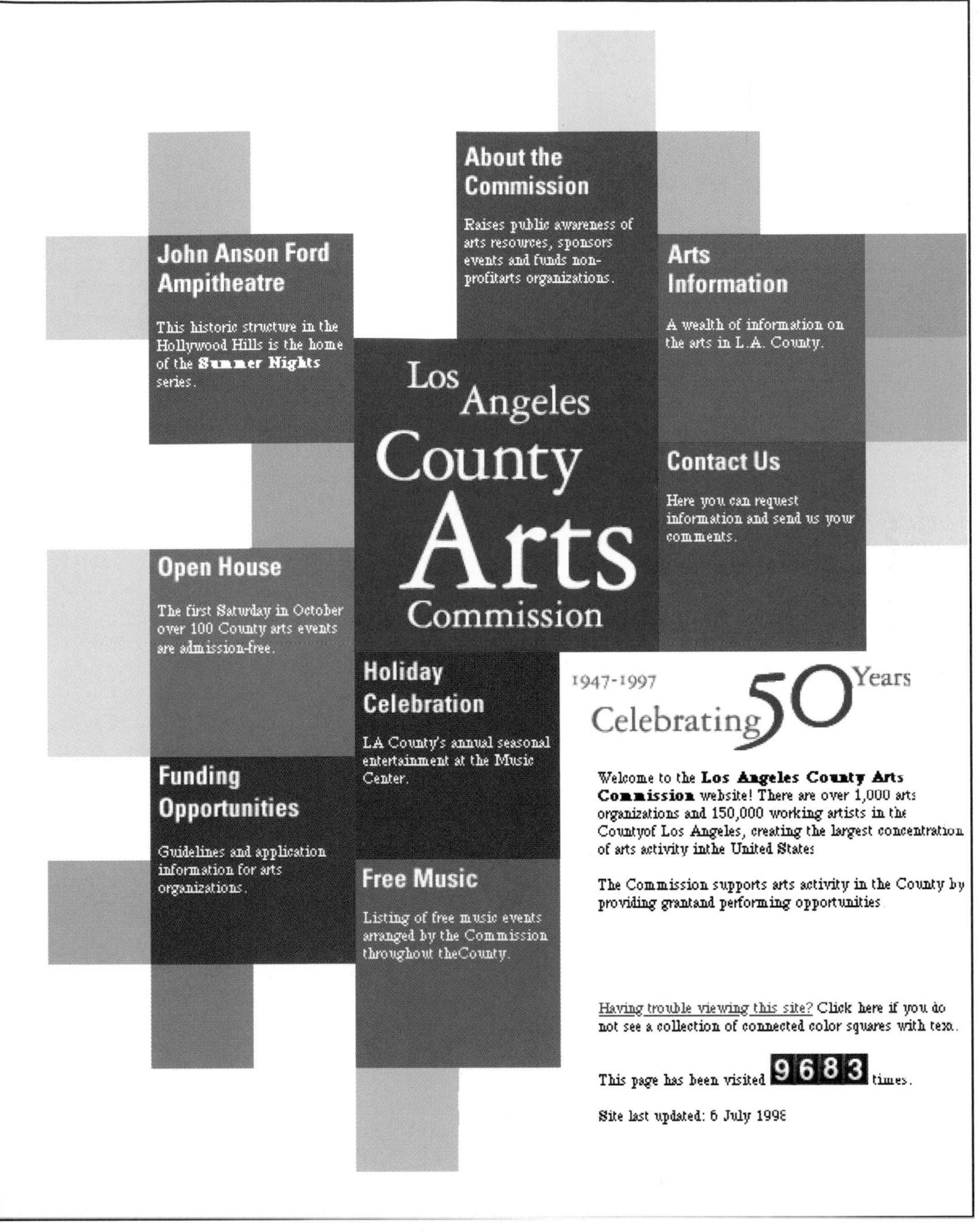

The LA County Arts Commission (http://www.lacountyarts.org) uses a lot of colors, but they look unified because the creator paid close attention to the value of each color. Because the values are similar, even the many different hues look harmonious.

summary Color Aesthetics

My hope is that this chapter helped you better understand what creates an effective color scheme and how to go about picking one that's right for your material. The key points are summarized here:

- Understanding color terminology is helpful in breaking down how to pick an effective scheme. In particular, hue, value, and saturation are key factors in making color choices.
- The value (lightness or darkness) of your color choice effects the readability of the end result. It's important to strive for high contrast in areas you want to pop off the page.
- One technique for training yourself to think in terms of value is to design first in grayscale, and then assign colors to the gray values.
- Effective color schemes have much more to do with color relationships than with picking a specific hue (a color within the spectrum). Examples in this chapter showed the use of analogous, split complementaries, and monochromatic color schemes.
- Color can be used to create a hierarchy of information on your site. Think about the "reads" of your message (i.e., first read, second read, etc.). You can assign different colors or values to your most important information to make it pop out or blend. Color is an excellent visual communication device and you need to understand its powers.

Introduction

Color HTML Tags

Chapter Topics

- HTML Color Attributes
- BODY Colors
- LINK Colors
- Color Names
- FONT Color
- Coloring TABLE Cells

10

When you work with color on the Web, you have two choices: to create colored artwork or to specify color in your HTML. Other chapters have focused on graphics; this one concentrates on the tags that produce colored backgrounds, text, and table cells.

Adding color via HTML really is the easy part. It's understanding the aesthetic prinicples of color design and cross-platform differences that makes color on the Web a complex subject.

Many of you will be using HTML editors that support color design without making you write the code by hand. That's totally acceptable, but this chapter will give you that "under the hood" understanding of what the HTML editors are doing for you. Others might discover that your HTML editor doesn't support every color attribute you want. It's always possible to begin a page in a WYSIWYG editor and then later edit the source code in a text editor in order to add additional color attributes.

For those who write code in text editors, this should provide a handy guide for referencing that specific tag or attribute you know existed, but couldn't remember!

Default Colors

If you don't specify any color attributes in your HTML, the page will display in default colors:

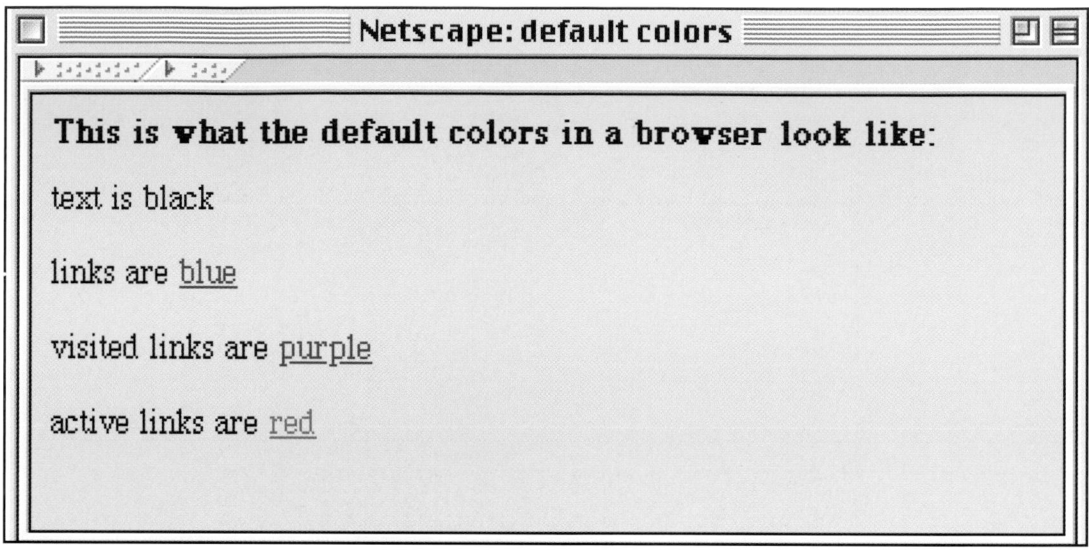

In order to change these default colors, you must learn a bit about color attributes that are allowed within HTML tags. The following sections will show examples of how to code color changes this way.

Color Attributes

If you want to change the colors in HTML, you will want to know which tags can be affected by color attributes. The following sections will go through the BODY, FONT, and TABLE tags and show how you can modify colors with HTML.

Tag	Attribute(s)	Description
BODY	BGCOLOR, TEXT, LINK, VLINK, ALINK	Sets colors for the document background/text/links/visited links/active links, respectively.
FONT	COLOR	Sets the color of the font.
TABLE	BGCOLOR	Sets the background color for the entire table.
TR	BGCOLOR	Sets the background color for the table row.
TD	BGCOLOR	Sets the background color for the table cell.
TH	BGCOLOR	Sets the background color for the table heading.

The BODY Tag

The BODY tag of your document affects the background, text, links, visited links, and active links. If you add a color attribute to this tag, it is possible to alter the color scheme of your HTML page.

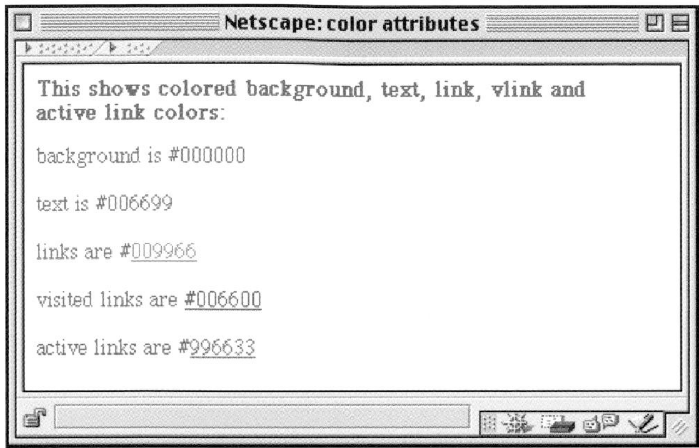

code

```
<BODY BACKGROUND="#FFFFFF" TEXT="#006699"
LINK="#009966" VLINK="#006600" ALINK="#996633">
```

Here's a list of possible attributes that can be modified using color within the BODY tag.

BGCOLOR	Color of the background of the Web page.
TEXT	Color of the text.
LINK	Color of the link.
VLINK	Color of the link after it's been visited.
ALINK	Color of the active link while the mouse is pressed down.

Link Colors

Link color can affect the border color around linked images or the color of linked text. Here's an example of how to set this up in an HTML document.

code

```
<HTML>
<HEAD>
<TITLE>Adding Color to My Page</TITLE>
</HEAD>
1 <BODY BGCOLOR="000000" TEXT="CCCCFF"
LINK="CCFF00">
<H1>Here's an example of a
<AHREF="http://www.monkeyland.com">
text-based hyperlink</A>.
<P>
Here's an example of a linked graphic
with a fat, colored border: </H1>
<P>
2 <A HREF="http://www.monkeyland.com">
<IMG SRC="monkeyland.jpg" BORDER=10></A>
</BODY>
</HTML>
```

code deconstruction

1. The LINK attribute within the BODY tag establishes the color for the linked text or graphic. The <A HREF></A> tag produces linked text.

2. The IMG SRC tag inserts an image, and the BORDER attribute enables you to set a width for the border, measured in pixels. **Note:** If you don't want a border, you can set this to BORDER=0.

Here's an example of creating colored links. The border around the graphic was made wider with the BORDER attribute.

Using Color Names Instead of Hex

You don't have to use hexadecimal numbers inside the color attribute tags; you can use words, too. Here's a list of color names that will work in Netscape.

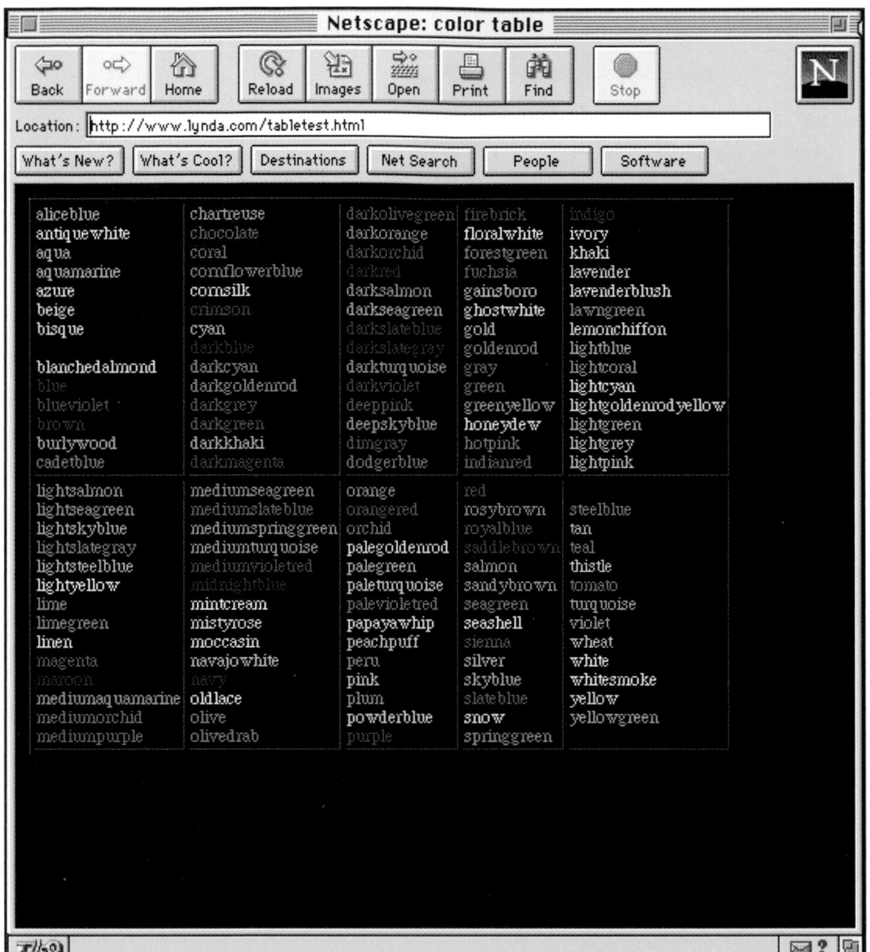

warning

Color Names Are Rarely Browser Safe

Out of all the possible color names, only ten of them are browser safe!

Aqua	Black	Blue	Cyan	Fuschia	Lime	Magenta	Red	White	Yellow
0000FF	000000	0000FF	00FFFF	FF00FF	00FF00	FF00FF	FF0000	FFFFFF	FFFF00

Color Attribute in Netscape

You don't have to use hexadecimal numbers inside the color attribute tags; you can use words, too.

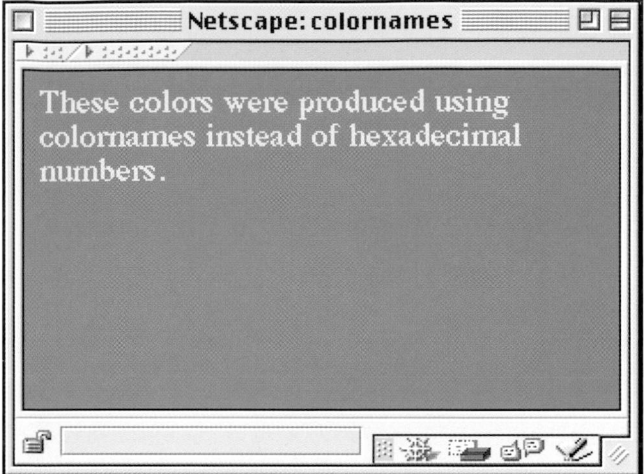

Using any of the names inside the color COLOR attribute tags will generate colored text in Netscape.

code

```
<HTML>
<HEAD>
<TITLE>colornames</TITLE>
</HEAD>
1 <BODY BGCOLOR="darkgreen" TEXT="lightblue">
<H1>These colors were produced using colornames
instead of hexadecimal numbers.
</H1>
</BODY>
</HTML>
```

code deconstruction

1. You don't have to use hexadecimal numbers to define color—certain color names work as well. Here's an example of using "darkgreen" and "lightblue" as color names within the BODY tag.

The FONT Tag

You can also assign specific colors to individual lines of text by using the FONT tag.

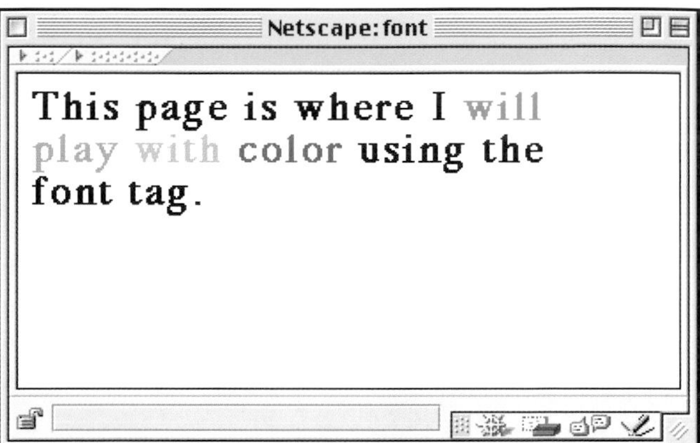

Here's an example of using the FONT tag to insert color attributes so that individual words or letters can be colored.

code

```
<HTML>
<HEAD>
<TITLE>Adding Color to My Page</TITLE>
</HEAD>
<BODY BGCOLOR="#FFFFFF">
<H1>This page is where I
1 <FONT COLOR="#99FFFF">will </FONT>
<FONT COLOR="#CCFF99">play </FONT>
<FONT COLOR="#CC99CC">with </FONT>
<FONT COLOR="#CC0000">color </FONT>
using all the nifty color tags I
can learnthe font tag.
</H1>
</BODY>
</HTML>
```

code deconstruction

1. The FONT tag can contain a color attribute, which can be specified by using color names or hex numbers. It must be closed with a /FONT tag each time you want the specific colored text attribute to end.

The TABLE Tag

The BGCOLOR attribute works in table cells as well as the body of the HTML document.

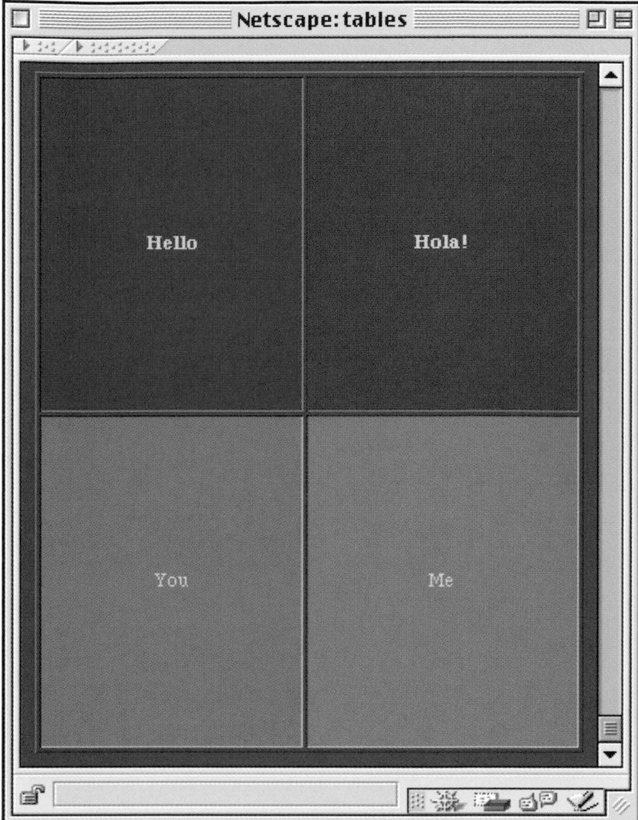

Here's an example of coloring cells within a table by using the BGCOLOR attribute within the TABLE tag.

code

```
<HTML>
<HEAD>
<TITLE>tables</TITLE>
</HEAD>
<BODY BGCOLOR="#660099" TEXT="#CCCCFF">
1 <CENTER>
2 <TABLE BORDER=1>
3 <TR><TH BGCOLOR="#003366" HEIGHT="200"
WIDTH="200">Hello</TH>
<TH BGCOLOR="#990033" HEIGHT="200"
WIDTH="200">Hola!</TH>
<TR><TD BGCOLOR="#666600" HEIGHT="200"
width="200" ALIGN=MIDDLE>You</TD>
<TD BGCOLOR="#996666" HEIGHT="200"
width="200" ALIGN=MIDDLE>Me</TD>
</TABLE>
</CENTER>
</BODY>
</HTML>
```

code deconstruction

1. The CENTER tag instructs the table to be centered in the page.

2. The TABLE tag establishes the beginning of the table command. The BORDER attribute assigns an embossed border to the table. In this example, the border is set to 1 pixel, but you could turn it off using a value of 0, or increase it's size by specifying a larger number.

3. TR initiates a table row. TH stands for table header. Everything within the TH tag will automatically be bold and centered. The BGCOLOR attribute allows a color to be established within the table cell and can be specified by using hexadecimal color or color names. The HEIGHT and WIDTH attributes assign dimensions to the table cells by using pixel-based measurements. The ALIGN=middle attribute centers the text within the table cells.

summary Color HTML Tags

Fortunately, HTML allows you to change colors so we aren't stuck with the boring defaults. The HTML is fairly simple; here's a little review of this chapter:

- You can change the default colors of your page using the BODY tag attributes: bgcolor, text, link, alink, vlink.
- You can change the text color within the body of your HTML text using the FONT tag.
- You can change your tables to contain color using the TABLE BGCOLOR element.

Introduction

Linking Basics

Chapter Topics

- Creating Links
- Turning Off Borders
- WIDTH and HEIGHT
- ALT
- Thumbnails
- Linking to Other Media

11

The "hyper" portion of the term **H**yper**T**ext **M**arkup **L**anguage (HTML) refers to linked images, text, and media. The fact that clicking on a text, image, or medium can transport you to other text, images, or media is what separates the Web from other communication mediums. This process offers a non-linear way of presenting information, which is more akin to the way our thoughts travel from one subject to another.

The challenge in Web design is to make purposeful choices about how to present information and graphics. Some of these choices are controlled by HTML, others by visual design. This chapter addresses these choices and offers advice on ways to invite visitors to your Web site to click on your hypertext and images.

There are several methods required to create linked text, images, and media. I will cover how to program HTML linking behavior and the different options for visually indicating that a link exists. This chapter will also teach how to control borders around images, and the importance of the ALT, WIDTH, and HEIGHT attributes in the IMG tag.

Identifying Links

If an image is static (has no linking HTML tags), it is often referred to as an inline graphic. Inline means it's embedded as part of your page and has no other purpose except to be visible. When a graphic is linked, it is referred to as a map, link, hyperlink, or interactive button. All these words describe the same thing; clicking on such an image will transport you elsewhere.

Images that are linked have certain visual markings that are different from inline graphics. Typically, a border appears around an image that links you somewhere else, and this border defaults to a blue color in most browsers. If your audience has had any experience on the Web, they will be trained that any time they encounter a border around an image, it means that image can be clicked on as an active link.

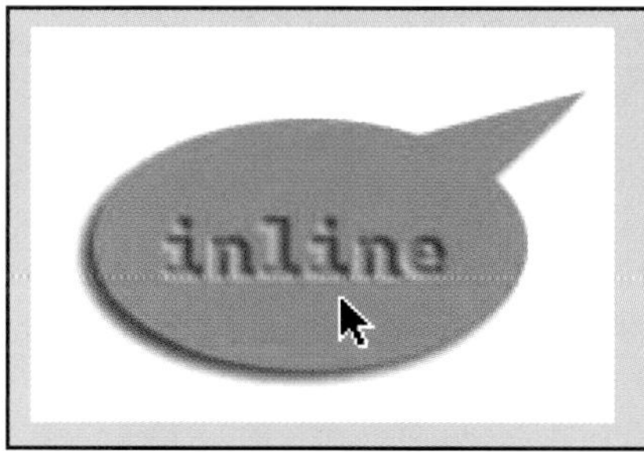

Inline Web graphics don't affect or change the mouse cursor. If you click on them, nothing happens.

Linked Web graphics often have a blue border around them, and the cursor changes to the hand symbol. If you click on a linked image, you will be directed to a new image, page, or downloadable item.

There are some instances when a linked image will not have a telltale border around it. If you'd prefer that your graphic be without one, this chapter will describe how to program the border to be "invisible." The only way a viewer will know to click on these types of borderless hot images is if your graphic invites them to bring their cursor closer. In most browsers, once the viewer's cursor passes over a linked image boundary, it changes from an arrow pointer to a hand cursor. This indicates, just like the border symbol, that an image is a clickable button, instead of a static inline graphic.

Linked Images

The easiest way to create a link that connects one graphic to another Web source is to use the anchor tag container <A HREF></A> with an IMG SRC tag nested inside.

This combination of tags automatically defaults to putting a border around the graphic. Here's an example of this standard HTML code:

```
<A HREF="http://www.lynda.com">
<IMG SRC="flowermonk.gif"></A>
```

Turning Off Image Borders

Sometimes that pesky blue border around an image is totally wrong for the page it was designed for. If you've gone to a great deal of trouble to make an irregular shaped image float freely on a background, using techniques described in Chapter 13, "Transparent Artwork," you aren't going to want to ruin the illusion you worked so hard to achieve by having a glaring rectangular shape around your graphic.

To eliminate the border:

```
<A HREF="http://www.lynda.com">
<IMG SRC="flowermonk.jpg"
BORDER=0></A>
```

Just as you can make the border disappear, you can also make it appear stronger. The following Netscape-specific code gives a thicker border to the image:

```
<A HREF="http://www.lynda.com">
<IMG SRC="flowermonk.jpg"
BORDER=10></A>
```

Sometimes your page has a specific color theme and the standard blue rectangle doesn't fit in. You can also change the color of your borders, if you program the links on your page to include hexadecimal values inside the BODY tag and LINK attribute (see Chapter 10, "Color HTML Tags," for detail on this feature). The following code changes the border color of the current image:

```
<BODY LINK="33CC33">
<A HREF="http://www.lynda.com"><IMG SRC="flowermonk.jpg"
BORDER=10></A>
</BODY>
```

Importance of Width and Height

By adding WIDTH and HEIGHT attributes to images within HTML, you are giving the browser information about the size of your graphic. This is a good thing, for a couple of reasons. First of all, the browser doesn't have to calculate the image size because you've supplied the information for it, which saves time. It also allows the text to load before the images, which can be a good thing with large images. Audiences will get something to look at while they're waiting!

So then, here's the way to implement the WIDTH and HEIGHT attributes:

```
<A HREF="http://www.lynda.com">
<IMG SRC="flowermonk.jpg" BORDER=0
HEIGHT="150" WIDTH="113"></A>
```

The values you put inside the WIDTH and HEIGHT attributes reflect how large the image is, measured by pixels. You can even resize an image if you put values that are larger or smaller than the image! Basically, the browser uses your information for the image size instead of looking to the image itself for size information.

In this example, I added WIDTH and HEIGHT attributes that were larger than the image. This stretched the pixels and created a distorted effect. My code looked like this:

```
<A HREF="http://www.lynda.com">
<IMG SRC="flowermonk.jpg" BORDER=0
HEIGHT="300" WIDTH="300"></A>
```

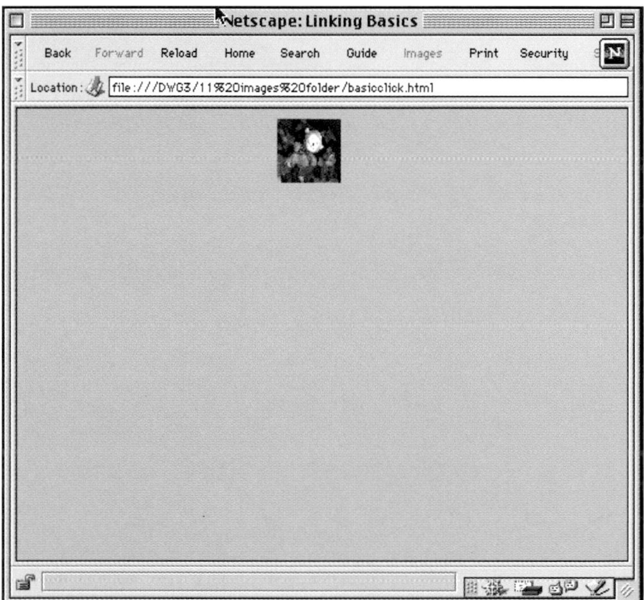

In this example, I shrunk the image by using WIDTH and HEIGHT attributes that were smaller than the image. This scaled the image to smaller than its original size. My code looked like this:

```
<A HREF="http://www.lynda.com">
<IMG SRC="flowermonk.jpg" BORDER=0
HEIGHT="100" WIDTH="100"></A>
```

warning

Shrinking and Enlarging Bitmaps

The most popular image formats for the Web—GIF, JPEG, and PNG—are bitmap formats, as you might have learned in Chapter 5, "Web File Formats." Whenever you scale a bitmap, it invariably loses quality. It's a bit akin to taking a small image and blowing it up on a copier machine. In that example, the image will lose a lot of detail and quality. When you blow up or reduce pixels on the Web, the resulting image will either look very pixelated or it will lose a lot of quality. It's always best that you scale the image to the size you want in your image editor. Sometimes people use the wrong WIDTH and HEIGHT tags for the intentional purpose of distorting an image, but if that is not your intent I suggest avoiding the technique.

Visual Effects with WIDTH and HEIGHT

Making your image bigger than its original dimensions will always distort the image. Sometimes the effect is intentional, however. My husband, Bruce, created a very small animation of Photoshop icons for my opening page and then increased their dimensions using WIDTH and HEIGHT tags. It was only because the browser did the scaling that the smaller image didn't take up much disk space. This animation was on the front page of my site for close to a year. More on GIF animation in Chapter 21, "GIF Animation."

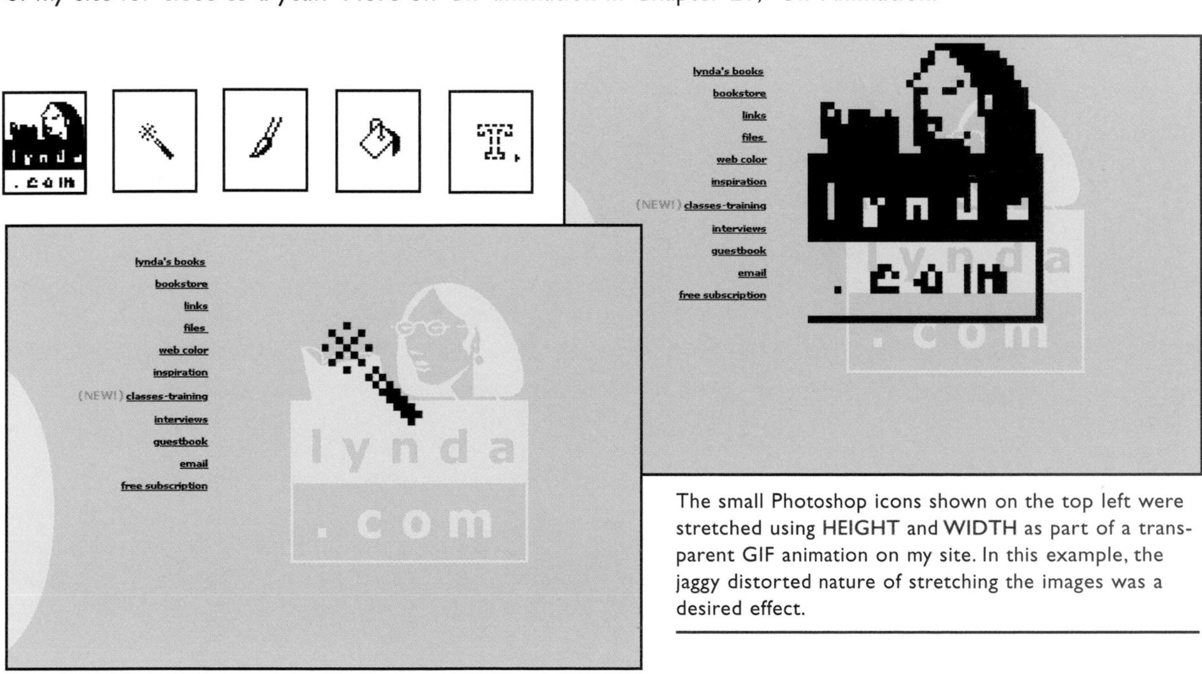

The small Photoshop icons shown on the top left were stretched using HEIGHT and WIDTH as part of a transparent GIF animation on my site. In this example, the jaggy distorted nature of stretching the images was a desired effect.

Importance of ALT

Suppose visitors who want to see your site arrive with browser software such as Lynx, which doesn't recognize images? Or they've turned off their images because they're in a hurry? Or they're disabled (yes, visually impaired people use the text-based Web; there are devices that can "read" the pages to them)? All these situations can be accommodated by adding one simple ALT attribute to your HTML. The ALT element allows you to put text in place of the image so readers have an idea of what the image is without having to view it.

Using the same example one more time, here's where the tag would be included:

```
<A HREF="http://www.lynda.com">
<IMG SRC="flowermonk.jpg" BORDER=0
ALT="monkey image"></A>
```

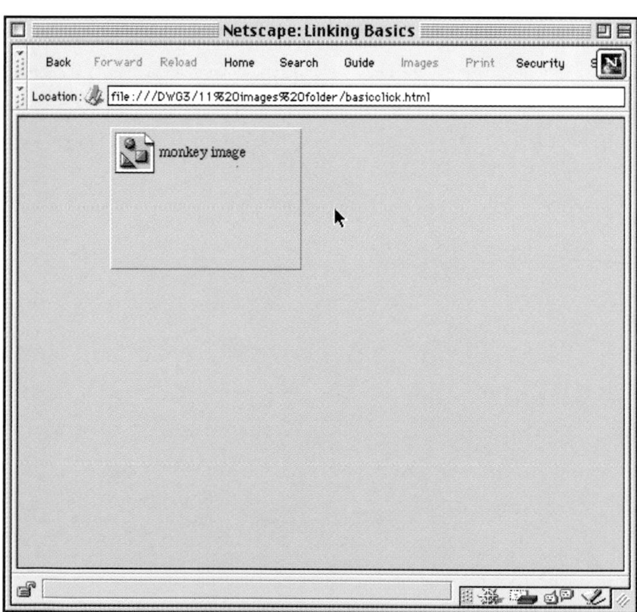

If someone has his or her graphics turned off, they will see (or read) the description of the image because of the ALT attribute.

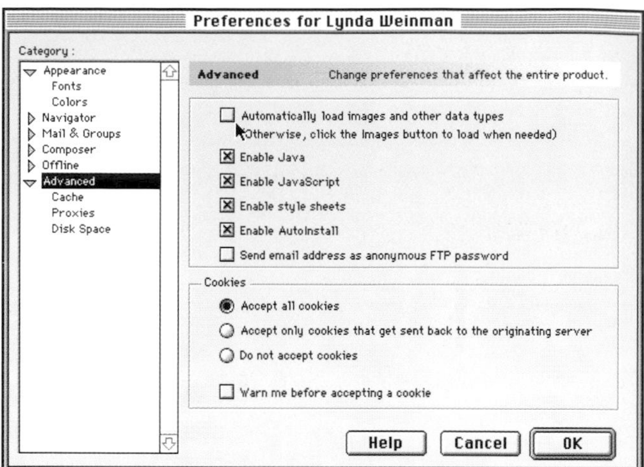

I recommend that you run a test on your site and view it with images turned off. In **Netscape 4.0**, choose **Edit:Preferences: Advanced** and uncheck the **Automatically Load Images** box.

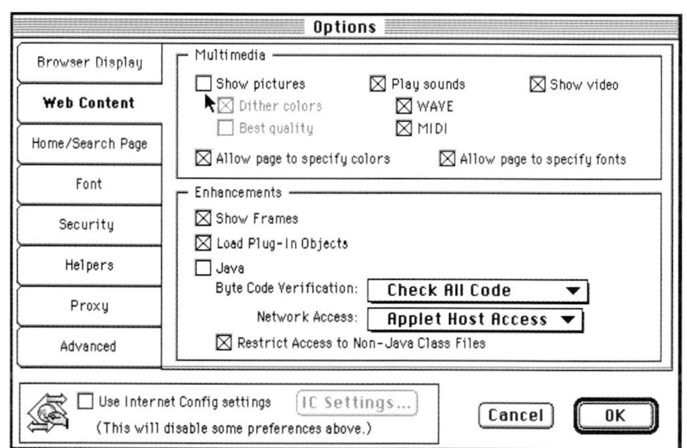

In **Explorer 3.0**, choose **Edit:Options** and uncheck **Show Pictures**. In either product, quit the browser and relaunch, or the change will not take effect.

Once you look at your site through text-only glasses, you might find yourself in an unnavigatable mess! I'm just as much at fault as the next Web designer when it comes to the lack of ALT text on my site. Because I personally maintain more than 1,000 pages, it's a pretty big chore to go back over my entire site and fix every graphic with ALT text. The point is not to tag every graphic, it's to tag every graphic that is critical to navigation or understanding the content of your site.

For a not-always-gentle wake-up call, run your site through **Josh Krieger's Bobby program** (http://www.cast.org/bobby). It checks for errors in your code that range from missing ALT text for images, imagemaps, and Java applets to using too many words in linked text. It gives you the option to check your site's compatibility with 13 browsers and returns a report that details slow downloading bottlenecks and HTML errors.

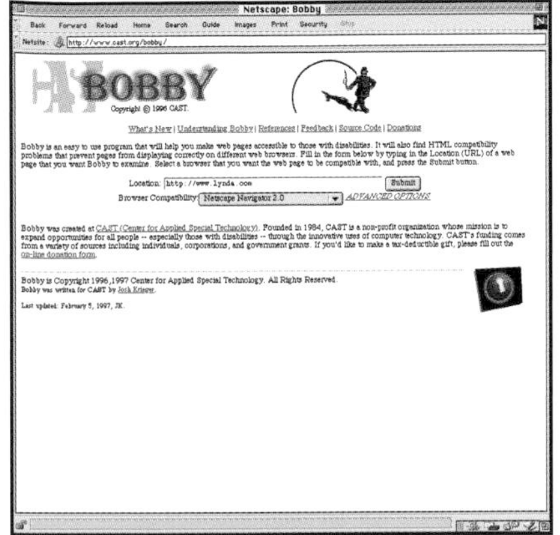

Step1: When you arrive at Bobby, enter your URL.

Step2: It will return tagged with problems.

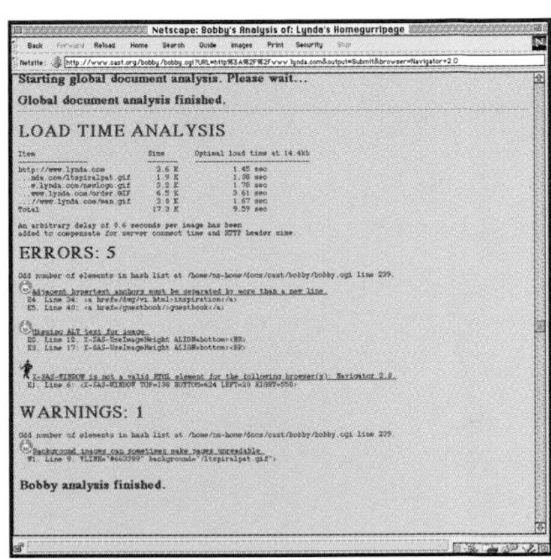

Step3: Click on the blue handicapped symbols to see potential accessibility problems.

The bottom line is, you may be a wonderful Photoshop artist or perfect HTML coder, but there's more to Web design than the tools and technologies you choose to use. The standards by which your site is judged include speed and readability. It's time to transcend our egos as artists and programmers and take the challenge to become communicators who reach as many people as this Web medium allows.

note

American Disabilities Act

It is estimated that 49 million people in the United States have a legal disability. Currently, the law does not require that you make sites accessible to handicapped visitors, but the possibility is clearly there. The **A**mericans with **D**isabilities **A**ct (ADA) protects the rights of all U.S. citizens to access public documents. It seems only a matter of time before the Web will fall under legal jurisdiction to become accessible to disabled individ-uals. Government and information-based sites will need to be especially sensitive to the needs of the disabled audience. Accessibility is something non-disabled people don't necessarily think about, so it has historically become a function of our government and society to make sure this group doesn't go unprotected.

Crystal Water's excellent book *Universal Web Design: A Comprehensive Guide to Creating Accessible Web Sites* includes chapters on legal and accessibility issues, plus it offers an exhaustive list of URLs and resources on these subjects. It is a must-have for anyone who wishes to create sites that are usable by all people.

Universal Web Design
Crystal Waters
New Riders Publishing
ISBN: 1-56205-738-3
$39.99

National Center for Accessible Media
http://www.boston.com/wgbh/ncam/

Thumbnails and Large Image

There are times when you might need to show a thumbnail representation of an image that leads viewers to an optional larger image, if they choose to go there. This technique involves making the same image in two sizes: one small and one large. Here's an example of what **Apple Computer** does for press releases.

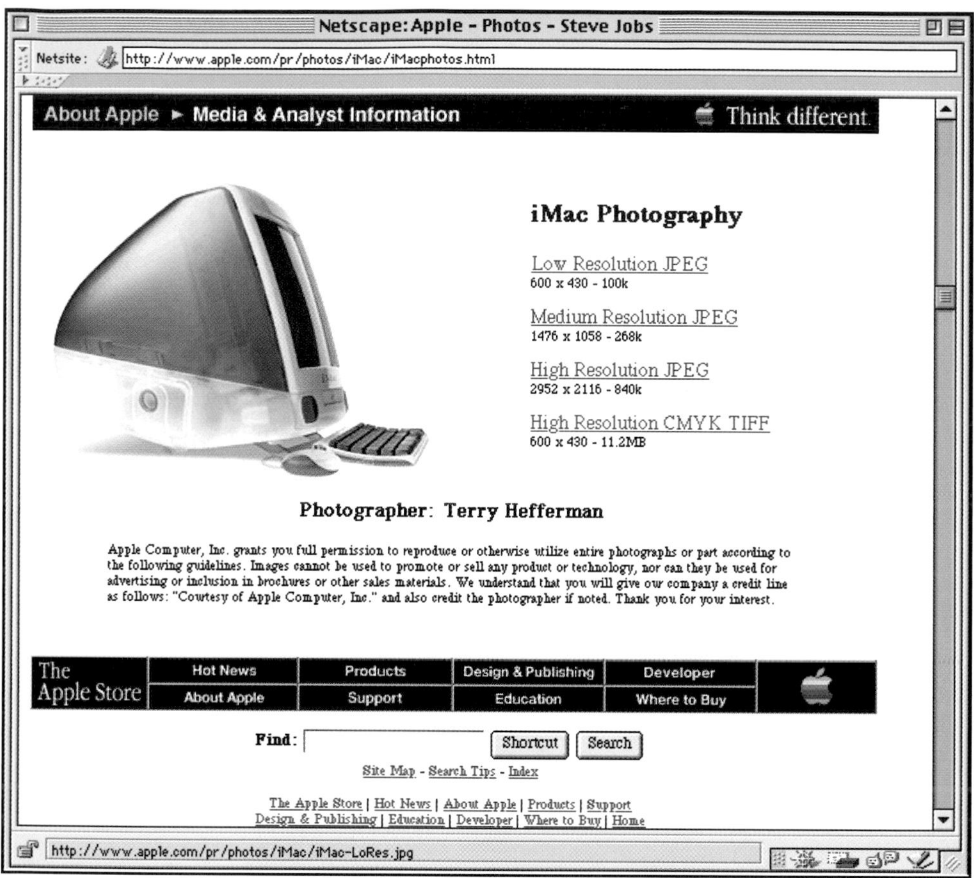

The Apple PR site has an excellent example of thumbnailing images. The list of links includes information about the dimensions and downloading size of each choice. This is an excellent service for reporters who might need a high-resolution image for an article. Note that the photographer, Terry Hefferman, is also cited, and the terms of use are listed below the image.

Low-res image

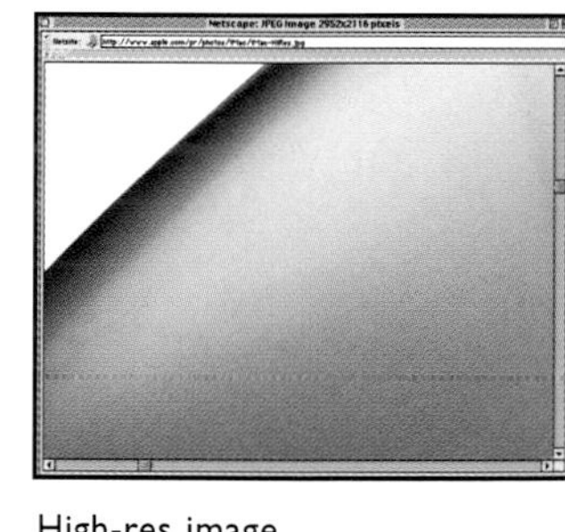

Medium-res image

High-res image

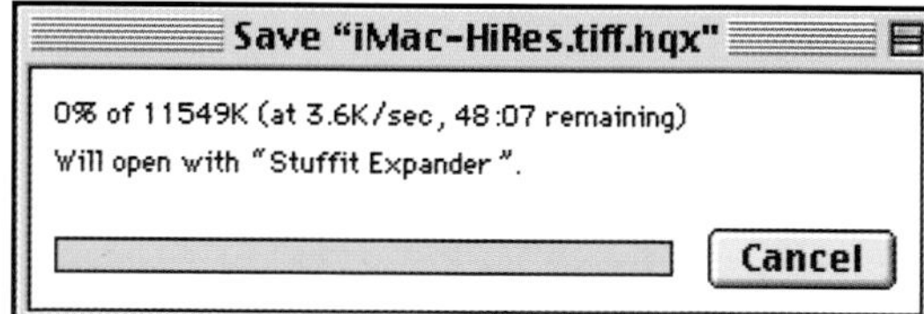

When clicking on the last option—the high-res CMYK Tiff image (not supported as an inline file format by browsers)—the image downloads instead. On my Macintosh, this dialog box shows up to let me know the image is being downloaded to my hard drive instead of appearing inside my browser window. More information on linking to other "media" follows in the next section.

Hallmark Cards uses thumbnails to sell their electronic greeting card line. This is another excellent example of using thumbnail images effectively.

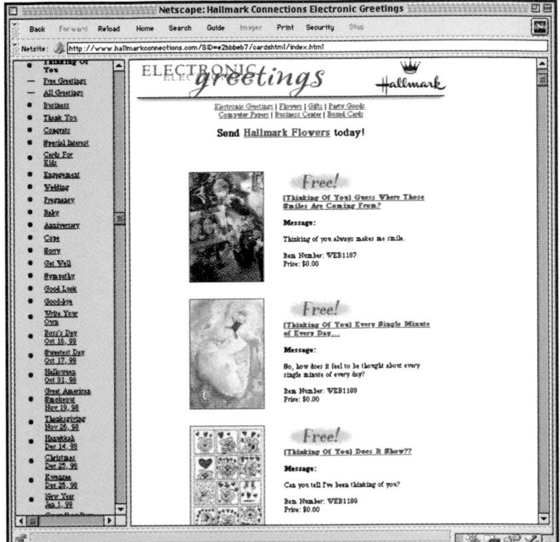

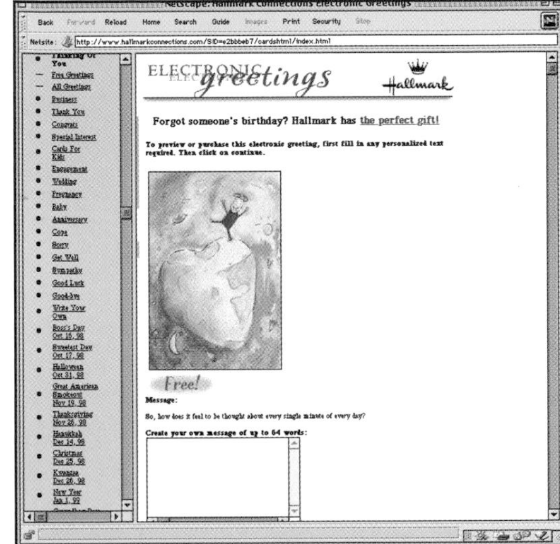

At http://www.hallmark.com, you can choose from 1,700 card designs. It makes sense that most of their images are thumbnails that link to larger views.

My husband, **Bruce Heavin**, uses his site to show art directors and fans a huge amount of images. He has a scrolling list of thumbnails and loads the larger image into a frame on the same page.

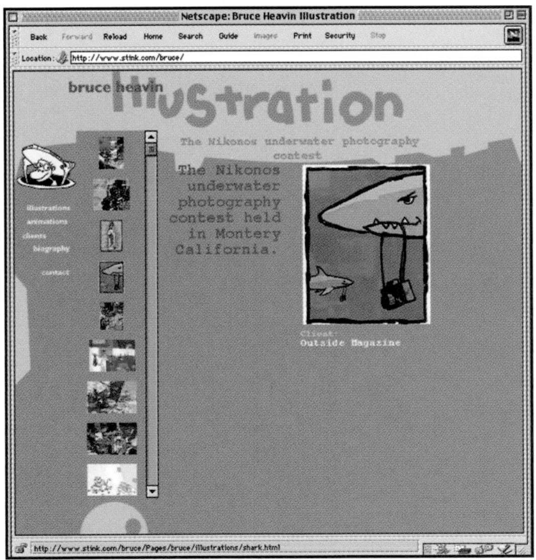

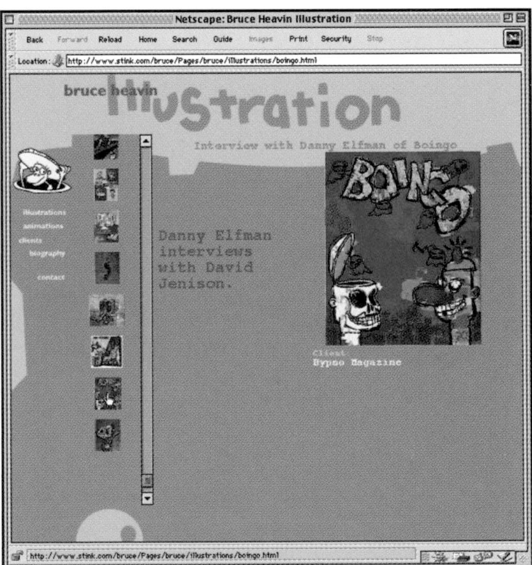

These examples show the use of thumbnails on a site using frames. The TARGET attribute is used to load the image inside a different frame region on the same page.

Linking to Other Media

When you link to something that isn't a known MIME type, the document will download to your hard drive instead of inside your browser window. MIME stands for **M**ultipurpose **I**nternet **M**ail **E**xtensions. Initially, this protocol was developed for sending attachments to email. Now, browsers honor predefined MIME types as well, meaning that the browser recognizes certain file formats by their extensions. For example, the file format and file name extension ".gif" is a known file format to all browsers. Whenever a GIF file is included in an HTML document, it appears in the browser window without the need for an external "player" application.

But what happens when you want to link to a document that isn't a known MIME type? Let's say you want to send a QuarkXPress document over the Net? Or an Excel spreadsheet? Because these aren't known MIME types, the documents will appear scrambled if someone downloads them in their native file formats. It's best if you compress the document first, which will result in a known MIME extension, such as .zip for PC or .hqx, .sit, or .sea for Macintosh. The most widely used compression tool is **StuffIt** (http://www.aladdinsys.com) for the Mac and **PKWare** (http://www.pkware.com) for the PC. If you are creating content for Mac and PC users, you will have to create two different versions of the downloadable file.

Another great use for this procedure is if you want someone to be able to download multiple documents in one click. Let's say you have a lot of family photos you want to transfer or images you want to get client approval for. StuffIt and PKWare can both create one file out of multiple files, which means your end user can point and click to download without ever viewing the files on-screen. You can also encrypt the files with a password, which is a neat way of making a financial transaction. Let's say you charge someone for a file. This way, they could not uncompress the file to see it without the password you supply (after payment, of course!).

MAC: In order to include links to these types of files, you would include them in HTML like this:

```
<A HREF="http://www.domain.com/filename.sit">
<IMG SRC="icon.gif"></A>
```

PC: In order to include links to these types of files, you would include them in HTML like this:

```
<A HREF="http://www.domain.com/filename.zip">
<IMG SRC="icon.gif"></A>
```

If you want to include an embedded sound or movie file, here are a few file types which are recognized by the major browsers.

Sound and Movie File Embedding			
Graphics	GIF	JPEG	*PNG
Video	QuickTime	AVI	
Audio	AU		

*PNG has been supported only within newer Web browsers.

File Types and HTML	
GIF, JPEG, *PNG	.gif, .jpg, .png
QuickTime, AVI	.mov, .avi
AU/μLAW, WAVE, AIFF/AIFC	.au, .wav, .aif

In order to include links to these types of files, you would include them in HTML like this:

```
<A HREF=http://www.domain.com/filename.xxx>
<IMG SRC="icon.gif"></A>
```

Aesthetic Cues for Linked Graphics

It's easy to rely on blue linked borders or the hand symbol to signify a link, but most designers are looking to do something that is more integrated into the look and feel of a site rather than rely on set conventions. There are dangers in this approach if your site visitor doesn't "get" what you meant, but there are dangers in being boring, too.

Many designers, myself included, have grown weary of predictable beveled 3D buttons on Web pages. If you're tired of the 3D look, however, there are other signals that imply a linked image. Drop shadows are often used, as are colored shapes. I fooled around in Photoshop for a while with this image of me and one of my stuffed monkeys to show a few other ideas. Photoshop techniques for these approaches are found in Chapter 14, "Rules, Buttons, & Bullets."

The left image was the original. You might not know where to click to visit my monkey collection! The studies on the right show that if you treat a graphic with a filter or unexpected shape that it will look more like a clickable piece of art than if you leave photographs with no visual cues that they are linked.

summary Linking Basics

Linked images and media are an integral part of any Web site. This chapter reviewed HTML methods for creating links and working with WIDTH, HEIGHT, and ALT attributes. Here's a summary:

- Using HTML BORDER attributes, you can control whether linked graphics have borders or not, what color they are, and what size they are.
- Be sure to include WIDTH and HEIGHT information about each graphic, because the browser will not have to calculate as much data and the text and images will display more quickly.
- ALT attributes are helpful to people who browse their site through text-based browsers or with images turned off. Be sure to check your site without images to see if key graphics contain ALT attributes, especially navigation graphics.
- Use .zip or .sit compression on media that is not standard, and it will be downloaded to your visitor's hard drive.
- If you choose to eliminate link borders around your graphics, make them look clickable through image editing enhancements so that they cue your visitor that you have linked content.

Introduction

Background Tiles

Chapter Topics

- Tiling Backgrounds
- Pattern Sizes
- Full-Screen Backgrounds
- Background Code
- Seamless Tiles
- Photoshop Techniques
- ImageReady Techniques

12

Sometimes the most simple enhancements to a Web site can make all the difference between an average design and exceptional one. The power of background tiles in Web design is often underestimated. This chapter will show compelling examples of how tiles can create richly layered pages that take up much less bandwidth than you might expect.

Perhaps you think it would take way too long to download an image that fills a viewer's browser screen and that it would be irresponsible to prepare images of this size for Web graphics. Making full-screen, wall-to-wall graphics on the Web would seem to be an impossible feat given the slow modems and phone lines most of us squeeze connections through. Not to mention the fact that full-screen graphics can mean one thing to a compact portable computer Web user and another to someone with a 21" monitor!

Repeated, tilable background patterns are the solution to many of these issues. This chapter covers an HTML tag called BODY BACKGROUND, which allows a single small image to be repeated endlessly so that it fills an entire Web page, regardless of size. These single small images will be referred to in this chapter as background tiles. They have the advantage of being small, so they load fast, and are able to repeat over the size of whatever Web screen they appear on. Because small graphics load faster than big ones, this technique works well to cover a lot of real estate on a Web page without incurring a lot of overhead in downloading time.

Tiling Backgrounds

The BODY BACKGROUND tag enables the browser to repeat a small graphic and turn it into a full-screen graphic. It accomplishes this effect by taking a single image and tiling it, creating a repeating image that will fill any size screen regardless of computer platform and browser area. The browser needs to load only a single source file for the pattern, and once it's downloaded, it fills the entire Web page. This saves time because the wait time is for a single small image, even though the result is that the entire screen fills with an image. Repeated tiles are a great solution for creating full-screen graphics for low-bandwidth delivery systems such as the Web.

This is the source artwork for the tile.

Once the tile is repeated in a browser window, you can't really see the source tile anymore.

Bandwidth limitations aren't the only problem that tiled background patterns solve. One of the great frustrations most Web designers share is HTML's inability to allow for images to be layered. If you consider that layering is a main feature of programs such as Photoshop, QuarkXPress, and PageMaker, you will understand why the this feature in HTML is sorely missed. Cascading Style Sheets are the answer to some designer's layering needs (see Chapter 19, "Cascading Style Sheets"), but using tiled background patterns is still a much easier and more backwards compatible method to achieve layering multiple images.

HTML allows text, links, and images to go on top of tiled backgrounds, making it an extremely useful and economical design element. The HTML code for this tiling effect is quite simple. The real challenge is making the art look good and controlling whether the seams of each repeated image are obvious or invisible.

Determining Tiled Pattern Sizes

One of the first questions that comes to mind is how big the tiled image should be. HTML puts no restrictions on the size of a source for a background tile. The image has to be in a square or rectangular, however, because that's the native shape of any computer file.

The size of the image is entirely up to you. You should realize that the size of a tile is going to dictate how many times it repeats. If a viewer's monitor is 640×480 pixels and your tile is 320×240, it will repeat four times. If it were 20×20 pixels, it would repeat 32 times.

If your tile has images that repeat on each side, it will not show visible seams and the viewer will not know how many times it repeats. If the image has an obvious border around it, the border will accentuate the fact that the image is being tiled. The size of your tile is up to you and the effect you are striving for.

Be aware, however, that file size restrictions must still be honored. If you create a tile that takes up a lot of memory, it will take the same amount of time to load as any other kind of huge graphic you put on the Web. If need be, refer back to Chapter 6, "Low-Bandwidth Graphics," for methods to minimize file sizes.

If you use an image source that has large dimensions, it will not repeat as often. If it is large enough, it will not repeat at all. In that event, the speed advantages of having a small image load once and automatically repeat with out incurring any additional downloading time would not exist. On the other hand, if you could make a large graphic in dimensions and not file size, then loading it in as a background image instead of a regular graphic could have its merits. Sometimes the pixel size count of a document and the amount of memory they take up are not relational, as Bruce proved in the above image!

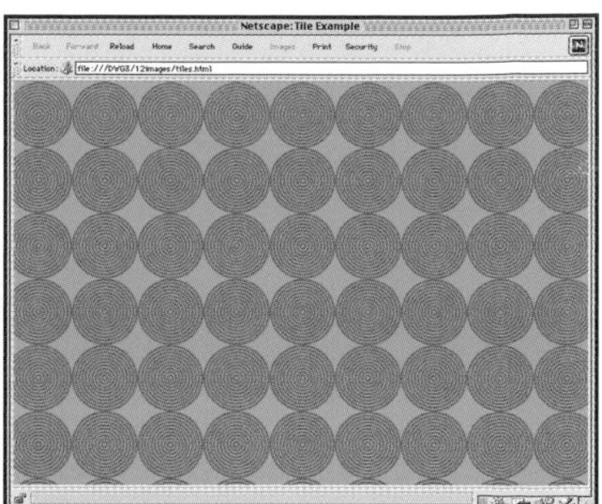

Small Source File

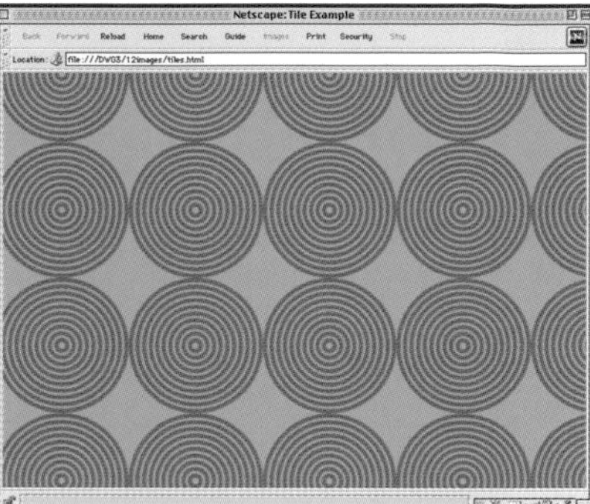

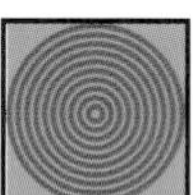

Medium Source File

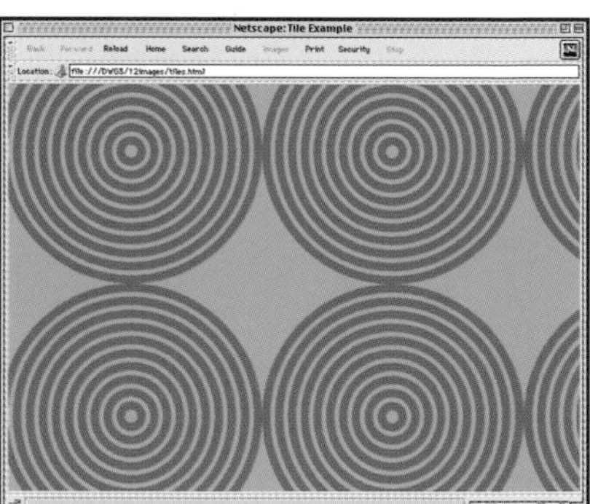

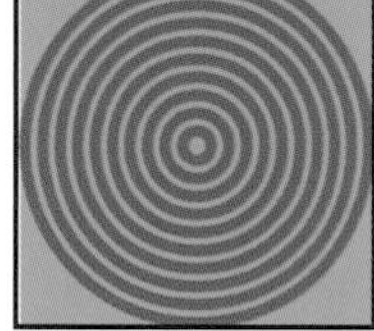

Large Source File

Full-Screen Body Backgrounds

Why would you use an image with large pixel dimensions as a tiled background, as it seems to defeat the point? Because it could go behind other images and text, making full-screen backdrop to other images on your page. HTML doesn't easily let you put text or images over regular images. The easiest way around this restriction is to use a background tiled graphic.

Here's an example of a 1080×720 background for my site which is only 5k. It only has two colors and has a lot of areas of solid color, so it compressed extremely well as a GIF even though the image was so large.

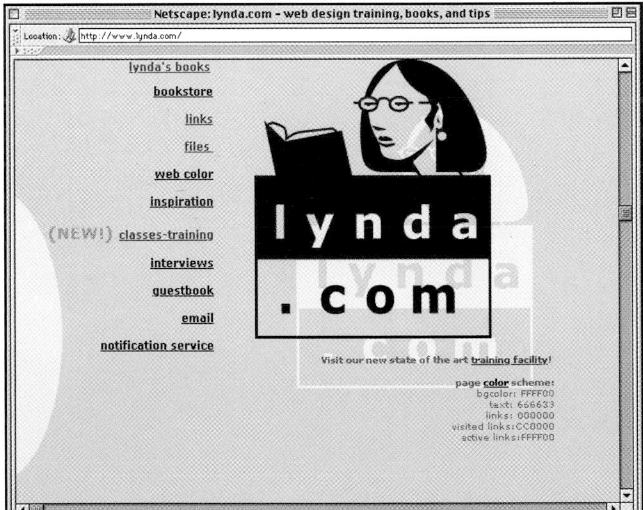

Combined with HTML text, this page looks rich and layered, and is not too large to download.

The background tile for the Fountains site (http://www.si.edu/ndm/) looks oversized. It is 1200×1200 pixels and weighs 49k.

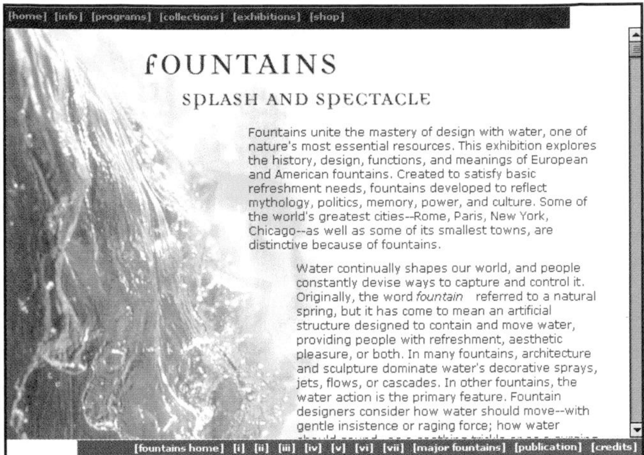

Combined graphical typography (Chapter 16, "Web Typography") and HTML type create a beautiful layout using a very simple technique.

Here is the source file for http://www.refuge. amnesty.org; it utilizes photography and graphics. It is 800×700 and weighs 23k.

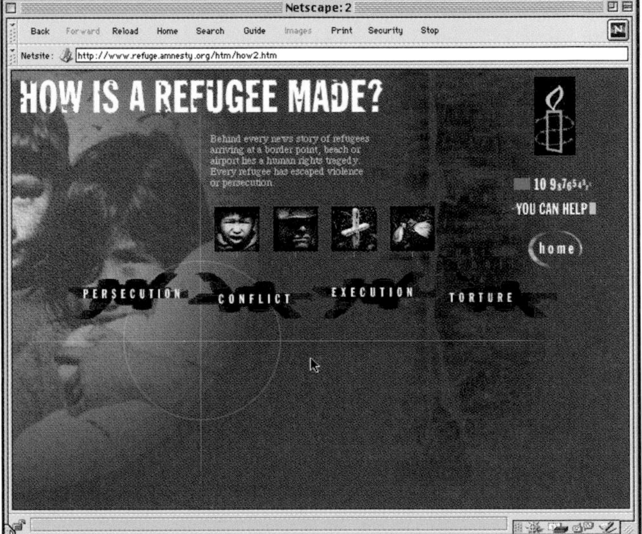

The foreground graphics in this site are so well tailored to the background tile that you can barely see where one ends and the other begins. It is a seamless effect.

File Formats for Patterned Tiles

GIFs and JPEGs are standard file formats for the Web, and tiled patterns are no exception. Just remember to follow the kilobyte rule. Every kilobyte of file size represents one second of download time for your viewer. The full size of the background pattern gets added to the download! If you have a background that's 60k and two images that are 10k each, the total file size of your page will be 80k. You would have just added a minute of download time to your page! Therefore, tiled backgrounds that take up a lot of memory are extra annoying to your audience during download.

Be careful if you are trying to match foreground and background tile images. They must both be the same file format—GIF and GIF or JPEG and JPEG—if you want the colors to match perfectly.

As usual, always save your file names in lowercase and use the extensions **.jpg** or **.gif** to let the HTML code know what kind of image it has to load. I usually put the word "**pat**" somewhere in a pattern file name, just for my own reference. That way I know what I intended to use the file for when I search for it in a text list, such as my server directory!

The Code, Please!

It is very simple to include a patterned background in an HTML document. Here's the minimum code required:

```
  <HTML>
1 <BODY BACKGROUND="pat.gif">
  </BODY>
  </HTML>
```

1. The BODY BACKGROUND tag enables you to add a background tile to the page. The "pat.gif" is the name of the image being tiled in this example.

pat.gif image

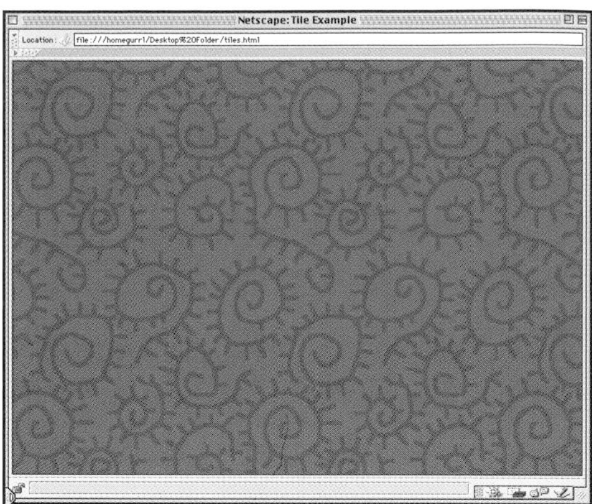

Here's the result of using the BODY BACKGROUND ="pat.gif" tag.

If you wanted to have an image lay over a background, the code would look like this:

```
  <HTML>
  <BODY BACKGROUND="pat.gif">
1 <IMG SRC="tile.gif">
  </BODY>
  </HTML>
```

1. The IMG SRC tag enables you to include an image that will lay over the background tile.

The finished Web page with the <IMG SRC="tile.gif"> tag.

Seams or No Seams, That Is the Question

The next sections take a look at two different ways to present your background tile on your Web page: with or without seams.

Seams

When an image has obvious seams—it looks tiled on purpose, some Web pages look great wallpapered with an obvious border. Andy Warhol first earned his notoriety by making images of repeating soup cans on a single canvas. Video walls are often built on the power of images repeating in squares. There's nothing wrong with making patterns that have obvious borders and repeats, especially if that's what you had in mind. Making a tiled pattern with an obvious repeating border is fairly simple.

Make sure that the tile you create has a border.

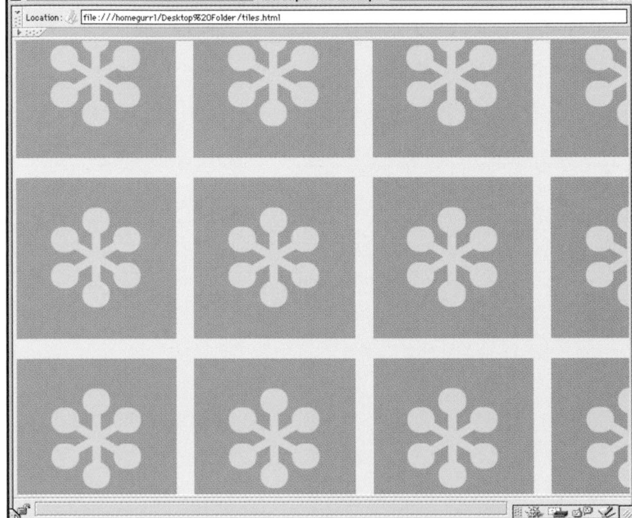

The border around the image makes this repeated background much more obvious.

No Seams, the Photoshop/ImageReady Way

When "seamless" patterns are described, it means the border of the pattern tile is impossible to locate. There aren't any pros or cons to using seamless or seamed tiles; it's purely an aesthetic decision. Seamless tiles, however, are much trickier to make.

The following section has a step-by-step example of a technique my husband, Bruce, developed, using Photoshop or ImageReady.

Seamless Tiles in ImageReady

The procedure in ImageReady is very similar to that of Photoshop, but because ImageReady is a Web graphics editor, it has a few extra bells and whistles that make it better.

If you're working with a lot of pasted images, like I am in this example, ImageReady (and Photoshop) automatically create multiple layers. The problem with the Offset filter is that it offsets only a single layer at a time. For this reason, I turned off the pink background and merged all the visible layers into one layer. When I used the Offset filter, it offset the single, merged layer.

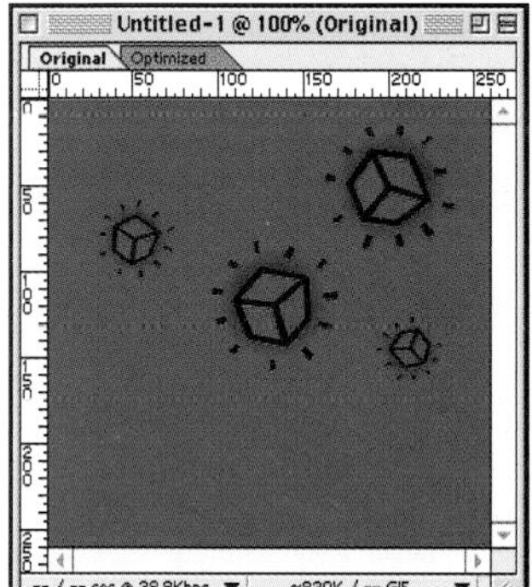

I started with our Digital Arts Center logo and pasted it into this ImageReady document (also 260×260 at 72 dpi).

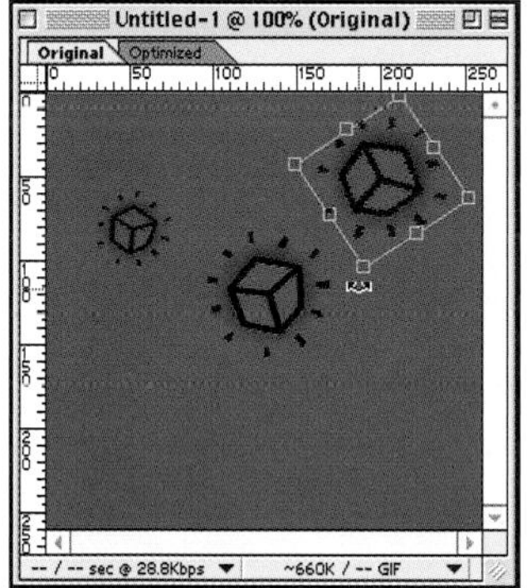

Using the transform commands in ImageReady, I rotated and scaled each paste in order to achieve a random positioning.

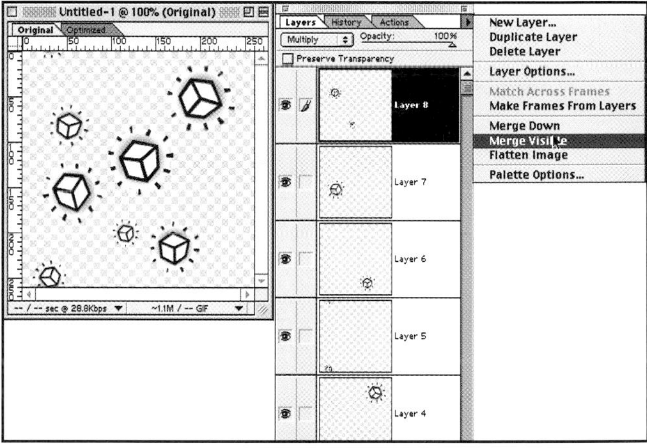

I filled the upper section of the image before using the Offset filter.

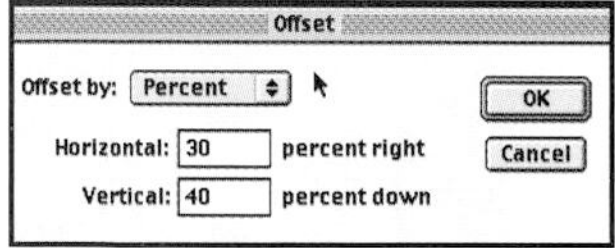

The **Offset filter** in ImageReady is simpler than Photoshop. It was designed specifically for this purpose, whereas Photoshop's Offset filter has other uses. The number of pixels, or in this case (the percentages), is somewhat arbitrary. It's safest to offset the image in uneven increments so that you avoid too much symmetry in the pattern.

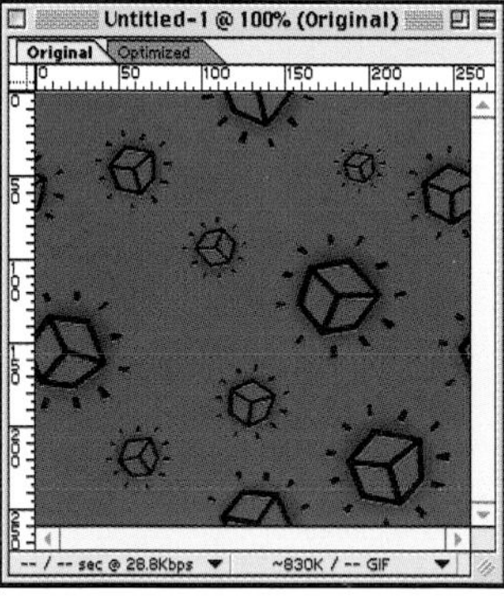

The finished tile.

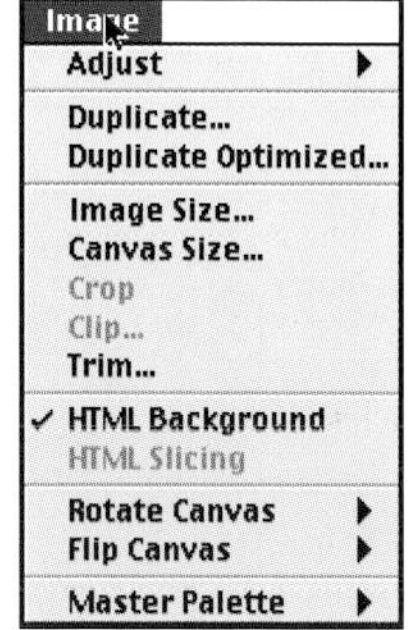

Check **Image: HTML Background**, it allows you to preview the pattern within a browser.

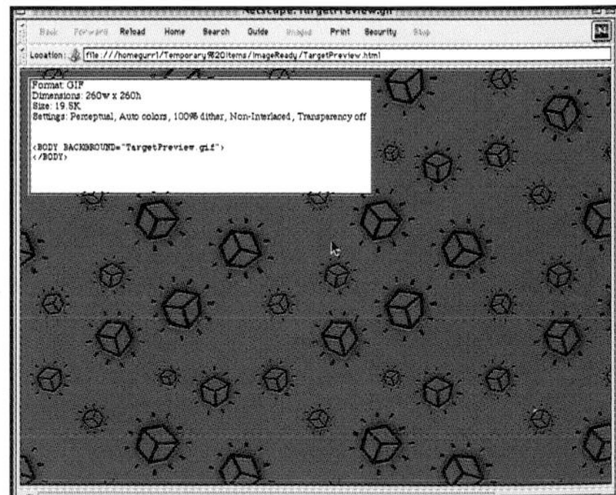

Choosing **File:Preview In Browser** causes ImageReady to write a temporary Preview file. You can then copy and paste the code in the white box into an HTML editor.

Seamless Tiles in Photoshop

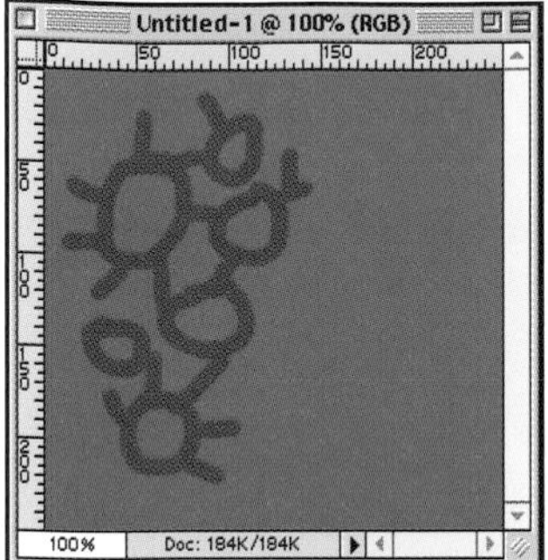

This source tile is 260× 260 pixels at 72 dpi. I started drawing shapes intentionally in one corner of the image.

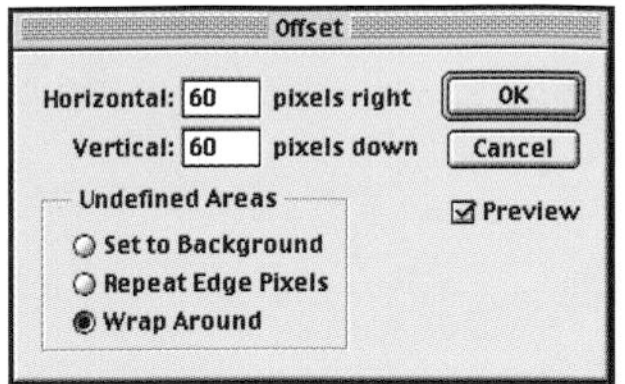

Using the Offset Filter in Photoshop (under **Filter:Other: Offset**), I entered the settings 60 pixels right, with 60 pixels down, using the Wrap Around method under Undefined Areas.

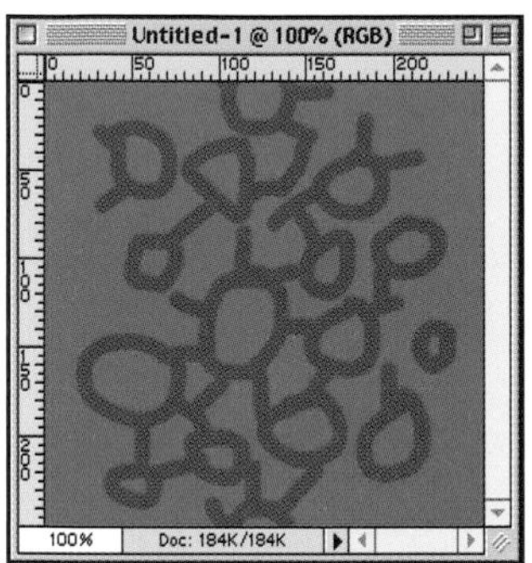

This caused my original drawing to shift position, and I added to the artwork.

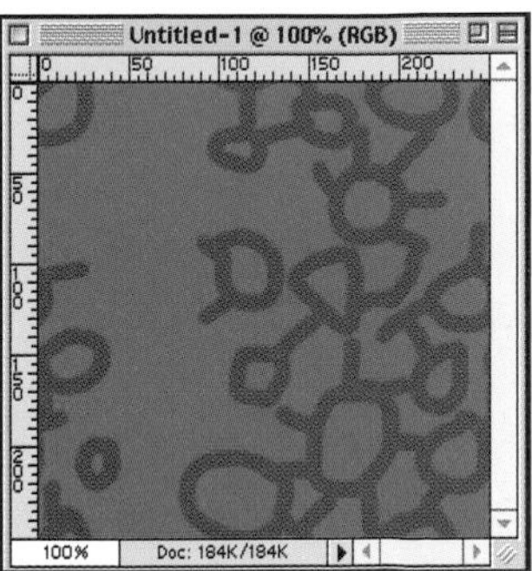

I reapplied the same Offset filter, which caused my artwork to shift again, revealing gaps in the areas that were unpainted.

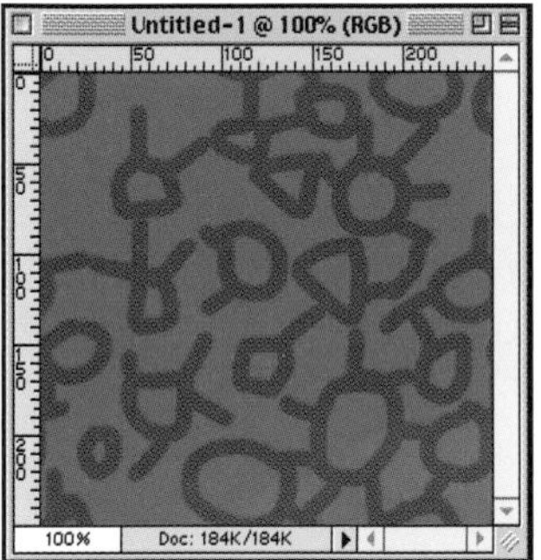

The objective is to fill all the gaps and to keep repeating the use of the Offset filter until you've painted every area there is to paint. The Offset filter reveals parts of the image that are hidden at the seams.

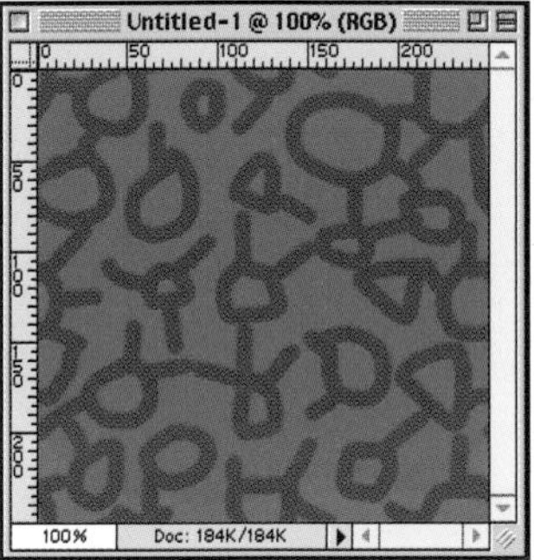

Here is the finished tile.

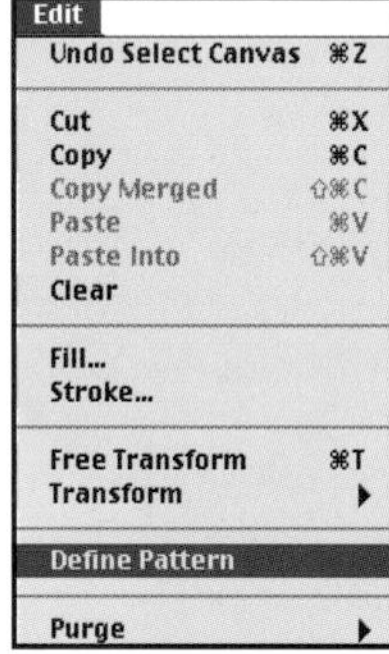

In order to preview my tile, I chose **Edit: Define Pattern**.

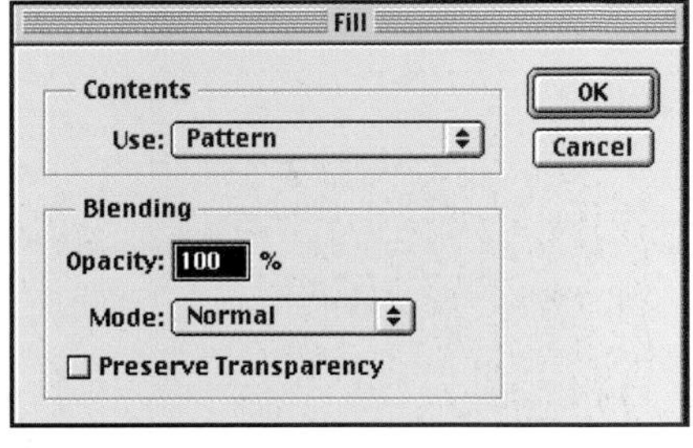

I created a larger preview file and chose **Edit:Fill:Pattern**. This allowed me to preview in Photoshop before I wrote the final background tile HTML.

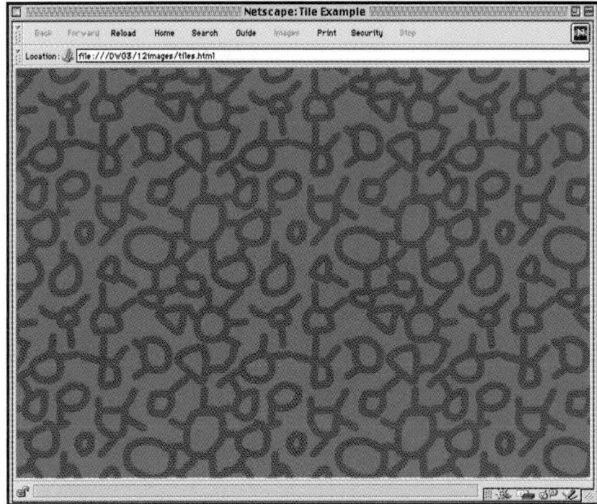

The finished result in Netscape.

Directional Tiles

It's possible to make skinny and tall tiles, or fat and short tiles, for directional tile effects. A tile in a horizontal shape will fill the browser window from top to bottom, and a tile in a vertical shape will fill the browser from left to right.

I'm sure you've seen tiles all over the Web with borders on the left. This tile is a nice twist on that technique, and creates a right and left border with soft edges. It was designed by Ammon Haggerty.

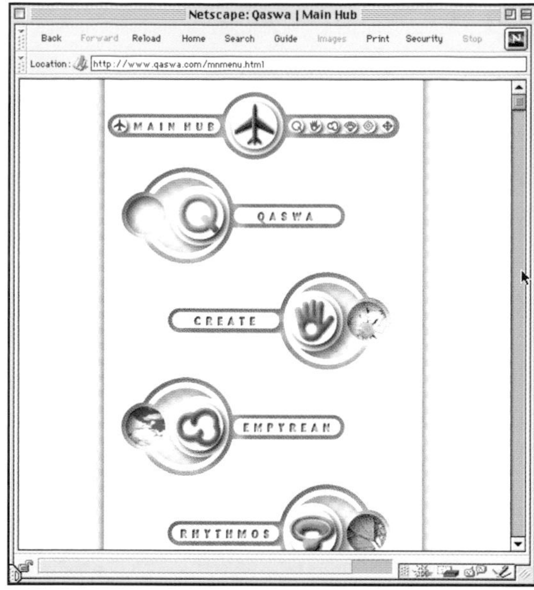

The finished effect is more impressive than the lone tile!

National Design Museum's designer Elizabeth Roxby developed this tall tile, which fills the screen in a horizontal motion as it loads.

The effect is spectacular once other images and typography are laid over the simple tile.

Aesthetics of Backgrounds

Always pay attention to contrast and value (lights and darks) when creating background tiles. If you have a light background, use dark type. If you have a dark background, use light type. If you aren't going to change your browser's default colors for text, links, visited links, and active links, use a light background—about the same value as the default light gray you see as the background color of most browsers. The light background will ensure that the default colors of black, blue, and purple text will read against your custom background.

When making art for pattern tiles, try to use either all dark values or all light values. If you have both darks and lights in a background, neither light nor dark type will work consistently against them. This is a basic, simple rule to follow, and your site will avoid the pitfalls of poor background tile aesthetics. Using either all dark values or all light values seems like common sense, but tour the Web a bit and you'll soon see rainbow-colored backgrounds with unreadable black type everywhere.

Make sure your images read. I don't mean your tiles should go to school to learn phonetics or anything; instead, I'm talking about readability of image versus background.

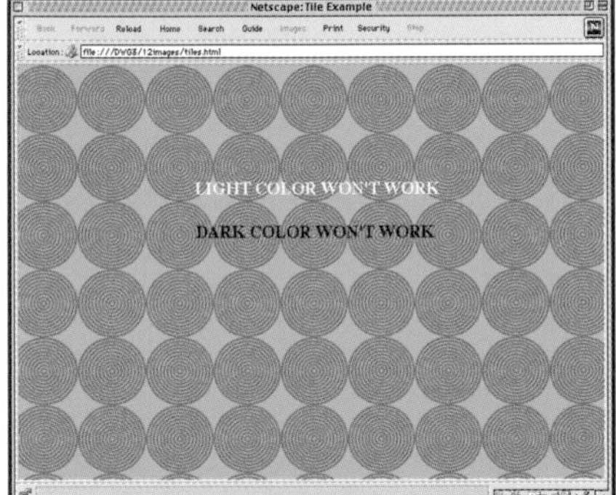

When the background has high contrast, HTML text will not read well on top of it.

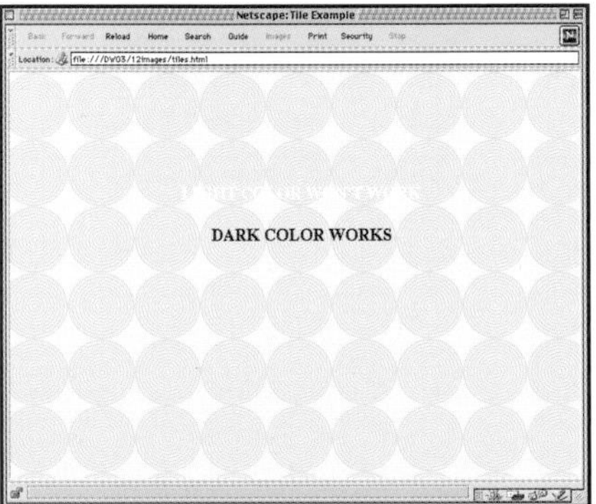

Dark and medium value colors will read over a light background.

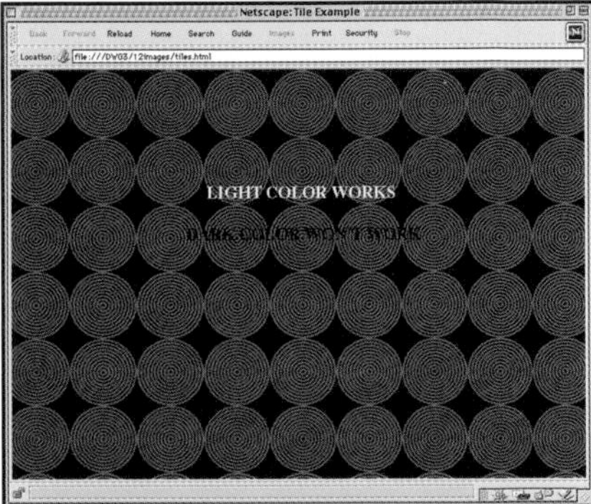

With a dark background, the reverse is true. It's not enough to make a cool-looking background tile. Always check to ensure your type reads over it as well! If it doesn't read, make the necessary adjustments to the color or contrast of the background image.

summary Background Tiles

I hope this chapter inspired you to think about background tiles as an important element in your Web graphics repertoire. Tiles can offer a very big effect for very low overhead. Here's a review of the principles described in this chapter:

- There is no "correct" size for a background tile. The size will affect the visual effect however, in terms of how many times the tile repeats before it fills the browser screen.
- Full screen backgrounds can add a lot of visual interest to a boring page.
- Pay attention to contrast and readability. It's easy to get carried away with complicated, high contrast backgrounds that result in unreadable Web pages.
- You can control the direction in which the background tile loads if you make a thin horizontal tile or a fat vertical shaped tile.
- ImageReady, a new Web graphics tool from Adobe, makes the creation of background tiles easier than any other program on the market.

Introduction

Transparent Artwork

Chapter Topics

- What Is Web Transparency?
- Faking Transparency
- GIF Transparency
- Problems with Glows
- Tools & Techniques
- PNG Transparency

13

Most of us don't think about the fact that computer images are always stored in square or rectangular files. It doesn't matter if you make a graphic on a transparent layer in Photoshop, ImageReady, Fireworks, or any other image editor; if you save and reopen it in another program, it will be in a rectangle. What's wrong with rectangles? Nothing. But they become mighty boring and predictable after a while.

The Web especially suffers from an abundance of rectangular shapes. The browser window is in a rectangle, frames are in rectangles, and buttons and graphics are often in rectangles, too. I call this problem "rectangle-itis." Too many rectangles on a page can make your visitors feel boxed in and claustrophobic.

The solution to the rectangle problem is to learn about transparency on the Web. Transparent graphics include masks with which you can obscure or reveal parts of an image, creating the illusion of an irregular shape.

There are a few different methods for implementing transparency on a site. You can fake it (my favorite method), create a transparent GIF file, or use the even newer type of Web format—a transparent PNG. This chapter covers all these methods (of course!) and discusses some of the newest tools and techniques available for this purpose.

What Is Transparency?

Transparency is the term used on the Web for masked images. Creating transparent images is a tricky business because the standard masking procedures for print or imaging applications don't apply to Web images.

A Web page without transparency can look boxy and unsophisticated.

GIF transparency removes parts of the image you want to mask out.

Of the two most popular Web image formats, GIF and JPEG, only GIF supports transparency fetures. Therefore, in order to make irregularly shaped Web images, you must either make GIF images or learn to fake transparency with the GIF or JPEG format. This chapter will also discuss PNG transparency, which will come into vogue when PNG is more widely supported.

Faking Transparency

There are two types of transparency: One involves masking, and the other involves trickery. The easiest one to use is the latter, which is pretty easy to explain.

Masking

Let's say you want a shape to appear to be free-floating even though it must be stored in a rectangular computer file. Make the background behind the shape the same color as your Web page. If you put the two together, there should be no obvious rectangular border. Sound simple? It is.

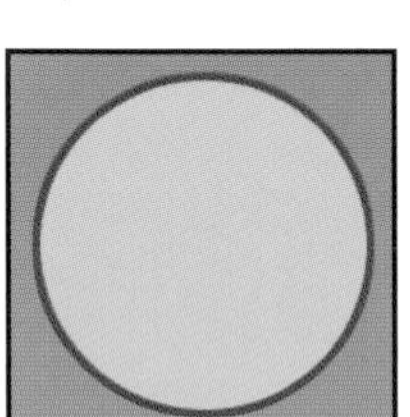

Image alone.

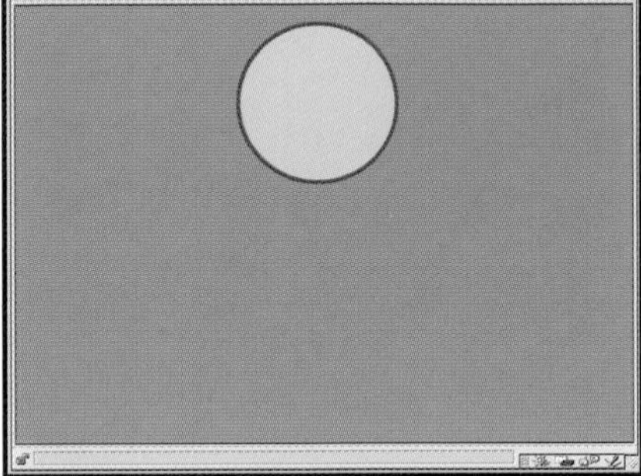

Image with matching background color.

You can easily create the illusion of an irregularly shaped image by making the foreground artwork include the same color as the target background on your Web page.

Trickery

There are two ways to achieve the fake transparency technique. You can use the BODY BACKGROUND or the BODY BGCOLOR tag and attribute.

1. The **BODY BACKGROUND** attribute involves making another small graphic with the same solid color as the background color of the shape.

code

```
<HTML>

<HEAD>

<TITLE>transparency</TITLE>

</HEAD>

<BODY BACKGROUND="bluebg.gif">

<CENTER>

<IMG SRC="circle.gif">

</CENTER></BODY></HEAD
```

Here's an example showing a small block of color saved as a GIF image. It's called **"bluebg.gif."**

2. To use the **BGCOLOR** attribute, you select the same color as the background, find its hexadecimal equivalent (visit Chapter 10, "Color HTML Tags," for more information), and insert that code into your HTML.

code

```
<HTML>

<HEAD>

<TITLE>transparency</TITLE>

</HEAD>

<BODY BGCOLOR="#6699FF">

<CENTER>

<IMG SRC="circle.gif">

</CENTER></BODY></HEAD>
```

warning

Browser Preferences

It is important to be aware that if your visitor has changed his or her browser settings to override the colors you've chosen, the illusion you create will be automatically broken.

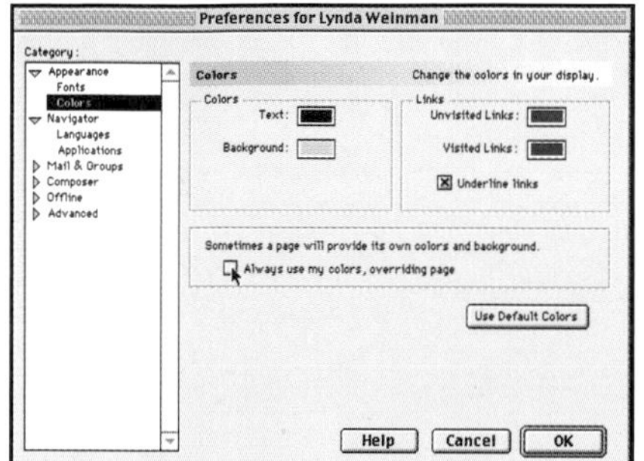

It's kind of scary that although Web designers count on background colors they pick achieving the illusion of irregularly shaped images, end viewers can check **Always Use Mine**, which will override the specified color choices! To view sites as the designers intended them to be seen, make sure **Let Document Override** is always checked instead.

There's No Faking Patterned Tiles

The method you just learned works beautifully if you have a solid background color. The minute you put a pattern behind the image, the illusion is ruined.

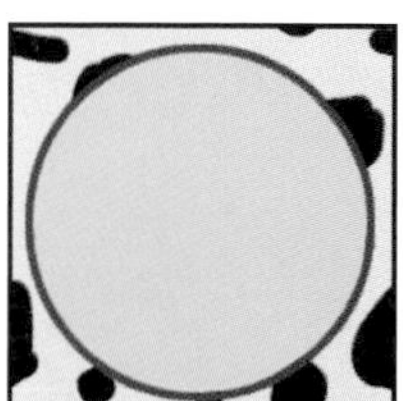

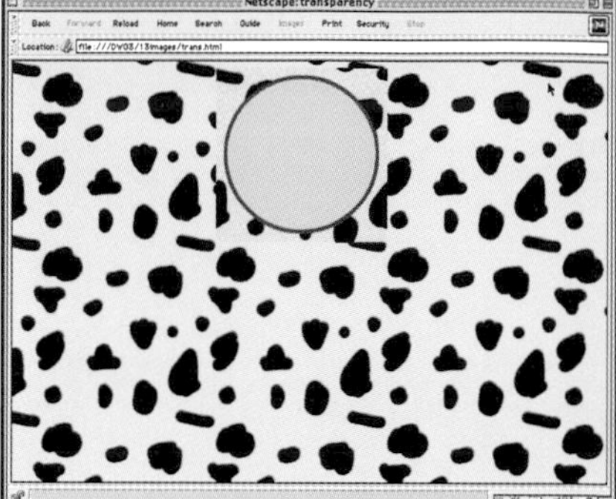

Notice the mis-registration between the circle graphic and the background tile? This is one of the hazards of "faking" transparency with a pattern background tile.

Even if you apply the same pattern to the circle document, it won't line up with your HTML background tile. Why? There's a different offset in the way foreground images and background images are aligned. Two potential solutions to this will be discussed later in this book (in Chapter 19, "Cascading Style Sheets," and Chapter 18, "Frames"). Meanwhile, the simple solution is to use true transparency instead of faking.

GIF Transparency

The GIF file format supports transparency (masking). GIF transparency is challenging because the file format is limited to 1-bit masking (whereas Photoshop transparency supports 8-bit masking). What this means in plain English is that you are restricted to creating a mask with a single value: on or off. Photoshop, on the other hand, allows you to use up to 256 values of on or off, which is why you can easily layer images with feathered edges, glows, and drop shadows. In a 1-bit GIF transparency world, such subtlety is not possible.

It's important to understand the 1-bit masking limitation, because if you aren't careful, the results of your transparency efforts can easily go awry, and you'll end up producing images with unwanted halos and edges.

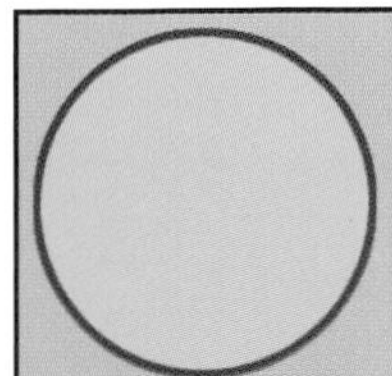

GIF is able to store a 1-bit mask. The mask is not visible until it's loaded into a Web browser.

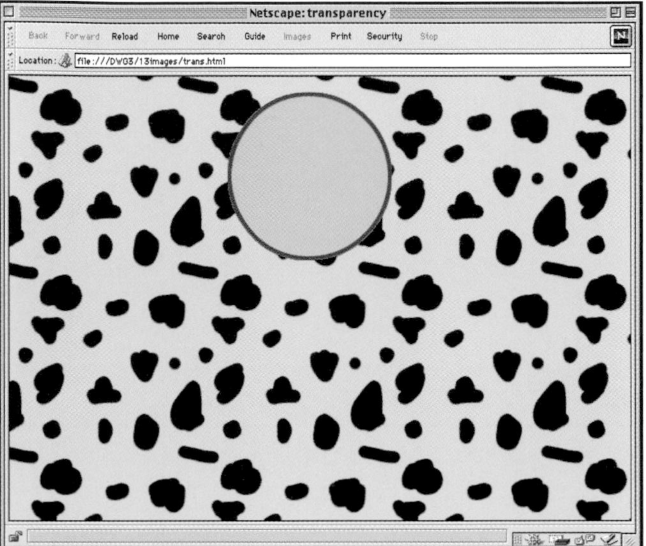

Here's the transparent GIF in the browser window. If you look closely at the edges, you will see an unwanted lighter-colored halo. This was caused by anti-aliasing, which is described in the next section.

Pro and Anti-Aliasing

Most well-trained digital artists would never think to work without anti-aliasing. We've been conditioned to make everything look as smooth and perfect as possible. Anti-aliasing was designed to hide the fact that computer graphics are made of square, jagged pixels. The computer screen is a pixel-based medium, so our compulsion to hide this fact in print and other media is not always appropriate for computer screen-based design, such as the Web and other multimedia delivery systems like CD-ROMs. Low-resolution Web graphics are much more forgiving with aliasing than are their print graphic counterparts.

Because the original was anti-aliased to the blue and the masking in GIF is only 1-bit, the edge of the masked image contains bits of the blue edge.

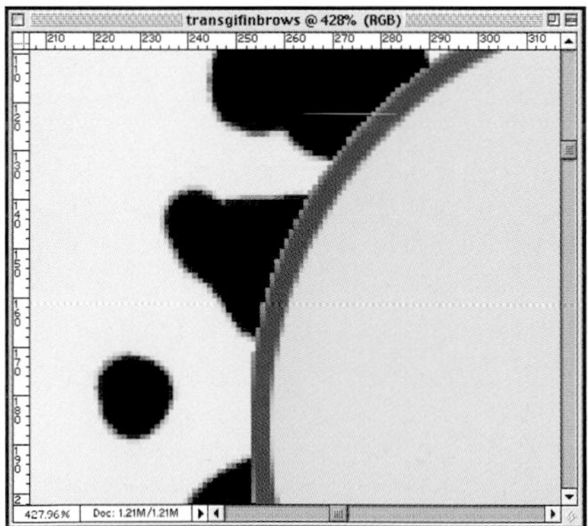

Here's a blow-up of the halo problem in the image to the right.

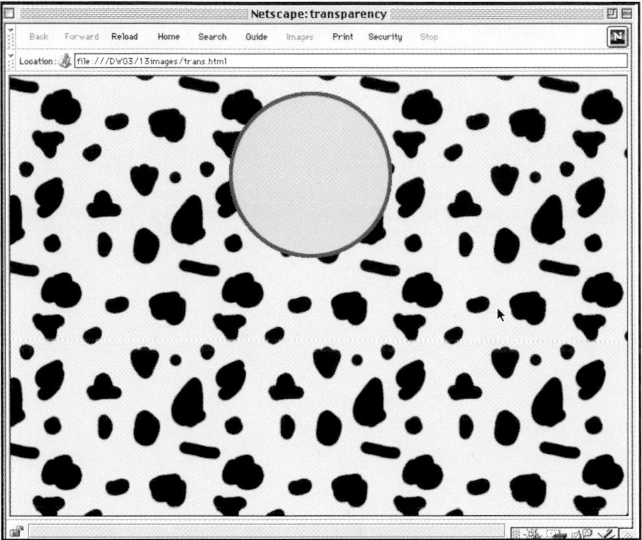

If you don't anti-alias the edges of your transparent GIF image, it will not show any unwanted halo effects.

On the Web, anti-aliasing is not always the best approach. Creating clean transparent GIFs is one of the exceptions wherein aliased graphics create the fewest problems.

The anti-aliased blended edge is precisely what causes fringing problems when the graphic is converted to a transparent GIF. Because transparent GIFs drop only one color out of your image, you will see all the remaining colors along the blended edges of anti-aliased artwork—even when what you really desire is for all of them to disappear. There is no way to avoid this because the GIF file format does not support masking for more than one color. Methods for creating aliased transparency will be addressed in the following sections.

Glows, Soft Edges, and Drop Shadows with GIF Transparency

Because of the problems anti-aliasing introduces in GIFs, artwork with glows, soft edges, and drop shadows can look awful as transparent GIFs. One popular solution is to build your artwork against the same color background it will be seen against in the Web browser. The artwork will look terrible when you make it, but it will look fine when it's displayed against the final background in a Web browser.

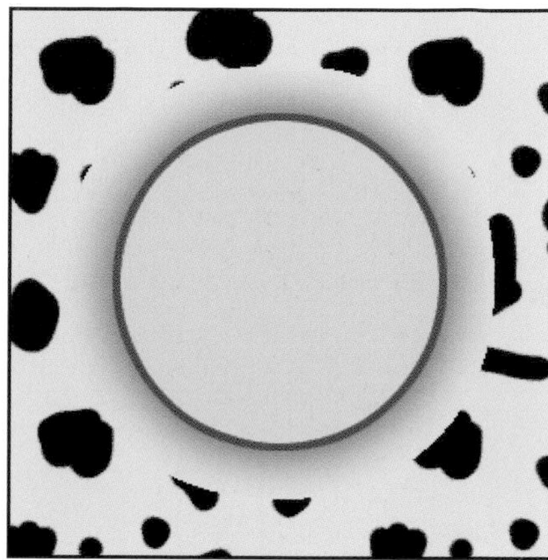

One popular solution is to build artwork against the same color background that is predominant within the pattern.

When the transparency is being created, the file looks terrible. It won't look good until it is placed over the pattern. If you prepare an image this way, you will correct the image's predisposition to favor any other color, which will eliminate unwanted fringes, halos, and matte lines.

The artwork will look terrible when you make it, but it will look acceptable (though not perfect) when it's placed against the final background in a Web browser.

Tools and Techniques for GIF Transparency

So far, we've covered the principles of transparency. The next section will describe production methods for producing transparent GIF graphics. As usual, there are many tools for this job. My favorite is Adobe ImageReady because I know of no other tool that helps artists with this task as much as ImageReady does.

GIF Transparency in ImageReady

ImageReady represents transparency the same way Photoshop does—with a checkerboard background. Anytime you have an image with a checkerboard background, creating a transparent GIF is as simple as checking a Transparency check box. You then have several useful matting options at your command.

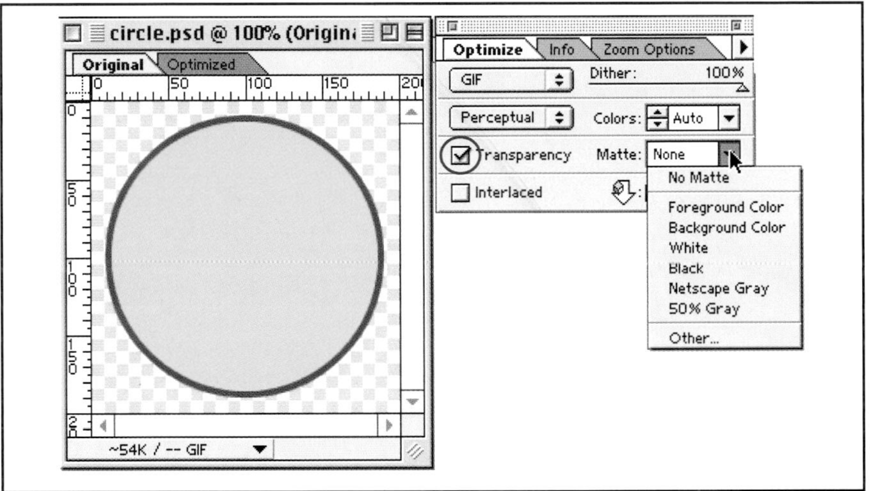

The matting features in ImageReady are very helpful for avoiding unwanted halos. I usually use the **Matte None** option, which creates an aliased edge but leaves the internal areas of the image anti-aliased. If I want to anti-alias to a specific color, I make sure the color is in my foreground color swatch and choose **Matte:Foreground Color**.

The **Matte None** option retains all the anti-aliasing inside the image's content, but creates aliased outer edges.

In this example, I chose a peach color as my foreground color. See how ImageReady anti-aliased to this color for me?

In ImageReady, you can make a photograph transparent even if it has a complex background by erasing the background away. This technique involves the use of a layer mask. You create a layer mask by clicking on the **Layer Mask icon** at the bottom of the Layers palette. A layer mask allows you to paint with white or black to erase or restore an image. If you make a mistake and erase too much, you can paint on the layer mask with the opposing color to restore the erasure. When you've erased the image to your liking, you can create a transparency as shown in the above example by accessing the **Optimize palette** and clicking the **Transparency check box**.

GIF Transparency in Fireworks

In Fireworks, you create transparency by using the Export module of the program. If you want to predispose the anti-aliasing to a specific color, you must fill the background of your image with that particular color.

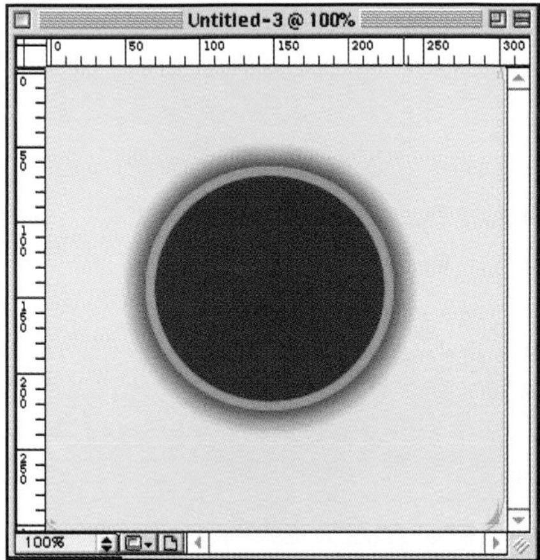

You could create the shape of a solid color that fills the background. Fireworks is a vector program, so it requires the use of a filled shape instead of a background fill color.

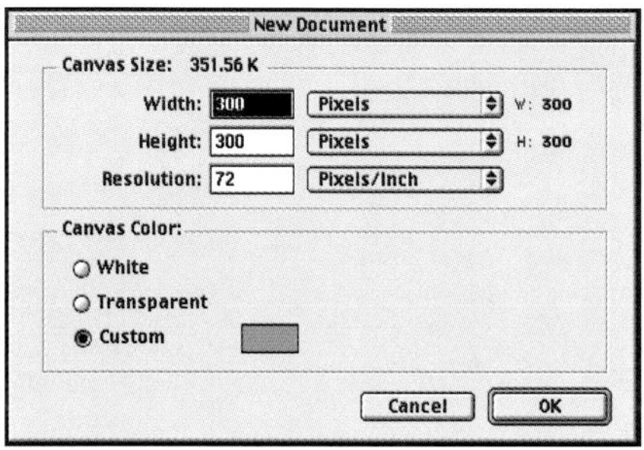

Alternatively, when you request a new document, you can set the background color to a custom choice. This is accessed by the menu **Modify:Document:Canvas Color**.

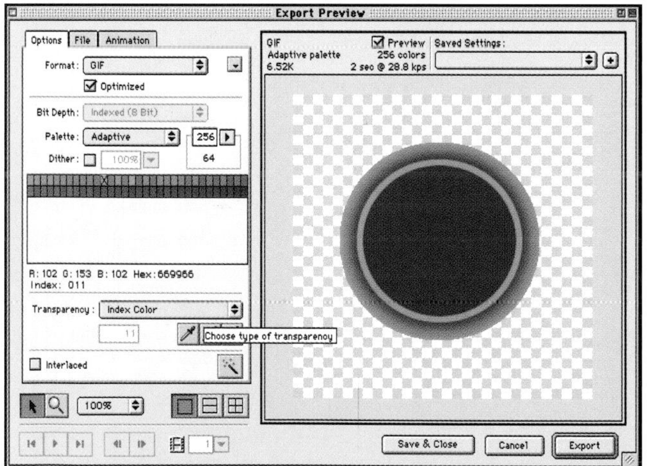

In the Export Preview, you can choose **Transparency** to use the Index Color. This selects whatever color is in the upper-left corner of the image and removes it.

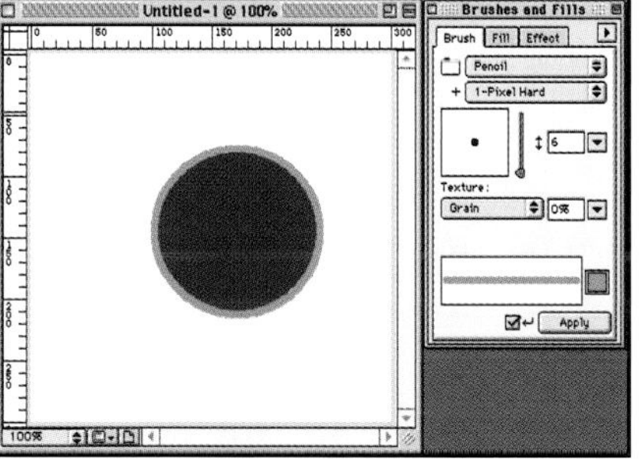

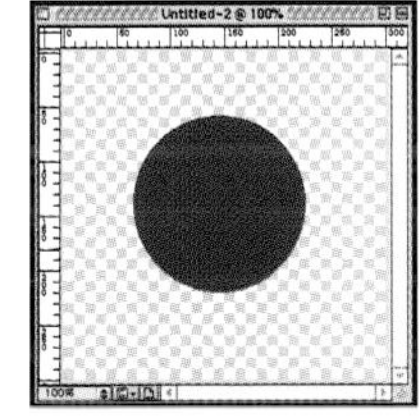

There are a couple of ways to create aliased images in Fireworks. If you have a **stroked graphic**, you can set the Stroked Brush setting to 1-Pixel Hard. If you want to adjust the pixel setting (as I have here), type in higher values or move the value slider. If you have a shape with no stroke (brush weight), you can select the shape and choose **Modify:Edge:Hard Edge**. This converts the fill from its default state of anti-alias to an aliased edge.

GIF Transparency in Photoshop 5.0

There are several methods for creating transparent graphics in Photoshop 5.0. First, however, it's important for you to understand that a GIF must be an 8-bit file. So before you can make a transparent GIF, you must convert your file to 8-bit. The transparency plug-in in Photoshop enables you to convert a 24-bit image to 8-bit, but I've found the palette controls to be less robust than if you first convert the image yourself by selecting **Mode:RGB:Indexed Color**.

Photoshop 5.0 handles transparency by using an Export plug-in. Most Photoshop plug-ins are found under the Filter menu, but the Export plug-in is located under the File menu. To access the GIF89a plug-in, choose **File:Export:Gif 89a Export**.

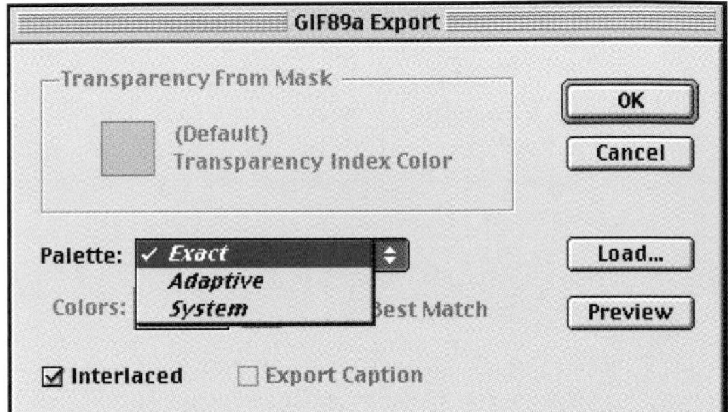

The first task in making a GIF transparency in Photoshop is to convert your 24-bit RGB image to an 8-bit Indexed Color image. If you do this from the GIF89a Export dialog box, you don't get as many options as you do if you convert the image first.

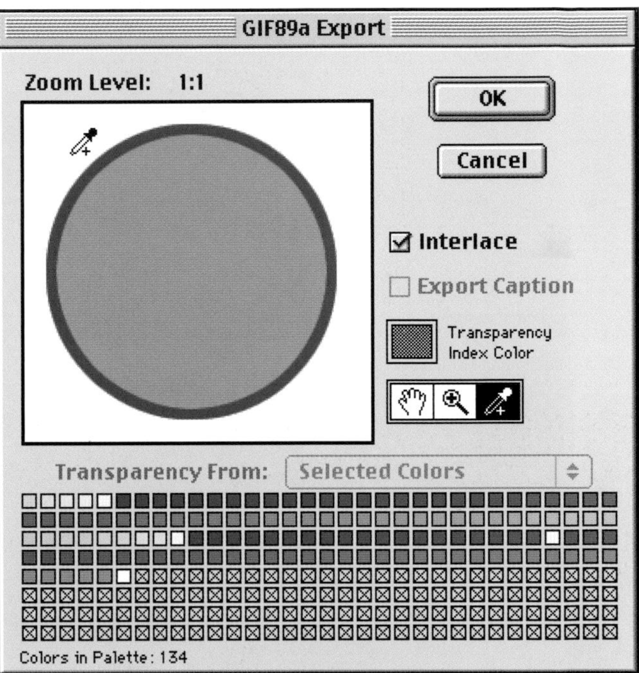

By using the **Mode:RGB:Indexed Color** command in Photoshop 5.0, I converted this graphic to 8-bit. Afterward, I selected **File: Export:GIF89a Export**. From there, you assign transparency by using the Eyedropper tool and clicking on the color(s) you want to remove. (**Hint:** If you hold down the Shift key, you can remove more than one color!) This dialog box offers more features than the plug-in conversion method does.

note

What Is GIF89a?

Photoshop calls its GIF transparency tool the GIF89a Export filter. This refers to the formal specification of GIF that enables transparency: GIF89a. A filter called GIF87a preceded GIF89a; you might occasionally read about it (most likely in the history of the GIF file format). Basically, Photoshop engineers chose to use the formal specification terminology instead of the more common terminology of "transparent GIF." Why? I dunno. But don't let it scare you off. Engineers are like that sometimes. ;-)

Photoshop also allows you to use an alpha channel mask for transparency. An alpha channel mask offers permanent storage of a mask region in Photoshop. Here are simple step-by-step instructions on how to create one.

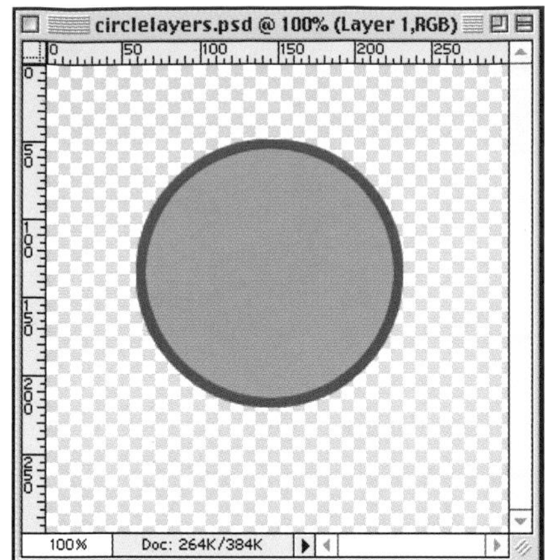

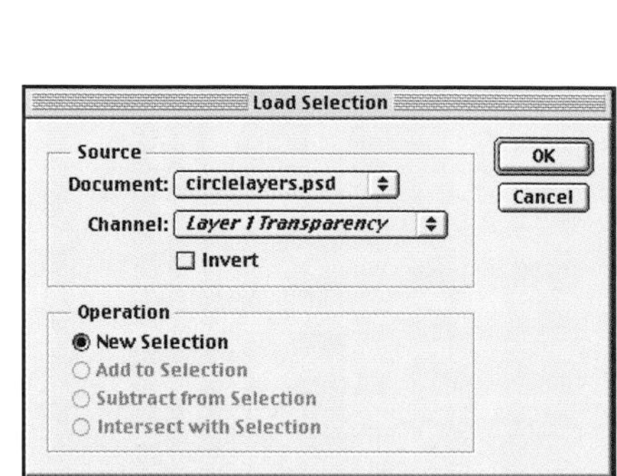

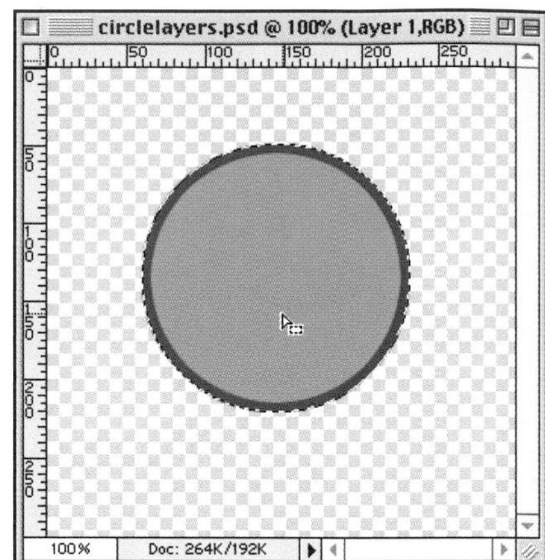

If you highlight a layer in Photoshop that uses transparency (has a checkerboard background), you can access its transparency layer by choosing **Select:Load** and then selecting **Channel:Layer x Transparency** from the Load Selection dialog box. Click OK, and you will see the loaded selection because it will contain marching ants. Marching ants is a cutesy term that means a selection is active in Photoshop; this effect appears as animated dotted lines around your selection.

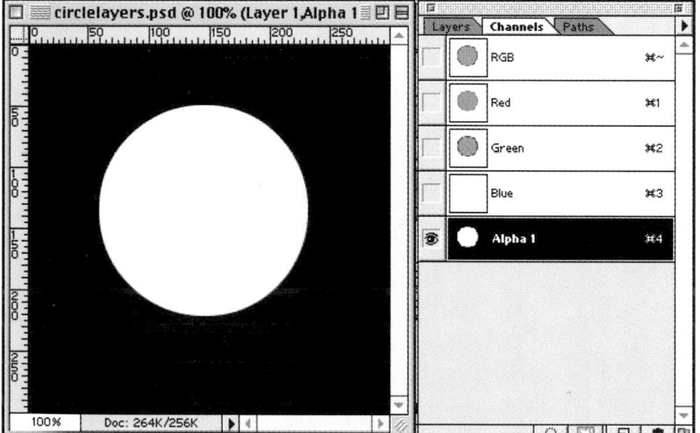

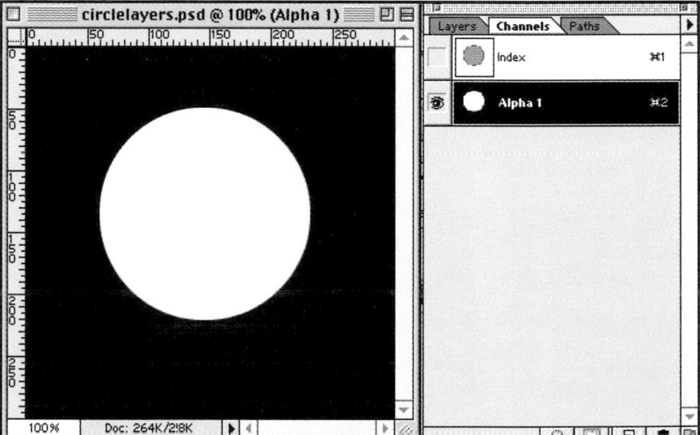

When you see marching ants around an image, choose **Select:Save** and you will be able to store the selection in an alpha channel. The alpha channel is stored as the fourth channel (and higher if you have multiple channels). Because the Red, Green, and Blue channels take up the first three slots, the alpha channel mask is stored in slots four and above. If you convert the image to Indexed Color mode (choose **Image:Mode:Indexed Color**), you can store this same alpha mask in the second channel. The first is reserved for the 8-bit color image.

If you have an image in Photoshop that contains an alpha channel and has been converted to Indexed Color mode, you can choose to base the selection on the alpha instead of using the Eyedropper tool. This means that even if you have complex colors in a background, your alpha mask could remove them (instead of painting them out like I've shown in the ImageReady and Fireworks examples).

PNG Transparency

I discussed the impressive capabilities of the PNG file format in Chapter 5, "Web File Formats." One of the coolest features of PNG is the fact that it supports 8-bit alpha channel transparency. What this means is that it can use any of the 256 color slots for varying degrees of opacity, unlike GIF, which can use only a single black or white for masking and uses all 256 slots for color.

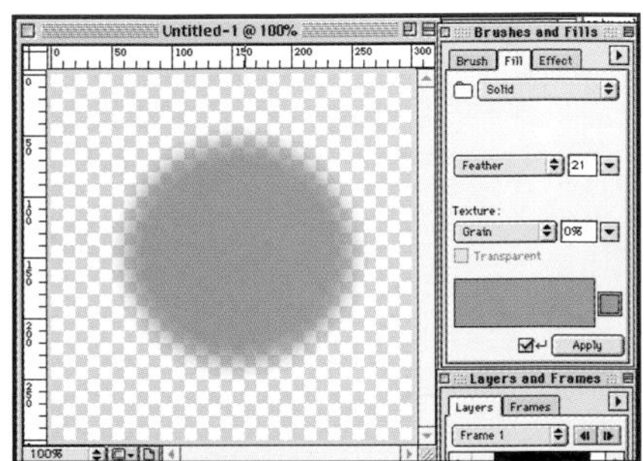

In Fireworks, I created a soft-edged circle by using a Fill Feather of 21 pixels.

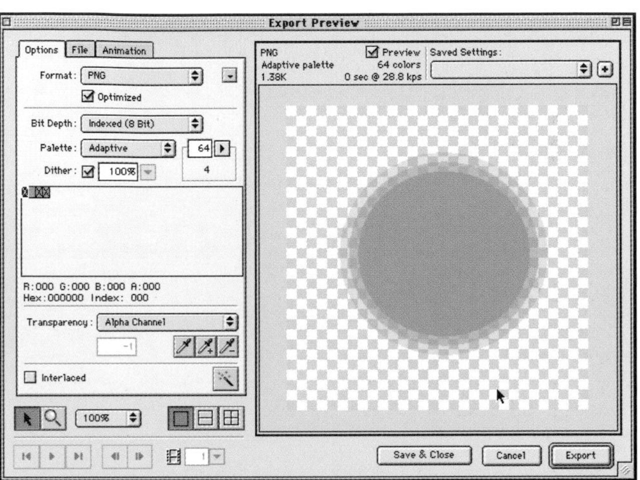

By choosing **File:Export**, I was able to select the PNG file format and choose **Alpha** transparency.

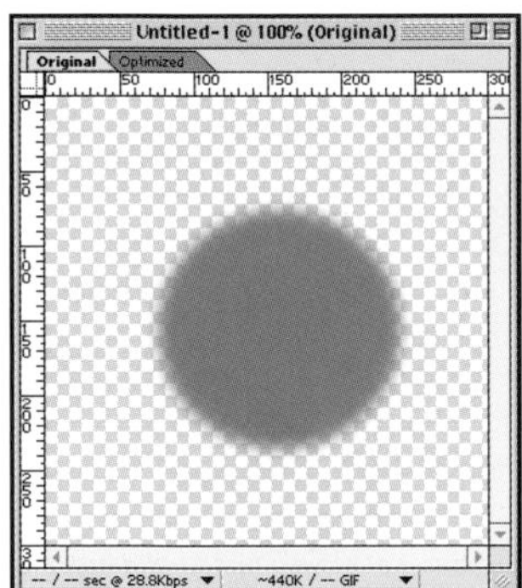

Original in ImageReady.

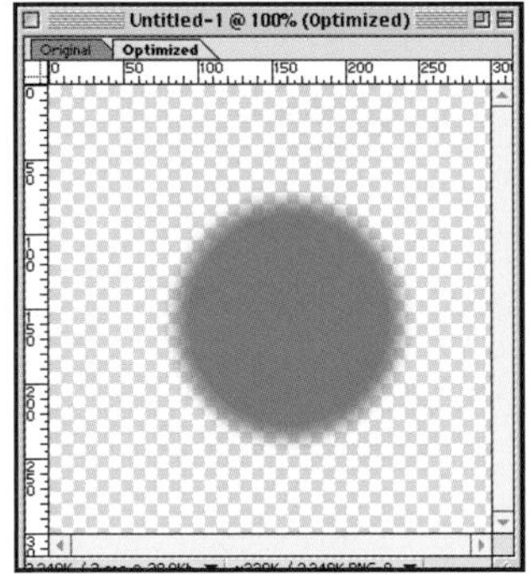

PNG Transparency in ImageReady.

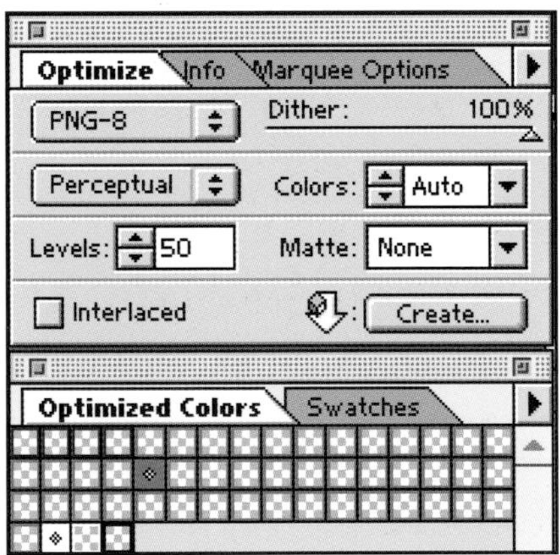

I set **Matte to None** and **Levels to 50** to achieve 50 slots of transparency for one single color.

Both ImageReady and Fireworks allow you to create PNG transparency. With these great tools, the techniques for creating PNG transparency are not difficult. The real problem is finding a browser that can display PNG transparency. If any of you have good contacts at Netscape or Microsoft, let them know that we designer folks would really love a better transparency solution than GIF.

summary Transparent Artwork

Adding transparent graphics to your site will undoubtedly result in a more visually appealing page. The trick is to know how to avoid the unwanted halos and edges that can easily result from anti-aliasing. Here's a summary of the key points in this chapter:

- If you are creating an irregularly shaped graphic against a solid background color in your HTML, don't bother with GIF transparency at all. Use the faking method described earlier; just be sure to match file formats (such as GIF on top of GIF or JPEG on top of JPEG).
- Using aliased edges on your artwork will eliminate the possibility of unwanted halos and edges.
- For glows, drop shadows, and soft-edged artwork, be sure to anti-alias to the target background color.
- If you are going to use a pattern background, anti-alias to the predominant color within the pattern.
- PNG transparency is cool, but it's not supported by the browsers.

Introduction

Rules, Buttons, & Bullets

Chapter Topics

- Rules with HTML
- Rules with Graphics
- Clip Art Rules
- Bullets with HTML
- Bullets with Graphics
- Using Layer Effects
- Button Clip Art

14

This chapter covers how to make rules, bullets, and buttons with standard HTML tags and/or custom graphics. These types of images and conventions have a purpose other than decoration, although a well-designed rule, button or bullet can easily have visual appeal as well as function. The point of making these types of graphics and HTML tags is to create order, hierarchy, and visual cues for navigation.

You will find rules and bullets in print design, but the techniques for creating them are different for the Web. In print, you can easily highlight information using multiple colored inks, or a splash of color behind some text. This is possible on the Web, too, but might involve code instead of picture boxes and text effects.

The area of rules, buttons, and bullets offers a creative playing field,—you can use just about any style graphic for these types of effects. In addition to HTML code and examples, this chapter will cover a variety of imaging techniques for creating "clickable" graphics.

Horizontal Rules

A horizontal rule that serves as a page divider is something you'll rarely see in print design. These divider rules are commonly observed across Web sites the world over, however, because they are part of the formal HTML specification. Some are embossed, some are thick, some are thin, and some are colored or have different shapes. The Web term for these lines is horizontal rule, and they are used for many things:

- Defining a page break
- Completing an idea
- Beginning a list
- Separating one picture from another

Horizontal rules are used often—some might even say too often. That's no wonder, if you ask me. Web pages have no set length like printed pages. The visual techniques and metaphors available to print designers—such as using a block of color behind text or images, changing the text color in an isolated paragraph or sidebar, or using a different screened-back image or picture frame to separate an idea or theme—are possible on the Web, but not nearly so easy as a simple HTML rule.

If you want to add horizontal rules to your pages, you have some choices. You can use HTML code, or you can insert your own artwork to make custom horizontal rules, and vertical rules, too. When all else fails, there are also libraries of horizontal rule clip art.

Horizontal Rules, the HTML Way

The basic HTML standard horizontal rule tag looks like this: <HR>. Here it is in the context of code.

```
<HTML>
<BODY>
Some Text
<HR>
Some More Text
</BODY>
</HTML>
```

Some Text

Some More Text

This will put an embossed, double-pixel line horizontally through your page at whatever point you insert it into an HTML document. If you stretch your browser window wider, the horizontal rule will get wider; vice versa if you narrow your window. Horizontal rules have no set width, except to fill the horizontal distance of your browser screen.

Sometimes you might want to add some breathing room because the horizontal rule will butt up underneath whatever text or image that was in the HTML code before it. The following code adds a row of empty space above and beneath the rule.

```
<HTML>
<BODY>
Some Text
<P>
<HR>
<P>
Some More Text
</BODY>
</HTML>
```

Some Text

Some More Text

If you want to add more breathing room between your text and rules, insert a paragraph break with the P tag.

Fancier Horizontal Rule Tags

An advanced course in horizontal rule-making:

- Changing the rule's width
- Changing the rule's weight (thickness)
- Changing both the rule's width and weight
- Left-aligning the rule
- Eliminating fake emboss shading

Notice that if you define a width, the resulting horizontal rule is automatically centered. Any value you put after the = (equals) sign tells the rule how wide to be in pixels.

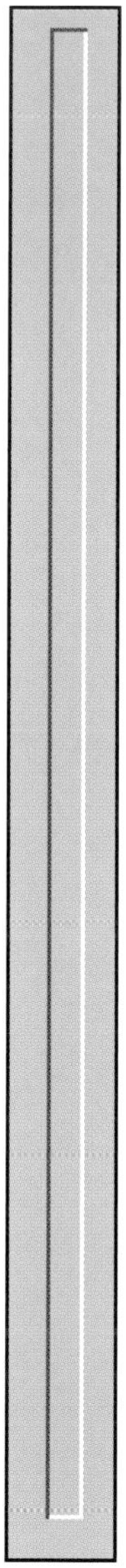

<HR WIDTH=10 SIZE=400> Horizontal rules don't have to be horizontal, if you know how to change the width and size.

Here is the code which tells the rule to be 25 pixels wide:

```
<HR WIDTH="25">
```

Using a WIDTH attribute can adjust the length of the line. Notice that if you define a width, the resulting horizontal rule is automatically centered. Any value you put after the = (equals) sign tells the rule how wide to be in pixels.

The following code changes the weight, or thickness, of the line. Notice that this stretches the length of a page:

```
<HR SIZE="10">
```

By changing the SIZE attribute, the entire line gets thicker.

The following code changes the thickness and width at the same time. Here's an example that shows the results of code specifying the rule to be a square (equal height and width):

```
<HR SIZE="25" WIDTH="25">
```

By changing the size and width together, you can make other rectalinear shapes like this square.

The following aligns the square left and sizes it at 10 pixels high and 10 pixels wide:

```
<HR ALIGN=LEFT SIZE="10" WIDTH="10">
```

You can use alignment tags on horizontal rules, too.

Look Ma, no fake emboss shading:

```
<HR NOSHADE>
```

The NOSHADE attribute creates a black line.

Horizontal Rules and Background Tiles

If you include a background tile on your Web page and insert horizontal rules, the embossed effect will show through the tile.

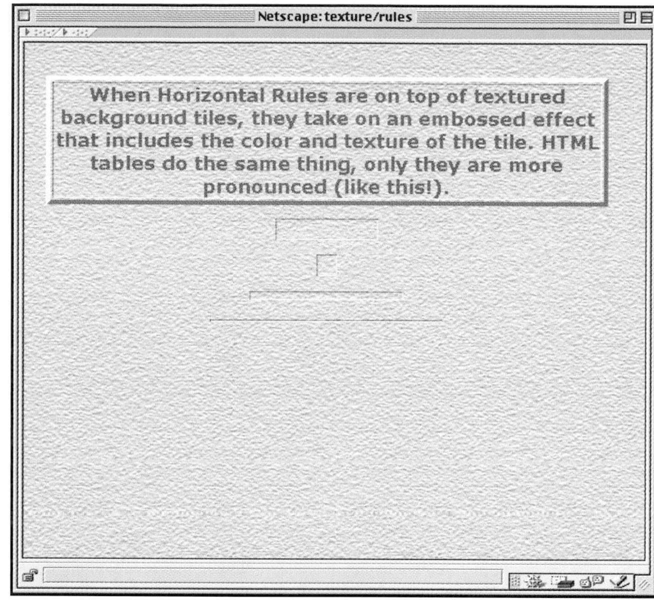

This example shows the source tile and the HTML page in which it was used, along with horizontal rules and tables.

Horizontal Rules the Do-It-Yourself Way

Anything gets old when you see it too often, and horizontal rules are no exception. If you want to be a little more creative, here are some tips to creating custom artwork to design your own rules. When you create your own horizontal rule art, your artwork dictates the length, width, and height. It's a graphic like any other graphic. It can be aliased, anti-aliased, a GIF, a JPEG, interlaced, transparent, blurred, 2D, 3D—you name it. If you know how to make it, it can be a horizontal rule.

To include a graphic as a horizontal rule, the HTML code would be

```
<IMG SRC="your_horizontal_rule_art_here.gif">
```

Using Photoshop 5.0 to Create Custom Rule Art

The latest version of Photoshop supports many interesting techniques for horizontal rule making. The following exercises will teach you a variety of methods.

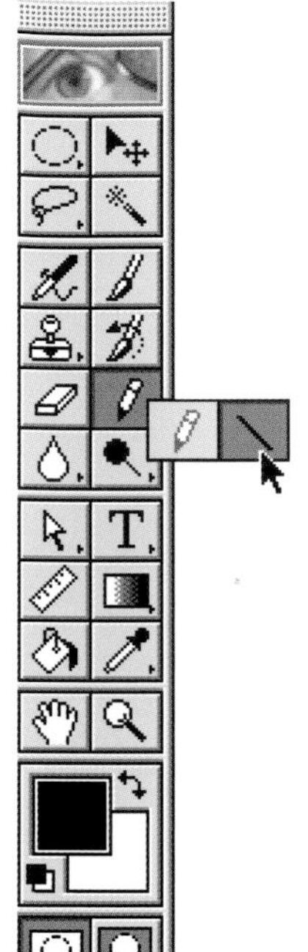

The **Line tool** is hid den as a pop-out menu from the Pencil tool. Double-clicking on the **Line** tool (once selected) brings up the **Line Options** palette.

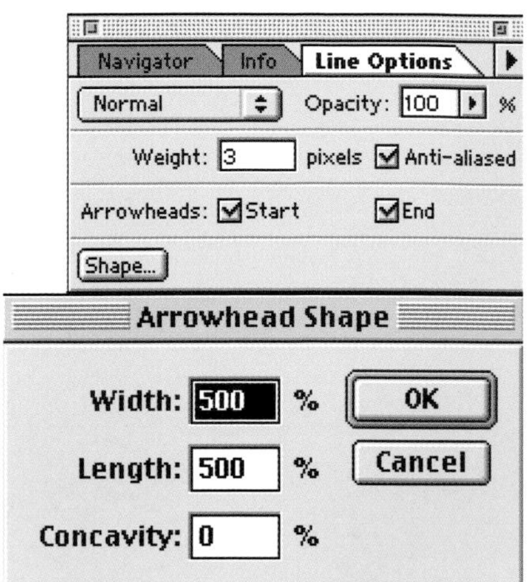

The **Line Options palette** allows you to set up the weight of the line and will also enable Arrowheads. By clicking the **Shape** button, the Arrowhead Shape window appears where you can set custom values.

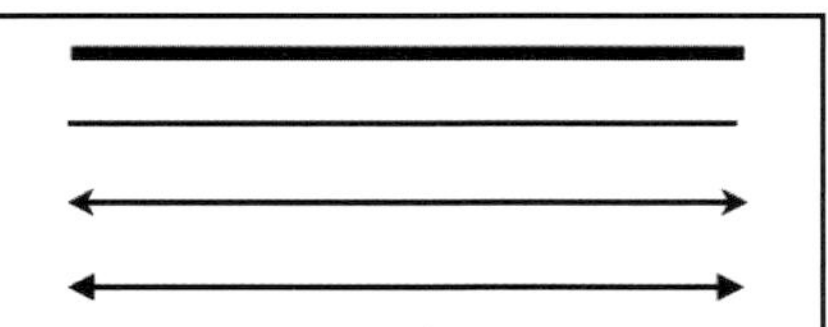

If you draw your horizontal lines on a transparent layer in Photoshop, you will have the maximum amount of design flexibility.

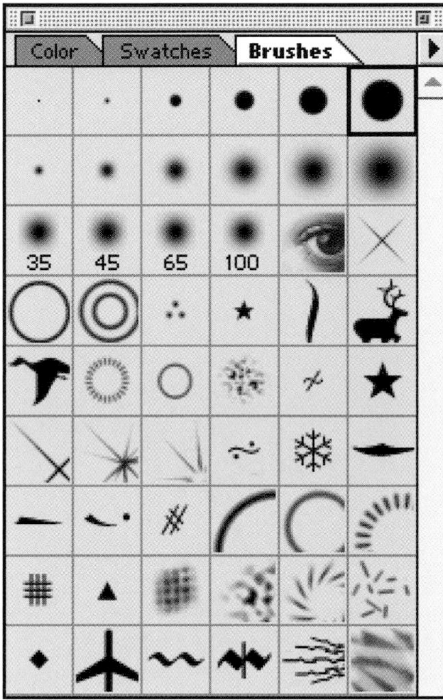

In Photoshop, you can load **multiple brush sets**. The version shown here ships free with the program. If you use the upper right arrow to access the pop-up selection menu, you can locate this brush set. Find the Photoshop 5.0 folder, and then select **Goodies:Brushes:Assorted Brushes**.

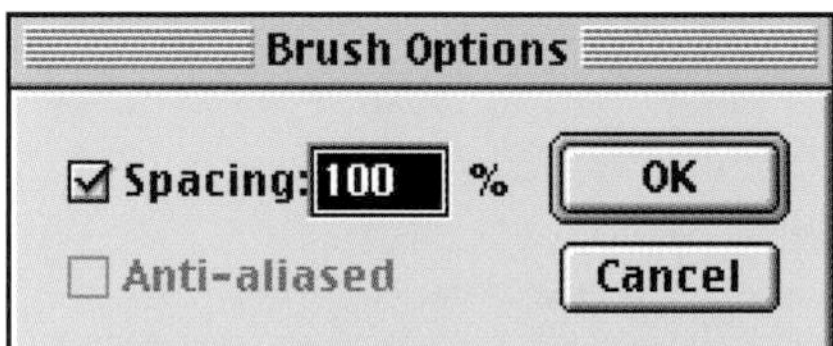

By double-clicking on a single brush shape, you access the **Brush Options dialog box**. Change the spacing to 100% and try drawing a straight line with your brush tool. **Hint:** The Shift key will constrain the horizontal movement to produce a perfectly straight line. The results will produce a dotted line with a custom brush.

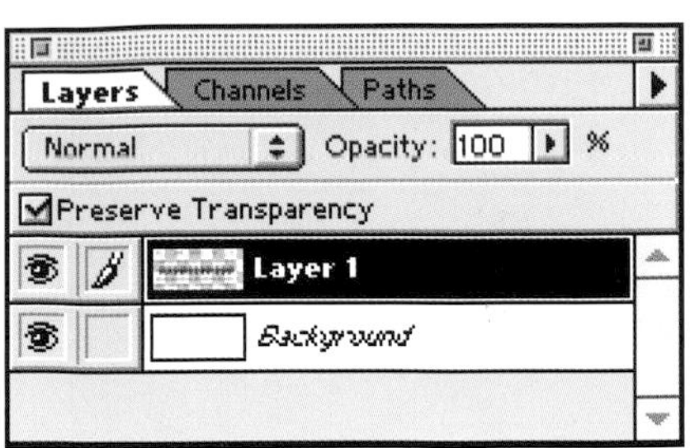

Notice how **Preserve Transparency** is checked? This allows me to recolor black-and-white brush artwork.

Using a paintbrush, I was able to color these examples after I had created them in black, white, and grayscale.

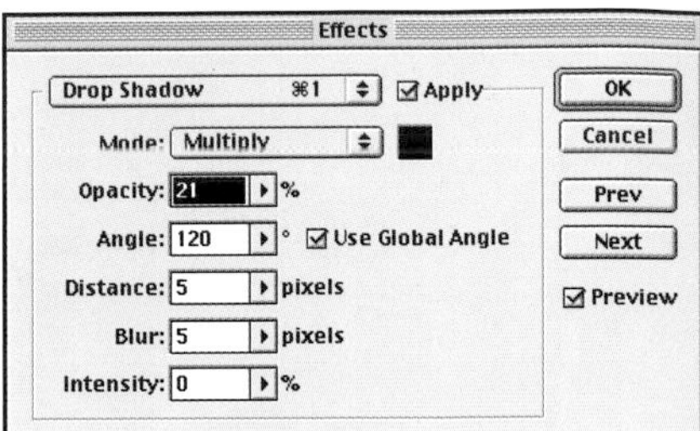

By choosing **Layer:Effects:Drop Shadow**, I was able to apply a **drop shadow** to the artwork at these settings. Had the artwork been on a nontransparent layer, this would not have worked.

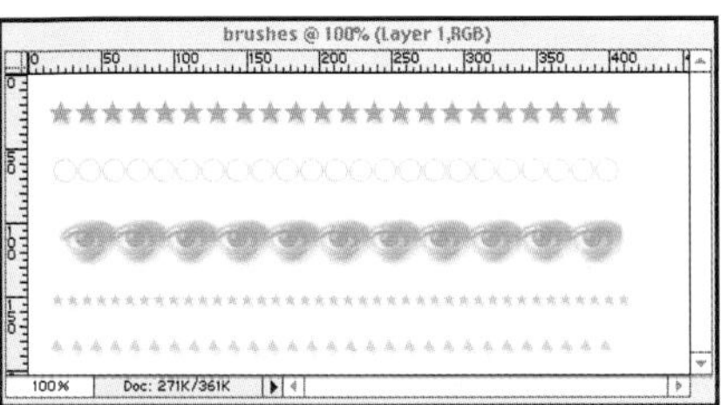

The finished result is more dimensional than the version without a drop shadow.

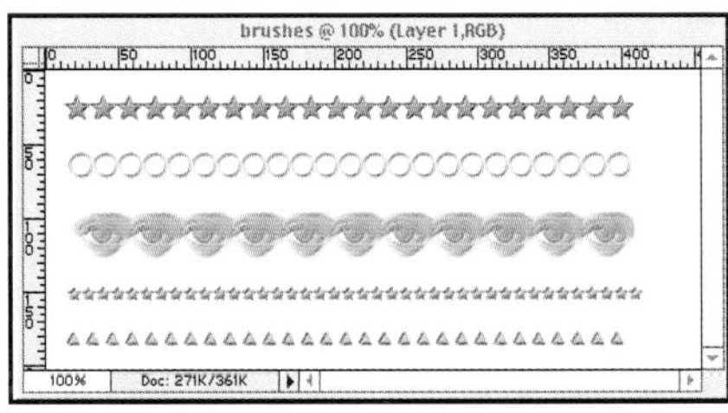

This shows the same artwork with the **Pillow Emboss** setting is under the **Layer:Effects:Emboss** setting.

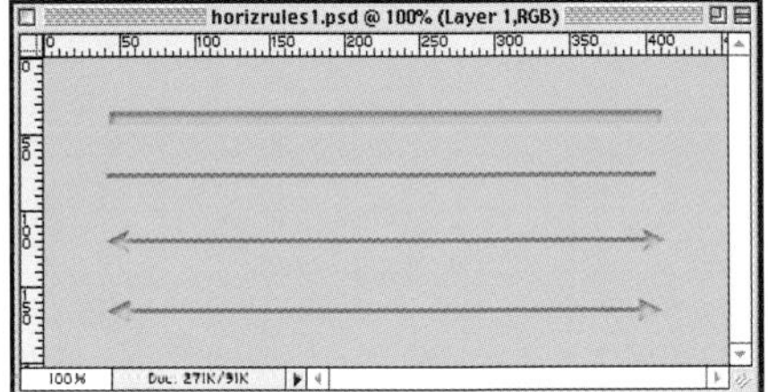

The **Inner Shadow** setting is under the **Layer:Effects:Inner Shadow** menu.

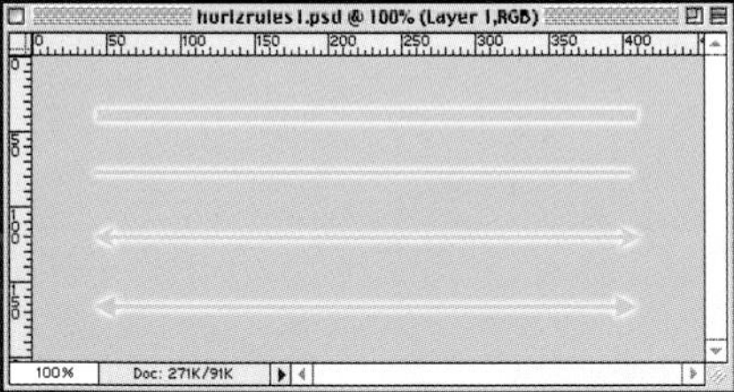

The **Outer Glow** setting is under the **Layer:Effects:Glow** menu with "Outer Glow" selected.

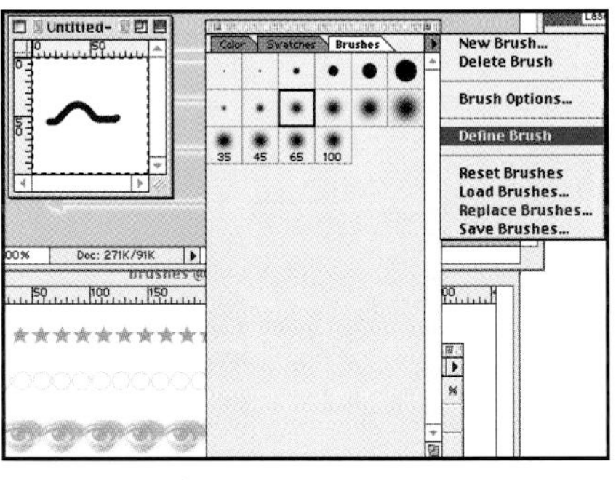

If you want to create your own **custom brushes** in Photoshop, it's very easy. Draw a shape in grayscale and select it. Click on the Brushes palette pop-up menu to select **Define Brush**. The new brush will be stored inside whichever brush set is open.

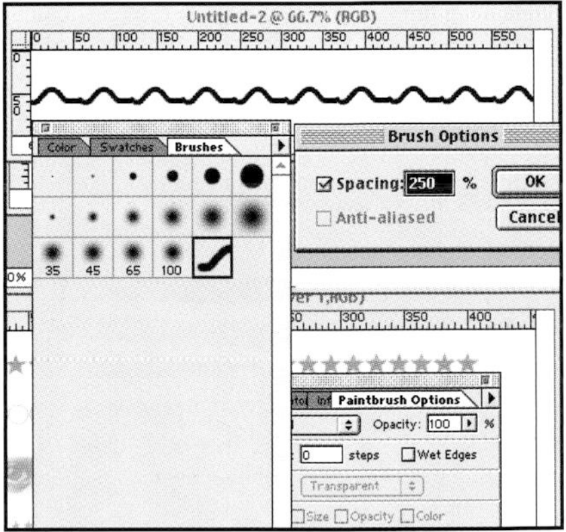

By adjusting the Brush Options setting to a custom setting, this new brush can be adjusted for a tiled effect, such as shown above.

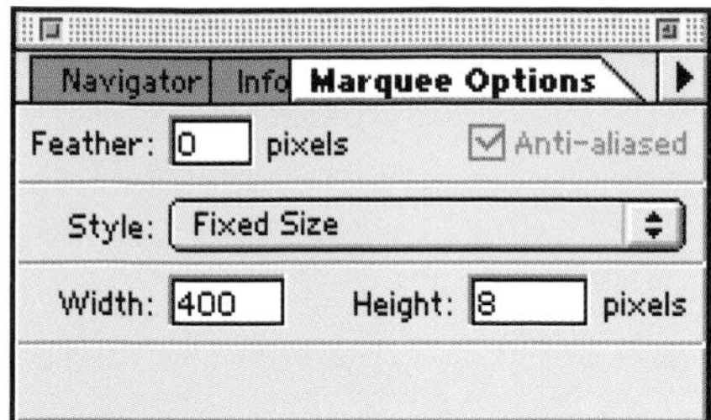

By double-clicking on the selection marquee tool, I chose to work with a fixed size. Using the **Linear Gradient tool**, I created a dimensional bar. Because the Photoshop gradient only has a Foreground to Background setting, I created a top and bottom selection so I could fill from gray to white and then change the direction from white to gray on the second selection. This created a rounded-looking shape to the straight line.

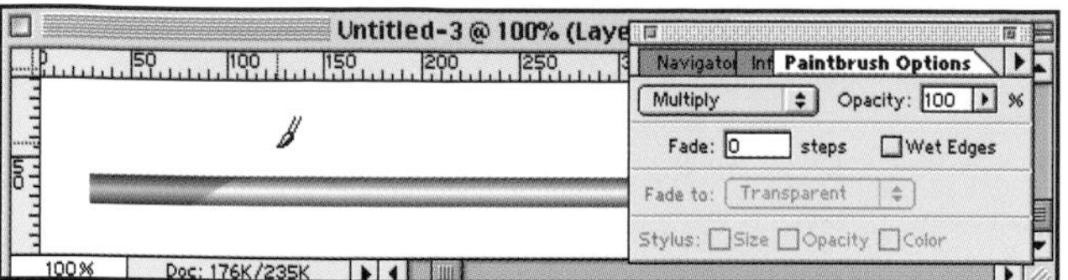

Once you have this shape made, you can paint on top of it. If you use the **Multiply mode**, the paint will show through the rounded line. **Hint:** Multiply will not change the color of pure white or pure black. I intentionally made this artwork using dark and light grays so that I could recolor it more successfully using this method.

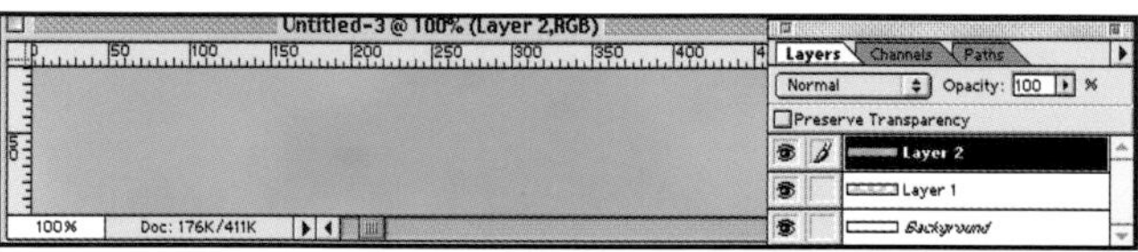

Create or import a layer above layer of a pattern or texture.

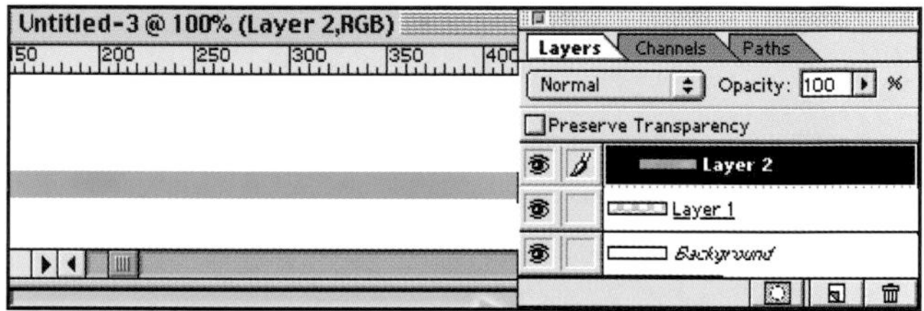

Hold down the **Option key between the two layers**. Your cursor should change to indicate you are in the correct spot. When you click there, a dotted line should appear between the layers.

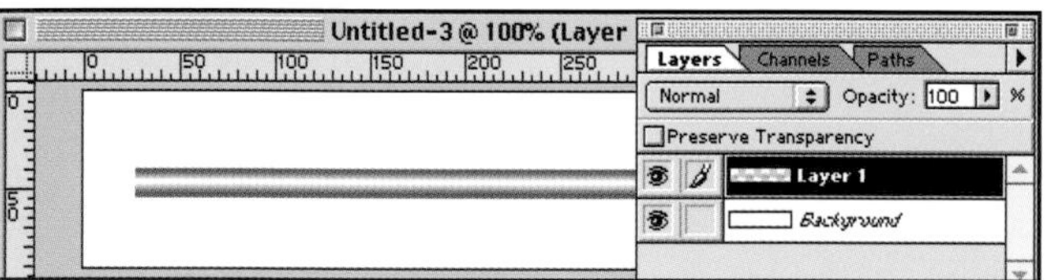

Another effect works with Clipping Layers. Begin with a grayscale dimensional rule, such as this one.

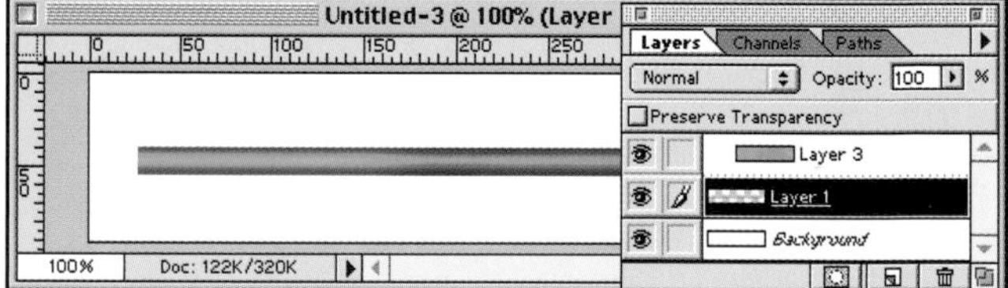

If you turn the top layer to **Multiply mode**, the textured effect will show through. Once again, it's best not to work with pure blacks or whites because they will not recolor using the Multiply effect.

Vertical Rules

Creating vertical rules is not an easy task in the land of Web graphics. Making the custom artwork is identical to making any other custom artwork in this chapter; that is not the problem.

Vertical lines can be aligned with HTML tables, or you can make a background tile with a single stripe down the left side.

How do you get vertical lines aligned to a Web page? There is no easy way to assign vertical columns using HTML! Check out the lesson on how to position vertical ruled lines in Chapter 17, "Alignment & Tables."

Clip Art Rules, Too

There are many kind, generous souls on the Web who lend their wares for free. Or other gifted souls who might charge for their art so that they can do what they're good at—satisfy you and me—and still feed themselves and their families. Clip art is a wondrous thing in a pinch, and with tools like Photoshop (and many other image editors), there's no end to the cool ways you can personalize clip art files. Make sure that the images are royalty free in the respective licensing agreements if you are going to modify them. Some authors have stipulations that must be honored. Read the readmes! Here are some popular clip art collections:

Gifs R Us

Jay Boersma's prolific image collection:
http://www.ecn.bgu.edu/users/gas52r0/Jay/home.html

Sandra's Clip Art Server

A great resource for clip art over the Net
http://www.cs.yale.edu/homes/sjl/clipart.html
http://www.cbil.vcu.edu:8080/gifs/bullet.html

Yahoo Search for Clip Art

A great bet to find the best and latest clip art listings:
http://www.yahoo.com/Computers_and_Internet/Graphics/Clip Art

Bullets

Lists of one type or another are pretty popular in all forms of publishing, including Web publishing. Bullets are often used to emphasize list items. On the Web bullets can look standardized, with solid circles in front of text (much like those generated by a word processor), or they can include custom artwork that looks more typical of a CD-ROM or magazine page layout. Creating custom bullets is similar to creating custom horizontal rules. Basically, any artwork that you're capable of creating is a candidate for bullet art.

When designing bulleted lists for the Web, you can choose from either HTML bullets or image-based bullets. **HTML bullets** are created by using code tags that identify the type of list you are creating; such bullets appear as basic circles or squares. **Image-based bullets** are those you generate from clip art or your own artwork, and they can be used to enhance a list or provide added functionality, such as links.

HTML Bulleted Lists

Using HTML-based bullets is certainly less work than creating your own custom artwork. Simple and clean design often looks best without a lot of custom artwork on a page. There will be many instances where an HTML-based bullet or indent will do the job more effectively than custom bullet artwork.

To create a list with solid circle bullets, use the UL tag, which stands for Unordered List. To create such a bulleted list within text items, use the UL tag along with the LI (List Item) tag, as shown in the following code:

```
<P>
<UL>
<LI> The first thinga-dingy
<LI> The second thinga-dingy
<LI> The third thinga-dingy
</UL>
```

Using the "unordered" list tags , and "list item" tags produces this result:

- The first thinga-dingy
- The second thinga-dingy
- The third thinga-dingy

The results of using the <UL> tag.

Lists can be nested by inserting a new tag where you want the list to indent or move to another level. The following code uses an additional UL tag to create a bulleted list nested within another bulleted list:

```
<P>
<UL>
<LI> The first thinga-dingy
<LI> The second thinga-dingy
<LI> The third thinga-dingy
<UL>
<LI> More types of thinga-dingies
<LI> Yet More types of thinga-dingies
<LI> Even more types of thinga-dingies
</UL>
```

You can nest lists within lists, by repeating the "ordered" or "unordered" list tags. The results look like this:

- The first thinga-dingy
- The second thinga-dingy
- The third thinga-dingy
  - More types of thinga-dingies
  - Yet More types of thinga-dingies
  - Even more types of thinga-dingies

You can nest bulleted points by adding multiple UL tags before the close /UL tag.

You can have the items in your list be links to other pages or sites by using the <A HREF></A> tag within an organized list or an unordered list. The following code shows how to use link tags to include links within a bulleted list:

```
<P>
<UL>
<LI> <A HREF="http://www.domain.com">The first
thinga-dingy</A>
<LI> <A HREF="http://www.domain.com">The second
thinga-dingy</A>
<LI> <A HREF="http://www.domain.com">The third
thinga-dingy</A>
</UL>
```

Including links within a list is a matter of using link tags within lists. The results look like this:

- The first thinga-dingy
- The second thinga-dingy
- The third thinga-dingy

The items in your list can be straight text or hypertext by changing a few tags.

Creating Ordered and Definition Lists

At times, you might not want your lists to be preceded with bullets. When creating a list of steps to be followed in order, for example, using numbers rather than bullets will help get your point across. Such numbered lists are called ordered lists. Likewise, lists such as glossaries can appear with indents rather than bullets or numbers. These lists are known as definition lists.

To make a list that automatically generates numbers in front of its items, use the OL (**o**rdered **l**ist) tag. The following code lines show how to use the OL code to produce a numbered list:

```
<P>
<OL>
<LI> The first thinga-dingy
<LI> The second thinga-dingy
<LI> The third thinga-dingy
</OL>
<P>
```

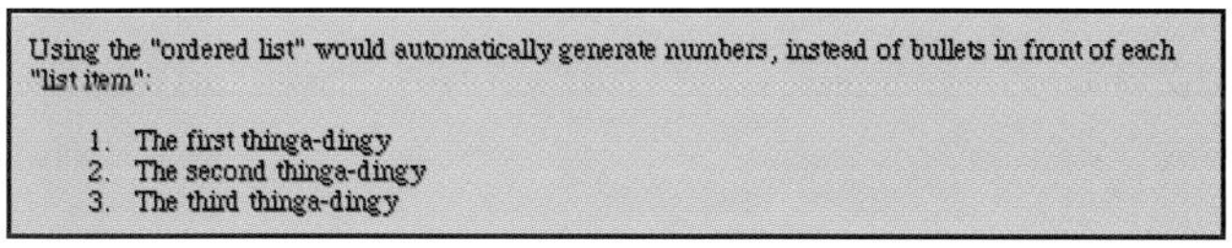

Using the "ordered list" would automatically generate numbers, instead of bullets in front of each "list item":

1. The first thinga-dingy
2. The second thinga-dingy
3. The third thinga-dingy

The OL tag generates ordered (numbered) lists.

If you want to indent items in a list without seeing a bullet shape, you may want to use a DL (Definition List) tag instead of creating an organized list or unordered list. You use the DT tag for the flush left items and the DD tag for the indented items, as shown in the following code:

```
<DL>
<DT>
Thingy Dingies<P>
<DD>The first thinga-dingy
<DD>The second thinga-dingy
<DD>The second thinga-dingy
</DL>
```

Thingy Dingies

The first thinga-dingy
The second thinga-dingy
The second thinga-dingy

Using the DL definition list tags creates indented lists.

If you want to change the shape of the automatically generated bullets, you can use the TYPE=circle or TYPE= square tags, as shown in the following code:

```
<UL>
<LI TYPE=circle>Circle-shaped Bullet
<LI TYPE=square>Square-shaped Bullet
</UL>
```

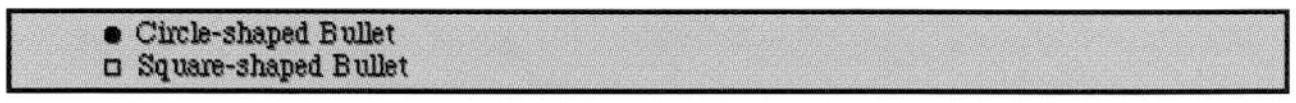

● Circle-shaped Bullet
□ Square-shaped Bullet

Using the TYPE attribute, you can change the shape of HTML generated bullets.

You can also set up organized lists by using alphabetic and Roman numeric criteria by adding the variations shown in the following table:

Organized Lists		
Tag	**Type**	**Example**
TYPE=1	Numbers	1, 2, 3
TYPE=A	Uppercase letters	A, B, C
TYPE=a	Lowercase letters	a, b, c
TYPE=I	Uppercase Roman numerals	I, II, III
TYPE=i	Lowercase Roman numerals	i, ii, iii

The following code shows variations of the TYPE tag, which produces these results:

code

```
<OL>
<LI TYPE=1> Thingy One
<LI TYPE=1> Thingy Two
<LI TYPE=1> Thingy Three
<p>
<LI TYPE=A> Thingy One
<LI TYPE=A> Thingy Two
<LI TYPE=A> Thingy Three
<p>
<LI TYPE=a> Thingy One
<LI TYPE=a> Thingy Two
<LI TYPE=a> Thingy Three
<p>
<LI TYPE=I> Thingy One
<LI TYPE=I> Thingy Two
<LI TYPE=I> Thingy Three
<P>
<LI TYPE=i> Thingy One
<LI TYPE=i> Thingy Two
<LI TYPE=i> Thingy Three
```

Variations on the "type" tag.

1. Thingy One
2. Thingy Two
3. Thingy Three

D. Thingy One
E. Thingy Two
F. Thingy Three

g. Thingy One
h. Thingy Two
i. Thingy Three

X. Thingy One
XI. Thingy Two
XII. Thingy Three

xiii. Thingy One
xiv. Thingy Two
xv. Thingy Three

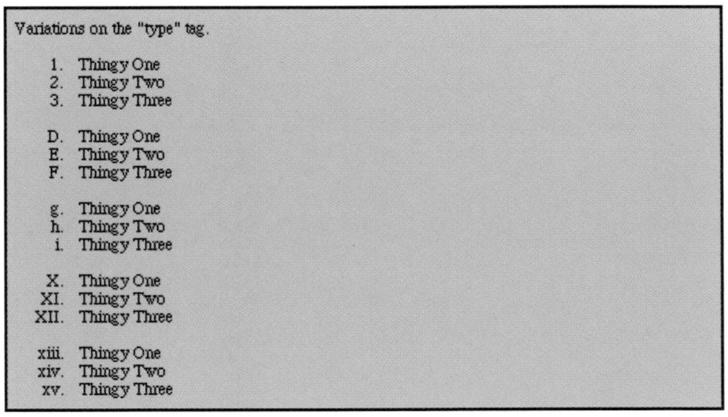

An example of all the different types of HTML-generated bullets.

Creating Custom-Made Bullets

If you want to use bullets that show more creativity than the basic square or circle, or if you need added linking functionality, you can create your own custom-made bullets. Custom-made bullets can be ornamental, where their sole purpose is to decorate the beginning of a list item. Or they can be functional, where they serve as icons that link you to another page or site.

If you plan to make your own artwork or use clip art for buttons, you'll need to use different HTML tags to make the art behave as you want. For visual enhancement only, use the IMG SRC tag to include image-based bullets at the front of a list, as shown in the following code example. You won't use the OL or the UL tags because the image itself is what is creating both the bullet and the indent. Note that you do have to put a BR tag at the end of each list item to tell the browser to jump to a new line for the next entry in the list. This wasn't necessary when working with the HTML tags because it's a built-in part of the list functionality. I've also used an alignment tag (see Chapter 17, "Alignment & Tables") to flow the type properly next to the artwork. Here's the code.

```
<IMG SRC="rarrow.gif" ALIGN=
MIDDLE> Important Item One<BR>
<IMG SRC=" rarrow.gif" ALIGN=
MIDDLE > Important Item Two<BR>
<IMG SRC=" rarrow.gif" ALIGN=
MIDDLE> Important Item Three<BR>
<IMG SRC=" rarrow.gif"ALIGN=
MIDDLE> Important Item Four<BR>
```

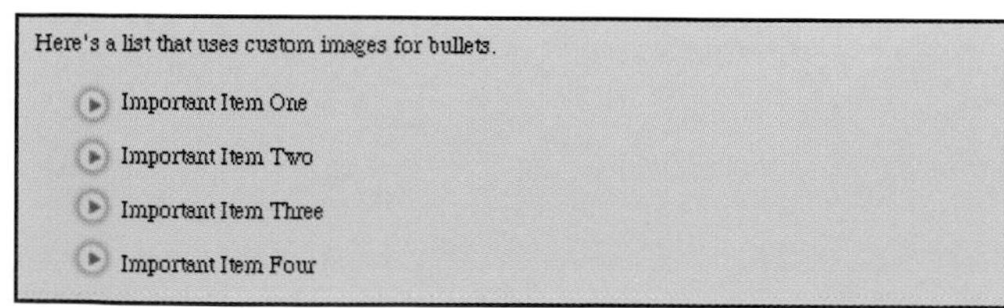

This example shows the result of using an IMG SRC instead of HTML-generated bullets. The red arrow (rarrow.gif) is a separate piece of art that's been used multiple times on this page.

If you want to use the bullets as icons to link to another site or page, use the <A HREF></A> tag, as shown in the following code example. Because linked images typically have a blue border around them, you'll want to use the BORDER="0" tag inside the IMG SRC tag. (Read more about this in Chapter 11, "Linking Basics.") Note the hand-shaped cursor on the snake in the following image. Your viewer's cursor will change to this when gliding over a linked image to let the viewer know the image is a link.

```
<P>
<A HREF><IMG SRC="lynda.gif" ALIGN=MIDDLE BOR-
DER="0"></A> Lynda<BR>
<A HREF><IMG SRC="jamie.gif" ALIGN=MIDDLE BOR-
DER="0"></A> Jamie<BR>
<A HREF><IMG SRC="stinky.gif" ALIGN=MIDDLE BOR-
DER="0"></A>Stinky<BR>
<A HREF><IMG SRC="elmers.gif" ALIGN=MIDDLE
BORDER="0"></A> Elmers<BR>
<A HREF><IMG SRC="jasonjr.gif" ALIGN=MIDDLE BOR-
DER="0"></A> Jason Jr.<BR>
<A HREF><IMG SRC="climber.gif"
ALIGN=MIDDLE BORDER="0"></A>Climber<BR>
<A HREF><IMG SRC="sam.gif"
ALIGN=MIDDLE
BORDER="0"></A>Sam (whose tail is growing back)<BR>
```

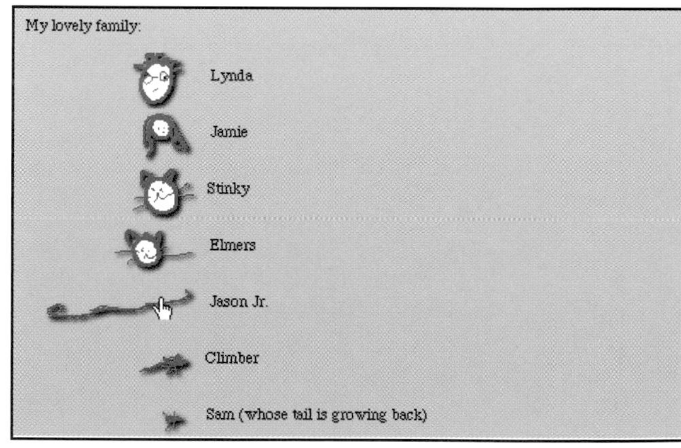

This example shows using the IMG SRC tag again, but changing the artwork inside each tag.

Creating Custom Bullet Art

Any paint program provides a good experimentation ground for making custom bullet artwork. There are no specific guidelines except to keep in mind the scale of the type the bullets will precede. It's very difficult to design anything with much detail that is small enough to match the scale of 12-point type, such as those typically generated by HTML. If you want to make larger icons for custom bullets, be sure to enlarge the type in the list as well. More info on controlling type size is available in Chapter 16, "Web Typography."

Here are some tips I can share from my bullet-making explorations, but please don't let them limit your imagination.

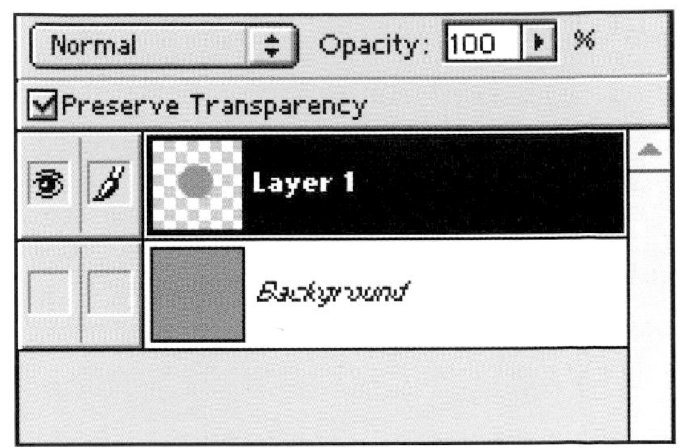

The source artwork for all the examples here was a solid background with the same color circle on a layer above.

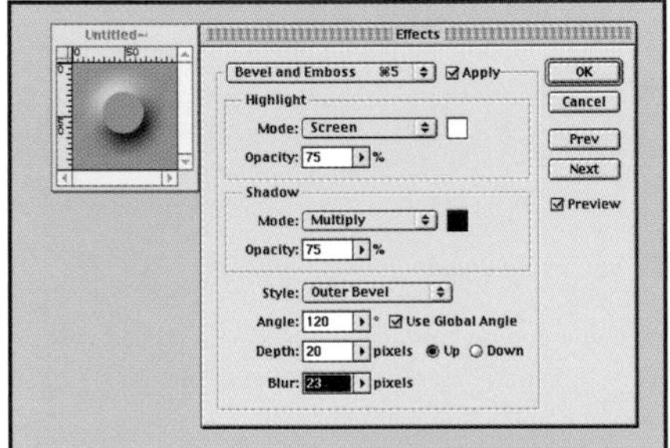

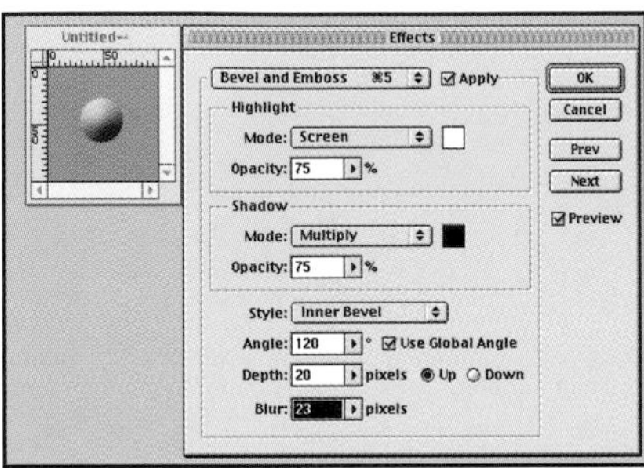

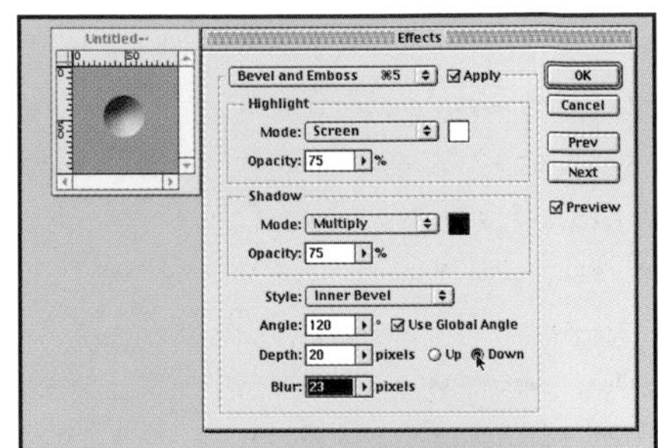

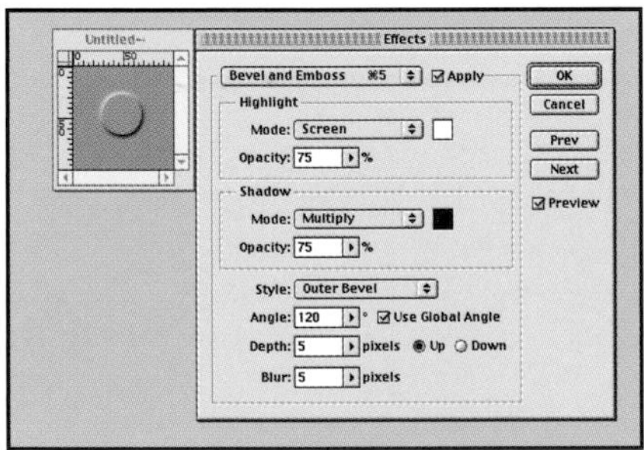

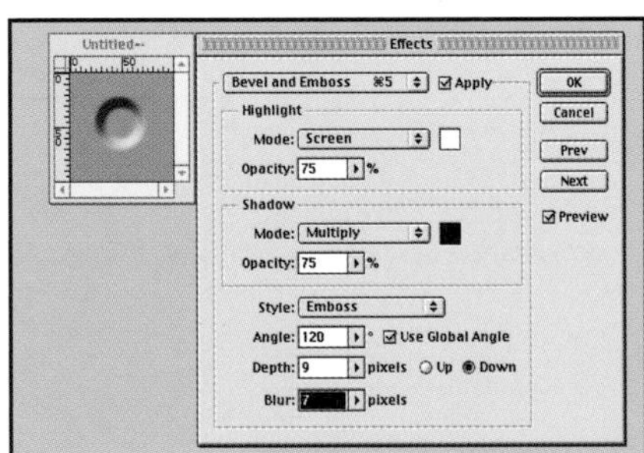

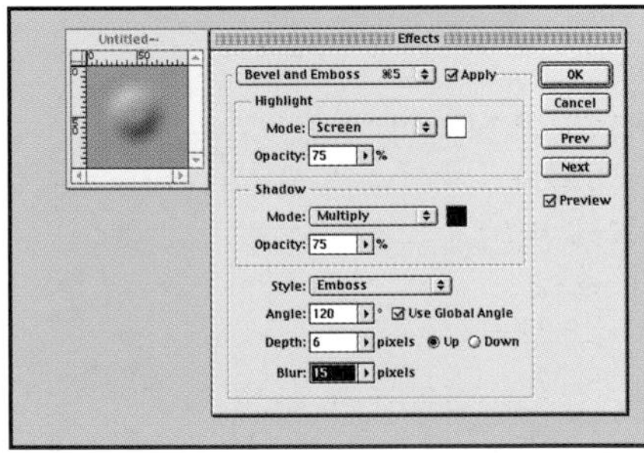

The preceding button examples were created using the **Layer:Effects** menu. By changing the Blur and Depth settings, you can see the possibilities for many variations on a theme.

Buttons Using Photoshop's Layer Effect Settings

A button is usually larger than a bullet and has the larger purpose of navigation instead of simply highlighting a point within a list. Buttons come in all varieties and shapes, and there is no one right or wrong way to make them.

Photoshop's Layer Effects automate many of the imaging processes that are popular for making buttons. The following examples include the source artwork and Layer Effect settings so that you can try these techniques on your own. Don't be afraid to play with the presets on the Layer Effect settings. If you look closely at the values and settings in these examples, you'll see a variety of alterations to the defaults.

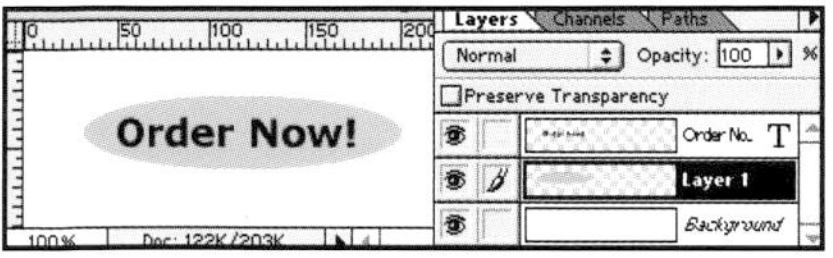

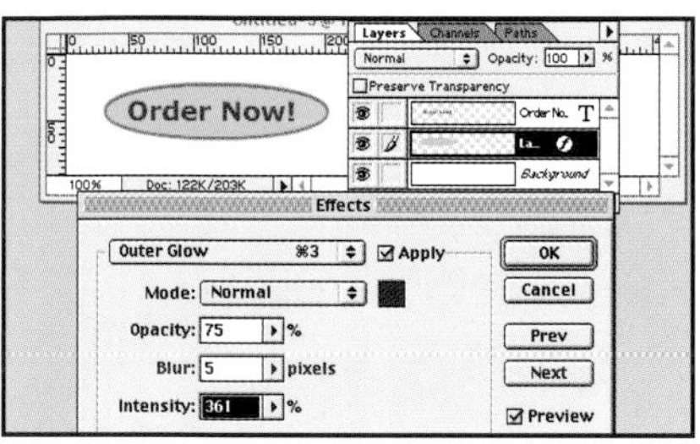

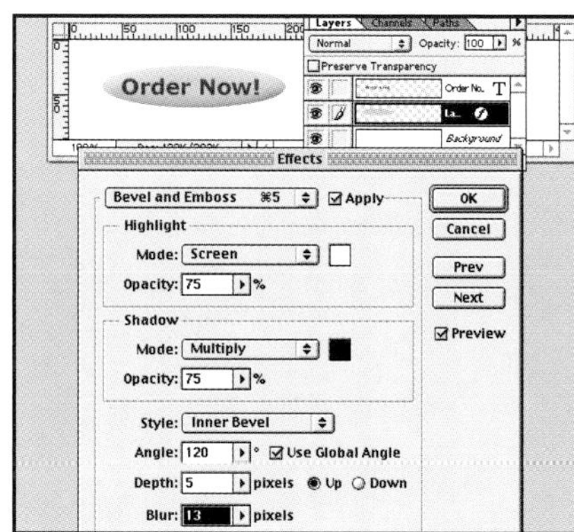

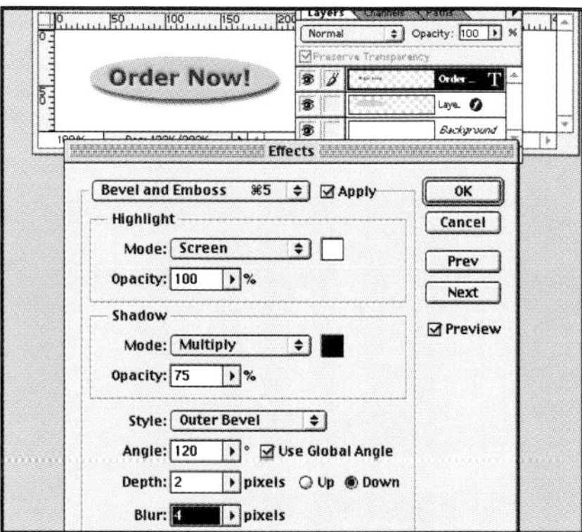

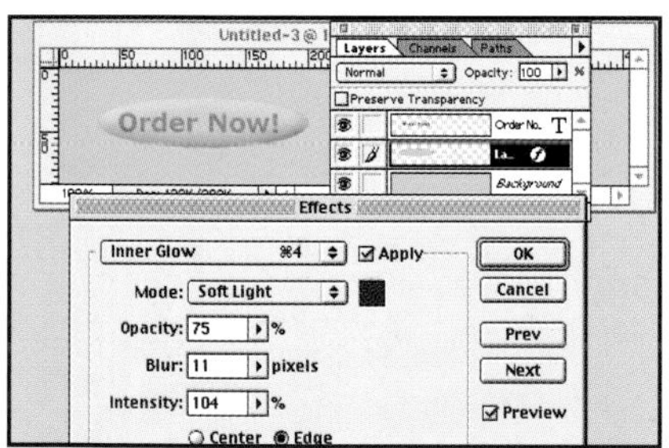

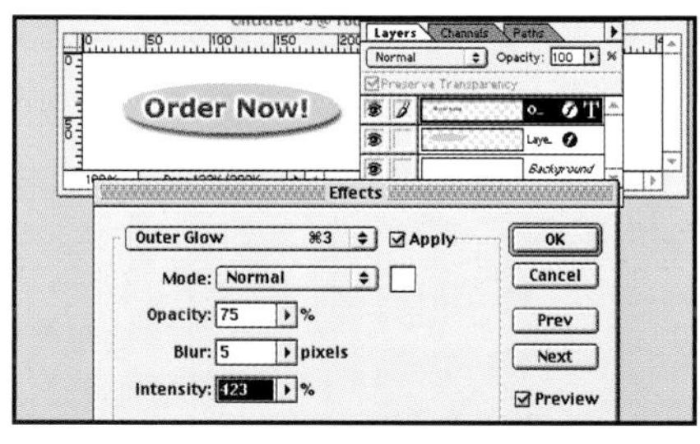

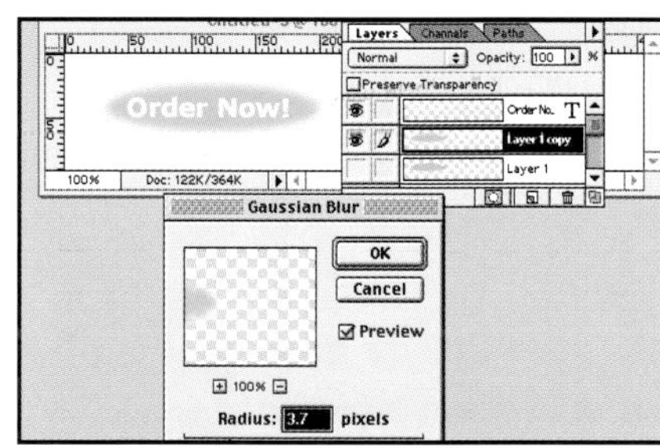

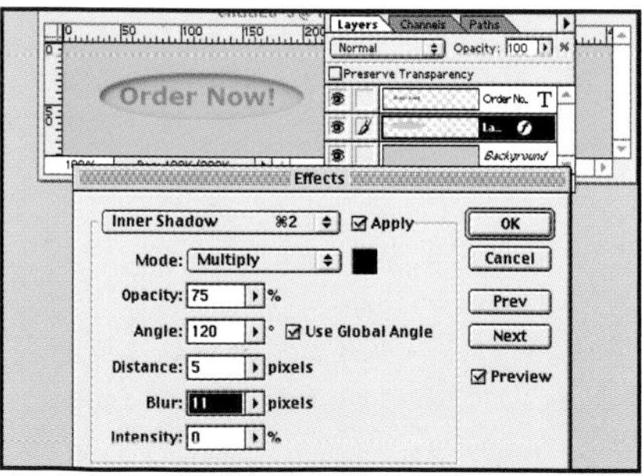

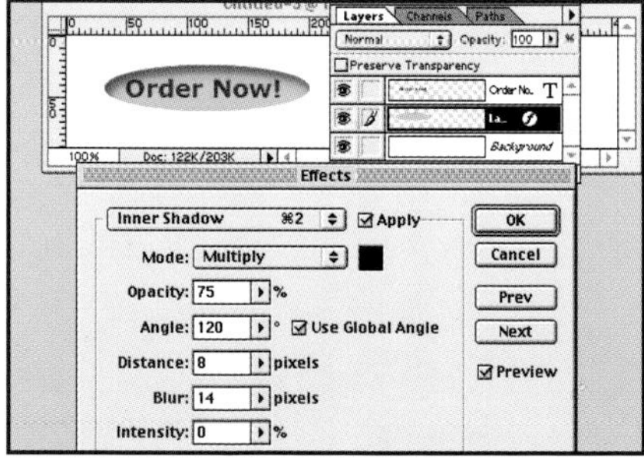

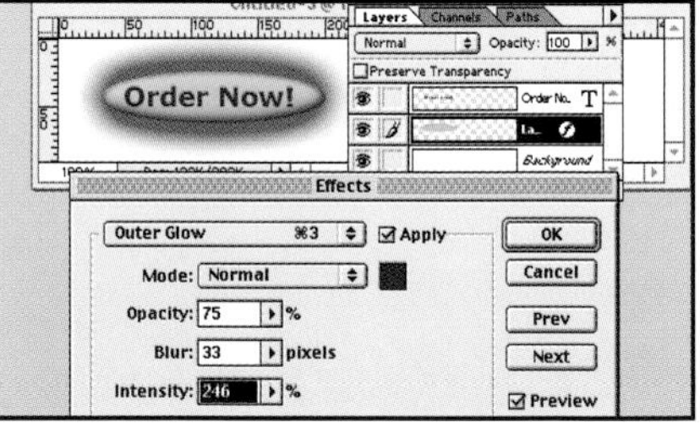

Here are examples of different layer effects and a variety of settings.

Button Clip Art

You'll find clip art for buttons all over the World Wide Web. Clip art buttons follow the same rules for custom bullet art; use the IMG SRC tag if you want the button for decoration only and the <A HREF=""><IMG SRC="" BORDER="0"></A> tag if you want them to link. Clip art typically already exists in Web file formats GIF or JPEG, and if not, you can use Photoshop to convert them.

Bullets can be abstract, such as dots and cubes, or they can be icons that actually mean something. **Michael Herrick**, of http://www.matterform.com, has invented something called QBullets, after "cue-bullet," or bullets that cue you to their hint or function. These buttons are part of a proposed interface standard that his site discusses in detail. I agree with the principle of his idea, but I prefer to let people explore their own artwork than rally around the standard of someone else's.

Basically, the idea is that QBullets let your audience know what the subject of your list is by using visual metaphors. The email button is a miniature envelope, the download button looks like a floppy disk, a new item has the word "new item," and so on. Herrick's opinion is that bullets should inform your reader about what is at the other end of the link: large download, outside Web site, ftp, telnet, form, and so on.

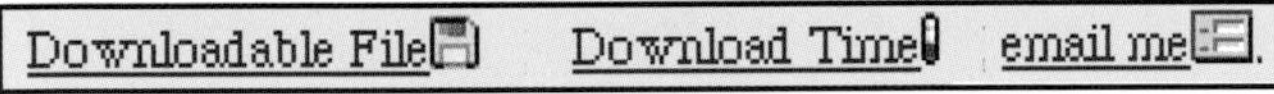

A close-up view of some of the QBullets Herrick has created.

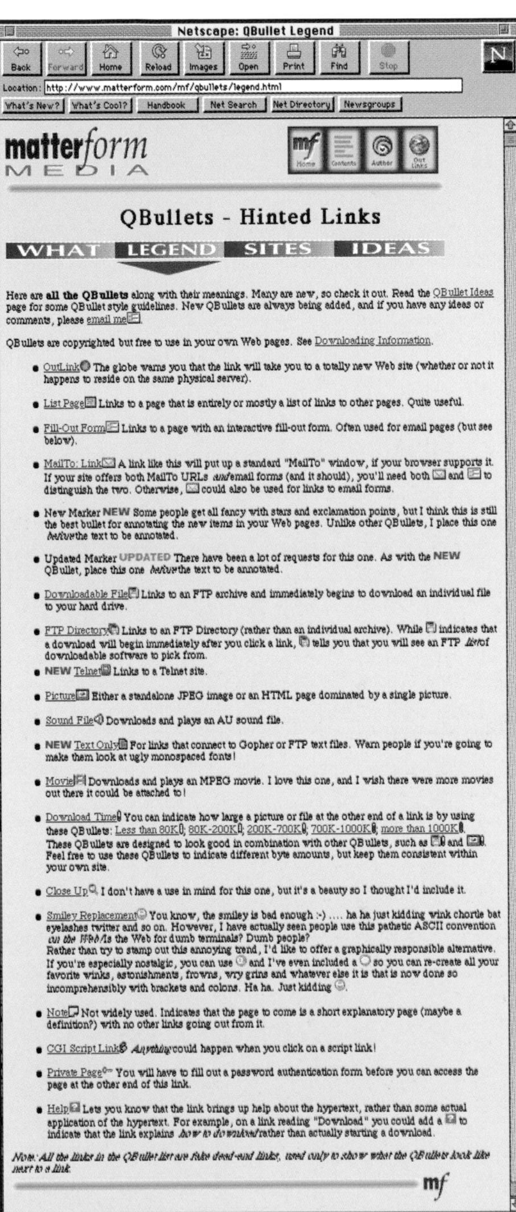

Here's a sample image that shows the Legend page from the QBullets site. QBullets can be used free of charge in exchange for a credit and a link to his page (http://www.matterform.com).

summary Rules, Buttons, & Bullets

As you can see from this chapter, there are many ways to design rules, bullets, and buttons on the Web. Techniques covered here included:

- There are many different settings in HTML for customizing horizontal rules by adjusting the SIZE and WIDTH attributes.
- If you use a background tile on your Web page and there is a horizontal rule, the tile will show through the emboss.
- You can use any kind of artwork for custom horizontal rules; just insert the artwork into your page using the IMG tag.
- HTML bulleted lists can include numbered, indented, or bullet symbols, depending on whether you use ordered lists, definition lists, or line item lists.
- Photoshop 5.0's Layer Effects feature makes button and bullet creation as simple as a single click.

Imagemaps Introduction

Chapter Topics

- What Are Imagemaps?
- Client-Side Imagemaps
- Server-Side Imagemaps
- Using Both Server- & Client-Side
- Imagemaps in Fireworks
- Imagemaps in ImageReady
- Imagemap Resources

15

The graphics we've discussed so far in this book have been of two varieties: linked or static. An imagemap is a linked graphic that contains multiple links instead of one. The imagemap is defined by coordinates (they define linked regions) that are stored in your HTML, or on your server in a separate map definition file, or both.

At many Web sites, you will see a list of underlined text links on a page (often referred to as a hotlist). This is simply a list of multiple URLs assigned to multiple text objects. Instead of using multiple text links, however, the designer could have attached the list of URLs to a single image object.

You see, an imagemap is actually just a fancy way of presenting a list of links. It takes a little longer to download than a hotlist because of the added time required to load the graphic. Most of the time, it's worth the wait because imagemaps are a more convenient, more visual way to present multiple choices to your audience.

This chapter covers a variety of methods for making imagemap graphics, assigning the map coordinates, and including the coordinates in your HTML.

Client-Side and Server-Side Imagemaps

There are two types of imagemaps: client-side and server-side. Before you begin constructing your imagemap, you will need to decide which type you want to use on your site, or decide if you want to use both types.

Client-side imagemaps are easier to make than server-side maps, and they are also easier for the browser to execute. Anytime you hear the term "client-side," it means that the information is contained within your HTML and the browser does not have to access the server to deliver the file to the end user. This puts much less stress on the server, which means your client-side imagemap will be more responsive and quicker to download.

For a client-side imagemap, all the coordinates for the imagemap are stored within the HTML document. For a server-side imagemap, the coordinates for the imagemap are saved in a "map definition file," which is stored on a server and accessed by a CGI script. In general, setting up a server-side imagemap is far more complicated than setting up a client-side imagemap. Server-side imagemaps work very differently on different systems—even on different systems using the same brand of server!

Another difference is how the two types of imagemaps display data within the Netscape browser. A server-side imagemap shows the coordinates at the bottom of the screen, whereas a client-side imagemap shows the actual URL at the bottom of the screen, which is much nicer.

Most people prefer client-side imagemaps to server-side imagemaps, but some older browsers still don't support the tags. That's why many Webmasters include both types of imagemaps in their documents.

In general, it's more complicated to create an imagemap than it is to code single linked images using the <A HREF> <IMG SRC></A> tag. Imagemaps are complicated on a number of fronts. You must determine and document each region's coordinates in pixels. The regions have to be put into a document in a specific manner, and if a comma, space, or coordinate is wrong, the map won't work properly. If you want to create a client-side map, you place the coordinates in the HTML; if you want to create a server-side map, you store the coordinates in an outside file. To top off the fun, coordinates for server-side and client-side maps are presented differently. The rest of the chapter outlines these differences and offers methods for creating both types of maps.

```
<html>
     <head><title>clientside imagemap</title></head>

  <body>
     <img src="/images/sign.gif" width="200" height="200" usemap="#sig
     <area coords="126,117,126,117,130,105,152,127,127,139,126,131,104
     href="http://www.lynda.com/books/">
     <area coords="62,111,62,111,44,109,47,101,20,116,35,131,44,124,62
      href="http://www.lynda.com/classes/">
      <area coords="56,33,100,61" shape="rect"
      href="http://www.lynda.com"></map>
  </body>

</html>
```

Client-side imagemap data is always located inside your HTML. You can tell that this code is for a client-side imagemap because it uses the attribute USEMAP. The numbers separated by commas indicate coordinates that define the regions of the imagemap.

```
<html>
<head><title>server-side</title></head>
   <body>
   <a href="/images/sign2.map">
      <img src="/images/sign2.gif" width="200" height="200"  border="0" ismap>
         </a>
   </body>
</html>
```

Notice that there aren't any coordinates in this HTML? Server-side map coordinates are stored in a map definition file, not in the HTML. Note the ISMAP attribute; it signifies a server-side imagemap, whereas USEMAP signifies a client-side imagemap. In this example, the file **sign2.map** is the definition file, and the file **sign2.gif** is the image.

```
rect http://www.lynda.com/classes/ 16,100 59,138
rect http://www.lynda.com/books/ 105,103 154,142
poly http://www.lynda.com 64,59 63,47 54,47 79,33 85,39 89,27 92,32 92,41 98,46
94,49 92,47 86,61 86,49 80,52 82,61
default http://www.lynda.com
```

The server-side map definition file is stored on a server. In this example, it's called **sign2.map**. Note that the coordinates are defined differently here than they were in the client-side example.

```
<a href="image/sign2.map">
<img src="sign2.gif" width="200" height="200"
 usemap="#sign2" ismap alt="imagemap" border="0" >
</a>

<map name="sign2">
<area shape="poly" coords="60,128" href="http://www.lynda.com" >
<area shape="poly" coords="60,128,60,113,42,111,42,99,24,115,39,133,40,124"
href="http://www.lynda.com/classes/" ><area shape="poly"
coords="105,116,104,129,127,129,126,137,153,126,131,109,131,118"
href="http://www.lynda.com/books/" >
<area shape="poly"
coords="58,56,60,49,52,47,74,30,82,36,84,29,89,30,89,39,97,41,96,44,93,45,91,55,86,56,84,47,77,47,77,55"
href="http://www.lynda.com" >
<area shape="rect" coords="0,0,200,200"
href="http://www.lynda.com" ><AREA SHAPE="DEFAULT" NOHREF>
</map>
```

Here's an example of an HTML document with both types of imagemaps.

http://www.razorfish.com/bluedot/typo/menu.map?105,70

Here's an example of a server-side imagemap reading on the bottom navigation bar of Netscape. It shows the position coordinates.

http://www.cgibook.com/links.html 

Here's an example of a client-side imagemap reading on the bottom navigation bar of Netscape. It shows the URL! Much better.

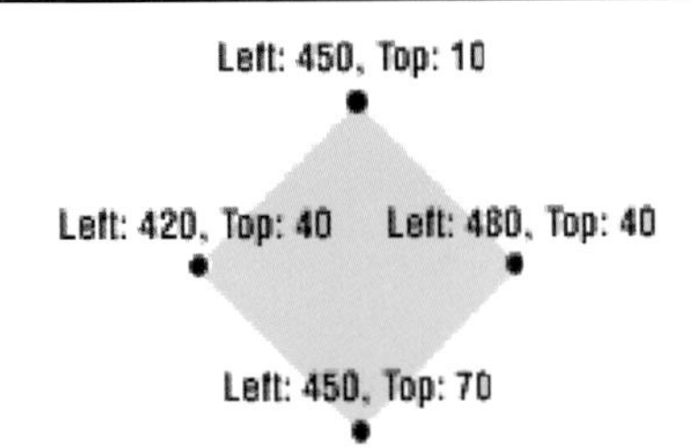

This image is taken from Bob Schmitt's excellent article about imagemaps, which you can read at: http://webreview.com/wr/pub/98/08/28/studio/index.html. This graphic shows the coordinate locations on this example of a diamond-shaped polygon.

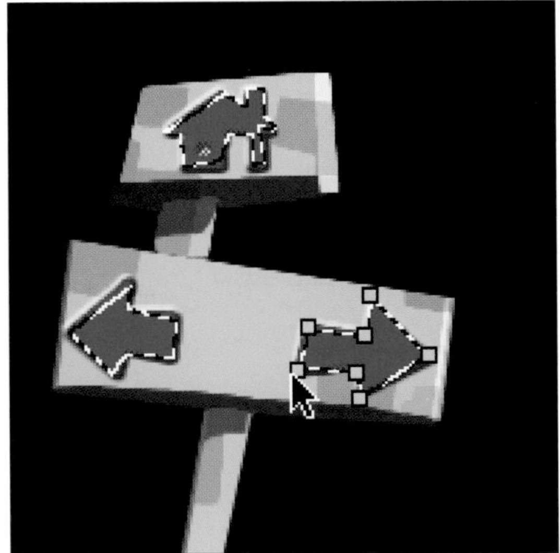

Regardless of whether it is client-side or server-side, an imagemap must contain coordinate and hyperlink information. Here's an example of what the regions look like when they're defined in an imagemap editor.

Client-Side Imagemap Code

Creating client-side imagemaps (and server-side imagemaps) involves documenting the regions of the map and creating a list of coordinates. This type of code is typically created in either an imagemap program or an HTML editor. Later in this chapter, you'll find step-by-step guidelines for creating imagemaps with Fireworks and ImageReady. For the moment, it's first useful to understand the code that is required for an imagemap. In this client-side imagemap example, the coordinates are stored in the HTML, which is not the case in a server-side imagemap file.

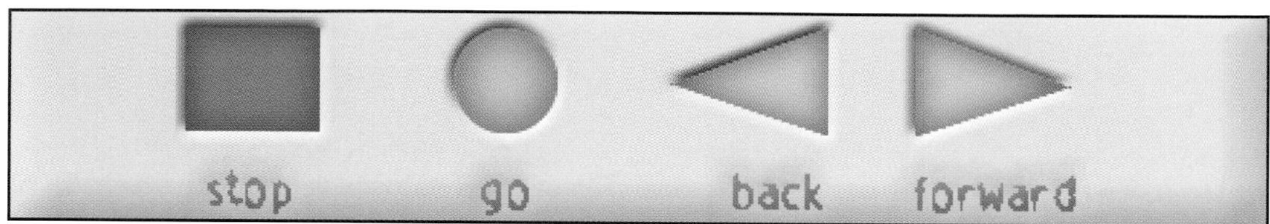

The artwork controls.jpg is the source artwork for this imagemap example.

code

```
1 <IMG SRC="controls.jpg" WIDTH="500" HEIGHT="100"
2 USEMAP="#controls"
3 ISMAP ALT="imagemap" BORDER="0">

4 <MAP NAME="controls">
5 <AREA SHAPE="poly" COORDS="419,41,360,16,360,61"
  HREF="http://www.controller.com/forward.html">
  <AREA SHAPE="poly" COORDS="263,40,322,17,325,60"
  HREF="http://www.controller.com/back.html">
6 <AREA SHAPE="circle" COORDS="197,39,22"
  HREF="http://www.controller.com/go.html">
  <AREA SHAPE="rect" COORDS="70,17,126,60"
  HREF="http://www.controller.com/stop.html">
7 <AREA SHAPE="rect" COORDS="0,0,500,100"
  HREF="http://www.controller.com">
8 <AREA SHAPE="DEFAULT" NOHREF>
9 </MAP>
```

code deconstruction

1. IMG SRC defines the artwork for the imagemap.

2. The USEMAP="#controls" indicates that the MAP NAME "controls" is being used.

3. ALT is the ALT tag for the imagemap image (controls.jpg). If people have their images turned off, they will not be able to see the imagemap, but they will be warned that it is there!

4. The MAP NAME is first requested in the USEMAP tag, but it is defined here in the MAP NAME element. It's a good idea to use a file name that corresponds to your image. In this example, the image "controls.jpg" uses the MAP NAME "#control".

5. AREA SHAPE describes which shape is being used by the imagemap. In this example, it is a polygon. The COORDS show how the polygon is defined, starting from the top left coordinate.

6. Notice that this AREA SHAPE is a circle?

7. This AREA SHAPE is "rect" for a rectangle.

8. This AREA SHAPE equals "DEFAULT" NOHREF, which means that if the end user clicks outside of a region, the URL HYPERLINK http://www.controller.com will be contacted.

9. As is true of many HTML elements, the closing tag is required for MAP.

Server-Side Imagemap

In the case of a server-side map, the coordinates must be stored in an imagemap definition file. This definition file is composed slightly differently depending on which kind of server your Web site uses.

The server is where your artwork and HTML are stored. There are two types of servers—**NCSA** and **CERN**—and they require slightly different imagemap definition file codes. This means that you have to ensure that the way you coded the imagemap is compatible with the type of server your site is stored on. The first step toward deciding how to build your imagemap is to call the online service provider with whom you have your Internet account and Web site to find out what kind of server they use. To insert a server-side imagemap into your HTML, you would use the following code:

code

```
1 <A HREF="controls.map">
2 <IMG SRC="controls.jpg" WIDTH="500"  HEIGHT="100"
3 ALT="imagemap"
4 BORDER="0"
5 ISMAP>
  </A>
```

code deconstruction

1. The <A HREF> element specifies the location of the map definition file. The "controls.map" file is the map definition. It's stored in the root directory.

2. The IMG SRC element specifies where the file "controls.jpg" is located. Its WIDTH and HEIGHT attributes are defined next.

3. The ALT attribute tells the browser to display the text "imagemap" if the end user is viewing this document from a text-only reader or if he or she has images turned off.

4. The BORDER="0" element turns off the border of the "controls.jpg" linked file.

5. The ISMAP element specifies that this imagemap is a server-side file.

Did you notice there were no coordinates in this example? That's because they're stored in the imagemap definition file. The file looks like this:

```
poly http://www.controller.com/forward.html
419,41 360,16 360,61
poly http://www.controller.com/back.html
263,40 322,17 325,60
circle http://www.controller.com/go.html 197,39 22
rect http://www.controller.com/stop.html 70,17 126,60
default http://www.controller.com
```

This uses the same coordinates as the server-side imagemap, but they are presented in a different syntax. This file must be stored on your server. You defined the path to it in Line 1 of the preceding code.

Combining Server- and Client-Side Imagemaps

code

```
<HTML>
<HEAD>
<TITLE>controls</TITLE>
</HEAD>
<BODY BGCOLOR="#FFFFFF">
<A HREF="controls.map">
<IMG SRC="controls.jpg" WIDTH="500" HEIGHT="100"
1 USEMAP="#controls"
2 ISMAP ALT="imagemap"
BORDER="0" >
</A>
<MAP NAME="controls">
<AREA SHAPE="poly" COORDS="419,41,360,16,360,61"
HREF="http://www.controller.com/forward.html" >
<AREA SHAPE="poly" COORDS="263,40,322,17,325,60"
HREF="http://www.controller.com/back.html" >
<AREA SHAPE="circle" COORDS="197,39,22"
HREF="http://www.controller.com/go.html" >
<AREA SHAPE="rect" COORDS="70,17,126,60"
HREF="http://www.controller.com/stop.html" >
<AREA SHAPE="rect" COORDS="0,0,500,100"
HREF="http://www.controller.com" >
<AREA SHAPE="DEFAULT" NOHREF>
</MAP>
</BODY>
</HTML>
```

code deconstruction

1. Note that the USEMAP element is present. This indicates the beginning of a client-side imagemap. Below that, however, you can see all the coordinates that represent a client-side map as well.

2. Note that the ISMAP element is present. The "controls.map" file is also specified. This enables the browser to execute the server-side map.

It's always safest to include both types of maps. If someone visits your site using an older browser that doesn't recognize the client-side map, the browser will display the server-side map. This is definitely the most foolproof method.

Importance of the ALT Tag

The ALT tag provides alternative information to images that can be read by text-based browsers. Some users might visit your site using browser software that does not recognize imagemaps, or maybe they've turned off their images because they're in a hurry or because they're disabled and can't see them. (Yes, even visually impaired people can and do use the text-based Web; there are devices that can "read" the pages to them.) Adding one simple ALT tag to your HTML can accommodate all these situations.

Using our example one more time, here's where the tag would be included:

```
<A HREF="http://www.domain.nam/cgi-bin/filename.map">
<IMG SRC="imagename.gif" ALT="this is an image of my bla bla"
BORDER="0"
ISMAP>
```

Importance of Width and Height Attributes

By adding WIDTH and HEIGHT attributes to image tags within HTML, you give the browser information about the size of your graphic. This is good for a couple of reasons. First of all, the browser doesn't have to calculate the image size because you've supplied it with the information, which saves time. It allows the text to load before the images, which can be a good thing with large images; audiences have something to look at while they're waiting! MSIE actually requires that you use the WIDTH and HEIGHT attributes or the client-side imagemap tags don't even work.

So then, here's the way to implement the WIDTH and HEIGHT attributes:

```
<A HREF="http://www.domain.nam/cgi-bin/filename.map">
<IMG SRC="imagename.gif" WIDTH="350" HEIGHT="200" ALT="this is an image of my bla bla"
BORDER="0"
ISMAP>
```

The values you put inside the WIDTH and HEIGHT attributes reflect how large the image is, in pixels. You can even resize an image if you enter values that are larger or smaller than the image! Basically, the browser uses your information for the image size instead of looking to the image itself for size information.

Do You Really Need an Imagemap?

It's always important to carefully analyze whether you really need an imagemap or whether there's some other way to accomplish the same goal. For example, if your image is composed of rectangles or can be seamed together by using rectangular shapes (transparent irregular shapes, see Chapter 13, "Transparent Artwork," and Chapter 17, "Alignment & Tables"), it might be easier for you to load multiple single graphics with independent links than to load one graphic with multiple links.

All over the Web you will see examples of imagemaps used on opening menu screens. Sometimes an imagemap is used even when the menu bar is composed of rectangular shapes. Some sites do this because the one image loads faster than multiple images would. This is a valid reason to use an imagemap, but even so, the difficulty of creating and maintaining one might outweigh the performance increase.

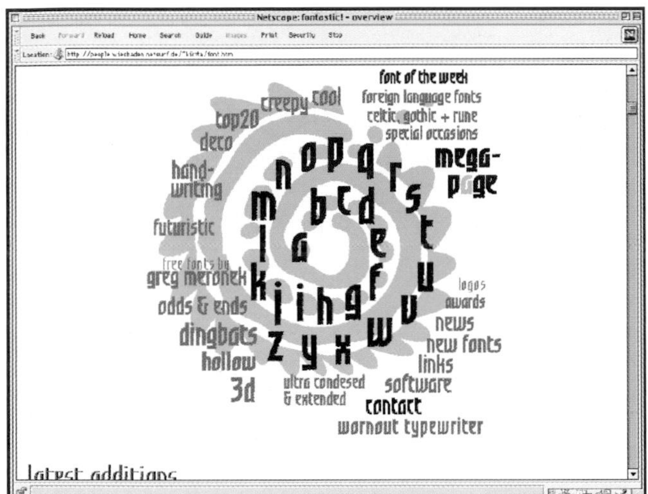

If you have an image, such as those shown above, that don't have obvious rectangular regions which you can cut apart as individual images, an imagemap is your only choice.

What's a Comment?

Comments are parts of HTML code that the browser ignores. This is useful because you can put notes to yourself or others within your code using comments. That's why Macromedia uses them in the code that Fireworks generates. You set up a command by putting your message between these symbols: <!---!>. That's all there is to it.

Creating an Imagemap with Fireworks

One of my favorite tools for creating imagemaps is Macromedia's Fireworks. That's probably because I am an artist—not a coder—by nature. What's nice is that you can create the imagemap from an imaging program and you never have to write a line of code! The first step, of course, is to create the artwork. You can create it in Fireworks, or you can create it elsewhere and open it in Fireworks.

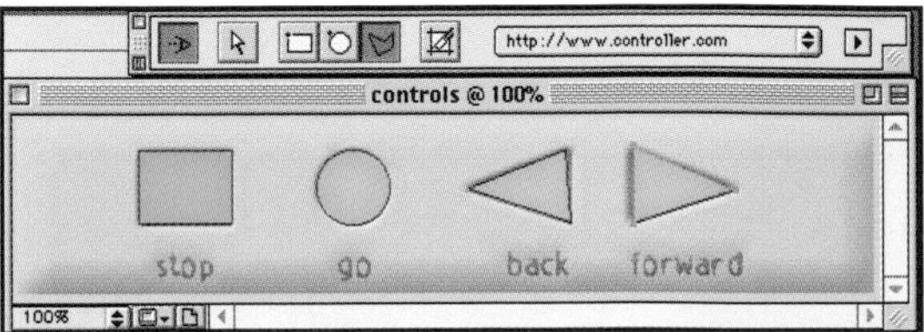

Step 1: After the image is open, you use the URL toolbar to plot the imagemap regions. By clicking on the **Panel Options** pop-up menu, you can access various options and set the URL destinations for each region of the map.

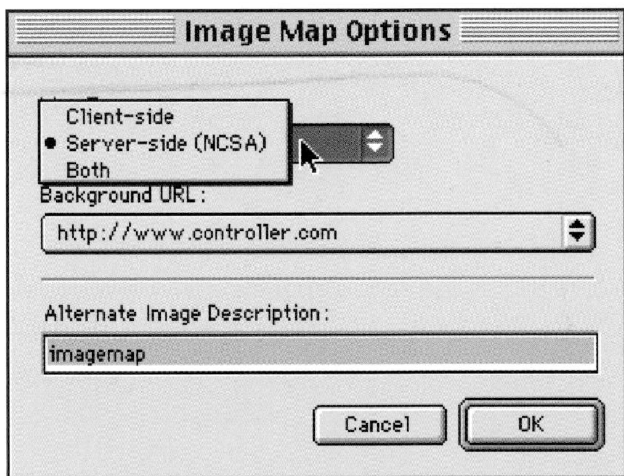

Step 2: By choosing **Image Map Options** from the Panel Options pop-up menu, you can choose whether you want the program to create a client-side imagemap, a server-side imagemap, or both.

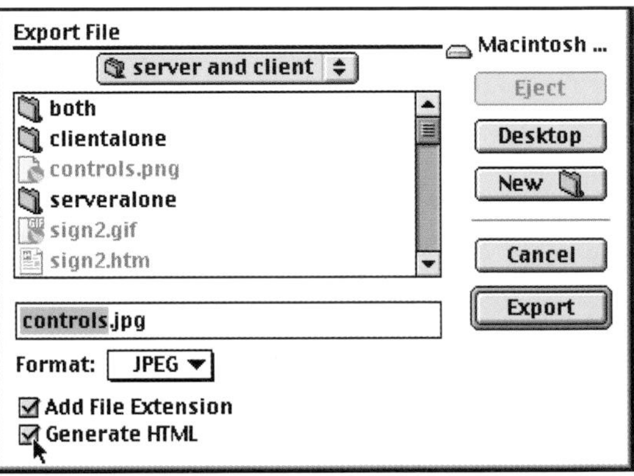

Step 3: When you optimize the graphic, you can choose whether you want JPEG or GIF. After you specify the file format, you are presented with the Save dialog box. You can indicate whether or not you want the program to generate the HTML.

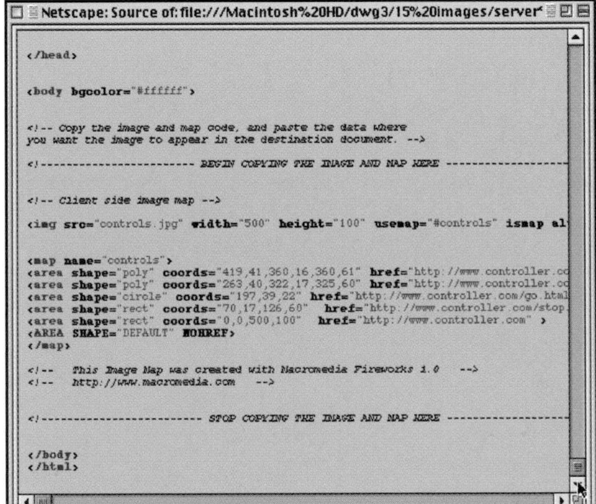

Step 4: Notice how the code contains comment tags that let you know where to copy and paste the imagemap data that Fireworks generated? Sure beats coding by hand, I tell ya!

Creating an Imagemap with ImageReady

If you create a lot of images using Photoshop or ImageReady, making imagemaps doesn't even require you to draw shapes around the regions anymore. The only drawback to using ImageReady to make imagemaps is that it only saves client-side maps and will not generate a map definition file for a server-side map. Other than that, you simply can't beat it!

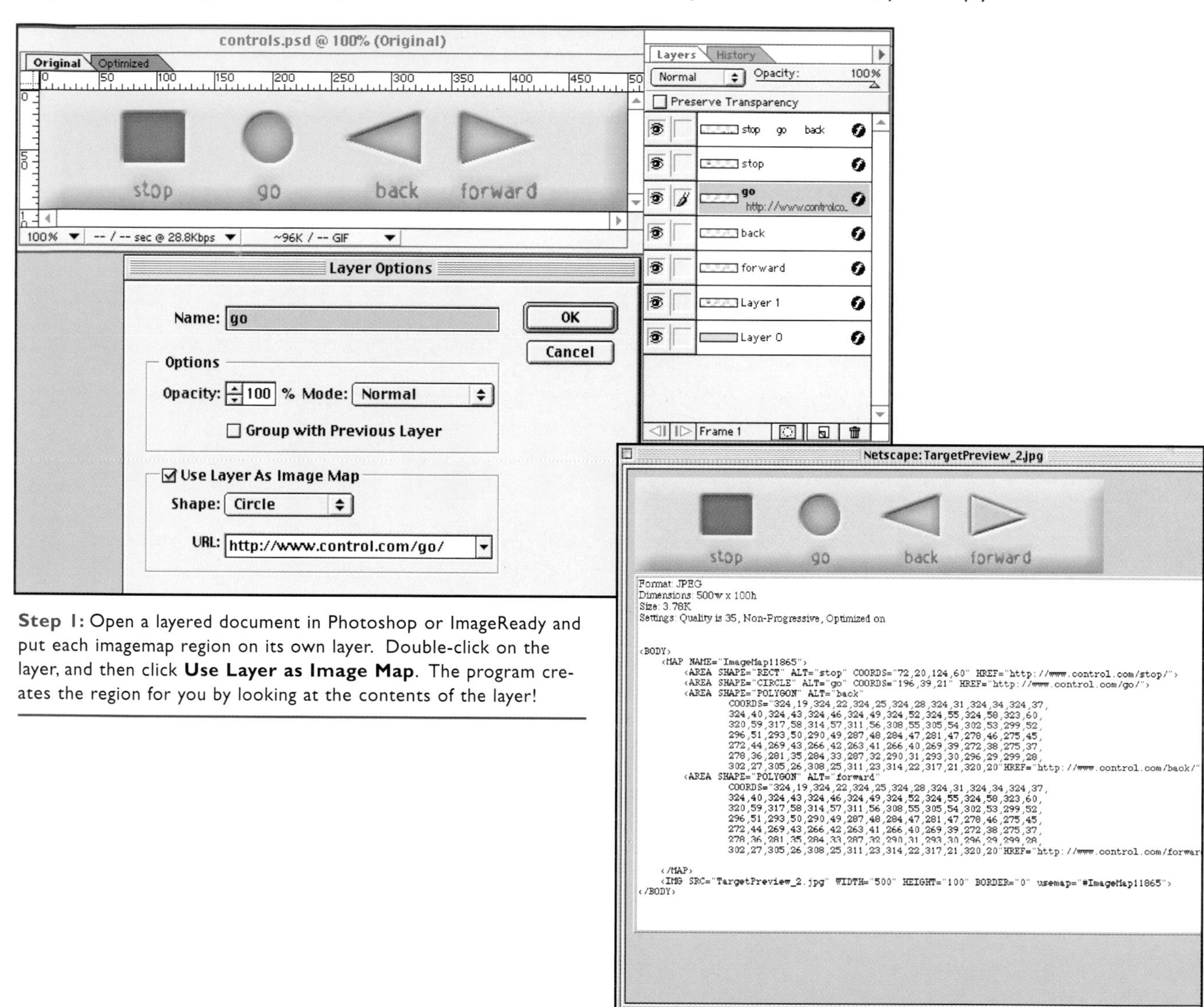

Step 1: Open a layered document in Photoshop or ImageReady and put each imagemap region on its own layer. Double-click on the layer, and then click **Use Layer as Image Map**. The program creates the region for you by looking at the contents of the layer!

Step 2: You can choose **File:Preview In:Browser**, and the program will create the HTML code for the client-side imagemap. Then you can copy and paste the code into your favorite text or HTML editor. Sweet!

tip

Other Imagemap Resources

I chose to profile ImageReady and Fireworks in this chapter, but there are many, many other imagemap software utilities available. Most HTML editors include imagemap functionality as well. Here's a short list of additional imagemap resources.

Imagemap Tutorial URLs

http://www.ihip.com/
http://webreview.com/wr/pub/98/08/28/studio/index.html
http://www.cris.com/~automata/tutorial.shtml

Imagemap Software Tools

MapEdit (Windows, PC, Mac, and UNIX)
http://www.boutell.com/mapedit/

LiveImage (Windows)
http://www.mediatec.com/

Glenn Fleishman's Server-Side to Client-Side Online Converter
http://www.popco.com/popco/convertmaps.html

summary Imagemaps

Imagemaps enable you to assign multiple URLs to a single image. Making an imagemap is not terribly complicated, but here are some things to keep in mind:

- Before you begin, decide whether you need a client-side or server-side imagemap. You might decide to use both because not all browsers support client-side maps.
- If you create a server-side map, check with your Internet service provider or presence provider before you begin. You will need to know whether to create a CERN or NCSA map definition file. You also need to know which directory to put this map definition file in. (Some ISPs and PPs have special CGI bins on their servers for this purpose.)
- Some graphics are well suited to be cut apart, but others require the use of imagemaps. It's important to assess whether an imagemap is the appropriate technique for the job at hand. Sometimes it's easier to create multiple images and link them individually than to create an imagemap.
- To tell which type of imagemap someone's HTML code contains, just look for the USEMAP and ISMAP tags. If you find USEMAP, you're looking at a client-side imagemap; if you find ISMAP, it's a server-side imagemap. If it contains both, you have both!

Web Typography

Introduction

Chapter Topics

- HTML Based Typography
- Verdana & Georgia
- Graphic Based Typography
- What About Font Embedding?
- TrueType Embedding & OneType
- What About Font PDF?
- What About Flash?

16

Written words are one of the most important communication vehicles of our culture. Type, therefore, is one feature that most Web sites must have, yet the issues surrounding type are not obvious at first glance.

Many designers do not think of type as text; instead, they use fonts and typefaces as devices and vehicles to communicate visually. Most of us look at type as an aesthetic medium and take for granted that type's purpose is also to represent text-based data. HTML-based text is used for search engines, data analysis, email transmissions, automated language translations, and text readers for the visually impaired. Unfortunately, the Web has many facets to it, and what is design to one person can easily become unusable to another.

Visual design is about control. Typography is an incredibly powerful visual design medium, but good typography requires much more control than HTML currently affords. HTML is about display flexibility and cross-platform distribution of information. The tension between these two contradictory missions is discussed here in detail.

This chapter focuses on the controversies, aesthetics, functionality, and techniques of Web type. It examines HTML-based type, image-based type, and type embedding. Information about CSS (**C**ascading **S**tyle **S**heets) and its relation to typography can be found in Chapter 19, "Cascading Style Sheets."

Glossary of Key Typographic Terms

Before you venture too far into the subject of Web type, let's establish a common vocabulary. The following examples will cover many of the basics of type terminology.

Most web browsers default to a serif typeface.

This is a serif typeface!

Serif: A serif typeface has a stroke attached to the beginning or end of one of the main strokes of each letter. Many people think this style of type is the easiest to read as body copy. The default font in most browsers is a serif typeface: Times Roman on Macs and Times New Roman on PCs.

You can specify san-serif fonts too.

This is a san-serif typeface!

Sans-serif: A sans-serif typeface has no slab attached. To use a sans-serif typeface on the Web, you must include special tags, requesting that your end user's is browser display a graphic picture of type instead of HTML. Sans-serif type is specified with the FONT FACE tag, which is described fully later in this chapter.

monospace

proportional

Monospace: A monospace font uses the same amount of horizontal width for every character, unlike a standard proportional font, which uses a different amount of space for each character. The top example shown here is set in Courier and could be accomplished in HTML with the PRE tag. You can specify monospace typefaces with the PRE, CODE, or TT tags.

regular leading regular leading regular leading regu
regular leading regular leading regular leading regu
regular leading regular leading regular leading regu
regular leading regular leading regular leading regu

Default leading: Leading (pronounced ledding) is the measurement of space between lines of type. The origin of the word leading dates to early days of typography when lead type was used. Blank pieces of lead were used between rows as spacers. This figure shows standard leading in HTML using no custom tags.

ing looser leading looser leading looser leading looser leading looser leading looser le

ing looser leading looser leading looser leading looser leading looser leading looser le

looser leading looser leading looser leading looser leading looser leading looser leadi

Looser leading: This looser leading in HTML was created by using the paragraph break tag, P.

this text has default word spacing

this text has word spacing of 125%

Spacing: This is the amount of space between each letter of a word.

DROP CAPS CAN BE KEWEL

Drop cap: A drop cap is used with all capital letters to indicate that the first letter of a word should appear in a larger size. In HTML, you can create a drop cap by using the FONT SIZE tag.

FOR HOTWIRED MEMBERS
Test Patterns presents pet projects that kept us up nights: MiniMind, KHOT, and the amazing Beta Lounge.

Small caps: HotWired uses small caps on its front page at http:// www.hotwired.com/frontdoor/.

fe palette, as I so named it, is the actual p
within their browsers. The palettes used by t
s. This palette is based on math, not beauty.
ors in this palette, but Netscape, Mosaic and

Body text: The body text, or body copy, of a document is the main block of text.

The Browser Safe Color Palette

By Lynda Weinman

Headline text: A headline is used to break up information. It can do so by being larger in size, a different color, or a different font. It might have an underline, bold, or other visual treatment, which will cause it to stand out.

Glossary of Elements Not Possible with HTML

Baseline shift: Enables you to change the position of a single character up or down.

Kerning: Enables you to adjust the spacing between individual characters.

Leading adjustment: Enables you to specify a particular leading by using point size measurements.

Looser leading adjustment: Enables you to specify a particular leading by using point size measurements.

Word spacing: Enables you to adjust the space between words.

Tracking: Enables you to adjust the global spacing between letters.

note

CSS Can Do!

Many of the typographic functions listed above that are not possible with HTML, are possible with CSS, which will be addressed in Chapter 19, "Cascading Style Sheets".

Type 101

Does type fascinate you, but you really don't know much about it? It is a fascinating subject indeed and a rather complex science (like just about anything if you go deep enough). I've selected some excellent resources for you to use to train yourself in type terms and issues.

There are a number of interactive type education-based sites on the Web; two of my favorites can be seen below.

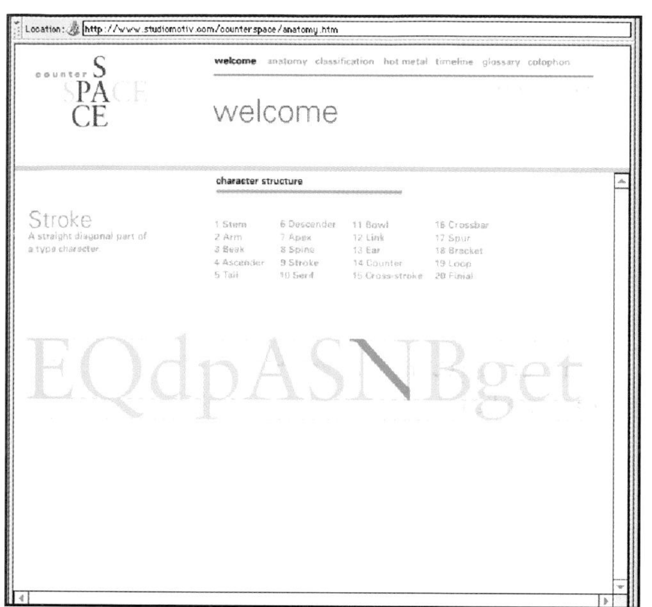

counterSPACE: (http://wwwstudiomotiv.com/counterspace/).

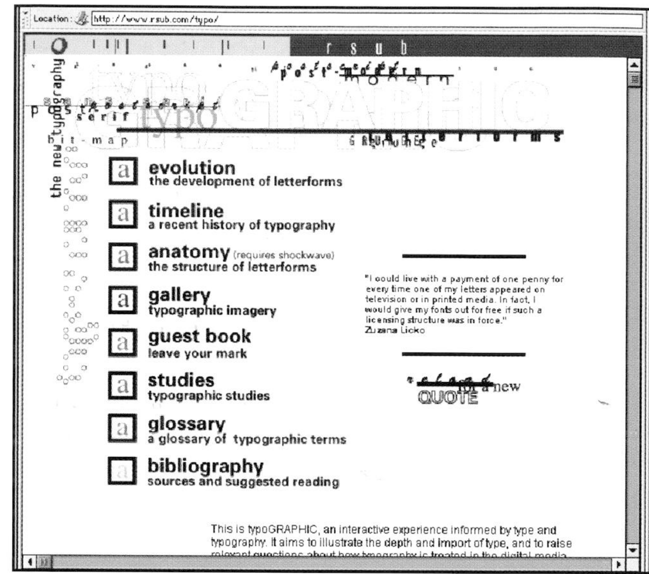

typoGRAPHIC: (www.rsub.com/typo).

Microsoft Typography:

An Excellent Essay on **Hinting**. Don't know what it is? Read this article!
http://www.microsoft.com/typography/hinting/hinting.htm

The Microsoft Typography **Glossary** (a disagreeably facetious type glossary!), which includes the low-down on all the type jargon you can possibly absorb:
http://www.microsoft.com/typography/glossary/content.htm

Daniel Will-Harris Choosing and Using Type & prolific verbiage:
http://www.will-harris.com/use-type.htm
http://webreview.com/wr/pub/Fonts

CounterSPACE is a beautifully executed interactive study in type created in Macromedia Flash:
http://www.studiomotiv.com/counterspace/

Creative Alliance, sponsored by Agfa, highlights the development of new faces:
http://www.agfahome.com/archive/features/agfatype/

Aesthetic Considerations

I think the Web is an incredibly great way to gather information. Typically, when I find a page with a lot of text on it though, I print the page on my printer instead of sitting and reading through the text on my screen. Who wants the light of a monitor blaring in her face while she is doing recreational reading? Give me crisp type on paper over that any day! I feel the same way about all computer-based text delivery systems, such as CD-ROMs and interactive kiosks. If I'm going to read a lot of text, I'd rather do so on paper. As designers, we have to recognize that computer-based presentations pose distinct challenges, and we should not treat our type-ridden Web pages the same way we would print.

I advocate breaking up type into small paragraphs. Also, use different weights, such as bold and italic, to make it possible for the reader to skim the page easily and catch the important points. Adding hypertext (text that links you from one spot to another, which typically appears underlined or bold depending on the way the viewer's browser preferences are set) is another way to break up screen text into more digestible portions. The idea is to break up blocks of text as much as possible. Assume your readers are skimming, and make it easy for them to do.

Understand that you're asking a lot of your end user to sit and read page upon page of type on a screen. It's your job to invent ways to hold his or her interest and to bring out the important ideas. You can do so by using either HTML or graphic-based text.

note

Printing Web Pages

As if there aren't enough things to think about in Web design, here is another wrench thrown your way. If you intend to have your audience print information from your pages, you should design your pages with that in mind. Many people don't realize, for example, that if they set up a dark Web page background with white type, the background will not be printed with the file. What results? White type on white paper, or as some might say—nothing!

I am not suggesting that you have to always use light backgrounds with dark type on every page, but if you know you want your audience to print a specific page, test print it yourself to see whether it is legible! Creating a PDF (**P**ortable **D**ocument **F**ormat) file is another option described at the end of this chapter.

HTML-Based Typography

The advantages of using HTML for most body type is that the memory and download time required for using native text is much lower than that used for graphics. Many sites are text-intensive, and HTML-based type is the only choice for presenting large quantities of written information in a timely and efficient manner.

The following examples and code demonstrate how to use HTML type tags.

Headings

Headings are created using the H and /H tags. The heading tags always have to be in the HEAD part of an HTML file. Here's some sample heading code.

```
<HTML><HEAD>
<H3>Welcome to this Site!</H3>
<H4>Welcome to this Site!</H4>
<H5>Welcome to this Site!</H5>
</HEAD>
</HTML>
```

Bold

Here are a couple of ways to make type bold.

```
<HTML>
Talk <B>LOUD!</B><P>
Talk <STRONG>LOUD!</STRONG>
</HTML>
```

Italic

Here are a couple of ways to italicize type.

```
<HTML>
Are you <I>ever going to shut up?  </I> <P>
Are you <EM> ever going to shut up?  </EM>
</HTML>
```

Preformatted

Preformatted text usually shows up in Courier or monospace type. Here's the code.

```
<HTML>
<PRE> When are you   g   o   i   n   g   to be
QUIET?</PRE>
</HTML>
```

Blinking Text

Use with caution! Many end viewers find this tag annoying.

```
<BLINK> flash news!</BLINK>
```

Changing Font Sizes

You can change font sizes by using the FONT SIZE and /FONT tags. Here's how.

```
<HTML>
Do you ever <FONT SIZE="5">listen</FONT>
to directions anymore?
</HTML>
```

Drop Cap

Here's the code for creating drop caps.

```
<HIML>
<FONT SIZE="4">D</FONT>ROP <FONT SIZE="4">C</FONT>AP
</HTML>
```

Small Cap

Use the following whenever you want small caps.

```
<HTML>
<FONT SIZE="1">SMALL CAPS </FONT>
REGULAR CAPS
</HTML>
```

Centering Text

You center text by using the CENTER tag.

```
<HTML>
<CENTER>
I'm in the middle...
</CENTER>
</HTML>
```

HTML Font Choices

Chances are, the person looking at your Web page is using the default settings for whatever browser he or she is viewing the page from. Most browsers use a Times Roman font by default. I've seen sites that include instructions to the viewer to change the default font to some other typeface. Good luck! I know very few Web visitors who would take the time to change their settings to see one single page. If you want your HTML type to be something other than Times Roman, don't count on asking your viewer to change his or her Web browser settings as a fool-proof method. In fact, I imagine an extremely low percentage of viewers would actually act on the suggestion. As an alternative, try the FONT FACE tag described next.

FONT FACE Tag

In case you want your audience to see your body copy in a font other than their browser's default font settings, an HTML attribute comes to the rescue. FONT FACE was originally developed by Microsoft but is now part of the standard HTML spec.

The FONT FACE element enables you to specify which font your page will be displayed in. The main caveat about using this is that your end user must have the font you request installed, or the tag will not work.

Microsoft has a free Mac or PC Web fonts package that can be downloaded from http://www.microsoft.com/typography/fontpack/default.htm.

The WebFonts Package includes Arial, Arial Bold, Arial Italic, Arial Bold Italic, Arial Black, Comic Sans MS, Comic Sans MS Bold, Courier New, Courier New Bold, Courier New Italic, Courier New Bold Italic, Impact, Times New Roman, Times New Roman Bold, Times New Roman Italic, and Times New Roman Bold Italic.

The odds are that even though Microsoft offers the free WebFonts Package to Mac and PC users, most of your Web audience won't know about it or take the time to install fonts that don't ship on their system. For that reason, it's safest to go with the basic fonts, which ship with every Mac and PC.

Note, however, that the WebFonts Package are installed on any system that contains Internet Explorer. That includes every PC that shipped with Win95 installed, as well as many new Macintosh computers (G3s and iMacs). Therefore, you could conceivably rely the use of Arial, Arial Bold, Arial Italic, Arial Bold Italic, Arial Black, Comic Sans MS, Comic Sans MS Bold, Courier New, Courier New Bold, Courier New Italic, Courier New Bold Italic, Impact, Times New Roman, Times New Roman Bold, Times New Roman Italic, and Times New Roman Bold Italic on your Macintosh-targeted Web pages.

Basic Fonts	
PC	**Mac**
Arial	Helvetica
Courier New	Courier
Times New Roman	Times

Here is some sample code using the FONT FACE tag.

```
<HTML>
<FONT FACE ="helvetica, arial"> TESTING,
</FONT> one, two, three.
</HTML>
```

To add size variation, add the SIZE attribute to the tag.

```
<HTML>
<FONT FACE="helvetica, arial" SIZE="5"> TESTING,
</FONT> one, two, three.
</HTML>
```

To change the color, add the COLOR attribute to the tag.

```
<HTML>
<FONT FACE ="helvetica, arial" SIZE="5"
COLOR="#CC3366">TESTING,
</FONT> one, two, three.
</HTML>
```

Verdana and Georgia

Until now, most Web publishers and designers have lived in a chocolate and vanilla typographical world. Web browsers have defaulted to using two typefaces: a serif font for standard text and a monospace font for code.

The trouble is, the basic font choices in browsers are bland at best. Arial and Helvetica suck! They are UGLY. In fact, all the fonts that ship as default fonts on the various platforms are UGLY. What makes them UGLY? Here's a short lesson in identifying the ugly factors.

Digital type is generally not well hinted (the uniform spacing between letters) for the screen. Letters often touch one another, making them hard to read—especially in very small sizes (9 pt. and below). Serifs (the slabs at the ends of lines on each type character) improve readability when printed at high resolution, but they actually interfere with readability on the screen. Italics are even more problematic and are almost illegible in many sizes and on many platforms.

For us to get a wider range of choices for type on the Web, fonts must be created from the ground-up that are designed for the screen. Microsoft has taken a leadership role in this endeavor by hiring renowned type designer **Matthew Carter** (ITC Galliard, Snell Roundhand, Charter, and Bell Centennial—the font used in phone books) to develop two screen-based font families for them.

Matthew Carter's two fonts (Verdana and Georgia) are part of a larger Web font library that Microsoft distributes for free (http://www.microsoft.com/fontpack/default.htm).

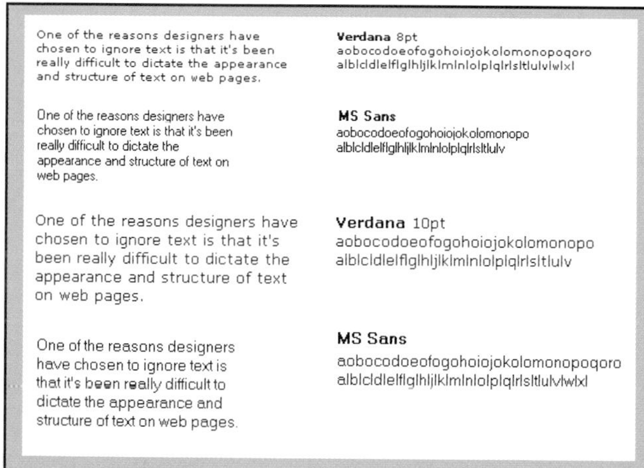

This figure shows a comparison between Carter's Verdana and its counterpart, MS Sans.

Georgia at text sizes, compared with Times Ne... - Microsoft Internet Explorer
File Edit View Go Favorites Help
One of the reasons designers have chosen to ignore text is that it's been really difficult to dictate the appearance and structure of text on web pages.
Georgia 10pt
aobocodoeofogohoiojokolomonopoqoro
alblcldlelflglhljlklmlnlolplqlrlsltlulvlwlxl
One of the reasons designers have chosen to ignore text is that it's been really difficult to dictate the appearance and structure of text on web pages.
Times New Roman 10pt
aobocodoeofogohoiojokolomonopoqoro
alblcldlelflglhljlklmlnlolplqlrlsltlulvlwlxl
One of the reasons designers have chosen to ignore text is that it's been really difficult to dictate the appearance and structure of text on web pages.
Georgia 12pt
aobocodoeofogohoiojokolomonopoqo
alblcldlelflglhljlklmlnlolplqlrlsltlulvlwlxl
One of the reasons designers have chosen to ignore text is that it's been really difficult to dictate the appearance and structure of text on web pages.
Times New Roman 12pt
aobocodoeofogohoiojokolomonopoqoro
alblcldlelflglhljlklmlnlolplqlrlsltlulvlwlxl

This figure shows Georgia compared to Times New Roman.

The differences between these font families make up a primer on what features work for screen-based typography. They were designed with a larger x-height (the size of ascenders, such as the letter d, and descenders, such as the letter g). Letter combinations such as fi, fl, and ff were designed clearly so they do not touch. Uppercase characters are a pixel taller than their lowercase counterparts when displayed at key screen sizes to improve readability. In addition, the spacing between characters is much looser, making it easier to scan quickly.

It took Matthew Carter two years to create these typefaces, and Microsoft gives his fonts away for free. Microsoft has done the online community a great service, but giving away fonts won't work for people who earn their living designing type. You can read more about this subject later in the chapter when I cover font embedding.

To read an excellent article about **Verdana and Georgia**, visit http://webreview.com/wr/pub/97/11/07/feature/screen/georgia-verdana.html or read an interview with Matthew Carter at http://webreview.com/wr/pub/97/11/07/feature/screen/fontdesigners.html.

warning

Font Size Differences Between Macs and PCs

No, you are not nuts. If you have both a Mac and a PC, you will notice that standard 12-point default fonts look different on the two platforms. Fonts display larger on PCs than they do on Macs. Sigh. I know you don't want to hear this, but this is one of the cross-platform-discrepancy things for which there is no real solution—except perhaps to serve different pages to Mac and PC end viewers, which is more than a bit too labor-intensive for most site designers. Remember to always check your pages on both platforms. You can adjust glaring problems accordingly.

Mac/Explorer

Mac/Netscape

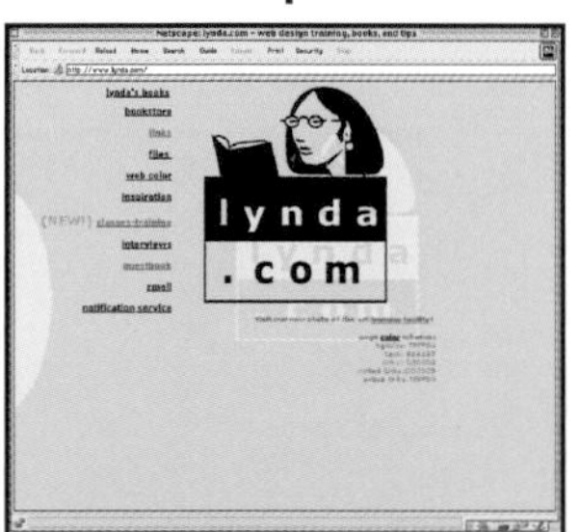

PC/Explorer

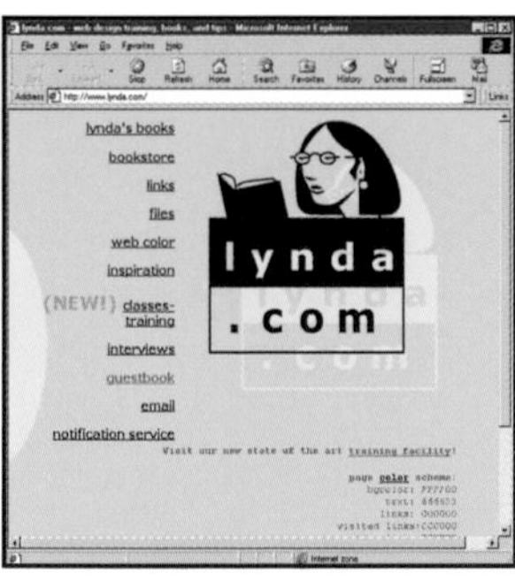

PC/Netscape

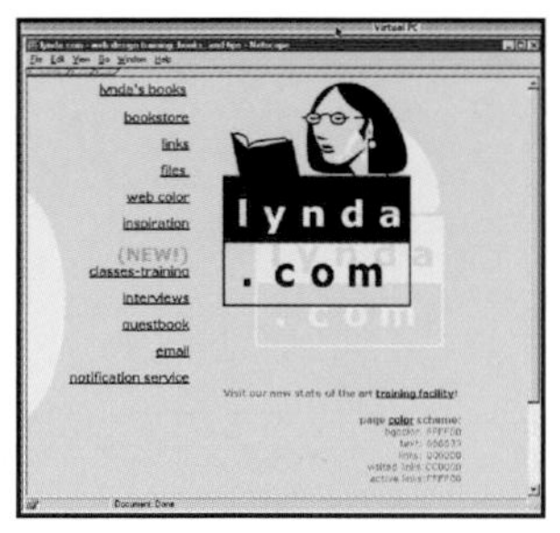

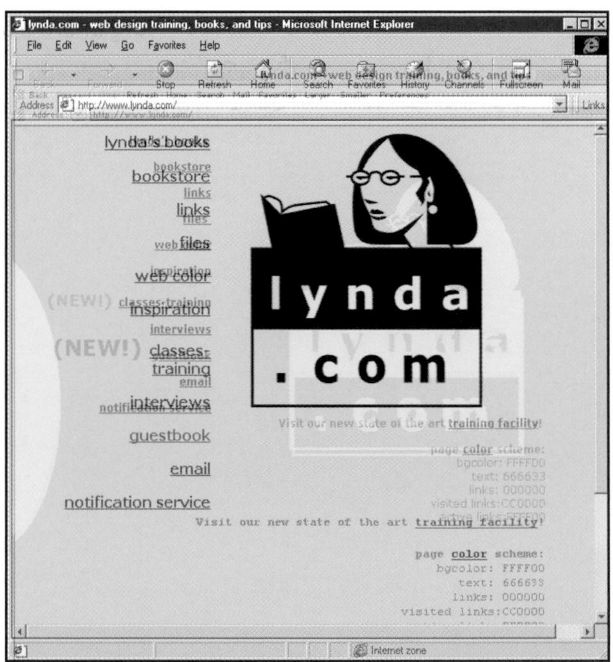

For fun (not), I made a composite of the Mac and PC versions of my site in Photoshop using partial transparency so you could see through to the bottom level. I lined up the black graphic; however, notice how different the type sizes are. Grrrr.

Graphics-Based Typography

You've just examined many HTML possibilities; now it's time to move on to graphics-based text. Using graphics for text instead of HTML is where you get the chance to flash your type design aesthetic touch for the world to see. You'll be able to use any font your heart desires and add special effects such as drop shadows, glows, and blurs. A great advantage to using this technique is that the end user will not have to own the font you used or have it installed on his system. Because it's a graphic, it shows up like any other graphic—regardless of what system your end viewer uses.

Some of the earlier chapters demonstrate techniques that I recommend you combine with your text-based graphics. Using transparency and solid colors that match the background color of your page are two processes that can be employed in combination to achieve some of the effects described here.

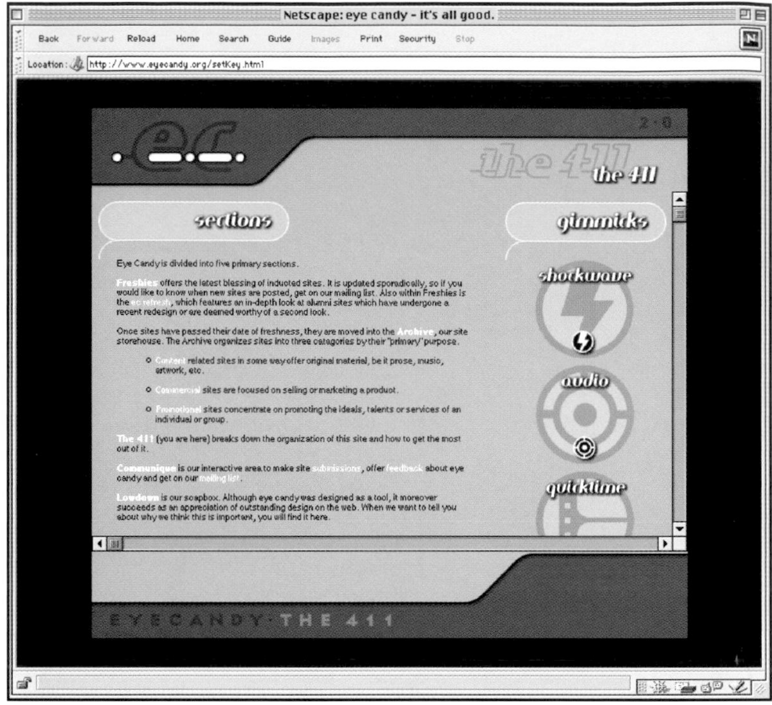

Here's a good example of graphics-based text used in combination with HTML body text. This site was designed by **Josh Ulm** (http://www.eyecandy.org).

warning

Aliasing or Anti-Aliasing

Most digital artists prefer the way anti-aliasing looks, but anti-aliasing is not always the best technique with typography.

Very small type actually looks worse and quite mushy if it's anti-aliased. Think about HTML type, the type on your computer desktop, and the type in a word processor. Very small type sizes (12 pt. and smaller) do not look good anti-aliased.

which looks better to you?

which looks better to you?

The top version is anti-aliased, and the bottom is aliased. Which looks better to your eye? I prefer aliased type at small point sizes and often find anti-aliasing difficult to read.

Using Fireworks for Type Design

Fireworks is an ideal environment for creating type and graphic Web elements. The various Effects settings enable you to create all kinds of special type effects for headlines that you can use on the Web. The editable text feature lets you set up one look and then change certain words that will take on the same appearance. This is great for creating navigation buttons!

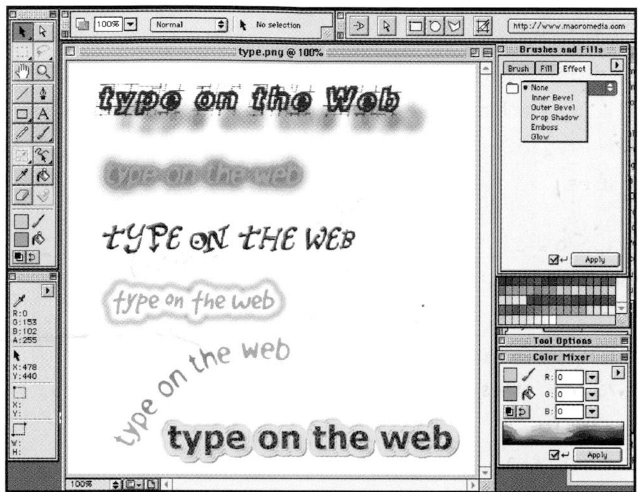

Fireworks offers a host of effects (similar to the Photoshop 5.0 Layer Effect feature). The fonts shown above were all downloaded for free from the Web from Fontastic, Fonthead Designs, and Chank Diesel (http://www.fonthead.com).

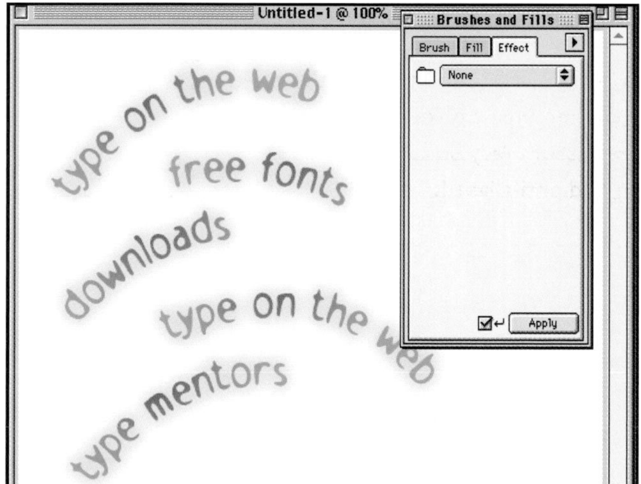

Once you set up a style you like in Fireworks, you can duplicate it and change the words. You can also copy and paste appearances, which is really handy if you change your mind (or if your client changes his or hers!).

Great Resources for Online Fonts

There are tens of thousands of PostScript and TrueType fonts available to personal computer users. It's a great benefit to be able to view and order fonts online—especially during those late nights when you're designing something that's due the next day and you need a specific font you don't yet own. If you're looking for new fonts, check out the following URLs. Some of these font developers distribute their wares for free, and some do not. Regardless, all of these sites are worth visiting.

Fontastic
http://rover.wiesbaden.netsurf.de/~kikita/

Nekkton
http://www.donbarnett.com/

Fonthead Designs
http://www.fonthead.com

Emigre Fonts
http://www.emigre.com

Letraset and ITC
http://www.letraset.com/itc/fonts/index.html

Chank Diesel
http://www.chank.com/

Just van Rossum and Erik van Blokland
http://www.letterror.com

House Industries
http://www.houseind.com/

Handwriting Fonts
http://www.execpc.com/~adw/

Daniel Will-Harris' Personal Favorites
http://www.will-harris.com/faces98/

Adobe's Type Browser (do not miss!)
http://www.adobe.com/type/browser/

Writing HTML to Place Text Graphics

Placing graphics on a Web page is addressed in depth in Chapter 14, "Rules, Bullets, & Buttons." The most basic way to insert a graphic on a page is to use the IMG SRC tag. Here's how to insert the drop shadow artwork, created earlier, on a page.

```
<HTML>
<BODY>
<IMG SRC="dropshad.jpeg">
</BODY>
</HTML>
```

If you want to link the drop shadow image to another source, combine the IMG SRC tag with an <A HREF> tag. Here's how.

```
<HTML>
<BODY>
<A HREF="http://www.domain.com">
<IMG SRC="dropshad.jpeg"></A>
</BODY>
</HTML>
```

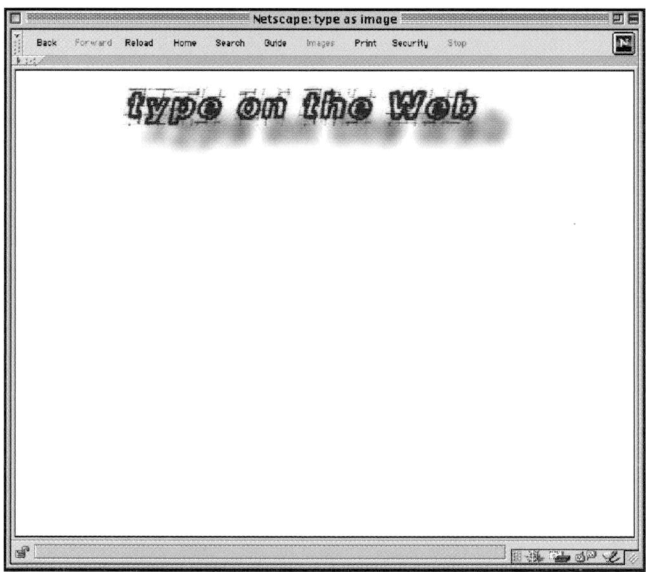

This page uses a text graphic inserted with HTML.

What About Font Embedding?

Wouldn't it be cool if you could specify and download a certain font with your HTML without the end user needing to install anything? That's actually possible today using a technique called type embedding. It should be no surprise that Netscape and Explorer are duking it out in the type arena, each offering different proprietary embedded font directions. Sigh. It makes a Web designer's job very difficult to have to make decisions between which spec to support. We'll look at both of them.

TrueDoc

Netscape supports the TrueDoc font files, which were developed by Bitstream, a major supplier of digital type (http://www.bitstream.com). The idea is that dynamic fonts will be downloaded along with an HTML page just as GIF and JPEG images are. A browser that can display TrueDoc font files will render the fonts on the screen (or on a printer). Browsers that cannot display TrueDoc fonts will use alternate fonts on the user's system.

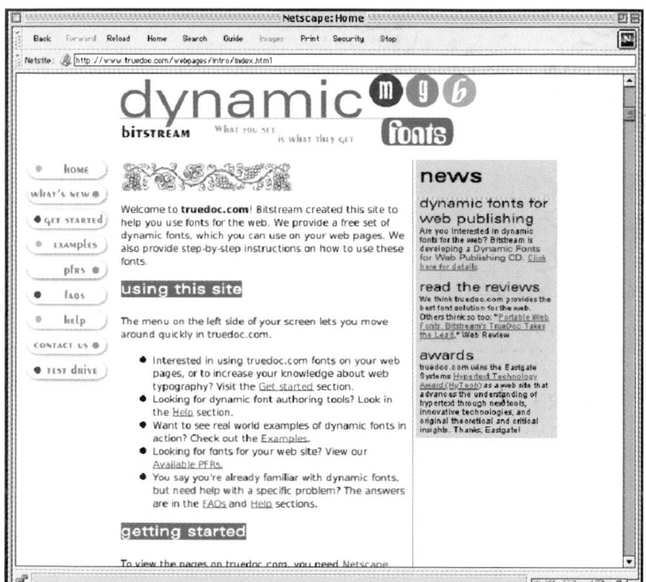

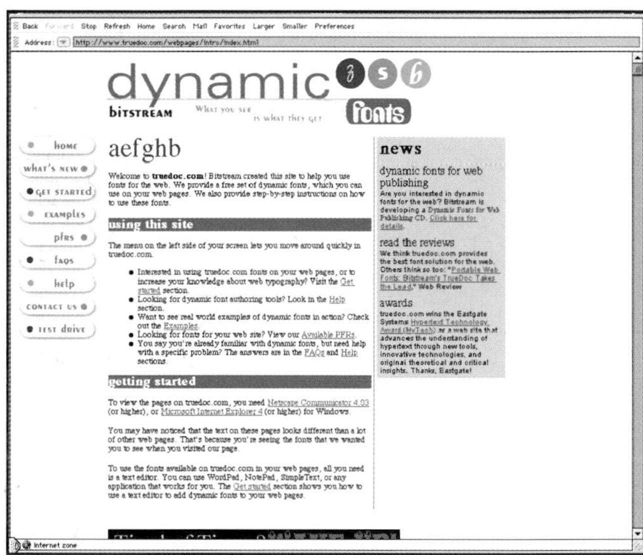

The biggest problem of all is that Netscape's solution doesn't work inside an Explorer browser window and vice-versa.

If you are creating Web pages and want to use dynamic fonts, you will need a TrueDoc-enabled authoring tool that will generate a PFR (**P**ortable **F**ont **R**esource) document to which HTML can link (by using the FONT FACE tags or Cascading Style Sheets). TrueDoc requires that fonts are generated with a CSR (**C**haracter **S**hape **R**ecorder) and rendered with a CSP (**C**haracter **S**hape **P**layer). Many authoring tools license this technology, including Macromedia, Corel, Sausage, SoftQuad, and InfoAccess.

So far, the only tool available for creating PFRs is HexMac (http://www.hexmac.com). To read a how-to tutorial on using HexMac, visit http://webreview.com/wr/pub/97/11/07/feature/hexweb.html. It is rumored that ActiveX Control will soon support the delivery of TrueDoc technologies to Windows browsers.

TrueType Embedding and OpenType

Microsoft is promoting a new format jointly developed with Adobe called **OpenType** (http://www.adobe.com/aboutadobe/publicrelations/HTML/9704/970423.admictyp.html). This format compresses and encrypts the font for delivery with HTML to browsers. On the end user's end, fonts are installed in their system for use only in the browser (supposedly).

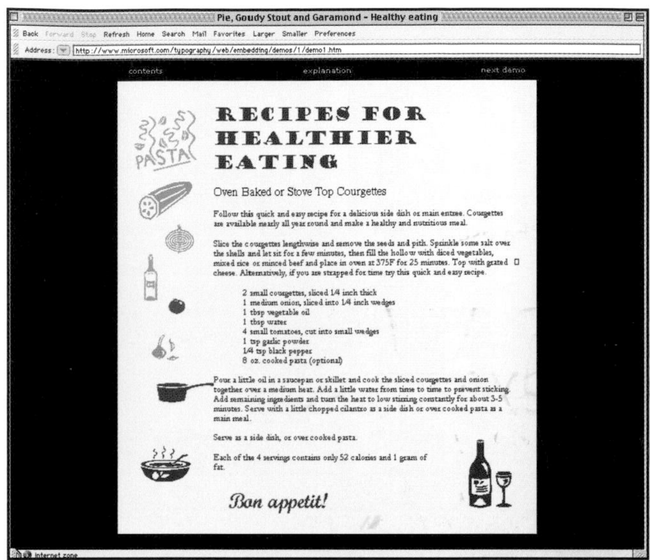

Here's an example of OpenType in Explorer.

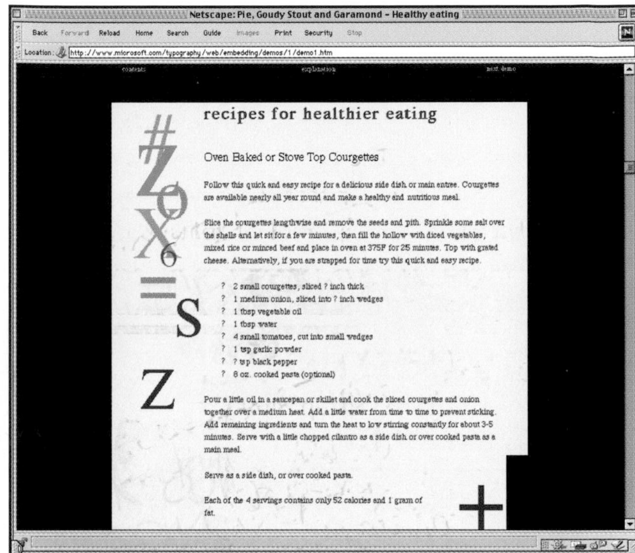

In Netscape, the page falls apart.

OpenType is available through the use of WEFT the (**W**eb **E**mbedding **F**ont **T**ool). A great online tutorial for using WEFT is located at http://www.microsoft.com/typography/web/embedding/weft/default.htm.

In the near future, TrueType Embedding will support Type1 fonts (the more popular format among graphic designers), which utilize PostScript. Unfortunately, the WEFT tool is Windows-only, leaving Mac developers (still the highest population of Web designers) unable to author this type of content.

Security Measures

Security for Bitstream's TrueDoc is provided through their technology called DocLock. This system uses encryption and tagging properties to record who owns a font. PFRs are tied to domains—so if you own a certain typeface, your PFR is tied to you. This allegedly prevents someone from looking at your HTML code, seeing where your PFRs are stored, and then linking to your server. Bitstream's TrueDoc doesn't include a font's outlines (the guts of the font—sort of like the digital mold); instead, it renders only the characters present in the document.

Security for TrueType Embedding is based on settings located within the embedding bit of the font itself. With TrueType fonts (and most Type1 fonts too), standard licensing policies allow for a font to be used by only one machine. Font embedding, on the other hand, ties the font to the document and not to the user. TrueType fonts contain permissions (called the embedding bit) determined by the original creator of the font, which can include embedding restrictions. Now, whenever you buy a TrueType font, you might find yourself asking first about its embedding levels!

Microsoft ships an extension (http://www.microsoft.com/truetype/property/property.htm) which enables you to view the properties of a TrueType font to check its embedding bit level. Possible settings include INSTALLABLE, EDITABLE, PRINT/PREVIEW, or RESTRICTED. A RESTRICTED embedding bit level would mean the font could not be embedded in online documents. OpenType, just like TrueType, promises to honor the embedding bit level of fonts. Because no one can even create OpenType until some tools are available, little is known about how many typefaces will include restrictions. Both OpenType and TrueType transmit the font's outlines which causes the type designer's skin to crawl. In fact, you might want to read http://news.i-us.com/wire/index-ie4font.htm to discover why designer's fears are well-founded.

Type Designers Against Embedding

Acclaimed type designers Just van Rossum and Erik van Blokland from **LetteRRor** (http://www. letterror. com/ LTR_central.html) don't like any of these solutions. They claim that hackers can easily steal the outlines from TrueType and OpenType embedded documents, and that the recorded character sets from TruDoc can be collected via automated font-stealing robots. They advocate a solution that is pixel-based, and have a spec for it on their site (http://www.letterror.com/LTR_ WrapSample.html). Another interesting pixel-based proposal comes from SGI's creative scientist **Paul Haeberli** at http://reality.sgi.com/grafica/ webfonts/. An organization called **TypeRight** has also been created to inform the public about the ethics of type (http://www.typeright.org).

The stakes are high in this game and we—the authors and designers of Web pages, who want to use fonts—are delighted that companies are working feverishly to make it possible. The developers of these embedding products have big bucks shining in their eyes, however, and seem to be eager to get a product out even if it contains questionable security holes. The font designers have a lot to protect, too, and they are certainly the underdogs here. Font designers predict copyright infringement and doom before the security measures are tested. It's a pivotal time, and the font designers appear to be losing their battle at the moment.

Don't discount the importance of font designers. It can easily take years (!) to create a good font design. If the Web renders designers' efforts for free, chances are few will be able to survive economically. This could result in the death of a very important art form.

If this embedding technical gobbledy-gook has your head spinning (mine is!), perhaps it's time to step back for a moment and let the dust settle. Most of these reported embedding options are not very developed yet, and the tools and tags are too new to work reliably. The ever-changing Web specs rage on, and we—the eager spectators of this embedded font war—are hoping to have our fonts and make sure the type designers can eat their cake, too.

What About PDF?

PDF stands for **P**ortable **D**ocument **F**ormat. It was developed long before the Web existed as a means of transporting documents to end users who didn't own the software applications the documents were created in. If, for example, I wanted to send a client a PageMaker document, and he or she didn't own PageMaker, my client could still see my layout with all the correct fonts and images intact.

PDF files are created with software available from Adobe, called Acrobat. Once you have the PDF authoring tool installed on your computer, you can choose to print to your printer or to a PDF document. If you print to PDF, it creates a file instead of a printout. You could upload the PDF to your Web site (using the IMG tag and the extension .pdf), and as long as your end user has the PDF Web browser plug-in called the Acrobat Reader, he or she can see your document. Trouble is, the plug-in is a hefty 3-4 megabytes. If you own any Adobe products, you'll find that most of the CD-ROMs include their reader; but, nevertheless, it is hefty for those who don't already have it.

PDFs are great if you have forms or documentation that need to uphold formatting. The IRS uses PDF forms to make tax reporting forms available online. I use PDF forms for the registration information for the workshops I teach from my training center. PDF is a great solution for transferring, but it's not a substitute for HTML or online delivery. For more information, visit: http://www.adobe.com/prodindex/acrobat/adobepdf.html.

What About Flash?

Flash is a vector-based authoring program and Web plug-in that allows you to create animation, interactive content, and Web pages. Because it works with vector data instead of bitmaps (like GIF and JPEG), the information is much smaller and downloads more quickly than any other format on the Web. It is possible to create entire Web sites in Flash that use any font you want, and those fonts will be accurately displayed to any visitor who has the plug-in installed.

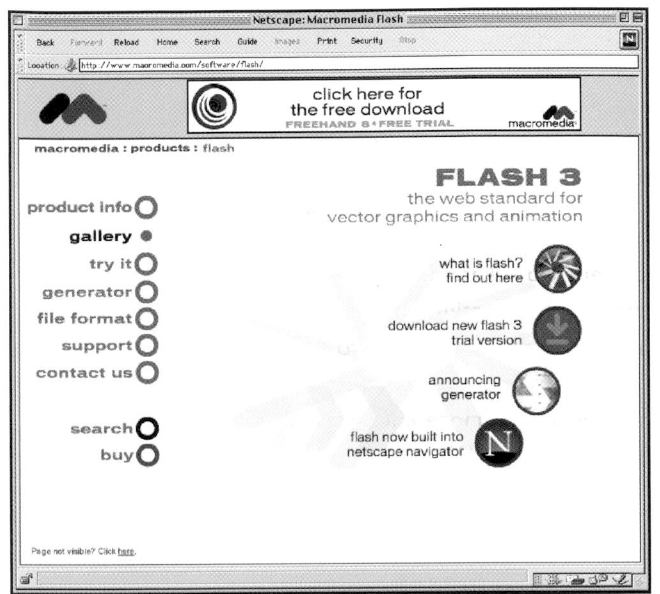

One of the best places to view Flash content is the Macromedia site. If you haven't seen the Macromedia site or Flash before, expect your mind to be blown. This is the Web that we all wish for.

The authoring tool has the ability to work with any font that you have installed in your system. You can make the type animate, fade, scale, and/or rotate over time, creating much more dynamism than GIF and JPEG could ever hope to possess. The authoring tool lets you assign sounds and rollovers to type as well, and you can create links that jump to other Flash scenes (meaning your visitor might view your entire site without ever seeing a single HTML ASCII font).

One of the major drawbacks to Flash has been its reliance on a plug-in. While the plug-in is small (118k), it is still a deterrent to many. Fortunately, Netscape 4.5 now includes the plug-in with its shipping version. In addition, Windows 98 supports Flash as a native file format. Many are speculating (and hoping) that the barriers to using Flash are going away and that this very exciting file format will be available to the general Web viewing public soon.

I think Flash holds incredible promise as an HTML alternative. It gives designers the design control they want without forcing them to learn any programming. There is also a new product, called Flash Generator, which allows you to use Flash with database-driven content. You could set up a template in Flash, for example, and have dynamically changing content conform to the template. Very exciting stuff.

The drawback to Flash is its reliance on a plug-in (which is destined to change), it's challenging authoring tool (which has an unusual interface), and the fact that Flash content is not searchable by search engines or text readers. I think Flash is here to stay, and it offers one of the most promising multimedia technologies the Web has seen so far. To read more about it, visit http://www.macromedia.com/software/flash/.

summary Web Typography

Typography is one of the most exciting design mediums at our disposal, yet the Web has been weak to support much more than two fonts. This chapter reviewed the different techniques available to help you gain more creative control over your typography on the Web. To summarize:

- The FONT FACE attribute allows you to specify fonts. Just be careful that your end user has the font you request.
- Verdana and Georgia are two typefaces that were designed for screen-based delivery. Use them in your Web pages if you'd like; chances are your visitors will have these fonts if they've installed Win95 or Internet Explorer.
- Font embedding sounds neat, but due to competing standards, it really isn't ready for prime time. You can try out the font embedding tools on the market today by following the URLs found in this chapter.
- PDF is useful if you have online documentation or forms that require exact positioning and fonts. It should not be used as an HTML substitute.
- Flash is an alternative font-delivery method that offers absolute design control plus interactivity and animation. You might try downloading the free trial to see if you like it.

Introduction

Alignment & Tables

Chapter Topics

- Web Page Size
- HTML for Alignment
- Text Alignment Tags
- Image Alignment Tags
- Spacers
- Tables for Data
- Tables for Images

17

In most layout software for print applications, such as QuarkXPress and PageMaker, you simply place an image or text block where you want it, and there it stays. Unfortunately in HTML, alignment is one of the trickiest challenges of all.

Part of the problem is that unlike paper, a Web page has no fixed size. Some browsers have predefined sizes that the viewing window fits to; others let you size the screen to fill your monitor. Some members of your audience will see your page through tiny portable computer screens. Others will have 21" monitors. In addition, some of your viewers will change the font size defaults, which will make everything line up differently than you planned. It's no wonder alignment is hard, given these variables.

This chapter looks at various alignment options within basic HTML, including the use of tables, spacers, and images. (It's also possible to establish alignment using Cascading Style Sheets, discussed in Chapter 19, "Cascading Style Sheets.") This chapter will demonstrate that it is possible to beat the odds and create interesting layouts using standard HTML. What is possible, however, is not always easy to remember. Unfortunately, HTML was never intended to be a page layout description language.

How Big Is a Web Page?

Because you can scroll a Web page vertically or horizontally, there is no set length or width restriction on a Web document. The amount of text and artwork you choose to place on any given page dictates its size. If you position artwork that is so wide it spans horizontally or so tall it spans vertically, the page will fit to the size of your artwork. Scrollbars appear in most browsers automatically when the artwork is oversized in either direction.

Your first page creates the most important impression because that is where most of your visitors will make the decision to either enter your site or wander elsewhere. If you want your opening graphic to be visible on most computer monitors, you will probably want to know what size to make your artwork.

It's a difficult question to answer because computer monitor sizes and resolutions vary. Most portable computer screens today are 800x600, though older models are as small as 640x400. On top of that, you need to take into account the default size of the browser window. On a Macintosh, Netscape's opening screen defaults to 505 pixels across, which is more narrow than the default size of Netscape when viewed on Windows.

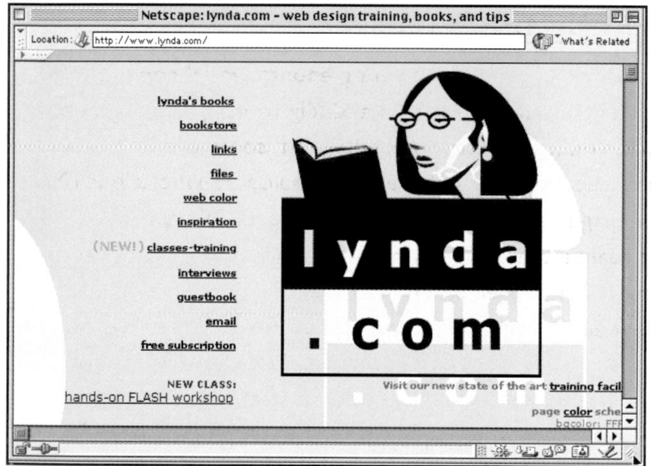

640x480

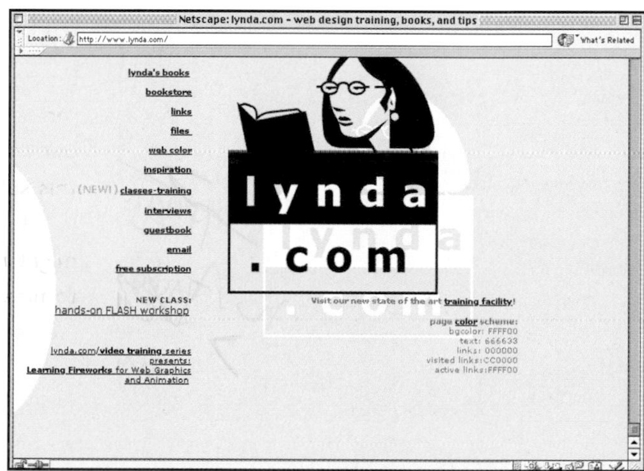

800x600

I've personally settled on 480x350 pixels as a good width and height for an opening graphic or splash screen. This rule is not cast in stone, and I realize it will seem far too conservative for many of your Web sites. I have based this size preference on the many possible conditions my site might be viewed from.

Some artists choose to make their screens wider than my conservative estimate of 480 pixels. There are lots of clever ways to tell your audience how wide to open the browser window, as shown by the next example. After you establish the size of your pages, move on to the following sections, which will examine techniques for lining up artwork within them.

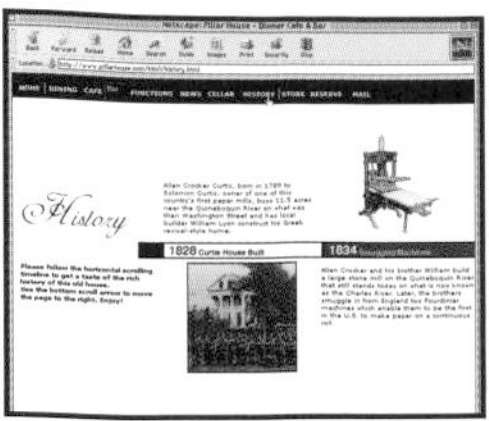
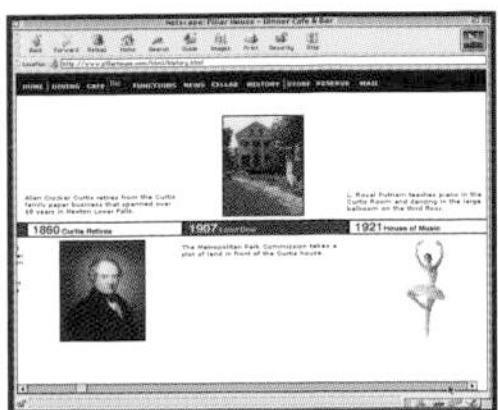
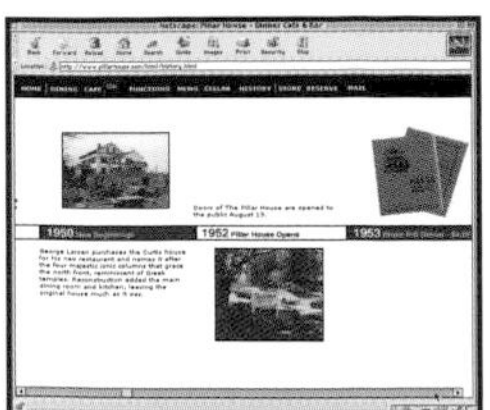
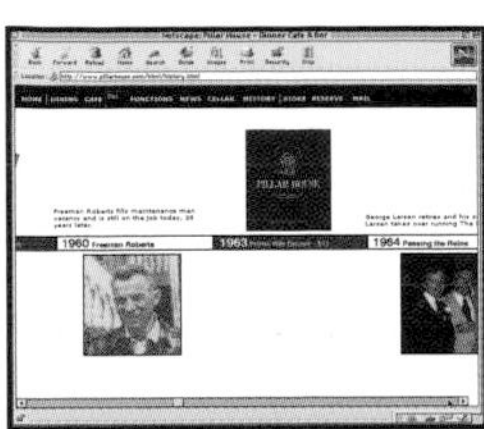
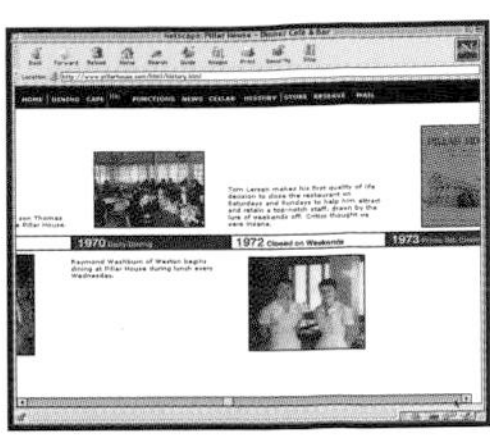
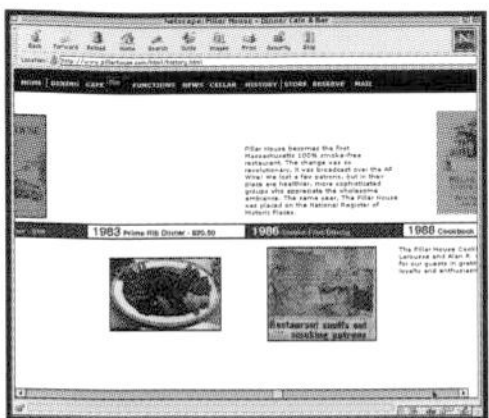
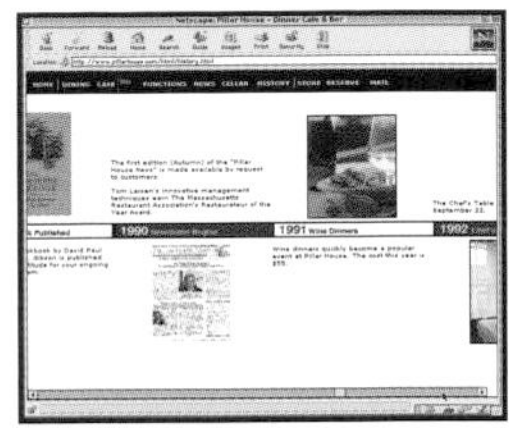
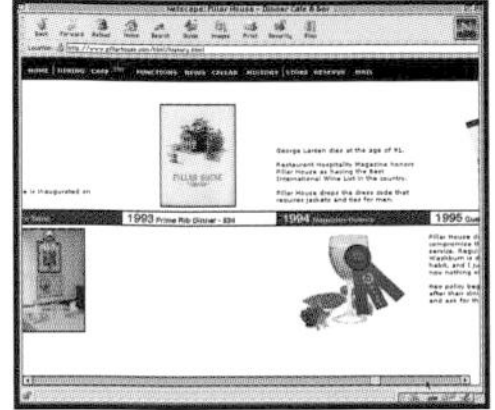
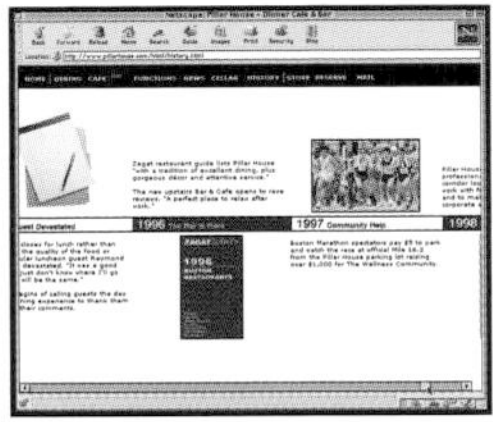
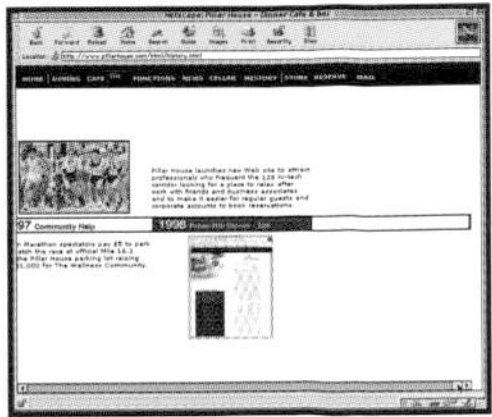

At http://www.pillarhouse.com, the history section uses a horizontal scrolling method that takes 10 browser screens to complete. This page was made wide by writing the HTML code to place a lot of images to the right, thus making the page open wide to display all the images. That is the only way to make a wide page (except by using JavaScript, which will be covered later).

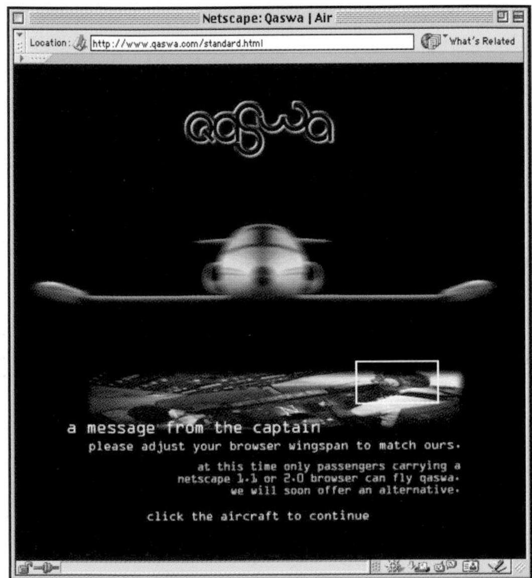

Ammon Haggerty (http://www.qaswa.com) uses the wings of a spacecraft as a visual metaphor for setting browser width at his site.

Using HTML for Alignment

If you hang around this industry long enough, you'll soon realize that many HTML purists don't take kindly to using HTML for layout. In fact, you'll encounter hostility from some authorities in this subject because they believe that developers who use HTML to "design" pages are ruining the founding principles of HTML. You might not realize that HTML was intentionally designed to be customized by the end user to provide changeable font sizes, colors, and window sizes, and that precise layout interferes with this feature. That is why Netscape and Internet Explorer—instead of the W3C Standards committee—initiated most of the alignment tags and attributes that are in vogue today. There is a movement underfoot to separate the structure of an HTML document (i.e., headers, body text, lists, etc.) from the formatting characteristics (such as whether the text is centered or colored or the size of a font).

Many predict that someday Cascading Style Sheets (see Chapter 19, "Cascading Style Sheets") will specify the formatting of HTML documents, and that HTML will return to its earliest roots of a structural-only language. This could be a good thing, especially because CSS affords a lot more precise control than many of the solutions this chapter covers. For the moment, however, CSS is not supported consistently between browsers, and very little of it is usable unless you decide to do a Netscape-only or Explorer-only site.

Therefore, if you want alignment control over your pages today, you'll have to learn to milk HTML for every alignment workaround it can provide. The following section reviews some of the HTML alignment tags.

Text Alignment Tags and Attributes

These tags relate to text elements. The following is an example of how they look on a Web page.

Paragraph breaks: Insert this tag where you want spaces between paragraphs:

<P>

This is a line of type separated by a paragraph break

This is a line of type separated by a paragraph break

Line breaks: Put this tag where you want the text to wrap to the next line but not create any extra space:

This is a line of type separated by a
This is a line of type separated by a

Centering text: Use this tag before you center text and/or images and use the closed tag when you want text below it to return to left-justified formatting:

<CENTER>

this
type is
aligned with
<CENTER>

Preformatted text: Preformatted text typically uses a different font, such as the typewriter-style Courier, instead of the default Times Roman. The PRE tag lets you set the spacing and indents of your type. (For more examples of the PRE tag, check out Chapter 16, "Web Typography," and Chapter 26, "HTML for Visual Designers."

<PRE></PRE>

```
p r e  formated text
             will use whatever spacing

you  s e t as you t      y       p       e
```

No break: Use this tag if you want the browser width to dictate where the text breaks. The closed tag signifies when you want the no break formatting to end.

<NOBR></NBR>

you can insert

extra paragraph spaces by

adding extra paragraph returns after the

no break space entities element

note

Leading with HTML

Leading is a typographic term for the amount of space between multiple lines of text. Creating extra space between lines of type in HTML isn't obvious unless you know about a couple of workarounds. If you add multiple P tags, for example, you will only get a single line of space between carriage returns because HTML recognizes only one P tag at a time. For multiple lines of space, there are two techniques: using the PRE tag or using the P tag with the entities element . The   element stands for "no break space."

```
you can insert


extra paragraph spaces by




adding extra paragraph returns after the

no break space entities element  
```

This above example used the following code:

```
<P>you can insert
<P> 
 <P>extra paragraph spaces by
<P> 
 <P> 
<P>adding extra paragraph returns after the
<P>no break space entities element &amp;nbsp;
```

This technique allows you to insert extra P tags because it recognizes the string   as invisible content and inserts a paragraph break after it anyway. The & entity displays an ampersand in the browser.

An alternative method would use the PRE tag. In this instance, just create multiple carriage returns while you are typing, and extra leading will appear.

```
You can use PRE to

insert multiple carriage



returns, and it will honor whatever
spacing you type on the keyboard.
```

Here's the code for the above example using PRE:

```
<PRE>You can use PRE to

insert multiple carriage



returns, and it will honor whatever
spacing you type on the keyboard.</PRE>
```

If you want more precise control over leading, you need to use CSS, which is described in a later chapter.

Image Alignment Tags

These tags cause text to align in relationship to the images it's next to. Note that the ALIGN attribute is associated with the IMG tag, not the text.

Top Alignment

About Ducks In A Row

Ducks In A Row sells custom designed wholesale rubber stamps to retail stores. If you'd like to find a retail location where our stamps are sold, click here. If you are a retail store and would like to carry our stamps you can fax us for a catalog at (805) 646.5299. Joan Farber is the illustrator who created the artwork for Ducks In A Row. Her artists representative for national/international advertising campaigns and private commissioned fine art is: 630 5th Avenue 20th floor Rockefeller Center, NY NY 100111 212.332.3460 fax - 212.332-3401.

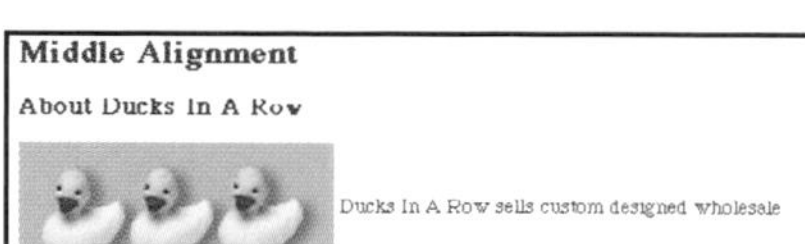

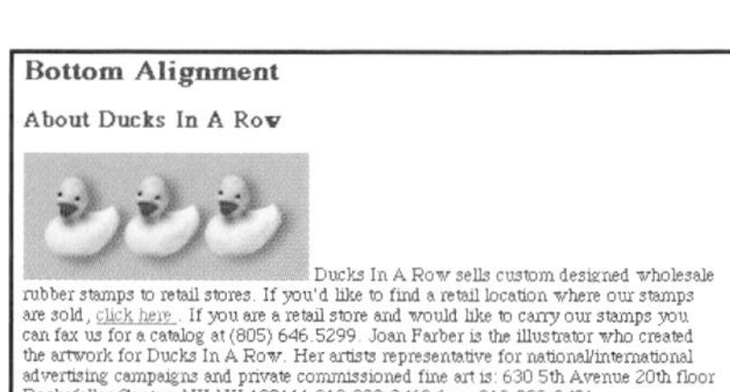

ALIGN=TOP Aligns the text to the top of your image:

```
<IMG SRC="duckies.jpg"
WIDTH="170" HEIGHT="76"
ALIGN=top>
Ducks In A Row sells custom
designed wholesale rubber stamps
to retail stores.  If you'd like
to find a retail location where
our stamps are sold, <A
HREF="sales.html">click here</A>.
If you are a retail store and
would like to carry our stamps
you can fax us for a catalog at
(805) 646.5299.  Joan Farber is
the illustrator who created the
artwork for Ducks In A Row.  Her
artists representative for
national/international advertising
campaigns and private commis-
sioned fine art is: 630 5th
Avenue 20th floor Rockefeller
Center, NY NY 100111 212.332.3460
fax - 212.332-3401.
```

ALIGN=MIDDLE Aligns the text to the middle:

```
<IMG SRC="duckies.jpg"
WIDTH="170" HEIGHT="76"
ALIGN=middle>
Ducks In A Row sells custom
designed wholesale rubber stamps
to retail stores.  If you'd like
to find a retail location where
our stamps are sold, <A
HREF="sales.html">click here</A>.
If you are a retail store and
would like to carry our stamps
you can fax us for a catalog at
(805) 646.5299.  Joan Farber is
the illustrator who created the
artwork for Ducks In A Row.  Her
artists representative for
national/international advertising
campaigns and private commis-
sioned fine art is: 630 5th
Avenue 20th floor Rockefeller
Center, NY NY 100111 212.332.3460
fax - 212.332-3401.
```

ALIGN=BOTTOM Aligns the text to the bottom:

```
<IMG SRC="duckies.jpg"
WIDTH="170" HEIGHT="76"
ALIGN=bottom>
Ducks In A Row sells custom
designed wholesale rubber stamps
to retail stores.  If you'd like
to find a retail location where
our stamps are sold, <A
HREF="sales.html">click here</A>.
If you are a retail store and
would like to carry our stamps
you can fax us for a catalog at
(805) 646.5299.  Joan Farber is
the illustrator who created the
artwork for Ducks In A Row.  Her
artists representative for
national/international advertis-
ing campaigns and private
commissioned fine art is: 630 5th
Avenue 20th floor Rockefeller
Center, NY NY 100111 212.332.3460
fax - 212.332-3401.
```

Left Alignment

About Ducks In A Row

Ducks In A Row sells custom designed wholesale rubber stamps to retail stores. If you'd like to find a retail location where our stamps are sold, click here. If you are a retail store and would like to carry our stamps you can fax us for a catalog at (805) 646.5299. Joan Farber is the illustrator who created the artwork for Ducks In A Row. Her artists representative for national/international advertising campaigns and private commissioned fine art is: 630 5th Avenue 20th floor Rockefeller Center, NY NY 100111 212.332.3460 fax - 212.332-3401.

ALIGN=LEFT Aligns the text to the left side:

```
<IMG SRC="duckies.jpg" WIDTH="170"
HEIGHT="76" ALIGN=right>
Ducks In A Row sells custom
designed wholesale rubber stamps
to retail stores.  If you'd like
to find a retail location where
our stamps are sold, <A
HREF="sales.html">click here</A>.
If you are a retail store and
would like to carry our stamps
you can fax us for a catalog at
(805) 646.5299.  Joan Farber is
the illustrator who created the
artwork for Ducks In A Row.  Her
artists representative for
national/international advertising
campaigns and private commissioned
fine art is: 630 5th Avenue 20th
floor Rockefeller Center, NY NY
100111 212.332.3460 fax -
212.332-3401.
```

Right Alignment

About Ducks In A Row

Ducks In A Row sells custom designed wholesale rubber stamps to retail stores. If you'd like to find a retail location where our stamps are sold, click here. If you are a retail store and would like to carry our stamps you can fax us for a catalog at (805) 646.5299. Joan Farber is the illustrator who created the artwork for Ducks In A Row. Her artists representative for national/international advertising campaigns and private commissioned fine art is: 630 5th Avenue 20th floor Rockefeller Center, NY NY 100111 212.332.3460 fax - 212.332-3401.

ALIGN=RIGHT Aligns the text to the right side:

```
<IMG SRC="duckies.jpg"
WIDTH="170" HEIGHT="76"
ALIGN=right>
Ducks In A Row sells custom
designed wholesale rubber stamps
to retail stores.  If you'd like
to find a retail location where
our stamps are sold, <A
HREF="sales.html">click here</A>.
If you are a retail store and
would like to carry our stamps
you can fax us for a catalog at
(805) 646.5299.  Joan Farber is
the illustrator who created the
artwork for Ducks In A Row.  Her
artists representative for
national/international advertis-
ing campaigns and private
commissioned fine art is: 630 5th
Avenue 20th floor Rockefeller
Center, NY NY 100111 212.332.3460
fax - 212.332-3401.
```

Horizontal and Vertical Space Tags

The horizontal and vertical space tags allow you to insert empty space around a graphic, creating breathing room.

HSPACE & VSPACE: The HSPACE and VSPACE attributes position the image with breathing room around the type. In this case, a value of 40 pixels was used, leaving 20 pixel spaces on the right and left sides and at the top and bottom of the image.

Left Alignment with Horizontal and Vertical Space

About Ducks In A Row

Ducks In A Row sells custom designed wholesale rubber stamps to retail stores. If you'd like to find a retail location where our stamps are sold, click here . If you are a retail store and would like to carry our stamps you can fax us for a catalog at (805) 646.5299. Joan Farber is the illustrator who created the artwork for Ducks In A Row. Her artists representative for national/international advertising campaigns and private commissioned fine art is: 630 5th Avenue 20th floor Rockefeller Center, NY NY 100111 212.332.3460 fax - 212.332-3401.

```
<IMG SRC="duckies.jpg" WIDTH="170" HEIGHT="76"
ALIGN=left HSPACE="40" VSPACE="40">
Ducks In A Row sells custom designed wholesale rub-
ber stamps to retail stores.  If you'd like to find
a retail location where our stamps are sold, <A
HREF="sales.html">click here</A>.  If you are a
retail store and would like to carry our stamps you
can fax us for a catalog at (805) 646.5299.  Joan
Farber is the illustrator who created the artwork
for Ducks In A Row.  Her artists representative for
national/international advertising campaigns and
private commissioned fine art is: 630 5th Avenue
20th floor Rockefeller Center, NY NY 100111
212.332.3460 fax - 212.332-3401.
```

Width and Height Attributes

These attributes work by allowing you to specify the width and height values (in pixels) of a graphic. This can accomplish two things: It causes the text on the page to load before the graphic, and it makes space for the graphic to come into the proper location. Using width and height attributes within HTML is very important for downloading speed, and many plug-in EMBED tags require that you include width and height information. (See Chapters 11 and 25 for more information on plug-ins and embedding.)

There's a lesser known feature of WIDTH and HEIGHT, however. If you put in values that are larger or smaller than the physical dimensions of your original image, they will actually enlarge or shrink your image. In the following example, the actual dimension of the ducks image is 170x76 pixels. By entering a value of 347x216 scaled it larger. By entering a width of 80 and height of 36, I shrunk the image. This doesn't always look good, but it is nevertheless used from time to time as a visual effect. The following images illustrate these alignment tags.

<IMG SRC="duckies.jpg" WIDTH="347" HEIGHT="216">

<IMG SRC= "duckies.jpg" WIDTH ="80" HEIGHT="36">

It is also possible to put percentages into the WIDTH and HEIGHT attributes.

<IMG SRC="duckies.jpg" WIDTH="100%" HEIGHT="100%">
Using percentages with the HEIGHT and WIDTH tags will distort the image, but it will also cause it to respond to the shape of the browser window instead of the image's native size. In this example, the image stretches to 100% of the browser size and changes depending on how wide your browser is opened.

If you use the actual size of the image for the HEIGHT and WIDTH values, your page will load faster because the browser doesn't have to assess the size on its own. It is recommended that you always put the desired HEIGHT and WIDTH values into your HTML, unless you are going after a visual effect of scaling or shrinking.

This exhausts the alignment possibilities offered by widely supported HTML tags. Next, we move on to alignment techniques that don't use HTML code—they involve making custom artwork that serves to align images.

Alternatives to HTML Using Artwork

Using images for custom alignment involves creating spacer art. This art exists on the Web page for the sole purpose of making spaces between text and images. For the spacer art to be invisible, you have two options: to make the spacer art the same color as your background or to make the spacer artwork a transparent GIF that contains only one color (making the entire graphic transparent).

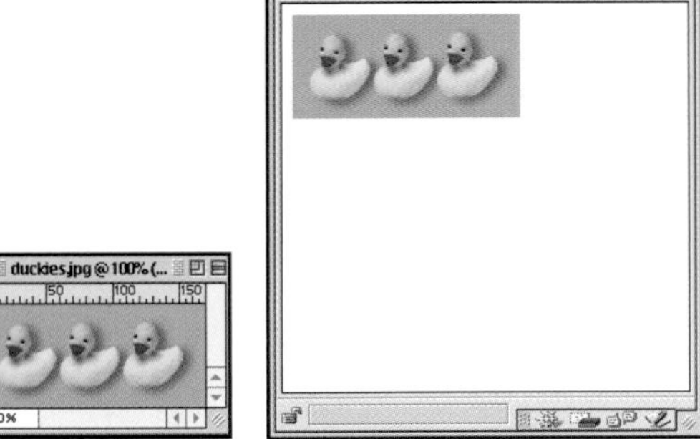

The original image.

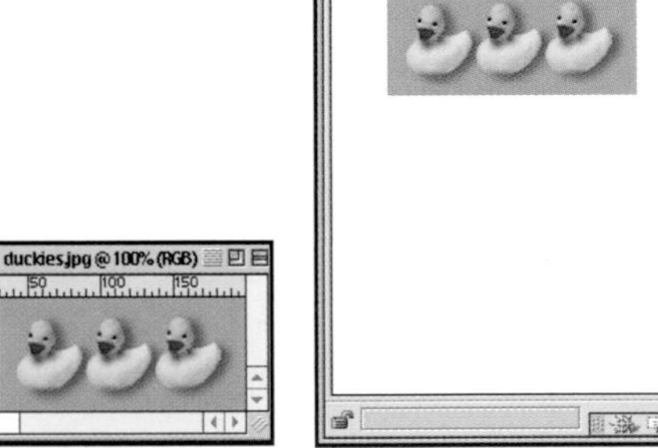

Here is the image with 20 pixels of white space inserted to the left.

note

WIDTH and HEIGHT Attributes for Spacers

Using the WIDTH and HEIGHT attributes, you can stretch a single pixel GIF to any size you wish. **David Siegel** is the master of the single pixel GIF trick. Check out his instructions at the following site:

http://www.dsiegel.com/tips/wonk5/single.html

Tables for Alignment

Tables for the Web were originally conceived to produce columns of text or numbers in individual cells, much like a spreadsheet or chart. Even though tables were invented to support text and numbers, you can put graphics inside table cells, too. All the graphic tags I've described so far work within the table tags. Because of this, I've made a distinction in this chapter between data tables and graphic tables.

A Web designer who knows how to use tables for page layout control will be a much happier camper than one who doesn't. Learning to program tables will offer lots of formatting options that HTML doesn't directly support.

Data Tables

Data-based tables are probably what the HTML standards committee (http://www.w3c.com) had in mind when they published the code. These are the typical kinds of tables you see on most sites. They contain text and numbers, links, and occasionally graphics. They have telltale borders around the cells, which look slightly dimensional, and are created by employing embossed lines of varying width to divide individual chart sections.

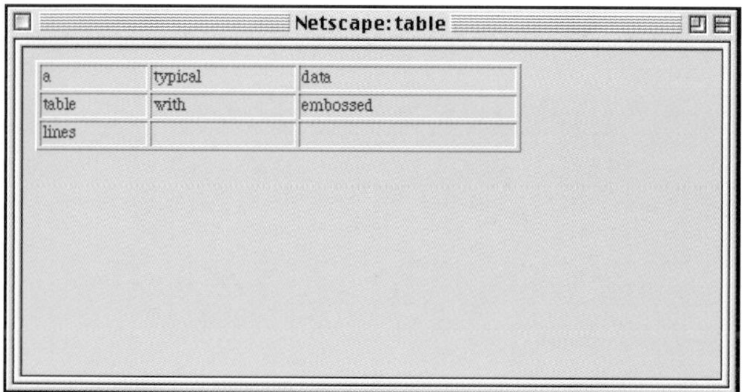

By default, data tables use embossed lines to divide up all the cells and sections.

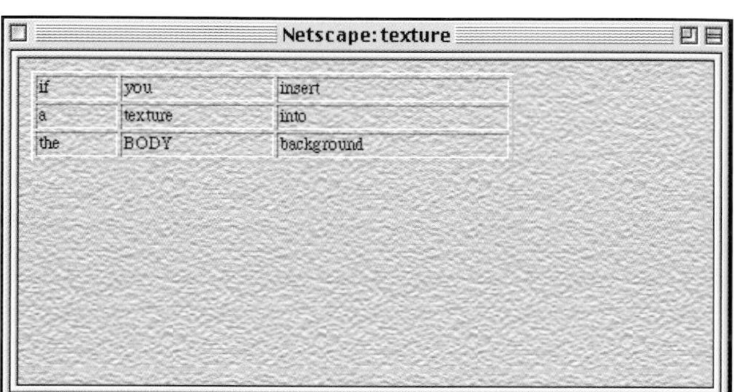

If you use a pattern background or solid color background, the embossing shows through and looks as if it's a lighting effect.

Table borders are similar to horizontal rules on steroids: The HTML code magically manufactures vertical and horizontal lines of different widths and thicknesses with a few choice strokes of code and tags. They seem complicated by appearance, but you will probably be surprised at how easy they are to create and use.

HTML Table Tags

When creating data or graphics tables for the Web, you work with the same HTML tags. The table tags allow you to put information inside individual cells. Understanding the tag structure for data tables enables you to work with the graphic tables later in this chapter.

You always begin a table with TABLE and end it with the /TABLE tag. The TR and /TR tags indicate the start and end of a new row. The TD and /TD tags mark the content of each data cell.

Upper Left	Upper Right
Bottom Left	Bottom Right

```
<TABLE><TR><TD>Upper Left</TD>
<TD>Upper Right</TD></TR>
<TR><TD>Bottom Left</TD>
<TD>Bottom Right</TD></TR></TABLE>
```

By adding the TH attribute, you can add header information to tables, which is displayed in most browsers as bold headlines.

Upper Left	**Upper Right**
Bottom Left	Bottom Right

```
<TABLE>
<TR><TH>Upper Left</TH>
<TH>Upper Right</TH></TR>
<TR><TD>Bottom Left</TD>
<TD>Bottom Right</TD></TR></TABLE>
```

The TABLE BORDER tag gives the table an embossed look and feel. Here's an example of such code, with the HTML below:

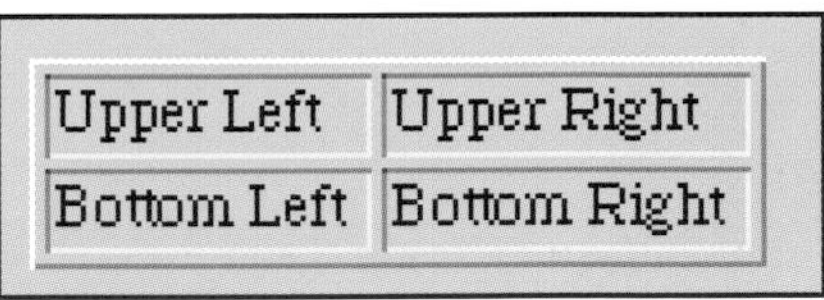

Upper Left	Upper Right
Bottom Left	Bottom Right

```
<TABLE BORDER>
<TR><TD>Upper Left</TD>
<TD>Upper Right</TD></TR>
<TR><TD>Bottom Left</TD><TD>
Bottom Right</TD></TR></TABLE>
```

The COLSPAN tag allows one row to fill more than one column. Here's an example of such code, with the HTML below:

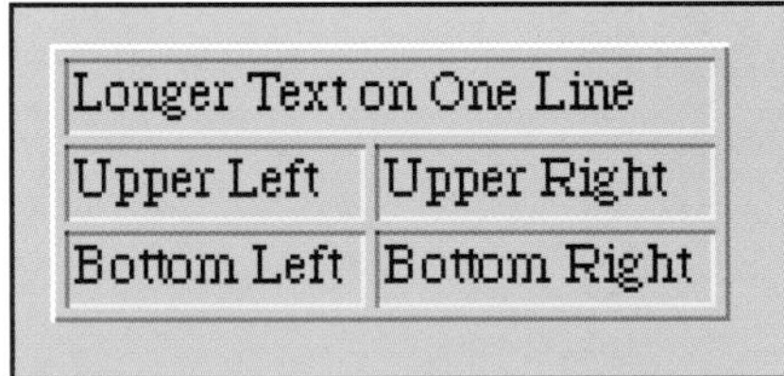

Longer Text on One Line	
Upper Left	Upper Right
Bottom Left	Bottom Right

```
<TABLE BORDER>
<TR><TD COLSPAN=2>
Longer Text on One Line</TD></TR>
<TR><TD>Upper Left</TH><TD>
Upper Right</TH></TR>
<TR>Bottom Left</TD>
<TR><TD>Bottom Right</TD></TR></TABLE>
```

The ROWSPAN tag takes up columns and rows. It is not any specific size or shape; the dimensions are dictated by the content you insert. Here's an example of such code, with the HTML below:

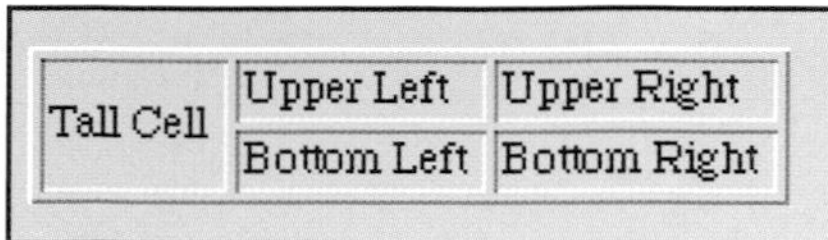


```
<TABLE BORDER>
<TR><TD ROWSPAN=2>
Tall Cell</TD>
<TD>Upper Left</TD>
<TD>Upper Right</TD></TR>
<TR><TD>Bottom Left</TD>
<TD>Bottom Right</TD></TR></TABLE>
```

WIDTH and HEIGHT attributes can include pixel-based or percentage-based values. The two images below show the same code in two different browser windows. When the browser is dragged out to be larger, the WIDTH attribute, which is using percentage values, stretches with it.

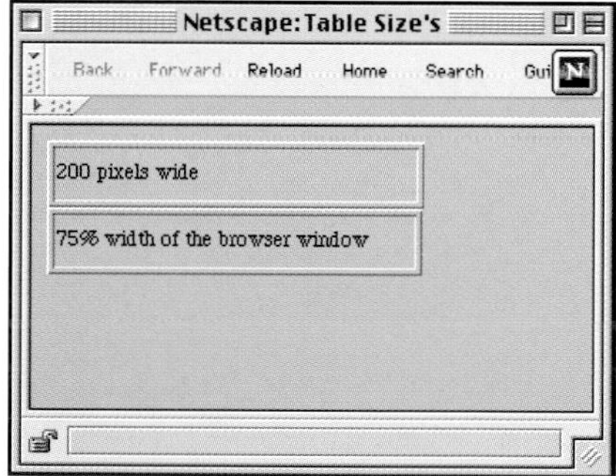

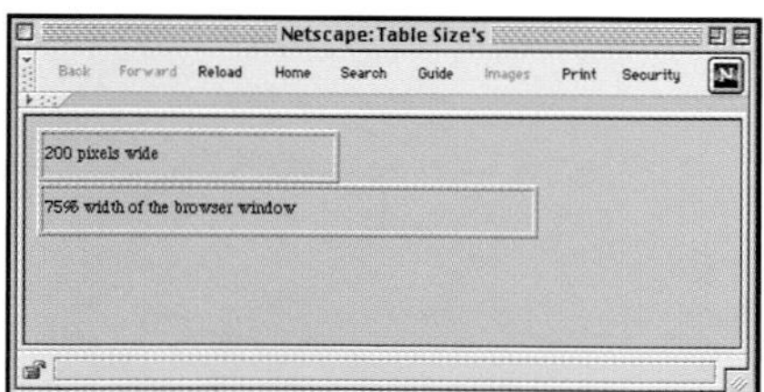


```
<TABLE BORDER WIDTH=200 HEIGHT=35>
<TR><TD>200 pixels wide</TD></TR></TABLE>
<TABLE BORDER WIDTH=75% HEIGHT=35>
<TR><TD>75% width of the browser window
</TD></TR></TABLE>
```

The <TABLE WIDTH=# of pixels> and <TABLE HEIGHT =# of pixels> tags let you dictate the shape of the table by pixels (or percentages, as shown next). Here's an example of such code, with the HTML below:

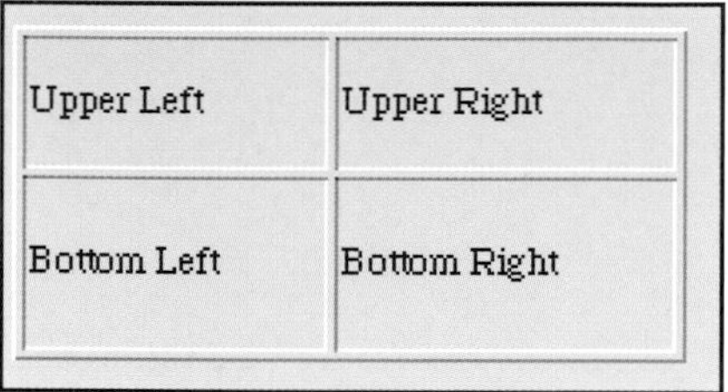


```
<TABLE BORDER WIDTH=200 HEIGHT=100>
<TR><TD>Upper Left</TD>
<TD>Upper Right</TD></TR>
<TR><TD>Bottom Left</TD>
<TD>Bottom Right</TD></TR></TABLE>
```

The <TABLE CELLPADDING=# of pixels> tag puts a uniform space inside the cells, governed by the number of pixels entered after the = (equal) sign. Here's an example of such code, with the HTML below:

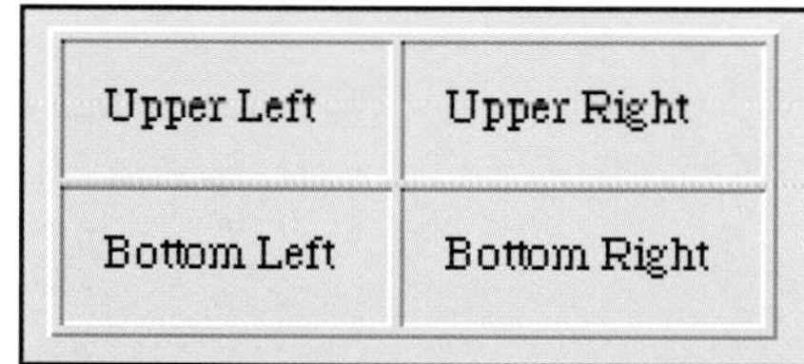


```
<TABLE BORDER CELLPADDING=10>
<TR><TD>Upper Left</TD>
<TD>Upper Right</TD></TR>
<TR><TD>Bottom Left</TD>
<TD>Bottom Right</TD></TR></TABLE>
```

The tag <TABLE CELLSPACING=# of pixels> puts a thicker line weight around the cells. Here's an example of such code, with the HTML below:

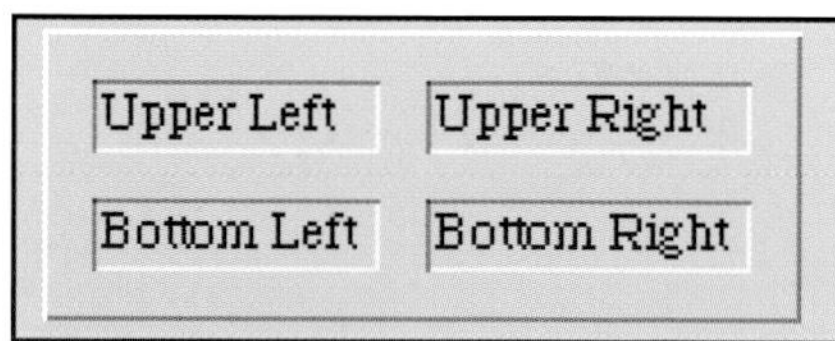


```
<TABLE BORDER CELLSPACING=10>
<TR><TD>Upper Left</TD>
<TD>Upper Right</TD></TR>
<TR><TD>Bottom Left</TD>
<TD>Bottom Right</TD></TR></TABLE>
```

You can adjust the alignment of data inside cells by using the VALIGN tag, which allows you to specify top, middle, bottom, and baseline alignments. Here's an example of such code, with the HTML below:

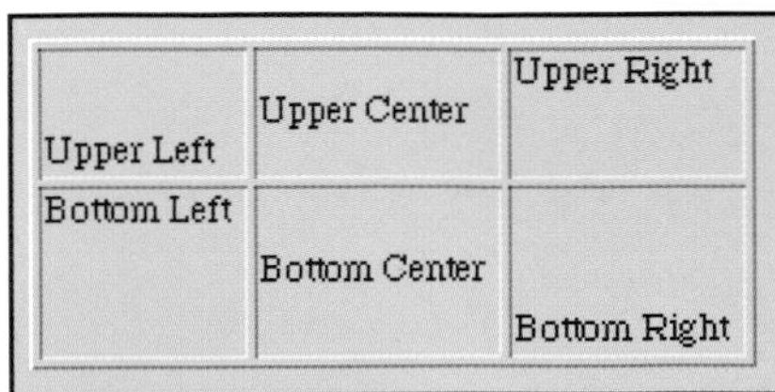

Upper Left	Upper Center	Upper Right
Bottom Left	Bottom Center	Bottom Right

```
<TABLE BORDER HEIGHT=100>
<TR><TD VALIGN=bottom>Upper Left</TD>
<TD VALIGN=middle>Upper Center</TD>
<TD VALIGN=top>Upper Right</TD></TR>
<TR><TD VALIGN=top>Bottom Left</TD>
<TD VALIGN=middle>Bottom Center</TD>
<TD VALIGN=bottom>Bottom Right</TD></TR></TABLE>
```

You can also specify, right, left, and middle alignment values within the TR, TH, and TD tags by using the word align. Here's an example of such code, with the HTML below:

Upper Left	Upper Center	Upper Right
Bottom Left	Bottom Center	Bottom Right

```
<TABLE BORDER HEIGHT=100>
<TR VALIGN=top>
<TD>Upper Left</TD>
<TD>Upper Center</TD>
<TD>Upper Right</TD></TR>
<TR VALIGN=bottom>
<TD>Bottom Left</TD>
<TD>Bottom Center</TD>
<TD>Bottom Right</TD></TR></TABLE>
```

You can also put graphics inside tables by using the IMG SRC="name.gif" tag instead of text or values. Here's an example of such code, with the HTML below:

```
<TABLE BORDER><TR><TD>
<IMG SRC="duckies.jpg"></TD></TR></TABLE>
```

The following example shows how you can mix text and graphics inside cells of a table; the code follows:

	QUACK!!		
	QUACK!		QUACK!!!

```
<TABLE BORDER>
<TR><TD rowspan=2>
<IMG SRC="ducky.jpg"></TD>
<TH colspan=3>QUACK!!</TH></TR>
<TR><TD>QUACK!</TD>
<TD><IMG SRC="ducky.jpg"></TD>
<TD>QUACK!!!</TD></TR></TABLE>
```

This last example showed how to insert graphics into your tables by using the IMG SRC tag. The following section explains how you can work with graphics more seamlessly, by eliminating the telltale border around table cells.

Graphic Tables for Page Layout

Table support was the first real hook designers had for being able to control layout of page design. If you use tables to create a design grid, all the things that basic HTML has kept you from doing are suddenly possible. You want a vertical row of linked type in the middle of your page or a vertical rule graphic? No problem! You want your graphics aligned left or right to a specific grid defined by pixels? No problem! You want to define the size of your page and not let the browser do that for you? No problem! Basically, if you're used to working with PageMaker or QuarkXPress, you're used to working with design grids. Tables take more effort, but if you do some planning, you can use them much the same way.

Percentages Versus Pixels

One of the key principles of using tables for alignment is understanding the differences and power of using percentages and/or pixels. Tables based on percentages scale to the size of your browser, and tables based on pixels are fixed in size.

Percentage-Based Tables

One of my favorite tricks is to center a graphic or text using tables so it remains centered regardless of the size of the browser. You do this with percentages and alignment attributes. Here's the code and the effect it produces:

```
<TABLE><TABLE BORDER="0" CELLPADDING="0" CELLSPACING="0" WIDTH="100%"
HEIGHT="100%"> <TR>
<TD ALIGN="center" VALIGN="middle"><IMG SRC="odac3.gif" WIDTH="162"
HEIGHT="225"></TD></TR></TABLE>
```

This code established that the table was 100 percent of the browser size, and the image contained within was centered on the horizontal and vertical axes.

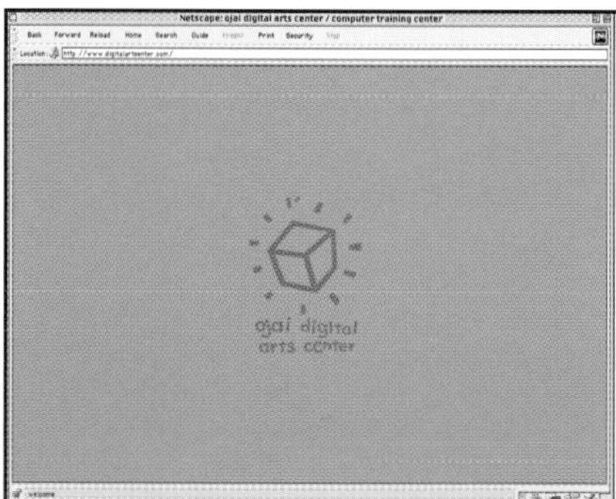

Regardless of how wide my browser is opened, this image will always stay centered because of the table trick I'm using.

Pixel-Based Tables

Pixel-based tables are useful for creating large graphics, cutting them apart, and reassembling them with a table. This is done for a few reasons. First, you could create a large graphic that contained artwork that was soft and hard edged. By slicing the image up and reassembling it into tables, you could compress various regions differently. You could also include animation or rollovers inside some of the table regions.

This image, found at http://www.movielink.com, is actually composed of lots of little images that have been reassembled seamlessly using table code in HTML.

<table>
<tr><td>JPEG</td><td rowspan="2">animated GIF</td><td>JPEG</td></tr>
<tr><td>GIF</td><td>GIF</td></tr>
</table>

This allowed the designer, Elizabeth Roxby (http://www.roxx.com), to combine JPEG, GIF, and animated GIF elements into what looked like a single large image. It also allowed for the site's content to be easily changed.

You can achieve a table of fixed pixel widths (like the example shown below) by knowing the exact size of each graphic and reassembling it using tables. In our book *Creative HTML Design*, my brother and I show the following example:

This shows the image inside Photoshop, with guides turned on. The guides show where the images were cut apart. Using the info palette, with Preferences set to **measure in pixels**, not inches, I was able to get the exact dimension for each region of the table in order to piece this back together again. Animated GIF files were used for the two circle regions, and the rest of the images were saved as GIF files.

The code to piece them together again looked like this:

```
<TABLE BORDER=0 CELLSPACING=0 CELLPADDING=0>
  <TR>
    <TD><IMG SRC="cutapart1.gif"></TD>
    <TD><IMG SRC="cutapart2.gif"></TD>
    <TD><IMG SRC="cutapart3.gif"></TD>
  <TR>
    <TD><IMG SRC="cutapart4.gif"></TD>
    <TD><IMG SRC="cutapart5.gif"></TD>
    <TD><IMG SRC="cutapart6.gif"></TD>
  <TR>
    <TD><IMG SRC="cutapart7.gif"></TD>
    <TD><IMG SRC="cutapart8.gif"></TD>
    <TD><IMG SRC="cutapart9.gif"></TD>
</TABLE>
```

Terminate Your Tables!

A common problem that many people encounter when they make tables for the purpose of assembling images is either forgetting to terminate their tables (close the TD tag) or putting the close tag on a separate line. Here are two bad examples, both of which leave spaces between the images and break the illusion of this technique.

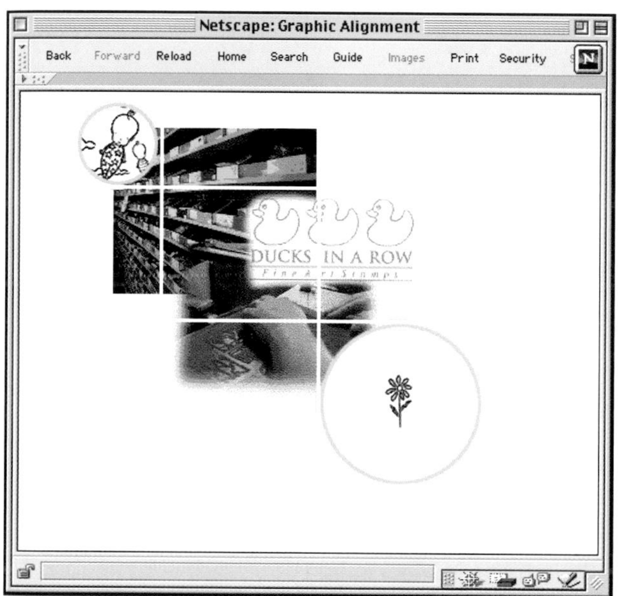

No Termination Example:

```
<TABLE BORDER=0 CELLSPACING=0 CELLPADDING=0>
  <TR>
    <TD><IMG SRC="cutapart1.gif">
    <TD><IMG SRC="cutapart2.gif">
    <TD><IMG SRC="cutapart3.gif">
  <TR>
    <TD><IMG SRC="cutapart4.gif">
    <TD><IMG SRC="cutapart5.gif">
    <TD><IMG SRC="cutapart6.gif">
  <TR>
    <TD><IMG SRC="cutapart7.gif">
    <TD><IMG SRC="cutapart8.gif">
    <TD><IMG SRC="cutapart9.gif">
</TABLE>
```

Termination in the Wrong Place Example:

```
<TABLE BORDER=0 CELLSPACING=0 CELLPADDING=0>
  <TR>
    <TD><IMG SRC="cutapart1.gif">
    </TD><TD><IMG SRC="cutapart2.gif">
    </TD><TD><IMG SRC="cutapart3.gif">
  <TR>
   <TD><IMG SRC="cutapart4.gif">
    </TD><TD><IMG SRC="cutapart5.gif">
    </TD><TD><IMG SRC="cutapart6.gif">
  <TR>
    <TD><IMG SRC="cutapart7.gif">
    </TD><TD><IMG SRC="cutapart8.gif">
    </TD><TD><IMG SRC="cutapart9.gif">
</TABLE>
```

Indents Using Tables

If you ever want to create some space in your layout that creates an indent, use a table. Here is the example and the code:

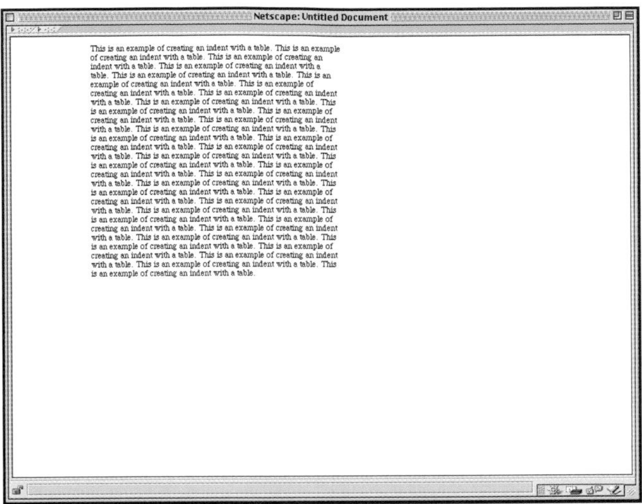

code

```
<table width="443" border="0">
  <tr>
    <td width="100"></td>
    <td width="339">This is an example of creating an indent with a table.  This is an example of creating
an indent with a table.  This is an example of creating an indent with a table.  This is an example of
creating an indent with a table.  This is an example of creating an indent with a table.  This is an exam-
ple of creating an indent with a table.  This is an example of creating an indent with a table.  This is
an example of creating an indent with a table.  This is an example of creating an indent with a table.
This is an example of creating an indent with a table.  This is an example of creating an indent with a
table.  This is an example of creating an indent with a table.  This is an example of creating an indent
with a table.  This is an example of creating an indent with a table.  This is an example of creating an
indent with a table.  This is an example of creating an indent with a table.  This is an example of creat-
ing an indent with a table.  This is an example of creating an indent with a table.  This is an example of
creating an indent with a table.  This is an example of creating an indent with a table.  This is an exam-
ple of creating an indent with a table.  This is an example of creating an indent with a table.  This is
an example of creating an indent with a table.  This is an example of creating an indent with a table.
This is an example of creating an indent with a table.  This is an example of creating an indent with a
table.  This is an example of creating an indent with a table.  This is an example of creating an indent
with a table.  This is an example of creating an indent with a table.  This is an example of creating an
indent with a table.  This is an example of creating an indent with a table.  This is an example of creat-
ing an indent with a table.  This is an example of creating an indent with a table.  This is an example of
creating an indent with a table.  </td>
  </tr>
</table>
```

WYSIWYG Tables

It should be noted that almost all WYSIWYG HTML editors let you create tables without programming the code. It's so much easier to use them—instead of hand coding—that it's really worth your time to invest in one of them. It's important to understand how tables in HTML work, however, because it's still necessary from time to time to edit the automatic code WYSIWYG editors generate.

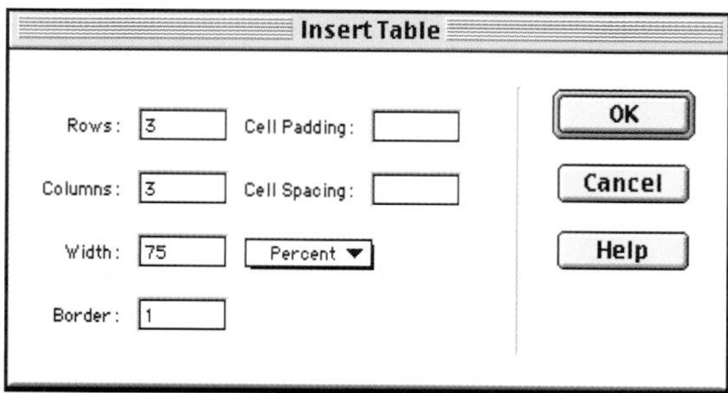

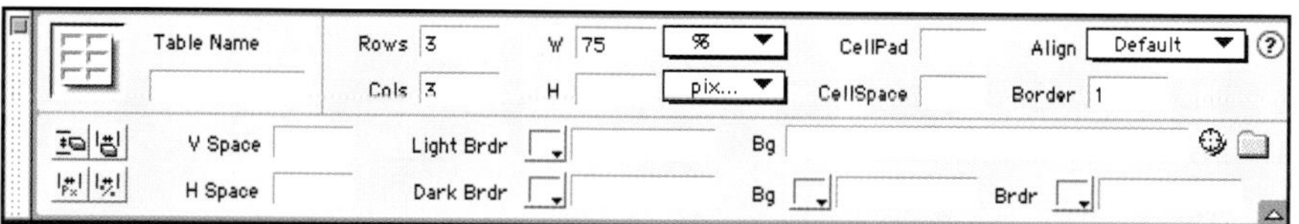

It's possible to create tables easily with the help of WYSIWYG editors. Shown above is Dreamweaver 2.0, which will generate or edit a table based on the values entered into helpful inspector palettes.

Imaging Software Tables

One of the coolest new trends in imaging software is the ability to generate table code from an image editor instead of from an HTML editor. Of the tools available to do this today, Fireworks 1.0 is my favorite.

Using the Slice Toolbar, the Slice tool is selected.

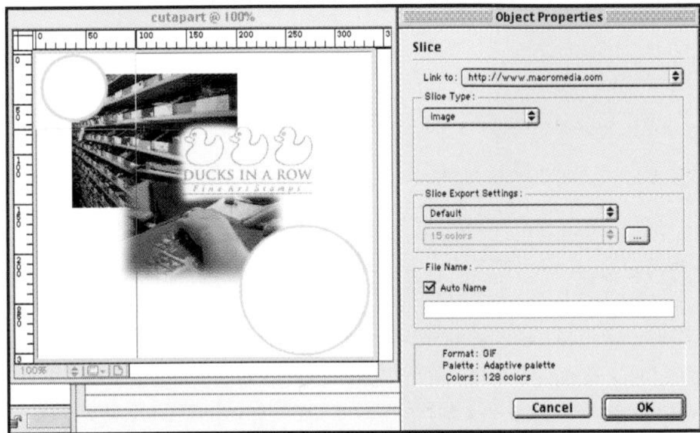

When you drag out a slice, the regions of the table are shown in yellow and red. Each slice can be independently named and compressed. You can set up the links, the type of image (rollover or still image), the compression settings, and the name of the slice all from the Object Properties palette.

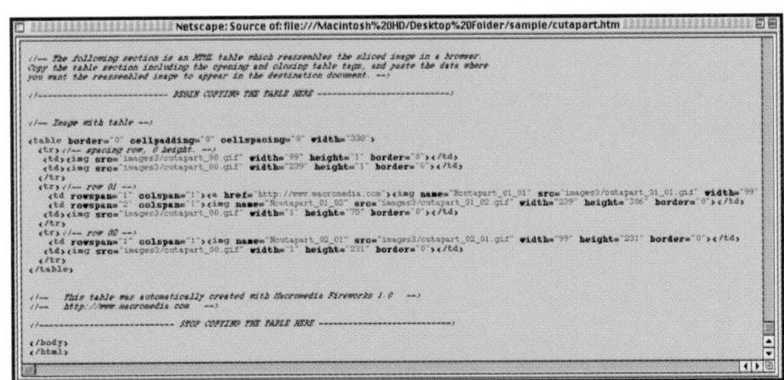

In this case, the Fireworks program wrote the HTML table, without me ever writing a line of code or entering an HTML editor. This is an exciting new trend in imaging software, which will hopefully continue and become more robust. Perhaps a day will come when artists won't have to code at all?

summary

Alignment & Tables

Alignment in HTML is very challenging. This chapter should help you as a reference when you want to program specific types of alignment of text or images. Here's a summary of what this chapter covered:

- Alignment tags and attributes enable you to align text and images by specifying center, left, right, top, bottom, and middle alignment.
- It's recommended that you use tables to align artwork and text because they offer much greater control than alignment tags and elements.
- Tables can contain absolute pixel dimensions, or they can base the shape and content on percentages. This chapter shows good examples of both types of tables.
- You can slice and reassemble images to create optimization settings for each graphic or to include dynamic media such as rollovers or animations.
- WYSIWYG and image editors are both making table creation less about math and more about design.

Frames

Introduction

Chapter Topics

- What are Frames?
- Pros & Cons
- Frames Basics
- Programming Frames
- Frames Targets
- No Frames Content
- Fun with Frames

18

Like most of you, I've watched the Web evolve over the past five years and I have to admit that the first time I saw frames, I was horrified. I read one review that referred to them as "Mondrian on LSD," and somehow that description has never failed to amuse me. When Netscape announced version 2.0, they proudly previewed their site showcasing frames, and there was such an outpouring of outrage that they ultimately changed their site and have never returned to that version.

To this day when I lecture, I often poll my audience to see who "hates frames." To this day, many hands still raise, and frames are still a subject of heated controversy and disagreement. What's the deal? What's good about frames and what's bad? What are they and how do you make them? How do you offer alternate content for those who don't like framed sites, and how do you avoid the serious pitfalls?

This chapter covers these issues and more. While frames are the subject of disagreement, they are also incredibly useful for a variety of things—from navigation to visual effects. I'll cover the pros and cons, and the how, what, why and when. By the end of this chapter, you should have a good handle on how to make frames and whether or not you want to bother.

What Are Frames?

When we teach workshops, my husband Bruce likes to use a silly analogy for frames. He has our students imagine TV dinner trays as the frameset, and uses peas, corn, the entrée, and desert tray as the metaphors for the frame content. While it usually produces a few chuckles, I mention it here, because I think it actually helps describe the simple (yet complex!) nature of frames. You see, frames contain multiple HTML pages. The main frame container is called the frameset, because it holds all the other HTML pages. It is, in Bruce's terms, the TV dinner tray for the HTML courses.

When you're programming frames, it can get very confusing, because you are dealing with multiple HTML documents. Each document contains all the various features we've described so far—background colors, tiles, images, imagemaps, type, tables, etc. It's one thing to manage these items on a single page, and quite another to manage multiples of them in a single page. Not to mention that you can "target" areas on a framed site, and targets are rarely used on single pages.

Before we get into how you make frames and targets, you might understandably wonder why anyone would use frames to begin with. Frames enable regions of a page to stay stationary, while other regions of a page change. This is useful for navigation, because it allows you to set up navigation links which will be present on every page of your site without substituting the entire page, which is what would happen if you tried to program navigation on standard non-frame pages. Consistent navigation is something CD-ROM multimedia developers have always taken for granted, but has proven much more difficult in Web development.

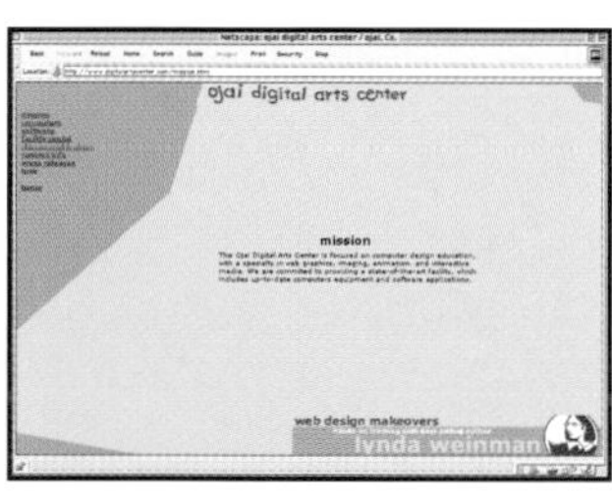

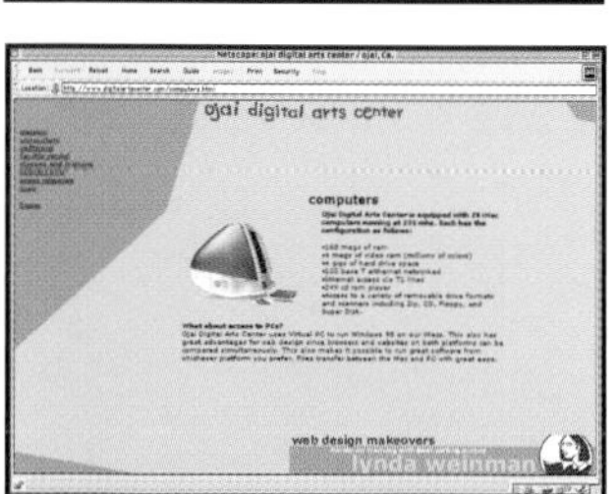

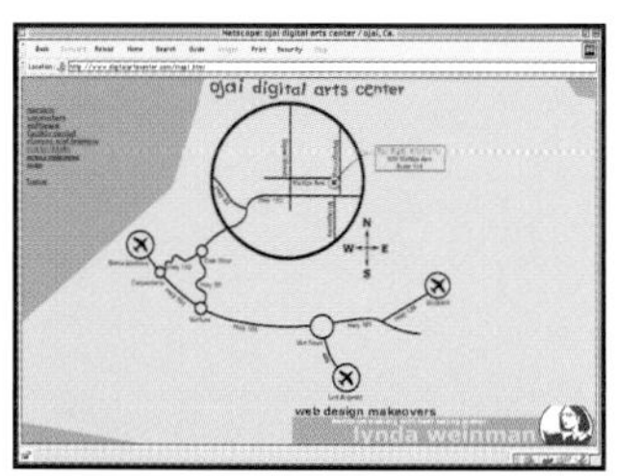

These examples at http://www.digitalartscenter.com illustrate why frames are useful and why many Web developers choose to use them. If you click on the left-hand navigation bar of this site, the middle of the screen changes, but nothing else does. This is the result of frames. This example shows frames with no borders, and different background tiles inside each frameset which blend into the appearance of a single background tile.

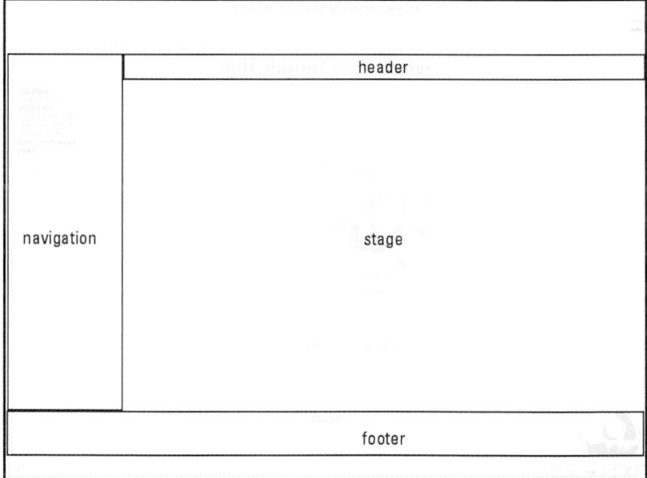

This example illustrates the frame regions of the **Ojai Digital Arts Center** (http://www.digitalartscenter.com). By dividing this screen into four separate pages, the middle "stage" can change, while the other three regions are anchored and locked. By clicking on an item in the "navigation" region, the "stage" is updated through a method called "targets." In practice, any region of a framed site can be made to lock or substitute content.

Frames Pros and Cons

So, why are frames so controversial? The function of a frames-based site is very practical, but the implementation is often plagued with problems. In other words, an unsuspecting and inexperienced Web developer can seriously abuse frames without an understanding of the pitfalls.

To backtrack a moment, when frames were introduced in 1997 by Netscape, they were implemented poorly. There was no way to turn off borders of frame regions, leaving ugly scrollbars and lines all over anyone's site who programmed them. It was impossible to print or bookmark a frame, and the back button would usually take you to the last site you visited rather than the last frame you visited.

Given that a Web page is already a small amount of real estate to work with, dividing it up with lots of lines and scrollbars can understandably annoy your end user. That is one reason why frames have a bad reputation—if you don't hide all the lines and scroll bars, it can actually present a more confusing presentation than not. Therefore, the very thing that a frames-based site should be good at (navigation) is actually something it can royally mess up if handled poorly.

Today, frames can be transparent if you know all the tricks (which of course you'll be learning in this chapter)! Most of the early complaints are unfounded, but there are still a few serious gotchas. If it's critical that your audience print one of your pages, you might still shy away from frames. The frame will print if your end user last clicked within it (making it active)—but if not, the browser might print another region. As a safeguard—it is good to include a PDF file, and/or a page that removes itself from the frameset (again, you'll learn how in this current chapter). Bookmarking a framed site is still problematic—the bookmark will refer to the frameset (remember that TV dinner tray?), and not the specific page or frame region that one might expect.

My company, **Lynda.com**, LLC recently had a problem where we had a secure ordering page for electronic commerce inside a frames-based site. Though that page was indeed secure, the taletell sign of a secure server (the little lock icon in the bottom left-hand corner) was not showing. We received numerous complaints that our server was not secure (which it was), and that we should fix it. Our solution? We took the secure ordering page out of the frameset. You'll see how to do this later in the chapter when I describe target practices.

So, after reading all this, you might wonder if you should use frames at all. I used to avoid them like the plague, but now that you can turn off borders, and make them transparent under most conditions (if printing, security, and bookmarking are not an issue to you) then you might grow to like using them, as we have on our training site.

Whatever you decide, be prepared for people to like and dislike your decision. There is no middle ground when it comes to frames!

Frames Basics

I've explained the TV dinner metaphor; let's put it to action. Frames require multiple HTML documents. Each HTML document is like any other HTML document, in that it must contain the proper basic structure—with an HTML, HEAD, and BODY tag. The frameset that we used on the digitalarts-center.com site contained five HTML documents—a container that holds them all together, a header, a footer, a navigation area and a stage area.

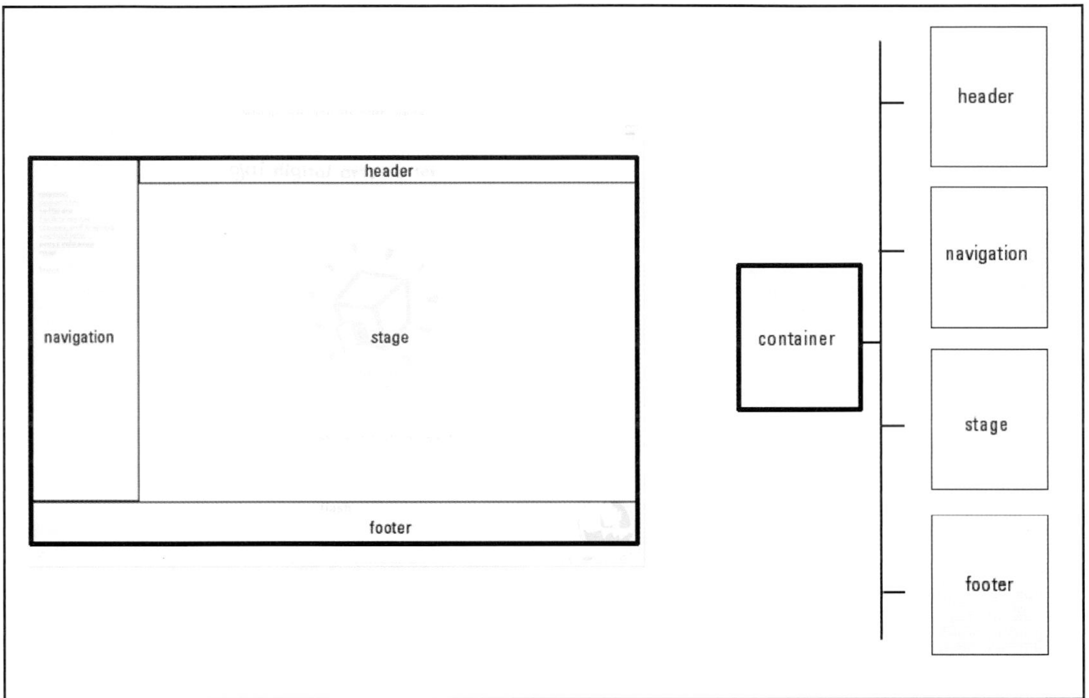

This example illustrates the relationship between a finished frames-based page and what is behind the scenes. The container HTML document holds the other four HTML documents in this example.

When you view the source of a frames-based site, you will likely be viewing the source code for the outer container. It's difficult to view the source of each interior frame, so it's difficult to teach yourself how to program frames by viewing the source of framed sites that you like.

Learning Frames

Rather than work further with the digitalartscenter.com site which offers a relatively complex example of frames, I believe it would be best to start with a simple two frame screen (which you might guess by now means that there would need to be three HTML documents).

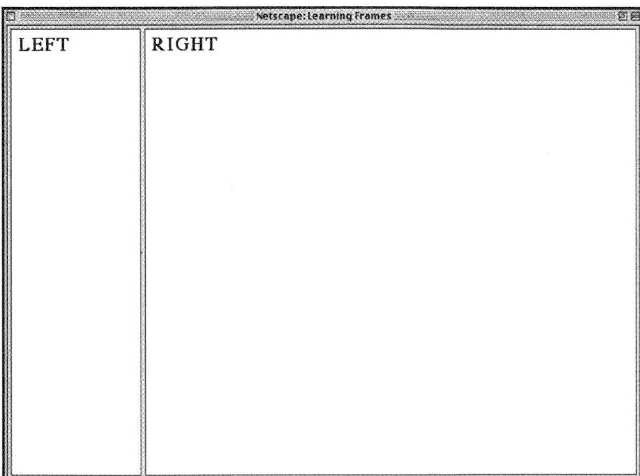

This figure shows a simple frameset. The code follows below.

code for a frameset

```
<HTML>
<HEAD>
<TITLE>Learning Frames</TITLE>
</HEAD>
<FRAMESET COLS="129,468">
  <FRAME SRC="left.html">
  <FRAME SRC="right.html">
</FRAMESET>
</BODY></HTML>
```

Notice that the FRAMESET and FRAME tags are inside this main document. The following two documents don't require any frame tags—they are just standard HTML documents nested inside the container frameset.

In this example, the borders are on (they default to on) and they can also be resized by the end user. We will proceed through a series of examples using this same document which show changing the frame borders.

The **left HTML** would look like this:

```
HTML>
<HEAD>
<TITLE>LEFT FRAME</TITLE>
</HEAD>
<BODY BGCOLOR="#FFFFFF">
<H1>LEFT </H1>
</BODY>
</HTML>
```

The **right HTML** frame would look like this:

```
<HTML>
<HEAD>
<TITLE>RIGHT FRAME</TITLE>
</HEAD>
<BODY BGCOLOR="#FFFFFF">
<H1>RIGHT</H1>
</BODY>
</HTML>
```

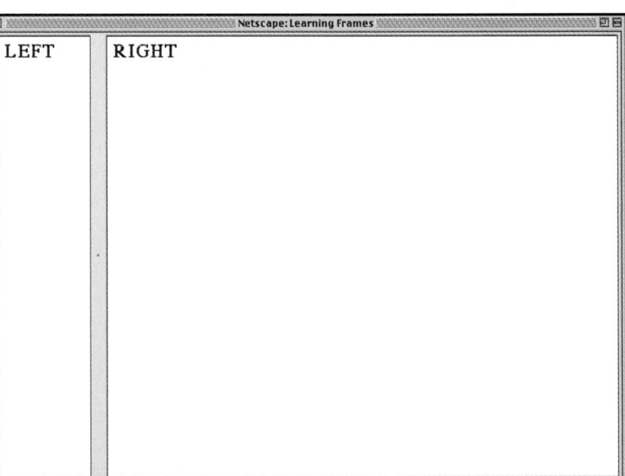

This figure shows the result of increasing the size of the frame border, which you can do with the following code.

code for increasing border size

```
<FRAMESET COLS="129,468" FRAMEBORDER="YES"
BORDER="20" FRAMESPACING="20">
  <FRAME SRC="left.html">
  <FRAME SRC="right.html">
</FRAMESET>
```

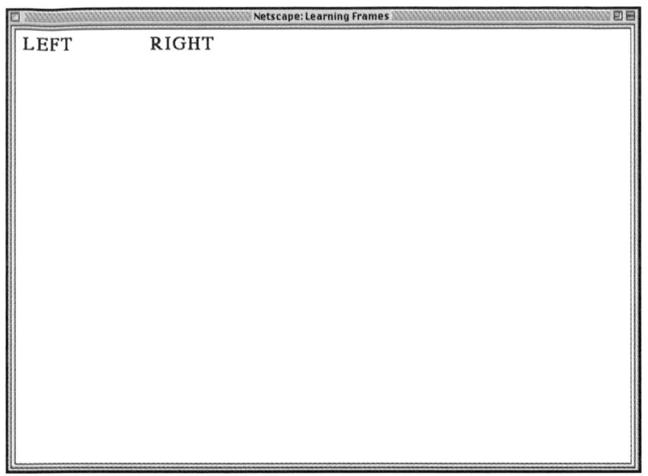

This figure shows you the result of putting a 0 value inside the frame border element.

code for zero border

```
<FRAMESET COLS="129,468" FRAMEBORDER="YES"
BORDER="0" FRAMESPACING="0">
  <FRAME SRC="left.html">
  <FRAME SRC="right.html">
</FRAMESET>
```

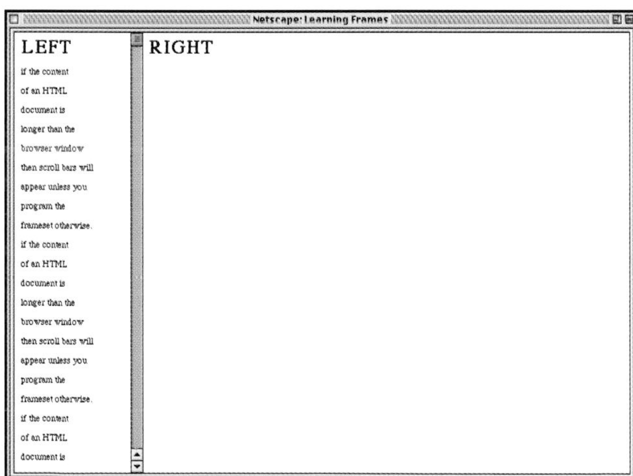

The identical code will result in a scrollbar if the content of one of the frames extends further than the size of the browser window.

You can clip the content that extends beyond the size of the browser with the NOSCROLL element, shown below.

code for clipping the content

```
<FRAMESET COLS="129,468" FRAMEBORDER="NO"
BORDER="0" FRAMESPACING="0" >
  <FRAME SRC="left.html" SCROLLING="NO">
  <FRAME SRC="right.html">
</FRAMESET>
```

It's also possible to use relative positioning (as opposed to absolute positioning with pixels). If you want to set one part of your frameset to be fixed (the left side), but allow the right side to be sized to whatever size the end user's browser is set, use the asterisk (*) symbol to signify a wild card. For example, FRAMESET COLS="129,*" would instruct the browser to keep the left side fixed at 129 pixels, but scale the right side to whatever size the window scales to.

code for relative positioning

```
<FRAMESET COLS="25%,75%" >
  <FRAME SRC="left.html">
    <FRAME SRC="right.html">
</FRAMESET>
```

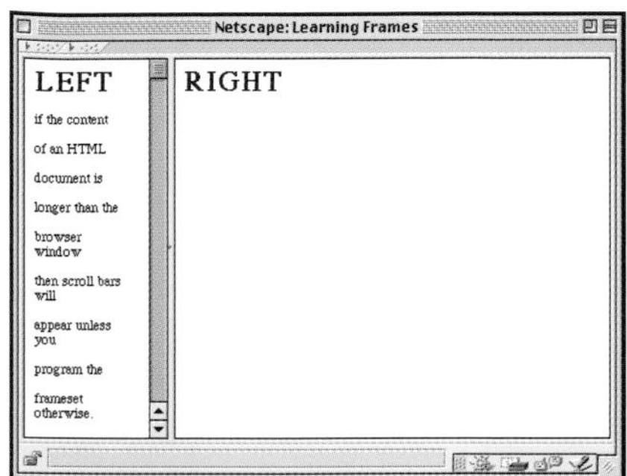

These examples show setting the size with percentages instead of pixels. Regardless of how wide or big I open my browser in this condition, the frame regions will always be 25%:75% of my screen.

code for nested frames

```
<FRAMESET COLS="129,468"
FRAMEBORDER="YES" >
  <FRAME SRC="left.html"
NAME="" SCROLLING="NO">
  <FRAMESET ROWS="229,229">
    <FRAME SRC="right.html">
    <FRAME SRC="bottom.html">
  </FRAMESET>
</FRAMESET>
```

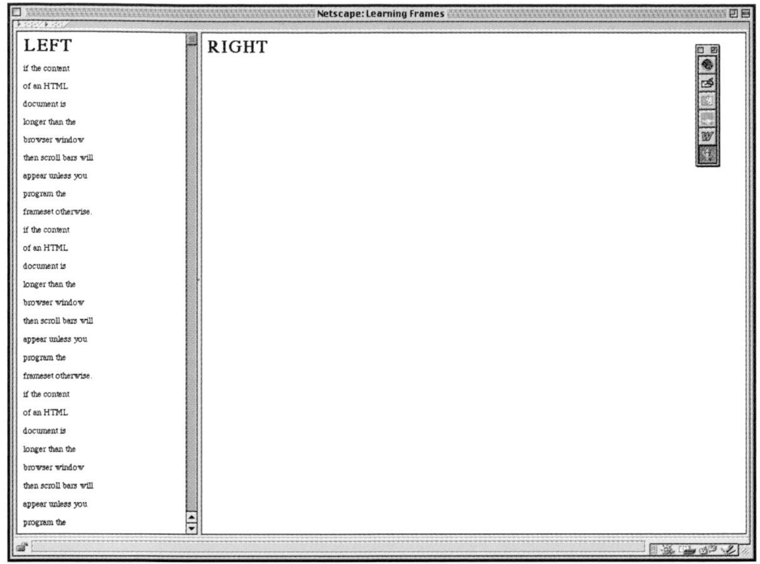

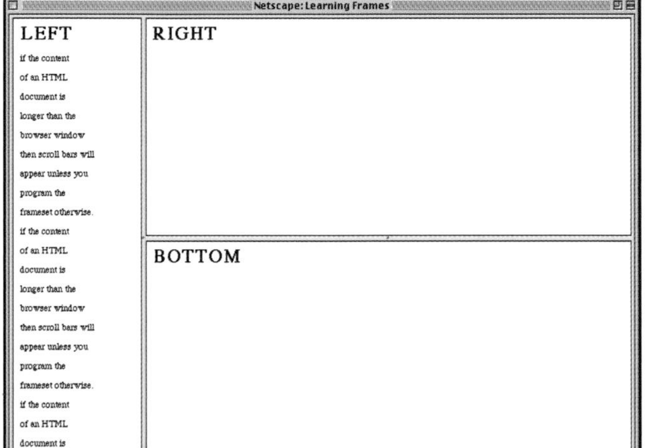

You can also nest framesets inside each other, as this example shows. Notice in the HTML code to your left that there are two sets of opening and closing FRAMESET tags. This is required when you nest frames for complex framesets. The **digitalartscenter.com** example was a nested frameset. Why would you nest frames? Whenever you need to divide regions in two directions with ROWS and COLS, like shown above.

Target Practice

Once you've learned how to program frames, the next step is to learn to program targets. Targets enable additional links or HTML pages to load into specific regions of your frameset. The following examples will demonstrate how to use targeting in your framesets.

The first step to using targets is to name your frames. You can name them Fred, Wilma, or even Bozo—but it's better to name them something that is meaningful. In our example I've chosen the boring, but useful names "left" and "right." I am going to work with linking my site in the following examples.

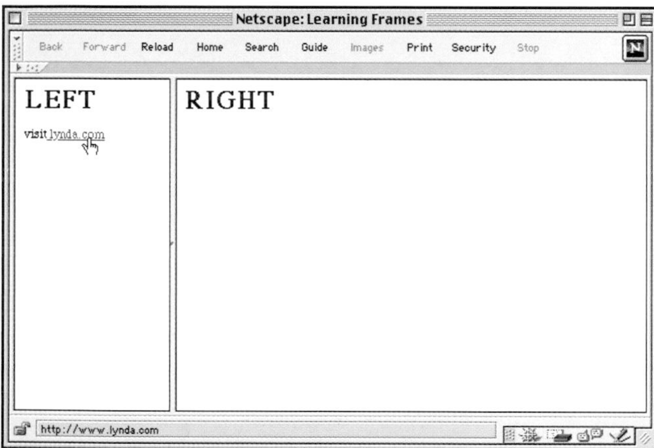

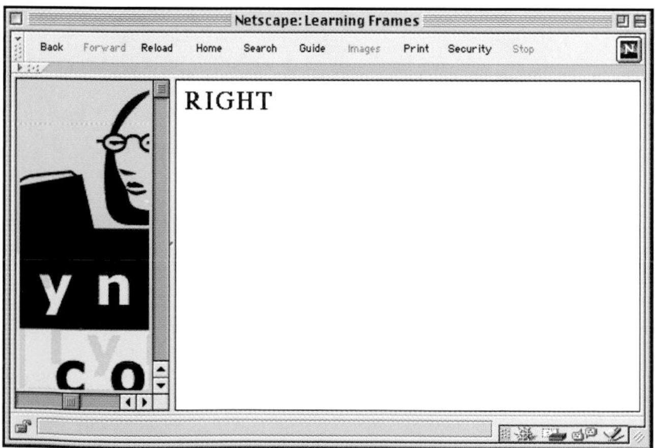

If all I do is insert a link to my site in the **left.html** document, once I click on that link the browser thinks I want to put my site into the same HTML document that contained the link.

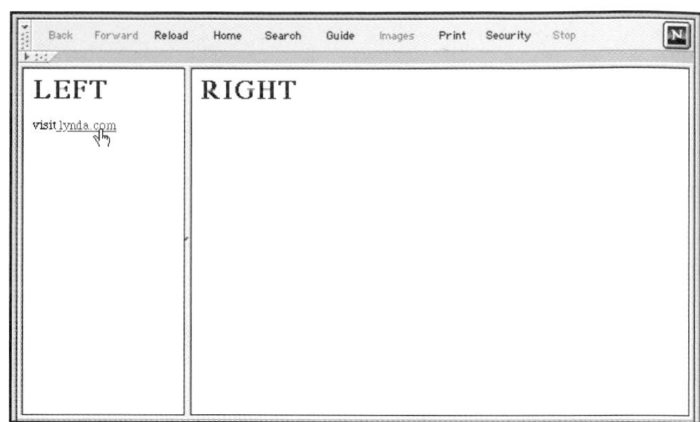

If, instead, I wanted to have my document load into the right frame, I would need to name my frame so I could use it as a target.

code inside the container.html

```
<FRAMESET COLS="25%,75%" >
  <FRAME SRC="left.html" NAME="left">
    <FRAME SRC="right.html" NAME="right">
</FRAMESET>
```

code inside the left.html

```
<HTML>
<HEAD>
<TITLE>LEFT FRAME</TITLE>
</HEAD>
<BODY BGCOLOR="#FFFFFF">
<H1>LEFT </H1>
<P>visit<A HREF="http://www.lynda.com"
TARGET="right"> lynda.com</A>
</BODY>
</HTML>
```

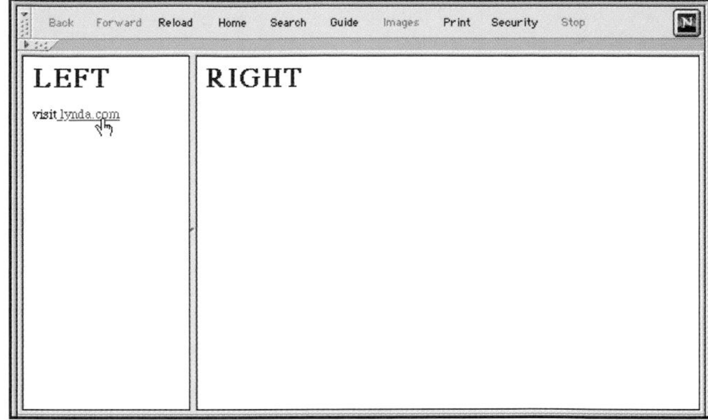

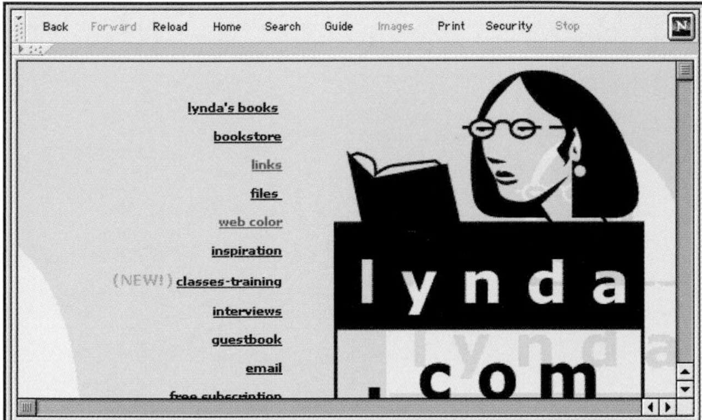

If, instead, I wanted to have my document load into the right frame, I would need to name my frame so I could use it as a target.

code for using your frame as a target

```
<HTML>
<HEAD>
<TITLE>LEFT FRAME</TITLE>
</HEAD>
<BODY BGCOLOR="#FFFFFF">
<H1>LEFT </H1>
<P>visit<A HREF="http://www.lynda.com"
TARGET="_blank"> lynda.com</A>
</BODY>
</HTML>
```

If I wanted to load my site, and replace the entire frameset with my site by itself, I would program TARGET ="_ parent". The identical effect would be achieved by choosing TARGET="_top".

code for replacing the frameset

```
<HTML>
<HEAD>
<TITLE>LEFT FRAME</TITLE>
</HEAD>
<BODY BGCOLOR="#FFFFFF">
<H1>LEFT </H1>
<P>visit<A HREF="http://www.lynda.com" TARGET
="_parent"> lynda.com</A>
</BODY>
</HTML>
```

Here's a list of all the target tags, and what they'll do:

Target Tags for Frames	
_self	Loads the HTML into the same frame as the link.
_blank	Launches a new browser window.
_parent	Replaces the frameset with the HTML that was linked to.
_top	Loads the HTML into the full window that's open.

Fun with Frames

Now that a lot of the technical barriers of frames have been solved, such as the ability to print a specific frame from a browser and navigate between frames with the back button, I've seen a lot more acceptance and creative uses of frames in the past year. I'd like to share some of the cool techniques I've seen used for frames in this section.

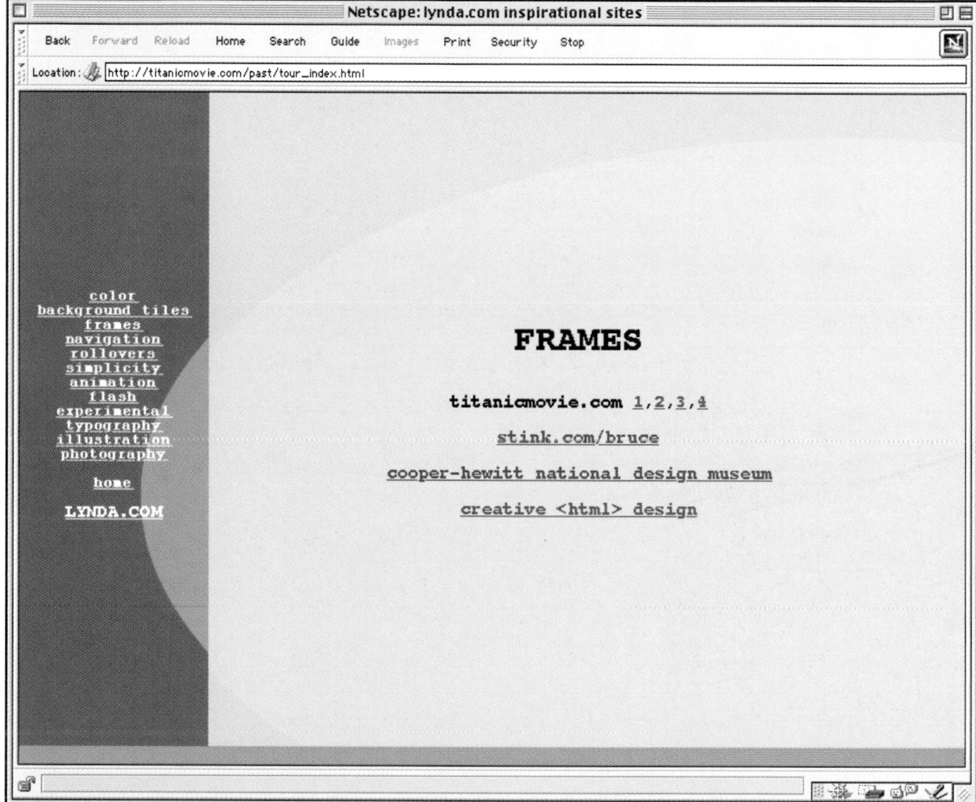

Here is an example of using background tiles in frames. The same background is used in different regions, and matches up by setting the frame regions to perfectly line up to the artwork. The next few examples will show you how this was accomplished.

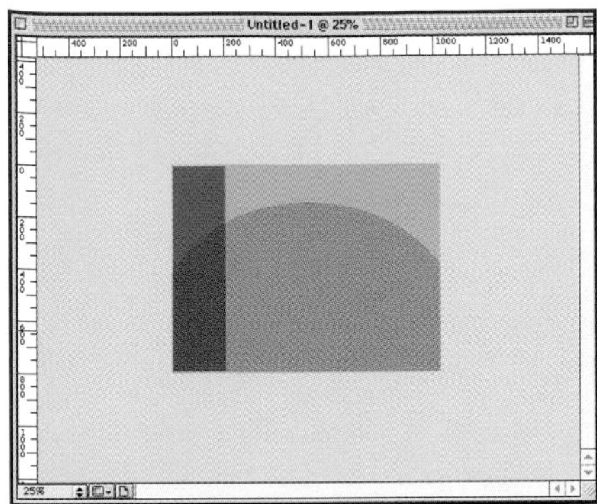

Want to try this yourself? Cut it into two slices, and note the exact size of each region. In this example, I've made the left side 200 pixels wide in Fireworks. I used the slicing capabilities to make two images—one that was 200 pixels wide, and the other that was 824 pixels wide. These images were named **left.gif** and **right.gif**.

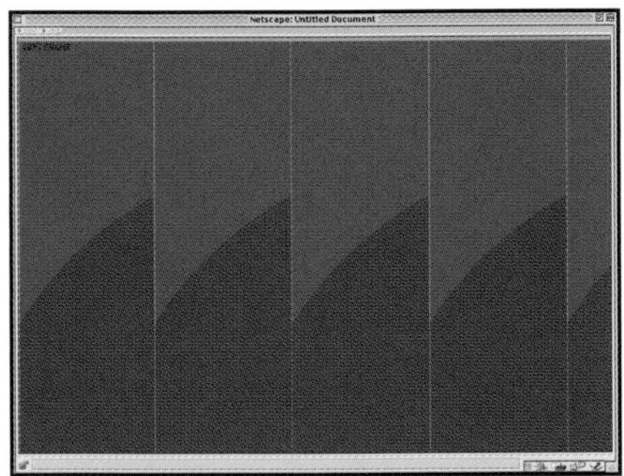

The **left.html** document looked like this. You will find the HTML shown at the end of this section.

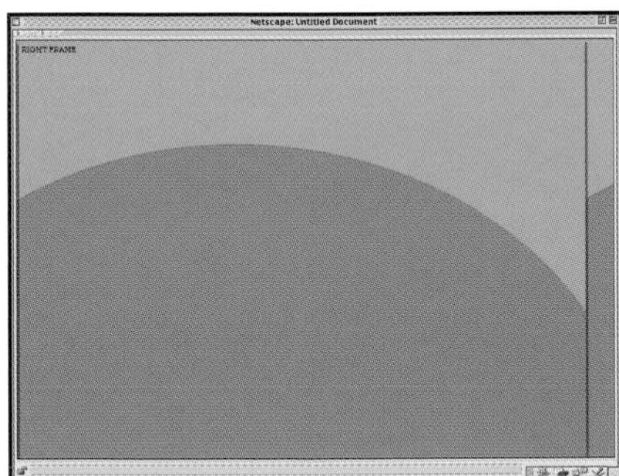

The **right.html** document looked like this. You will find the HTML shown at the end of this section.

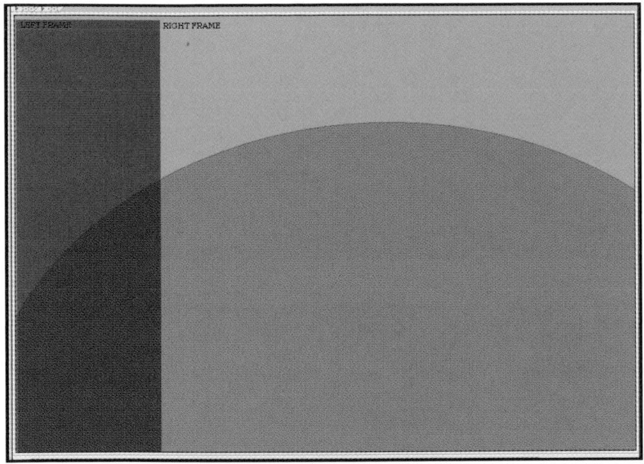

Here's the finished result of reassembling the background tiles into a frameset. The code for this is called container.html.

code inside the left.html

```
<BODY BGCOLOR="#FFFFFF" BACKGROUND="right.gif">
RIGHT FRAME
</BODY>
```

code inside the right.html

```
<BODY BGCOLOR="#FFFFFF" BACKGROUND="right.gif">
RIGHT FRAME
</BODY>
```

code inside the container.html

```
<FRAMESET COLS="200,*" BORDER="0" FRAMESPACING="0">
  <FRAME SRC="left.html">
  <FRAME SRC="right.html">
</FRAMESET>
```

The COLS was set to 200 fixed pixels and used a wild card (*) which puts the right side of the frameset into percentages.

My brother **Bill Weinman** programmed this interesting frameset based on a design by **Don Barnett** for his site, http://www.webmonster.net. You can see the code for his site on the following page.

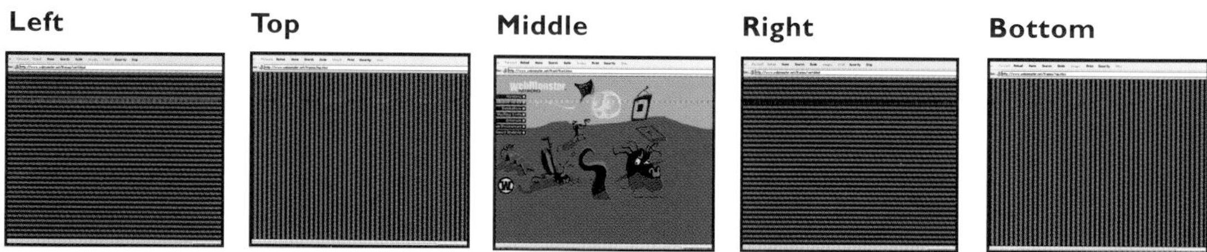

It contains six frames—the outer container, four separate sets for the borders, and one interior set for the central content. The striped borders are actually tiny frame regions that contain a striped background tile. Here's how the pages look separated.

code for my brother's frameset

```
<head>
<title>WebMonster Networks</title>
</head>
<frameset cols="*,616,*" border=0 frameborder=0 framespacing=0>
  <frame src="/frames/black.html" scrolling=no marginheight=0 marginwidth=0>
  <frameset rows="*,416,*" border=0 frameborder=0 framespacing=0>
    <frame src="/frames/black.html" scrolling=no marginheight=0 marginwidth=0>

    <frameset cols="8,*,8" border=0 frameborder=0 framespacing=0>
      <frame src="/frames/vert.html" scrolling=no marginheight=0 marginwidth=0>
      <frameset rows="8,*,8" border=0 frameborder=0 framespacing=0>
        <frame src="/frames/top.html" scrolling=no marginheight=0 marginwidth=0 name=content>

        <!-- content goes here -->
        <frame src="/front/front.html" scrolling=no marginheight=0 marginwidth=0>

      <frame src="/frames/horiz.html" scrolling=no marginheight=0 marginwidth=0>
      </frameset>
      <frame src="/frames/vert.html" scrolling=no marginheight=0 marginwidth=0>
    </frameset>

    <frame src="/frames/black.html" scrolling=no marginheight=0 marginwidth=0>
  </frameset>
  <frame src="/frames/black.html" scrolling=no marginheight=0 marginwidth=0>
```

Bleeding Borders Simplified

Here's an example of what my brother did, using solid background colors, not artwork.

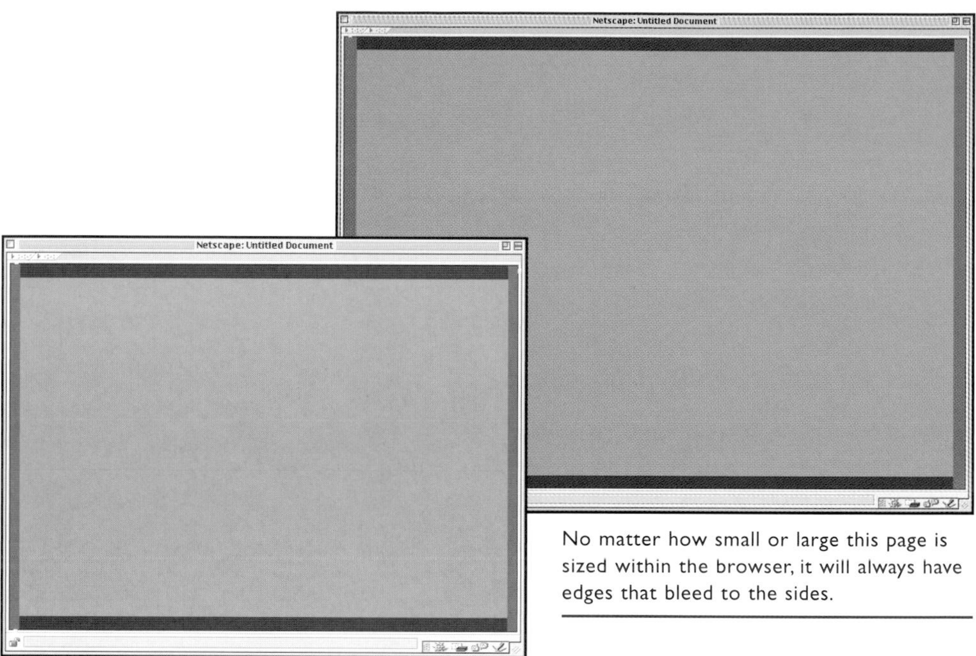

No matter how small or large this page is sized within the browser, it will always have edges that bleed to the sides.

code for a frameset using solid backgrond colors

```
<FRAMESET COLS="20,*,20" ROWS="*" BORDER="0" FRAMESPACING="0" FRAMEBORDER="NO">
  <FRAME SRC="left.html">
  <FRAMESET ROWS="*,20" COLS="*" FRAMEBORDER="NO" BORDER="0" FRAMESPACING="0">
    <FRAMESET ROWS="20,*" COLS="*">
      <FRAME SRC="top.html" SCROLLING=NO>
      <FRAME SRC="inside.html" SCROLLING=NO>
    </FRAMESET>
    <FRAME SRC="bottom.html" SCROLLING=NO>
  </FRAMESET>
  <FRAME SRC="right.html" SCROLLING=NO>
</FRAMESET>
```

The main trick to this technique is to combine absolute pixel values (in this case 20 pixel borders) with the wild card (*) for whatever percentage is left to fill.

note

No Frames!

I highly recommend that you create alternate content for those people who might come to your site with older browsers that cannot see frames. It's pretty simple to do by using the NOFRAMES tag:

```
<HTML>
<HEAD>
<TITLE>Learning Frames</TITLE>
</HEAD>
<FRAMESET COLS="25%,75%" >
  <FRAME SRC="left.html" NAME="left">
    <FRAME SRC="right.html" NAME="right">
</FRAMESET>
<NOFRAMES><BODY BGCOLOR="#FFFFFF">
```

Insert your no frames content here.

```
</BODY></NOFRAMES>

</HTML>
```

Whatever you put into the BODY of the NOFRAMES content will appear to people who are not able to see frames.

summary Frames

This concludes the chapter on frames. As I've stated here, frames are something most people either love or hate. I happen to have personally shifted from hating them in Netscape 2.0 to loving them in 4.0 browsers. Most of the problems of frames have been worked out by the browsers; now it's just a matter of knowing how to handle frames so you don't fall prey to the pitfalls. Here's a summary of what to do:

- Use frames when you want to use a consistent navigation device throughout your site. Frames allows that region to remain stationary, while other content can change around it.
- If possible, turn the borders and scrollbars off of your frames. There is already a limited amount of real estate on a Web page, and too many frames can create confusing navigation and a boxed-in aesthetic.
- Use TARGET to control where linked content appears within your frames.
- You can create interesting special effects with background tiles and fills using frames. Combining fixed pixel dimensions and percentage dimensions allows some regions to stay fixed, while others scale with the size of the browser window.

Cascading Style Sheets

Introduction

Chapter Topics

- What Is a Style Sheet?
- Anatomy: Declarations & Selectors
- Using Comment Tags
- External, Internal & Inline Styles
- Typography
- Absolute Positioning
- Layering Text & Images

19

OK, I admit it; I'm a CSS curmudgeon. CSS (**C**ascading **S**tyle **S**heets) hold the promise to offer more design control over Web pages, so as a designer you might find my attitude surprising. My main criticism of style sheets is not what they promise to do, but that they are poorly supported by browsers. If you go to the effort to learn a new way to specify the appearance of your Web page, it would be nice if the rest of the world would somehow benefit. In my opinion, style sheets are not well enough supported to make the effort involved in learning and using them worthwhile.

Therefore, Cascading Style Sheets will be described in this chapter from a practical perspective in terms of what is supported, and what is promised. I don't advocate that you use style sheets just yet, but at some point (when the browsers get their act together) they will potentially offer greater design control than standard HTML.

DHTML (**D**ynamic **HTML**) will be discussed in a later chapter, and you will then note that CSS is an important component that makes DHTML capable of exact positioning of media and text elements. For this reason, once you have a basic understanding of CSS, you will be able to better understand all the capabilities of DHTML.

There is no need to learn to program style sheets from scratch—many HTML editors now generate style sheets automatically. Still, a base knowledge of style sheets is necessary in order to know how to specify what you want in these WYSIWYG editors. This chapter offers descriptions of the main elements within CSS to help you out!

What Is a Style Sheet?

If you've ever used QuarkXPress, Pagemaker, or even Word, you might have used style sheets. Style sheets allow you to specify certain styles for text, such as font, color, and formatting. This is similar in principle to style sheets found elsewhere, except that CSS specifically controls styles for Web pages.

In principle, the promise of style sheets is a wonderful thing. Designers want pixel-precise control, better layout options and more robust typographic control. HTML purists believe the structure of a document should be separated from the presentation, so that HTML pages can be accessed by anyone, by any device, or on any browser. Style sheets separate the display properties of an HTML document from the structure, which would seemingly give everyone what they wanted. Until the browsers support style sheets in a uniform manner however, that promise will not be met.

The W3C supports a style sheet specification—one for formatting and the other for absolute positioning. If you want to read about the specs, you will find them at

W3C's CSS Positioning Specification
http://www.w3.org/TR/WD-positioning

CSS Test Suite
http://www.w3.org/Style/CSS/Test/current/sec10.htm

Anatomy of a Style Sheet

The anatomy of a style sheet includes some terminology that is likely new to you, such as declarations and selectors. Here are some examples of how these terms relate to style sheet programming.

```
<STYLE TYPE="text/css">
<!--
H1 {
  font-family: Verdana
  }
-->
</STYLE>
```

In this example, the STYLE element is a container that goes in the HEAD section of your HTML document. The TYPE attribute specifies the type of style sheet being used, which in this case is text/css. The STYLE element can contain any number of different styles. This style element contains one style, which applies to the H1 tag, changing its font to Verdana. H1 is the selector, font-family is the property, and Verdana is the value.

The curly braces ("{" and "}") enclose the body of the style. Within the body of the style are lines with properties and values. The word on the left side of the colon is called a property, and the right side is the value assigned to the property. In this example, the font-family property is given the value Verdana, which effectively tells the browser to use the Verdana font for H1 elements in this document.

You can group selectors together, such as

```
H1, P, BLOCKQUOTE { font-family: verdana }
```

This element specifies that all text within H1, P, and BLOCKQUOTE tags will display in the Verdana font.

note

Cascading Defined

What does the Cascading stand for in CSS? Cascading means that the style sheet specification has a hierarchy to it. Style sheet commands can be combined, but the cascading nature of the specification means that the browser will interpret the commands in a certain order, making it possible to "cascade" commands.

Hiding Styles from Older Browsers

If you enclose your style sheets inside HTML comments, browsers that don't understand the STYLE tag wil be prevented from seeing it. Those browsers that do understand the style sheet will ignore the comment tag and apply the style sheet to the page.

```
<HEAD>
<TITLE>CSS Examples</TITLE>
<STYLE TYPE="text/css">
<!--
H1 {
  font-family: Verdana
  }
-->
</STYLE>
</HEAD>
```

Because the style sheet itself is enclosed in HTML comments, browsers that don't understand the STYLE tag are prevented from displaying the style sheet in the browser window (that's one of the rules of HTML: Ignore the tags you don't understand). Browsers that do understand the style sheet will ignore the comment tags and apply the style sheet to the page.

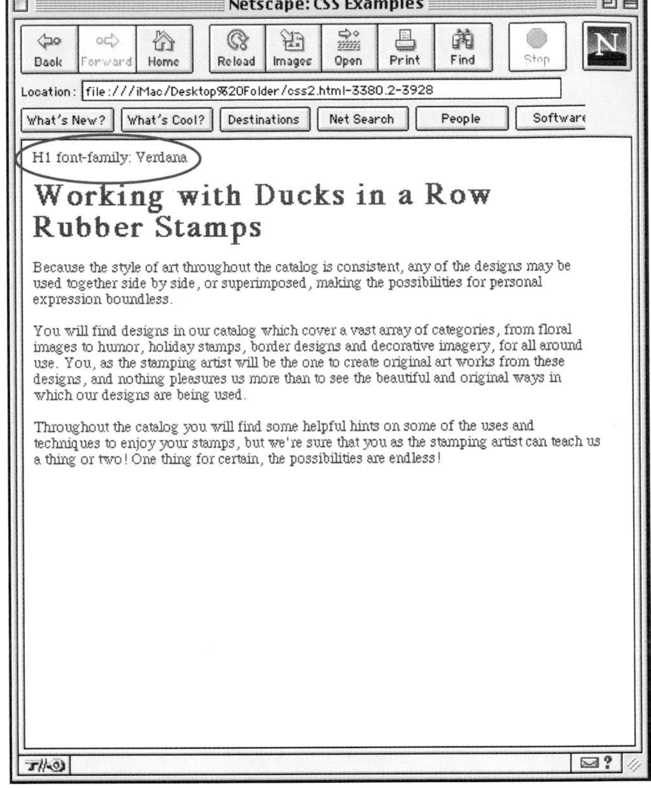

Here is an example in Netscape 3 showing a style sheet that was not hidden within any comment tags.

External, Internal and Inline

There are three flavors of stylesheets, those which are inside an HTML document and apply only to that document or parts of that document, and those which are outside and can be referenced by multiple documents.

External

An external style sheet can be referenced by multiple HTML pages, which is signified by the LINK tag within the HEAD.

```
<HTML>
<HEAD>
<TITLE>Accessing an External Style Sheet</TITLE>
<LINK REL=stylesheet HREF="external.css"
TYPE="text/css">
</HEAD>
<BODY>
<H1>Check it Out!</H1>
<P>My style is cool, daddy-o</P>
</BODY>
</HTML>
```

The file this document references is called "external.css". You can name the .css anything you want; just be sure to save it in text-only mode (just like HTML) and upload it to the same directory as your HTML (or set the link to whichever directory in which it lives). You don't have to put an external style sheet inside a comment tag. The **.css** document might look something like this:

```
H1 { color: FFCC33; font-family: san-serif }
P { background: black; font-family: verdana }
```

It doesn't need to contain anything else but this, no HEAD elements or closing tags.

When would you use an external style sheet? If you wanted the styles to apply to multiple HTML documents, as opposed to a single HTML document.

Internal

An internal style sheet only applies to the HTML document it's contained within, which is signified by the STYLE tag inside the HEAD element.

```
<HEAD>
<TITLE>CSS Examples</TITLE>
<STYLE TYPE="text/css">
<!--
H1 {
  font-family: Verdana
  }
-->
</STYLE>
</HEAD>
```

When would you use an internal style sheet? When you wanted the style to only apply to a specific HTML page.

Inline

An inline style sheet only applies to the parts of an HTML document which are specified.

```
<HTML>
<HEAD><TITLE>My First Stylesheet</TITLE>
</HEAD>
<BODY>
<H1 STYLE="color: orange; font-family:
impact">Stylesheets: The Tool of
the Web Design Gods</H1>
<P STYLE="background: yellow; font-family:
courier">Amaze your friends!
Squash your enemies!</P>
</BODY>
</HTML>
```

When would you use an inline style sheet? Whenever you wanted a style to affect only a portion of an HTML page.

The disadvantage to this method is that you have to add the inline style code every single time you want to use it. The next H1 text after this one would revert back to the default browser display unless you add yet another STYLE attribute.

Type and Measurements

In order to work with style sheets, it's important to understand the types of measurement units that can be specified. Measurement units in electronic type is tricky, because when you specify a "twelve-point" typeface, it probably won't mean the same thing across computer platforms. Anyone who has ever looked at type on the same Web page inside a Windows and Macintosh browser can attest that the same code does not produce the same results across platforms.

With that in mind, let's look at some measuring units. In the following table, you'll see a list with the English name, the CSS name, and a short description for each measurement unit.

English	CSS	Description
Pixel	**px**	A pixel is the distance from one dot to the next on a computer screen (the word literally means picture element).
Point	**pt**	A point is 1/72 inch. How many pixels that is depends on the resolution of your screen, but it is one pixel on 72 dpi systems.
Pica	**pc**	12 points.
Em	**em**	The "body size" of the font. That is, if the font size is 12 points, one em is 12 points.
En	**en**	1/2 em. The height of a lowercase "x".
Inch	**in**	2.54 centimeters or 1/3 meter.
Centimeter	**cm**	1/100 meter.
Millimeter	**mm**	1/1,000 meter.

Because most Web-based graphics are a fixed number of pixels wide and a fixed number of pixels high, I recommend that you use pixel measurements most of the time. That way, you can always be sure that your page will look more-or-less uniform relative to the size of the graphics on the page.

Working with Typography

CSS defines a number of different properties for working with text. The font-family property, for example, lets you specify a particular font family, either by name (like Verdana) or by generic type (like sans-serif).

Property: font-family
Values: Name of the font family, like Verdana or Georgia, or one of the following generic names:
- serif
- sans-serif
- cursive
- fantasy
- monospace

You can also give a list of values for font-family:

```
H1 {
  font-family: Verdana, Helvetica, sans-serif
  }
```

In that case, the system would try to use Verdana, or if that's not available, Helvetica; otherwise, it will use whatever sans-serif font is available.

Another useful text-related property is line-height. This property affects the space between lines, also called after the strips of lead used to provide the spaces between lines of metal type.

Property: line-height
Values:
number
default
Sets the amount of between lines of text

The line-height is measured from the baseline of one line to the baseline of the next. The special value default will set the line-height to the default of the browser, which is probably about the same as 1.2 em.

```
P {
  font-family: Georgia;
  font-size: 12px;
  line-height: 1.5em;
  }
```

This will set the line-height to 1.5 em. Remember: 1em is the same as the font-size, so 1.5 em is one-and-a-half times the body size of the type.

Selectors

So far, we've been using the selector to specify what tag the style will apply to, but the selector can do more than that! You can also use the selector to apply to only some instances of a particular tag.

For example, what if you wanted every paragraph except the first to have an indent on the first line.

```
P {
  font-family: Georgia;
  font-size: 12px;
  line-height: 1.5em;
  text-indent: 1.5em;
  }
```

The text-indent property indents just the first line of a paragraph. Our P style now has a 1.5 em indent for the first paragraph.

Now we add another style with a class selector like this:

```
.first {
  text-indent: 0;
  }
```

A class selector always starts with a dot (.).

Now you can use the CLASS attribute in your HTML to apply that style in addition to the existing style on the paragraph tag:

```
<P CLASS="first">Because the style of art
throughout the catalog is consistent, any
of the designs may be used together side
by side, or superimposed, making the poss-
ibilities for personal expression boundless.
```

The potential of this for simplifying Web sites and reducing bandwidth is truly exciting! It used to be that you needed to trick HTML into indenting your paragraphs and adding space between the lines by using single-pixel transparent GIFs. Now you can do it with style sheets!

CSS style sheets are going to be a very powerful mechanism for enhancing the presentation quality of text on the web. Though not ready for prime time yet, there is good reason to believe that CSS will become a useable feature of mainstream browsers in the not-so-distant future.

Using CSS, you will be able to format your text in manners much closer to that of the printed page, and expect your layouts to work consistantly within certain limits—across platforms, browsers, and differing sizes and resolutions of displays.

note

ID Versus CLASS

On the surface, the ID and CLASS selectors seem so similar that it might make you wonder why there are two different methods for the same thing!

As best as I can determine, the only difference is that it is considered an error to use the same ID selector more than once. Validation engines—and some future browsers—may flag errors on duplicate ID selectors.

Absolute Positioning

Designers have long complained that it's not possible to absolutely position a graphic on a page using HTML. CSS offers a solution for this complaint, allowing designers the first real ability to position objects accurately inside the Web brower window.

To implement absolution positioning, it's necessary to introduce another type of selector, the ID selector, and a few new properties:

code

```
1  #smduck1 {
2  position: absolute;
3  top: 0px;
4  left: 0px;
5  z-index: 1;
   }
```

code deconstruction

1. The ID selector always begins with a hash mark (#) and must be unique within the document. That means that you can only define it once, and you can only use it once (see the note to your left, "ID vs. CLASS"). It works almost like the class selector (.), but is usually used for absolute positioning of objects on a page, where only one object will have any single position.

2. The position property can be either absolute or relative. Use absolute for objects that you want to have at a specific position on the page and relative for objects that you want to position relative to wherever they would have otherwise fallen. Absolute position-ing was used in this example to position the graphic at a specific point on the page. An example of relative will be given a little later.

3.4. The top and left properties are used to position the object. These measurements are absolute measurements from the top-left corner of the screen, leaving no padding between the graphic and the edge of the screen. This style will place the graphic in the absolute upper left-hand corner of the screen.

5. Objects that are put on the screen with absolute positioning can be laid on top of each other. The z-index property tells the browser which objects should be on top of (or under) which other objects. Higher-numbered objects will overlay lower-numbered objects.

Here's a page that uses the style we just defined in **5**.

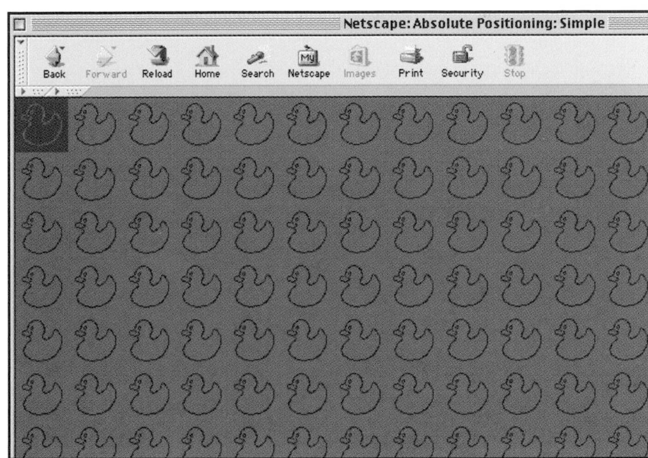

code

```
<HTML>
<HEAD>
<TITLE>Absolute Positioning: Simple</TITLE>
<STYLE>

#smduck1 { position: absolute; top: 0px; left:
0px; z-    index: 0; }

</STYLE>
<BODY>

1  <DIV ID="smduck1"><IMG SRC=revgreentile.gif
WIDTH=50 HEIGHT=50></DIV>

</BODY>
</HTML>
```

1. Notice the use of the DIV element that encloses the IMG. The DIV tag has a new attribute called ID, which is used to specify the selector in the style. The DIV element is necessary to make the absolute positioning work.

DIV and Absolute Positioning

According to the specification, you should be able to forgo the DIV tag and use the ID attribute directly in the IMG tag, but the current crop of browsers will not perform absolute positioning without the DIV tag. This is one of those areas that will change in the next generation of browsers.

One of the most common frustrations with HTML is the inability to accurately align a foreground image against a background tile. Using absolute positioning, this is no longer a problem.

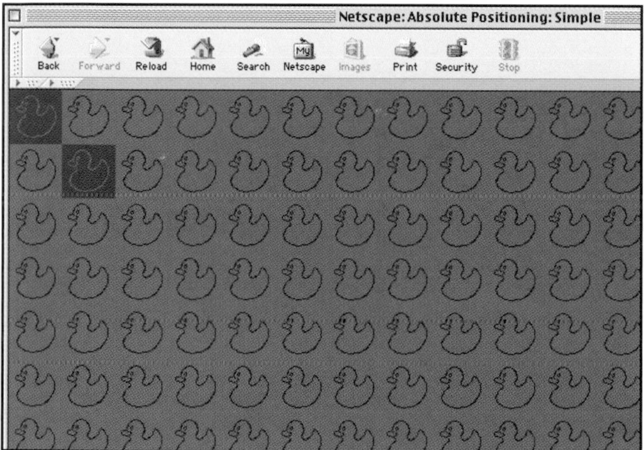

In this example, you can see how nicely images can line up against a repeating background.

The tiny image in the example to your lower left is 50×50 pixels, so we should be able to lay another one right on its lower-right corner by positioning it exactly 50 pixels in and down:

code

```
<HEAD>
<TITLE>Absolute Positioning: Simple</TITLE>
<STYLE>

#smduck1 { position: absolute; top: 0px; left:
0px; z-index: 0; }
#smduck2 { position: absolute; top: 50px; left:
50px; z-index: 0; }

</STYLE>

<BODY BGCOLOR="#999966" BACKGROUND="greentile.gif">

<DIV ID="smduck1"><IMG SRC=revgreentile.gif
WIDTH=50 HEIGHT=50></DIV>
<DIV ID="smduck2"><IMG SRC=revgreentile.gif
WIDTH=50 HEIGHT=50></DIV>

</BODY>
```

Layering Text and Images

By extending these same techniques to a mixture of text and graphics, you can create a nice effect with a number of overlapping lines of text and a simple graphic and use very little bandwidth since the browser only has to download the image or text one time. This example is a little complex, but keep in mind that the techniques involved have already been described in a more simple context.

Let's take a look at the result, and then see what it takes to do this.

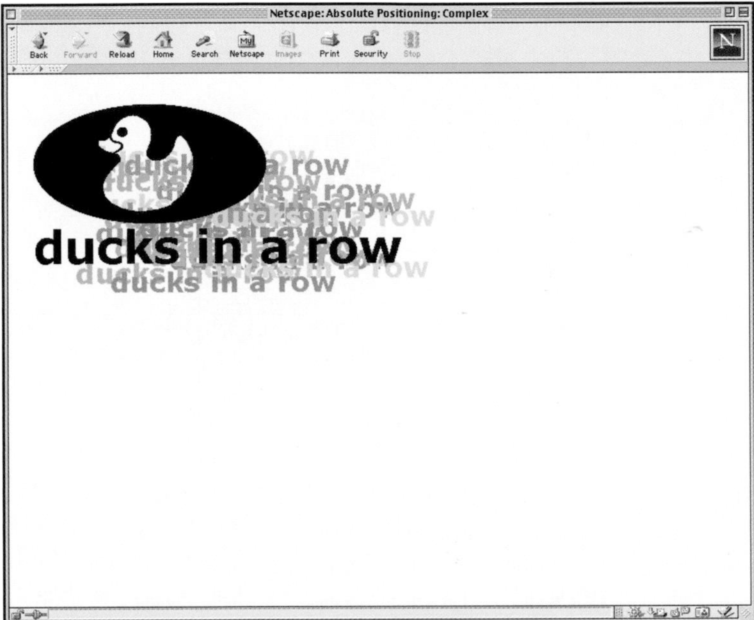

Overlapping text and a simple graphic make a catchy splash page with very low bandwidth overhead. This example only uses one graphic, and HTML-based text colored and sized differently.

This example is basically just 20 copies of the string "ducks in a row" using the Verdana font and a number of different browser-safe colors, all overlapping and covered with a black oval cutout duck and one more "ducks in a row" in black.

code for layering text and image

```
<HTML>
<HEAD>
<TITLE>Absolute Positioning:
Complex</TITLE>

<STYLE TYPE="text/css">

1  H1 {
     font-family: verdana;
     font-weight: bold;
     font-size: 52px;
     color: black;
     }

2  H2 {
     font-family: verdana;
     font-weight: bold;
     font-size: 32px;
     }

3  #words1 {
     position: absolute;
     top: 50px;
     left: 50px;
     z-index: 1;
     }
4  #words2 {
     position: absolute;
     top: 60px;
     left: 90px;
     z-index: 2;
     }
5  .ovalduck {
     position: absolute;
     top: 35px;
     left: 30px;
     z-index: 3;
     }
6  .ducktitle {
     position: absolute;
     top: 130px;
     left: 0px;
     }
7  .duck1 { color: #999900; }
   .duck2 { color: #FFCC00; }
   .duck3 { color: #FF9933; }
   .duck4 { color: #FF6633; }
   .duck5 { color: #FF9933; }

8  #w00 { position: absolute; top: 112px; left: 52px; }
   #w01 { position: absolute; top: 24px; left: 45px; }
   #w02 { position: absolute; top: 95px; left: 62px; }
   #w03 { position: absolute; top: 142px; left: 138px; }
   #w04 { position: absolute; top: 128px; left: 74px; }
   #w05 { position: absolute; top: 63px; left: 122px; }
   #w06 { position: absolute; top: 79px; left: 36px; }
   #w07 { position: absolute; top: 158px; left: 29px; }
   #w08 { position: absolute; top: 83px; left: 146px; }
   #w09 { position: absolute; top: 42px; left: 12px; }
   #w10 { position: absolute; top: 112px; left: 52px; }
   #w11 { position: absolute; top: 24px; left: 45px; }
   #w12 { position: absolute; top: 95px; left: 62px; }
   #w13 { position: absolute; top: 142px; left: 138px; }
   #w14 { position: absolute; top: 128px; left: 74px; }
   #w15 { position: absolute; top: 63px; left: 122px; }
   #w16 { position: absolute; top: 79px; left: 36px; }
   #w17 { position: absolute; top: 158px; left: 29px; }
   #w18 { position: absolute; top: 83px; left: 146px; }
   #w19 { position: absolute; top: 42px; left: 12px; }

</STYLE>

</HEAD>
<BODY BGCOLOR="#FFFFCC" TEXT="#663333" LINK="#006699"
VLINK="#006699">
```

```
9  <DIV ID="words1">
     <H2 CLASS="duck1"><SPAN ID="w00">ducks in a row</SPAN></H2>
     <H2 CLASS="duck2"><SPAN ID="w01">ducks in a row</SPAN></H2>
     <H2 CLASS="duck3"><SPAN ID="w02">ducks in a row</SPAN></H2>
     <H2 CLASS="duck4"><SPAN ID="w03">ducks in a row</SPAN></H2>
     <H2 CLASS="duck5"><SPAN ID="w04">ducks in a row</SPAN></H2>
     <H2 CLASS="duck1"><SPAN ID="w05">ducks in a row</SPAN></H2>
     <H2 CLASS="duck2"><SPAN ID="w06">ducks in a row</SPAN></H2>
     <H2 CLASS="duck3"><SPAN ID="w07">ducks in a row</SPAN></H2>
     <H2 CLASS="duck4"><SPAN ID="w08">ducks in a row</SPAN></H2>
     <H2 CLASS="duck5"><SPAN ID="w09">ducks in a row</SPAN></H2>
   </DIV>
10 <DIV ID="words2">
     <H2 CLASS="duck5"><SPAN ID="w10">ducks in a row</SPAN></H2>
     <H2 CLASS="duck1"><SPAN ID="w11">ducks in a row</SPAN></H2>
     <H2 CLASS="duck4"><SPAN ID="w12">ducks in a row</SPAN></H2>
     <H2 CLASS="duck2"><SPAN ID="w13">ducks in a row</SPAN></H2>
     <H2 CLASS="duck3"><SPAN ID="w14">ducks in a row</SPAN></H2>
     <H2 CLASS="duck5"><SPAN ID="w15">ducks in a row</SPAN></H2>
     <H2 CLASS="duck1"><SPAN ID="w16">ducks in a row</SPAN></H2>
     <H2 CLASS="duck4"><SPAN ID="w17">ducks in a row</SPAN></H2>
     <H2 CLASS="duck2"><SPAN ID="w18">ducks in a row</SPAN></H2>
     <H2 CLASS="duck3"><SPAN ID="w19">ducks in a row</SPAN></H2>
   </DIV>

11 <DIV CLASS="ovalduck">
     <IMG SRC="blackoval.gif" width=269 height=136>
     <H1><SPAN CLASS="ducktitle">ducks in a row</SPAN></H1>
   </DIV>

   </BODY>
   </HTML>
```

This HTML file for our "ducks in a row site" is only 3k and the GIF is only 900 bytes! There are no techniques used here that you haven't already seen in this chapter.

code deconstruction

1. This defines the style for the H1 element, used for the black "ducks in a row" on the top.

2. This defines the base style that is used for all the overlapping "ducks in a row" strings.

3. This defines the ID used for the first layer of words in **[9]**.

4. This defines the ID used for the second layer of words in **[10]**.

5. This defines the position used for the black oval duck image and black type in **[11]**.

6. This positions the title relative to the image in **[11]** to your right.

7. These classes define colors for the overlapping "ducks in a row" strings.

8. These are all the positions for the "ducks in a row" strings.

9. There are two layers of overlapping strings, and this is the first one. The DIV element is used to position the block absolutely on the page. Each of the SPAN elements position an individual string within the block. The H2 elements have the font and size for the strings, and the duck 1–5 classes have the varying colors.

   Since there is no z-index property, the layering occurs in same the order that the text appears in the HTML file. You only need to use z-index when you need to specify a particular order. In this example, the order of the layers doesn't matter.

10. This works exactly like **[9]** and gets overlapped on top of it to provide a more random appearance than just one layer of 10 strings.

11. Finally, the oval duck and the black letters are layered on top of the rest of the type and artwork, using the classes from **[5]** and **[6]**.

Note: This is a complex example that applies all the elements covered by this chapter so far. It is intended to demonstrate the power of style sheets, but is not really intended for a production Web site. There are still too few browsers that understand CSS; many believe that the specification will change significantly before it is really ready for widespread use.

WYSIWYG Editors

My two favorite HTML editors, Dreamweaver and CyberStudio, both support CSS. You still have to know what you are doing however, because there is no way for the HTML editor to decide for you whether to choose between an ID or a CLASS, pixels or inches. CSS is another challenge in the Web publishing curve. Just when you thought HTML was finally manageable!

Hopefully, this chapter will familiarize you with CSS so you can make these decisions within HTML browsers. Here are some other helpful references for CSS:

WebMonkey's CSS Tutorials
http://www.hotwired.com/webmonkey/stylesheets/

WebReview's Style Sheet Tutorials
http://webreview.com/wr/pub/Style_Sheets

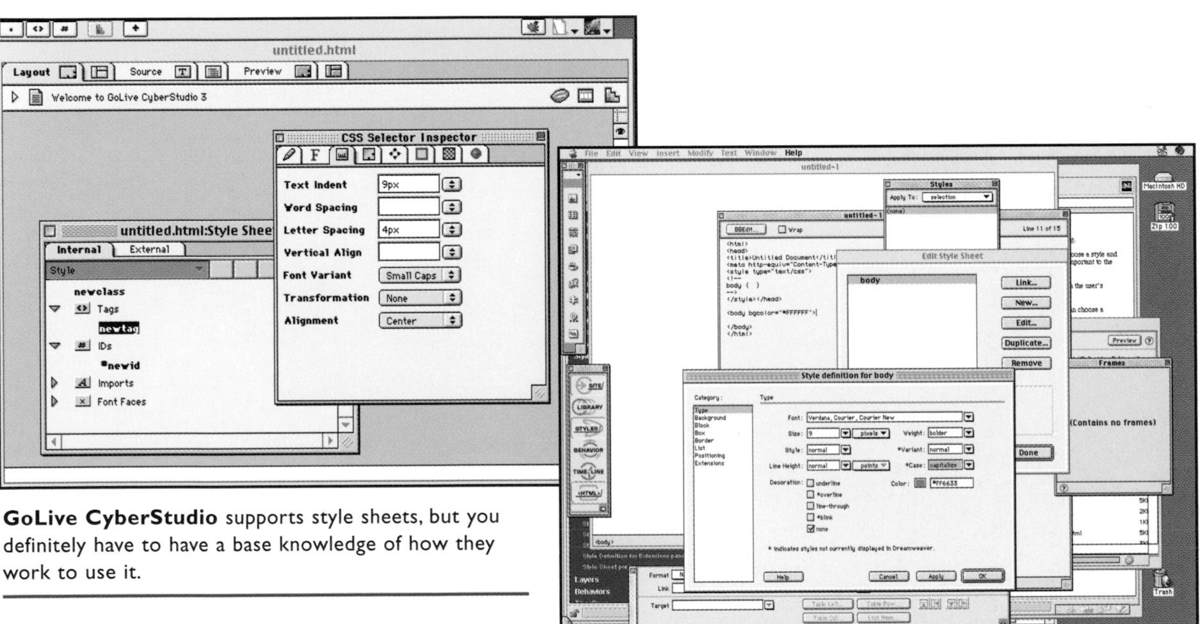

GoLive CyberStudio supports style sheets, but you definitely have to have a base knowledge of how they work to use it.

Macromedia Dreamweaver supports style sheets too, but you must know what you are doing to use the WYSIWYG capabilities.

summary Cascading Style Sheets

CSS style sheets are going to be a very powerful mechanism for enhancing the presentation quality of text on the Web. Though not ready for prime time yet, there is good reason to believe that CSS will become a useable feature of mainstream browsers in the not-so-distant future.

- Using CSS, you will be able to format your text in manners much closer to that of the printed page, and expect your layouts to work consistently—within certain limits—across platforms, browsers, and differing sizes and resolutions of displays. This chapter covered the basic principles of style sheets, so that you can use them now, or wait until they are supported more widely.
- Internal style sheets are used within a single HTML document.
- External style sheets are used by multiple HTML documents.
- Inline style sheets only apply to part of an HTML document.
- It's best to use pixel measurements for specifying type, since it will produce the most reliable results.
- Be sure to put your style sheet commands within comment tags, so browsers that don't support CSS will ignore the code.
- While WYSIWYG editors support style sheets, you still need to understand what to specify within the various choices.

Introduction
Scanning for the Web

Chapter Topics

- Scanning Resolution
- Scanning Terms
- Scanning Equipment
- Digital Cameras and DV
- Photo CDs
- Eliminating Moirés
- Photoshop 5.0 Imaging Techniques

20

When I used to teach digital imaging full-time at Art Center College of Design, teaching students to scan was often much more challenging than teaching them Photoshop or other imaging programs. This was because scanning for print involves lots of rules and variables that have to do with dot screen, print resolution, and colored ink selection. Thankfully, scanning for the Web is a much more simple science!

Scanning is easier to learn for the Web because of the fixed resolution (72 ppi, or 72 pixels per inch) and the fact that RGB doesn't have to get translated into printed inks; it is simply delivered via computer screens around the world.

This chapter, therefore, concentrates a little on scanning and much more on the creative aspects of getting your scanned images to look good. I should warn you, however, that this chapter is Photoshop-centric, since Photoshop is unarguably the best professional tool for the task.

In this chapter, I will cover techniques that will eliminate dot patterns and moirés, help you balance your images with levels, and teach you to select isolated areas of a graphics to enhance or edit. Luckily, at 72 ppi, scanning for the Web is more about creativity and purpose than overcoming technical complexity.

What Resolution?

When scanning for the Web, it isn't necessary to scan your original image any larger than 72 ppi. Anyone who has ever scanned for print will find this very hard to believe, and you will distrust my advice immediately. The first step to believing me will be understanding an extreme difference between Web and print.

When designing for print, it's critical to know at which resolution your artwork will ultimately be published. If you knew, for example, that your piece would be published at 150 lines per inch, you would likely scan your original at 300 dots per inch. On the Web there is but one answer to the dpi question, and it is 72 pixels per inch. If you scan an original at 300 dots per inch, you will simply need to further reduce the size in Photoshop to 72 ppi.

Although some people swear that you get better quality if you scan at a high resolution and then use Photoshop to reduce the size to 72 dpi, I have rarely found this to be the case. You have a choice: either scan at 72 dpi in the first place or reduce the work you do scan to 72 ppi after scanning.

I know it's hard for quality-conscious designers to accept that a low resolution scan is good enough quality. You basically have to throw away the print designer mentality for this medium. A printed piece will improve in appearance if it is high resolution. That's because high resolution printers can take that data and output it. When you're printing to computer screens, high resolution doesn't do you any good. In fact, it hurts you.

If you were to put a 300 dpi image on the Web, it would simply display at 72 ppi and quadruple in size. It would be too big by bandwidth standards, as well as dimensions of a normal computer display. I dare you to try it to prove me right, if you so insist!

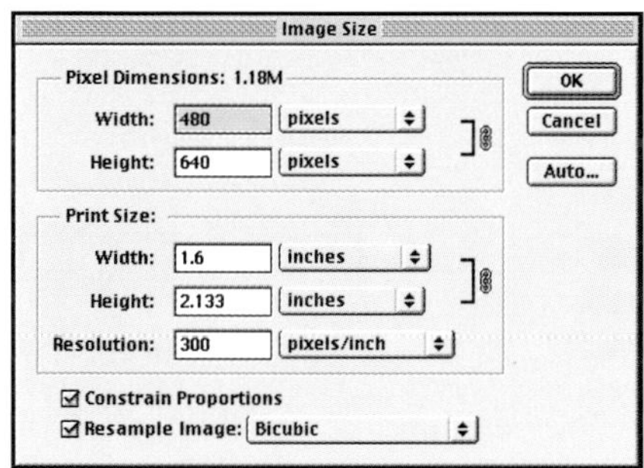

The only result of setting high resolution on the Web will be an image that is too large and bulky for Internet delivery.

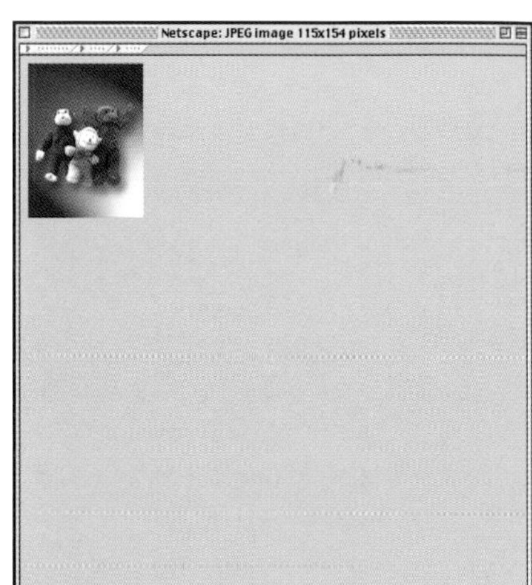

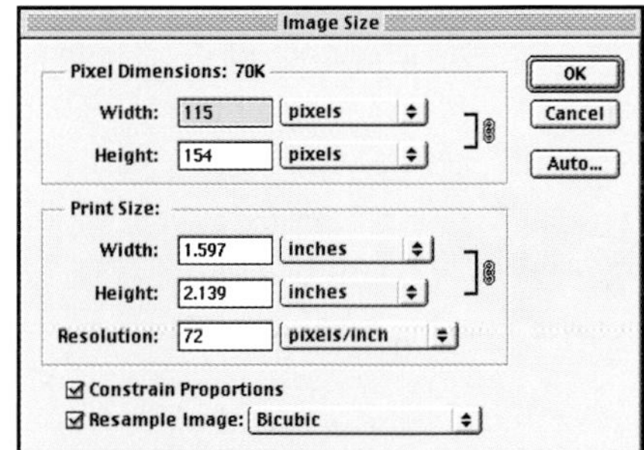

If I intended for this image to be 1.5×2", but set my dpi to 300, this is the result. When stored at 72 ppi, the image is exactly the size I intended.

Dictionary of Scanning Terms

DPI (Dots Per Inch): A measurement relating to the number of halftone dots per inch; used for printers.

LPI (Lines Per Inch): Used to measure halftone dot screens.

PPI (Pixels Per Inch): How many pixels describe an inch.

Resolution: Measurement of how many pixels, dots, or lines per inch are used by images, printers, and screens.

Moiré pattern: An unwanted dot pattern that creates a noticeable screen that degrades the scanned image. It is caused by scanning artwork that contains a pre-existing halftone dot pattern.

Scanning Equipment

There are all kinds of scanners at all kinds of price points: high-resolution scanners, scanners that scan transparencies (including slides and film negatives), hand-held portable scanners, and digital cameras that double as scanners. It's a confusing group of choices, but as an experienced screen-based designer, I'll share my hard-earned wisdom and advice.

First of all, if you already own a scanner, you don't have to buy a different one for Web design. The Web probably makes the lowest demands of any other medium you might use a scanner for. Because everything you'll do is for screen resolution, not print, you don't have to care so much about the quality of the scans. That might sound blasphemous, but with all the great imaging programs out there, it's really not necessary to have the best-quality original scan. You can fix a lot of things in post-processing, especially if you use Photoshop. I'll share a lot of my favorite imaging techniques later in this chapter.

I always look to the speed of the scanner as the highest consideration when purchasing a system for screen-based artwork (Web, multimedia, or video). I have found that what really counts the most is how fast you can get the scanner to capture an image. This is especially true if you are scanning a high volume of images. A slow scanner can really eat away at productivity. There are lots of fantastic scanners on the market that are fast. You may want to find one that scans the red, green, and blue pass at once instead of the slower models that take a full pass for each color. A good place to research scanners is, you guessed it... on the Web.

ZD Net-Scanner Buyer Guide
http://www.zdnet.com/products/scanneruser/index.html

Scanner Comparison Table
http://www.hsdesign.com/scanning/table/scanner_table2.html

The last equipment comment I'll make is about SCSI (pronounced scuzzy; hence, one my personal favorite computer terms) chain conflicts. A SCSI device requires a special SCSI cable, which should come standard with most scanners. Most scanners for both Macs and PCs are SCSI-based devices. I've experienced a lot of trouble in my day with SCSI conflicts and bad SCSI cables. Be sure to use a high-quality cable, and the thicker and shorter the better. If you experience problems with your scanner, try hooking it up directly to your computer and unhooking any other external devices, such as hard drives or CD-ROM drives. If you continue to have problems, check to see whether you have outdated scanner software. As operating systems change, scanner software changes, too. Most of the major scanning manufacturers have Web sites where you can download software updates.

Digital Cameras and DV

Digital cameras are the rage today, even though the quality of these cameras is dubious at best. When dealing with the Web, however, low quality has its appeal since most of the images you'll work with will be small in dimensions and will contain significant compression. Because you are working at low quality to begin with, the allure of a digital camera can be quite compelling.

One major warning about digital cameras: most of them use JPEG compression to begin with. The bad thing about that is if you do anything to the resulting image (such as sharpening, scaling, editing, etc.), you will have to resave it with JPEG. Because JPEG is a lossy compression method, it continues to lose quality each time it is compressed. If you can find a camera that supports megapixels, you will be able to start with a larger image that you can later reduce. This can potentially help with compression problems because you can scale the image, which will eliminate some of the compression artifacts.

Depending on what you are using your camera for, a digital camera can prove more useful than a flatbed scanner. Let's say you're trying to grab a quick picture of your car to sell through an Internet classified ad, or you want to send pictures of your grandkids home to their mom and dad. There are plenty of reasons why a digital camera is handy, even if the quality is low and the compression issues are high.

As an alternative, my husband Bruce and I decided to buy a DV (**D**igital **V**ideo) camera instead of a digital still camera. Most DV cameras will take live action and still images, and the great thing is that they don't employ any compression. We figured, for slightly more money (alas, isn't it always the case?), we could capture moving digital images as well as have higher quality digital still images.

The caveat to the DV versus digital camera decision is that most digital cameras ship with the cables and software to get the images into your computer easily. If you get a DV camera, like we did, you'll need to additionally purchase a Firewire card and cable system. It's a much more expensive route to be sure, even though the quality and flexibility of DV is indisputable.

DV URLs

http://www.zdnet.com/products/
http://www.promax.com
http://www.radius.com

tip

Photo CDs Instead of Scans

Often times I work with Photo CDs instead of scans. Whenever I have transparencies to scan, it's cheaper for me (because I don't own a transparency scanner) to have my transparencies converted to Photo CDs. Each image is scanned by a local Kodak Photo CD service provider and stored at many different resolutions to a CD-ROM disc. For Web-based images, you can almost always use the lowest resolution from the CD, and the images will look great.

For more info:
http://www.kodak.com

Photo CD Books

The Photo CD Book
Heinz von Buelow
Verbum Books
ISBN: 1-55755-195-2
$29.95

The Official Photo CD Handbook
Michael Gosney
Peachpit Press
ISBN: 1-56609-172-1
$39.95

Photo CD: Quality Photos at Your Fingertips
John Larish
Micro Publishing News
ISBN: 0-941-84509-5
$27.95

Start with a Scan
Janet Ashford and John Odam
Peachpit Press
ISBN:0-201-88456-9
$34.95

Resizing Images in Photoshop 5.0

Understanding how to resize images is important when working with scans, clip art, and Web images. You want to ensure that your images are 72 dpi with Web-bound graphics and photographs. Many scanners default to scanning at higher dots per inch settings, meaning it's up to you to scale the images down to Web-appropriate size.

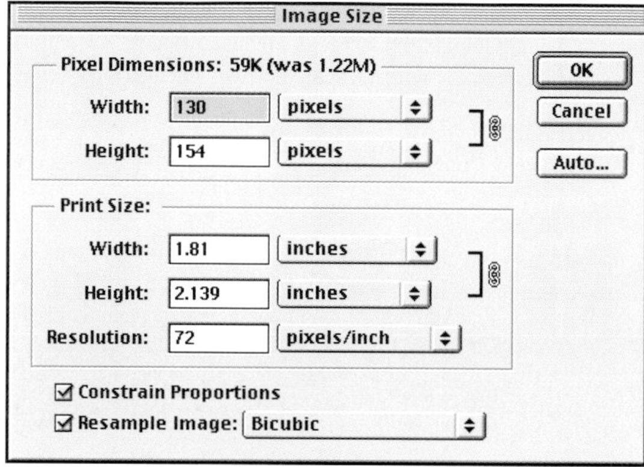

Under Image, select **Image Size**. Make sure you check Resample Image and Constrain Proportions (unless you want to intentionally distort the image).

Nearest Neighbor
Bilinear
✓ Bicubic

When you choose to resize an image, you have different interpolation methods to select from.

Bicubic: Usually the best quality type of reduction method. Adds anti-aliasing, which is sometimes not desired.

Bilinear: In-between quality is faster and lower quality than bicubic, but better quality than nearest neighbor.

Nearest neighbor: Much faster than bicubic, lower quality—unless you want to retain an aliased edge.

Original size

Enlarged image

When enlarged with bicubic interpolation, notice how the right image becomes soft and out of focus. Never scale up in size, or this will be the result. Scan large and reduce, rather than scanning small and enlarging.

Nearest Neighbor Interpolation

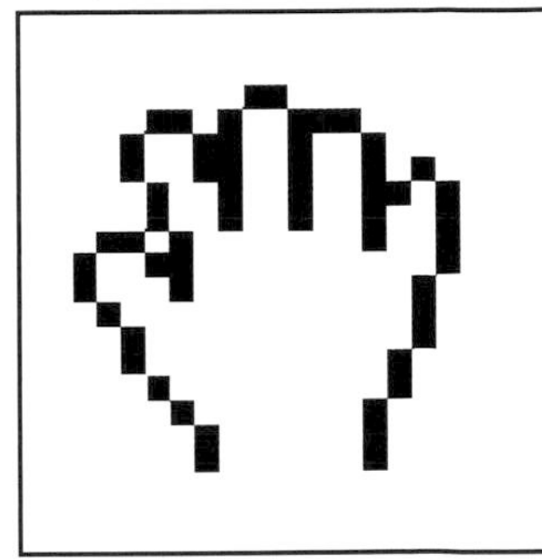

Sometimes, you might be going for an intentionally pixelated appearance—starting from a small image and wanting to retain the pixels. In this event, use nearest neighbor.

warning

Do Not Resize in Indexed Color!

Be careful when you scale images to make sure the Photoshop mode is RGB and not Indexed Color. If you open a GIF, let's say, in Indexed Color mode, when you go to resize it, no amount of finesse will improve the image because the image won't shift color outside its fixed color table. Go to **Image:Mode**, and select **RGB**, and everything will work beautifully.

Dot Screen Patterns and Moirés

If you plan to use images out of a book or catalog, beware of the moiré monsters! Unfortunately, there is an inherent problem with this technique because it almost always results in unwanted dot patterns and moirés. This section covers techniques to correct this problem.

Scanned images from printed sources have specific problems when converted to RGB. The printing inks CMYK (**C**yan, **M**agenta, **Y**ellow, and Blac**K**) result in patterns of dots that are visible and unattractive when scanned. A close-up of a dot pattern is shown here to demonstrate this common scanning problem.

Here's a scanned image from my book *Coloring Web Graphics*. Because I scanned this image from a book, it contained a dot pattern. The moiré problem is clearly visible.

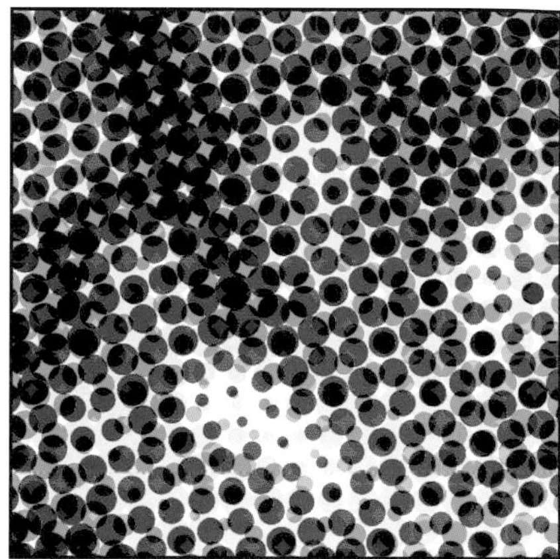

A simulation of CMYK printing inks that form a dot pattern.

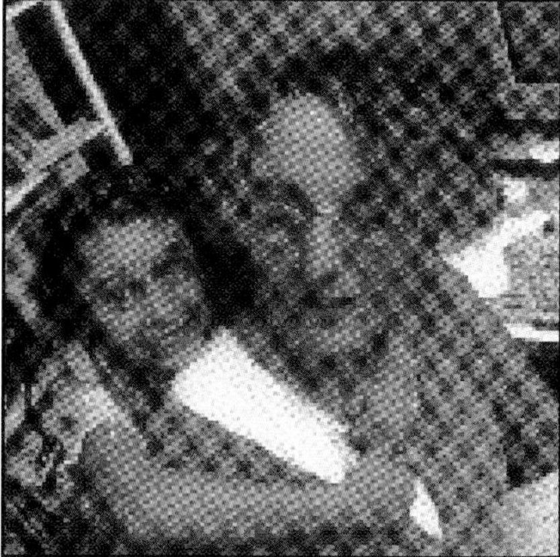

After this image is scaled, the dot patterns get more or less objectionable. The dot patterns change with each resize. The best approach to this problem is to get rid of the dot pattern that appears on the image before doing any resizing. Here are some techniques for getting rid of the dots.

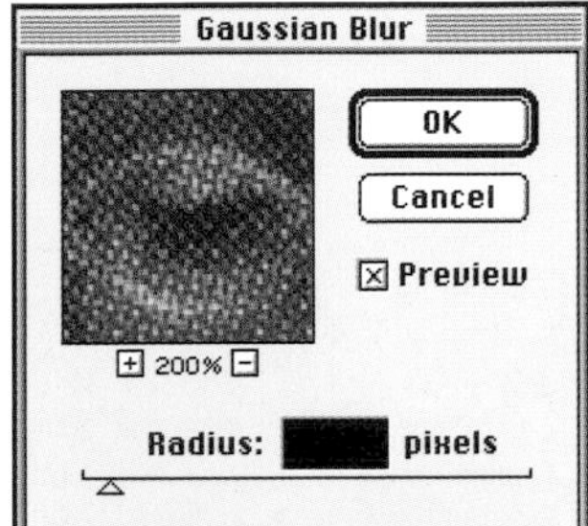

Under **Filters**, select **Gaussian Blur**. This filter causes the image to blur depending on what setting is chosen. The idea isn't to completely blur the image, but to get rid of the printing dots. The printing dots are visible within the preview window of this filter.

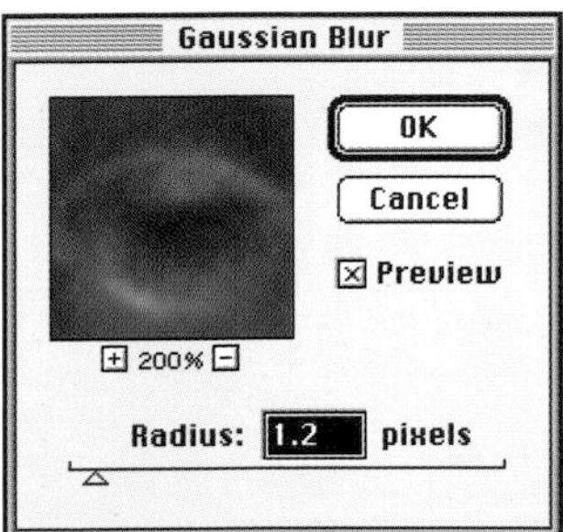

The blur setting at 1.2 pixels. No more printing dots! A higher blur setting will start to degrade the image. This will be a judgement call that you will have to make, and it will differ for every single image you work with.

The resulting image has no dots, but it's blurry.

The trick is to resize the image smaller. This will cause the blurry appearance to become sharper and less noticeable.

At this point, you can add a **sharpening filter** to eliminate some of the blur. You should have no evidence of the dot pattern! The Sharpen filter increases the contrast between light and dark areas, so I suggest you use it sparingly.

Voilà! This image is perfectly acceptable for the Web. You may choose to add a little extra saturation to the image using techniques described earlier.

Image Processing Techniques

Photoshop offers a wonderland of image processing techniques to fix or stylize any type of photograph or graphic. I'm covering some of my favorites here, found under the Image:Adjust menu.

Levels

I choose to use this process the most for scanned images. You can access it through **Image:Adjust:Levels**.

Adjusting the **black point** will result in all the blacks becoming darkened.

Adjusting the **middle slider** will adjust the midpoint in the image.

Adjusting the **white point** will make all the whites in the image brighter.

By moving the **Output Level black slider** to the right, you can create a screened-back image. This is the equivalent of tinting all the colors with white.

By moving the **Output Level white slider** to the left, you can create a toned-back image. This is the equivalent of toning all the colors with black.

Hue/Saturation/Brightness

My second favorite image processing technique is to colorize photographs using **Image:Adjust:Hue/Saturation**.

By clicking on the **Colorize checkbox**, you can create monotones of images very easily. Try this one, and you'll never stop using it! It's a magic fix for any type of photograph that doesn't look its best.

summary

Scanning for the Web

I hope this chapter answered your questions about working with scanned images. I outlined many of the gotchas that have "gotten" me and made suggestions that should result in great-looking scans and images. Here's a brief summary:

- Always scan at 72 ppi, or reduce your images to that resolution after you've scanned them.
- Bicubic interpolation lends the best quality to most resized images, unless you are striving for a pixelated look on purpose, in which case you should use nearest neighbor interpolation.
- The most important choice in selecting a scanner is how fast it scans, because the quality for Web graphics is not nearly as critical as for print.
- Using the features found under the Photoshop Image:Adjust menu can fix almost any scan.
- Getting rid of moirés for scanned images involves a combination of filters and scaling techniques.
- Digital cameras are handy for Web graphics, but they often use JPEG compression, which can be problematic.

Introduction

GIF Animation

Chapter Topics

- Aesthetics of Animation
- Glossary of Terms
- GIF Animation Resources
- ImageReady Techniques
- Fireworks Techniques
- Other GIF Animation Tools

21

There are many ways to add animation to a Web page, but the most popular method by far is through using the simple GIF file format. No extra programming knowledge is required whatsoever because the same IMG tag that inserts regular GIF files into Web pages works for animated GIF files as well.

Making animated GIFs involves using a software application that can create the format for you. This chapter will outline the use of several different GIF animation applications and utilities. It will also review techniques for certain effects that are commonly requested or used in animation.

Animation can add a lot of spice to a Web page, but many people don't realize that if applied gratuitously, animation can detract from your message as well. This chapter reviews animated GIF files from an aesthetic and technical perspective, and offers advice on when and when not to use this feature on your site.

The Aesthetics of Animation

Before we get into the what, where, how, and why of animation, I think it's important to consider the broader issue: the aesthetics of animation. With the exception of multimedia, the Web is the first medium to combine animation and body text on a single page. For this reason, it's no wonder that many people struggle to use animation effectively.

Adding animation to a site can be great, but it can also have the reverse effect of annoying your audience or detracting from what your page is trying to say. During a recent conference I attended, Ben Olander, Creative Director at **Angry Monkey** (http://www.angrymonkey.com) commented, "Most animation you see on the Web is the equivalent of the BLINK tag." I agree with him, but I also see this as a natural outgrowth of artists and developers who are first working with a new tool.

Here are some very general, personal guidelines I would like to share:

- Animation calls attention to itself much more than static images on a page. Make sure that the content of your animation is, in fact, something you want the most attention called to on your page. If it isn't, the animation will effectively detract from what you're trying to communicate.
- In most instances, animation that cycles or loops endlessly will eventually become annoying. This chapter will teach you how to set up loops, or a finite number of repeats, but you must be the judge of when loops are appropriate. You might test the page on some friends or colleagues first to get their feedback.
- If you use more than one animation on a single page, the effect may be overwhelming to the end viewer instead of impressive.
- Make sure your animation loads quickly. You'll learn guidelines to achieve fast downloading speeds in this chapter. If you make your audience wait too long for the animation to load, they'll move onward before ever seeing it.

Animated GIF Format

This chapter uses the term "animated GIF," but the technical term for this type of file is GIF89a. Animated GIFs have been in existence since the late 1980s, but they weren't originally supported by early Web browsers. The great news is that all the major Web browsers now support this spec, making it possible to include these types of files in Web pages without worry of excluding any potential end viewers.

The GIF89a file format allows for multiple images to be stored inside a single GIF document. When displayed within browser software that recognizes the multiple images, the artwork streams in to the Web page in a predetermined sequence, creating a slide-show style animation. The file format supports looping (the capability to repeat multiple images indefinitely) and timing delays between frames of artwork. The GIF file format also supports limited masking, meaning that GIF animations can use the same type of transparency supported by static GIF images.

Animated GIFs require no plug-ins and no programming, and they don't even require a live Web connection, making them perfect for Intranets and testing locally on your machine. Animated GIFs are simple to make, easy to include in HTML, and effortless for your Web-viewing audience to see. They are one of the most elegant solutions for adding Web animation and lack only in that they cannot include interactivity or sound. For an animated logo or button, however, animated GIFs are a pretty smart option.

To include animated GIFs on Web pages, you'll use the standard IMG SRC element. A simple example of the code would look like this:

```
<IMG SRC="my_animation.gif">
```

Animated GIF Tech Notes

Animated GIFs can include the following features:

- Set looping, or number of repeats
- Set delays between individual frames
- Different disposal methods to optimize the graphics
- Palettes
- Transparency
- Interlacing

tip

Animated GIF Resources

Specific tools that create animated GIFs are discussed later in this chapter. Here are some recommended resources for learning how to create and code animated GIFs:

Hotwired's Animation Express
The best inspirational gallery of Web animation
http://www.hotwired.com/animation/

Webmonkey Animation Tutorial
http://www.hotwired.com/webmonkey/multimedia/tutorials/tutorial1.html?tw=multimedia

Yves Piguet's Site
(author of GIFBuilder) Great tutorials
http://iawww.epfl.ch/Staff/Yves.Piguet/clip2gifhome/GifBuilder.html

GIF Animation Studio
Full Color book w/CD
Richard Koman
O'Reilley
Price: $39.95

Glossary of GIF Animation Terms

There are many terms in animation that might be unfamiliar to you or specific to GIF animation. Here's a glossary:

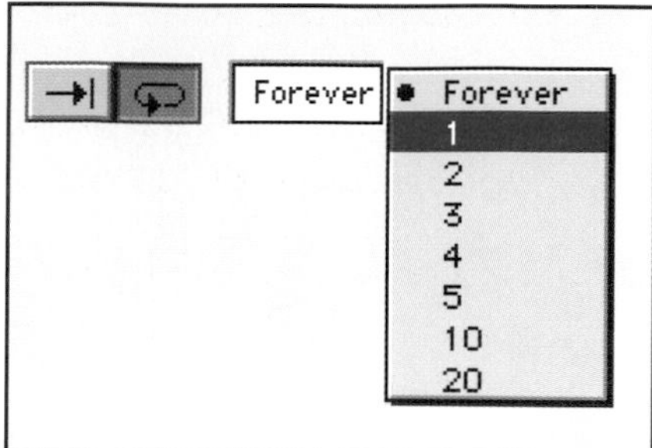

This example, taken from Macromedia's Fireworks program, shows how looping can be set when creating animated GIF files.

Looping: Looping is the process of repeating an animation over and over and over. If the animation is 10 frames long and is looped three times, the end user will see 30 frames of the animation, with three repeats. The animation itself would still be 10 frames; however, it would contain a setting that would tell it to play the same animation three times. **Tip:** As stated earlier, be careful of unlimited looping animations as they can annoy your audience.

300

Frame 1	U	20	/100
Frame 2	U	20	
Frame 3	U	300	
Frame 4	U	20	

You can set the timing of an animated GIF, which is most commonly measured in units of 100, which approximately equals one second depending on processor speed. In this example (again from Fireworks), frame 3 has the value of 300, meaning it will hold for approximately three seconds while the other frames will play back at 1/5th of a second.

Frame delays: Frame delays can be used to alter the timing of animations. The common unit of measuring the timing is 100. In a loose way, 100 is supposed to equal one second of play time. The problem is that faster processors will play animated GIFs more quickly than slower processors; the Web is not like film or video, which have a set playback rate. Loosely, a good guide to follow is that 100 will equal one second. If you want your first frame to last five seconds, your next three to last one second each, and the last frame to last 15 seconds, your frame delays would look something like this:

Frame 01=500
Frame 02=100
Frame 03=100
Frame 04=100
Frame 05=1500

Download speeds: The initial download time of the animated GIF will depend on your end user's connection speed, but once the animation has fully downloaded, it will depend on the processor speed of his or her computer. This can make for wildly different frame delay timings on different systems, regardless of what frame delays you program. Almost all GIF animation software packages support frame delays.

Optimization: Animated GIFs can be optimized, just like regular GIFs. The same rules that applied to file size savings in Chapter 6, "Low-Bandwidth Graphics" apply here. Like other GIFs, you want to make sure that you use as few colors as needed and try to avoid dithering or noise in your image.

Transparency and disposal methods: Disposal methods are a scary sounding term for how the animation is displayed in terms of its transparency. With a static GIF image, this is a non-issue. A transparent static image shows through to its background, and that's the end of the story.

With a multiple-frame GIF, however, this presents a bigger issue. Let's say I have an animated ball that's bouncing. If I make the ball transparent, and the image before it has already loaded, the transparency might show part or all of the frame before. Instead of the illusion of motion, the result would be the non-illusion resulting in each frame of my ball bouncing animation being visible at the same time.

Disposal methods are used to specify how you want to display your transparent animated GIFs.

The disposal method is what instructs the GIF animation on how to display preceding frames of the animation. Disposal methods are set within whatever GIF animation authoring software package you're using.

Unspecified: Use this disposal method when you aren't using transparency. It will simply present each frame in its entirety and will not yield any added optimization to the file. If I had an animation that changed images every single frame, such as a slide show of changing visuals, I would use this disposal method.

Do not dispose: This disposal method would reveal each preceding frame of an animation. Let's say I wanted to create an animation of my name handwriting itself on the screen. If I left the L to draw itself only once and then used the subsequent frame to draw the Y, I would be creating a smaller file size. Use this method when you want the prior frames to show through and you want to enjoy some file savings with no penalty to image quality.

Restore to background: Instead of displaying the previous frame, the animation is set to show the background color or tile image of your Web page.

Restore to previous: This function is almost the same as Do Not Dispose except the first frame always stays visible underneath the rest of the animation. Netscape has known problems with supporting this disposal method.

Palettes: Most GIF animation software allows you to specify bit-depth values. Lower bit-depth settings will result in smaller, faster animated GIFs. One problem palette management issues in animated GIFs suffer from is that often the software or browser defaults to accepting a different palette for each frame, which causes palette flashing (a psychedelic feast for the eyes, to be sure)—most likely not the effect you were wishing to see.

The best way to avoid GIF animation palette problems is to map each frame of your animation to a common palette. Some programs do this automatically, and others require that you load a palette to achieve this result. This technique is called creating a "super" or "global" palette.

Creating a super or global palette is handled automatically by the tools reviewed in later sections of this chapter. If you need to do this by hand, try pasting all your animation frames into a single Photoshop document and then changing the Mode to Indexed Color. Select **Mode:Indexed Color:Color Table**, and save the table. This table can be loaded into many different animation tools.

Interlacing: Interlaced GIFs were discussed in Chapter 5, "Web File Formats." Adding the interlace feature to a single or multiple GIF image will cause it to look blocky until it comes into focus. Personally, I dislike the effect, and especially dislike the effect in the context of animation. It sort of breaks the illusion of motion to see each individual frame come into full focus, don't you think?

How to Create Animation Content

There are lots of different animation tools and technologies, but what about the animation content itself? If you've never made animation before, you might be asking what exactly constitutes animation, per se?

Animation is actually the illusion of motion. It's really composed of a series of still images—shown in quick succession—the process of which tricks our minds into thinking that stationary artwork is truly moving. It's all fake! Making artwork for animation is an exercise in understanding how to fake motion through presenting changing artwork over time.

There are all kinds of ways to generate animation files or sequential images that change in appearance from frame to frame. Any number of animation software packages can generate sequential images in PICT, PICs, GIF, or QuickTime formats; most of the Web animation tools can import standard PICTs, GIFs, or QuickTime formats.

You can make animation without a dedicated animation program, too. If you use an image editor, such as Photoshop, try running a filter in incremental amounts over a still image. Try drawing the same artwork three times and it will appear to jitter subtly, or not so subtly depending on how much each version changes. Try changing the opacity over multiple images, and you'll create artwork that appears to "fade up."

If you want to get ideas for animation, start by looking at existing animation on a VCR and single-framing through it, or try loading other people's animated GIFs into animating GIF programs to reverse-engineer what you like. Just be sure that reverse-engineering doesn't mean stealing. The same copyright laws that apply to images apply to movies.

Common Animation Terminology

If you are new to animation, you might find many unfamiliar terms. Here is a short list of terms and their meanings:

Keyframe: A keyframe is an extreme point of motion. If you were to make an animation enter on screen left and exit on screen right, the keyframes would identify the start and stop positions.

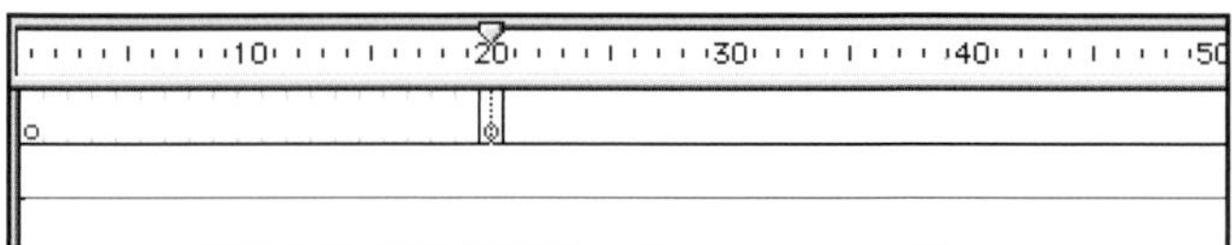

Timeline: A timeline usually keeps track of frames. In this example, there are two keyframes; one on Frame 1, and the other on Frame 20.

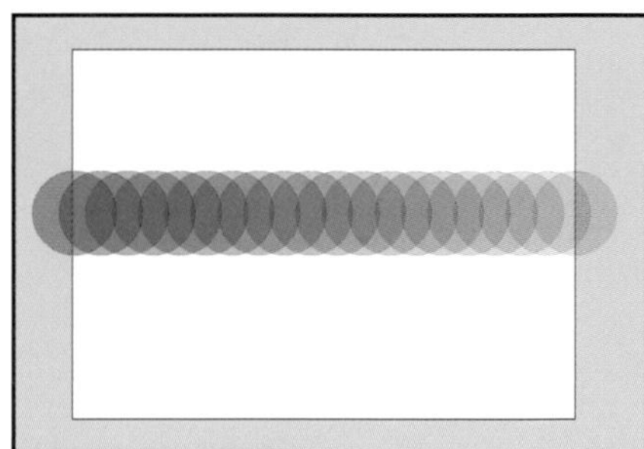

Inbetween or tween: Many programs that use keyframes also produce inbetweens or tweens. In this case, there are 20 inbetween frames between the two keyframes shown earlier. They are all shown at once on this page because a feature called "onion skinning," which shows all the frames at once, has been turned on. In reality, each position of each circle is on an individual frame that would play back one at a time. In character animation, like what you see in "Snow White" or "Rugrats," drawings are inbetweened by hand drawing each frame of artwork.

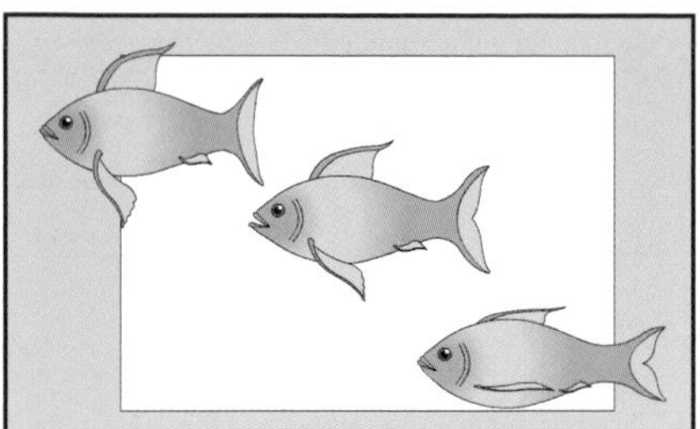

Frame-by-frame animation: Artwork that changes every single frame. Here's an example of frame-by-frame animation, with three frames showing at once.

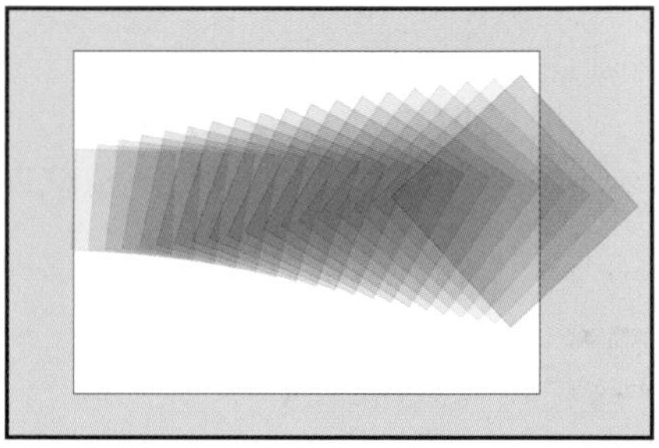

Motion graphics: Motion graphics involves taking one piece of artwork and moving it's with position, scale, rotation, or changing its opacity.

Tools and Techniques for Frame-by-Frame GIF Animation

There are many, many tools with which to create frame-by-frame GIF animations. Some are free, and some are not. I've concentrated on ImageReady and Fireworks, two excellent tools which are not free, but you can download free demos of either program to try these exercises.

Frame Animation in ImageReady

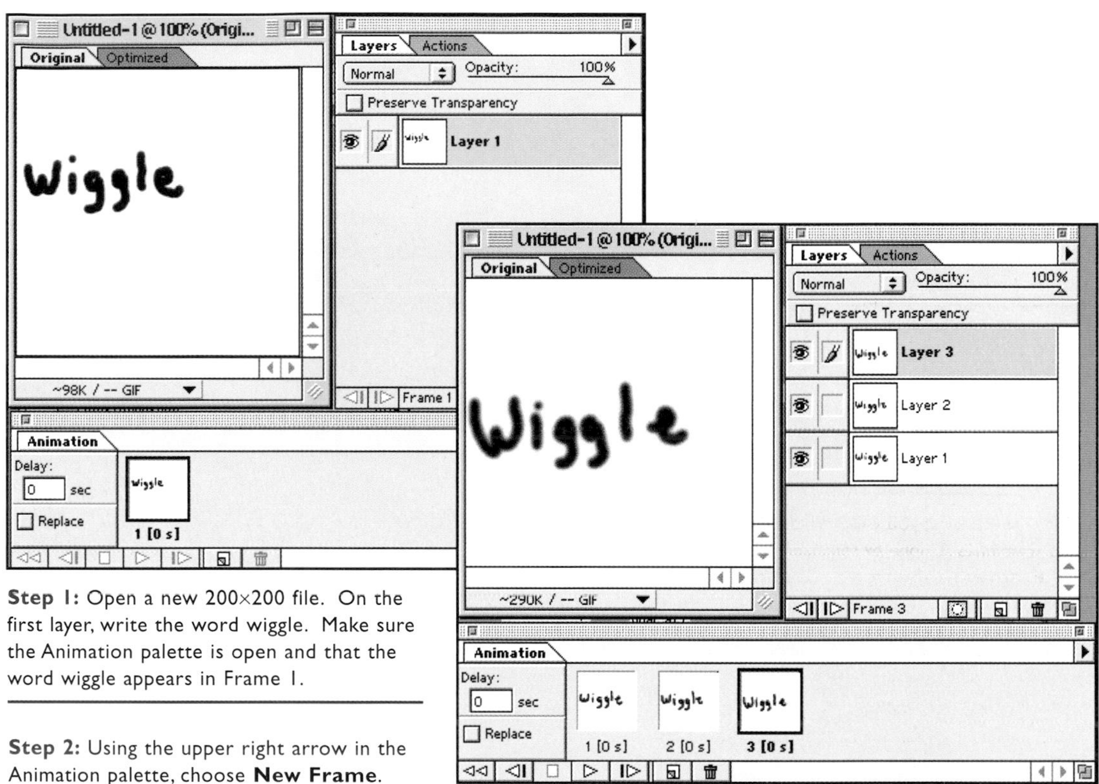

Step 1: Open a new 200×200 file. On the first layer, write the word wiggle. Make sure the Animation palette is open and that the word wiggle appears in Frame 1.

Step 2: Using the upper right arrow in the Animation palette, choose **New Frame**.

Step 3: In the Layers palette, click on the **New Layer** icon. Fill it with white, and then write the word wiggle again in black (color suggestions are optional). Repeat this step for a third frame. Click the Play button to preview the animation in ImageReady.

Step 4: Use the upper right arrow of the Animation palette to select **Play Options**. You can set the animation to loop, play a specific number of times, or play only once. In the Optimize palette, be sure to GIF as the file format (other file formats will not produce animations). You can preview the whole thing by selecting **File:Preview** in the browser.

Frame Animation in Fireworks

Creating animation in Fireworks involves the use of Frames and Export.

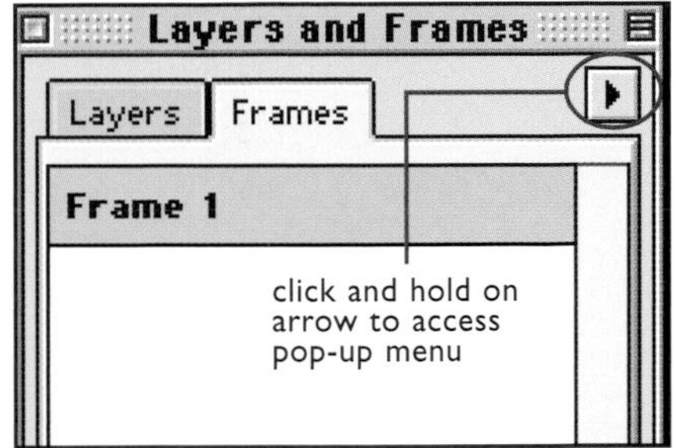

Step 1: To access Frames, make sure to open the Layers and Frames palette (select **Window:Frames.**) Use the right upper arrow to access the Frames pop-up menu.

Step 2: Using the pop-up menu, you can add, duplicate, or delete frames. Copying to frames is done by selecting an object and then choosing **Copy to Frames**. If you have multiple objects selected, you can choose **Distribute Selection**, which will put each object in a separate frame.

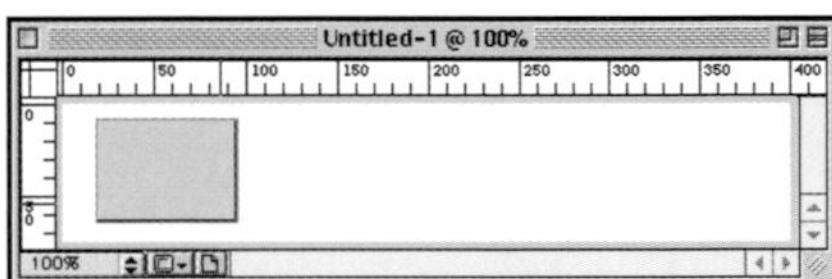

Step 3: Create a new document and draw a shape.

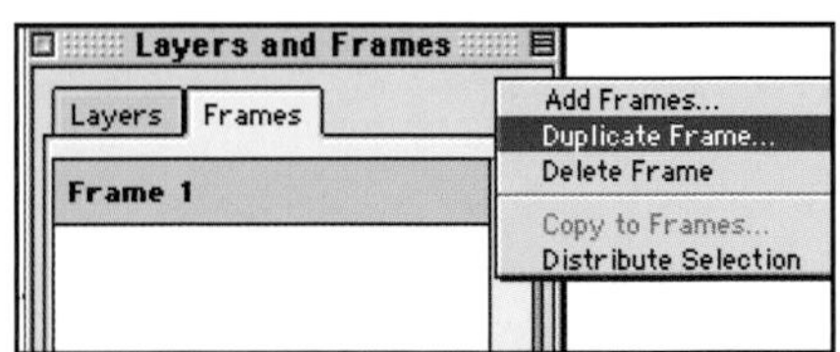

Step 4: Choose Duplicate Frame from the upper-right arrow pop-up menu.

Step 5: In the dialog box that appears, choose After current frame.

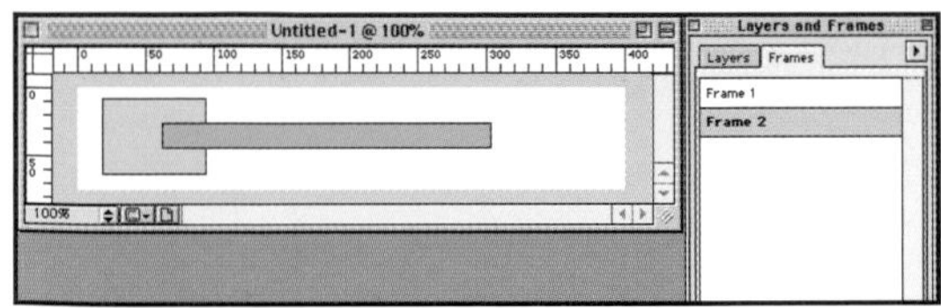

Step 6: Draw another shape and repeat the process. Keep adding artwork until you have five or six frames. By selecting all the objects you've created and choosing **Duplicate Frame** each time, the objects will be copied to the duplicate with each new graphic you create.

Step 7: When you're ready, choose **File:Export**.

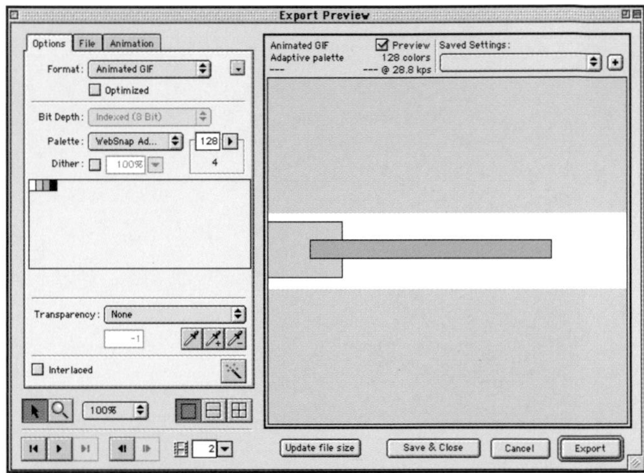

Step 8: With the **Options tab** selected, make sure the file format **Animated GIF** is selected.

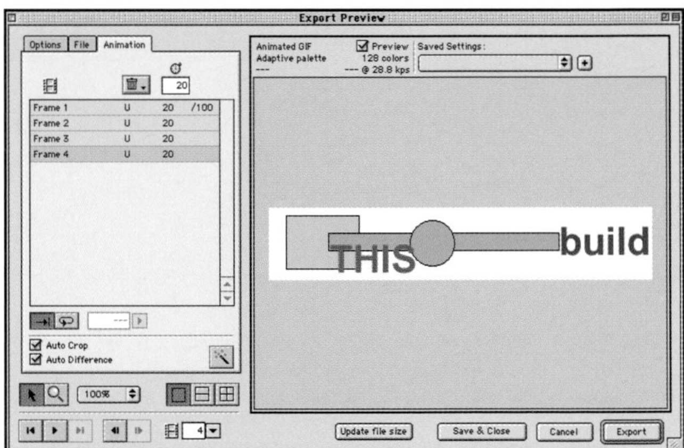

Step 9: Click on the **Animation tab**, and you can create your settings for delays. Once you're happy with the settings, click **Export**, and Fireworks will write the GIF file.

Motion Graphics in ImageReady

Although many people use Photoshop for animation purposes, the product itself (as of version 5.0) does not support the creation of animated GIF files. Adobe's ImageReady does, however, and it uses the Layers palette in conjunction with the Animation palette to do so.

This next exercise shows how to create motion graphics using ImageReady. It involves setting up a file with three layers: a background (shown here in solid white), a circle, and the word circle, each on its own layer.

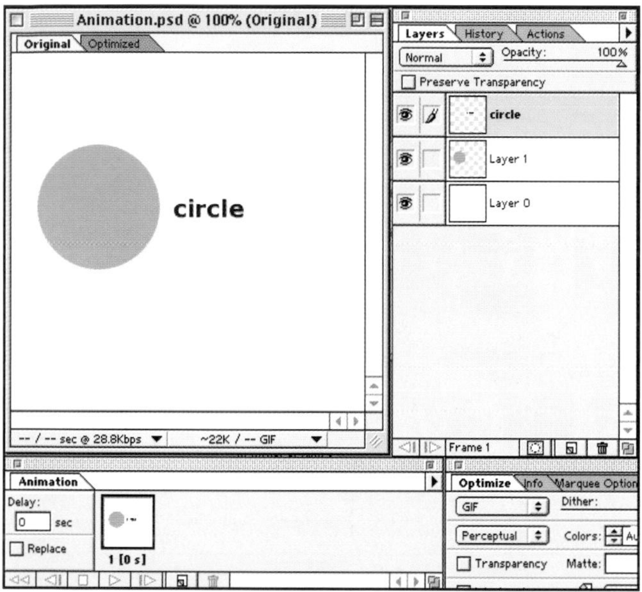

Step 1: Choose **Window:Show Animation** to bring up the Animation palette. You should see a single frame composite of all the layers in Frame 1.

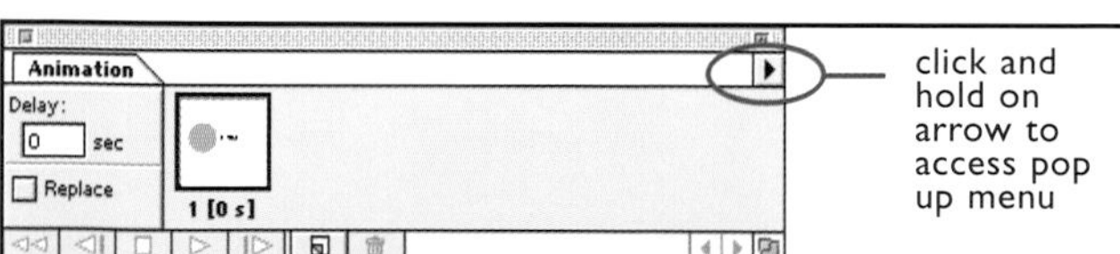

Step 2: Click on the upper-right arrow of the Animation tab to select **New Frame** to make a duplicate frame. By highlighting the circle and the circle text inside the Layers palette, move the images over each other using the **Move tool**. You should have two frames in the Animation palette, with the objects in two different positions.

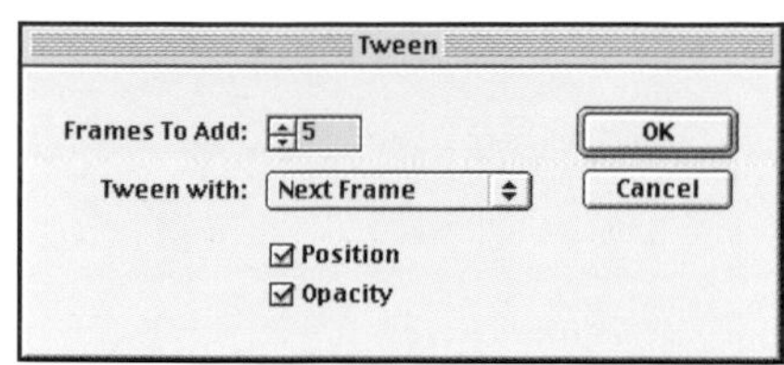

Step 3: Highlight the first frame in the Animation tab. Click on the upper-right arrow again and select Tween.

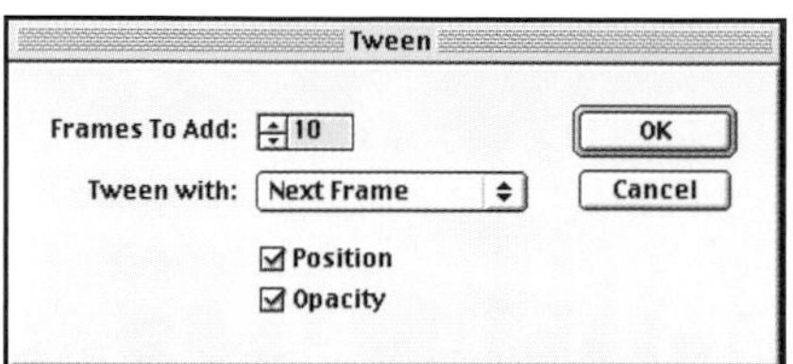

Step 4: Add 10 frames.

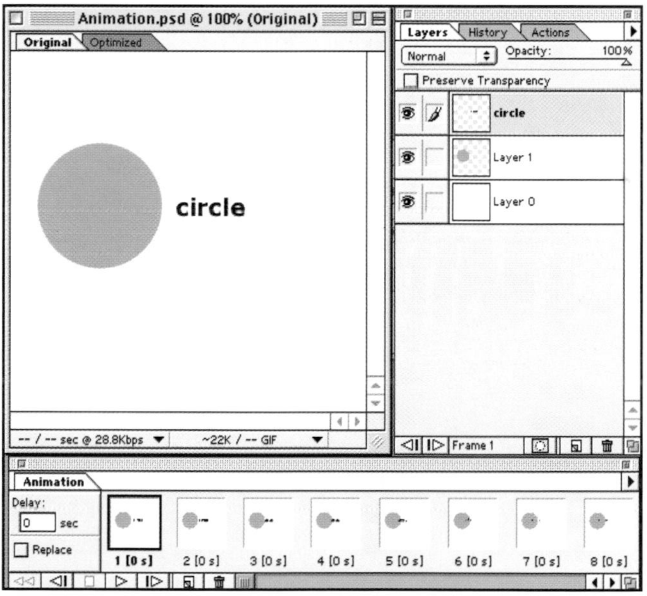

Step 5: The setting above produced the result of the circle and text moving together.

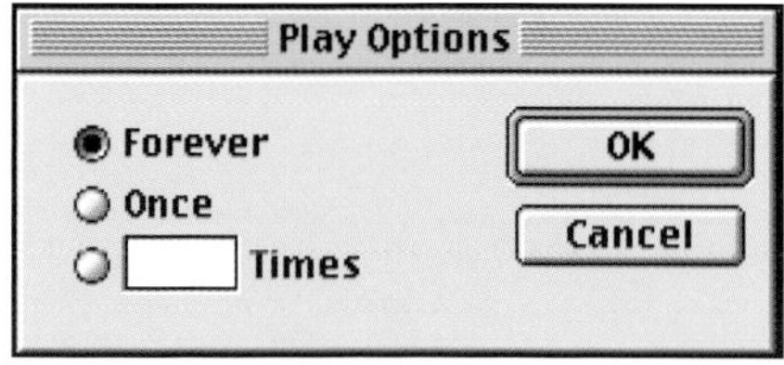

Step 6: Repeat **Step 4** from the previous exercise on page 340 to play the file.

Using Instances and Tweening for Animation in Fireworks

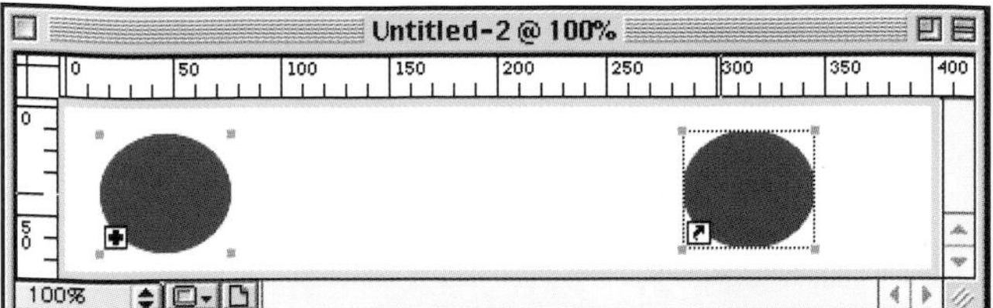

Step 1: Create a shape in a Fireworks document.

Step 2: Under **Edit:Symbols**, choose **Make Symbols**. A symbol will always appear with the plus sign. Next, select the symbol, and copy and paste it. Move the pasted duplicate to the other side of the screen. It should appear with an arrow on it. The plus sign signifies that the object is a symbol, whereas the arrow signifies that it is a copy of the symbol.

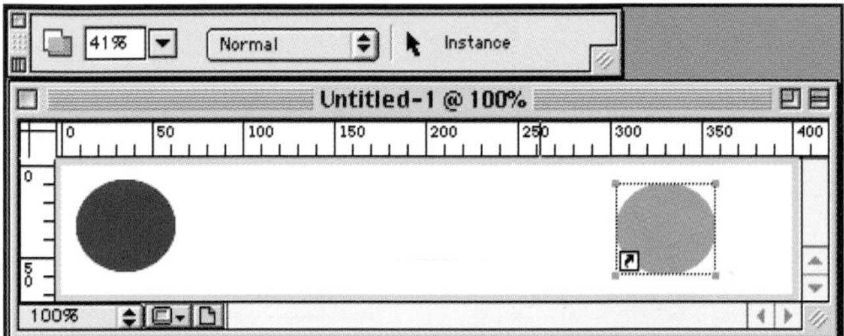

Step 3: Modify the copy of the symbol. In this case, I changed its opacity. Notice how the Opacity value is set to 41% and the copy of the symbol is selected.

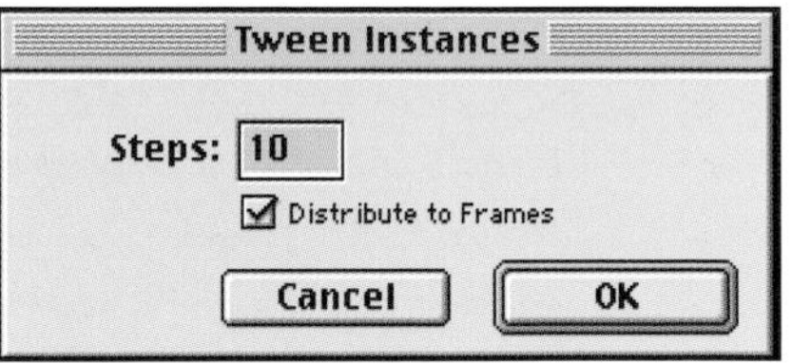

Step 4: Select both objects and choose **Edit:Symbols**, **Tween Instances**. Choose 10 steps and **Distribute to Frames**.

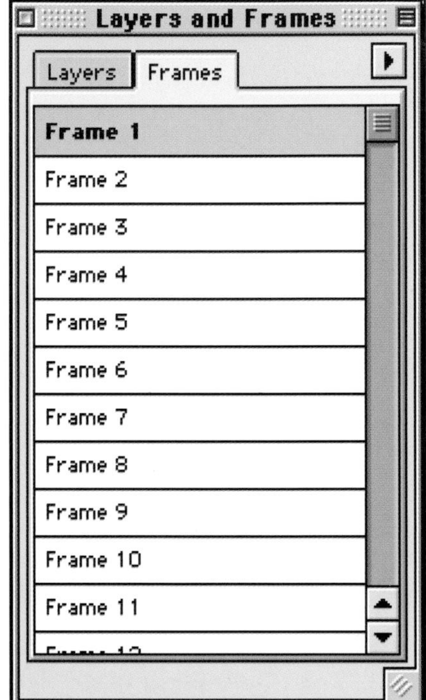

Step 5: This puts all the steps into separate frames. Repeat the export steps from page 341 to view the animation.

Other GIF Animation Tools of Note

I can't cover every tool in this chapter due to space limitations and the fact that I don't use all of these different products regularly to give them justice here. I would like, however, to mention some other noteworthy animation tools to check out:

PhotoDisc Animation Series (Mac/PC Compatible)PhotoDisc, Inc.
http://www.photodisc.com

Animation clip art is usually pretty mundane. The folks at PhotoDisc (a leading digital stock photo agency), however, went many steps ahead of the competition and published the work of renowned designer **Clement Mok** (http: //www. studioarchetype.com/) to create some superb clip animation sequences. The two series, Metaphorically Blinking and EveryDay Objects Live, include photo-realistic animations of such things as chattering teeth toys and shaking alarm clocks. This product comes in two varieties: the basic version, with animations saved out as Animated GIFs and Shockwave documents with rollover and sound built-in, and the Pro Versions, which include the necessary Director files to allow end users to customize and edit the animations. The price is a little high for some, but the quality is worth it. The fact that the professional version lets you edit the Director files is a great bonus.

GifBuilder (Mac Only)
Written by Yves Piguet
http://iawww.epfl.ch/Staff/Yves.Piguet/clip2gif-home/GifBuilder.html

GifBuilder is a free standalone animation application that allows you to import Photoshop layers, QuickTime movies, and sequential GIFs or PICTs as source artwork for animations. It saves animated GIFs with a simple, no-programming-required "save" command, and lets you set frame delays, transparency, load custom palettes, and display methods to boot. GifBuilder also supports built-in transitions, meaning you can add fades or wipes without having to create them from scratch. This can cut file size significantly. Altogether, an awesome product at an awesome price (free!). GifBuilder is for everyone who uses a Mac, from novices to professionals.

Ulead GIFAnimator 3 (PC only)
http://www.webutilities.com/ga/ga_main.htm
$39.99 or 15-day free trial

Ulead GIF Animator 3 includes the ability to create optimized animations, global palette building, support for Photoshop compatible plug-ins, automated moving sprites, and integrated transitions.

Totally Hip's WebPainter (Mac and Windows)

http://www.totallyhip.com/Link/ProductsWP3.html
$89.95

A standalone application that writes animated GIFs and QuickTime movies, this program works with vector and bitmap artwork, contains auto-transitions, uses multiple layers, and comes with Photoshop (Mac only). WebPainter also includes a "cel" animation interface that lets you use onion skinning (the computer equivalent of tracing paper), multiple cel editing, and foreground/background drawing cels. It saves the files as PICs, QuickTime movies, GIF89a's, and sequential GIF files. The product lacks sophisticated animation features found in more high-end packages, but it is useful for anyone wanting to learn how to create cel-style character animation. Because the product saves animation in so many formats, it is not hindered by any plug-in constraints. At the time this chapter was written, a free trial version was available from the Totally Hip Web site.

BoxTop Software's GIFmation

http://www.boxtopsoft.com/gifmation.html
$49.00 or free limited-time demo

This Photoshop plug-in includes the capability to optimize and check browser compatibility. It also provides support for onion skinning, coordinate image positioning, automatic image alignment, image editing and palette creation tools, and scale, crop, and flip features. GIFmation has excellent preview options, and many formats are supported for import.

Digital Frontier's HVS Animator Pro

http://www.digfrontiers.com/anim.html
Visit Web site for pricing

You can build GIF animations from single-frame GIFs, and add, delete, and reorder frames. In addition, you can view exact sizes for each frame, the overall animation, and the optimized animation. HVS Animator Pro computes minimum recommended color depth, and offers precise control over frame delay, disposal, offsets, and transparency. Many preview options, batch importing, and an illustrated, hyperlinked manual in HTML format are included.

summary GIF Animation

GIF animation is easy to create in a variety of software applications and easy to code in HTML. This makes it an ideal format for Web page animation, although it does lack the capability to include sound and/or interactivity. Here is a summation of the principles covered in this chapter:

- GIF animation is supported by all browsers and is simple to implement. It is important to understand that animation draws a lot of attention and to use animation where appropriate on your site.
- Understanding the principles of GIF compression will help you make smaller animated GIFs. The same factors of color depth and noise reduction that will affect static GIF files also affect moving GIF files.
- Understanding terminology such as motion graphics, tweening, and frame-by-frame animation will help you use tools for creating animated GIFs.
- Beware of endless looping animations. They can easily annoy your audience, and can serve to send people away instead of inviting them in.

Introduction

JavaScript: Rollovers & More

Chapter Topics

- Short History of JavaScript
- Learning JavaScript
- Creative Rollover Artwork
- Rollovers in Fireworks
- Rollovers in Dreamwork
- Multiple Rollover Events
- Browser Detection & Sizing

22

If you've followed the history of the Web, you know the story by now: HTML was created for one purpose, and its capabilities were unofficially extended by browser vendors such as Mosaic, Netscape, and Explorer as much-wanted features that were slow to come from HTML standards committees. JavaScript is an outgrowth of this movement, originally invented by Netscape, and later adopted by Explorer.

JavaScript is a scripting language that extends the capabilities of HTML, enabling many features never before possible. There are many different programming languages to enhance HTML—such as the most popular and widely used Perl, AppleScript, and/or Java. The absolute beauty of JavaScript, however, is that you can view, copy and paste the source code to teach yourself how to use it, just like you can with HTML. Not only that, but some popular HTML editors, such as Dreamweaver 2.0, write JavaScript so that you don't have to know how to program the language yourself.

This chapter focuses on how to use JavaScript for rollover buttons, browser detection, and window resizing. I am not a JavaScript programmer, so I will be highlighting many tools which allow the automatic generation of JavaScript. The emphasis here will be on the practical implementations of using JavaScript to enhance your Web pages, not on teaching you the language. There are many fine resources for that, which will be noted throughout the chapter.

The Short History of JavaScript

The term "JavaScript" has nothing to do with the popular programming language that Sun Microsystems developed called Java. Originally, in fact, JavaScript was slated to be called "LiveScript." The name was changed for marketing reasons because it was believed at the time that anything with the word Java in it would be embraced by the Web development community with ease. Ironically, Java's promise of cross-platform compatibility and widespread use has fallen flat so far, but JavaScript's promise of extended functionality to HTML has far exceeded many people's expectations.

JavaScript, in its most simple sense, is a scripting language that can be used to extend and enhance HTML. A simple comparison between HTML and JavaScript might deem HTML as the "static" medium, and JavaScript as the "dynamic" medium. That's because JavaScript can do many things that HTML cannot, such as sequencing and moving images (animation), responding to interaction (multimedia), and triggering other extensions, such as ActiveX, Java, and plug-ins.

Unlike other popular programming languages, such as Perl, C++, and Java, JavaScript is client-sided; which in this case means that JavaScript is built into the browser and requires no additional compiling. In simple terms, this means that JavaScript can co-exist inside basic HTML pages, and can be studied, copied, and pasted, just like HTML. Other programming languages get "compiled," which is a post-processing technique that renders the code usable by computers. By the time you see the compiled code, you can no longer break it apart or deconstruct it. One of the great advantages to JavaScript is that browsers understand it without the need for this extra compiling step.

While it is possible to study, copy, and paste other people's JavaScript code into your own, it is widely accepted that you credit other people's JavaScripts if you use them. Comments are different in JavaScript than they are in standard HTML because JavaScript comments are introduced with a pair of slashes (//). Everything following the pair of slashes to the end of the line is ignored by the browser, such as

```
// Bill Weinman's Common JavaScript Rollover Engine
```

If the next line of code does not have the pair of slashes (//), it is no longer treated as a comment by the browser. If you copy someone's code, and they have credited themselves or someone else, leave these comments intact.

JavaScript has many uses in Web design. I will focus on rollovers, browser resizing, and browser detection as three areas of attention in this chapter.

Learning JavaScript

Like HTML, many people wonder if they have to learn it. While I advocate you will be much happier if you do understand the basics of HTML, in this chapter I use Dreamweaver to write my JavaScript code. That's because I do not know how to write it from scratch.

Is it better to know how than not to? Probably! Those people who write their own JavaScript look at the code from WYSIWYG editors, such as Dreamweaver, and consider it to be "verbose." By that, I mean that it's longer and not as streamlined as it could be. My feeling is, if it works and spares me the effort of learning a new language, I'm all for it. But I'm an artist, not a programmer! It's probably the equivalent of using "clip art" in graphics (which I would rarely consider doing!).

Of course, there are great resources for learning JavaScript. Some of my favorite **JavaScript references**:

URLs
http://www.webreference.com/js/
http://www.webcoder.com/scriptorium/index.html

Designing With JavaScript
Nick Heinle
ISBN 1-56592-300-6
O'Reilly
$29.95

Rollovers

In past chapters, I've discussed the aesthetics of buttons, and have shared visual design methods for creating images that look "clickable." No other method, in my opinion, is as successful for indicating that a graphic is linked than rollovers. Rollovers are a term used for graphics that change when the mouse rolls over them—hence the word "rollover." They are also sometimes referred to as "mouseovers," which is a JavaScript syntax term, or "image swaps," which is the type of JavaScript event invoked for rollovers. For simplicity's sake, I'm gonna call'em rollovers in this chapter!

Making the artwork for a rollover is a different process than coding it. Successful rollovers require two parts: the correct artwork and the correct code. I'm going to focus on a variety of tools and techniques for creating rollovers and code. First, let's look at making the artwork.

Creating Rollover Artwork

There are many types of rollovers, but I am going to identify three styles for the purposes of this chapter: replacement, pointing, and multiple. Replacement is the most simple type of rollover, where the original artwork is replaced by new artwork when the mouse rolls over it. Pointing is the term I'll use for leaving the original artwork the same, but making an additional piece of artwork appear to its side, such as a dot or an arrow. A multiple rollover is when the mouse rolls over one piece of artwork, triggering its replacement of new artwork and additional artwork somewhere else on the page. If this description is confusing, please see the images below.

Replacement: Where the rollover artwork is replaced with other artwork.

Pointing: Where another graphic appears to follow your mouse.

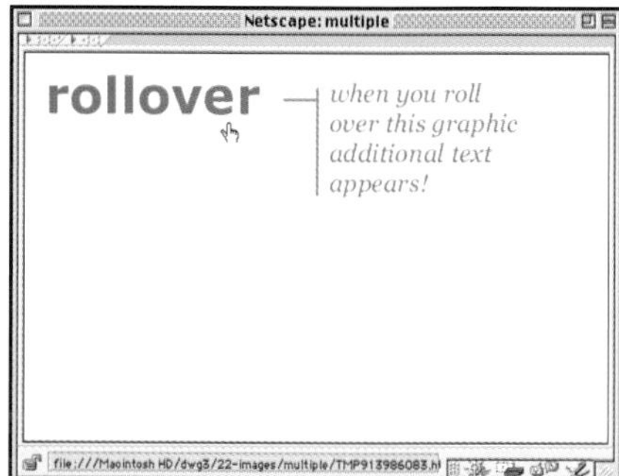

Multiple: Upon the rollover, additional artwork appears somewhere else on screen.

When creating artwork for JavaScript-based rollover buttons, it's essential that the artwork is the same size, even when it appears different. For the examples above, the artwork on the following page was used.

Replacement Example

The replacement example requires two pieces of artwork, identically sized.

When the mouse rolls over the word "rollover," this new artwork replaces it.

Highlight Example

Pointing examples require three pieces of art.

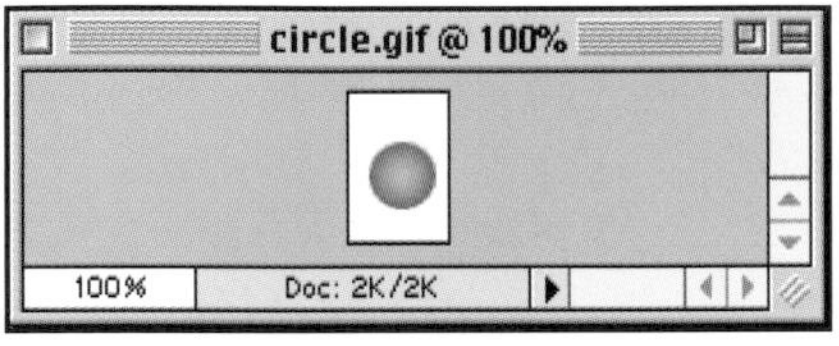

The red circle appears when the mouse rolls over the word "rollover."

Before the mouse rolls over the word, a blank image is showing. When the mouse rolls over the word "rollover," this blank image is replaced with the red circle image.

Multiple Example

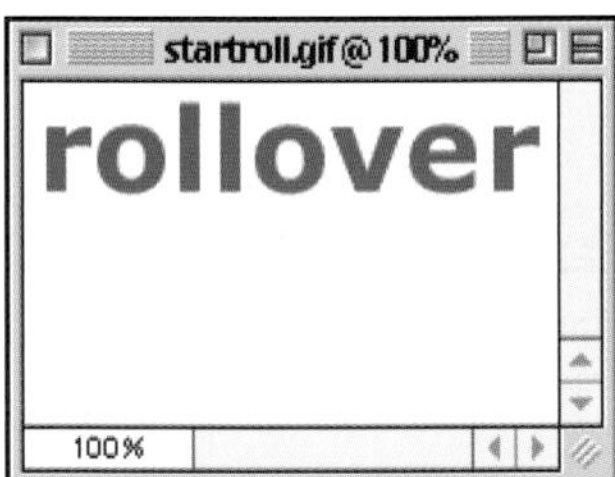

The multiple example requires four pieces of artwork. The blue artwork is what shows before the mouse rolls over it.

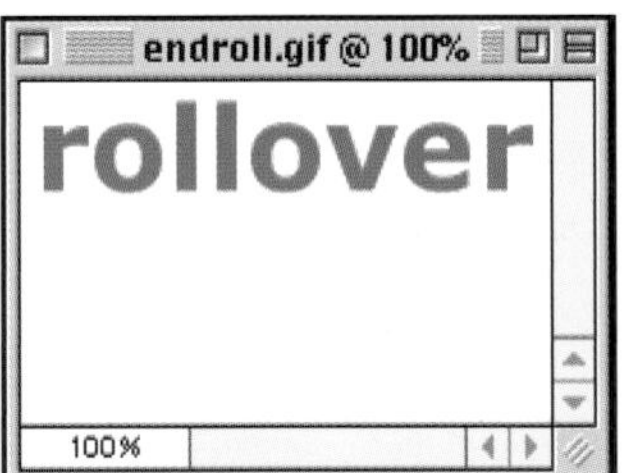

When the mouse rolls over the blue artwork, it is replaced with the green artwork.

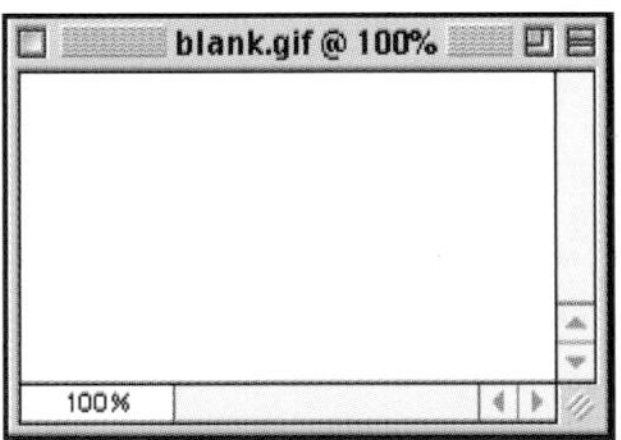

Before the rollover, this blank image is a placeholder for where the green text will appear next.

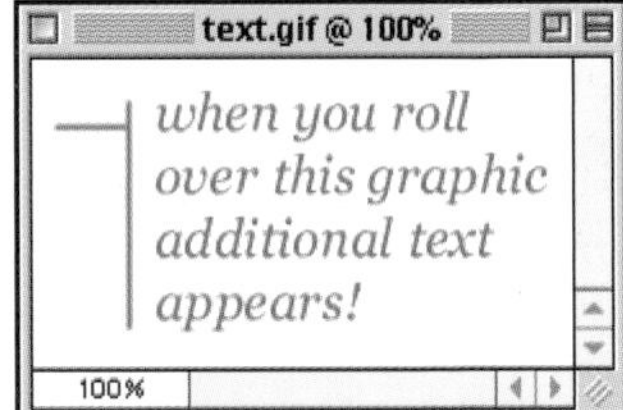

When the mouse rolls over the blue word "rollover", the green text appears and replaces the blank placeholder.

There are many software applications which will create images for rollovers. I am going to cover Photoshop, ImageReady and Fireworks in the following sections. Later, this chapter will cover how to create the JavaScript code using Dreamweaver 2.0.

Photoshop Layers for Rollovers

Rollovers require a minimum of two different images—an image for the unclicked state and another for the clicked state. A great thing about Photoshop is that the layers help you maintain registration between states of the rollover.

This example shows a single image with two layers in Photoshop. By clicking the eye icon in the left hand column of the Layers palette, you can pre-visualize the effect of the rollover.

Cutting the Rollovers Apart

If you **Show Rulers** in Photoshop, you can drag grid lines onto your screen for cutting apart images. This is useful for rollovers and other web graphics (such as cutting apart a large image to later rebuild inside an HTML table). Once you have set up rule lines, the left hand marquee selection tool will snap to the grid lines. These grids are very useful in helping you select the same size icon for both the on and off layers.

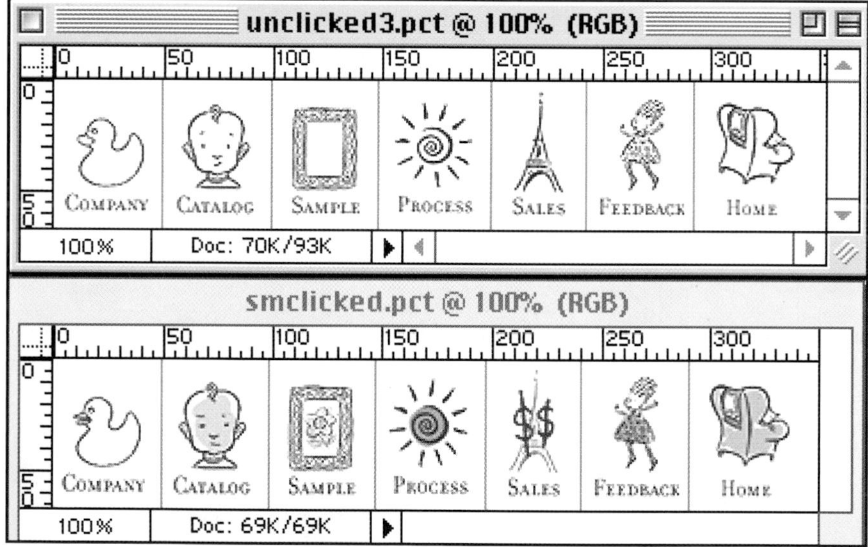

The two versions of icons with Guides turned on for cutting purposes.

Once you've selected a single icon, Copy and Paste into a new document. The image can be a GIF or a JPEG, depending on what technology you use for the rollover. A good rule of thumb is to name the files with a suffix of "on" or "off." For example, if you select the Company icon, name it **company-on.gif**. The rollover files you create can now be accessed by scripting languages or other authoring tools.

ImageReady for Slicing and Optimization

ImageReady is far better than using Photoshop for slicing up images because it will actually do the cutting for you, as well as write the HTML code for the resulting table. You can open an existing Photoshop layer file into ImageReady, or create one there.

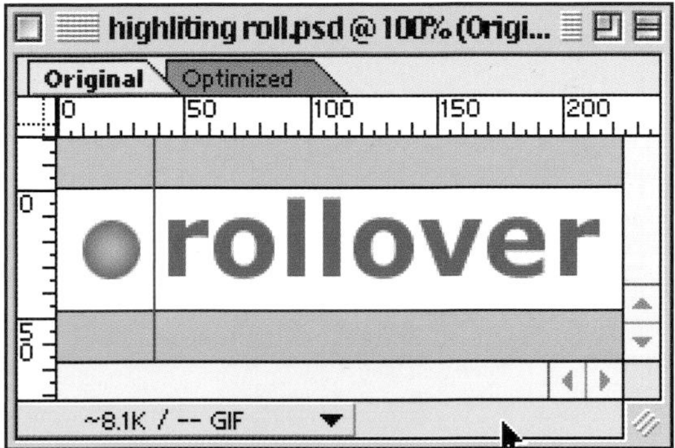

Here's an example of a file brought over from Photoshop into ImageReady. Notice the blue guide? That tells ImageReady where to slice this image.

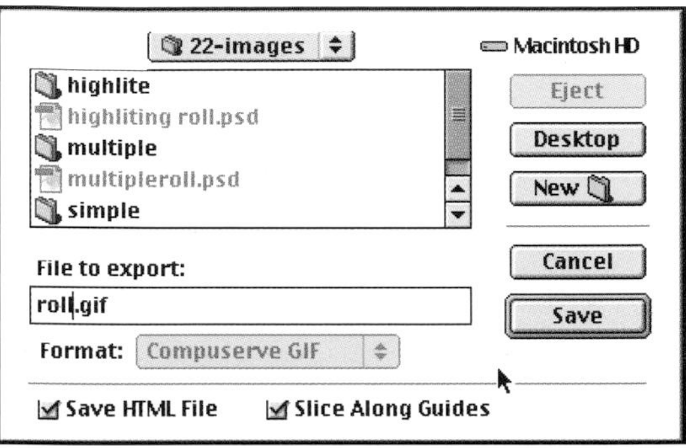

When you choose **Save Optimized As**, ImageReady gives you the option to slice along guides and save an HTML file. By checking the **Save HTML File** box, ImageReady will write an HTML table in addition to saving the slices. This won't write the JavaScript code for the rollover, but it will construct a table that pieces the artwork together. By choosing the **Slice Along Guides** checkbox, ImageReady knows to create two images. Whatever name you assign, the image will be reflected in the resulting HTML file and image files.

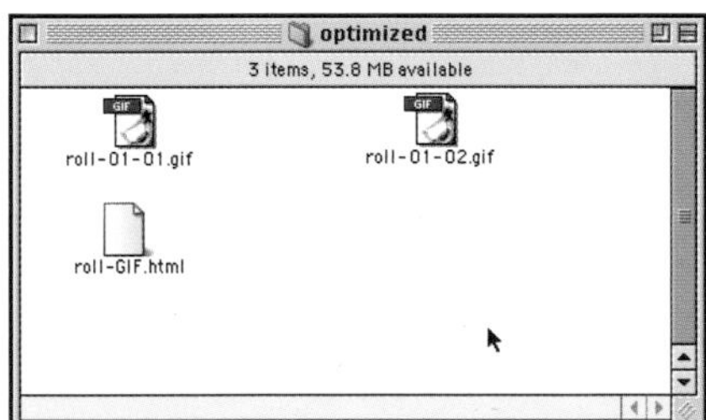

ImageReady will automatically write three files. In this example, the red circle image is **roll-01-01.gif** and the word "rollover" is **roll-01-02.gif**. The HTML file is called **roll-gif.html**.

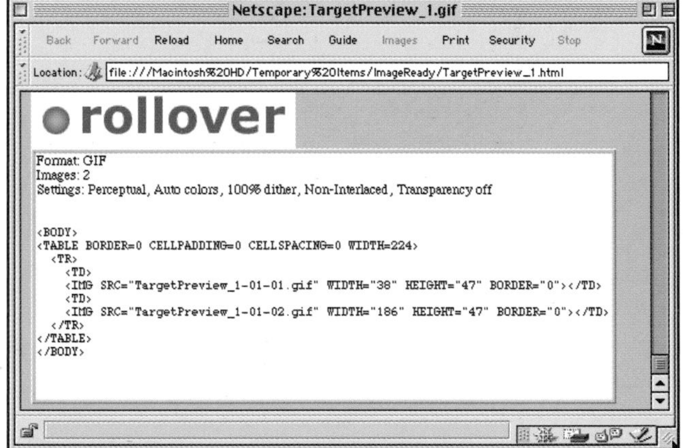

This is the **roll-gif.html file** that ImageReady writes for you. It can now be taken into another application, such as Dreamweaver, where the rollover JavaScript can be added.

Simple Rollover in Fireworks

The following steps show how to create a simple replacement rollover in Fireworks:

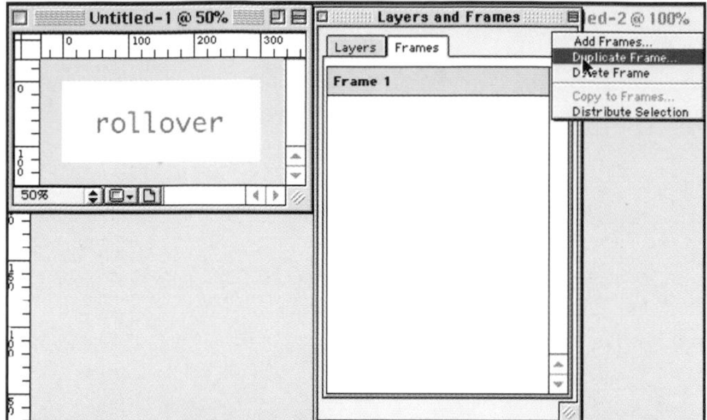

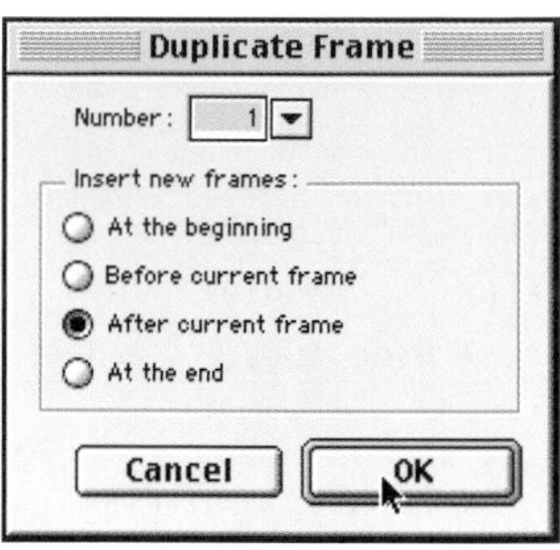

This dialog box appears. Select **After current frame**.

Step 1: Using the type tool, write the word "rollover." With the Frames palette open, choose **Duplicate Frame**.

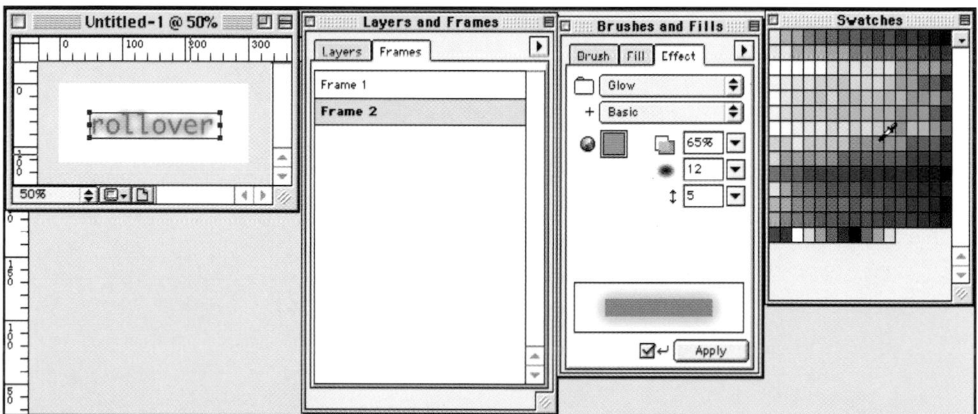

Step 2: With the "rollover" text selected on Frame 2, add an effect from the **Effect tab** (within the Brushes and Fills palette). I chose glow, and changed the glow color to a cyan color.

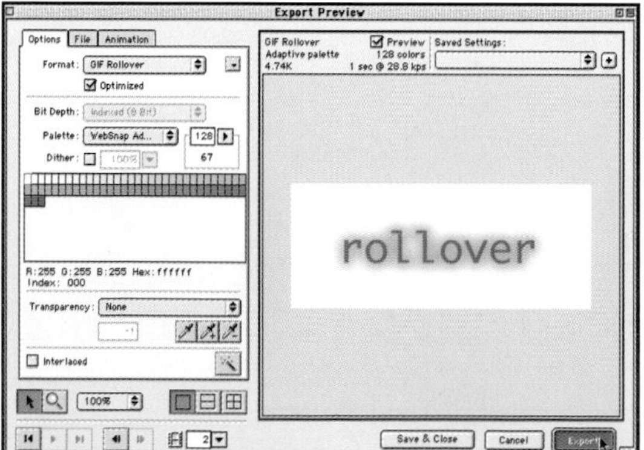

Step 3: Under **File:Export**, choose **GIF Rollover** as the file type and click **OK**.

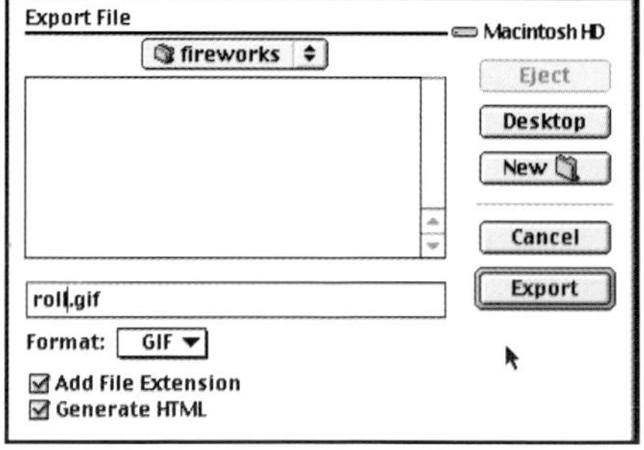

Step 4: The above dialog box appears. Be sure to check **Generate HTML**—this will create the JavaScript rollover code. Open the resulting file in a Web browser and just watch it work!

Firework's rollover code

```
<!-- To put this html into an existing HTML document, you must copy the JavaScript and
paste it in a specific location within the destination HTML document.  You must then copy
and paste code for the image in a different location.  -->
<html>
<head>
<title>roll.gif</title>
<meta http-equiv="Content-Type" content="text/html; charset=iso-8859-1">
<meta name="description" content="Fireworks Rollover">
<!-- Copy the JavaScript code including the opening and closing script tags, and paste it
into the head section of the destination document.  If the destination document already
contains a script section, do not include the script tags when copying.  -->
<!------------------- BEGIN COPYING THE JAVASCRIPT SECTION HERE ------------------->

<script language="JavaScript">

<!-- hide this script from non-javascript-enabled browsers

// pre-cache 'filename' button state images

if (document.images) {
var Nroll_up = new Image(300,124)
Nroll_up.src = "roll_up.gif"

var Nroll_over = new Image(300,124)
Nroll_over.src = "roll_over.gif"

}
// function that displays status bar message

function dm(msgStr) {
  document.returnValue = false;
  if (document.images) {
     window.status = msgStr;
     document.returnValue = true;
  }
}
// functions that swap images

function di(id,name){
  if (document.images) document.images[id].src=eval(name+".src");
}
// stop hiding -->
</script>
<!------------------------ STOP COPYING THE JAVASCRIPT HERE ------------------------>
```

```
</head>

<body bgcolor="#ffffff">

<!-- Copy the code that embeds the image including the anchor tags, and paste the data
where
you want the image to appear in the destination document.  -->
<!------------------------- BEGIN COPYING THE IMAGE TAG HERE ------------------------->
<a href="http://www.macromedia.com" onMouseOver="di('Nroll', 'Nroll_over' ); "
onMouseOut="di('Nroll','Nroll_up');"  ><img name="Nroll" src="roll_up.gif" width="300"
height="124" border="0"></a>
<!---------------------------- STOP COPYING THE IMAGE HERE --------------------------->
</body>
</html>
```

note

Rollovers in Fireworks

Not only does Fireworks allow you to create artwork for rollovers, it generates the HTML for the tables and the JavaScript for the rollover behaviors! It's the only image editor on the market at the time this chapter was written that can do all of this at once.

The following examples assume that you know how to use Fireworks' drawing and Frames tools. I will give a brief primer in this chapter, but I highly recommend the following resources if you want to learn more:

Fireworks Visual Quickstart
Sandee Cohen
Peachpit Press
ISBN: 020135361X
$19.95

Learning Fireworks with Lynda Weinman
VHS or PAL
http://www.lynda.com/video/fireworks/

Rollover in Tables Using Fireworks

Fireworks takes rollovers, JavaScript, and HTML tables a bit further—setting all these attributes within a single document.

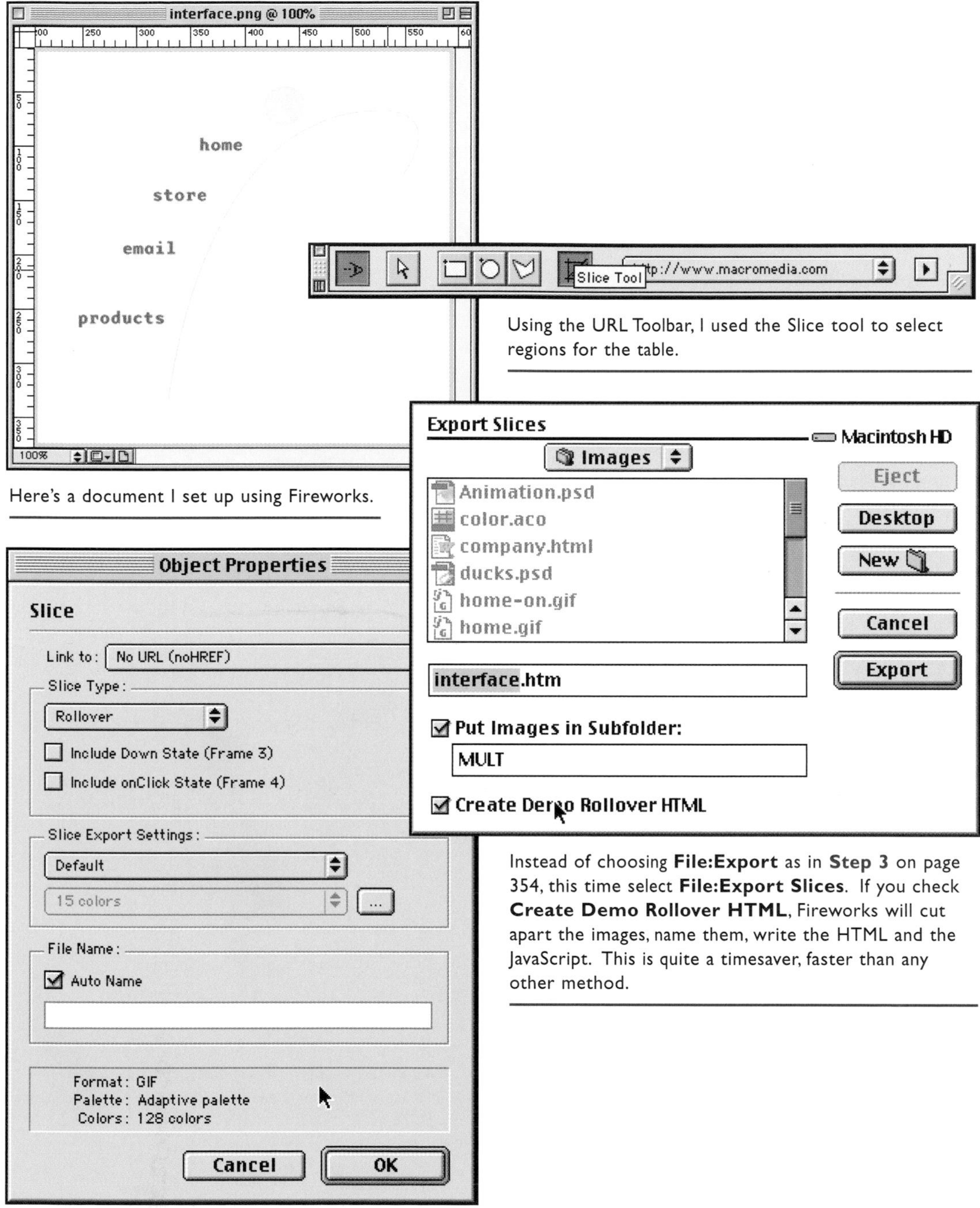

Here's a document I set up using Fireworks.

Using the URL Toolbar, I used the Slice tool to select regions for the table.

The Objects Properties dialog allows me to set up what type of slice I want. In this case, I've requested that each slice contain a rollover.

Instead of choosing **File:Export** as in **Step 3** on page 354, this time select **File:Export Slices**. If you check **Create Demo Rollover HTML**, Fireworks will cut apart the images, name them, write the HTML and the JavaScript. This is quite a timesaver, faster than any other method.

Rollovers in Dreamweaver 2.0

While creating the artwork can be done in Photoshop, ImageReady or Fireworks, complex rollovers, such as those used in the pointing and multiple examples shown earlier, require the use of a more powerful tool.

I know of a few different WYSIWYG editors that create JavaScript, but my favorite is Dreamweaver 2.0. I will go through the steps of how to use this tool for the three examples shown earlier: replacement, pointing, and multiple.

Dreamweaver's Replacement Rollovers

For simple replacement rollovers, Dreamweaver 2.0 has a built-in feature on the Object bar.

Insert Rollover Image

Original Image: roll1.gif Browse...

Image Name: Image1

Rollover Image: roll2.gif Browse...

Link: # Browse...

Preload Images

OK

Cancel

Help

Step 2: All you do is click the **Browse button** to locate the rollover artwork for the off state, and then browse for the rollover image and click **OK**—Dreamweaver will write the code and the rollover will perform beautifully.

Step 1: The Insert Rollover Image is part of the Object tool bar in Dreamweaver. Click on this image to bring up the Insert Rollover dialog box.

Dreamweaver's rollover code

```
<html>
<head>
<title>replacement rollover</title>
<meta http-equiv="Content-Type" content="text/html;
charset=iso-8859-1">
<script language="JavaScript">
<!--
function MM_swapImgRestore() { //v2.0
  if (document.MM_swapImgData != null)
    for (var i=0; i<(document.MM_swapImgData.length-
1); i+=2)
      document.MM_swapImgData[i].src =
document.MM_swapImgData[i+1];
}
function MM_preloadImages() { //v2.0
  if (document.images) {
    var imgFiles = MM_preloadImages.arguments;
    if (document.preloadArray==null)
document.preloadArray = new Array();
    var i = document.preloadArray.length;
    with (document) for (var j=0;
j<imgFiles.length; j++) if
(imgFiles[j].charAt(0)!="#"){
      preloadArray[i] = new Image;
      preloadArray[i++].src = imgFiles[j];
  } }
}
function MM_swapImage() { //v2.0
  var i,j=0,objStr,obj,swapArray=new
Array,oldArray=document.MM_swapImgData;
  for (i=0; i < (MM_swapImage.arguments.length-2);
i+=3) {
    objStr =
MM_swapImage.arguments[(navigator.appName ==
'Netscape')?i:i+1];
    if ((objStr.indexOf('document.layers[')==0 &&
document.layers==null) ||
        (objStr.indexOf('document.all[')   ==0 &&
document.all   ==null))
      objStr =
'document'+objStr.substring(objStr.lastIndexOf('.'),
objStr.length);
    obj = eval(objStr);
    if (obj != null) {
      swapArray[j++] = obj;
      swapArray[j++] = (oldArray==null ||
oldArray[j-1]!=obj)?obj.src:oldArray[j];
      obj.src = MM_swapImage.arguments[i+2];
  } }
  document.MM_swapImgData = swapArray; //used for
restore
}
//-->
</script>
</head>
<body bgcolor="#FFFFFF"
onLoad="MM_preloadImages('roll2.gif','#913984936133'
)">
<a href="#" onMouseOut="MM_swapImgRestore()"
onMouseOver="MM_swapImage('document.Image1','docu-
ment.Image1','roll2.gif','#913984936133')"><img
name="Image1" border="0" src="roll1.gif" width="228"
height="89"></a>
</body>
</html>
```

Dreamweaver's Pointing Rollover

The pointing rollover involves the use of Dreamweaver Behaviors because it is more complex than simply switching out two pieces of art, like the first replacement example. Dreamweaver Behaviors are a module inside Dreamweaver that automate the creation of certain effects (like rollovers)! In the example below, I used three pieces of artwork.

roll.gif **circle.gif** **blankcircle.gif**

Name the image using the Property bar.

Step 1: I created a two column, one row table, and assigned it to have a **border=0** so the borders wouldn't show. Next, I inserted the artwork "blankcircle.gif" into the left cell, and "roll.gif" into the right cell.

Step 2: I assigned the file "roll.gif" a name "roll", and the fill "blankcircle.gif" the name "blank."

Step 3: I opened the Behaviors palette (by clicking on the **Behavior button** in the Launcher palette).

Step 3: I clicked on the "roll. gif" image inside my table, added the Behavior Swap Image by clicking on the **plus sign** inside the Behaviors palette, and then choosing **Swap Image**.

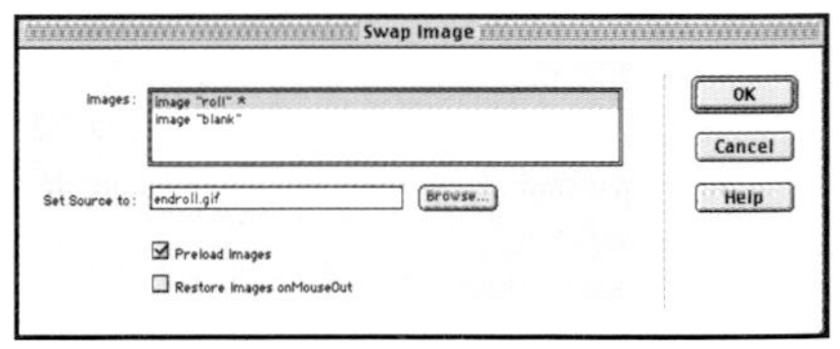

Step 4: Making sure that the "blank" image was selected, I clicked the **Browse button** to select the image "circle.gif." The reason I selected the "blank" image is because I was instructing Dreamweaver to understand that upon rolling over the image "rollover" that the "circle.gif" image would swap out. That's it, let Dreamweaver write the code!

Dreamweavers pointing rollover code

```
<html>
<head>
<title>pointing rollover</title>
<meta http-equiv="Content-Type" content="text/html;
charset=iso-8859-1">
<script language="JavaScript">

<!--
function MM_preloadImages() { //v2.0
  if (document.images) {
    var imgFiles = MM_preloadImages.arguments;
    if (document.preloadArray==null)
document.preloadArray = new Array();
    var i = document.preloadArray.length;
    with (document) for (var j=0;
j<imgFiles.length; j++) if
(imgFiles[j].charAt(0)!="#"){
      preloadArray[i] = new Image;
      preloadArray[i++].src = imgFiles[j];
  } }
}
function MM_swapImgRestore() { //v2.0
  if (document.MM_swapImgData != null)
    for (var i=0;
i<(document.MM_swapImgData.length-1); i+=2)
      document.MM_swapImgData[i].src =
document.MM_swapImgData[i+1];
}
function MM_swapImage() { //v2.0
  var i,j=0,objStr,obj,swapArray=new
Array,oldArray=document.MM_swapImgData;
  for (i=0; i < (MM_swapImage.arguments.length-2);
i+=3) {
    objStr =
MM_swapImage.arguments[(navigator.appName ==
'Netscape')?i:i+1];
    if ((objStr.indexOf('document.layers[')==0 &&
document.layers==null) ||
        (objStr.indexOf('document.all[')   ==0 &&
document.all   ==null))
      objStr =
'document'+objStr.substring(objStr.lastIndexOf('.'),
objStr.length);
    obj = eval(objStr);
    if (obj != null) {
      swapArray[j++] = obj;
      swapArray[j++] = (oldArray==null ||
oldArray[j-1]!=obj)?obj.src:oldArray[j];
      obj.src = MM_swapImage.arguments[i+2];
  } }
  document.MM_swapImgData = swapArray; //used for
restore
}
//-->
</script>
</head>
<body bgcolor="#FFFFFF"
onLoad="MM_preloadImages('circle.gif','#913985442683
')">
<table width="32%" border="0">
  <tr>
    <td width="5%"><img src="blankcircle.gif"
width="34" height="51" name="blank"></td>
    <td width="95%"><a href="#"
onMouseOut="MM_swapImgRestore()"
onMouseOver="MM_swapImage('document.blank','docu-
ment.blank','circle.gif','#913985442683')"><img
src="roll.gif" width="186" height="51"
name="rollover" border="0"></a></td>
  </tr>
</table>
</body>
</html>
```

Dreamweaver's Multiple Rollover

Programming the multiple rollover took a bit more work than the other two examples. Here's a blow-by-blow account of what I did. It's helpful to once again see the different pieces of art involved, and their names so you can reference what was done.

startroll.gif

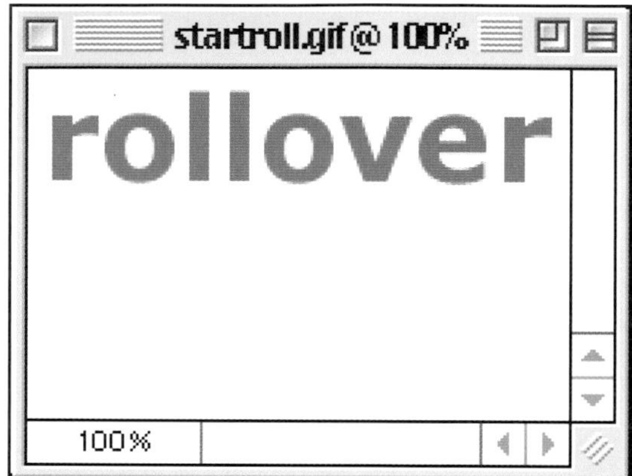

endroll.gif

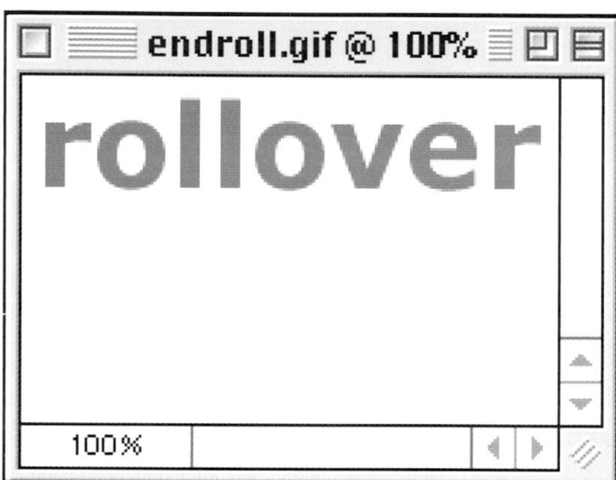

blank.gif

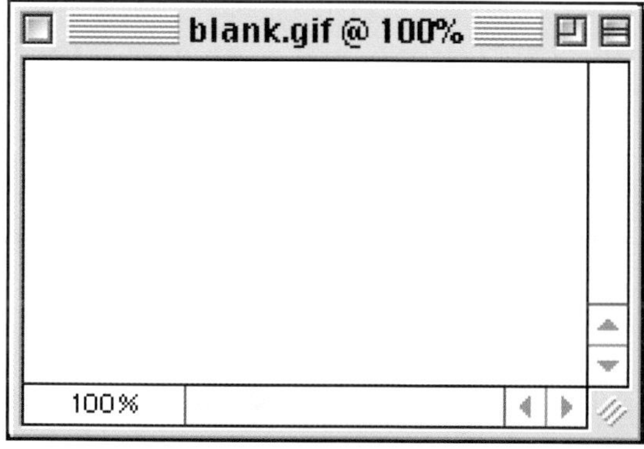

text.gif

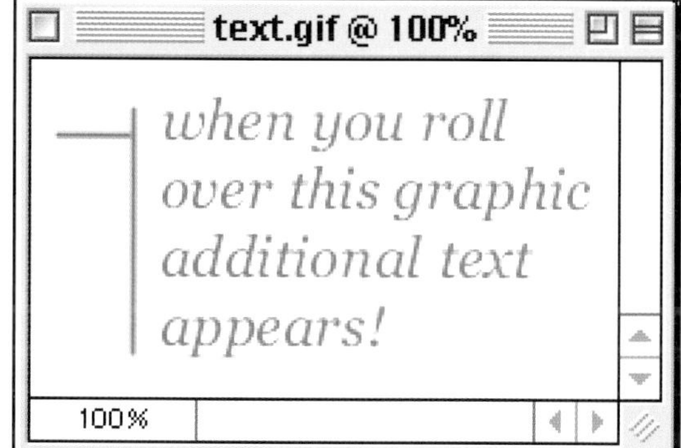

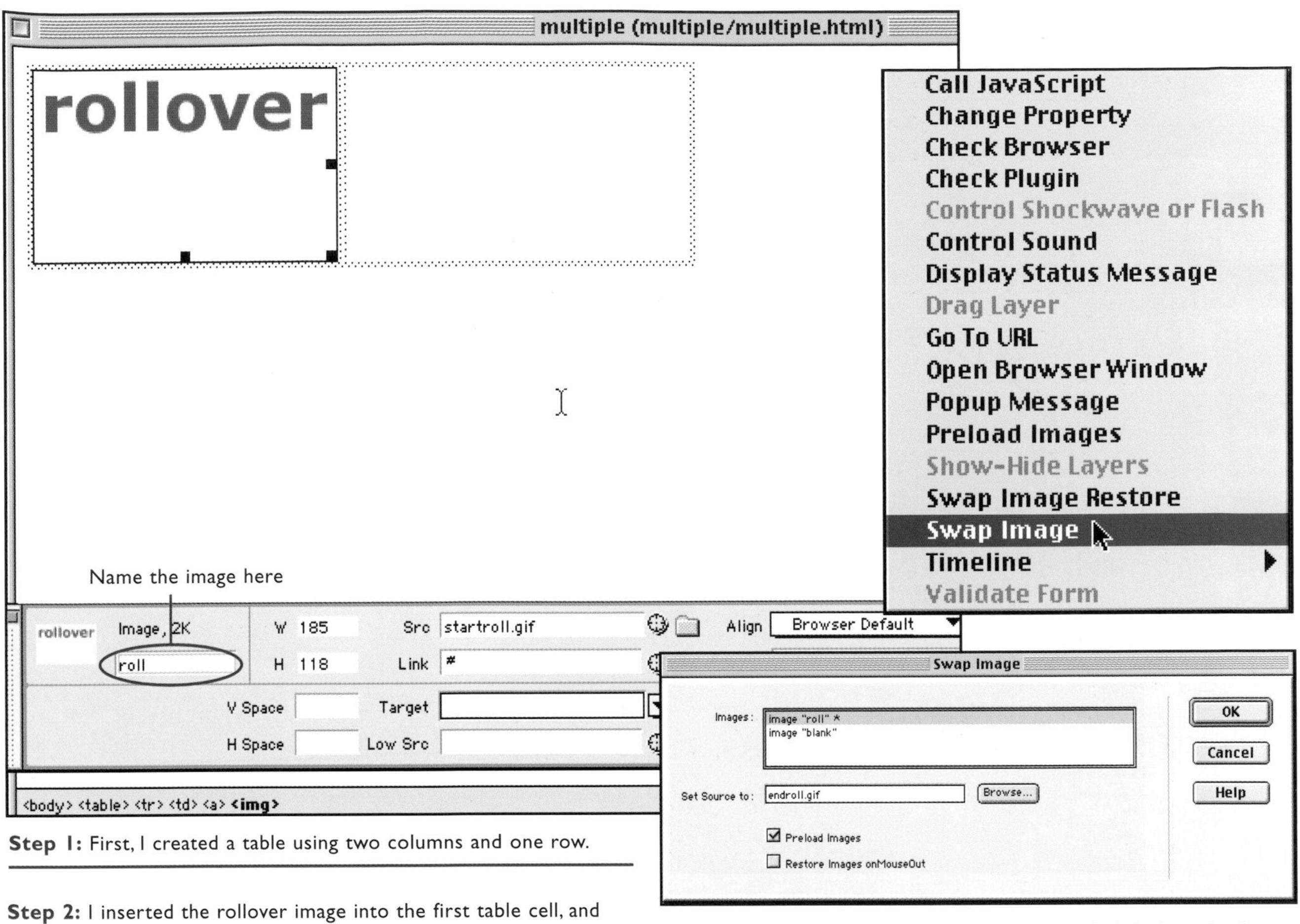

Step 1: First, I created a table using two columns and one row.

Step 2: I inserted the rollover image into the first table cell, and the blank image into the next.

Step 3: I highlighted the entire table and inserted a **border=0** property to turn off the borders on the table.

Step 4: I named the rollover image by selecting it and entering the name "roll" into the Property bar. I named the blank image "blank" by highlighting it and entering it into the Property bar.

Step 5: I selected the "start-roll.gif" image and clicked on the **Behaviors button** to launch the Behaviors window. I chose to make this 4.0 browser compatible, and clicked on the **plus sign** to select **Swap Image**.

Step 6: I selected the Image roll and browsed to find the replacement artwork "**endroll.gif**." Next, I selected the image "blank' and browsed to select the file called **text.gif**.

Dreamweaver's multiple rollover code

```
<html>
<head>
<title>multiple</title>
<meta http-equiv="Content-Type" content="text/html;
charset=iso-8859-1">
<script language="JavaScript">

<!--
function MM_preloadImages() { //v2.0
  if (document.images) {
    var imgFiles = MM_preloadImages.arguments;
    if (document.preloadArray==null)
document.preloadArray = new Array();
    var i = document.preloadArray.length;
    with (document) for (var j=0; j<imgFiles.length;
j++) if (imgFiles[j].charAt(0)!="#"){
      preloadArray[i] = new Image;
      preloadArray[i++].src = imgFiles[j];
  } }
}
function MM_swapImgRestore() { //v2.0
  if (document.MM_swapImgData != null)
    for (var i=0; i<(document.MM_swapImgData.length-1);
i+=2)
      document.MM_swapImgData[i].src =
document.MM_swapImgData[i+1];
}
function MM_swapImage() { //v2.0
  var i,j=0,objStr,obj,swapArray=new Array,oldArray=doc-
ument.MM_swapImgData;
  for (i=0; i < (MM_swapImage.arguments.length-2);
i+=3) {
    objStr = MM_swapImage.arguments[(navigator.appName
== 'Netscape')?i:i+1];
    if ((objStr.indexOf('document.layers[')==0 && docu-
ment.layers==null) ¦¦
        (objStr.indexOf('document.all[')   ==0 && docu-
ment.all   ==null))
      objStr =
'document'+objStr.substring(objStr.lastIndexOf('.'),objS
tr.length);
    obj = eval(objStr);
    if (obj != null) {
      swapArray[j++] = obj;
      swapArray[j++] = (oldArray==null ¦¦ oldArray[j-
1]!=obj)?obj.src:oldArray[j];
      obj.src = MM_swapImage.arguments[i+2];
  } }
  document.MM_swapImgData = swapArray; //used for
restore
}
//-->
</script>
</head>
<body bgcolor="#FFFFFF"
onLoad="MM_preloadImages('endroll.gif','#913986006633');
MM_preloadImages('startroll.gif','#913986019066');MM_pre
loadImages('text.gif','#913986042933');MM_preloadImages(
'blank.gif','#913986063616')">
<table width="37%" border="0">
  <tr>
    <td width="33%" height="2"><a href="#"
onMouseOver="MM_swapImage('document.roll','document.roll
','endroll.gif','#913986006633');MM_swapImage('docu-
ment.blank','document.blank','text.gif','#913986042933')
"
onMouseOut="MM_swapImage('document.roll','document.roll'
,'startroll.gif','#913986019066');MM_swapImage('docu-
ment.blank','document.blank','blank.gif','#913986063616'
)"><img src="startroll.gif" width="185" height="118"
name="roll" border="0"></a></td>
    <td width="67%" height="2"><img src="blank.gif"
width="208" height="118" name="blank"></td>
  </tr>
</table>
</body>
</html>
```

Backwards Compatibility

My friend and JavaScript mentor **Michael Macrone** (http://www.atlasmagazine.com) contributed this helpful advice to those who are concerned about backwards compatibility with rollovers (otherwise known as "image swaps"):

Image swaps are perhaps the most popular JavaScript applications on the Web today. But, like most other interesting scripts, image swaps aren't possible in older browsers, and attempts to use them can produce JavaScript errors.

Using Dreamweaver 2.0's Behaviors, as Lynda describes later in this chapter, to automate image swapping will ensure compatibility with older browsers because Macromedia builds in a test that blocks incompatible browsers from running the code. But if you're going to write the rollover script yourself, there are a few things to know.

First, the image swap technique depends on the JavaScript Image object, which Netscape introduced with JavaScript 1.1 (Netscape Navigator 3.0). Microsoft never supported the Image object in Windows versions of Internet Explorer 3.0, even though version 3.02 shipped with a scripting engine that claimed to be JavaScript 1.1-compliant. However, Explorer 3.01 on the Macintosh does support the Image object. And both Explorer 4.0 and Netscape 4.0, as well as later versions of both browsers, completely support the Image object.

To guard against JavaScript errors, you must test for support of the Image object before attempting to preload or swap an image. (And swapping works seamlessly only if all the relevant images are preloaded into the user's browser cache.) Since the browser version is an unreliable guide, you should just test for the object directly—or rather, you should test for properties a document will have if the browser supports the object.

One such property is the images[ ] array, which belongs to the Document object. The array, which contains references to all the images in your document, is represented this way:

```
        document.images
You can test the array thus:
        if (document.images)
```

which returns "true" if the array exists, and "false" if it doesn't. You can use this result to sidestep errors on older browsers.

For example, let's say there's an image on your page called "image1.gif," and that you'd like to swap in "image2.gif" whenever a user rolls over the image. (Both images should be the same size or the second will appear distorted.) The first thing to do is preload both images and assign them to JavaScript variables. (Technically, "image1.gif" doesn't need to be preloaded, since it's automatically loaded along with the page, but you should still assign it to a variable, which is the same as preloading it.)

Let's assign the original image to the JavaScript Image object "out," and the second image to the object "over." We'll only do this if the Image object is supported. The code would look like this:

```
var over, out;
if (document.images) {
        out = new Image(); out.src = "image1.gif";
        over = new Image(); over.src = "image2.gif";
}
```

If the Image object isn't supported, then "over" and "out" remain null.

To make the swap work, the original image must be named in your HTML code, so that your script will know which object to swap. The IMG tag should look something like this:

```
<IMG Name="rollover" SRC="image1.gif">
```

The name "rollover" can now be used to identify the image in your script:

```
document.images["rollover"]
```

and its source will be indicated as

```
document.images["rollover"].src
```

Swapping the image is as simple as reassigning its "SRC" property to the variable containing the second image. But there are two things you should do first: Make sure both images have completely loaded, and make sure the browser supports image swaps.

Both images will have completely loaded once the entire document has loaded. When this happens, JavaScript receives a "load" event, and it can be trapped with an "onLoad" handler in the BODY tag. To make this work, declare some variable in your JavaScript and set its value to "true" once the document has loaded:

```
<HEAD>
<SCRIPT Language="JavaScript">
<!--
var loaded = false;
// -->
</SCRIPT>
</HEAD>
<BODY onLoad="loaded=true;">
```

Then create an image swap function that tests the value of "loaded" and the existence of "document.images":

```
function swapImageIn() {
        if (loaded && document.images)
                document.images["rollover"].src = over.src;
}
```

If the browser doesn't support image swaps, nothing will happen—not even an error.

A complete document using these techniques might look something like this:

```
<HTML>
<HEAD>
<TITLE>Image Swap</TITLE>
<SCRIPT Language="JavaScript">
<!--
var over, out, loaded = false;
if (document.images) {
        out = new Image(); out.src = "image1.gif";
        over = new Image(); over.src = "image2.gif";
}
function swapImageIn() {
        if (loaded && document.images)
                document.images["rollover"].src = over.src;
}
function swapImageOut() {
        if (loaded && document.images)
                document.images["rollover"].src = out.src;
}
// -->
</SCRIPT>
</HEAD>
<BODY onLoad="loaded=true;">
<A HREF="#"
        onMouseOver="swapImageIn(); return true;"
        onMouseOut="swapImageOut();"><IMG
        Name="rollover" SRC="image1.gif"></A>
</BODY>
</HTML>
```

Notice that the onMouseOver and onMouseOut event handlers are placed in an enclosing anchor tag (A). This is because Netscape versions 3 and 4, as well as Explorer 3, do not support event handlers in the IMG tag.

This example isn't the most interesting or efficient, but it demonstrates a completely reliable way of producing seamless image swaps, without browser errors.

Browser Detection

There are times when you might want to serve two different pages to your audience, and Dreamweaver has a built-in JavaScript device to help you detect which browser is viewing your page. The giant caveat to this is that in order for this method to work successfully, your end user must have a Java-enabled browser. Some people have older browsers (before 3.0) or have turned JavaScript off in their browser preferences. Even though this method works, it is not fool-proof.

Regardless, it might be useful to some of you, and it's easy to set up.

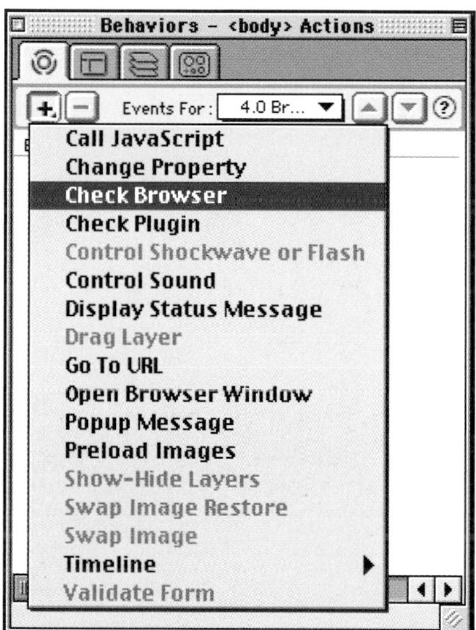

Step 1: Choose **Check Browser** as the Behavior.

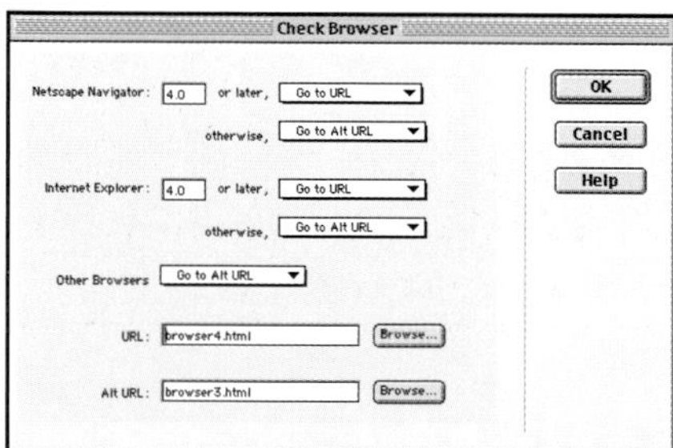

Step 2: Use the browse buttons at the bottom of this window to select your URL and alternate URL. The first URL would be the one that you would show to 4.0 browsers, and the ALT URL would be the alternative 3.0 browser page.

browser detection code

```
<HTML>
<HEAD>
<TITLE>check browser</TITLE>
<META HTTP-EQUIV="Content-Type" CONTENT="text/html;
charset=iso-8859-1">
<SCRIPT LANGUAGE="JavaScript">
<!--
function
MM_checkBrowser(NSvers,NSpass,NSnoPass,IEvers,IEpass
,IEnoPass,OBpass,URL,altURL) { //v2.0
  var newURL = '', version =
parseFloat(navigator.appVersion);
  if (navigator.appName.indexOf('Netscape') != -1) {
    if (version >= NSvers) {if (NSpass>0) newURL =
(NSpass==1)?URL:altURL;}
    else {if (NSnoPass>0) newURL =
(NSnoPass==1)?URL:altURL;}
  } else if (navigator.appName.indexOf('Microsoft')
!= -1) {
    if (version >= IEvers) {if (IEpass>0) newURL =
(IEpass==1)?URL:altURL;}
    else {if (IEnoPass>0) newURL =
(IEnoPass==1)?URL:altURL;}
  } else if (OBpass>0) newURL =
(OBpass==1)?URL:altURL;
  if (newURL) {
    window.location = unescape(newURL);
    document.MM_returnValue = false;
  }
}
//-->
</SCRIPT>
</HEAD>
<BODY BGCOLOR="#FFFFFF"
onLoad="MM_checkBrowser(4.0,1,2,4.0,1,2,2,'check.htm
l','browser3.html');return document.MM_returnValue">
</BODY>
</HTML>
```

Launching Another Window

You might have come to some sites that trigger a smaller browser window with no controls on the top. This is done using JavaScript. I'm not sure I personally like this trend, since I prefer the comfort of seeing a Back button and familiar navigation symbols, but if it's something you want to do, this section describes how, using Dreamweaver.

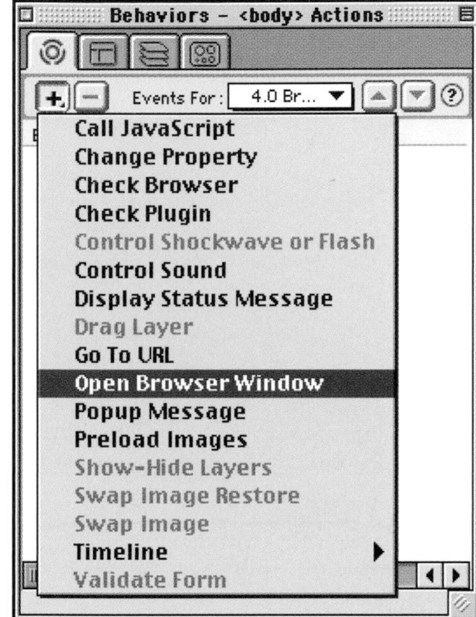

Step 1: Create the HTML document that you want to load into the separate window first. I called mine "**load.html**." Choose the Behavior "**Open Browser Window**."

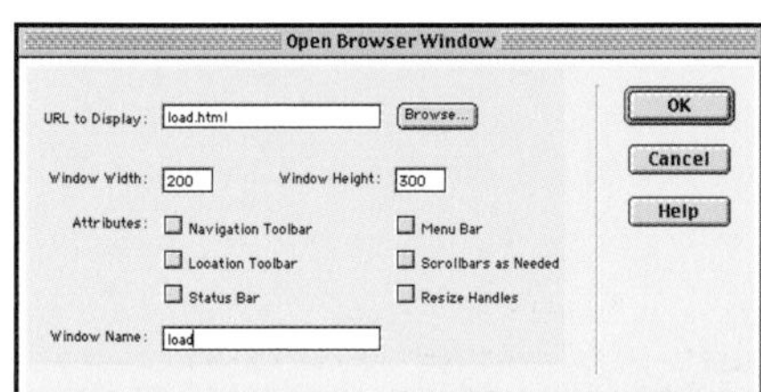

Step 2: Fill in the blanks in the preceding dialog box. Whichever attributes you assign will be there. I suggest that you leave some of the Attribute buttons checked, but it isn't necessary, as you can see by this example.

code to launch another window

```
\
<HTML>
<HEAD>
<TITLE>newwindow
</TITLE>
<META HTTP-EQUIV="Content-Type" CONTENT="text/html;
charset=iso-8859-1">
<script language="JavaScript">
<!--
function MM_openBrWindow(theURL,winName,features) {
//v2.0
  window.open(theURL,winName,features);
}
//-->
</script>
</HEAD>

<BODY BGCOLOR="#FFFFFF"
onLoad="MM_openBrWindow('load.html','load','width=20
0,height=300')">
A smaller window should launch now.
</BODY>
</HTML>
```

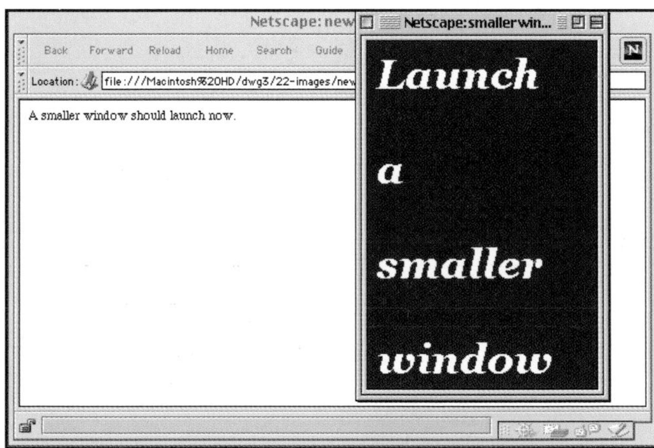

Here's the little browser window it launched for me.

summary JavaScript: Rollovers & More

JavaScript is useful for extending the capabilities of HTML. This chapter focused on three things that JavaScript makes possible: rollovers, browser detection, and launching presized browser windows. Here's a brief recap of the key issues:

- Rollover graphics are a great device to indicate that a graphic is linked. It is necessary to make correct artwork and code for Rollovers to work.
- Whenever you make artwork for rollover graphics, it's important to remember that the on and off states be exactly the same dimensions; otherwise registration will be problematic.
- Making complex rollovers involves giving your artwork a name that JavaScript can reference. You can trigger multiple events with a rollover by using the Name attribute.
- Browser detection with JavaScript is very easy with Dreamweaver; just be aware that it will only work on JavaScript-enabled browsers.
- Launching a predetermined sized browser window is possible with JavaScript, and once again Dreamweaver makes it easy.

Introduction

Dynamic HTML

Chapter Topics

- DHTML Overview
- Layers
- Animation
- Drag & Drop
- Helpful URLs

23

DHTML stands for **D**ynamic **H**yper**T**ext **M**arkup **L**anguage. Dynamic HTML is a loosely defined term that describes enhancements to standard HTML such as animation, sound, rollovers, and better control over typography. These enhancements are achieved by combining various types of existing technologies, such as JavaScript, ActiveX, CSS (**C**ascading **S**tyle **S**heets), plug-ins, DOM (**D**ocument **O**bject **M**odel), and proprietary methods that the competing browser giants have invented privately.

The huge challenge before DHMTL is that same huge challenge that faces any Web developer: overcoming browser and platform differences. Some JavaScripts work on Netscape and not on Explorer. ActiveX works only on PC versions of Explorer, not Mac versions. If you delve into the nitty gritty, it's horrifying to discover what works where and what doesn't. You could literally spend all your time testing tags and browsers and forget about ever making any Web content at all.

Unfortunately, DHTML knows no standards yet—and so competing methods for creating this type of content abound between the warring browserlords. Netscape and Microsoft have pledged future support for a standard that is currently being decided by the **W**orld **W**ide **W**eb **C**onsortium (W3C), but we've all heard that one before. Meanwhile, life goes on without standards, as usual.

Regardless, many think DHTML is the future of the Web. I am not necessarily in agreement, but if the features were to be standardized and widely available, I would be terrifically excited about using it. It's one of those not-quite-ready-for-prime-time things that excites me more in terms of its potential, not reality.

DHTML Overview

Our drive to enhance HTML is natural and unavoidable. Because modern computers are capable of rich multimedia delivery, it's only a matter of time before the browsers and tags catch up with the capabilities. Dynamic HTML is the latest contender for creating multimedia content, and here's an overview of a few of its underlying technologies:

Cascading Style Sheets

Cascading **S**tyle **S**heets (CSS) are used to define the way in which content can appear on Web pages. You can define such attributes as text margins positioned with pixel accuracy, color for specific fonts or specific-sized text, or pixel-based leading (the space between lines of type). It's also possible to position artwork on top of itself, creating layered effects. Rollovers can be achieved this way, by displaying one layer on mouseover or another on mousedown.

Cons: The problem with CSS, from my point of view, is that it requires a whole new understanding of how to program it—separate from HTML. This is compounded by the fact that CSS is implemented differently by the two major browsers. While programs like Dreamweaver and Cyber-Studio make programming CSS less painful, it's still supported in a very limited manner.

Pros: You can create a single style sheet that can link to multiple HTML documents. This means that I could change my site very easily by changing a single document. This will be a great timesaver for many Web design tasks—though it will work better for sites that have style formulas rather than for freeform designed sites.

JavaScript

JavaScript is a scripting language that resides inside HTML documents. This means that, unlike Java, the code is not compiled beforehand. What I like about JavaScript is that it can be copied and pasted like HTML, and it's easy to learn by studying other Web sites' source code. It is not proper netiquette, however, to use someone else's JavaScript without crediting him or her. JavaScript can be used for all types of Web-based applications; the most popular ones for DHTML include animation, sound, and rollovers.

Cons: JavaScript is sensitive to browser interpretation, and Netscape and Internet Explorer handle the code differently. This makes it extremely difficult to use on a cross-browser compatible site. Fortunately, some of the WYSIWYG editors, such as Dreamweaver and Cyber-Studio, perform some of the cross-browser compatibility checks for you.

Pros: Everything within JavaScript is client-sided. This means that server delays are not present to access the scripts. It also means that you can study, copy, and paste JavaScript, just like HTML.

Plug-Ins

Plug-ins can be included as content for style sheets. This means that Shockwave or Flash documents can be treated as objects for pixel accurate positioning and layering within CSS. Netscape and Internet Explorer embed plug-ins for use within style sheets by using two different HTML tags: OBJECT and EMBED.

Cons: Netscape and Internet Explorer use different tags to embed plug-ins for use within style sheets using two different HTML tags: OBJECT and EMBED. It's possible to combine the two in one document, but that adds to the complexity of programming them by hand.

Pros: Plug-in content can add greater interactivity and more robust features than straight DHTML or HTML can.

DOM

The **D**ocument **O**bject **M**odel (DOM) specifies how text and graphics can be controlled as objects within DHTML. Basically, the DOM enables anything to be controlled by a script. Unfortunately, DOM is handled slightly differently by Explorer and Netscape. This is one of the key problems with the current implementation of DHTML.

Cool Things with DHTML

Once again, because I'm not a programmer, I'm going to default to showing some things that Dreamweaver can do with DHTML. I'll focus on some of the things that can't be done with any other means—for example, hiding and showing layers, animation, and drag and drop.

One of the neat things about Dreamweaver is that you can target specific browsers, and the program will write the code so it works on Netscape and Explorer, just Netscape, just Explorer, all 3.0 browsers, or whatever you specify.

Dreamweaver also has a mechanism to warn you if something is not compatible with an older browser.

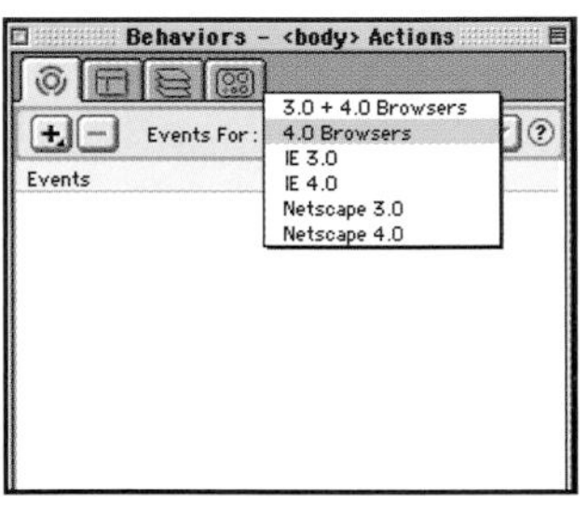

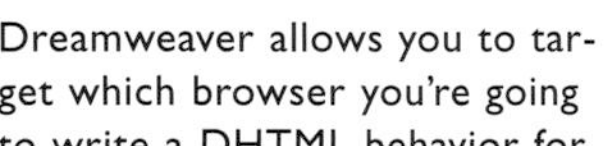

Dreamweaver allows you to target which browser you're going to write a DHTML behavior for.

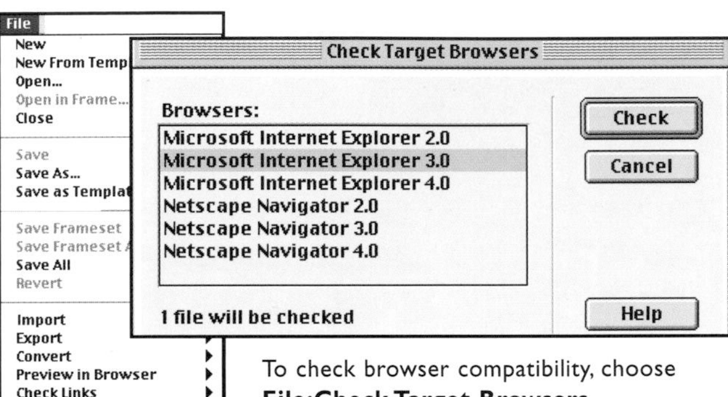

To check browser compatibility, choose **File:Check Target Browsers**.

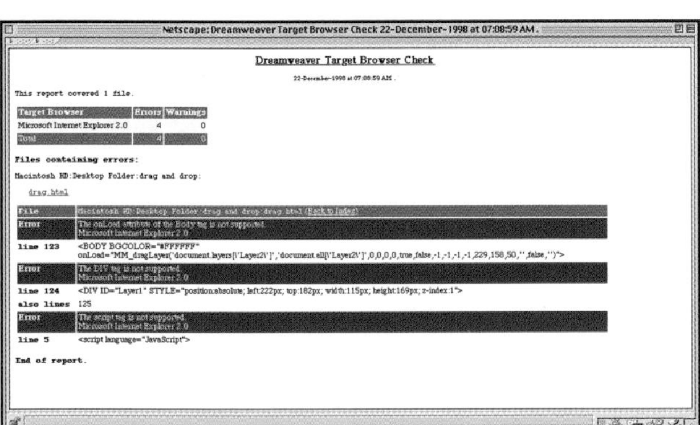

The results of checking a sample DHTML page on an older browser from Dreamweaver.

note

Appropriate Uses of DHTML

I am not a huge advocate of DHTML, even though it's quite fun to learn and experiment with. If you know for certain, though, that your audience has a 4.0 browser, it can be worthwhile to set your site up with dynamic features such as those presented in this chapter. Some such scenarios might be if you are creating an intranet or an extranet, and you can be sure that your end users have a specific 4.0 browser. In that case, go to town. Otherwise, carefully consider making alternative content for your non-4.0 browser visitors.

Layers

Showing and hiding layers is a very powerful thing in DHTML. In this example, I have put some text into a layer. As I roll the mouse pointer over the text, the text appears, and as I roll off the link, it disappears.

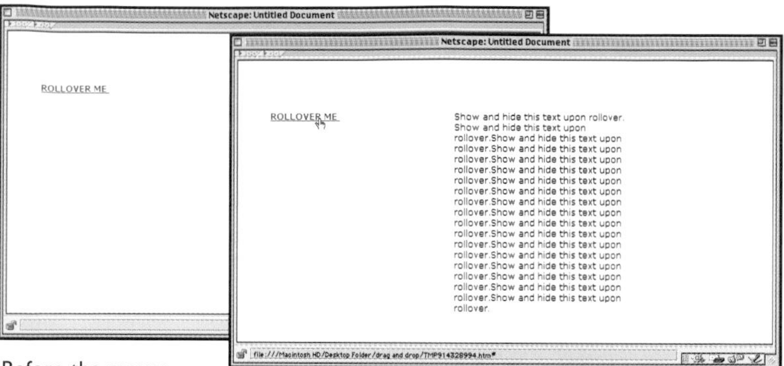

Before the mouse rolls over the link, nothing is there but the link.

When the mouse rolls over the link, additional text appears. This was accomplished with show and hide layers in Dreamweaver 2.0.

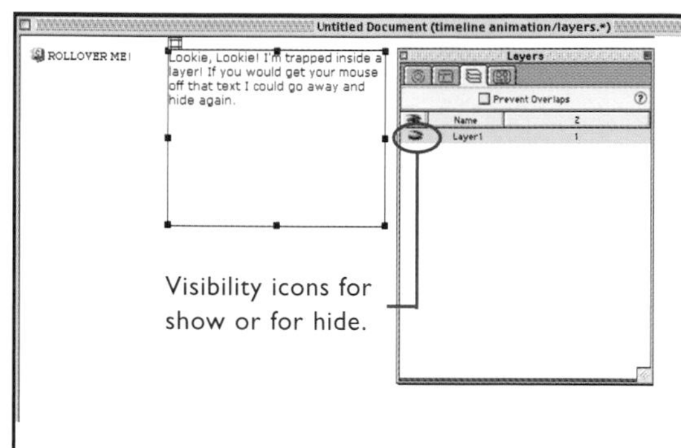

Step 1: Type out the rollover text and make it a link by using the Properties bar and inserting a URL into the Link cell. Next choose **Insert:Layer**. Write some additional text inside the layer. Choose **Window: Layers** to open the Layer palette. Notice the column with the eyes? This is where visibility is set. Because I want the layer to be hidden when this page is loaded, I have clicked the eye icon twice—until it has shut closed (meaning hidden).

Step 2: Select the link at the bottom left hand corner of the Dreamweaver window and click on the **Behaviors** button on the Launcher. Select **Show-Hide Layers**.

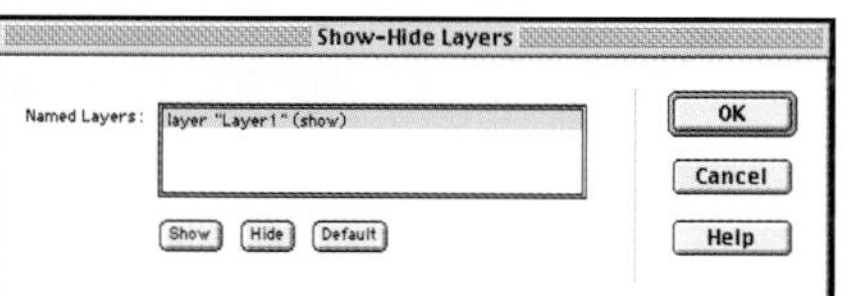

Step 3: Click on the **Show button** and click **OK**.

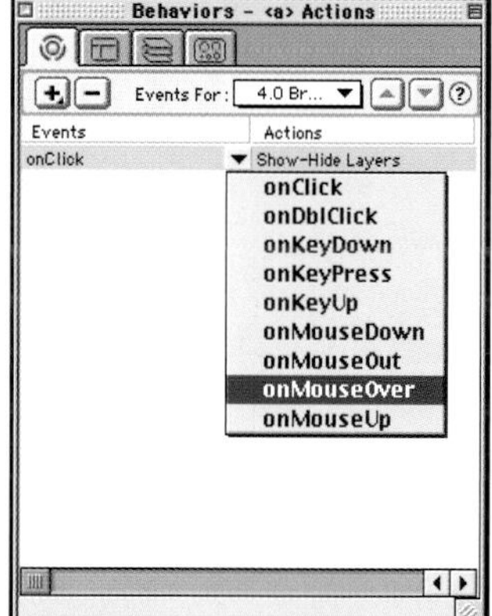

Step 4: The Show-Hide Layer Behavior defaults to using onClick as its trigger. Let's change this to **onMouseOver** by holding down the pop-out arrow and selecting it (as shown above).

Step 5: Make sure the link, or <a>, is still selected and add another Show-Hide Layer action. This time choose to hide the layer. Change onClick to **onMouseOut**.

Preview the results with the F12 key. Here's the code that Dreamweaver generated:

code

```
<HTML>
<HEAD>
<TITLE>Untitled Document</TITLE>
<META HTTP-EQUIV="Content-Type" CONTENT="text/html; charset=iso-8859-1">
<script language="JavaScript">
<!--
function MM_showHideLayers() { //v2.0
  var i, visStr, args, theObj;
  args = MM_showHideLayers.arguments;
  for (i=0; i<(args.length-2); i+=3) { //with arg triples (objNS,objIE,visStr)
    visStr   = args[i+2];
    if (navigator.appName == 'Netscape' && document.layers != null) {
      theObj = eval(args[i]);
      if (theObj) theObj.visibility = visStr;
    } else if (document.all != null) { //IE
      if (visStr == 'show') visStr = 'visible'; //convert vals
      if (visStr == 'hide') visStr = 'hidden';
      theObj = eval(args[i+1]);
      if (theObj) theObj.style.visibility = visStr;
  } }
}
//-->
</script>
</HEAD>
<BODY BGCOLOR="#FFFFFF">
<DIV ID="Layer1" STYLE="position:absolute; left:152px; top:15px; width:228px;
height:184px; z-index:1; visibility: hidden"><FONT FACE="Verdana, Courier,
Courier New">Lookie,
  Lookie! I'm trapped inside a layer! If you would get your mouse off that text
  I could go away and hide again.</FONT></DIV>
<A HREF="#" onMouseOver="MM_showHideLayers('document.layers[\'Layer1\']','docu-
ment.all[\'Layer1\']','show')"
onMouseOut="MM_showHideLayers('document.layers[\'Layer1\']','document.all[\'Laye
r1\']','hide')">
ROLLOVER ME! </A>
</BODY>
</HTML>
```

Animation

For this example, I've made some titles that fly into place.

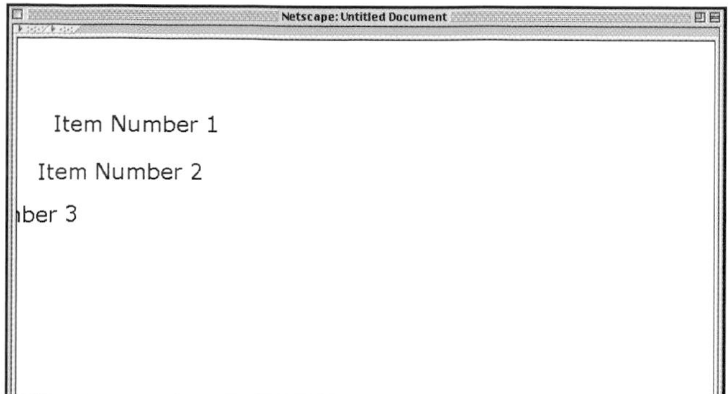

Each line of text flies into place using JavaScript animation and the Dreamweaver 2.0 timeline.

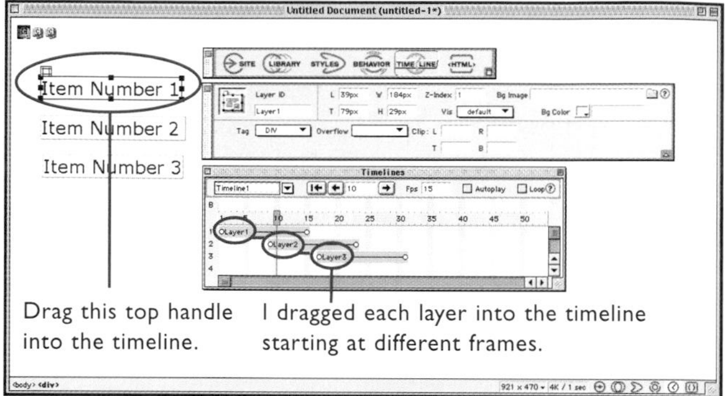

Step 1: Choose **Insert:Layer** three times and type words into each layer. Click on the Timeline button on the Launcher. Then drag each layer into the timeline by the top handle. Notice how I dragged each layer in at a different starting frame? I did that on purpose because I want the effect of these titles to fly in one at a time.

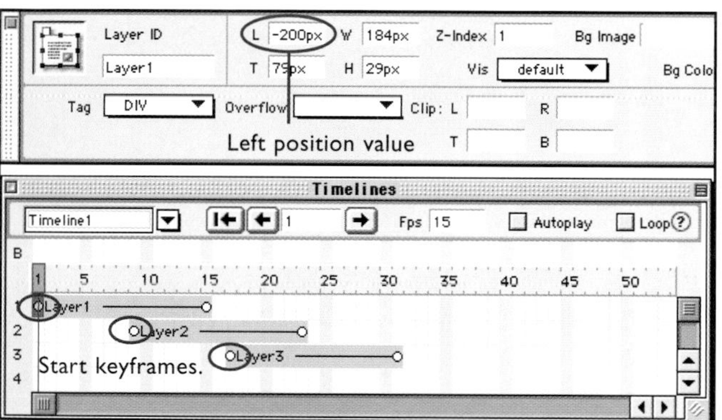

Step 2: Set the key frames: Select the layer, go to the first dot on the timeline, and set a -200px value into the **L** position value. Repeat the same setting for each layer. This sets their start point outside of the browser screen.

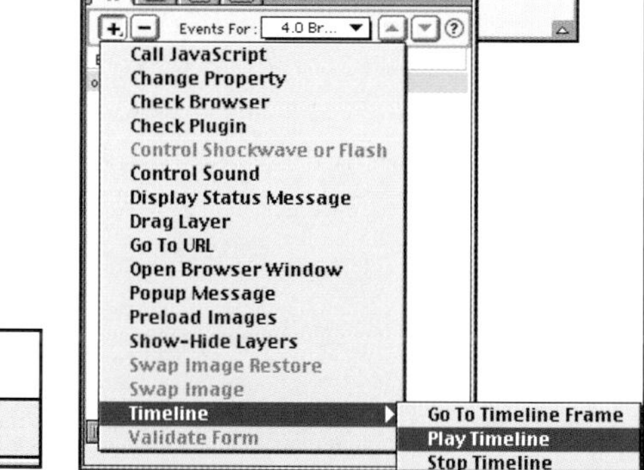

Step 3: Click on the Behaviors button on the Launcher and select the body of the document by going to the bottom left-hand corner of the Dreamweaver window and highlighting <body>. Click on the add button in the Behaviors palette to select **Timeline:Play Timeline**.

Save this, and then use the F12 key to preview! It was that simple. Here's the code that Dreamweaver generated:

code

```
<HTML>
<HEAD>
<TITLE>Untitled Document</TITLE>
<META HTTP-EQUIV="Content-Type" CONTENT="text/html; charset=iso-8859-1">
<script language="JavaScript">
<!--
function MM_timelinePlay(tmLnName, myID) { //v1.2
  //Copyright 1997 Macromedia, Inc.  All rights reserved.
  var i,j,tmLn,props,keyFrm,sprite,numKeyFr,firstKeyFr,propNum,theObj,firstTime=false;
  if (document.MM_Time == null) MM_initTimelines(); //if *very* 1st time
  tmLn = document.MM_Time[tmLnName];
  if (myID == null) { myID = ++tmLn.ID; firstTime=true;}//if new call, incr ID
  if (myID == tmLn.ID) { //if Im newest
    setTimeout('MM_timelinePlay("'+tmLnName+'",'+myID+')',tmLn.delay);
    fNew = ++tmLn.curFrame;
    for (i=0; i<tmLn.length; i++) {
      sprite = tmLn[i];
      if (sprite.charAt(0) == 's') {
        if (sprite.obj) {
          numKeyFr = sprite.keyFrames.length; firstKeyFr = sprite.keyFrames[0];
          if (fNew >= firstKeyFr && fNew <= sprite.keyFrames[numKeyFr-1]) {//in range
            keyFrm=1;
            for (j=0; j<sprite.values.length; j++) {
              props = sprite.values[j];
              if (numKeyFr != props.length) {
                if (props.prop2 == null) sprite.obj[props.prop] = props[fNew-
firstKeyFr];
                else        sprite.obj[props.prop2][props.prop] = props[fNew-
firstKeyFr];
              } else {
                while (keyFrm<numKeyFr && fNew>=sprite.keyFrames[keyFrm]) keyFrm++;
                if (firstTime || fNew==sprite.keyFrames[keyFrm-1]) {
                  if (props.prop2 == null) sprite.obj[props.prop] = props[keyFrm-1];
                  else        sprite.obj[props.pr op2][props.prop] = props[keyFrm-1];
        } } } } }
      } else if (sprite.charAt(0)=='b' && fNew == sprite.frame) eval(sprite.value);
      if (fNew > tmLn.lastFrame) tmLn.ID = 0;
  } }
}
```

```
function MM_initTimelines() {
    //MM_initTimelines() Copyright 1997 Macromedia, Inc.  All rights reserved.
    var ns = navigator.appName == "Netscape";
    document.MM_Time = new Array(1);
    document.MM_Time[0] = new Array(3);
    document.MM_Time["Timeline1"] = document.MM_Time[0];
    document.MM_Time[0].MM_Name = "Timeline1";
    document.MM_Time[0].fps = 15;
    document.MM_Time[0][0] = new String("sprite");
    document.MM_Time[0][0].slot = 1;
    if (ns)
        document.MM_Time[0][0].obj = document["Layer1"];
    else
        document.MM_Time[0][0].obj = document.all ?  document.all["Layer1"] : null;
    document.MM_Time[0][0].keyFrames = new Array(1, 15);
    document.MM_Time[0][0].values = new Array(2);
    document.MM_Time[0][0].values[0] = new Array(-200,-183,-166,-149,-132,-115,-98,-81,-
63,-46,-29,-12,5,22,39);
    document.MM_Time[0][0].values[0].prop = "left";
    document.MM_Time[0][0].values[1] = new
Array(79,79,79,79,79,79,79,79,79,79,79,79,79,79,79);
    document.MM_Time[0][0].values[1].prop = "top";
    if (!ns) {
        document.MM_Time[0][0].values[0].prop2 = "style";
        document.MM_Time[0][0].values[1].prop2 = "style";
    }
    document.MM_Time[0][1] = new String("sprite");
    document.MM_Time[0][1].slot = 2;
    if (ns)
        document.MM_Time[0][1].obj = document["Layer2"];
    else
        document.MM_Time[0][1].obj = document.all ?  document.all["Layer2"] : null;
    document.MM_Time[0][1].keyFrames = new Array(9, 23);
    document.MM_Time[0][1].values = new Array(2);
    document.MM_Time[0][1].values[0] = new Array(-200,-183,-166,-149,-132,-115,-98,-81,-
63,-46,-29,-12,5,22,39);
    document.MM_Time[0][1].values[0].prop = "left";
    document.MM_Time[0][1].values[1] = new
Array(131,131,131,131,131,131,131,131,131,131,131,131,131,131,131);
    document.MM_Time[0][1].values[1].prop = "top";
    if (!ns) {
        document.MM_Time[0][1].values[0].prop2 = "style";
        document.MM_Time[0][1].values[1].prop2 = "style";
    }
```

```
    document.MM_Time[0][2] = new String("sprite");
    document.MM_Time[0][2].slot = 3;
    if (ns)
        document.MM_Time[0][2].obj = document["Layer3"];
    else
        document.MM_Time[0][2].obj = document.all ?  document.all["Layer3"] : null;
    document.MM_Time[0][2].keyFrames = new Array(17, 31);
    document.MM_Time[0][2].values = new Array(2);
    document.MM_Time[0][2].values[0] = new Array(-200,-183,-166,-149,-132,-115,-98,-81,-
63,-46,-29,-12,5,22,39);
    document.MM_Time[0][2].values[0].prop = "left";
    document.MM_Time[0][2].values[1] = new
Array(177,177,177,177,177,177,177,177,177,177,177,177,177,177,177);
    document.MM_Time[0][2].values[1].prop = "top";
    if (!ns) {
        document.MM_Time[0][2].values[0].prop2 = "style";
        document.MM_Time[0][2].values[1].prop2 = "style";
    }
    document.MM_Time[0].lastFrame = 31;
    for (i=0; i<document.MM_Time.length; i++) {
        document.MM_Time[i].ID = null;
        document.MM_Time[i].curFrame = 0;
        document.MM_Time[i].delay = 1000/document.MM_Time[i].fps;
    }
}
//-->
</script>
</HEAD>
<BODY BGCOLOR="#FFFFFF" onLoad="MM_timelinePlay('Timeline1')">
<DIV ID="Layer1" STYLE="position:absolute; left:-200px; top:79px; width:184px;
height:29px; z-index:1"><FONT FACE="Verdana, Courier, Courier New" SIZE="6">Item
  Number 1</FONT></DIV>
<DIV ID="Layer2" STYLE="position:absolute; left:-200px; top:131px; width:189px;
height:30px; z-index:2"><FONT FACE="Verdana, Courier, Courier New" SIZE="6">Item
  Number 2</FONT></DIV>
<DIV ID="Layer3" STYLE="position:absolute; left:-200px; top:177px; width:183px;
height:28px; z-index:3"><FONT FACE="Verdana, Courier, Courier New" SIZE="6">Item
  Number 3</FONT></DIV>
<P> </P>
<P> </P>
<P> </P>
</BODY>
</HTML>
```

Drag and Drop

Assigning drag and drop features to a Web page is something that standard HTML does not allow you to do. In this example, I created two pieces of art: the top and bottom to an eggshell. Using Dreamweaver, I programmed a drag and drop so you could cover the chick back up with its eggshell. There are many more practical applications of this technique, but this shows a very basic example of what you can do.

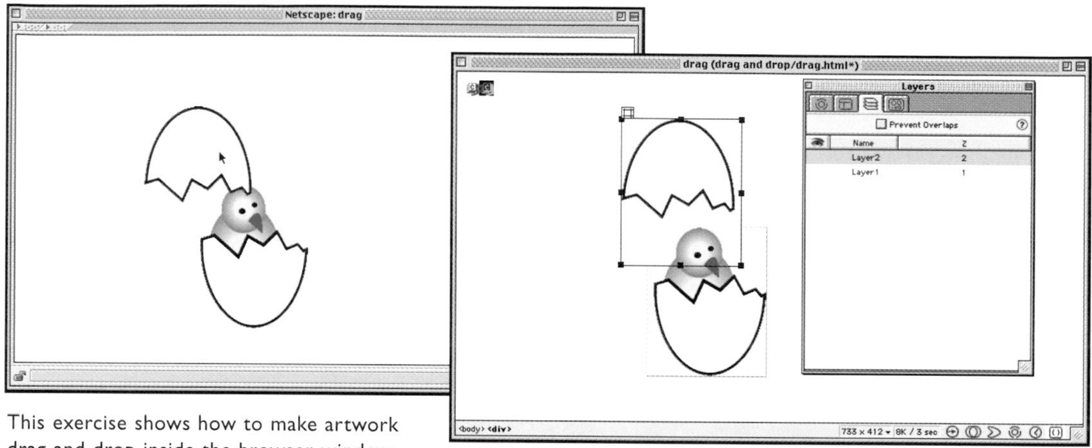

This exercise shows how to make artwork drag and drop inside the browser window.

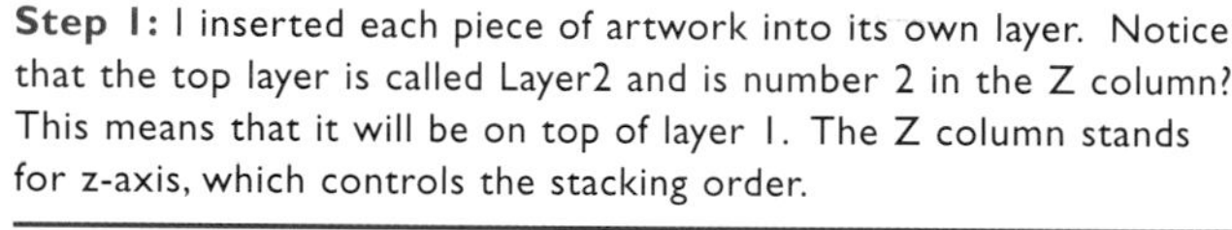

Step 1: I inserted each piece of artwork into its own layer. Notice that the top layer is called Layer2 and is number 2 in the Z column? This means that it will be on top of layer 1. The Z column stands for z-axis, which controls the stacking order.

Step 2: I positioned the eggshell on top of the bottom layer perfectly. Then making sure that the <body> element was selected in the lower left-hand corner of Dreamweaver's browser window, I added the Drag Layer behavior.

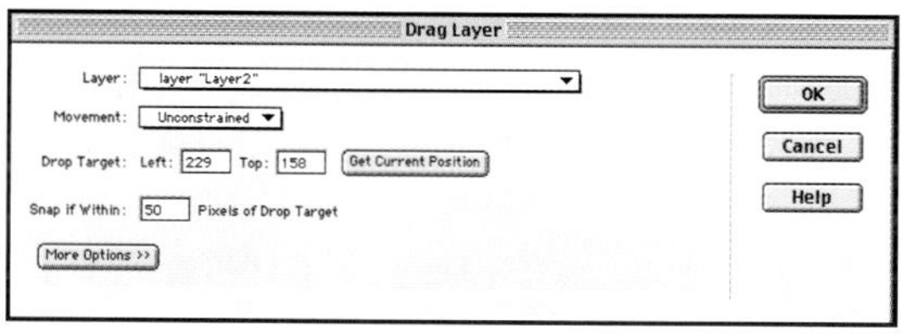

Step 3: Because Layer 2 is the layer I want my end user to be able to place perfectly, I selected **Layer:Layer2**. Then I clicked **Get Current Position**. This put the pixel accurate position into the Drop Target cells. Now click **OK**.

Step 4: I dragged the top eggshell layer off the bottom eggshell and positioned it where I wanted the layer to appear when the page loads.

Click F12 to preview the effect. You can drag the top layer onto the bottom, and they fit perfectly. Here's the code:

code

```
<HTML>
<HEAD>
<TITLE>drag</TITLE>
<META HTTP-EQUIV="Content-Type" CONTENT="text/html; charset=iso-8859-1">
<script language="JavaScript">
<!--
function
MM_dragLayer(objNS,objIE,hL,hT,hW,hH,toFront,dropBack,cU,cD,cL,cR,targL,targT,tol,dropJS,
et,dragJS) { //v2.0
  //Copyright 1998 Macromedia, Inc.  All rights reserved.
  var i,j,aLayer,retVal,curDrag=null,NS=(navigator.appName=='Netscape'), curLeft, curTop;
  if (!document.all && !document.layers) return false;
  retVal = true; if(!NS && event) event.returnValue = true;
  if (MM_dragLayer.arguments.length > 1) {
    curDrag = eval((NS)?objNS:objIE); if (!curDrag) return false;
    if (!document.allLayers) {
      document.allLayers = new Array();
      with (document) {
        if (NS) {
          for (i=0; i<layers.length; i++) allLayers[i]=layers[i];
          for (i=0; i<allLayers.length; i++) {
            if (allLayers[i].document && allLayers[i].document.layers)
              for (j=0; j<allLayers[i].document.layers.length; j++)
                allLayers[allLayers.length] = allLayers[i].document.layers[j];
        } } else {
          for (i=0; i<all.length; i++)
            if (all[i].style != null && all[i].style.position)
              allLayers[allLayers.length] = all[i];
    } } }
    curDrag.MM_dragOk=true; curDrag.MM_targL=targL; curDrag.MM_targT=targT;
    curDrag.MM_tol=Math.pow(tol,2); curDrag.MM_hLeft=hL; curDrag.MM_hTop=hT;
    curDrag.MM_hWidth=hW; curDrag.MM_hHeight=hH; curDrag.MM_toFront=toFront;
    curDrag.MM_dropBack=dropBack; curDrag.MM_dropJS=dropJS;
    curDrag.MM_everyTime=et; curDrag.MM_dragJS=dragJS;
```

```
    curDrag.MM_oldZ = (NS)?curDrag.zIndex:curDrag.style.zIndex;
    curLeft= (NS)?curDrag.left:curDrag.style.pixelLeft; curDrag.MM_startL = curLeft;
    curTop = (NS)?curDrag.top:curDrag.style.pixelTop; curDrag.MM_startT = curTop;
    curDrag.MM_bL=(cL<0)?null:curLeft-cL; curDrag.MM_bT=(cU<0)?null:curTop -cU;
    curDrag.MM_bR=(cR<0)?null:curLeft+cR; curDrag.MM_bB=(cD<0)?null:curTop +cD;
    curDrag.MM_LEFTRIGHT=0; curDrag.MM_UPDOWN=0; curDrag.MM_SNAPPED=false; //use in your
JS!
    document.onmousedown = MM_dragLayer; document.onmouseup = MM_dragLayer;
    if (NS) document.captureEvents(Event.MOUSEDOWN¦Event.MOUSEUP);
  } else {
    var theEvent = ((NS)?objNS.type:event.type);
    if (theEvent == 'mousedown') {
      var aLayer, maxDragZ=null;
      var mouseX = (NS)?objNS.pageX : event.clientX + document.body.scrollLeft;
      var mouseY = (NS)?objNS.pageY : event.clientY + document.body.scrollTop;
      document.MM_maxZ = 0;
      for (i=0; i<document.allLayers.length; i++) {
        aLayer = document.allLayers[i];
        var aLayerZ = (NS)?aLayer.zIndex:aLayer.style.zIndex;
        if (aLayerZ > document.MM_maxZ) document.MM_maxZ = aLayerZ;
        var isVisible = (((NS)?aLayer.visibility:aLayer.style.visibility).indexOf('hid')
== -1);
        if (aLayer.MM_dragOk != null && isVisible) with (aLayer) {
          var parentL=0; var parentT=0;
          if (!NS) {
            parentLayer = aLayer.parentElement;
            while (parentLayer != null && parentLayer.style.position) {
              parentL += parentLayer.offsetLeft;
              parentT += parentLayer.offsetTop;
              parentLayer = parentLayer.parentElement;
          } }
          var tmpX=mouseX-(((NS)?pageX:style.pixelLeft+parentL)+MM_hLeft);
          var tmpY=mouseY-(((NS)?pageY:style.pixelTop +parentT)+MM_hTop);
          var tmpW = MM_hWidth;  if (tmpW <= 0) tmpW += ((NS)?clip.width :offsetWidth);
          var tmpH = MM_hHeight; if (tmpH <= 0) tmpH +=
((NS)?clip.height:offsetHeight);
```

```
      if ((0 <= tmpX && tmpX < tmpW && 0 <= tmpY && tmpY < tmpH) &&
         (maxDragZ == null || maxDragZ <= aLayerZ)) {
        curDrag = aLayer; maxDragZ = aLayerZ;
  } } }
  if (curDrag) {
    document.onmousemove = MM_dragLayer;
    if (NS) document.captureEvents(Event.MOUSEMOVE);
    curLeft = (NS)?curDrag.left:curDrag.style.pixelLeft;
    curTop = (NS)?curDrag.top:curDrag.style.pixelTop;
    MM_oldX = mouseX - curLeft; MM_oldY = mouseY - curTop;
    document.MM_curDrag = curDrag;  curDrag.MM_SNAPPED=false;
    if(curDrag.MM_toFront) {
      eval('curDrag.'+((NS)?'':'style.')+'zIndex=document.MM_maxZ+1');
      if (!curDrag.MM_dropBack) document.MM_maxZ++;
    }
    retVal = false; if(!NS) event.returnValue = false;
} } else if (theEvent == 'mousemove') {
  if (document.MM_curDrag) with (document.MM_curDrag) {
    var mouseX = (NS)?objNS.pageX : event.clientX + document.body.scrollLeft;
    var mouseY = (NS)?objNS.pageY : event.clientY + document.body.scrollTop;
    newLeft = mouseX-MM_oldX; newTop  = mouseY-MM_oldY;
    if (MM_bL!=null) newLeft = Math.max(newLeft,MM_bL);
    if (MM_bR!=null) newLeft = Math.min(newLeft,MM_bR);
    if (MM_bT!=null) newTop  = Math.max(newTop ,MM_bT);
    if (MM_bB!=null) newTop  = Math.min(newTop ,MM_bB);
    MM_LEFTRIGHT = newLeft-MM_startL; MM_UPDOWN = newTop-MM_startT;
    if (NS) {left = newLeft; top = newTop;}
    else {style.pixelLeft = newLeft; style.pixelTop = newTop;}
    if (MM_dragJS) eval(MM_dragJS);
    retVal = false; if(!NS) event.returnValue = false;
} } else if (theEvent == 'mouseup') {
  document.onmousemove = null;
  if (NS) document.releaseEvents(Event.MOUSEMOVE);
  if (NS) document.captureEvents(Event.MOUSEDOWN); //for mac NS
  if (document.MM_curDrag) with (document.MM_curDrag) {
    if (typeof MM_targL =='number' && typeof MM_targT == 'number' &&
```

```
        (Math.pow(MM_targL-((NS)?left:style.pixelLeft),2)+
         Math.pow(MM_targT-((NS)?top:style.pixelTop),2))<=MM_tol) {
      if (NS) {left = MM_targL; top = MM_targT;}
      else {style.pixelLeft = MM_targL; style.pixelTop = MM_targT;}
      MM_SNAPPED = true; MM_LEFTRIGHT = MM_startL-MM_targL;
      MM_UPDOWN = MM_startT-MM_targT;
    }
    if (MM_everyTime || MM_SNAPPED) eval(MM_dropJS);
    if(MM_dropBack) {if (NS) zIndex = MM_oldZ; else style.zIndex = MM_oldZ;}
    retVal = false; if(!NS) event.returnValue = false;
   }
   document.MM_curDrag = null;
  }
  if (NS) document.routeEvent(objNS);
 }
 return retVal;
}
//-->
</script>
</HEAD>
<BODY BGCOLOR="#FFFFFF"
onLoad="MM_dragLayer('document.layers[\'Layer2\']','document.all[\'Layer2\']',0,0,0,0,tru
e,false,-1,-1,-1,-1,229,158,50,'',false,'')">
<DIV ID="Layer1" STYLE="position:absolute; left:222px; top:182px; width:115px;
height:169px; z-index:1"><IMG SRC="eggbottom.gif" WIDTH="141" HEIGHT="175" NAME="bot-
tom"></DIV>
<DIV ID="Layer2" STYLE="position:absolute; left:46px; top:77px; width:135px;
height:172px; z-index:2"><IMG SRC="eggtop.gif" WIDTH="141" HEIGHT="122" NAME="top"></DIV>
</BODY>
</HTML>
```

DHTMLzone

The thing about all this multimedia stuff is that it's harder to create than you think. Even a really cool visual editor like Dreamweaver can't change the basic challenges of coming up with compelling content and appropriate aesthetics.

I was really impressed with the site that Macromedia put together to showcase DHTML technology. At the **DHTMLzone** site (http://www.dhtmlzone.com), they have a sample site called **SuperFly Fashions** (designed by Akimbo Designs), which features some very hot-looking cross-platform compatible DHTML. Besides a snazzy demo, each page within the site includes step-by-step tutorials of how it was created. (You'll need a 4.0 browser, as will your end users if you decide to adopt DHTML on your Web site.) Be sure to check out this site and the demo version of Dreamweaver.

tip

Other Great DHTML Resources

You can get third-party Dreamweaver behaviors from the following sites:

http://www.macromedia.com/support/dreamweaver/upndown/objects/

http://people.netscape.com/andreww/dreamweaver/

http://home.att.net/%7EJCB.BEI/Dreamweaver/

http://www.yaromat.com/

http://www.cybernet.ch/users/massimo/

summary Dynamic HTML

DHMTL can do very cool things that standard HTML is not capable of. It's very complex to code DHTML, however, due to the variety of browser standards (or lack thereof!). I have used Dreamweaver in this chapter to demonstrate some of the possibilities within DHTML. Here's a summary:

- DHTML is not a technology unto itself, but a combination of technologies. It combines HTML, JavaScript, CSS, and DOM.
- DHTML is supported only by 4.0 browsers right now, and it is supported differently by each of them.
- If you are going to use DHTML on your site, it's important that you understand that people using older browsers will not be able to see the effects of your labor. You should consider creating alternate content for those viewers and using a browser-sniffing JavaScript (covered in Chapter 22, "JavaScript: Rollovers & More") or some other means to offer alternative content.
- Dreamweaver is a WYSIWYG HTML editor that not only writes DHTML, but helps you target browsers that can see the results.

Introduction

QuickTime 3.0

Chapter Topics

- Quicktime Web Advancements
- Poster Movies
- Text & Sprite Tracks
- Multiple Data Rate Movies
- Image Format Support
- Digital Video Terms Glossary
- QuickTime HTML Commands

24

Why write an entire chapter about QuickTime? Because it's the movie format of choice for the Web. Yes, there are other movie technologies, plug-ins, and streaming video options. And some people might disagree with me and think some other format is going to come along to outdo QuickTime. I, however, believe in this format. Perhaps you might understand why after reading this chapter.

I remember the first time I saw a QuickTime movie played back on a computer. It was postage-stamp size, sputtering and skipping along at a snail's pace, with really bad sound and even worse sync. Everyone around me was really excited about it, but frankly, I thought they were nuts. I didn't "get" that the movie format I was looking at would someday change the history of filmmaking, multimedia, and now the Web.

Today, QuickTime movies are on almost every CD-ROM in existence because of pioneering advancements in digital movie and sound compression, sound sync, and impressive data rate speeds. Once Quick-Time conquered the CD-ROM market, it took the film and video market by storm. That postage-stamp size movie capacity grew to support 4,000 x 4,000 pixel resolution, which matches the resolution of feature film quality film recorders. In the broadcast video world, QuickTime applications began outperforming systems that cost hundreds of thousands of dollars. Through the wonders of QuickTime, individuals on personal computers with the right equipment and software could actually produce feature films, music videos, industrials, and television commercials. QuickTime single-handedly created the desktop video explosion, which is still sending shock waves through video/film post houses and high-end equipment supply houses.

QuickTime 3.0 is now poised to take the Web on by storm. If you need to put movies on the Web, there is no better choice around.

QuickTime Basics

What exactly is a QuickTime movie? Just like animated GIF files, QuickTime movies can contain multiple frames. The content can be cartoons, vectors, or live action.

How do you make a QuickTime movie? There are numerous ways. If you have a copy of MoviePlayer, you can open the following file formats and instantly convert them to QuickTime movies: MPEG audio and video; AVI video; AIFF, AU, WAV, and MIDI audio; GIF animations; and GIF, JPEG, SGI, Photoshop (PSD), BMP, MacPaint, PNG, Targa, and FLC images.

It's recommended that you download **QuickTime Pro** (http://www.apple.com/quicktime/upgrade/) if you plan to do serious QuickTime Web authoring. It offers many extra features, and it's a bargain at $29.99.

There are also many QuickTime movie creation tools. Some of those include Adobe After Effects, Adobe Premier, Macromedia Director, Terran Interactive's Movie Cleaner, Totally Hip's WebPainter, Lari Software's Electrifier Pro, and Equilibrium's DeBabelizer.

After you make a QuickTime movie, here's how you embed it into your Web page:

```
<EMBED SRC="placeholder.mov" HEIGHT=176 WIDTH=136>
```

Replace the name **"placeholder.mov"** with the name of your movie, and replace the values for height and width of the movie with your movie dimensions (add 16 to the height of the movie for the default movie controller unless you plan to turn it off with a **CONTROLLER= FALSE** command).

The QuickTime controller (circled) can be hidden or visible, with the CONTROLLER=FALSE or TRUE command. This example is at http://www.apple.com/quicktime/samples/stream/kane.html. The song listings shown above are using static images as "Poster" movies, which are described later in this chapter.

Web Advancements

QuickTime 1.0 started out as a Mac-only file format, but QuickTime 2.0 included a Windows version as well. The QuickTime 1.0 plug-in was one of the only contenders to make it into the default plug-in folder of MSIE, Navigator, and Communicator. Not only did this mean that QuickTime became cross-platform through the Web, but it also meant that even though it was a plug-in, most people did not have to endure the bother of installing it. The QuickTime 1.0 plug-in included features for doing a few nifty things on a Web page: embedding a video or sound clip, hiding the controllers, and playing without a controller and loop, for example. Its Web functionality wasn't earth-shattering, but it didn't exactly suck either.

In the wake of doomsday predictions and market share losses, it seems that Apple woke up and decided to put some major programming muscle behind their QuickTime brainchild. The results are QuickTime 3.0 and a QuickTime 2.0 plug-in, both of which include an awesome new feature list.

QuickTime 3.0 Web Features

The new Web features list for QuickTime 3.0 is long and impressive. In order to view the results of QuickTime 3.0, the end user must have the latest QuickTime 2.0 plug-in installed. To install it on your system, go to http://www.apple.com/quicktime/download/index.html.

"Poster" Movies

Ever notice that when you encounter a plug-in on the Web, a little promotional graphic for the plug-in type appears? I'm sure everyone has seen the Macromedia logo for Shockwave and the QuickTime logo for QuickTime content.

"Poster" movies come to the rescue here. It's possible now for a movie to replace itself with another movie when it's clicked on. You can specify that a small single-frame movie (in other words, a still frame) with no audio be downloaded instantly instead of the annoying little QuickTime logo. When the user clicks on the poster movie, the real movie will play (if it's had a chance to load enough material). A poster movie looks like a regular picture, but because it is a QuickTime movie, the QuickTime plug-in responds to mouse clicks on the movie and can load a new movie in its place.

For a complete tutorial on creating poster movies for QuickTime, visit http://www.apple.com/quicktime/authors/posterht.html. To see a sample of a poster movie, visit http://www.apple.com/quicktime/samples/interactive-mm/poster.html.

Poster movies should be only one frame in length. To embed a poster movie in your page, you need to add an EMBED tag to your HTML code. Here's an example:

```
<EMBED SRC="poster.mov" BGCOLOR="#FFFFFF"
CONTROLLER=false HEIGHT="216" WIDTH="320"
HREF="real.mov" >
```

The path after "SRC=" points to the poster movie, and the path after "HREF=" points to the movie you want downloaded after the user clicks on the poster.

HREF, Sprite, and Text Tracks

QuickTime, from its inception, has allowed you to link to outside URLs, creating a movie file that functions like any other hyperlink. Now you can add URLs to text tracks and have a different link from each frame in a movie.

From the QuickTime site of a movie containing a text track.

A text track is something that's written and assigned to the movie in HTML. You can set long text strings or simple HREFs to outside URLs, depending on how you code your page. Detailed instructions and syntax for this feature are available online at the QT developer's site (http://www.apple.com/quicktime/developers/).

The site shows another example in which a text track is associated with a movie. An "Auto URL" feature causes HTML text to appear within a frameset on the same page that changes over the course of the movie. The HTML text is triggered by the movie and almost works like an HTML version of closed-captioning.

A "Sprite Track" can also be linked to outside URLs. This means that if a movie contains several sprites (see the glossary), each sprite could be linked to a separate URL, like an imagemap inside a movie!

Multiple Data Rate Samples

The QuickTime plug-in has just become savvy about connection speeds! If you author and post multiple movies at different sizes, the browser can detect which one to display. This means that you could provide a large movie with a highdata rate for end users with T1 lines, and a smaller movie for 14.4 modem visitors. There is also an override feature, which enables someone on a slower connection to choose to view or download the bigger movie.

A free utility called **MakeRefMovie** (available for Macs and Windows) helps you easily author movies for multiple platforms. You can download this free software from http://www.apple.com/quicktime/developers/tools.html.

Also look to outside developers, such as **Adobe** (Premiere and After Effects) and **Terran Interactive** (Movie Cleaner Pro), for tools that render multiple movies at different sizes. This is a nice solution—if only Web images could easily take this same tack!

Large (least compressed)
(672 kBytes)

If you click on the bottom right arrow of a QuickTime movie in your browser, you can get the plug-in settings information.The next window prompts you to select a connection speed.

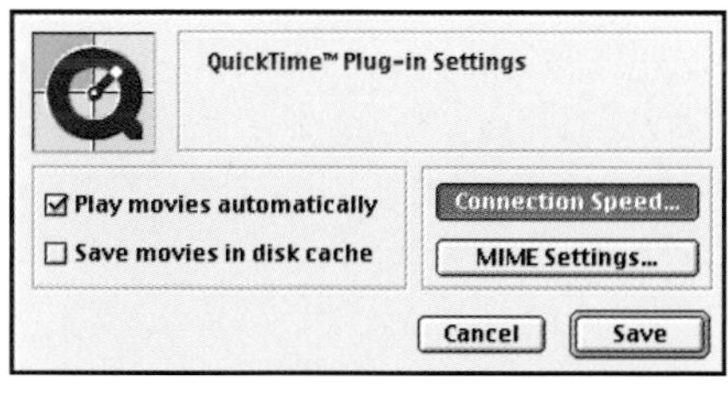

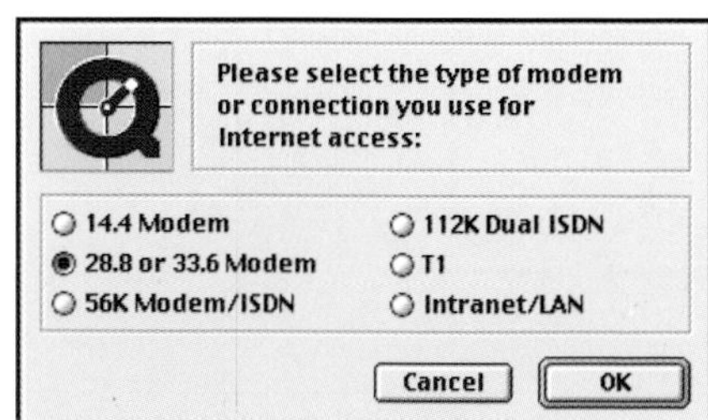

Which size movie is presented depends on your responses to these two dialog boxes.

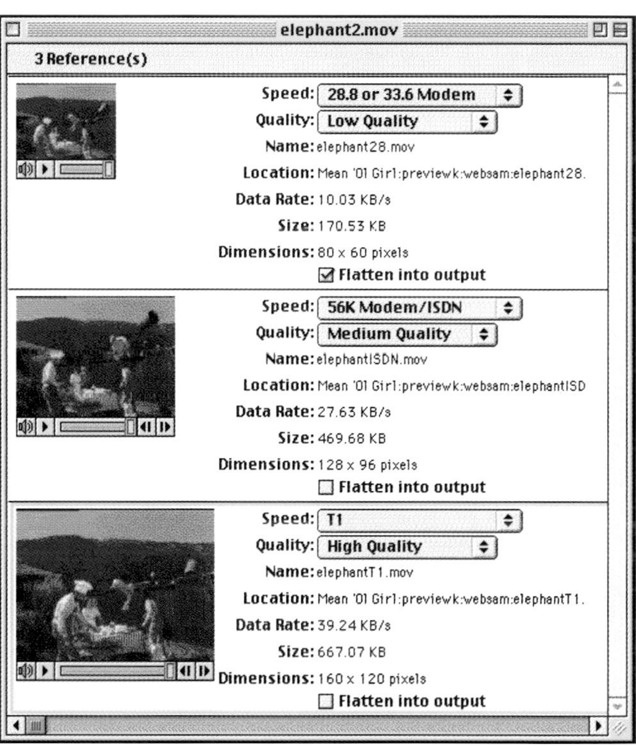

This shows the authoring tool **MakeRefMovie** and how it handles the creation of three different-sized reference movies.

Streaming (Sort Of)

QuickTime claims that it streams now. Well, it streams better than it did before, but the movie still has to download enough at the front end before it will display a single moving pixel. It's forgivable and definitely more livable than the previous version. QuickTime is able to achieve faster streaming through three newly supported codecs:

Sorenson Video is considered to be a replacement for Cinepak. It boasts much higher compression. A sample on the QT site showed a 6.7 second movie that was only 11k (although it had a lot of compression artifacts that weren't that attractive, imho). To buy the codec straight from Sorenson (http://www.s-vision.com/), the cost to developers is $499. Or, you could purchase the excellent MediaCleaner Pro Developer's Edition for $499, which includes the codec and MediaCleaner Pro, and is available at (http://www.terran.com).

QDMC (**Q** **D**esign **M**usic **C**odec) provides high-fidelity audio at greatly reduced bit-rates, giving Web publishers access to a level of audio compression for music unavailable anywhere else. I heard it at MacWorld, and it ruled (as I drooled). You can hear a sample at http://www.apple.com/quicktime/samples/stream/index.html#music.

QUALCOMM's PureVoice™ enables Web authors to publish voice-based content suitable for any modem connection speed. PureVoice compresses the spoken word, such as a newscast, to a compact digital format, yet still delivers an extremely high, nearly land-line voice quality experience for the listener. Look out RealAudio; this format sounds waaaay better for voice-overs and narration sound tracks. You can visit http://eudora.qualcomm.com/purevoice/ for more information.

Image Format Support

The QuickTime 2.0 plug-in supports the following file for- mats: BMP (Windows Bitmap), GIF, JFIF/JPEG, Mac-Paint, Photoshop, PNG, QuickDraw Picture (PICT), QuickDraw GX Picture, QuickTime Image File, Silicon Graphics Image File, Targa Image File, and TIFF. I was able to drag and drop a Photoshop image into my browser and see it for the first time on the Web. Oh joy! Note that all these formats need to be in RGB. It choked on my CMYK TIFFs.

DV Camcorder Support

QuickTime 3.0 enables you to takes DV video direct from a DV camcorder or DV recording deck and save it as a QuickTime movie. This is going to be awesome news to the zillions of consumers who are expected to run out and buy DV decks and cameras as soon as the prices fall lower. I'm sure there will be plenty of other issues, such as what firewire hardware and software, hard disk storage and speed specs, and authoring tools to buy. Nevertheless, it's cool in theory!

QTVR Support

It used to be that you needed an additional plug-in to view QuickTimeVR, a 360-degree panoramic movie format that can contain imagemap-like hyperlinks. The new QT2.0 plug-in will display QTVR movies now, too. Not only that, but the QTVR (http://www.apple.com/quicktime/samples/qtvr/) format capabilities have also improved. Check out their site!

Common QuickTime Commands	
HEIGHT WIDTH	Specifies the size of the movie in Web pages.
HIDDEN	Allows sound-only movies to play in the background without affecting the look of a Web page.
AUTOPLAY	Starts the movie playing automatically.
LOOP	Loops movie playback automatically.
CONTROLLER	Specifies whether or not to display the QuickTime movie controller bar.
HREF	Indicates which URL to link to when the movie is clicked.
TARGET	Provides a frame target for the URL, specified in an HREF tag.
CACHE	Indicates whether the movie should be cached (Netscape Navigator 3.0).
BGCOLOR	Sets a background color for the movie display.
SCALE	Scales the movie display automatically.
VOLUME	Sets the default playback volume (QuickTime VR only).
CORRECTION	Specifies this image Correction mode.
PAN	Sets the initial pan angle.
TILT	Sets the initial tilt angle.
FOV	Sets the initial field of view angle.
NODE	Sets the initial node.

Cons of QuickTime

QuickTime 3.0 still doesn't rival the streaming capabilities of RealVideo, NetShow, or Vxtreme for longer movies. If you want to do Webcasting, QT is not a contender. It is, however, a good choice for shorter movies under 10 minutes long (which includes the majority of Web video and audio content). In addition, it has a distinct advantage over those other guys: It is free and doesn't require any server-side proprietary software. All in all, QuickTime may give some of its streaming audio and video competitors a very hard run for their money.

Another difference between QT and other streaming technologies is the fact that it will not degrade according to modem speed. A QT movie is pre-rendered, and the image quality is what was rendered, not what the connection speed can support. This is both good and bad. It means that a certain level of quality is guaranteed. However, it can also mean that if there are connection bottlenecks, the file format might not perform responsively.

The QuickTime Developer's site (http://www.apple.com/quicktime/developers/tools.html) offers an impressive array of tips, techniques, HTML syntax and examples. If you want to learn how to program QuickTime 3.0 effects into your HTML, you won't want to miss this site.

Digital Video Terms Glossary

If you're new to digital video and sound terminology, you might need this handy glossary:

Codec: Software that translates video or audio between its uncompressed form and the compressed form in which it is stored. Two common video codecs are **Cinepak** and **Indeo**. A new codec of great interest to Web developers is **Sorenson**, which results in much smaller file sizes than Cinepak or Indeo. For a wonderful comparison of codecs: http://www.terran-int.com/CodecCentral/bigpic.html.

Data rates: Amount of information per second used to represent a movie. A single-speed CD-ROM movie would be created at a data rate of 100 Kilobytes per second (Kbps), whereas a movie for broadcast television would be created at 27 Megabytes per second (Mbps). The data rate is established when the movie is captured or recompressed.

Frames differencing: Frames that contain only changes from the previous frames. Some compression algorithms rely on frames differencing to achieve smaller file size.

Keyframes: If you author a QuickTime movie, you will set "keyframes." The keyframes could be considered the fixed non-changing points if the movie had to drop certain frames in order to play quickly enough. If you put in too many keyframes for the computer processor or Internet connection to handle, the movie will play slowly and will not look smooth or fluid.

DVD-ROM: A DVD-based alternative to the CD-ROM, which will hold up to 10 times the amount of current CD-ROM content.

Flattening: A post-processing pass that "flattens" the Mac resource fork of a QuickTime movie and makes the file cross-platform.

kHz: Kilohertz is the measure of audio samples per second (the equivalent of "data rate" for video). Higher sample rates yield better sound quality and larger file sizes.

Sample size: Audio sample sizes are generally 8-bit or 16-bit. The higher the bit depth, the better the sound and larger the file.

Sample rate: The number of samples per second for audio. The higher the sample rate, the larger the sound file.

Sprite: A QuickTime track that is made up of small graphic elements, which are assigned position and time information. A bouncing ball could be used as a sprite: Only the ball graphic and its location would be stored over time, instead of a series of full-frame images.

Streaming: Movie or audio data that is visible in real time while it is downloading.

Tracks: Different media types that compose a movie. A movie can include an audio and video track, or text tracks, sprite tracks, or midi tracks (and more varieties that are yet to come).

Transcode: Transferring one file format to another without recompressing the data. If you wanted to change an AVI movie into a Cinepak movie, you could transcode the data so it wouldn't have to be recompressed.

summary QuickTime 3.0

The latest QuickTime Web developments are welcome news to small publishers who can't afford proprietary server software and expensive solutions to movie authoring. The new feature set is filled with innovative ideas and interesting possibilities. It has been a pleasure to watch Web-based QuickTime come of age and to remember that it was just a tiny stuttering postage stamp a few short years ago. One can only imagine what to expect a few short years from now. Here's a review of this chapter:

- QuickTime comes pre-installed in all new browsers, making the plug-in barrier non-existent.
- You can author QuickTime movies by using a variety of free tools or any one of a number of high-end professional tools.
- You can visit the QuickTime developer's site for in-depth lessons on making QuickTime Web content.
- The new QuickTime 2.0 plug-in also supports QuickTime VR.

Introduction

Flash & Shockwave

Chapter Topics

- Plug-In Reliabilty
- Flash File Format
- Learning Flash
- HTML for Flash
- Shockwave Content
- Director 7
- Aftershock for Director & Flash

25

Plug-ins have been the only alternative to basic HTML for a long time. Things are progressing, however, and some plug-ins such as QuickTime, RealAudio, Shockwave, and Flash are preinstalled in newer browsers. In the case of Flash and Shockwave, the file format is now part of the newest Mac and PC operating systems, which means that for these products, future plug-ins at the browser level won't even be necessary.

Pioneering vendors like Macromedia have believed in an immersive Web experience similar to that of a movie or a CD-ROM and have pushed long and hard to create alternatives to the limitations of HTML. This chapter focuses on their two plug-in technologies of note: Flash and Shockwave.

Flash and Shockwave offer unparalleled amounts of interactivity and dynamic content. While this is exciting to all of us, plug-ins do have their dark side. Many end users resent having to download plug-ins and don't want to wait for movies or sounds to load in order to get to their beloved content. As with anything on the Web, one must carefully weigh the benefits and disadvantages of choosing the plug-in path.

Plug-In Reliance

Plug-ins are an outgrowth of a desire to extend basic HTML. They were introduced with Netscape 2.0, and today thousands of plug-ins are available for download. If you want to see one big list of all the plug-ins the Web has to offer, visit http://browserwatch.internet.com/plug-in.html/.

Plug-ins must be downloaded and installed by the end user. Some plug-ins download very quickly, but others do not. For installation, your end user must often quit his or her browser, install the plug-in, and relaunch the browser. Then he or she can locate your URL again to see your content. While this might not seem like a big deal to you as a Web developer, many end users aren't up for the task.

Newer browsers that support Java enable the end user to install or update plug-ins automatically without quitting the browser. If you've ever experienced this, it is a lot better than manual installation, but it still isn't pretty. Many people resent plug-ins, and plug-ins aren't appropriate for every type of site. As a rule, I think Flash and Shockwave are great for entertainment- and education-based sites. For information-based sites and commerce-based sites, I would be very careful not to impose unnecessary barriers that might prevent the reader from getting quickly to the content.

For the above reasons, I recommend that you don't require a plug-in for the very front page of your site. Give your end user the option of downloading the plug-in before entering, and even better, offer some alternative content in case she or he doesn't want to download it.

AOL users can't make the choice of whether or not to download a plug-in. While the plug-ins discussed in this chapter are available to AOL users who have the latest version installed, more obscure plug-ins are not.

If you want to use Shockwave or Flash on your site, you will need to educate yourself on plug-in management. I'm sure you've seen many sites on the Web that instruct users to get the plug-in before entering. Many of these sites present alternative content as well, which is recommended unless you have a controlled environment such as an intranet or extranet. In those cases, you can dictate the end user's software configuration and can ensure that she'll see the plug-in content.

Sending Visitors to Plug-In Pages

If your end user doesn't have the necessary plug-in, you can write HTML code that will send him to the appropriate page when he clicks on the broken plug-in icon.

For Flash:

```
<EMBED SRC="xxx.swf"
PLUGINSPAGE="http://www.macromedia.com/shockwave/download/"
TYPE="application/x-shockwave-flash" WIDTH="xx" HEIGHT="xx">
 </EMBED>
```

For Shockwave:

```
<EMBED SRC=".dcr"
PLUGINSPAGE="http://www.macromedia.com/shockwave/download/"
TYPE="application/x-director" WIDTH="xx" HEIGHT="xx">
 </EMBED>
```

Flash File Format

Flash was the first vector file format for the Web. As you learned in Chapter 5, "Web File Formats," vectors often offer much smaller file sizes than their bitmap counterparts. Because the vector format of Flash was developed specifically for online delivery, a Flash document can contain movement, interactivity, and sound, as well as static images, and can still be smaller than many standard HTML Web pages.

The caveats? First, the authoring tool needed to create Flash content has a high learning curve, and second, you still face the plug-in barrier (which we've already discussed). Fortunately, newer browsers are coming with Flash (and Shockwave) preinstalled, and the Flash/Shockwave Player is also now a part of Windows 98 and Mac OS 8.5. Recent announcements have also reported that AOL CD-ROM editions of their browser and @home networks will be distributing the Flash player. Also, beta Flash/Shockwave players for Linux and UNIX systems based on the Solaris operating system are available.

Overlooking the aforementioned drawbacks, some of the most exciting sites on the Web today are being created using Flash. One of the really cool things about Flash is that it is resolution independent. This means that it can be scaled to play back large on a 1,024×768 monitor or small on a 640×480 system.

You would set up the HTML for Flash content to scale to the browser with this HTML code:

```
<EMBED SRC="xxx.swf" WIDTH="100%" HEIGHT="100%">
```

The percentages tell the browser to display the content at 100% of its size, and the vector artwork renders out at whatever size the browser window appears.

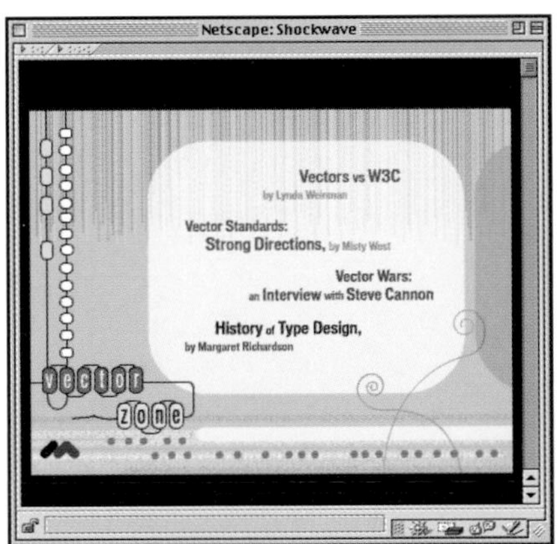

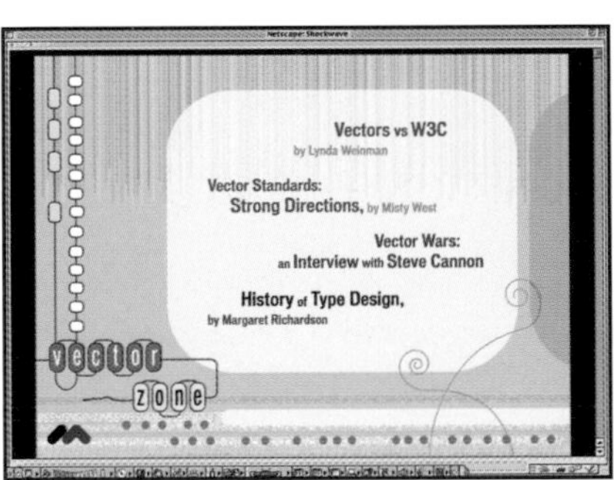

This page from the excellent and informative site http://www.vectorzone.com can be seen in two sizes here. The vector content scales to fit the browser window.

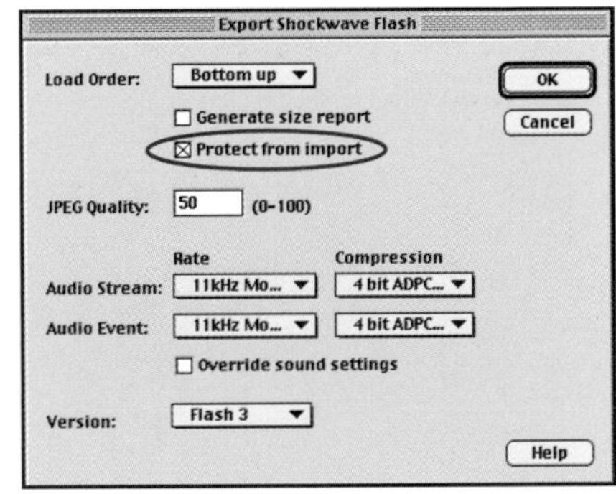

Another really cool thing about Flash is that, unlike HTML content, you can lock people out from viewing the source files. When you're exporting Flash content, you can check **Protect from Import**, and Flash will be unable to reopen the .SWF file.

Learning Flash

Learning Flash can be challenging (it was for me!). But once you know it, like anything you know in life, it becomes a lot easier to use. I'll share a few of the basics with you in this chapter, but the best way to learn is to download the product and dive right in.

The file format for a Flash project is .FLA, and the file format for a flash Web movie is .SWF. If you view the source of a page and see that it includes a SRC="xxx.swf" file, you will know it's Flash content instead of HTML content. A short overview of the authoring tool follows.

Flash Resources

Learning Flash
VHS or PAL Video
Lynda Weinman
http://www.lynda.com/video/
2 hours

Flash 3—Creative Web Animation
Darryl Plant
Peachpit Press
ISBN 0-201-35368-7
$29.99

Web Sites
http://www.vectorzone.com
http://www.flasher.net/flashpad.html
http://www.users.bigpond.com/xtian/welcomenew.html

Drawing in Flash

Flash is unlike any other vector program you've ever used, so it's best to clear your mind of any preconceptions, such as the way FreeHand, Illustrator, or CorelDraw create vector artwork. When you draw, your artwork replaces what's there (like what you would find in a traditional bitmap-oriented drawing program); it doesn't draw a separate stroke.

Flash defines shapes by color. If you paint with one color over another, it will actually divide the image with the new color. If you draw on a separate layer, your artwork won't intersect with the artwork on the other layers. Coloring artwork involves using different tools, and which you use depends on whether the artwork is a stroke, a fill, text, or a Symbol.

Scenes and Symbols

When you first open Flash, you will find yourself in the Main Scene area of the program. In order to create content, you will need to generate or import artwork, media, and sound elements. The program ships with libraries of buttons, graphics, and movies. These are located under the Libraries menu. If you create your own Symbols (more on this later), you will create your own library items. Those personal library items will be stored under the **Window: Library** menu.

To access the default Symbol libraries, go to the Libraries menu.

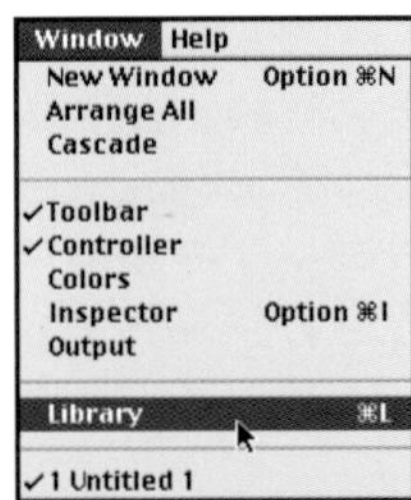

If you want to access a Symbol library you've created, go to the Window menu and select **Library**.

Symbols: Symbols are objects that you will be able to use over and over, and they will save file space. There are also certain features in Flash, such as motion tweening (animating scale, rotation, and color effect), that can be applied only to Symbols.

Making Symbols

There are three types of Symbols: graphics, buttons, and movie clips. Each is described in the following list. To create a Symbol, select **Insert:Create Symbol**.

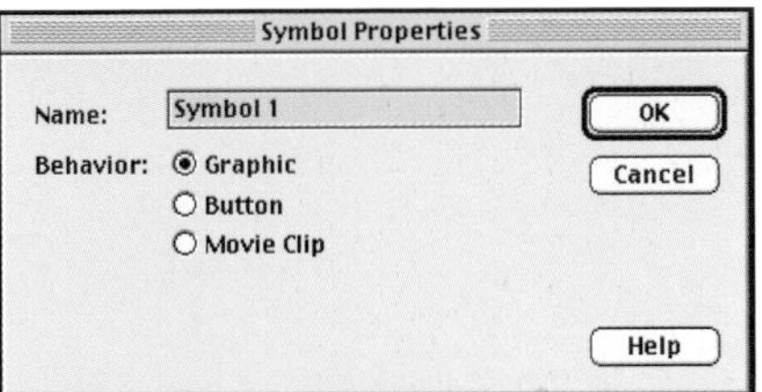

Graphic Symbol: Can be used for static or moving images.

Button Symbol: Has behavior states associated with it, such as a rollover. It can also be assigned "actions" (such as stop, play, go to, and load movie), which make Flash movies interactive.

Movie Clip Symbol: Can animate independently of the timeline of the Scene/Symbol it is placed in. If you wanted to build an animated rollover, for example, it would include a movie clip. You can also assign actions within movie clips.

Managing Symbols and Scenes

Symbols and scenes appear as tabs along the side of your screen. It is possible to have an unlimited number of Symbols and scenes.

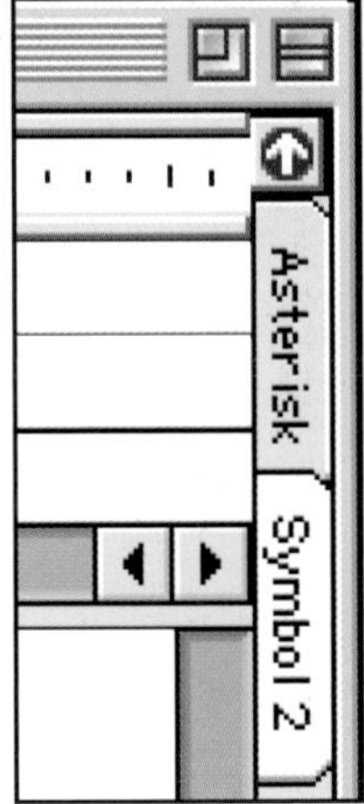

Click on the arrow above the Symbol tab to return to the scene.

Timeline and Keyframes

Learning to use the timeline involves working with artwork or Symbols, setting up keyframes, and tweening.

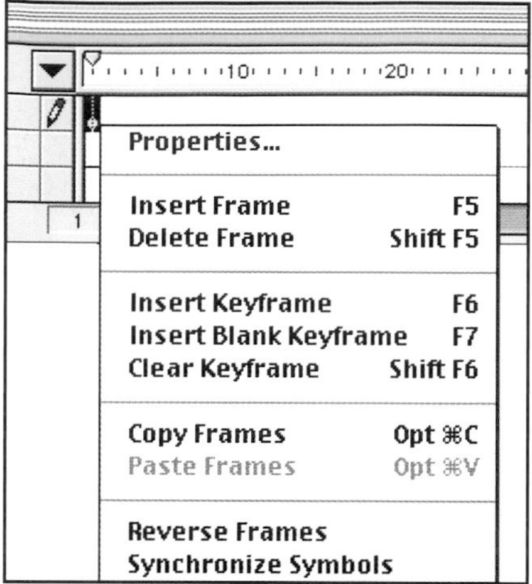

In order to work with the timeline, you have to either Control-click or click and hold the mouse down on a timeline frame (**Mac**) or right-click on a frame (**PC**) to access the pop-up menu shown above.

This pop–up menu offers the following commands:

Insert Frame: Create a new frame.

Insert Keyframe: Insert a frame that will signify a change in the animation.

Insert Blank Keyframe: Create an empty keyframe.

Tweening is a process that takes two keyframes and interpolates their movements. (This is very similar in principle to the tweening I wrote about in Chapter 21, "GIF Animation.")

Rollover Buttons

You already know how to make rollovers with JavaScript, but you can make rollovers in Flash, too. Here's how:

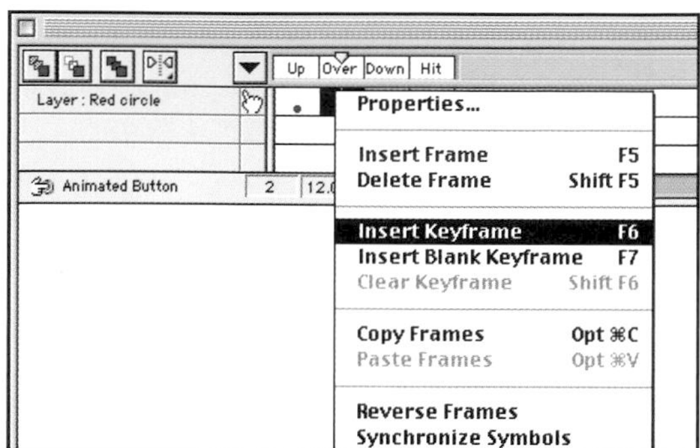

Step 1: Choose **Insert:Create Symbol:Button**. The button Symbol automatically generates four states: Up, Over, Down, and Hit.

Step 2: Draw something on the **Up** state. Click in the **Over** state area and choose Insert Keyframe.

Step 3: Draw something new on this frame.

Step 4: Click in the **Down** state area, choose **Insert Keyframe**, and draw something on that frame.

Step 5: When you finish, return to the Stage by clicking on the arrow above the Symbols tab.

Note: The **Hit** state is invisible; it's the region that defines the "hot" part of the graphic (similar to an image-map region in HTML). Because the end user won't ever see the **Hit** state, it doesn't matter what colors you use. But remember to think of it in terms of what makes the button turn on and off. Whatever you draw in the **Hit** state turns the button on when a user places his cursor over it on a Web page.

Step 6: Drag this new button Symbol onto the Stage. Under the Control menu, choose **Enable Buttons**. Now Position your mouse over your new button and try it out!

Add a Sound to the Button

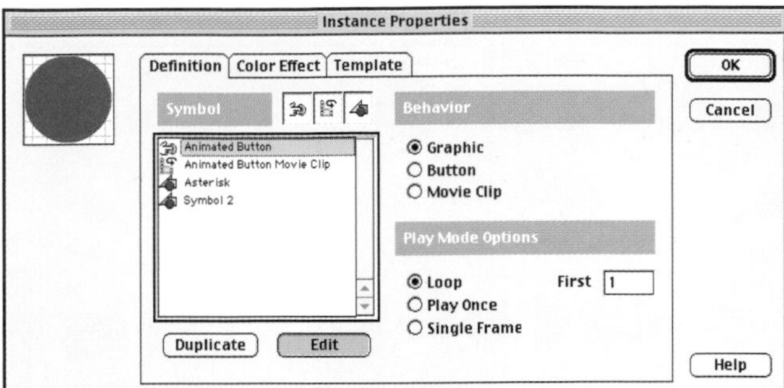

Step 1: Open the button library that ships with Flash by selecting **Library:Buttons**. Drag a button from the Buttons library into an empty scene. Double-click on the button item to open instance properties of that button, and then click the **Edit** button on the Definition tab to edit it.

Step 2: Select **Libraries:Sound**. Play the sound files until you find one you want. Move the playback head of your button timeline to whichever state you want the sound to play on (Up, Over, Down, or Hit) and drag it onto the artwork for the Symbol. **Note:** Make sure you have a current layer selected in the button Symbol's layers list (as indicated by a pencil icon next to the frames in the timeline).

Step 3: Use your cursor to click and drag the image of the sound waves from the Sounds library's preview window to the drawing area of the button you are currently editing. When you release the mouse button to drop the sound onto the drawing area, Flash adds that sound to the current keyframe in the timeline.

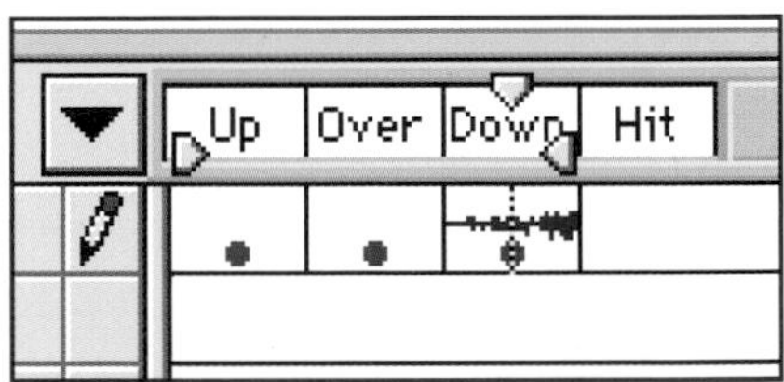

Step 4: You should see the sound waves on that frame as shown above. Double-click the **keyframe** to open the Frame Properties dialog box. Click on the **Sound** tab to check to see if it loaded.

Step 5: Return to the Stage and choose **Control:Enable Buttons** if it is not already checked. Try your button. It should have sound now.

Interactivity in Flash

Flash offers various levels of interactivity from simple to complex. It contains pre-built scripts that are accessible from the Actions palette. You can apply actions to frames (for example, telling frames in the timeline to play, go to a specific frame, or stop) or to button Symbols (for example, telling a Symbol to play or stop).

You can work with Actions in Flash in a variety of ways.

Actions in Flash include the following:

Go To: Can instruct the timeline to advance to a specific frame or label (marker).

Play: Plays the timeline.

Stop: Stops the timeline.

Toggle High Quality: Turns quality settings on and off.

Stop All Sounds: Does what the name says!

Get URL: If you assign a URL to a Flash button, clicking it in the Web browser will trigger the Web page.

FS Command: Enables a variety of JavaScript commands that work with Flash.

Load Movie: It is possible to load Flash movies within Flash movies.

Unload Movie: You can also unload Flash movies within Flash movies.

Tell Target: You can give a movie within Flash a name and add actions to that name (target).

If Frame Is Loaded: This allows the program to monitor whether images have loaded or not, so developers can give feedback to the end user about whether or not the file has finished downloading.

On MouseEvent: You can program your own rollover behaviors in Flash.

Flash Web Integration

Loading Flash movies into HTML is not terribly involved. In the most simple example, you could load a .SWF file into an HTML document using the embed or object tag. Dreamweaver 2.0 integration with Flash is excellent; there's even a Flash icon on the Object bar in Dreamweaver!

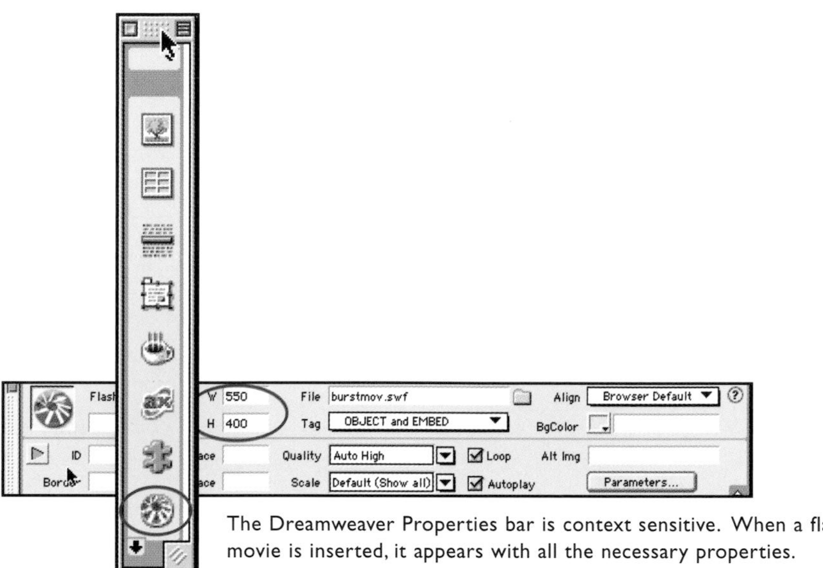

The Dreamweaver Properties bar is context sensitive. When a flash movie is inserted, it appears with all the necessary properties.

A Flash object (.SWF file) can be inserted easily into a Dreamweaver document by clicking the button marked above.

If you wanted to set the movie to fill the browser screen, for example, you would simply set the **W** (width) and **H** (height) cells to 100%.

You might want to set the Quality to High instead of Auto High because it will take less time to render on slower systems.

Dreamweaver automatically writes the following code:

```
<OBJECT CLASSID="clsid:D27CDB6E-AE6D-11cf-96B8-444553540000"
CODEBASE="http://download.macromedia.com/pub/shockwave/cabs/flash/swflash.cab#3,
0,0,0" WIDTH="550" HEIGHT="400">
 <PARAM NAME="SRC" VALUE="burstmov.swf">
 <PARAM NAME="QUALITY" VALUE="high">
 <EMBED SRC="burstmov.swf"
PLUGINSPAGE="http://www.macromedia.com/shockwave/download/" TYPE="application/
x-shockwave-flash" WIDTH="550" HEIGHT="400" QUALITY="high">
 </EMBED>
</OBJECT>
```

HTML Frames with SWF

In certain instances, such as with framesets, it's important that you define your site's structure before finalizing your .SWF file. If, for example, you have created a nav bar and you want to load other movies into named frame regions, you have to set up the target information in Flash before saving your movie. To do this, you have to have a master plan of how you were going to name your frameset.

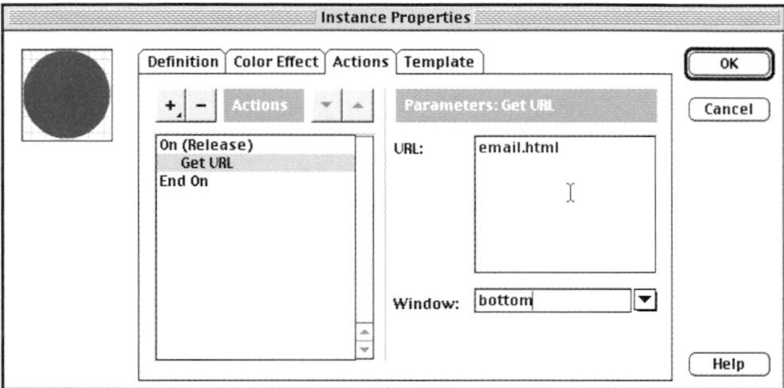

Double-click on the **nav bar** button in question to launch the Instances Properties dialog box. Click on **Actions**, and then choose **Get URL**.

It's important that you know, for example, the name of your target and the name of the HTML document to which you are linking. Be sure to save the file as a .FLA so you can open it again to make a change to the URL setting if you have to make a new .SWF file. The URL and target information is embedded into the Flash document. If you decide to change your site's structure and need to rename the **Get URL** information, you must re-access the project.

Shockwave Content

Macromedia Director has been around almost as long as personal computers have. Among most professionals, it's considered the premiere authoring tool for multimedia content, and it boasts more than 300,000 registered users. A few years ago, Shockwave was developed as a means of distributing Director movies over the Web.

Director is a very deep program that contains its own scripting language called Lingo. It has much deeper interactivity than Flash, in that complex "if" and "and" statements can be used to program all kinds of deep-level interactivity, such as that you might find in a game or a training application. Again, like Flash, Director has a high learning curve. This does not mean it's bad or something to be avoided, it just means that you wouldn't necessarily make a casual decision to use it on your site.

The thing about multimedia is that what looks simple to the end user is generally very difficult to create. It's one of the great ironies in this type of work. Although it's totally possible to program small interactive pieces in Director, most large projects are developed by teams of people.

Saving Shockwave Files

You can save Director content for Web delivery by exporting it as a Shockwave movie. This file format uses the .DCR extension.

When I saved a simple animation created in Director, it automatically created the following code:

```
<OBJECT CLASSID="clsid:166B1BCA-3F9C-11CF-8075-444553540000" CODE-
BASE="http://download.macromedia.com/pub/shockwave/cabs/director/
sw.cab#version=7,0,0,0" WIDTH="640" HEIGHT="480">
        <PARAM NAME="src" VALUE="hello.dcr">
 <EMBEDSRC="hello.dcr" PLUGINSPAGE="http://www.macromedia.com/
shockwave/download/" WIDTH="640" HEIGHT="480"></EMBED>
 </OBJECT>
```

Intro to Director 7

Macromedia Director's initial focus was multimedia for disk-based delivery. Eventually, when CD-ROMs came of age, Director became the premiere authoring tool for interactive content.

Director is based on a variety of interface elements that all work together. As the program has matured, so have its capabilities. This product is now one of the richest multimedia applications in the world. The interface is described in the next section, which shows how the different areas work together.

Over the years, the emphasis on CD-ROM delivery has shifted towards online delivery. Director 7 is the first version of this product to be predominantly oriented towards Web delivery—yet it is still capable of creating CD-ROM and DVD titles as well.

The learning curve for Director is both easy and steep. This is an incredibly deep program, but some of its features are so easy to learn that you can get instant gratification for creating animation and interactive content.

The real powerhouse lies in Director's scripting capabilities. Depending on what level programmer you are, you can write entire CD-ROM or Web-based applications in Director that are incredibly complex. If you have only simple ideas and simple skills however, the product is still within your reach.

Director Interface

Director is based on a variety of concepts and interface elements. A pictorial overview follows:

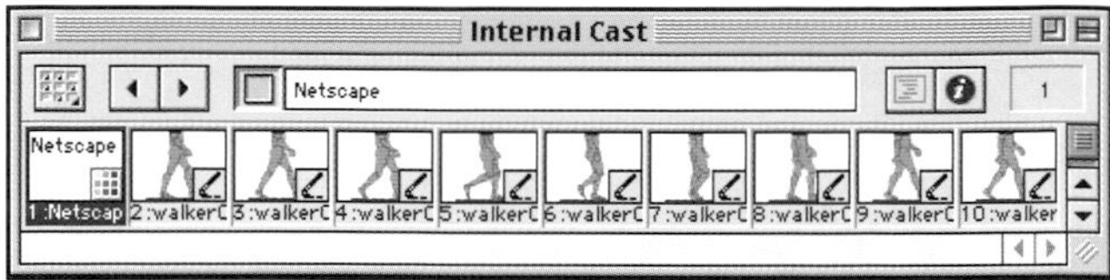

The **Cast** is where artwork, sounds, animations, and media are stored for projects.

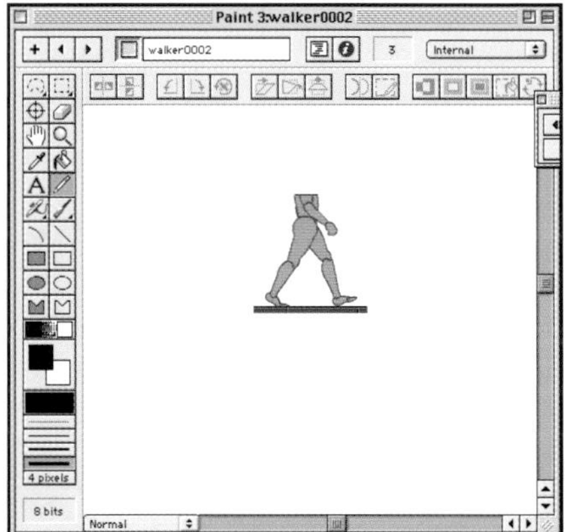

A **Paint Interface** enables you to create artwork from scratch or edit imported artwork.

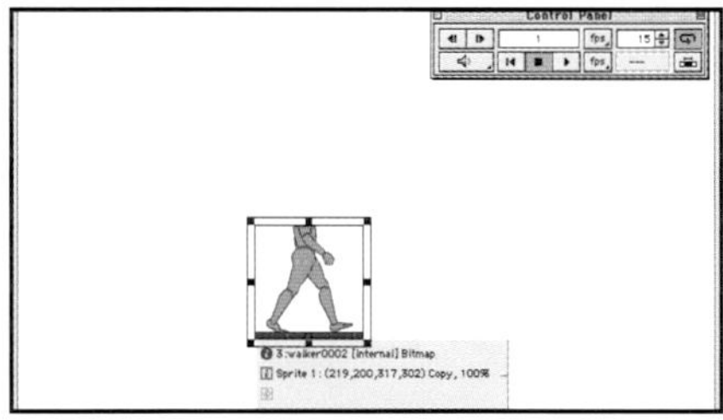

The **Stage** is where movies are composed. Artwork from the cast is placed here, and when the artwork is highlighted, Director offers information about its properties.

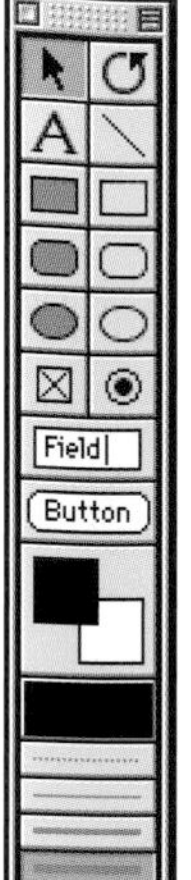

The **Tool Palette** offers primitive shapes and buttons (similar to HTML forms) with which you can draw directly on the stage. If you want to create artwork that is more complex than simple shapes and lines, it's best to import artwork that you've created elsewhere or to draw the artwork in the Paint or Vector Paint window.

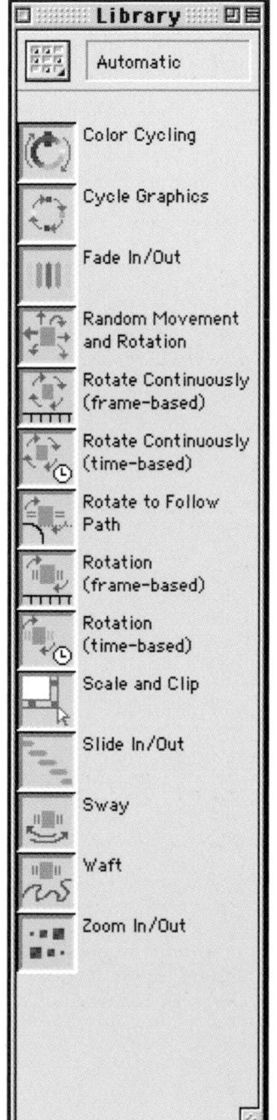

The **Library Palette** is new to Director 7. It allows you to assign properties to artwork or animations by dragging and dropping them onto the stage.

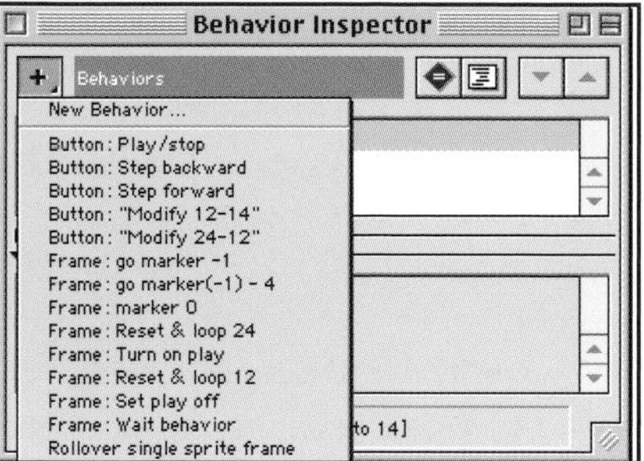

The **Behavior Inspector** offers another easy way to assign properties to artwork or animation.

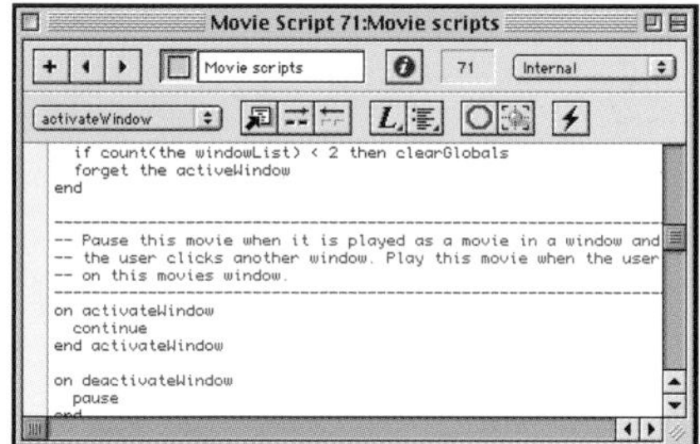

The **Script Window** is where Lingo is written. Lingo is Director's proprietary scripting language that is used to program interactivity.

Note: Director now allows you to draw vector artwork inside a new Vector Paint window. These shapes remain vectors (similar to Flash content) on the Web. For some types of artwork, vectors will be much smaller in file size than bitmaps are.

New Web Features

As stated earlier, Director 7 focuses on Web delivery more than any other version of the product. Here is a list of new Internet features:

Shockwave 7: Director projects that are destined for the Web are turned into Shockwave movies. There's even a part of the Macromedia site called "Shocked Site of the Day," which refers to this process. To view Shockwave content, you or your end user must have the Shockwave plug-in installed. Director 7 installs this plug-in at the system level instead of the browser level. This means that updates for future versions can be automatically received, so you don't have to intentionally download and install them. Presumably, this is a much less intrusive way to deliver the plug-in.

Save As Java: You can now save Director projects as Java applets, and the program ships with a variety of Java behaviors as well.

XML Support: You can import XML data into Director, and you can script its contents with Lingo.

Multiuser Server: Director ships with a multiuser server, which enables users to create and distribute chat environments, white boards, and shared Web navigation.

Internet Protocol Support: Built-in support for HTTP, FTP, HTTPS, and CGI Post. This means that you can build e-commerce applications or Web applications right in Director. This also means that you can create hyperlinks to any Web page within a Director movie.

Internet Behavior Library: Many Lingo commands are now available from a library palette, which means that manual scripting can be replaced by the dragging and dropping of library elements.

Shocked CD Creation: You can create CD-ROM or DVD content that connects and interacts with the Web.

Preview in Browser: You can preview your Director movies in a browser now. Simply choose **Edit:Preview in Browser**, and Director automatically generates a Shockwave movie and the HTML code to present the movie within a browser.

Improved Streaming: The Shockwave player was rewritten to allow for much faster playback in a browser.

Selective Bitmap Compression: Either you can preserve compression settings from Fireworks content (Fireworks ships with Director 7), or selectively compress bitmap cast members that are present in your project.

Shocked Fonts: Director embeds any typeface you choose from your computer's system and compresses it 75% to 85% smaller than any TrueType font.

Aftershock for Director and Flash

After you create a Director or Flash movie, you need to generate an HTML document in order to run your movie in a browser.

Macromedia's Aftershock utility creates HTML files that display Shockwave movies, Flash player movies, Java applets, or JPEGs. Use the Aftershock interface to set all of the possible parameters for the OBJECT and EMBED tags that make the browser display a movie.

You can also use Aftershock to do the following:

Add a movie to or update the OBJECT and EMBED parameters in an HTML document that has already been converted by Aftershock.

Create a script to detect when the appropriate Shockwave plug-in or ActiveX control is missing and then either download or display a JPEG or Java applet instead of the movie.

Create a cookie that allows visitors to choose how to view your movies.

Create or update multiple HTML files that contain Director Shockwave or Flash player movies. Generate lists of the text and URLs used in the movie so that search engines can index the text and link verification tools can verify the links.

Aftershock is a post-processing application that enables you to convert Director content to Shockwave content. It offers a lot more controls than simply the **File:Save** as Shockwave command.

When you finish, you can still use HTML to modify the HTML document generated by Aftershock.

summary Flash & Shockwave

Macromedia has made the leap from the print age into the Web age. It has created two products that are extremely useful for the Web, though it has bypassed standard HTML in order to extend its limits. This makes Flash and Director content harder to see than HTML, but it also makes a compelling case for the use of plug-ins. Here's a review of key elements of this chapter:

- Don't include Flash or Shockwave content on a front page without warning your visitors. If they don't have the necessary plug-in, they won't get to see the content.
- Remember to include code in your Flash or Shockwave content that can send your end users to the correct page at Macromedia to download the plug-in if they don't have it.
- The Flash file format can be much smaller than many bitmap formats, such as JPEG and GIF files.
- Flash enables a high level of interactivity, which is more powerful than what HTML affords.
- Director uses Lingo, a proprietary scripting language with which you can build complex Web or multimedia applications.

Introduction

HTML for Visual Designers

Chapter Topics

- HTML Naming Protocols
- Common File Extensions
- Relative Versus Absolute Paths
- HTML Troubleshooting
- Checking
- Uploading
- Common Tags & Elements

26

This chapter is intended to serve as a quick reference for your HTML needs. It is not a definitive HTML reference; it's sole purpose is to help with quick questions or to remind you how to code something.

Why is it called for "visual designers"? Because these are the most commonly used tags and attributes for creating visual layouts. The focus here is on layout, color, tables, frames, targets, and linking elements.

This is also where I've stuck a lot of short HTML tips. Feel free to read through the chapter, skip around, or save it for when you need it.

HTML Naming Protocols

Spaces in file names will result in broken links. If you have spaces between the title of your document, as in my document name.extension, either string the name together as in mydocumentname.extension or use underscores as in my_document_name.extension.

If you are working with files that are going to be downloaded by your audience, such as audio and video files, remember to abbreviate names so that they contain eight characters or less in the main title, and leave room for a period and three-letter extension such as mydocunm.ext. This is called the 8.3 (eight dot three) convention, and will be a courtesy to your visitors who are using Windows 3.1 or earlier, which did not support longer file names.

Common File Names

You must give images and media the proper file name extensions so the browser reading your HTML can display them properly. The following is a list of the most common file types.

File Extensions	
Name	**Extension**
HTML text document	.html, htm
JPEG	.jpg
GIF	.gif
QuickTime	movie.mov, .qt
Shockwave	.dcr
Flash	.swf
Video for Windows	.avi
MPEG Video	.mpg
MPEG Audio	.mp2
AU/μlaw	.au
AIFF/AIFC	.aiff
WAV	.wav

Relative Versus Absolute Path Names

An absolute path name gives the entire http header information, such as http://www.lynda.com/image.gif. This would instruct a server to locate my domain and find an image inside the main directory folder of my site.

If I know someone is already linked into my site, however, I do not need to give them all that same information. I could write a link that requested image.gif. This tells the file to look for the image.gif within the current directory.

Some people have messy rooms and offices, and others are neat. I fall in the first category and have been known to build an entire site leaving every file in one folder. This is not the best way to work, but it does work! The better, more organized way would be to have folders for different areas of the site. Here are some example scenarios:

In our **first scenario**, this is what existed on my site:

```
index.html
image1.gif
page2.html
other.gif
goodbye.html
last.gif
```

If I wanted to link from index.html to page2.html, I could write "page2.html" into my document and the file would be found. If I wanted to link to an image, I could write "last.gif" and the image would be found:

In our **second scenario**, everything is organized into neat folders

folder1
```
   index.html
   image1.gif
```
folder2
```
   page2.html
   other.gif
```
folder3
```
   goodbye.html
   last.gif
```

If I wanted to link index.html to page2.html, I would need to write the following:

```
"../folder2/page2.html"
```

Notice how the request included two dots and a slash (../)? This told the HTML to jump outside the folder that index.html was in and go inside another folder.

In the **third scenario**, let's imagine I have everything loaded into neat folders but my index.html is sitting in the root directory:

```
index.html
```

folder1
```
   image1.gif
```
folder2
```
   page2.html
   other.gif
```
folder3
```
   goodbye.html
   last.gif
```

If I wanted index.html to link to page2.html, it would look like this:

```
folder2/page2.html
```

It doesn't require the (../) this time because **index.html** is sitting in the root directory. It can go inside the **folder2** directory to find **page2.html** because of the slash dividing them.

Troubleshooting

If your page tested properly off your local hard drive but not when you posted the files to the server, make sure the file names you requested in your HTML match the names of the actual document. Unix is case-sensitive, meaning if your file is saved **JPG** and your HTML calls for it as **jpg**, the code will not be able to read the file. Because your local files are most likely not on a Unix platform, this problem will not surface until you post your files and view them from a browser.

If your file is named jamie.gif and your HTML reads <IMG SRC="jamie.GIF">, it won't work! Redo the IMG SRC tag to read <IMG SRC="jamie.gif">.

note

Checking Your Pages

You should always check your pages from your hard drive before you post them to your server. This way you will catch a lot of HTML and artwork mistakes before the rest of the world knows you made them. To test local files from your hard drive, open your browser and then open your HTML ascii (text only) file from there. All the images should load in properly and give an accurate preview of what your page will look like once it's on the Web. The only types of files that will not preview properly are those that require server-side code, such as server-side push, server-side imagemaps, CGI forms processing, and server-side include tags.

Uploading Your Pages

Most likely, you'll need a password and authorization name to access either your, or your client's, Web server. This would be obtained from your online service provider or your client.

Whenever you transfer elements for a Web page to your server, remember:

- Transfer the HTML document as Text Only (ascii).
- Transfer the image, sound, and movie files as Raw Data on Macs and as Image or Binary mode on PCs.
- The Basic Structure of an HTML Document:

```
<HTML>
   <HEAD>
     <TITLE><META>
   </HEAD>
   <BODY> or <BODY BGCOLOR><BODY BACKGROUND><BODY TEXT>
     Body of the document
     (all the text, images, links, etc.)
   </BODY>
</HTML>
```

- HTML is not case sensitive (upper- and lowercase). The tag HTML will be just as effective as the tag html.
- Always save an HTML document in **Text Only mode** (ascii) with the extension .html or .htm at the end.

Common HTML Tags

The following table shows the various HTML tags and what they are used for. The table is divided into sections containing HTML tag information for the various tag types:

Head Tags

Tag	Description
<HEAD></HEAD>	Enables you to use a HEADLINE or TITLE tag within the document.
<H#></H#>	Enables you to set sizes inside header tags (H1, H2, H3).
<TITLE></TITLE>	Enables you to name the HTML document. Whatever you put inside this tag will show up in the title bar of your browser.
META HTTP-EQUIV="refresh" CONTENT=# URL=#	Allows you to perform client pull effects where you automatically send your viewers to another URL without them having to request it.
META NAME="keywords" CONTENT="x"	Allows you to insert keyword information about your site to help search engines know how to categorize it.
META NAME="description" CONTENT="x"	Allows you to write a 10-word sentence description of your site for search engines to read.

Body Tags

Tag	Description
BODY bgcolor=link= #alink=#vlink=#	The following tags allow you to change the colors of your background, text, links and so on in browsers that support it.
TEXT="#xxxxxx"	Sets text color.
LINK="#xxxxxx"	Sets link colors for text and borders around images.
ALINK="#xxxxxx"	Sets the link color when the mouse is clicked in the down position.
VLINK="#xxxxxx"	Sets the visited link color for text and borders around images.
BODY BACKGROUND	Allows you to load tiled background patterns into your Web pages.

Alignment Tags and Attributes for Text

Tag	Description
<CENTER></CENTER>	Centers text or images inside this tag.

Text Tags

Tag	Description
<STRONG></STRONG>	Makes text bold.
<B></B>	Makes text bold.
<EM></EM>	Italicizes type.
<I></I>	Italicizes type.
<PRE></PRE>	Allows you to work with pre-formatted type.
<CODE></CODE>	Used for computer codes.
 	Denotes a line break.
<P>	Denotes a paragraph break.
<FONT SIZE=#></FONT>	Enables you to change font sizes.
<TT></TT>	Denotes the typewriter style (monospaced font).
<FONT COLOR=#></FONT>	Sets the color of type.

Horizontal Rule Tags

Tag	Description
<HR>	Creates a standard embossed horizontal rule.
<HR WIDTH=#>	Changes the length in pixels.
<HR SIZE=#>	Changes the height in pixels.
<HR WIDTH=# ALIGN= "left, right, or center">	Aligns a horizontal rule that's shorter than the distance of your entire page.
<HR NOSHADE>	Creates a plain black line.

Linking Tags and Attributes

Tag	Description
<A></A>	Anchors text.
<A HREF="URL"></A>	Links the image or text to an URL.

Alignment Tags and Attributes for Images

Tag	Description
<IMG SRC="#" ALIGN= "top, middle, bottom, left, right">	Aligns text to the top, middle, bottom, left, or right of the image inside this tag.

Image Tags

Tag	Description
<IMG SRC="#">	Contains an image.
<IMG SRC="#" ALT="#">	Contains an image and a text description for viewers who don't have graphical Web browsers.
<IMG SRC="#" HEIGHT=# WIDTH=#>	Allows for specifying image dimensions and causes the HTML text to load before large graphics.
<A HREF="#"><IMG SRC= "#"></A>	Contains a linked image and automatically generates a border around the image in whatever link color has been specified.
<A HREF="#"><IMG SRC="#" BORDER=0></A>	Ensures that there's no border on browsers that support this feature.
<A HREF="#"><IMG SRC="#" BORDER=#></A>	Depending on the value, puts a heavier or lighter border around the linked image.

List Tags and Attributes

Tag	Description
<UL>	Unordered list: Generates an indented list with bullets.
<OL>	Ordered list: Generates numbers in front of list.
<LI>	Puts a bullet in front of each item, indents the text, and creates a line break at the end of each item.
<DL>	Definition list: Produces an indented list with no bullets.
<DD>	Produces items in a definition list.

Comments Tag

Tag	Description
<!... >	Sets comments that appear as notes for the HTML document but won't show up on the actual Web page.

Table Tags

Tag	Description
<TABLE></TABLE>	Put at the beginning and end of tables.
<TH></TH>	Makes bold text or numbers and accepts table attributes.
<TD></TD>	Includes text, numbers, or images and accepts table attributes.

Table Tags and Attributes

Tag	Description
ALIGN="left, right, or center"	Aligns text or images in table.
VALIGN="top middle, bottom, or baseline"	Vertically aligns text or images in table.
ROWSPAN=#	Denotes the number of rows in a table.
COLSPAN=#	Denotes the number of columns in a table.
WIDTH=#	Specifies the width of the table by pixels.
CELLPADDING=#	Sets the space between the border and content of table.
CELLSPACING=#	Adjusts the thickness of the borders.

Frames Tags and Attributes

Tag	Description
<FRAMESET></FRAMESET>	Initiates frames.
COLS	Specifies the numbers of columns and widths in a frameset.
ROWS	Specifies the rows and their height in a frameset.
SCROLLING	Turn on or off scrolling when content is larger than the frame.
TARGET	Lets you set _blank, _self, _parent, or _top attributes.
FRAMEBORDER	Allows you to turn borders on or off.

notes

Designing Web Graphics.3

Introduction

Web Graphics Resources

Here is a collection of my favorite design resources for web and graphics. I hope this is something helpful that you can refer to when in need.

Chapter Topics

- Design Conferences
- Digital Arts Programs
- Web Galleries
- Design Magazines
- Helpful URLs

27

Design Conferences

American Center for Design
http://www.ac4d.org

Web Design and Development
http://www.mfiweb.com

International Design Conference
http://www.idca.org

TED
http://www.ted.com/

MacWorldExpo
http://www.macworldexpo.com/Seybold
http://www.seyboldseminars.com/

SIGGRAPH
http://www.siggraph.org/

Thunder Lizard
http://www.thunderlizard.com

Lynda.com Conferences
http://www.lynda.com/conferences/

Doors of Perception
http://www.doorsofperception.com

HOW Design Conference
http://www.howdesign.com/conference/index.htm

Milia
http://www.milia.com/flash.htm

CNET's builder.com Conference
http://www.builder.com/web.builder/

Macromedia Usercon
http://www.macromedia.com/macromedia/events/

AIGA Conferences
http://www.aiga.org/gr8/conferences.cfm

BDA Conferences
http://www.bdaweb.com/

Digital Art Programs

Art Center College of Design
(Pasadena, California)
http: //www.artcenter.edu/

California College of Arts and Crafts
(Oakland and San Francisco, California)
http://www.ccacsf.edu/

California Institute of the Arts
(Valencia, California)
http://www.calarts.edu/

College of Art and Design
(Detroit, Michigan)
http://www.ccscad.edu/

Cooper Union
(New York City, New York)
http://www.cooper.edu/

Emily Carr Institute of Art and Design
(Vancuouver, British Columbia)
http://www.eciad.bc.ca/

Herron School of Art
(Indianapolis, Indiana)
http://www.herron.iupui.edu/

Utrecht
(Netherlands)
http://www.hku.nl/

Interactive Telecommunications Program
(New York City, New York)
http://itp.nyu.edu/

MIT Media Lab
(Boston, Massachuset)
http://www.media.mit.edu/

Maryland Institute of Art
(Baltimore, Maryland)
http://www.mica.edu/

Minneapolis College of Art and Design
(Minneapolis, Minnesota)
http://www.mcad.edu/

Otis Institute of Art
(Los Angeles, California)
http://www.otisart.edu/

Parsons School of Art
(New York City, New York)
http: //www.parsons.edu/

Portfolio Center
(Atlanta, Georgia)
http://www.portfoliocenter.com/welcome.html

Pratt College
(Brooklyn and Manhattan, NY)
http://www.pratt.edu/

Rhode Island School of Design
(Providence, Rhode Island)
http://www.pratt.edu/

Royal College of Art
(London, England)
http://www.rca.ac.uk/

School of Visual Arts
(New York, New York)
http://www.schoolofvisualarts.edu/

Creative Circus
(Atlanta, Georgia)
http://www.creativecircus.com/

Acadamy of Art College
(San Francisco, California)
http://www.academyart.edu/

Miami Ad School
(Miami, Florida)
http://www.adschool.edu/

University of the Arts
(Center City, Philadelphia)
http://www.uarts.edu/

Ojai Digital Arts Center
(Ojai, California)
http://www.digitalartscenter.com

Anderson Arts Ranch
(Snomass, Colorado)
https://central-services.com/cgi-win/
snowtech.exe/get_sitezdoc_frst!60

Helpful URLs

Web Coder
http://www.webcoder.com

Web Review
http://www.webreview.com

Web Reference
http://www.webreference.com

Web Monkey
http://www.hotwired.com/webmonkey/monkey

Webop Æ dia
http://www.pcwebopaedia.com/

Meckler Media
http://www.mecklermedia.com

Step-by-Step Graphics
http://www.dgusa.com/index.aspe

Fuse
http://www.eFuse.com/

Lynda.com
http://www. lynda.com

Web Site Design Galleries

Communication Arts Web Site of the Week
http://www.commarts.com/interactive/index.html?sow_main.html

High Five
http://www.h5.comInspiration

Pages
http://www.lynda.com/paris/

Magazines

Graphis
http://www.graphis.com/

How Magazine
http://www.howdesign.com/

CMYK Magazine
http://www.cmykmag.com/

Adobe Magazine
http://www.adobe.com/publications/adobemag/main.html

Communication Arts
http://www.commarts.com

Glossary

#

8-Bit Graphic: A color or grayscale graphic or movie that has 256 colors or less.

8-Bit Sound: 8-bit sound has a dynamic range of 48 dB. Dynamic range is the measure of steps between the volume or amplitude of a sound.

16-Bit Graphic: A color image or movie that has 65,500 colors.

16-Bit Sound: Standard CD-quality sound resolution. A 16-bit sound has a dynamic range of 96 dB.

24-Bit Graphic: A color image or movie that has 16.7 million colors.

32-Bit Graphic: A color image or movie that has 16.7 million colors plus an 8-bit masking channel.

A

Active Navigation: Point-and-click navigation, where the end user guides the information flow.

Adaptive Dithering: A form of dithering in which the program looks to the image to determine the best set of colors when creating an 8-bit or smaller palette. *See also dithering.*

Additive Color: The term for RGB color space that uses projected light to mix color.

AIFC: A sound file format. AIFC is a new spec for the older **A**udio **I**nterchange **F**ile **F**ormat (AIFF). Both AIFF and AIFF-C files can be read by this format.

Aliasing: In bitmapped graphics, the jagged boundary along the edges of different-colored shapes within an image. *See also anti-aliasing.*

Animated GIF: Part of the GIF89a spec that supports multiple images. It streams and displays them sequentially.

Anti-Aliasing: A technique for reducing the jagged appearance of aliased bitmapped images, usually by inserting pixels that blend at the boundaries of adjacent colors. *See also aliasing.*

Artifacts: Image imperfections caused by compression.

Attributes: Modifiers to HTML tags. In FONT FACE, for example, the tag FONT has the attribute FACE. The FONT tag could also have other attributes, such as COLOR or SIZE.

Authoring Tools: Creation tools for interactive media.

AVI: **A**udio-**V**ideo **I**nterleaved. Microsoft's file format for desktop video movies.

B

Bit Depth: The number of bits used to represent the color of each pixel in a given movie or still image. Specifically, bit depth of 1=2 colors (usually black and white); bit depth of 2=4 colors; bit depth of 8=256 colors; bit depth of 16=65,536 colors; and bit depth of 24=16,777,216 colors.

Bitmapped Graphics: Graphics that are pixel based, as opposed to object oriented. Bitmapped graphics are what the computer can display because it's a pixel-based medium, whereas object-oriented graphics can be viewed in high resolution once they are sent to a printer. Graphics on the Web are bitmapped because they are viewed from a computer-screen-based delivery system.

Brightness: Adds white or tints an image, whereas lack of brightness adds black or tones an images.

Browser: An application that enables you to access World Wide Web pages. Most browsers provide the capability to view Web pages, copy and print material from Web pages, download files from the Web, and navigate throughout the Web.

Browser-Safe Colors: The 216 colors that do not shift between platforms, operating systems, or most Web browsers.

C

Cache: A storage area that keeps frequently accessed data or program instructions readily available so that you do not have to retrieve them repeatedly.

Chat: A real-time multiple user email environment.

Cinepak: Cinepak is a very high form of movie compression. The compression type is called "lossy" because it causes a visible loss in quality.

CGI: **C**ommon **G**ateway **I**nterface. A Web standard for extending the functionality of HTML. CGI always involves the combination of a live Web server and external programming scripts.

Client: A computer that requests information from a network's server. *See also server.*

Client Pull: Client pull creates a slide show effect with HTML text or inline images. It is programmed within the META tag.

Client Side: Client side means that the Web element or effect can run locally off a computer and does not require the presence of a server.

Client-Side Imagemap: A client-side imagemap is programmed in HTML, and does not require a separate map definition file or to be stored on a live Web server. *See also server-side imagemap.*

CLUT: **C**olor **L**ook**U**p **T**able. An 8-bit or lower image file uses a CLUT to define its palette.

Color Mapping: A color map refers to the color palette of an image. Color mapping means assigning colors to an image.

Color Names: Some browsers support using the name of a color instead of the color's hexadecimal value.

Complementary Colors: Created from opposing color hues on the color wheel.

Compression: Reduction of the amount of data required to re-create an original file, graphic, or movie. Compression is used to reduce the transmission time of media and application files across the Web. *See also lossy compression and lossless compression.*

Contrast: The degrees of separation between values.

Counter: Counts and displays the numbers of hits on a Web page.

CSS: Cascading **S**tyle **S**heets control the appearance of Web pages. Multiple style sheets can be applied to a single page, which is why CSS has the word "cascade" in it.

D

Data Rate: Data rate relates to how fast movie data was captured.

Data Streaming: The capability to deliver time-based data as it's requested, much like a VCR, rather than having to download all the information before it can be played.

DHTML: A collection of technologies, ranging from HTML, JavaScript, CSS, and DOM (**D**ocument **O**bject **M**odel) which create more dynamic possibilities than straight HTML.

Dithering: The positioning of different-colored pixels within an image that uses a 256-color palette to simulate a color that does not exist in the palette. A dithered image often looks noisy, or composed of scattered pixels. *See also adaptive dithering.*

DPI: Dots **P**er **I**nch. A term used mostly by print graphics-based programs and professionals, dpi is a common measurement related to the resolution of an image. *See also screen resolution.*

E

Extension: Abbreviated code at the end of a filename that tells the browser what kind of file it's looking at. For example, a JPEG file would have the extension .jpg.

Extranet: Like an Intranet, an Extranet is available only to exclusive members. Unlike an Intranet though, it is generally not protected by a firewall, and has membership-only access through passwords or a CD-ROM.

F

Firewall: A security system designed to keep intruders out of Web or file servers.

Fixed Palette: An established color palette that is fixed. When a fixed palette Web browser views images, it will convert images to its colors and not use the colors from the original.

Flash: A vector file format, a plug-in, and authoring tool from Macromedia.

Forms Processing: Forms that enable users to enter information on Web pages are created by using HTML and CGI, and their function is typically referred to as "forms processing."

FPS: Frames **P**er **S**econd. A movie contains a certain number of frames, and the fewer frames, the more jerky the motion and the smaller the file size.

Frames: Frames offer the ability to divide a Web page into multiple regions, with each region acting as a nested Web page.

FTP: File **T**ransfer **P**rotocol. An Internet protocol that enables users to remotely access files on other computers. An ftp site houses files that can be downloaded to your computer.

G

Gamma: Gamma measures the contrast that affects the midtones of an image. Adjusting the gamma lets you change the brightness values of the middle range of gray tones without dramatically altering the shadows and highlights.

Gamut: A viewable or printable color range.

GIF: A bitmapped color graphics file format. GIF is commonly used on the Web because it employs an efficient compression method. *See also JPEG.*

GIF89a: A type of GIF file that supports transparency and multi-blocks. Multi-blocks create the illusion of animation. GIF89a files are sometimes referred to as "transparent GIFs" or "animated GIFs."

Guestbook: A type of form that enables end-users to enter comments on a Web page.

H

Hexadecimal: A base 16 mathematics calculation, often used in scripts and code. Hexadecimal code is required by HTML to describe RGB values of color for the Web.

HTML: **H**yper**T**ext **M**arkup **L**anguage. The common language for interchange of hypertext between the World Wide Web client and server. Web pages must be written using HTML. *See also hypertext.*

HTTP: **H**yper**T**ext **T**ransfer **P**rotocol is the protocol that the browser and the Web server use to communicate with each other.

Hue: Defines a specific location on the color wheel or in the color spectrum.

Hybrid-Safe Colors: Pre-mixed, interlaced browser-safe colors which give the illusion of colors outside the 216 safe spectrum, but are still browser safe.

Hyperlink: Linked text, images, or media.

Hypertext: Text formatted with lines that enable the reader to jump among related topics. *See also HTML.*

I

Imagemaps: Portions of images that are hypertext links. Using a mouse-based web client such as Netscape or Mosaic, the user clicks on different parts of a mapped image to activate different hypertext links. *See also hypertext.*

Inline Graphic: A graphic that sits inside an HTML document instead of the alternative, which would require that the image be downloaded and then viewed by using an outside system.

Interlaced GIFs: The GIF file format allows for "interlacing," which causes the GIF to load quickly at low or chunky resolution and then come into full or crisp resolution.

Intranet: A Web site that is accessed exclusively by members and is usually protected by a firewall.

ISP: Acronym for **I**nternet **S**ervice **P**rovider.

J

Java: A programming language developed by Sun Microsystems which is cross-platform compatible and supported by some Web browsers.

JavaScript: A scripting language developed by Netscape which enables you to extend the capabilities of HTML.

JPEG: Acronym for **J**oint **P**hotographic **E**xperts **G**roup, but commonly used to refer to a lossy compression technique that can reduce the size of a graphics file by as much as 96 percent. *See also GIF.*

L

Links: Emphasized words in a hypertext document that act as pointers to more information on that specific subject. Links are generally underlined and may appear in a different color. When you click on a link, you can be transported to a different Web site that contains information about the word or phrase used as the link. *See also hypertext.*

Lossless Compression: A data compression technique that reduces the size of a file without sacrificing any of the original data. In lossless compression, the expanded or restored file is an exact replica of the original file before it was compressed. *See also compression.*

Lossy Compression: A data compression technique in which some data is deliberately discarded in order to achieve massive reductions in the size of the compressed file. *See also compression.*

M

Masking: The process of blocking out areas in a computer graphic.

MIME: **M**ultipurpose **I**nternet **M**ail **E**xtensions. An Internet standard for transferring nontext-based data such as sounds, movies, and images.

Moiré: A pattern that results when dots overlap.

MPEG: MPEG audio is a high-quality audio compression file format.

Multi-Blocks: *See GIF89a.*

O

Object-Oriented Graphics: A graphic image composed of autonomous objects such as lines, circles, ellipses, and boxes that can be moved independently. Object-oriented graphics are based on math instructions instead of pixel locations. This type of graphic is often used for print-based design because it can be printed at a higher resolution than a computer screen. *See also bitmapped graphics.*

Object Resolution: Relates to how many polygons form a shape. High object resolution includes many polygons, looks the best, and takes the longest to render. Low-resolution objects have fewer polygons and render faster.

P

Passive Navigation: Animation, slide shows, streaming movies, and audio. Basically anything that plays without the end user initiating the content.

Plug-In: Plug-ins are supported by some browsers, and extend the capability of standard HTML. They need to be installed in the end-user's plug-in folder, found inside the browser software folder.

PNG: An acronym for **P**ortable **N**etwork **G**raphics. PNG is a lossless file format that supports interlacing, 8-bit transparency and gamma information.

PostScript: A sophisticated page description language used for printing high-quality text and graphics on laser printers and other high-resolution printing devices.

PPI: **P**ixels **P**er **I**nch. A common measurement related to the resolution of an image. *See also screen resolution.*

Primary Colors: The theory behind primary colors is that these colors are the starting point from which any other colors can be mixed. On the computer, the primary colors are red, green, and blue because color mixing is additive (created with light). With pigment the primary colors are red, blue, and yellow because color mixing is subtractive.

Progressive JPEG: A type of JPEG that produces an interlaced effect as it loads and can be 30 percent smaller than standard JPEGs. It is not currently supported by many Web browsers.

Provider: Provides Internet access. *See ISP.*

Q

Quick Mask: A Photoshop technique for making masks. *See also masking.*

QuickTime: System software developed by Apple Computer for presentation of desktop video.

R

Raster Graphics: *See bitmapped graphics.*

Rollover: A type of navigation button that changes when the end-user's mouse rolls over.

S

Sample Rates: Sample rates are measured in kilohertz (KHz). Sound editing software is where the initial sample rate settings are established. Standard sample rates range from 11.025 KHz, 22.050 KHz, 44.10 KHz, to 48 KHz. The higher the sample rate, the better the quality. The sample describes its highs and lows.

Sampling Resolution: *See bit depth.*

Saturation: Defines the intensity of color.

Screen Resolution: Screen resolution generally refers to the resolution of common computer monitors. 72 dpi is an agreed upon average, although you will also hear of 96 dpi being the resolution of larger displays.

Search Engine: A type of application, commonly found on the Web, which enables you to search by keywords for information or URLs.

Server: A computer that provides services for users of its network. The server receives requests for services and manages the requests so that they are answered in an orderly manner. *See also client.*

Server Push: Server push is the method of requesting images or data from the server and automating their playback. It involves CGI and the presence of a live Web server.

Server Side: Server side means any type of Web page element that depends on being loaded to a server. It also implies the use of a CGI script.

Server-Side Imagemap: A server-side imagemap requires that the information about the imagemap be saved within a "map definition file" that needs to be stored on a server and accessed by a CGI script. *See also client-side imagemap.*

Shockwave: A file format for Macromedia Director content that can be displayed on the Web.

Spectrum: All the possible colors in a color space, such as RGB or CMYK.

Splash Screen: A main menu screen or opening graphic to a Web page.

Sprite: An individual component of an animation, such as a character or graphic that moves independently.

T

Tables: Tables create rows and columns, as in a spreadsheet, and can be used to align data and images.

Tags: ASCII text indicators with which you surround text and images to designate certain formats or styles.

Tint: The process of adding white to colors

Tone: The process of adding black to colors.

Transparent GIF: A superset of the original GIF file format that adds header information to the GIF file, which signifies that a defined color will be masked out.

True Color: The quality of color provided by 24-bit color depth. 24-bit color depth results in 16.7 million colors, which is usually more than adequate for the human eye.

U

μ-law: μ-law is a sound file format rendered by Unix platforms. The sound quality is generally much lower than other sound formats, but the files are much smaller, too.

URL: **U**niform **R**esource **L**ocator. The address for a Web site.

V

Value: The range of colors from light to dark in an image.

Vector Graphics: *See object-oriented graphics.*

Video for Windows: A multimedia architecture and application suite that provides an outbound architecture that lets applications developers access audio, video, and animation from many different sources through one interface. As an application, Video for Windows primarily handles video capture and compression, and video and audio editing. *See also AVI.*

W

WYSIWYG: Pronounced wizzy-wig, acronym for **W**hat **Y**ou **S**ee **I**s **W**hat **Y**ou **G**et. A design philosophy in which formatting commands directly affect the text displayed on-screen so that the screen shows the appearance of printed text.

DWG . 3

Index

Symbols

A

B

C

H

I

J

N

O

P

Q

R

S

<deconstructing web graphics.2>

Web Design Case Studies and Tutorials

Deconstructing Web Graphics.2 is the sequel to Lynda Weinman's successful book series which profiles top web designers and programmers in order to demystify and analyze how they make decisions, solve complex issues, and create exceptional web sites. Lynda Weinman and co-author Jon Warren Lentz walk you through how to read and understand the source code for each site, break down all of the technical elements, and describe the inside details straight from the designers and programmers who created the pages.

This conversational and information-rich guide offers insight into web design that is not found through any other means. Profiles of successful web designers, programmers, photographers, and illustrators allow them to share their tips, techniques, and recommendations. You'll bring your own web design skills to a higher level through studying their experiences and the step-by-step tutorials and examples found in *Deconstructing Web Graphics.*

Product and Sales Information

Deconstructing Web Graphics.2 By Lynda Weinman and Jon Warren Lentz
Available at your local bookstore or online
ISBN:1-56205-859-2 ▪ $39.99/USA ▪ 225 pages
Macmillan Publishing ▪ 1-800-428-5331

- http://www.lynda.com/decon/
- http://www.mcp.com/newriders

In this book, you'll learn about:

- DHTML
- Macromedia's Dreamweaver
- HTML 4.0
- Cascading Style Sheets
- Tables for Alignment
- Macromedia Flash
- Macromedia Shockwave
- Sites without Plug-Ins
- JavaScript Rollovers
- Browser Detection
- Innovative Background Tiles
- Artistic Use of Frames
- HTML Tricks and Workarounds
- Imagemaps
- Adobe Photoshop Techniques
- Storyboarding Web Sites
- Information Architecture
- Adobe Illustrator for the Web
- Multimedia Versus the Web
- Animated GIF Design
- Creating Strong Compositions
- Typographical Innovations

<deconstructing web graphics>

Web Design Case Studies and Tutorials

Deconstructing Web Graphics profiles top web designers and programmers in order to demystify and analyze how they make decisions, solve complex issues, and create exceptional web sites. Adding her own voice and digital design teaching experience to the book, best-selling author Lynda Weinman selects from her list of favorite designed web sites. She walks you through how to read and understand the source code for each page, breaks down all of the technical elements, and describes the inside details straight from the designers and programmers who created the pages.

This conversational and information-rich guide offers insight into web design that is not found through any other means. Profiles of successful web designers, programmers, photographers, and illustrators allow them to share their tips, techniques, and recommendations. You'll bring your own web design skills to a higher level through studying their experiences and the step-by-step tutorials and examples found in *Deconstructing Web Graphics*.

Product and Sales Information

Deconstructing Web Graphics By Lynda Weinman
Available at your local bookstore or online
ISBN:1-56205-641-7 ▪ $44.99/USA ▪ 250 pages
Macmillan Publishing ▪ 1-800-428-5331

- http://www.lynda.com
- http://www.mcp.com/newriders

In this book, you'll learn about:

- Low-bandwidth graphics
- Scanned imagery for the web
- Cross-platform colors
- Custom Photoshop brushes & patterns
- Artwork using ASCII
- Copyright issues
- Animated GIFs
- LOWSRC animation tricks
- Tables for alignment
- Invisible GIFs for spacers
- Frames for navigation
- HTML tricks and workarounds
- Java
- JavaScript
- CGI
- Forms processing
- Server push
- Client pull
- Shockwave & Macromedia Director
- Sound & video files
- VRML

<creative html design>

A Hands-On HTML 4.0 Web Design Tutorial

It's easy to make web pages with today's new WYSIWYG editors, but those programs don't teach you how to make fast-loading graphics, write accurate HTML that will endure for future browsers, or the necessary techniques involved in preparing your site for the web. Written by two of the industry's foremost experts, this definitive tutorial teaches you not just how to make a web page, but how to design web sites that are cross-platform compatible and work effectively within the web's distinct constraints.

Creative HTML Design walks you through all the phases of site design—from selecting an ISP and uploading files, to more advanced techniques like adding animation and rollovers. Step-by-step tutorials for Photoshop 4.0® and Paint Shop Pro™ teach how to design using "safe" colors, make distinctive background tiles, align your graphics, use tables and frames, include JavaScript rollovers, use CSS, as well as numerous other design and HTML features.

Product and Sales Information

Creative HTML Design
By Lynda Weinman and William E. Weinman
Available at your local bookstore or online
ISBN: 1-56205-704-9 ▪ $39.99/USA ▪ 434 pages
Macmillan Publishing ▪ 1-800-428-5331

- http://www.cgibook.com
- http://www.mcp.com/newriders

In this book, you'll learn about:

- How to build a finished web site with real-world examples and exercises
- The stages of creating a web site
- How to write and read HTML
- Choosing an Internet Service Provider or Presence Provider
- Creating speedy GIF, JPEG, and PNG files
- Working with safe, cross-platform colors that will not shift in web browsers
- Designing distinctive background tiles, with and without visible seams
- Typographic principles and type tricks for the web
- Cascading Style Sheets
- Creating artwork and code for JavaScript rollovers
- Using tables to align text and graphics
- How to use frames aesthetically and effectively
- Using forms aesthetically so they fit the look of the rest of your site
- Adding animation and sound
- Organizing your pages on a server using relative URLs and SSI
- Troubleshooting automatically-generated WYSI-WYG HTML
- A complete HTML 4.0 Reference

The cross-platform CD-ROM includes:

- All the necessary files for the tutorials in this book
- JavaScript rollover code and many other customizable scripts